THE TWENTIETH CENTURY AND BEYOND

A Brief Global History

Seventh Edition

RICHARD GOFF
WALTER MOSS
JANICE TERRY
JIU-HWA UPSHUR
MICHAEL SCHROEDER
Eastern Michigan University

Boston   Burr Ridge, IL   Dubuque, IA   Madison, WI   New York   San Francisco   St. Louis
Bangkok   Bogotá   Caracas   Kuala Lumpur   Lisbon   London   Madrid   Mexico City
Milan   Montreal   New Delhi   Santiago   Seoul   Singapore   Sydney   Taipei   Tor

The **McGraw·Hill** Companies

Mc Graw Hill **Higher Education**

Published by McGraw-Hill, an imprint of The McGraw-Hill Companies, Inc., 1221 Avenue of the Americas, New York, NY 10020. Copyright © 2008. All rights reserved. No part of this publication may be reproduced or distributed in any form or by any means, or stored in a database or retrieval system, without the prior written consent of The McGraw-Hill Companies, Inc., including, but not limited to, in any network or other electronic storage or transmission, or broadcast for distance learning.

This book is printed on acid-free paper.

1 2 3 4 5 6 7 8 9 0 DOC/DOC 0 9 8 7

ISBN-13: 978-0-07-320692-9
ISBN-10: 0-07-320692-X

Editor in Chief: *Emily Barrosse*
Publisher: *Lyn Uhl*
Sponsoring Editor: *Jon-David Hague*
Editorial Assistant: *Sora Kim*
Marketing Coordinator: *Clare Cashen*
Marketing Manager: *Leslie Oberhuber*
Project Manager: *Holly Paulsen*
Manuscript Editor: *Jan McDearmon*

Design Manager: *Cassandra Chu*
Cover Designer: *Ross Carron*
Art Editor: *Katherine McNab*
Senior Photo Research Coordinator: *Brian Pecko*
Production Supervisor: *Rich DeVitto*
Composition: *10/12 Berkeley Book by Techbooks*
Printing: *45# New Era Matte Plus,*
R. R. Donnelley & Sons

Cover: Robert Rauschenberg (1925–). *Estate.* 1963. Oil and silk-screened inks on canvas. 96 x 69-13/16 inches (243.8 x 177.3 cm). Gift the Friends of the Philadelphia Museum of Art, 1967. Photo © The Philadelphia Museum of Art/Art Resource, NY. Cover art © Robert Rauschenberg/Licensed by VAGA, New York, NY.

Credits: The credits section for this book begins on page 600 and is considered an extension of the copyright page.

Library of Congress Cataloging-in-Publication Data

The Twentieth century and beyond : a brief global history / Richard Goff—[et al.].—7th ed.
    p. cm.
    Includes bibliographical references and index.
    ISBN 13: 978-0-07-320692-9
    ISBN 10: 0-07-320692-X
    1.History, Modern—20th century. I. Goff, Richard D.

  D421 .T9 2007
   909.82—dc21

The Internet addresses listed in the text were accurate at the time of publication. The inclusion of a Web site does not indicate an endorsement by the authors or McGraw-Hill, and McGraw-Hill does not guarantee the accuracy of the information presented at these sites.

www.mhhe.com

ABOUT THE AUTHORS

Richard Goff is Professor Emeritus of History at Eastern Michigan University. He received his A.B. from Duke University and was a Woodrow Wilson Fellow at Cornell and a James B. Duke Fellow at Duke, where he received his Ph.D. He taught twentieth-century world history for more than a quarter of a century beginning in 1975. He is the author of *Confederate Supply* and of articles in the *Encyclopedia of Southern History* and the *Encyclopedia of Southern Culture*. He is the editor and co-author of two other college textbooks, *A Survey of Western Civilization* and *World History*.

Walter Moss is Professor of History at Eastern Michigan University, where he has taught history since 1970. He attended Xavier University in Cincinnati and received his Ph.D. from Georgetown University. He is the author of *A History of Russia,* 2 vols. (2nd ed.: 2002–2005) and *Russia in the Age of Alexander II, Tolstoy, and Dostoevsky*. He is co-editor, along with Terry and Upshur, of *The Twentieth Century: Readings in Global History*. He also co-authored *Growing Old* and edited *Humanistic Perspectives on Aging*. He has written over 100 book reviews and several articles on Russian history, literature, and philosophy and has traveled on many occasions to Russia, the former Soviet Union, and other parts of Europe. He is currently working on a book on the major global changes of the twentieth century.

Janice Terry is Professor of History at Eastern Michigan University with a specialty in the modern Middle East. She received her Ph.D. in history from the School of Oriental and African Studies, University of London. She is the author of *The Wafd, 1919–1952: Cornerstone of Egyptian Political Power; Mistaken Identity: Arab Stereotypes in Popular Writing;* and *U.S. Foreign Policy in the Middle East: The Role of Lobbies and Special Interest Groups*. She has also contributed to numerous anthologies and journals. She is the co-editor of *The Arab Studies Quarterly* and has lived and traveled extensively throughout the Middle East and Africa. She is co-author, along with Goff and Upshur, of the textbook *World History;* co-editor, along with Moss and Upshur, of *The Twentieth Century: Readings in Global History;* and co-editor, along with Upshur and Schroeder, of the seven-volume *Encyclopedia of World History*.

Jiu-Hwa Upshur is Professor of History at Eastern Michigan University. She received her B.A. from the University of Sydney and her Ph.D. in Chinese history from the University of Michigan, where she was a Rackham Prize Fellow. She is the author of book reviews and numerous articles on Chinese history and two catalogs on Chinese art. She is co-author, along with Goff and Terry, of *World History* and co-editor of *Lives and Times: Readings in World History* and (with Moss and Terry) *The Twentieth Century: Readings in Global History*. She is also co-editor of the *Encyclopedia of World History* to be published by Facts on File. She has chaired the College Board World History Committee and served on the Social Studies National Advisory Committee. She has lived and traveled extensively in East Asia, India, and Australia.

Michael J. Schroeder is an independent scholar who has taught U.S. and Latin American History at Eastern Michigan University and the University of Michigan–Flint. He received B.A.s in History and Economics at the University of Minnesota and his Ph.D. in History at the University of Michigan. He is the author of numerous articles and chapters on Nicaraguan history, including pieces on death squads, children and war, the question of aerial terrorism in the air war of the 1920s and 1930s, and his award-winning 1996 article in the *Journal of Latin American Studies*, "Horse Thieves to Rebels to Dogs," on Nicaraguan political violence. He is currently completing his book manuscript, *The Sandino Rebellion: Tragedy and Redemption in the Mountains of Northern Nicaragua*. He has also authored a middle school text on Mexican-American history and immigration and is co-editor of *Encyclopedia of World History*.

CONTENTS

PART IV

THE POST–COLD WAR PERIOD

APPENDICES

SPECIAL FEATURES

MAPS AND CHARTS

AUTOBIOGRAPHICAL BOXES

CORRELATION GUIDE

❻

THE TWENTIETH CENTURY AND BEYOND: A GLOBAL HISTORY (TC) AND THE TWENTIETH CENTURY: READINGS IN GLOBAL HISTORY (TCR)

TC Chapter	TCR Reading
1	
Part I	
2.	R1.1, R1.2, R1.3, R2.1
3.	R2.2
4.	R3.1
5.	
6.	R2.3, R3.2A
7.	R4.1
8.	R4.2, R4.3
Part II	
9.	R8.2
10.	R7.1, R7.2
11.	R3.2B, R6.1, R6.2
12.	R5.1, R5.2, R8.1, R9.1
13.	R10.2, R10.3A
14.	R10.1, R10.3B
15.	R11.1, R11.2
16.	R9.2, R12.1, R12.2
17.	R13.1, R13.2
18.	R13.3
Part III	
19.	R14.1, R14.2
20.	R15.1, R15.2
21.	R17.1, R17.2, R17.3
22.	R18.1, R18.2
23.	R19.1, R19.2
24.	R20.1
25.	R20.2A
26.	R16.1, R16.2, R16.3
27.	
28.	R18.3
29.	
30.	
31.	R15.3, R16.3
Part IV	
32.	R21.1
33.	R21.2B
34.	R20.2B, R21.2A

PREFACE

Now that we are halfway through the first decade of the twenty-first century, we have decided to modify the title of the seventh edition of our text to *The Twentieth Century and Beyond: A Global History*. We are also adding a new co-author, Michael Schroeder, an expert on Latin America. We have tried, however, to keep in mind the principles that have guided us in preparing the previous editions, beginning in the early 1980s. Thus, the five of us, with specialties in five different regions of the world, have retained a balanced global treatment regarding regions as well as different types of history and periods of the twentieth century and beyond. Believing that science, technology, economic forces, and culture have all been significant in this period, we continue to begin each major section of the text with an overview of developments in these spheres, as well as those of sociopolitical forces and international affairs. Unlike many other twentieth-century texts, we have also given ample treatment to the first few decades of the century. Another guiding principle from the beginning has been to make the text as user-friendly to students as possible. Thus, we have organized and written the book with this principle always utmost in our minds, and in this new edition have taken several new steps to further this goal, as discussed in the "What Is Different, and Why" section below. Although keeping the students' needs in mind, we have also written a text that allows instructors a great deal of flexibility. While providing sufficient analysis, we have done so as objectively as possible and shied away from any heavily interpretive or ideological type of approach. Thus, professors with differing viewpoints can use the text without it contradicting their own interpretation of twentieth-century history.

ORGANIZATION

The Twentieth Century and Beyond: A Global History combines thematic and chronological approaches, leading students from the late nineteenth century to the present with a firm sense of historical order. Chapter 1 introduces five important topics that are covered throughout the text: (1) science and technology, (2) economics, (3) political and social developments, (4) international relationships, and (5) cultural trends. These five key topics serve as an organizational thread that weaves together the important events and figures discussed in each chapter. Following Chapter 1, we have divided the "century and beyond" into three main periods and a shorter fourth one dealing with the post–cold war period. Each part opens with a "general trends" chapter that explains how the five main topics pertain to the period discussed in that part. The chapters that follow each general trends chapter deal with these topics where appropriate.

WHAT IS DIFFERENT, AND WHY

In the seventh edition we have updated and rearranged Part IV, expanding it from two to three chapters. Chapter 32 deals with the five key topics first introduced in Chapter 1, but now covers the post–cold war period up to 2005. Chapters 33 and 34 then deal with more specific events in this period, first in Europe and the Americas, and then in Asia, the Middle East, and Africa. With the addition of Michael Schroeder to our writing team, we have completely revised all of the American chapters (5, 12, 21, 27, and part of 33) and added a short section on Canada in each of these chapters. We have rewritten other sections for stylistic reasons and to incorporate new scholarly findings and have added more material on terrorism (beginning with Chapter 1) and the environment. We have also revised some of the maps and charts and replaced some of the boxed inserts and photos with new ones. The Suggested Sources section has been thoroughly updated to provide students with the most current source information. Because students are increasingly turning to the Internet to find additional historical materials, we have added several reliable and valuable Web Sources to the end of each chapter.

RETAINED FEATURES

Through all of our editions we have kept the student foremost in mind. Our text includes many learning aids such as numerous Maps, Time Charts, a Glossary, and Marginal Notes, which visually highlight themes throughout the text to help students identify important topics. Our text features a series of excerpts from autobiographies and diaries of significant twentieth-century figures, mainly as young adults. Short annotated lists of additional sources appear at the end of each chapter. These lists highlight well-written historical sources, relevant fiction, and films and television programs that students may view outside the classroom. Because most college students lack sufficient knowledge of geography, we have provided Appendix A, which briefly surveys world demographic and economic patterns.

In the absence of a uniform practice on transliteration of proper names, we have applied the system we considered most appropriate for the historical situation. For Chinese names, we have used the pinyin convention when referring to the People's Republic since 1949; otherwise, we have employed Wade-Giles and traditional usages. For Arabic names, we have generally employed the commonly accepted Western usage. For Russian names, we have most commonly used a variation of the Library of Congress system.

SUPPLEMENTS

For the Instructor and Students

Online Learning Center (www.mhhe.com/goff7)

Available for download at the Online Learning Center is the Instructor's Resource Manual. Co-authored by the text's author team, this manual is designed to help instructors explain historical trends to college students. For each chapter, except for the uniquely organized first chapter, this manual includes a chapter outline; a diverse set of test questions, including multiple-choice, matching, identification, and essay questions; suggested research paper topics; and a set of instructional resources, which lists key books and films that provide the basic insights for teaching the subject matter found in the chapter. The instructor's material is password-protected.

Also at the Online Learning Center, students can access a customized web site correlated to the text. The site is organized around the four parts that compose the texts, and provides students with key themes and objectives for each part.

Videos

A wide range of videos (on both CD and DVD) on contemporary topics in World History is available through the Films for the Humanities and Sciences collection (see www.films.com) and other sources. Instructors can illustrate and enhance lectures by selecting from a series of videos that are correlated to the course. Contact your local McGraw-Hill sales representative for further information.

ACKNOWLEDGMENTS

For the seventh edition, we are grateful for the support provided by the staff of McGraw-Hill, particularly our various editors, Lyn Uhl, Jon-David Hague, Liliana Almendarez, and Holly Paulsen. We would also like to thank the reviewers of the various editions for their helpful insights:

Michael Balyo
Chemeketa Community College

Lynda S. Bell
University of California, Riverside

Eric Dorn Brose
Drexel University

Frank Chiteji
Gettysburg College

William B. Cohen, Ph.D.
Indiana University

C. Stewart Doty
University of Maine–Orono

Laird Easton
California State University–Chico

Susan H. Farnsworth
Trinity College

Jennifer Reed Fry
King's College

Greg P. Guelcher
Morningside College

Louis Haas
Duquesne University

James R. Hagen
Frostburg State University

Katherine R. Jolluck
University of North Carolina–Chapel Hill

Louis Menashe
Polytechnic Institute of New York

William Morris
Shelby State Community College

Gersham Nelson
Frostburg State University

William Ochsenwald
Virginia Polytechnic University

Michael F. Pavkovic
Hawaii Pacific University

Brian A. Pavlac
King's College

Robina Quale
Albion College

Erik P. Rau
Drexel University

Barbara Reinfeld
New York Institute of Technology

Paul Scherer
Indiana University–South Bend

John Snetsinger
California Polytechnic State University

Christopher S. Stowe
The University of Toledo

Shuping Wan
Montgomery College

Martin W. Wilson
East Stroudsburg University

John B. Wiseman
Frostburg State University

We remain indebted to Sally Marks, Professor Emerita of Rhode Island College, for her encouragement.

In preparing the various editions of this text, we have been indebted to many people at Eastern Michigan University. In the early 1980s, Richard Abbott, Donald Briggs, Donald Disbrow, Della Flusche, James McDonald, and Lester Scherer were kind enough to read and comment on major portions of the original manuscript. In subsequent editions, Michael Homel, Richard Nation, John Wagner, Michael Schroeder, and Raymond B. Craib aided us on the Americas. Joseph Engwenyu was particularly helpful on Africa, and Roger Long on the Indian subcontinent. George Cassar, Louis Gimelli, Theodore Hefley, Neil McLarty, and Reinhard Wittke gave professional advice; James Waltz, Ira Wheatley, Margot Duley, Gersham Nelson, and Philip Schmitz provided administrative support; and Rich Goff, James Wolfe, Jennifer Yonan, Kristi Nowack, Dana Rogers, and Michael Pryplesh provided bibliographical and other assistance. We are especially indebted to Nancy Snyder, who has untiringly helped us prepare all seven editions, including earlier instructor's manuals for the first six editions. For the seventh edition we are most grateful to our colleague Robert Citino for offering us his considerable expertise on World War I and World War II and helping us to revise the chapters dealing with these topics. We would also like to thank Nora Faires, Department of History, Western Michigan University, for her work on the sections on Canada. Nancy Moss's many hours of proofreading are also appreciated.

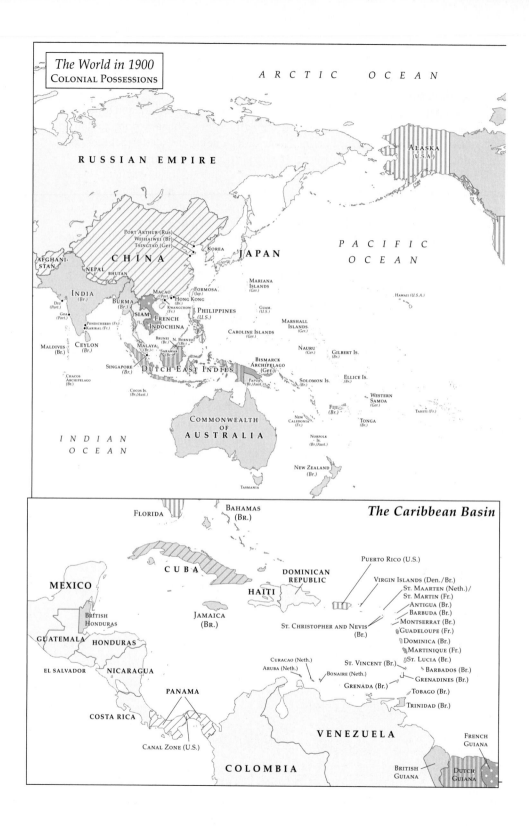

The World in 1900
Colonial Possessions

ARCTIC OCEAN

RUSSIAN EMPIRE

ALASKA (U.S.A.)

PACIFIC OCEAN

AFGHANI-STAN
NEPAL
BHUTAN
CHINA
PORT ARTHUR (Rus)
WEIHAIWEI (Br)
TSINGTAO (Ger)
KOREA
JAPAN
INDIA (Br.)
DIU (Port.)
GOA (Port.)
PONDICHERRY (Fr.)
KARIKAL (Fr.)
MALDIVES (Br.)
CEYLON (Br.)
BURMA (Br.)
SIAM
FRENCH INDOCHINA
MACAO (Port.)
HONG KONG (Br.)
KWANGCHOW (Fr.)
FORMOSA (Jap.)
PHILIPPINES (U.S.)
MARIANA ISLANDS (Ger.)
GUAM (U.S.)
HAWAII (U.S.A.)
MARSHALL ISLANDS (Ger.)
CAROLINE ISLANDS (Ger.)
NAURU (Ger.)
GILBERT IS. (Br.)
BRUNEI (Br.)
N. BORNEO (Br.)
SARAWAK (Br.)
MALAYA (Br.)
SINGAPORE (Br.)
CHAGOS ARCHIPELAGO (Br.)
DUTCH EAST INDIES
COCOS IS. (Br./Aust.)
PAPUA (Br./Aust.)
BISMARCK ARCHIPELAGO (Ger.)
SOLOMON IS. (Br.)
ELLICE IS. (Br.)
WESTERN SAMOA (Ger.)
FIJI (Br.)
TONGA (Br.)
TAHITI (Fr.)
NEW CALEDONIA (Fr.)
NORFOLK IS. (Br./Aust.)
INDIAN OCEAN
COMMONWEALTH OF AUSTRALIA
NEW ZEALAND (Br.)
TASMANIA

The Caribbean Basin

FLORIDA
BAHAMAS (Br.)
CUBA
DOMINICAN REPUBLIC
HAITI
JAMAICA (Br.)
MEXICO
BRITISH HONDURAS
GUATEMALA
HONDURAS
EL SALVADOR
NICARAGUA
PANAMA
COSTA RICA
CANAL ZONE (U.S.)
COLOMBIA
PUERTO RICO (U.S.)
VIRGIN ISLANDS (Den./Br.)
ST. MAARTEN (Neth.)/ ST. MARTIN (Fr.)
ANTIGUA (Br.)
BARBUDA (Br.)
MONTSERRAT (Br.)
GUADELOUPE (Fr.)
ST. CHRISTOPHER AND NEVIS (Br.)
DOMINICA (Br.)
MARTINIQUE (Fr.)
ST. LUCIA (Br.)
ST. VINCENT (Br.)
BARBADOS (Br.)
CURACAO (Neth.)
ARUBA (Neth.)
BONAIRE (Neth.)
GRENADINES (Br.)
GRENADA (Br.)
TOBAGO (Br.)
TRINIDAD (Br.)
VENEZUELA
FRENCH GUIANA
BRITISH GUIANA
DUTCH GUIANA

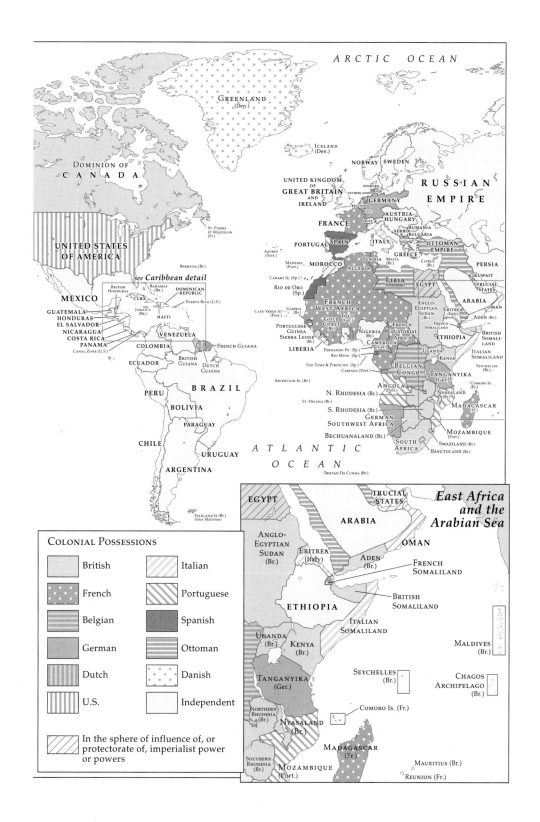

ARCTIC OCEAN

GREENLAND
(Den.)

DOMINION OF
CANADA

ICELAND
(Den.)

NORWAY SWEDEN

UNITED KINGDOM
OF
GREAT BRITAIN
AND
IRELAND

NETHERLANDS
DENMARK

BELGIUM

GERMANY

RUSSIAN
EMPIRE

AUSTRIA-
HUNGARY

FRANCE

SWITZ.

SERBIA
RUMANIA
BULGARIA

ST. PIERRE
ET MIQUELON
(Fr.)

PORTUGAL SPAIN

ITALY

GREECE

OTTOMAN
EMPIRE

UNITED STATES
OF AMERICA

AZORES
(Port.)

MADEIRA
(Port.)

MOROCCO

TUNISIA
ALGERIA

MALTA
(Br.)

CYPRUS
(Br.)

PERSIA

KUWAIT

see Caribbean detail

BERMUDA (Br.)

CANARY IS. (Sp.)

RIO DE ORO
(Sp.)

LIBYA
(Ottoman)

EGYPT

TRUCIAL
STATES

MEXICO

BRITISH
HONDURAS

BAHAMAS
(Br.)

CUBA

JAMAICA
(Br.)

DOMINICAN
REPUBLIC

PUERTO RICO (U.S.)

HAITI

CAPE VERDE IS.
(Port.)

GAMBIA
(Br.)

FRENCH
WEST AFRICA

TOGO
(Ger.)

ANGLO-
EGYPTIAN
SUDAN
(Br.)

ERITREA
(Italy)

ARABIA

OMAN

ADEN (Br.)

GUATEMALA
HONDURAS
EL SALVADOR
NICARAGUA
COSTA RICA
PANAMA

CANAL ZONE (U.S.)

PORTUGUESE
GUINEA

GOLD
COAST
(Br.)

SIERRA LEONE
(Br.)

NIGERIA
(Br.)

FRENCH
EQUATORIAL
AFRICA

CAMEROON
(Ger.)

FRENCH
SOMALILAND

ETHIOPIA

BRITISH
SOMALI-
LAND

VENEZUELA

LIBERIA

FERNANDO PO (Sp.)

RIO MUNI (Sp.)

UGANDA
(Br.)

KENYA

ITALIAN
SOMALILAND

COLOMBIA

FRENCH GUIANA

ECUADOR

BRITISH
GUIANA

DUTCH
GUIANA

SAO TOME & PIRINCIPE (Sp.)

CABINDA (Port.)

BELGIAN
CONGO

SEYCHELLES
(Br.)

PERU

BRAZIL

ASCENCION IS. (Br.)

ANGOLA
(Port.)

TANGANYIKA
(Ger.)

NYASALAND
(Br.)

COMORO IS.
(Fr.)

BOLIVIA

N. RHODESIA
(Br.)

MADAGASCAR
(Fr.)

PARAGUAY

ST. HELENA (Br.)

S. RHODESIA (Br.)

GERMAN
SOUTHWEST AFRICA

MOZAMBIQUE
(Port.)

CHILE

URUGUAY

BECHUANALAND (Br.)

SOUTH
AFRICA

SWAZILAND (Br.)

BASUTOLAND (Br.)

ARGENTINA

ATLANTIC
OCEAN

TRISTAN DA CUNHA (Br.)

FALKLAND IS (Br.)
(Isles Malvinas)

East Africa and the Arabian Sea

EGYPT

TRUCIAL
STATES

*East Africa
and the
Arabian Sea*

ARABIA

ANGLO-
EGYPTIAN
SUDAN
(Br.)

ERITREA
(Italy)

OMAN

ADEN
(Br.)

FRENCH
SOMALILAND

ETHIOPIA

BRITISH
SOMALILAND

ITALIAN
SOMALILAND

UGANDA
(Br.)

KENYA
(Br.)

MALDIVES
(Br.)

SEYCHELLES
(Br.)

CHAGOS
ARCHIPELAGO
(Br.)

TANGANYIKA
(Ger.)

NORTHERN
RHODESIA
(Br.)

NYASALAND
(Br.)

COMORO IS. (Fr.)

MADAGASCAR
(Fr.)

MAURITIUS (Br.)

SOUTHERN
RHODESIA
(Br.)

MOZAMBIQUE
(Port.)

REUNION (Fr.)

COLONIAL POSSESSIONS

- British
- French
- Belgian
- German
- Dutch
- U.S.
- Italian
- Portuguese
- Spanish
- Ottoman
- Danish
- Independent

In the sphere of influence of, or protectorate of, imperialist power or powers

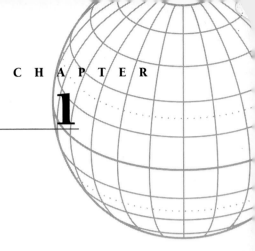

©1900: A Preview of the Twentieth Century

In 1900, on the sandy, breezy shores of Kitty Hawk, North Carolina, two bicycle mechanics from Dayton, Ohio, tested their first flying machine, a glider weighing 50 pounds. Within a few years, these brothers, Orville and Wilbur Wright, kept a powered airplane aloft for more than half an hour. Other aviation pioneers were right on their heels.

The Wrights' airplane symbolizes the emergence of a technology based on new scientific knowledge, a technology that became one of the central forces shaping twentieth-century life. In the following decades, scientists rapidly expanded their insights into the basic properties of chemistry, biology, and agronomy. Medical and sanitation practices based on these insights dramatically improved health and longevity. New concepts of mathematics, physics, space, and time revolutionized the thinking of many on the meaning of history and the nature of the universe.

THE WRIGHT BROTHERS AND SCIENCE AND TECHNOLOGY

This notable twentieth-century advance in scientific knowledge led to a spectacular technological explosion. Automobiles and airliners, motion pictures and television, atomic energy, plastics and synthetics, vaccines and antibiotics, satellites and space probes, missiles, lasers, and computers are only a few examples of the technological outpouring of the decades after 1900. The changes that resulted from twentieth-century science and technology came with increasing rapidity and ensured that each new generation lived in a world markedly different from that of preceding generations. Few living in 1900 imagined, for example, that by 1930 many would be spending evenings listening to voices coming out of a box or watching people moving and talking on a screen. Even fewer dreamed that in 1969 hundreds of millions of people around the world would sit in their homes and see men walking on the moon or that by 1999 vast numbers of people, especially in the more industrialized countries of the world, would be using something called computers to send and receive mail and access increasing amounts of information.

Unfortunately, scientific and technological breakthroughs frequently have had negative as well as positive consequences and have often strained humanity's capacity to adapt to them. By 1999 life expectancy for many people was double that of 1900, yet enough nuclear weapons still existed to extinguish all human life in a few hours.

At the same time that the Wright brothers were pursuing their dream, famine was destroying hundreds of thousands of lives in India. Observers wrote of the sunken eyes, hollow stomachs, and emaciated arms and legs of multitudes of suffering Indians. By the end of 1900 about 2 million had died in two years. According to one estimate, 15 million Indians died from famine in the years 1875–1900, 10 times the number who had died from hunger in the first 50 years of the nineteenth century. The British government tried to provide relief, blaming the tragedy primarily on rapid population growth, aggravated by drought.

INDIAN FAMINE AND ECONOMICS

In fact, the 1899–1900 famine in India dramatically illustrated the role that another force, economics, played in the twentieth century. Although the famine in India was immediately precipitated by drought, its more fundamental cause lay in the boardrooms of the cartels that operated in a global economic context far away from the stricken villages and urban slums of India. Even though food production had increased as a result of scientific and technological improvements, the companies or governments controlling the global supply of essential grains often created an unequal distribution of such foodstuffs.

In this context, Great Britain during the nineteenth century had encouraged the great landlords of India to produce export crops for Britain's global trading empire. The opening of the Suez Canal in 1869 and the rapid expansion of the Indian railroad network dramatically cut the time and costs of importing Indian products into Great Britain and other parts of the empire. Landowners were encouraged to utilize their lands and peasant labor for the production of jute, cotton, tea, and wheat for sale abroad rather than to cultivate food crops for the growing population. In 1901, when some were still perishing from hunger, landowners in India exported two and one-half times more food grains than they had in 1858. In addition, British-imposed land taxes and other agricultural policies were driving more and more Indian peasants into poverty.

As illustrated by the situation in India in 1900, a major economic theme of the twentieth century was the continuing disparity between the impoverished and the affluent areas of the world. Particularly in Asia, Africa, and Latin America, malnourished people remained tied to meager local economic resources, while at the same time the great international businesses that controlled the world's resources helped to create prosperity for a few favored nations, particularly in Europe, North America, and parts of East Asia and the Middle East.

Climatic conditions, overpopulation, political rivalries, civil war, and domestic economic policies also contributed notably throughout the twentieth century to the recurrent horror of famine, a tragedy that gripped nations of varying economic systems. In the 1930s, for example, millions starved in the Soviet Ukraine as a result of the policies of Joseph Stalin, even though Ukrainians produced enough food to feed themselves. Owing to a variety of governmental and international business policies and natural disasters in the decades following 1950, millions died of hunger in such varied nations as China, Nigeria, Bangladesh, India, Cambodia, Ethiopia, Mozambique, and Somalia. In the same period, on the other hand, the international marketing of an array of industrial and consumer products brought a comfortable standard of living not only to many in the United States, Canada, and western Europe but also to increasing numbers in Japan, South Korea, Taiwan, Hong Kong, Singapore, and the petroleum-rich states of the Middle East.

Economic inequality helped to stimulate another significant twentieth-century phenomenon: social and political conflict. No one personifies this better than Emma Goldman, a dynamic Russian Jewish émigré to the United States who was a major figure in the rise of anarchism. In the belief that the rich exploited the poor and that the state was merely a tool of wealthy interests, anarchists advocated doing away with all government. Leo Tolstoy, the famous Russian nobleman writer who was also an anarchist, urged the use of nonviolent means to bring about this goal, but most anarchists advocated violence. Some of them were the chief terrorists—a common term even then—of their day. For a while in the early 1890s, as anarchist bombs exploded in places such as a railway station café, a fashionable restaurant, and even in the French Chamber of Deputies, some Parisians feared to gather in public places, and fewer tourists visited the city. During the 1890s anarchist bombs also exploded in other European cities such as Barcelona, where one at an opera house in 1893 killed and wounded over 70 people.

In 1900 Goldman was a delegate to the Anarchist Conference in Paris. Sitting in a café one day, she read of the assassination of King Humbert of Italy by a fellow anarchist who had come from the United States to perform the deed. Her reaction was that such acts were inevitable as long as centralized governments continued to exist. King Humbert had been the fourth royal figure or chief of state to be assassinated within six years. In 1901 U.S. President William McKinley became a fifth victim, at the hands of a young man named Leon Czolgosz. Earlier in the year, Czolgosz had attended a Goldman lecture, and he allegedly stated later that her fiery rhetoric had influenced his decision to commit his bloody act.

EMMA GOLDMAN AND SOCIOPOLITICAL CONFLICT

Goldman viewed herself as a spokesperson not only for the economically downtrodden but for all oppressed people, including women. Although she criticized U.S. suffragists for seeking what seemed to her meaningless voting power and for ignoring the problems of working women, her thoughts on the liberation of women echoed down through the decades. Goldman argued that a woman had the "right to support herself; to live for herself; to love whomever she pleases, or as many as she pleases."[1]

Anarchism and women's rights became just two of the many ideas and ideologies stirring political waters after 1900. Nationalism, Marxism, liberalism, and conservatism were some of the others. Later in the century, communism, fascism, and Nazism became particularly powerful examples of the quest of men and women for political solutions to their various problems. Much blood flowed in many parts of the world as a result of the conflicts among these ideologies and the men and women who espoused them. By the end of the century, ethnic nationalism, which helped lead to World War I (see Chapter 7), was still a strong force in the world. Like most anarchists, Goldman was a strong critic of nationalism. Three years before World War I she wrote,

> Patriotism assumes that our globe is divided into little spots, each one surrounded by an iron gate. Those who have had the fortune of being born on some particular spot consider themselves better, nobler, grander, more intelligent than the living beings

---

[1]Quoted in Alice Wexler, *Emma Goldman: An Intimate Life* (New York: Pantheon Books, 1984), p. 94.

inhabiting any other spot. It is, therefore, the duty of everyone living on that chosen spot to fight, kill, and die in the attempt to impose his superiority upon all others. The inhabitants of the other spots reason in like manner.[2]

In 1900, nationalism was strongest in Europe and the United States, but, partly in response to imperialism, nationalist sentiments were also stirring in other parts of the world. The Boxer Rebellion in China was a good example.

BOXER REBELLION AND IMPERIALISM

The Boxer Rebellion in China was one of the most dramatic events of 1900. An antiforeign group known as the "Boxers" (the Society of Harmonious Fists) besieged the compound that housed the diplomatic community in Peking. Persistent Chinese hostility to predatory outsiders, a drought and other natural disasters in northern China, and patronage by a parochial dowager empress culminated in the Boxer fury. Almost two months after the beginning of the siege of the foreign legations, an eight-nation force rescued the survivors. Before his soldiers departed from Germany on this mission, the bombastic Kaiser Wilhelm II encouraged them to be as merciless as the barbarian followers of Attila the Hun. After occupying Peking, many soldiers from the invading armies did their best to live up to the kaiser's militant exhortations.

The Boxer Rebellion and its quick suppression illustrated another dynamic force of the twentieth century: turbulent international relations. For decades before the Boxer Rebellion, foreign powers had used imperialist policies and superior military might to impose unfair treaties on the Chinese and to carve China into spheres of influence. Even the Open Door policy of the United States was little more than a U.S. plan to gain a share of the wealth of helpless China. As the twentieth century proceeded, the international scene continued to be a key forum for the expression of nationalism, imperialism, and militarism.

Many great powers displayed the imperialism by which stronger countries imposed and maintained their rule over weaker nations. Early in the century, for example, France forced Morocco to accept its "protection," the United States took de facto control of a number of Caribbean nations, and Japan annexed Korea. After World War I Great Britain and France took over part of the Middle East. In the 1930s and 1940s Japanese militarists sought to impose their will on China, Hitler saw it as a German right to conquer and dominate the nations of Europe, and Stalin annexed the Baltic republics. Following World War II, the Soviet Union imposed its control over the states of Eastern Europe.

As China's twentieth-century resurgence from the Boxer defeat of 1900 indicated, however, the force wielded by powerful nations to impose their will on weaker states often failed to snuff out the nationalistic aspirations of conquered peoples to be free from outside controls. Thus, France failed to "assimilate" the Moroccans, and Latin Americans resisted "Yankee imperialism." A harsh Japanese colonial policy failed to turn Koreans into docile subjects, and the Soviet Union failed to turn the Baltic peoples into happy Soviet citizens or Hungarians into willing allies.

---

[2]Emma Goldman, "Patriotism, a Menace to Liberty," in *Anarchism and other Essays* (1917; reprint, New York: Dover Publications, 1969), pp. 128–129.

After World War II, one after another, colonial empires collapsed. Hundreds of millions of the peoples of Asia and Africa became citizens of new independent nations. Between 1989 and 1991 the "Soviet empire" also collapsed, and the subjugated states of Eastern Europe regained their independence.

In 1900 the philosopher Friedrich Nietzsche died in Weimar, Germany, at the age of 55. His ideas posed a major challenge to the traditional Western religious beliefs and morality of his day. At a time when Western imperialists thought of themselves (in the words of the poet Rudyard Kipling) as taking up the "white man's burden" to bring their civilization to "inferior" peoples in Africa and Asia, Nietzsche's writings undermined confidence in Western civilization itself. The son of a Lutheran minister, Nietzsche preached that religion was no longer credible, that "God is dead," and that Christianity—the "one great curse"—was a strategy of the weak, intended to enslave the strong. He advised individuals who dared to go "beyond good and evil" to become new "supermen." He had contempt not only for the spirit of Christianity, but also for much of the Western culture that had evolved from it. Nietzsche also despised democracy and the ideal of equality. He predicted a future of uncertainty, revolution, war, and turmoil.

Even after Nietzsche's death, his ideas lived on, testifying to the importance of culture—that is, philosophical ideas and cultural values—as another force that shaped the twentieth century. Many European poets, artists, playwrights, and composers fell under the sway of Nietzsche's ideas. During the twentieth century, a world interconnected by ever-more-effective communication systems presented individuals with an unprecedented array of often conflicting ideas and values. Both new ideas from thinkers in technologically advanced nations and older ideas from traditional cultures were propagated around the world. Although Nietzsche's ideas represented, for many, a very powerful challenge to traditional Western values, even more of the world's people in the twentieth century felt liberated—or threatened—by the theories of Charles Darwin, Karl Marx, and Sigmund Freud. Some observers repudiated what they considered to be the cultural and religious anarchy of the modern era, and throughout the century traditional religious believers continued to predominate in many parts of the world; others celebrated the multiplication of cultural and religious choices.

The discontentment with traditional Western values that Nietzsche stimulated led some to seek enlightenment from other cultures. The French artist Paul Gauguin, disenchanted with Western materialism, sought what he considered a nobler existence in Tahiti, while Nietzsche's friend Paul Deussen became a leading expert on the religious philosophies of ancient India. Later, some in Europe and the United States adopted Zen Buddhism or, like the boxer Muhammad Ali, converted to Islam.

To conclude, these five sketches from 1900—the Wright brothers at Kitty Hawk, the famine in India, Emma Goldman's activities in Paris, the Boxer Rebellion, and the death of Nietzsche—offer a preview of the years ahead. They illustrate the five major forces that this text will focus on throughout its discussions of the history of the twentieth century: rapid scientific and technological innovation, an increasingly global economy coupled with persistent economic inequality, continuing social and political conflict, aggression and reactions to it in international relations, and the broad dissemination of conflicting philosophical ideas and cultural values. These forces did not

NIETZSCHE AND THE CONFLICT OF RELIGIOUS AND CULTURAL VALUES

work in isolation but combined in unique patterns to create important results throughout the twentieth century. An example of how these factors intertwine is this Boxer leaflet that cites both technological change and the clash of cultural values in explaining the Boxers' hostility to outsiders:

> The arrival of calamities is because of the foreign devils. They have come to China to propagate their teachings, to build telegraph lines, and to construct railways. They do not believe in spirits and they desecrate the gods. It is the desire of the gods to cut up the telegraph lines, to rip up the railroads, and to cut off the heads of the foreign devils.[3]

This book will show how the forces underlying these five events combined in different ways to shape the history of the twentieth century.

---

[3]Quoted in William J. Duiker, *Cultures in Collision: The Boxer Rebellion* (San Rafael, Calif.: Presidio Press, 1978), p. 37.

THE ERA OF IMPERIALISM

TIME CHART I
1900–1918

Year	South & East Asia	Middle East & Africa	Europe	Western Hemisphere	Trends in Culture, Science, Technology
	AGE OF IMPERIAL DOMINATION			UNITED STATES PREDOMINANT IN LATIN AMERICA	INDUSTRIAL WEST
1900	Boxer Rebellion	Boer War, 1899–1902			
1901	Philippine insurrection, 1898–1913				
1902			Triple Alliance in effect (1882)		Growing influence of Darwinism, Marxism
1903					
1904	Russo-Japanese War 1904–1905				
1905	All-India Muslim League formed	First Moroccan crisis	Continuing British-German naval race	Roosevelt Corollary	Einstein's theory of relativity Decade of arms buildup
1906					Birth of modern art and music

8

Year				
1907		Triple Entente completed		
1908		Austria annexes Bosnia and Herzegovina	South Africa self-governing	
1909				Advent of motion pictures, airplanes, automobiles
1910	Japan annexes Korea			
1911	Manchus overthrown in China			
1912	French protectorate in Morocco	Balkan Wars, 1912–1913	Beginning of Mexican Revolution	
1913				Tagore first non-European to win Nobel Prize for Literature
1914		**WORLD WAR I**		Panama Canal completed
	Ottoman Empire joins Central Powers			
	German colonies taken by Allies, 1914–1918			Submarines, trench warfare
1915	Japan serves Twenty-One Demands on China			
1916				Dadaism founded
1917		Russian Revolution, 1917	United States enters WWI	
1918	United States-Japanese intervention in Siberia, 1918–1925	Allied intervention and civil war in Russia, 1918–1921		

⑥General Trends before World War I

The twentieth century opened on a world dominated by the West. Major European nations and the United States led the world in scientific discoveries and technological innovations and controlled most of the globe with overwhelming economic and military power. Japan adopted Western technology and competed with Western nations in international ventures.

**WESTERN CIVILIZATION
APPEARS DOMINANT**

For the West the future offered the prospect of continued progress and power. Westerners believed that their preeminent position was a reflection of their superior culture. By the beginning of the twentieth century, most Western peoples enjoyed an unmatched standard of living as well as the opportunity for better education, health care, and social services.

As it turned out, Western power was not as overwhelming as it seemed. Many Western nations were beset by ethnic and religious differences as well as by political conflicts. In addition, most European nations nursed hostilities toward their neighbors. These tensions stemmed in part from long histories of national rivalries in Europe and from competition for control of territory around the world.

SCIENCE AND TECHNOLOGY

The people of Europe and the United States took great pride in a wave of Western scientific discoveries and technological improvements in the nineteenth and early twentieth centuries. In biology, Charles Darwin's *On the Origin of Species by Means of Natural Selection* (1859) and *The Descent of Man* (1871) revolutionized perceptions of humanity's history. Darwin theorized that different animal species, including humans, originated through a process of natural selection whereby the "fittest" or most adaptable survived and flourished. His concept became widely accepted, although many could not reconcile it with the biblical account of creation. Darwin's ideas, along with advances in the study of geology and paleontology (study of fossils), led to further discoveries that explained the history of early humans and their societies.

Psychologists brought forth a new field of investigation that opened human mental functions to study and interpretation. At the beginning of the twentieth century, Sigmund Freud was in the vanguard of psychological practitioners. His theories revolved around his belief that humans were driven by unconscious pleasure-seeking forces such as sexuality. The conflict of these unconscious desires with other psychological forces more attuned to social "reality" often led to inner psychological conflict. To deal with serious cases, Freud developed psychoanalysis, a method of probing the unconscious mind, frequently by analyzing dreams. Freud's theories and methods were both supported and attacked by later experts in the field.

In 1895 Wilhelm Roentgen discovered a form of radiation that could penetrate opaque materials. These x-rays, as he called them, were gradually applied in many areas of physics and medicine. Meanwhile, Antoine Becquerel discovered the radioactivity of uranium. Starting from this discovery, Marie and Pierre Curie investigated other radioactive elements, discovering radium and polonium in 1898. Their work helped to provide a foundation for twentieth-century research in the composition of atoms.

A GREAT AGE OF THEORETICAL AND APPLIED SCIENCE

As Darwin changed thinking about the nature of humans, Albert Einstein, in the first two decades of the twentieth century, changed thinking about the nature of the universe. He demonstrated that energy is mass multiplied by the square of the velocity of light. Joined with the conclusion of Ernest Rutherford and others that the atom is a combination of particles moving at enormous velocity, Einstein's theorem suggested that useful thermal energy would be released if the nuclei of atoms could be altered.

In addition to his studies of the atom, Einstein's theory of relativity and his other discoveries changed scientific understanding of the forces that make up the universe. During the two centuries before 1900, scientists believed that the universe was a three-dimensional spatial arrangement and that its properties could be measured from an absolute point of reference. Einstein proposed that time was a fourth dimension interrelated with the other three. According to him, the velocity of light is the same whether or not the observer is in motion, and thus there is no absolute point of reference. Measurement is in that sense relative.

Westerners were particularly proud of advances in health and longevity. The work of Joseph Lister in the nineteenth century improved hygienic conditions in hospitals; puerperal fever, the main cause of death for women in childbirth, was eradicated. The introduction of anesthesia techniques enabled doctors to perform more complicated operations, which saved countless lives. Louis Pasteur and Robert Koch proved that bacteria were the cause of many previously incurable diseases and could be controlled through inoculations, medication, and hygienic measures. As a result, anthrax and rabies, which had destroyed many animals around the world, came under control, and four major causes of child mortality—smallpox, diphtheria, typhoid fever, and scarlet fever—appeared to be on the road to elimination in the Western world. Soon after 1900 chemists discovered vitamins and developed sulfa drugs, which helped to combat disease-causing bacteria.

ADVANCES IN HEALTH CARE AND THE CURE OF DISEASE

Improvements in health care and in the control of disease contributed to a marked population increase late in the nineteenth century, not only in Europe and the United States but throughout much of the world. The population of Europe more than doubled between 1800 and 1900, primarily because of a lowered death rate. On the other hand, population increases often created overcrowding in Western cities. As better health care spread through the rest of the world to countries such as India and

An age of science: Marie Curie, twice a recipient of the Nobel Prize, in her laboratory.

China, it, too, contributed to population increases that often outstripped the available food supply.

Scientific insights spawned a multitude of technological breakthroughs. Thomas Edison pioneered the development of electricity, including electric lighting, and for those living early in the twentieth century who had access to electricity, no single invention was more important. Engineers who developed turbines and dynamos dramatically accelerated the production of electropower. New petroleum-refining techniques produced gasoline and diesel fuels to power the new internal combustion engines. The chemists and technicians who produced rayon and artificial dyes in the laboratory brought in a new era of synthetic materials, while their discovery of new metal alloys promised greater diversity in manufactured products. Industrial innovators used interchangeable parts and created the assembly line to make production more efficient, thus making manufactured goods cheaper. The development of structural steel, reinforced concrete, and the electric elevator allowed cities to grow upward as well as outward.

By 1900 physicists studying electricity and its relationship to magnetic waves had already revolutionized concepts of communication. The telegraph had been well established in the nineteenth century, and underseas cables already linked the world's continents. The telephone began to make its impact in urban centers at the beginning of the twentieth century. Perhaps the most exciting development in communication came in 1895, when Guglielmo Marconi sent messages through space with a wireless transmitter. The age of the radio soon followed. Advances in photography created a new wonder, the motion picture.

In transportation, the advent in the nineteenth century of steam-driven locomotives and steamships had already greatly accelerated travel on land and water. After 1903, through the efforts of Orville and Wilbur Wright and many others, the age-old dream of air travel was realized. This achievement in aviation soon meant that people could traverse the world in a matter of days or hours instead of months or weeks. More important to the average Westerner was the development of the internal combustion engine, which led to the automobile. While only in its infancy in 1900, the automobile already promised to transform work and leisure patterns throughout the West and eventually around much of the world.

Ironically, the same spirit of scientific and technological advance that was enhancing the lives of human beings was also busily devising new means to destroy them. Scientists and metallurgists produced explosives and propellants such as cordite, TNT, and nitroglycerin. Their improvements in the techniques of rifling and metal casting brought forth a new class of artillery—howitzers, mortars, and long-range naval guns—and new or improved fragmentation weapons, such as shrapnel shells, antipersonnel mines, and hand grenades. These projectiles could now be delivered with great accuracy through new guidance systems, thus increasing the number of casualties per projectile expended. Technicians working on new fuel and hydraulic technology produced the submarine; additional propellants and guidance technology armed the submarine with a reliable torpedo. Applications of chemistry and physics created poison gas, the flamethrower, and the machine gun.

The military establishment also adapted a number of techniques originally developed for civilian use. Mass production of textiles and clothing, plus the invention of canning and refrigeration, meant that nations could raise, equip, and feed larger armies and navies. Utilizing new modes of transportation and communication, military leaders could move about, supply, and coordinate their forces around the world.

Whether for good or ill, there was an explosion of scientific and technological advances in this period. Indeed, it was difficult for many to see how this pace could be sustained. In 1899 the head of the U.S. Patent Office asked President William McKinley to abolish the bureau: "Everything that can be invented has been invented."

DEVELOPMENT OF ELECTRICITY AND THE TELEPHONE

DEVELOPMENT OF STEAM-DRIVEN TRANSPORTATION AND THE INTERNAL COMBUSTION ENGINE

ECONOMIC TRENDS

INDUSTRIALIZED NATIONS NEED MARKETS AND RAW MATERIALS, OFTEN FROM ABROAD

By the dawn of the twentieth century the West was in economic control of the planet. Before the eighteenth century, economic systems had been primarily local and regional, but by 1900 the rapid expansion of the Industrial Revolution, coupled with advances in transportation and communication, had created a worldwide economy. The heart of this new global economy lay in western Europe, particularly in Great Britain and Germany, and in the United States. These nations had created a complex of heavy industry in which iron ore, petroleum, and electricity provided power for the production of iron and steel, machinery, chemicals, and textiles. Great Britain had been the world's greatest industrial nation early in the nineteenth century, but by 1900 it was losing its lead to Germany and the United States.

The rise of industry in Western nations had a major impact on other areas of the world. As their industries outgrew local resources and markets, industrialized Western nations pursued a policy of imperialism (see later section), seizing economic control over parts of Latin America, Africa, and Asia in order to ensure a ready supply of raw materials for their factories and to gain secure markets for their surplus goods. The growing power and aggressiveness of the established industrial powers spurred some of the less developed nations such as Russia and Japan to protect themselves by commencing intensive industrialization programs of their own.

WESTERN NATIONS BUILD UP A WORLDWIDE INDUSTRIAL AND AGRICULTURAL NETWORK

Although European investors had built a few textile factories around the globe, overall there was little heavy industry outside Europe, the United States, and Japan. Mineral, fiber, and hide processing was the most common form of manufacturing in the British dominions and in the Latin American nations.

Paralleling their industrial expansion, Westerners had been developing a global network for producing and distributing agricultural products. By 1900 they had organized many areas of the world into large plantations, "agricultural factories" that poured out enormous quantities of foodstuffs. As a result, citizens in western Europe and the United States could sit at their dinner tables and enjoy Honduran bananas, Brazilian coffee, East Indian spices, Cuban sugar, Hawaiian pineapple, Ceylonese tea, and many other products from around the globe.

As the industrial and agricultural factory system spread around the world, people moved—or were forced to move—from continent to continent to provide the labor necessary for economic development. For centuries, Westerners had imported black Africans into the Western Hemisphere to work as slaves on plantations. By 1900 the slave trade had ended, but new human migrations were under way. Millions of Europeans were encouraged to settle in North and South America, Australia, and New Zealand. Chinese and Japanese—many of them contract laborers—went to work on the plantations of Hawaii and the railroads of North America. Indians worked in the mines of eastern and southern Africa and on Caribbean plantations. Many of them later rose in economic and social status in their new homes.

SUEZ AND PANAMA CANALS FACILITATE GLOBAL COMMERCIAL TRAFFIC

An effective worldwide economy would have been impossible without a concurrent revolution in the technology of commercial transportation. Ships of ever-greater capacity and speed, paced by the British merchant marine, hauled raw materials and finished products into every nook and cranny of the globe. Where water traffic was impeded by land formations, engineers constructed the Suez and Panama canals, created canal networks in western Europe and the United States, and built or enlarged harbors all over the world.

On land, the tremendous cargo-hauling capacity of steam-driven engines operating on rails gave an enormous boost to economic development by the early twentieth century. Railroads crisscrossed northwestern Europe, Japan, and much of North America. Elsewhere in the world, however, railroads were much rarer. The cargo-hauling potential of the internal combustion engine used in automobiles remained uncertain because no cheap permanent road surface had yet been developed.

The massive economic development under way around the world was fueled by investment money, and Great Britain was overwhelmingly dominant with London as the center of world finance, setting the standards in investment, banking, and insurance. "Insured by Lloyds of London" was the ultimate guarantee of protection.

SOCIAL AND POLITICAL TRENDS

The rapid transformation of the world economy had brought many social changes by the opening decades of the twentieth century, particularly in the nations of western Europe. These changes were also apparent in the United States and, to a lesser degree, in Latin America and Japan. As the century progressed, some of these social changes spread to other parts of the world.

Population Mobility and Social Classes

One social consequence of the industrialization process was that many people left the countryside to work where the factories were located. Old cities grew rapidly, and new ones appeared. The populations of new urban areas grew so rapidly that the authorities were technologically and psychologically unprepared to deal with the changes. Industrialized nations soon faced a host of problems—poor sanitation and housing, crime, a shortage of schools and hospitals, and many others—in their urban centers.

INDUSTRIALIZATION BRINGS SOCIAL PROBLEMS, ESPECIALLY CRIME

The impact of industrialization and worldwide commercial activity created major changes in the social classes in Western nations. The upper class now comprised an uneasy combination of the traditional titled, landed aristocracy (except in the United States) and a new group of wealthy industrial and commercial entrepreneurs. Whatever their background, the members of the upper class dominated their nations. In Great Britain, 5 percent of the population controlled 75 percent of the earnings from private property. Members of the European hereditary aristocracy still occupied most of the high civil and military posts, but an increasing percentage of the important government posts were also being filled by men with a "common," though often affluent, background. The new rich, although usually products of the work ethic, matched the traditional aristocrats in lifestyles of conspicuous consumption. They built and furnished mansions; consumed huge quantities of expensive food and clothing; bought technological marvels such as automobiles, phonographs, telephones, and radios; patronized the arts; and indulged in expensive travel and recreation.

GROWTH OF PROSPEROUS MIDDLE CLASS

The middle class, while sharply separated from the upper class in income and status, was growing in size, prosperity, and complexity. Traditionally, the middle class had consisted of shopkeepers, skilled artisans, and such white-collar professionals as academics, physicians, and clergymen. By the twentieth century it also included new professionals such as engineers, business managers, and architects. These newcomers were joined by a large mass of less affluent professionals, such as teachers, business clerks, and civil servants. Living in modest comfort, these groups saved money for a better home, for their children's education, and, if not protected by one of the new business or government pension plans, for retirement.

IMPROVEMENT IN WORKING-CLASS CONDITIONS

Perhaps the greatest social change brought about by the changing economy was the improvement in the condition of urban working classes. Mass production and improved agricultural techniques provided cheaper clothing, shoes, and food at the same time that wage increases were outstripping inflation. In western Europe just before World War I, two-thirds of the urban workforce, now rapidly outnumbering the rural labor force, earned wages above the subsistence level. A small minority of skilled workers and foremen enjoyed an income greater than some in the lower middle class. Many workers could afford to add meat, dairy products, and vegetables to a diet that had previously consisted almost entirely of bread and potatoes. Better nutrition and improved health care increased average life expectancy in western Europe from about 40 years in the mid-nineteenth century to about 50 years just before World War I. Increased wages and new laws forbidding child labor (although not in the United States) allowed children to go to school.

Despite improvements for the upper ranks of the working class, however, many problems remained. Housing was cramped and uncomfortable; workplaces usually remained noisy, unhealthy, and dangerous. One-third of urban workers, especially those employed in textiles, mining, hauling, and other relatively unskilled occupations, still eked out a living at a bare subsistence level. In 1900 in the United States, the average workweek was 59 hours at $13 a week. Some were no better off, and some were worse off, than farmers or peasants working on agricultural estates. It was estimated that in 1900 one-third of the inhabitants of New York and London lived in poverty.

INCREASED STATUS OF WOMEN

There were some modest shifts in the status of women. The advent of the typewriter and other office machines opened new opportunities for "respectable" women, especially single women, to work in business offices instead of remaining at home. Others became teachers or nurses. On the other hand, the rise in income for many working-class families allowed some wives to leave factory work and stay home to look after their children and households. The statement "My wife doesn't have to work" became a status symbol for many working-class husbands. Some upper- and middle-class women, particularly in the United States, obtained higher education and entered the professions. Many women wanted political power commensurate with their heightened economic and social status, and increasing numbers of them pushed for the right to vote.

In western and central Europe, two trends were under way in the countryside. First, farmers who already owned substantial land expanded their holdings and mechanized their operations. Along with the nobles on the great estates, many converted from producing grain to raising beef, dairy herds, and vegetables in order to meet the changing consumption patterns of the city dwellers. These farmers were able to maintain a comfortable lifestyle, but their incomes often barely kept pace with inflation. Secondly, at the same time, small farmers often lost their land and joined the mass of farmhands who were struggling to subsist in the countryside. Millions went to work in factories, where they had to make the difficult transition from the episodic work habits of the country to the continuous discipline demanded by the factory work routine. Millions more immigrated to the Western Hemisphere, where some secured farms of their own or worked as farm laborers. Most immigrants, however, stayed in the cities and worked in factories. At the turn of the century, especially in the United States, the flood of immigrants outpaced the growth of industry, and workers faced low wages and poor working conditions.

Outside the industrialized West, social changes came much more slowly. In Japan, and to a much lesser extent in China and India, partial industrialization had enlarged the traditional middle class and created a small class of factory workers. However, most of the people of the world remained workers or peasants living close to subsistence levels.

Competing Political Forces

The struggle between liberals and conservatives was a major source of dissension in the Western world. Conservatives usually came from the more privileged groups in society and supported existing class distinctions, autocratic government, and special economic privileges for the upper classes. They also generally defended institutions that embodied traditional practices and values—the established church, a divine-right monarchy, and a powerful military. Conservatism was still a powerful force in such central and eastern European nations as Germany and Austria-Hungary, and particularly in Russia.

LIBERAL-CONSERVATIVE STRUGGLES IN EUROPE

Liberals tended to come from the rising business and professional classes and wanted to change society so that they would have a secure and powerful place in it. They wanted freedom of speech, press, religion, and assembly; the right, for men with modest amounts of property, to vote and hold office; elected governments responsible to the voters; and commerce free from restrictions. Some who were very liberal wished to allow all adult males, even those without property, the right to vote and hold office. Americans had achieved this for white males by the middle of the nineteenth century. Generally speaking, liberalism had been gaining power in Europe since the French Revolution in 1789, and by 1900 it was a strong force in Great Britain and France, among some groups in Italy, and in some of the small western European nations. By the turn of the century, some liberals, hoping to avoid socialist revolution, advocated such welfare state programs as unemployment compensation and pensions.

Liberal-conservative differences were often contests between people of property, and such battles did not seem particularly relevant to many factory workers. One response of Western workers to their exploitation was to organize into trade unions to force improvements from their employers through collective bargaining, picketing,

URBAN WORKERS TRY TO ORGANIZE

strikes, and boycotts. Trade unionists were not necessarily interested in bringing an end to the capitalist system but instead concentrated on improving their wages and working conditions and on acquiring pensions and other forms of security. Trade unions were opposed by employers and their political allies, but they slowly gained strength, especially in Great Britain, after the turn of the century. Other people concerned with the plight of the workers turned to a more radical approach than trade unionism: the destruction of capitalism through socialism.

MARX PRODUCES INFUENTIAL IDEAS ABOUT ECONOMIC AND SOCIAL ISSUES

Karl Marx, who died in 1883, was one of the world's most important political theorists. The core of Marx's "scientific socialism," which he developed along with his fellow German Friedrich Engels, was the theory of historical or dialectical materialism. This theory proclaimed that such productive forces as technology, material resources, and labor determined economic relationships. According to Marx, these productive forces and economic relationships together made up the foundation of society and in turn determined the "superstructure" of government, laws, religions, and culture that the dominant class in any historical period used to strengthen its position.

Productive forces, Marx declared, had changed in the course of history. Therefore, economic relationships had changed, and, as a result, new classes had emerged to replace the old dominant classes and create new superstructures. However, no ruling class ever surrendered its power peacefully. It had to be overthrown by the rising class associated with the new productive forces; thus, class conflict was inevitable and would continue until the golden era of communism was established. In his own time, Marx believed that he was witnessing in western Europe the overthrow of the feudal landowning class by capitalist merchants and industrialists. Just as inevitably, said Marx, the industrial working class, or "proletariat," would associate itself with still newer productive forces even then evolving out of capitalist society. This working class would clash with the capitalist class and would eventually overthrow it. The working class would then establish a "dictatorship of the proletariat" in order to set up a new socialist system. That dictatorship and all the machinery of government would then wither away, to be followed by an age of equitable social relations, humanized labor, and increased leisure.

By the turn of the century, both trade unionism and Marxism in its various interpretations had numerous followers in the industrial nations. It was clear that both liberals and conservatives faced formidable political opposition. Despite their differences, Marxists and trade unionists influenced each other. Marx had stated that the conditions of workers under capitalism would grow worse and that they would become increasingly radical. On the contrary, salaries and working and living conditions in capitalist countries such as Great Britain and Germany began to improve as capitalist politicians instituted reforms to ward off socialism. Many workers became more interested in continuing such improvements, and perhaps in gaining a share of political power, than in overthrowing capitalism through revolution.

SOCIALIST PARTIES EMERGE

Before World War I, responding to the moderate outlook of most workers, many socialists in Europe and in the United States had decided to replace capitalism through the political party system rather than pursue violent revolution. In nations that allowed a popular vote, Marxist parties such as the German Social Democratic Party

Karl Marx, founder of one of the most influential modern ideologies.

increased rapidly in size. In the United States, the presidential candidate of the Socialist Party, Eugene Debs, twice received nearly a million votes.

As some socialist parties became less revolutionary, two other movements, anarchism and syndicalism, became more prominent. Anarchists believed that governments exploited people on behalf of the wealthier classes, and so they wished to destroy all governments and to reconstruct the social order without them. From 1894 to 1912 anarchists assassinated a president of France and one of the United States, two Spanish premiers, the king of Italy, and the empress of Austria. Syndicalists believed that a trade union–led general strike would paralyze society and destroy its government, after which the unions would be the basic organizing structures of society. The movement developed in France but influenced workers and radicals elsewhere. In the United States, the largest group that reflected syndicalist ideas was the Industrial Workers of the World (the "Wobblies").

Liberalism, conservatism, socialism, and other political movements also had some impact outside the West. At the start of the twentieth century, liberalism was already strong among Western-educated Indians, some of whom founded the Indian National Congress in 1885. At about the same time, some Japanese, influenced by Western ideas, advocated adopting a constitution, which was finally granted in 1889. Although Marxism eventually proved to be a potent influence among non-Westerners, it was a negligible force before World War I. A major example of Western influence in Asia was Sun Yat-sen, who overthrew the old regime in China in

WESTERN POLITICAL IDEAS INFLUENTIAL OUTSIDE THE WEST

1911 and attempted to replace it with one founded on democratic, liberal, and moderate socialist principles.

Although Western political ideas gained some ground in non-Western areas, most traditional leaders sought to perpetuate the old customs and cultures of their societies and often used religion as a powerful force to prevent or limit Westernization. Because these traditional leaders sought to maintain the status quo, they bore some resemblance to European conservatives.

Nationalism

MANY FORMS OF NATIONALISM APPEAR

Nationalism was another political force at work at the turn of the century. Concentrated in the West and in Japan in 1900, it spread around the world during the twentieth century. Nationalism is a learned emotional loyalty that individuals direct toward a group with which they perceive common bonds. It gives individuals a sense of membership and belonging. Nationalism is nurtured by a number of common bonds—language, religion, social and institutional traditions, territory, and history. The most recurrent basis for nationalism in recent times has been loyalty to one's ethnic group; however, it is not necessary for a national group to share all the bonds mentioned. Switzerland, for example, has a long national history, but it comprises several major language groups.

A common history is an important ingredient in nationalism. National groups and states glorify their past and sometimes create or rediscover a past history if one is lacking. For example, Germans sought to overcome regional, political, and religious differences by emphasizing triumphs in their distant tribal past. Nationalistic Indians, chafing under British rule, rediscovered Asoka, an emperor of the third century B.C.E., under whom the subcontinent was unified and made powerful. His insignia, the wheel and the lion, became the symbols of the newly independent state of India in 1947. After the 1910 revolution, Mexicans of predominantly Amerindian extraction stressed their Aztec and Mayan past rather than their Spanish heritage.

In nationalism, the nation itself is often glorified. Nationalists evoked old, even primitive, feelings based on myths that nations are eternal. As the Italian writer Joseph Mazzini expressed it, "Our country is our Home, the house that God has given us. In laboring for our own country, on the right principle, we labor for humanity."

NATIONALISM AS A UNIFYING FORCE

By 1900 nationalism as a unifying force was well established in western Europe and the United States. Leaders in these areas, where literacy was high, used the printed word and the educational system to indoctrinate individuals into supporting their government as the paramount symbol of their nation. Because of the heterogeneous population of the United States, nationalism in that country was a complex and contradictory phenomenon. There was the traditional doctrine of an ethnic and religious "melting pot" whose citizens gave primary allegiance to the concepts of economic opportunity and political democracy. This doctrine was counterbalanced, however, by a cultural tradition that reflected the values and prejudices of the politically and economically powerful persons descended from the ethnic groups of northern Europe.

In Europe the dramatic unifications of Germany and Italy in the 1860s and 1870s demonstrated the power of ethnic nationalism. Many Germans, however, considered their unification incomplete because millions of Germans still lived outside the boundaries of the new Germany. Demands by ultranationalistic Germans for *Anschluss* (union) of all Germans into a single state disrupted the history of Europe well into the twentieth century.

In many areas, nationalism was a divisive rather than a unifying force because it sometimes inspired a dominant group to persecute minorities within a nation. These actions were often based on ethnic antagonism, economic jealousy, and religious hatred. Pogroms (government-instigated mob attacks) in Russia against the Jews and Turkish suppression of the Armenians are examples of such persecutions at the beginning of the twentieth century.

NATIONALISM AS A DIVISIVE FORCE

Nationalistic sentiments were also divisive in another way. In some countries, certain populations that were under the dominance of other groups aspired to break away from that control, either to form their own independent nations or to join a neighboring nation governed by their kindred. Austria-Hungary and the Ottoman Empire, in particular, were torn by nationalistic dissension because these states governed a host of ethnic minority groups that were becoming increasingly nationalistic. The Austro-Hungarian Empire was largely held together by loyalty to the monarchy and the Catholic Church. When the dominant Germans and Magyars (Hungarians) began to stress that the empire was primarily a German one or a Magyar one, the Slavs and other minority ethnic groups within the empire responded by pushing for their own national states. The tensions and hatreds of nationalism made the Balkans the "Tinderbox of Europe." In the Ottoman Empire, which had been held together by a common belief in Islam, religious bonds were no longer sufficient; Arabs and Kurds, though Muslims, sought their own national independence from a state dominated by the Turks. Such local nationalisms and ethnic prejudices contributed to the collapse of both of these formerly great empires.

In the early part of the twentieth century, Western doctrines that asserted the inherent superiority of the so-called Aryan group and of Aryan nations and stressed the inferiority of other groups—Jews, Slavs, Gypsies—flourished. This was the clearest example of the use of racial myths to foster nationalism.

By 1900 nationalism in its different forms was also taking hold in Asia. The Japanese justified their aggressiveness in Asia by asserting that they were a superior race. A small Indian elite, influenced by the West, worked to throw off British rule by attempting to instill the concept of a united India into a population divided by ethnicity, language, and religion. In China another Western-influenced elite worked to rally the Chinese on two nationalistic crusades simultaneously. They channeled Chinese resentment of the ruling Manchu minority into plots to overthrow the Manchu dynasty and at the same time tried to rally all ethnic groups in China to resist Western and Japanese imperialism.

NATIONALISM SPREADS OUTSIDE THE WEST

INTERNATIONAL RELATIONS

At the beginning of the twentieth century, international relations around the world were poisoned by tensions emanating from a number of sources. New levels of nationalistic pride spilled over into international affairs, heightening existing fears and hostilities inherited from the past. Often, nationalism manifested itself in general feelings of national or racial superiority; the British referred to non-Westerners as "Wogs," to the French as "Frogs," and to the Germans as "Huns." Nations fought one another over territory and power while accusing their opponents of having a vicious character and a history of wrongdoing. "The policy of the German Empire . . . has always been one of undisguised blackmail," asserted a British official in 1899. Imperialist competition for the control of territories around the world added more fuel to the flames, driving nations to search for security in arms races, alliances, and plans for war.

Imperialism

A CHANGING CAST OF IMPERIALIST NATIONS

Imperialism, the process by which a small number of industrial nations extended their economic and political control over much of the rest of the world, was the main driving force in international relations at the turn of the century. As one of Great Britain's leading imperialists put it, "The day of small nations has passed away; the day of empires has come." Actually, the process was not new; from the fifteenth through the eighteenth century, searching for foods, fibers, and precious metals, Europeans had taken control of the entire Western Hemisphere, Australasia, large sections of Asia, and a few spots in Africa. Thereafter, although imperialist conquests never entirely ceased, they proceeded at a somewhat slower pace before imperialism intensified dramatically in the last third of the nineteenth century. The cast of imperialist nations changed. Spain, Portugal, and the Netherlands, three stalwarts of an earlier era, were no longer very active. However, three other traditional imperial powers, Great Britain, France, and Russia, were fully involved in the new era. They were now joined by Belgium, Germany, Italy, the United States, and Japan.

There were many reasons for the resurgence of imperialism, economic considerations being one of the most important. With new economic forces at work, Western and Japanese industrialists continually searched for new markets, cheap labor, industrial raw materials, agricultural products, and places for investment. Complex patterns of economic interdependence often developed. For example, British textile manufacturers encouraged the planting of cotton in India and Egypt, both crucial parts of the vast British Empire. Cheap local labor grew and harvested the cotton, which was shipped to Great Britain to be manufactured into cloth. Cotton cloth was then made into shirts and other articles of clothing that were in turn sold back to the laborers in India and Egypt. In such a fashion, industrialists not only enjoyed cheap labor and raw materials but also profited from new markets for their manufactured goods.

Imperialism was also fueled by nationalism, which engendered in many countries a relentless urge to compete with other nations to become the most powerful in the world. Frequently, special interest groups or such lobbyists as explorers and adventurers encouraged national governments to extend their influence.

Strategic imperialism, a concern for control of key waterways, ports, and military outposts, was another important factor leading nations to take over distant territories. The British government, for example, used a powerful navy operating out of strategically located bases to protect its international trade routes. The Suez Canal and the surrounding Middle Eastern territory, in particular, were viewed as crucial for controlling the lifeline to India and East Asia. The British took over Singapore, Aden, and other territories as bases to protect this vital trade route.

One complex aspect of imperialism, part motive, part rationalization, part result, has been termed *cultural imperialism.* On the basis of the alleged natural superiority of the white race, Westerners argued that it was the white man's burden to bring the benefits of "superior" Western civilization—its technology, its religion, its institutions—to the "inferior" nonwhites of the world living in "darkness and ignorance." The virulently imperialistic Kaiser Wilhelm II of Germany proclaimed, "God has called us to civilize the world. We are missionaries of human progress." A U.S. senator put it in a more folksy way: "We will lift Shanghai up and up, ever up, until it is just like Kansas City." Some Westerners went even further, arguing that nonwhites had few cultural or historical achievements to their credit and could never reach the cultural, political, or technical heights that the predominantly white societies of the West had attained.

Social Darwinists such as Herbert Spencer argued that biological evolution, which involved competition, elimination of the weak, and survival of the fittest, should be applied to competition among cultures, nations, and peoples. They argued that it was right or "natural" for "strong, superior cultures" to control or even to eliminate "weaker, inferior cultures"; thus, after France conquered Algeria, it attempted to eradicate local traditions, language, and religion. When the Algerians fought against the destruction of their society, the French responded that there was no such thing as an Algerian nation and that they were bringing the benefits of the superior French civilization to wandering, ignorant tribes.

Christian missionary zeal was another manifestation of cultural imperialism. It was often said that the flag followed the cross. Missionaries from Europe and the United States sought to spread Christianity in Africa and Asia, as they had earlier in Latin America. Often these missionaries and their converts became embroiled in misunderstandings and quarrels with adherents of the local culture. Imperial powers would then send military forces into the local area to protect the missionaries. In China, when a French missionary was killed by Chinese in the 1850s, Napoleon III seized on this incident to wage war against China and, as a result of France's victories, gained concessions.

For cultural, religious, and racial reasons, many imperialists believed that the West's domination over the globe would go on forever. Western nations attempted to re-create their empires in their own images. Entire societies in Africa, Asia, and Latin America were modified and, in some cases, totally destroyed. In virtually all instances of imperial domination, the conquered people were changed. In many instances, they tried, but failed, to overthrow outside control and to recapture control over their own destinies. On the other hand, Western encroachments and cultural claims gave impetus to Asians and others to reexamine their traditional values and to propose reforms.

Sometimes, imperialist competition led Western rivals to the brink of war. One dangerous situation in 1898 in Africa is a prime example. The British were interested in building a colonial empire, and perhaps a transcontinental railroad, that would extend from South Africa north to Egypt, from "Cape to Cairo." Equally enthusiastic French imperialists dreamed of a transcontinental empire extending from western

CULTURAL IMPERIALISM

BELIEF IN THE SURVIVAL OF THE FITTEST AMONG NATIONS

IMPERIALISM BRINGS THREATS OF WAR

BIOGRAPHY

The Outlook of a Young Imperialist

It did seem such a pity that . . . the age of wars between civilized nations had come to an end forever. If it had only been 100 years earlier what splendid times we should have had! Fancy being nineteen in 1793 with more than twenty years of war against Napoleon in front of one! However, all that was finished. The British Army had never fired on white troops since the Crimea, and now that the world was growing so sensible and pacific—and so democratic too—the great days were over. Luckily, however, there were. . . . Zulus and Afghans, also the [Mahdi's followers in] the Sudan. Some of these might, if they were well-disposed, "put up a show" some day. There might even be . . . a revolt in India. . . . These thoughts were only partially consoling, for

. . . fighting the poor Indians [was no comparison to taking part in a real European war.]*

. . .

Here Winston Churchill, a member of one of the great ruling families of Great Britain, recalls his outlook when he was a cavalry cadet in the 1890s. The confidence in Western superiority over non-Western peoples that young Winston displayed here reflects the attitude of cultural imperialism that typified the era before World War I. Churchill retained his imperialist attitudes throughout his career and resisted the dissolution of the British Empire after World War II.

*From *My Early Life: A Roving Commission* by Winston Churchill. Copyright 1930 Charles Scribner's Sons; copyright renewed ©1958 Winston Churchill. Reprinted by permission of Charles Scribner's Sons, an imprint of Macmillan Publishing Company.

Africa to the east coast. This rivalry brought about a confrontation in 1898 at the Sudanese village of Fashoda. The Fashoda crisis was an outstanding example of extreme nationalism, or jingoism, a term deriving from a British beer hall song of the day: "We don't want to fight, / But by Jingo! if we do / We've got the ships, / We've got the men / And got the money, too!" Goaded by articles in the new mass media of journals and newspapers, people in France and Great Britain rushed thoughtlessly to support their nations—"my country, right or wrong." Neither the French nor the British gave a thought to the Sudanese in the conflict. Only the intercession of more moderate diplomats, and second thoughts by the French, averted open warfare between Great Britain and France in 1898.

IMPERIALIST PROBLEMS USUALLY SETTLED BY DIPLOMACY

On a few occasions, imperialists went to war with one another to further their interests, but in most cases nations settled their rivalries peacefully. For example, Japan and Russia fought over Korea and Manchuria, and the British battled Dutch settlers in South Africa. For the most part, however, the imperialists preferred to hammer out diplomatic agreements in which territories were parceled out as in some gigantic Monopoly game. For example, 14 nations met at the Berlin Colonial Conference of 1885 to decide the fate of the Congo in Africa. No Congolese were included, and the European nations decided the fate of one of Africa's largest areas without ever asking the people of that region what they wanted.

Although major powers generally had not gone to war over imperialist claims, a number of them continued to nurse grievances. Japan, Germany, Russia, and Italy, in particular, believed they did not have their fair share of possessions and looked for ways to increase their global holdings. Other nations, such as Great Britain, France, and the United States, were essentially satisfied with the territories they had annexed and the areas of indirect economic control they had accumulated.

Arms Races, Militarism, and Alliances

In a period filled with nationalistic and imperialistic tensions, the major nations moved to strengthen their security. They stockpiled the new weapons of the era, built up the size of their military establishments, and made alliances. In the nineteenth century, Prussia had led the military buildup, creating a mass army of short-term conscripts. Men were drafted, trained, and then sent home to their civilian occupations. This procedure created a large reserve of trained men that could be called up to form a formidable army at the outbreak of war. Prussia also set up a general staff organization charged with planning and conducting future wars. In 1870 Prussia's large army of conscripts and reservists, well trained, equipped, and led, defeated France's smaller army of long-term professional soldiers. Learning from its defeat, France switched to the Prussian system and built up its own mass army. Such a system required huge amounts of money and disrupted the civilian occupations of a large percentage of a nation's population.

NATIONALIST FEARS
LEAD TO BUILDUP OF
MASS ARMIES

To protect itself from Western imperialism, Japan built up a Western-style military machine and demonstrated its strength by winning wars against China in 1895 and Russia in 1905. It won more praise from the West for these victories than for any other aspect of its modernization and gained equality in international affairs. Seeing that a strong military brought results, Japan steered an increasingly militaristic and imperialistic course. On the other hand, Great Britain and the United States, protected by the sea, regarded large standing armies as possible threats to representative government and thus maintained relatively small armies. By 1914, however, both nations were building up reserves and both had created general staffs.

The buildup in armies was matched by a naval arms race. Until the 1880s, the naval situation had been relatively stable. The British navy led in both size and quality. The French navy was a distant second, and France was not disposed to challenge Great Britain. Germany, however, began a naval building program in the 1890s, and the United States and Japan followed with more modest efforts. Both Germany and the United States were rapidly developing interests around the world and needed substantial navies to protect their supply lines. Japan also sought to protect its regional interests with a strong navy. Great Britain feared that the German naval building program was intended not only to protect German interests outside Europe but also to threaten Great Britain itself. As a consequence, the British launched a determined effort to keep well ahead of Germany. This naval race was enormously expensive and created a further strain on the economies of both nations.

The arms race, begun as a defensive measure, only created more tension and fear and led national leaders to the conclusion that if war should break out, the best protection would be to take the military offensive. Basing their calculations on the Austro-Prussian and Franco-Prussian Wars of 1866 and 1870, European military planners believed that the next war would be a short one of open maneuver, although

A symbol of the arms race: In 1906, the new British battleship *Dreadnought* made other battleships obsolete and spurred expensive naval building programs in several major nations.

the Civil War in the United States and recent wars in the Balkans suggested that the next war might be a long one of trenches and attrition.

The buildup of armies and navies was accompanied by the rise of militarism, the concept that military aspects of a society are the most important. The German general Friedrich von Bernhardi, reflecting the influence of Charles Darwin, wrote that war was a biological necessity, a law of nature. Darwin's ideas led the Russian writer Leo Tolstoy to lament in 1906 that science "has decided that the struggle and enmity of all against all is a necessary, unavoidable, and beneficent condition of human life." Friedrich Nietzsche wrote, "You say it is the good cause that hallows even war? I say unto you: it is the war that hallows any cause. War and courage have accomplished more great things than love of the neighbor."

RISE OF MILITARISTIC DOCTRINES

Advocates of militarism stressed that war was good because it developed the qualities of loyalty, cooperation, courage, and sacrifice that were important for the development of humanity. President Theodore Roosevelt and Kaiser Wilhelm II agreed on the bracing effect of war on a nation's population. Roosevelt said, "No triumph of peace is quite as great as the sublime triumphs of war." Japanese patriotic writings glorified both war and the warrior. This Japanese attitude owed much to the sense of solidarity and sacrifice among the samurai (the former hereditary warrior class). A code of conduct called *Bushido* (Way of the Warrior) governed samurai behavior. It taught service, loyalty, and willingness to die for nation and cause. Japanese leaders relied on the traditional respect accorded to samurai superiors to inculcate the same values in the ordinary citizen.

In addition to building up their military forces, European countries sought to obtain security in alliances or in a balance of power between blocs of nations. Long before 1900, European nations had made it a leading principle of diplomacy to balance their economic, military, and strategic power against competing nations so that a rival nation would not have a clear-cut advantage and use that advantage to attack. Often, a major power, unsure of having parity with a competitor, sought to create a balance by forming a partnership with a third nation. Great Britain, for example, traditionally maintained a balance of power by formulating understandings with other nations based on economic relationships.

ALLIANCE SYSTEMS

Other nations, such as the European rivals France and Germany, believed their security lay in constructing formal military alliances. Both nations built up an alliance system that was designed to deter their enemy from attacking. If war did break out, the alliance would add to their military power.

Occasionally, smaller nations used the concept of balance of power to protect themselves from more powerful ones. For many decades the Ottoman Empire, called the Sick Man of Europe, prevented Russia and others from taking its territory by playing off the competitors against each other. Thus, while Russia envisioned carting the Sick Man off to the undertaker, the British, fearing that a Russian defeat of the Ottoman Empire would upset the balance of power in the eastern Mediterranean region, wanted to keep the patient alive. The Ottomans were thereby able to retain vast amounts of territory that otherwise would have been lost to more powerful nations. Likewise, China resorted to a strategy of "using barbarians to control barbarians" in an attempt to play off the Western nations against one another and against Japan. Thailand remained independent because it served as a buffer state between British Burma and French Indochina. Similarly, Ethiopian emperors preserved their sovereignty by propagating the idea that if one European nation controlled Ethiopia, the balance of power in Africa would be destroyed.

The balance-of-power idea was also used in a global context. Great Britain, fearing growing German strength in East Asia, concluded a rare formal peacetime alliance with Japan in 1902. Leaving Japan to watch the Germans in East Asia, Great Britain concentrated its forces to meet opponents elsewhere in the world—for example, confronting Russia in Persia (present-day Iran).

BALANCE-OF-POWER DIPLOMACY TAKES DIFFERENT FORMS

At times, the attempt to achieve a balance of power fomented war rather than sustaining peace. Nations were not content to maintain the balance of power in all its various aspects—military, economic, and diplomatic; they also struggled to shift that balance in their own favor. Consequently, the balance-of-power concept became a source of ever-spiraling economic and military competition and, eventually, war.

Alliances, in theory constructed to deter war, in practice threatened to cause wars that otherwise might not have occurred. Nations backed by allies sometimes acted more aggressively than they would have alone. In some situations, such as in the summer of 1914, European nations in the German- and French-dominated alliance systems urged their allies to refuse compromises, thus creating an explosive situation.

PEACE ORGANIZATIONS SPRING UP TO COUNTER MILITARISM

In reaction to the atmosphere of nationalistic tensions pointing toward war, many people became interested in fostering a spirit of international cooperation to preserve the peace. In 1899 and 1907 delegates met at international peace conferences at the Hague in the Netherlands, where they worked on disarmament propositions and international arbitration techniques and established the Hague Tribunal for the arbitration of disputes. The presence of the tribunal induced a number of nations to settle their disputes through arbitration. The peace movement also benefited from the participation of prominent individuals. Alfred Nobel, the inventor of dynamite, instituted the Nobel Prize for Peace, among others. The iron and steel magnate Andrew Carnegie, whose steel helped to build the Great White Fleet, set up the Carnegie Endowment for International Peace and also built the Peace Palace at the Hague. Compared to the onrush of nationalistic hostilities, however, the international peace movement was feeble; the Hague Tribunal was given only insignificant cases such as technical boundary questions. Meanwhile, the major nations continued to put their energy and money into building up their war machines.

CULTURAL TRENDS

In the West, many significant new forms of expression developed in religion, literature, and the arts. Non-Western cultures were also modified by contacts with the West. Non-Western cultures had some impact in the West as well, but not nearly to the same degree.

SECULAR AND RELIGIOUS VALUES IN CONFLICT

The West before World War I witnessed a continual conflict between secularism and traditional religions. In Europe and the United States, secularists (people who wanted to limit the role of churches and their teachings in society) strongly challenged the privileged position of the established churches. Scientific and technological changes and urbanization disrupted traditional living patterns, which in turn affected religious customs and beliefs. Despite their differences, the ideas of Darwin, Marx, Nietzsche, and Freud all challenged, in whole or in part, long-standing religious beliefs.

Within Judaism and Christianity, some individuals tried to reconcile their religious beliefs with some of the new influences and ideas. Reform Judaism and liberal Protestantism were two such responses, but Orthodox Jews and Protestant fundamentalists were much less ready for compromise. The Catholic and Orthodox Churches also were usually not enthusiastic about modern ideas.

ARTISTS AND THINKERS DISAGREE AMONG THEMSELVES ABOUT HOW TO DEPICT REALITY

Another conflict in Western culture concerned differences among Western thinkers and artists about how to view and depict the world around and inside them. In the decades immediately before 1914 many began to question the dominance of an objective, scientific, and strictly rational approach to reality. Einstein's theory of relativity seemed to deny certainty in science. The French philosopher Henri Bergson emphasized intuition rather than reason, and Freud, preceded by Nietzsche, stressed the role of unconscious, nonrational motivation. Writers and artists increasingly questioned the realistic modes of artistic expression that had been dominant since the mid-nineteenth century and that tended to depend on an objective, scientific approach.

Picasso's *Young Ladies of Avignon* (1907) reflects the movement away from realistic representational art; it also shows the influence of primitive art on Picasso.

Modern art, music, and literature came out of this questioning and out of new ways of seeing and portraying the external world and the reality within oneself. Modern art embraced a range of expression, from the postimpressionist paintings of Paul Cézanne, Vincent van Gogh, Paul Gauguin, and Georges Seurat to the Fauvism of Henri Matisse, the cubism of Pablo Picasso, and the abstractionism of Wassily Kandinsky. In music, Arnold Schoenberg was the most significant innovator. Between 1906 and 1909, he developed what came to be called atonal music, a step that led the artist Kandinsky to write that Schoenberg had "discovered mines of new beauty in his search for spiritual structure." In literature, the symbolist poets of France and Russia, such as Stéphane Mallarmé and Alexander Blok, were among the most notable challengers of literary realism and naturalism. By using words as symbols, they attempted to suggest a more meaningful, mysterious, and hidden reality.

In addition to changes inside Western culture, another noteworthy trend was that non-Westerners sometimes altered their values after contacts with the West. The major religions and philosophies of Africa and Asia, such as Islam, Confucianism, Buddhism, and Hinduism, were confronted by Christianity, secularism, and other aspects of Western culture. Although some local religions were destroyed or transformed, in general the major world faiths were little affected before 1914. In India, Hindu reformers attempted to reconcile traditional teachings with modern science and with the concept of the equality of all human beings. Some Chinese scholars attempted a reinterpretation of Confucianism to accord with democratic ideals. In both instances, however, such attempts were rejected by the orthodox majority.

Although the influence of Western culture on the non-Western world was certainly greater than the reverse, there were also some notable non-Western influences on Western artists, writers, and thinkers. As a result of imperialistic expansion, Westerners became increasingly interested in foreign cultures. The publication of the first two volumes of Sir James Frazer's *The Golden Bough* in 1890 opened the world of "primitive" societies to many, including Freud and others, who eventually made use of Frazer's material in formulating some of their psychological theories. Some modern Western artists who rejected traditional Western perspectives were influenced by Japanese, South Pacific, and African art. Paul Gauguin, for example, went to Tahiti in 1891 and was influenced by its art. Vincent van Gogh was much indebted to Japanese woodblock prints. Picasso was studying African art when, along with Georges Braque, he founded Cubism in 1907–1908. By the mid-nineteenth century, religious ideas of India had already begun to influence such Western thinkers as the German philosopher Arthur Schopenhauer and the American writer Ralph Waldo Emerson. In 1912, the famous Irish poet William Butler Yeats called attention to the poetic writings of the Indian religious thinker and writer Rabindranath Tagore, who the following year would become the first non-European writer to win the Nobel Prize for Literature. Commenting on Tagore's writings, Yeats noted, "They stirred my blood as nothing has for years."

SUGGESTED   SOURCES

Betteman, Otto L. *The Good Old Days—They Were Terrible!* 1974. The founder of the Betteman Archive of picture libraries illustrates with excellent pictures why he thinks the "good old days" in the United States before 1900 were not so good.*

Churchill, Winston S. *My Early Life: A Roving Commission.* 1930. A recounting of Churchill's youthful experiences as a soldier and correspondent at home and abroad; gives insights into the British aristocracy and imperialism.* (also a film, *Young Winston.*)

Conrad, Joseph. *The Secret Agent.* 1907. A novel by one of Britain's great writers that deals with terrorists.*

Elon, Amos. *The Pity of It All: A Portrait of Jews in Germany 1743–1933.* 2004. Perceptive discussion of changing societal roles of Jews in Germany and elsewhere in Europe during the first part of the twentieth century.*

Hobsbawn, Eric. *Nations and Nationalism since 1780: Programme, Myth, Reality.* 2nd ed. 1992. A panoramic coverage of a complex and powerful force in history.

Kern, Stephen. *The Culture of Time and Space, 1880–1918.* New ed. 2003. Kern offers interesting reflections on the momentous changes in technology and culture in this era.*

Ledger, Sally, and Roger Luckhurst, eds. *The Fin de Siècle: A Reader in Cultural History, c. 1880–1900.* 2001. Includes sections titled "Degeneration," "Outcast London," "The Metropolis," "The New Woman," "Literary Debates," "The New Imperialism," "Socialism," "Anarchism," "Scientific Naturalism," "Psychology," "Psychical Research," "Sexology," and "Anthropology and Racial Science," primarily, though not exclusivly, from British sources.

Massie, Robert K. *Dreadnought: Britain, Germany, and the Coming of the Great War.* 1992. An engrossing study of a fatal rivalry.*

Mosse, George L. *The Culture of Western Europe.* 3rd ed. 1988. Standard cultural history, with analysis of links between romanticism and nationalism.*

1900 House. A four-hour PBS video of a 1999 English family spending several months in a Victorian house in London that has been restored to 1900 condition, including all the furnishings and appliances. The family attempts to duplicate the lifestyle of a middle-class 1900 family. (A companion book of the same title is also available.)

Palmer, Alan. *The Penguin Dictionary of Twentieth-Century History.* 5th ed. 1999. A useful and readable resource.

Ruis (Eduardo del Rio). *Marx for Beginners.* 1979. A humorous but sophisticated explanation of Marx by means of cartoons.*

Taylor, Edmund. *The Fall of the Dynasties: The Collapse of the Old Order, 1905–1922.* 1963. A comprehensive survey of one of history's great upheavals.

Toer, Pramoedya Ananta. *The Earth of Mankind.* 1990. This historical novel by a leading Indonesian writer, set in the Dutch East Indies around 1900, offers interesting insights into colonial rule and the reactions to it by the main character.*

Tuchman, Barbara W. *The Proud Tower.* 1972. A detailed and well-written look at politicians, anarchists, socialists, imperialists, nationalists, militarists, and leading figures in the arts in Europe and the United States from 1890 to 1914.*

Ward, Barbara. *Five Ideas That Change the World.* 1984. A survey of five important ideologies that have had and continue to have a significant impact.*

Ware, Caroline F., K. M. Panikkar, and J. M. Romein, eds. *History of Mankind: Cultural and Scientific Development.* Vol. 6, *The Twentieth Century.* 1966. A comprehensive overview of twentieth-century trends.

Watson, Peter. *The Modern Mind: An Intellectual History of the 20th Century.* 2001. Pt. 1. A wide-ranging treatment that deals not only with philosophers but also with writers, artists, scientists, social thinkers, theologians, and others.

WEB SOURCES

www.fordham.edu/halsall/mod/modsbook17.html. Excellent Fordham University source on nationalism's development during the nineteenth century; provides numerous links to other sources.

www.fordham.edu/halsall/mod/modsbook34.html. Excellent source on imperialism, primarily in the nineteenth and early twentieth century; provides numerous links to other sources.

www.marxists.org/archive/marx/index.htm. The Marx & Engels Internet Archive with links to their many writings and materials about them.

www.fordham.edu/halsall/mod/hs1000.html. This site provides excellent links to materials by or about Darwin, Freud, Einstein, Nietzsche, and modern art.

*Paperback available.

⑥The Great Powers of Europe

The history of the period before World War I can be best understood by examining the characteristics of the powerful European nations that dominated much of the globe. Although each of these nations had its unique historical experiences, strengths, and weaknesses, each was also heavily influenced by the major trends of urbanization, nationalism, militarism, and secularism discussed in the previous chapters. A brief description of European nations will begin with the more democratic nations in western Europe, then move eastward to focus on the more autocratic nations.

GREAT BRITAIN

In 1900 Great Britain was considered one of the most liberal and prosperous nations in the world. The British people enjoyed the benefits of a highly industrialized economy fed by raw materials shipped in from a huge colonial empire. The empire also supplied many vital foodstuffs, for Great Britain's large urban population needed much more food than the farmers of the small island nation could provide. Britain's widespread economic prosperity led both old landed aristocrats and new industrialists to agree that it was the "best of all possible worlds."

POLITICAL REFORMS AND WOMEN'S RIGHTS

Political life in Great Britain, a constitutional monarchy, was characterized by growing tendencies toward social reform and liberalism. Reform bills in the 1860s and 1880s had created virtually universal adult male suffrage. The Parliament Bill of 1911 in effect gave the House of Commons, the elected chamber of the British Parliament, control over the government budget. It also somewhat diminished the "gentlemen's club" atmosphere that had previously pervaded the Parliament. Before World War I, Emmeline Pankhurst, her two daughters, and many other women organized a suffragist movement to demand voting rights for women. Pankhurst adopted effective but controversial militant tactics such as processions to the Houses of Parliament, window smashing, and bombs in letter boxes to draw attention to the issue of women's rights. When they were arrested and jailed, the women suffragists went on hunger strikes. Prison authorities retaliated by brutally force-feeding the women. Then the British government adopted a cat-and-mouse strategy whereby the women were released from prison when their health was threatened by the hunger strikes and then rearrested when they had recovered. The war delayed the full franchise for women, which was not secured in Great Britain until 1928 (see Chapter 11).

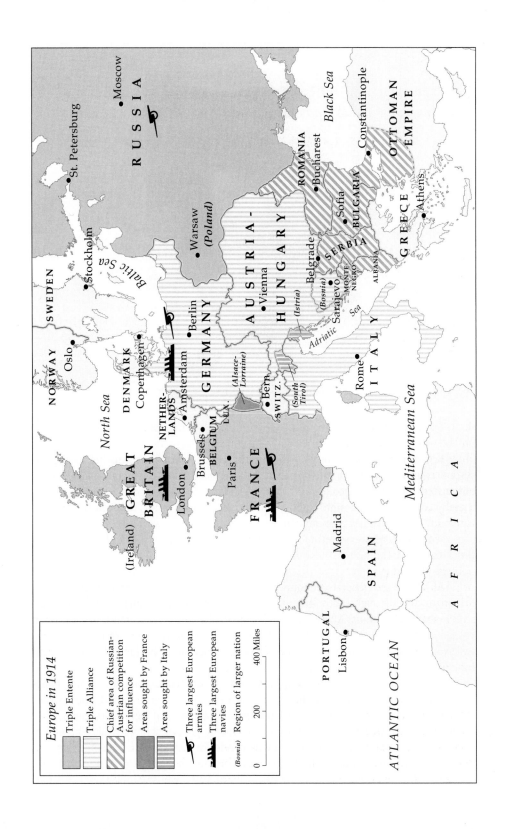

Europe in 1914

Triple Entente

Triple Alliance

Chief area of Russian-
Austrian competition
for influence

Area sought by France

Area sought by Italy

Three largest European
armies

Three largest European
navies

(Bosnia) Region of larger nation

0   200   400 Miles

NORWAY
Oslo
SWEDEN
Stockholm
St. Petersburg
RUSSIA
Moscow
Baltic Sea
North Sea
DENMARK
Copenhagen
Warsaw
(Poland)
Black Sea
GREAT
BRITAIN
(Ireland)
London
NETHER-
LANDS
Amsterdam
Brussels
BELGIUM
Berlin
GERMANY
AUSTRIA-
HUNGARY
Vienna
ROMANIA
Bucharest
Constantinople
OTTOMAN
EMPIRE
LUX.
*(Alsace-
Lorraine)*
Paris
FRANCE
Bern
SWITZ.
*(South
Tirol)*
Belgrade
(Bosnia)
Sarajevo
SERBIA
MONTE-
NEGRO
Sofia
BULGARIA
ALBANIA
GREECE
Athens
Adriatic
Sea
(Istria)
ITALY
Rome
Mediterranean Sea
AFRICA
SPAIN
Madrid
PORTUGAL
Lisbon
ATLANTIC OCEAN

33

Three London policemen arrest a suffragist
outside Buckingham Palace, 1914.

TWO-PARTY SYSTEM

British politics developed in a two-party context, in contrast to the multiparty system common in France and many other European nations. The two-party system eliminated the necessity of forming party coalitions to gain a governing majority. It thereby contributed to a more stable political system. As a result, the British were able to modify many of their economic and political institutions without bloody and divisive revolutions. However, ethnic separatist movements in Wales and Scotland and the struggle for "home rule" in Ireland placed continued demands on the centralized political structures.

Although the general economy was prosperous, the industrialization of Great Britain during the eighteenth and nineteenth centuries had brought with it oppressive working conditions. Many remained so poor that the poet Alfred Lord Tennyson could write, "White chalk and alum and plaster are sold to the poor for bread." Workers lived in small, dark, and unheated houses. In London, working-class apartment buildings did not have private indoor plumbing until years after World War I.

WORKERS STRUGGLE TO UNIONIZE

Workers demanded better pay, improved working conditions, and fringe benefits. In contrast, industrialists believed in a laissez-faire system in which the government kept a hands-off policy toward business, a system that permitted them to do precisely as they wished. Relatively unhampered by government controls, the industrialists tenaciously fought labor union demands for better working conditions. In spite of the owners' opposition, however, labor unions steadily gained power and influence. Workers rallied around the new Labour Party, whose rapid growth demonstrated the rising political power of workers and their supporters and threatened to displace the Liberals, one of the traditional gentry-dominated political parties. Labour politicians and their political friends in Parliament created legislation that limited monopolies, assisted the unemployed, and improved working conditions. They also made similar reforms in the fields of education and social welfare.

Beyond the British Isles, as a popular saying went, "The sun never sets on the British Empire." By 1900 Great Britain had amassed the largest collection of overseas possessions in the world. In Africa, Great Britain dominated Egypt, the vital Suez Canal, and the Sudan; it also held Nigeria and other territories in western Africa. In eastern and southern Africa, Great Britain had taken control of Kenya, Uganda, the Rhodesias, and South Africa. In Asia, it held Hong Kong, other concessions on the China coast, the Malay Peninsula, Burma, Ceylon, key areas along the Persian Gulf, and above all India, the "Jewel in the Crown." Halfway around the world, Great Britain had created two new "Britains" in Australia and New Zealand, almost completely displacing the indigenous populations and populating the areas with settlers from the British Isles and Europe. Through its control of Canada, extensive Caribbean possessions, and islands off South America, Great Britain also maintained a formidable presence in the Western Hemisphere. Self-governing dominions such as Canada, Australia, and New Zealand had their own armed services but relied on the British navy for overall protection and followed Great Britain's lead in foreign policy.

BRITAIN'S HUGE EMPIRE

This vast empire, vital to the survival of Great Britain, required a large navy to protect the supply lines from the colonies and to secure the British Isles from invasion. "Rule Britannia! Britannia rules the waves," the British sang as they spent millions of pounds to support their navy, the largest in the world. Conservatives seeking to increase the number of dreadnoughts, battleships with heavy-caliber guns, adopted the slogan, "We want eight and we won't wait." Naval units were stationed around the world at strategic outposts such as Gibraltar, Suez, the Cape of Good Hope, Aden, and Singapore. The British also used numerous islands in the oceans of the world as coaling, watering, and supply stations for the navy.

LARGE NAVY PROTECTS EMPIRE

In contrast to their enormous navy, the British maintained a small but efficient volunteer army. Protected primarily by the navy, the British had little need for a huge standing army of conscripts. Nor did the empire require large land forces. A surprisingly small number of British officers and men, supported by a substantial number of local troops commanded by British officers, kept the peace throughout the colonies. For example, only 4,000 Britons were stationed on the entire Indian subcontinent.

FRANCE

France was also an industrialized nation with a large empire. Compared with Great Britain, it had a much larger agricultural base but a less developed industrial system. Like Great Britain, France had been moving toward liberalization. French liberals advocating more democratic political forms clashed with conservatives, who tended to support more authoritarian policies. The multiparty system of French politics before World War I reflected many gradations of conservatism, liberalism, and radicalism

MULTIPARTY SYSTEM

and often made French governments unstable. After France's disastrous defeat in the Franco-Prussian War in 1870–1871, an essentially moderate, middle-class group of politicians founded the Third Republic. They were opposed both by the political Right, which wanted a return to conservative monarchy, or what was jokingly called the "man on horseback," and by forces on the Left, which wanted a more revolutionary, socialist government.

DREYFUS CASE AND ANTI-SEMITISM

The Dreyfus case, which dragged on from 1894 to 1906, reflected the deep divisions within French society. Alfred Dreyfus, a French Jew and a junior army officer, was wrongly convicted of selling military secrets to a foreign power. Many French people, including such noted intellectuals as Émile Zola, were convinced that Dreyfus was innocent and because of anti-Semitism (anti-Jewish prejudice) he had been used as a scapegoat to protect high-ranking judicial and military officials. The case became a cause célèbre and brought into serious question the extent to which French society had eradicated age-old privileges and prejudices. Dreyfus was finally found innocent in 1906. His exoneration resulted in the downfall of the conservative forces and the victory of the republicans and the socialists.

Successive liberal coalition governments reformed the military and subordinated it to the civilian government, while limiting the political power of the Catholic Church. One politician stated unequivocally, "Clericalism, there is the enemy." Organized labor sought to institute sweeping economic reforms and gained widespread political support. With increased power within the Chamber of Deputies, French radicals from 1905 to 1910 pushed through measures formally separating church and state and creating old-age pensions and other legislation to improve the lot of working people. However, before World War I, workers in Britain still had more basic rights than did those in France.

MILITARY WEAKNESS AND THE ALLIANCE SYSTEM

France also faced problems in international affairs. Its population was smaller than that of other major continental powers. In addition, French industry lagged behind that of Great Britain, Germany, and, later, the United States. These problems led to military weakness. The French army was smaller and less efficient than that of its neighboring enemy Germany, and its navy had fallen to fourth place behind those of Great Britain, Germany, and the United States.

To compensate for these weaknesses, the French government sought to create an alliance system to bolster French power. Concerned about further German expansion, France sought to limit German power on the Continent by finding allies to counterbalance Germany and its Triple Alliance. In 1894, France signed a secret convention with Russia whereby if France were attacked by Germany or Italy, Russia would attack Germany and, conversely, if Russia were attacked by Germany or Austria, France would move against Germany. France later enlarged this agreement by including Great Britain. Traditionally suspicious of European alliances, Great Britain hesitated before finally joining in an entente (informal understanding) with France in 1904 and Russia in 1907. With the resulting Triple Entente, which was actually no more than a gentleman's agreement, the French believed they had formed a powerful balance to Germany's growing strength in central Europe.

SECOND-LARGEST EMPIRE

France controlled the second-largest colonial empire. In North Africa, France held Algeria and Tunisia and, by 1912, Morocco. In sub-Saharan Africa, France dominated vast stretches of West and equatorial Africa. In Asia, the French held Indochina, which was subdivided into Vietnam, Laos, and Cambodia. In the Western Hemisphere, France possessed a number of Caribbean islands and French Guiana in South America. France also controlled numerous small islands in the South Pacific and in the Indian Ocean.

GERMANY

The opening of the twentieth century witnessed Germany's emergence as arguably the most powerful nation in Europe. Although not unified until 1871, Germany moved forward rapidly. It had a sound agricultural base and had used its large resources of coal and iron ore to develop into one of the world's top industrial nations. By and large, Germany's industrial plant was newer and more efficient than that of its major economic rival, Great Britain.

Politically, the German government reflected autocratic tendencies characteristic of the Prussian monarchy, the dominant entity within the federal system of German states. The German constitution provided the chancellor with wide executive powers in relationship to those of the German parliament. The Reichstag, elected by males above the age of 25, was never as powerful a voice for citizen representation as was the British House of Commons or the French Chamber of Deputies.

As in other industrialized nations, Germany's growing industrial strength caused a rapid movement toward unionization. Ironically, it was Otto von Bismarck, the conservative "Blood and Iron Chancellor" who had masterminded the unification of Germany, who brought about many of the changes the workers desired. Hoping to cripple the socialist movement in Germany, the conservative and paternalistic Bismarck inaugurated social welfare programs in the 1880s, several decades before the more liberal governments of France and Great Britain and half a century before the United States. Through his social welfare program, Bismarck instituted social insurance compensating workers for illness or accidents and providing the aged with pensions.

GROWING INDUSTRIAL POWER AND SOCIAL REFORMS

German successes in the Franco-Prussian War of 1870–1871 not only completed the unification of Germany but also shifted the center of European politics. Under the Treaty of Frankfurt, France was forced to surrender the provinces of Alsace-Lorraine to Germany, to pay an indemnity of about $1 billion, and to allow Germany to occupy key French fortresses until the amount owed was paid. Bismarck knew France would be set on revenge. Indeed, the unification of Germany was viewed with hostility and fear not only by the French but also by other European nations, particularly Russia and Great Britain.

VICTORY IN FRANCO-PRUSSIAN WAR

Fearing French retaliation, Bismarck set out to form new political and military alliances; he compared this diplomatic maneuvering to a giant chess game. To isolate France and to avoid fighting a two-front war against France and Russia, Bismarck sought alliances with Austria-Hungary and Russia. He failed to conclude a lasting agreement with Russia, but he did forge an alliance with the declining Austro-Hungarian Empire, which wanted support to protect itself from possible conflict with Russia. In 1879, Germany and Austria-Hungary signed a secret Dual Alliance whereby both would make war together if either were attacked by Russia, and if either were attacked by another power, the other would remain neutral.

DUAL ALLIANCE

TRIPLE ALLIANCE

Three years later, in 1882, the Dual Alliance was enlarged to include Italy. Under the secret terms of the Triple Alliance, all three nations would fight together if Italy or Germany were attacked by France; if any one of these nations were attacked by any two great powers, all three would give mutual assistance. The Italians, fearing British naval power, stipulated that the treaty did not apply if Great Britain was involved in any of the attacks. Italy was willing to align itself with Germany because it was angry over the 1881 French takeover of Tunisia and because Germany offered to assist in securing the North African territory of Libya for the Italian empire.

Bismarck also tried to prevent Austrian-Russian conflict in the Balkans, but such efforts were undermined by Austria-Hungary's ambitions for territorial gains there. Indeed, Austria's aggressive foreign policy against both Italy and the Balkan nations directly conflicted with the surging nationalism in these areas and contributed to the destruction of Bismarck's carefully constructed alliance system. Initially, Great Britain, secure with its naval superiority, remained aloof from these maneuverings. However, after Germany announced that it intended to build a first-class navy and in general to become a major industrial and military power, Great Britain's policy of isolation rapidly changed.

In 1890, Bismarck resigned under pressure from Kaiser Wilhelm II, who wanted to be his own chief minister. Wilhelm II sought to reestablish a more autocratic government, a move the German socialists opposed. Wilhelm also supported the growth of the German military and the stockpiling of armaments. With continued economic prosperity and successes in expanding the German empire, Wilhelm II had little difficulty keeping the Socialist Party from coming to power in the Reichstag.

SMALL GERMAN EMPIRE

Like Italy, Germany came late to the imperial scramble and had to pick up the leftover pieces. Germany acquired a block of islands in the western Pacific and a sphere of influence in China. The Germans also obtained several scattered territories in Africa: Togoland and Cameroon in western Africa, German East Africa (Tanzania), and German Southwest Africa (Namibia). Other imperial powers, hardly pacifists themselves, considered the Germans particularly aggressive in their prowling around the world looking for opportunities to expand their colonial power. The United States feared that the Germans were even trying to establish a base of power in the Western Hemisphere.

RUSSIA

To western European eyes, tsarist Russia was a gigantic backward nation. Territorially three times as large as the continental United States, it was overwhelmingly populated by peasants. Despite significant industrial growth in the preceding quarter century, by 1914 only about 3 million out of a population of approximately 170 million were industrial workers. Nor was it a homogeneous population. The Russians (or Great Russians) constituted less than half of the population of the empire. Ukrainians, Belorussians, Poles, Lithuanians, Latvians, Estonians, Finns, Jews, Armenians, Georgians, Muslim Turkish groups, and numerous smaller ethnic minorities made up the remainder. Most non-Russians had their own cultural and religious traditions and were held in the empire only by the greater strength

Tsar Nicholas II of Russia surrounded by his family. His only son, Alexei, was born in 1904.

of the Russians. The Russian school system had recently been expanded, but on the eve of World War I, less than half of the Russian population was literate.

CONSERVATIVE MONARCHY

Like his predecessors, Nicholas II, "Tsar of All the Russias" from 1894 to 1917, believed that he had been chosen by God to rule the Russian Empire. Only a revolt in 1905 persuaded him to permit the creation of a parliament with a lower-house Duma that had very limited legislative powers. Once the turmoil quieted, Nicholas promptly retreated from reforms. When he found the composition of the first two Dumas not to his liking, he changed the electoral law in 1907 so as to obtain more conservative representatives. Disparaging the determination of the tsar to remain an autocratic ruler, his opponents sarcastically grumbled, "The Duma is dead, long live the Duma." As a result of the tsar's interference, the next Duma was more cooperative and was allowed to serve the maximum five-year term. The Fourth Duma had almost completed a full term when the first 1917 revolution occurred. (The revolution is discussed in Chapter 10.)

EXPANSION INTO ASIA

Because geographic constraints made it difficult for the Russians to move overseas to acquire colonies, they expressed their imperialism by moving overland. By the mid-seventeenth century, the Russian Empire had expanded eastward to the shores of the Pacific. In the nineteenth century Russia moved southeastward, conquering Central Asia and holding it until the collapse of the Soviet Union in 1991. Russian growth eastward was in some ways comparable to the westward expansion of the United States across North America. Both American and Russian armed forces and settlers pushed aside indigenous resistance. Like the United States in dealing with Mexico, Russia also made extensive gains at the expense of established nations on its border. The Ottoman Empire, Persia, Afghanistan, and China all felt the power of Russian imperialist expansion. Although both the Austro-Hungarian and the

Ottoman empires had once been rich and powerful, both were now on the decline. The Ottoman Empire was so weak that it was popularly known as the Sick Man of Europe. Many nations, especially Russia, wished for the Sick Man to die, and during the nineteenth and early twentieth centuries the Ottoman Empire lost territories around the Black Sea and the Balkans to Russia and Austria. (See Chapter 15 for more on the Ottoman Empire.)

TRANS-SIBERIAN RAILWAY

In 1858 and 1860, Russia gained from China lands the size of Germany and France combined. In 1891, the Russian government began building the Trans-Siberian Railway from Moscow to Vladivostok to knit together the vast stretches of its domain. By 1904 Russian railroad workers completed their task, except for a final mountainous link around the southern shore of Lake Baikal. Most of the railway's eastern section, the Chinese Eastern Railway (CER), cut across northern Manchuria, and not until World War I would a Trans-Siberian railroad entirely in Russia be completed. Since Vladivostok was icebound for part of the year, Russia in 1898 forced China to allow a branch line of CER to run south to Russia's ice-free naval base at Port Arthur on the Yellow Sea. In Manchuria and Korea, Russian imperialism openly confronted Japanese imperialism, which sought to expand into the same territories.

SUMMARY

Before World War I, Europe was rich and powerful, but it was also plagued with internal problems. Domestically, all European governments struggled with the conflict among the forces of conservatism, liberalism, and socialism. In Great Britain, France, and even Germany, these internal political divisions resulted in reforms that improved the lives of middle-class and working-class people. In Russia, however, the conservative aristocrats continued to be the dominant political force. While both Britain and France were characterized by a trend toward liberalization, the more autocratic governments of Germany and Russia continued to maintain their ascendancy.

The mounting trend of nationalism also escalated old rivalries among the various European nations. These nationalist rivalries poisoned the atmosphere and led European nations to increase their armaments and to forge alliances in order to achieve security. Despite the known problems in creating and maintaining alliances, both Germany and France designed alliance systems that were as likely to cause war as to keep the peace. Increased arms stockpiles and the alliances added to tensions instead of providing a sense of calm or security.

Finally, Europeans felt superior to the Asians and Africans whom they were eagerly incorporating into vast empires. Great Britain and France had the largest empires. Having unified late in the nineteenth century, both Germany and Italy were relative newcomers and struggled to secure whatever territories remained independent in Africa and Asia. Russia was another major European imperialist power, whose interests clashed with those of Austria-Hungary in the Balkans. These imperialist rivalries added to the international tensions and further exacerbated hostilities among European nations.

SUGGESTED SOURCES

Gilbert, Felix. *The End of the European Era, 1890 to the Present.* 4th ed. 1991. A brief, general survey for students, with illustrations.*

Hale, Oron J. *The Great Illusion, 1900–1914.* 1971. A survey of technological, economic, cultural, and political developments in Europe before World War I.*

Hobsbaum, Eric. *The Age of Empire, 1875–1914.* New ed. 1996. A critical look at the motivations behind the European rush for imperial gains.*

Lukacs, John. *Budapest 1900: A Historical Portrait of a City and Its Culture.* 1988. An excellent depiction of one of the chief cities of Austria-Hungary.*

Massie, Robert K. *Nicholas and Alexandra.* 1967. A popular, sympathetic biography of the last Russian tsar and tsarina. Gives a feeling for the world of royalty before World War I.* (Also a film.) See also *Last of the Tsars,* PBS video on last tsar and his family.

Palmer, Alan Warwick. *Twilight of the Habsburgs: The Life and Times of Emperor Francis Joseph.* 1997. A very readable work by a historian who has written many fine historical biographies.*

Rich, Norman. *Great Power Diplomacy 1814–1914.* 1992. A survey of the often complex relationships among diverse European nations.*

Stone, Norman. *Europe Transformed, 1878–1919.* 2nd ed. 1999. A good overview of the period by a scholar who has authored many books and been a professor in both England and Turkey.*

When the Century Was Young: From Monarchy to Modernity and *Colonialism, Nationalism and Migration.* Films for the Humanities and Sciences. These two videos explore the political and social changes in Europe at the turn of the century and the consequences of imperialism, with extensive firsthand footage.

WEB SOURCES

www.fordham.edu/halsall/women/womensbook.html. This sourcebook on women's history has links to various nineteenth- and twentieth-century materials including selections from Emmeline Pankhurst.

www.alexanderpalace.org. A site offering numerous textual and visual materials associated with the last Romanov rulers of the Russian Empire.

www.friends-partners.org/partners/beyond-the-pale/english/25.html. A discussion of France's Dreyfus case and its place in the modern history of anti-Semitism; includes pictures.

---

*Paperback available.

4

⑥ The European Conquest of Africa

When the Suez Canal opened in 1869, Europeans directly controlled only a scattering of outposts on the African coast, Algeria in North Africa, and the southern tip of Africa. By 1912 several European nations had partitioned nearly all of the continent and incorporated vast areas into their empires.

Only two states in Africa, Liberia and Ethiopia, remained independent after the partition. Liberia was partly settled by former slaves from the United States and remained heavily dependent economically on U.S. companies such as Firestone. Ethiopia had the unique distinction of defeating a European nation when it repulsed an Italian attempt to conquer it in 1896.

AFRICAN SOCIETIES

The African continent in the late nineteenth century was home to many different ethnic groups that lived in a varied landscape of desert, rain forest, savannah, mountain, and coastal lands. These peoples had adapted their social and economic organizations to their environments; hence, some were hunters, while others were agriculturalists, nomads, food gatherers, or herders. Their political systems varied from large empires to tribal groupings, but some of Africa's greatest empires had existed centuries earlier. For example, in the early sixteenth century, the kingdom of Songhai dominated most of western Africa. Under its Muslim ruler the city of Tombouctou (in modern-day Mali) became a great commercial and cultural center with its own university.

EARLY MUSLIM AND EUROPEAN CONTACTS WITH AFRICA

From the eleventh century onward, Africa south of the Sahara had experienced an influx of newcomers from Islamic Arabicized North Africa and from western Asia. By the sixteenth century, Europeans were engaging in active trade with coastal African areas, and it was mainly Europeans who began shipping slaves to the Americas. Although African slave trading predated the European arrival, the insatiable demand of European slave traders greatly increased the capture and sale of slaves. From 1600 to 1870 many millions of Africans were enslaved and sent to the New World. During this same period some European nations controlled small portions of coastal African areas, but during the 1870s and 1880s the pace of European imperialism and its penetration of the African interior rapidly accelerated.

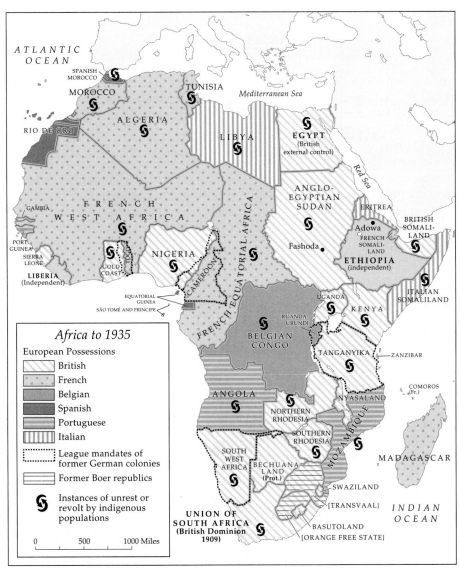

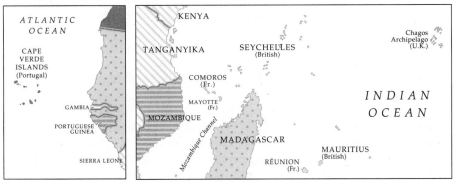

THE PARTITION OF AFRICA

The late-nineteenth-century European penetration of Africa owed much to the scientific and technological advances of the nineteenth century (see Chapter 2). Once convinced that quinine (taken from the bark of the cinchona tree) could defend against malaria, the Dutch and British empires began producing it in significant enough quantities to reduce the danger malaria had earlier posed for Europeans entering tropical areas. As technological advances increased industrial development, the demand for raw materials from Africa and elsewhere grew. Improvements in shipping reduced transportation costs, and steamships, telegraphs, railways, and superior guns and other military equipment, despite African resistance, facilitated European imperial control of the African interior. Besides economic incentives, nationalistic and strategic reasons also motivated the European conquest and competition for African territories. Also, most Europeans believed they were benefiting Africans by exposing them to European civilization and Christianity.

Leaders of several nations watched with particular interest the activities of a private commercial association organized by King Leopold II of Belgium in 1876 for the purpose of exploiting the resources of the Congo basin. As Leopold had commented, "I want my share of this wonderful African cake." The Congo Free State, the name given to the area controlled by Leopold's company, was headed by the king in his private capacity, although his prestige as king of the Belgians was crucial to the success of the association. The company's oppressive policies in the Congo Free State and its exploitation of the people justified accusations that modern colonization by Europeans was motivated only by economic greed. International outcry against Leopold's regime forced him to appoint a Commission of Inquiry in 1904. Its report horrified the world.

> Witness Ilange Kunda of M'Bongo: "I knew Malu Malu [Quickly Quickly, the African name for Force Publique Lieutenant Charles Masard]. He was very cruel; he forced us to bring rubber. One day, I saw him with my own eyes kill a native named Bongiyangwa, solely because among the fifty baskets of rubber which had been brought, he found one not full enough. Malu Malu ordered the soldier Tshumpa to seize [Bongiyangwa] and tie him to a palm tree. There were three sets of bonds: one at knee height, a second at stomach height, and a third crushing his arms. Malu Malu had his cartridge-pouch on his belt; he took his rifle, fired from a distance of about 20 meters, and with one bullet he killed Bongiyangwa. . . . I saw the wound. The unhappy man gave one cry and was dead."

In 1908 the Belgian government replaced the king's private regime in the Congo, which it continued to rule until 1960.

EUROPEAN RIVALRIES AND PARTITION OF AFRICA

Leopold's early success played a key role in sharpening the mutual suspicions of European nations about one another's intentions in Africa; these countries muscled in after 1880 to get what they wanted. At the Berlin West African Conference in 1884–1885, European colonial powers agreed on "first come, first served" as the basic rule of dividing Africa. Any power that effectively occupied an African territory and notified others would be recognized as having established sole possession. After 1884, the scramble intensified as the older colonial powers—Portugal, Spain, and particularly Great Britain and France—expanded inland from their original coastal outposts. Newly unified Italy and Germany also gained footholds on the African coast and

Herero warriors in German captivity.

pushed inland as well. By 1912 almost all of Africa was under European control. Between 1871 and 1900, Britain added about 4.3 million square miles of territory and 66 million people to its African empire, and France added about 3.5 million square miles and 26 million people. The possessions of the other imperial powers were smaller and less populous. Since Great Britain and France dominated the partition of Africa, their actions will be the focus of this chapter.

As Europeans sought to consolidate their holdings, Africans saw their traditional ways of life disrupted or destroyed. They resisted bitterly; there were at least 25 conflicts with Europeans before World War I. Besides the Ethiopians, other key resisters were the Ashante in present-day Ghana, the Hereros in South West Africa against Germany, and peoples in Islamic northern Africa. Two groups were most determined and fought for years. They were the followers of the Mahdi in the Sudan and the Zulus of southern Africa; both will be discussed later. In the end, all lost except for the Ethiopians, who skillfully used knowledge of the local terrain and the modern weapons they purchased.

The scramble to divide Africa created a number of intense hostilities among the imperialist nations, particularly among Great Britain, France, Germany, and Italy. However, problems were generally settled peacefully at conference tables in European capitals. After partitioning Africa, Europeans found that few areas could produce immediate wealth without large capital investment. Not surprisingly, most European governments thus lost some interest in their newly acquired possessions. The following will detail the partition of Africa by regions by major European powers in the late nineteenth century.

NORTH AFRICA

North Africa between the Mediterranean Sea and the Sahara Desert was a land of ancient civilizations. Since the eighth century C.E., most peoples of this region had become Muslim. This land was called the *Mahgrib,* meaning the West in Arabic, because it was the westernmost extension of Arab culture. North Africa came under British, French, and Italian control.

British Control of Egypt and the Sudan

THE SUEZ CANAL: STRATEGIC LINK BETWEEN EUROPE AND ASIA

Great Britain's interest in this region was primarily strategic, focused on the Suez Canal, which shortened the distance between Europe and Asia. Designed by a French engineer and built by an international company, it was opened in 1869. Because of their far-flung empire and global trading network, the British were the most interested in the canal. In 1875 Great Britain acquired control of the waterway when the ruler of Egypt sold his shares in the company to the British government to avert bankruptcy. To protect the canal, Great Britain looked for an opportunity to gain control over Egypt, making it into a de facto protectorate, in 1882. British advisers supervised all important Egyptian government offices and became the real rulers of the country, although it nominally remained a province of the Ottoman Empire.

Egypt claimed authority over the Sudan, which controlled the water supply of the Nile River. The Sudanese, who resented Egyptian and British expansion, rose in revolt in 1883 under the Mahdi (Rightly Guided One), the leader of a nationalist Muslim movement. Since Great Britain controlled Egypt, it too became involved in putting down the Sudanese uprising. Between 1896 and 1898, General Sir Herbert Kitchener undertook the reconquest of the Sudan. After its conquest, Great Britain and Egypt established joint rule over the land, which in effect meant British control.

GREAT BRITAIN GAINS CONTROL OF ENTIRE NILE VALLEY

In 1898 when British forces reached Fashoda, a village on the bank of the Nile in southern Sudan, they found a French expedition, which had arrived overland from the west, already established there. France hoped to control the Sudan so that its African empire might extend from the Atlantic Ocean to the Indian Ocean, and at the same time put pressure on the British downriver in Egypt by controlling the source of the Nile. The ensuing standoff was called the Fashoda incident. It ended when France backed down in 1899 and renounced all claims to the Nile valley in return for British recognition of its claims in the Sahara. This crisis illustrates the intensity of rivalries among the colonial powers in Africa.

The French Conquest and Settlement of North West Africa

Outside Egypt and the Sudan, France was the dominant colonial power north of the Sahara. France had conquered Algeria between 1830 and 1869, which it then used as a base for further advances into the Sahara. In 1881 the French had made Tunisia (situated to the east) a protectorate, against a strong claim by Italy, also anxious to build an empire in Africa. As in Egypt, a facade of native government was allowed to remain in Tunisia. The French also moved southward across the Sahara and finally westward into Morocco.

Unlike the British, who made no attempt to send settlers to Egypt, the French from the start encouraged the immigration of Europeans into Algeria, pushing Algerians off their best agricultural lands. By 1911, out of a total population of 5.6 million people in Algeria, 752,000 were Europeans. Tunisia had a European population of 130,000. In both Algeria and Tunisia, there was friction between the privileged European minority and the Arab majority. Under the circumstances, it is hardly surprising that a racial problem developed between the Europeans and Muslims. In no other part of the Islamic world were Muslims confronted with so large a number of foreigners settled in their midst.

FRANCE SETTLES EUROPEAN COLONISTS IN ITS NORTH AFRICAN TERRITORIES

In addition to economic advantages, the privileged European settlers enjoyed the right of political representation in the legislature of metropolitan France. Under the French constitution, the *colons* (French settlers) in Algeria sent six deputies and three senators to the French legislature in 1900. The Muslims had no representation. Established in a position of superiority, many *colons* regarded the Algerians with open contempt. "The Arab must accept the fate of the conquered," wrote one *colon*. "He must either become assimilated to our civilization or disappear. European civilization can have no sympathy for the life of the savage."

Gradually, the abuses of the colonial system became widely known in France, and a spirited debate on colonial policy ensued in the Chamber of Deputies (the lower house of the French legislature), which enacted limited reforms early in the twentieth century. Given the tenor of French thought, most reformers sought the assimilation of upper-class Algerian Muslims, who were encouraged to attend French schools and adopt French ways, for which they would be rewarded with a share in the power structure of the French empire.

FRANCE ATTEMPTS POLICY OF ASSIMILATION

The policy of assimilation failed, however, for three basic reasons. One was the resistance of most Algerians, who were not prepared to renounce their culture and Islamic law for those of their masters. Second, not all French opinion supported the assimilation plan, and it was therefore extremely limited in application. The *colons* were the third factor. Unwilling to give up their privileges, they vigorously opposed measures designed to lessen or dilute their power.

Morocco was the last French acquisition in North Africa. At the beginning of the twentieth century, it was an independent kingdom beset by internal problems. For a time, the government of Morocco was able to delay French imperialistic advances by exploiting the Franco-German rivalry in international affairs and appealing to the German government for help. Anxious to further its influence in Africa, Germany was at first happy to comply, but in the face of European opposition it eventually backed down and recognized Morocco as a French sphere of influence. In 1912, the sultan of Morocco was forced to sign a treaty that handed his country over to French protection.

WEST AFRICA

The huge territory of West Africa contained grasslands, tropical rain forests, and some of the harshest desert in Africa. Before European colonization, the peoples in this area lived in societies that ranged from large empires like that of the Muslim Hausa-Fulani peoples in today's northern Nigeria, through well-organized kingdoms like that of the Ashante in today's Ghana, to small groups who still lived by hunting and gathering in the equatorial rain forests. Except for those areas south of the Sahara that had become largely Islamic, traditional religions prevailed in West Africa.

Indirect Rule in Great Britain's Scattered Colonies

In West Africa, Great Britain ruled four colonies strung out on the coast and mostly surrounded by French possessions. The earliest was Sierra Leone, begun in the eighteenth century for freed slaves in British colonies, just as Liberia was later established for former slaves from the United States. The British opened mines and encouraged cash crops grown by African peasants. They made this development profitable by building railroads to connect the coast with the interior. The Gold Coast (Ghana) was the best example of a successful and prosperous colony. Here, the railroad system made it possible to exploit timber, open up cocoa farms, and develop gold mines in the hinterland. British-owned trading companies and their shareholders became rich from these operations. This economic process also provided jobs for some Africans, but it disrupted the previously self-sufficient economy.

GREAT BRITAIN APPLIES "INDIRECT RULE" IN WEST AFRICA

In administering Africa, the British applied no preconceived notions of colonial government but devised practical solutions to the problems of governing. The policy Great Britain eventually applied in West Africa was called "indirect rule," a system developed by Lord Lugard, governor-general of Nigeria, the largest and most populous British West African colony. Because the British administrative staff was small, local chiefs and advisers were delegated the task of running the day-to-day matters of government. They were supervised by a British official who also ensured that British interests in the area were upheld.

Climatic conditions and an already large population made West Africa unsuitable and unattractive for British immigration. The absence of a British immigrant group eager to compete for local jobs meant more opportunities for Africans. Many were anxious to acquire a Western education to qualify them for the new skilled positions opening up in a rapidly changing economy. British official opinion was responsive and sometimes even enthusiastic about West African demands for more schools and job opportunities. Sir Frederick Guggisberg, governor of the Gold Coast during World War I, appointed a committee that drew up a new educational plan for the colony. This plan provided a foundation for the modernization of the Gold Coast, paving the way for the independent nation of Ghana.

France's Vast West African Empire

By the twentieth century, France had also acquired a huge block of territory south of the Sahara that stretched 3,000 miles from the extreme west coast of Africa to the Congo River deep in central Africa. In Senegal, the oldest French colony in West Africa, the colonial administration encouraged the population to grow groundnuts as a cash crop. The peasants sold the nuts for cash, part of which they used to pay the head tax that was for many years the chief source of revenue for the government of Senegal. The French worked hard to implant French culture in Senegal, with some success. With its boulevards and shops filled with French-speaking Africans and Europeans, Dakar (the capital of Senegal) came to be called the Paris of Africa. Senegalese soldiers fought in the French army around the world. In France's other coastal colonies, Guinea, the Ivory Coast, and Dahomey, cash crops such as palm oil and cocoa were introduced and proved profitable.

FRANCE CONSOLIDATES ITS WEST AFRICAN HOLDINGS

The French colonies in the interior of West Africa were sparsely populated, limited in resources, and difficult to reach. Formidable rapids made the three major river systems in this area—the Congo, the Senegal, and the Niger—difficult to navigate. New cash crops, such as cotton in Niger, were introduced, but until railroads could be built to penetrate the interior, few products could be brought out. These colonies were therefore a financial drain on France.

Pending the completion of new railroads to move interior products to market, the quest for economic efficiency led the French government in 1904 to gather the West African territories into a single unit, called French West Africa, under a governor-general who ruled from Dakar. The economic benefits that emerged from the formation of French West Africa led the French government to follow the same policy in its territories in the Congo basin, joining them in 1910 into a single colonial unit called French Equatorial Africa, under a governor-general who ruled from Brazzaville. In both cases, the greater resources of a consolidated colonial government resulted in faster economic development.

BRITISH EAST AFRICA: THE ADVENT OF A MULTIRACIAL SOCIETY

ENGLISH COLONISTS SETTLE IN EAST AFRICA

Geographically, East Africa is dominated by mountains and high plateaus that extend southward from Kenya to the Cape of Good Hope. Although near the equator, the temperate climate of the uplands soon attracted British settlers. To the Colonial Office in search of revenue, the prospect of settlement by British farmers seemed a good step toward economic development. Up to World War I, the number of British settlers in East Africa and central Africa remained small—around 3,000 in what is now Kenya and a few hundred in Uganda. Although some English settlers congregated in what were previously sparsely populated lands, others took over lands already settled by Kikuyu tribes, displacing the people or making them tenant farmers. British colonists were a disruptive factor in the region, competing with Africans for land and exploiting labor. Many Africans were forced to become migrant laborers on European farms. This development caused political and social problems in the next generation.

The racial tensions of East Africa were further inflamed when the British government allowed large numbers of emigrants from India to settle as indentured laborers to build railroads or work as clerks in government offices and commercial companies. Indians settled in towns and villages, and many became traders. In the early decades, Europeans resented the numerous and resourceful Indians in their midst. In a later era, as a result of growing African nationalism, Indian British subjects were ousted by African majorities who did not think Indians belonged in Africa. Thus, in British East Africa, a pluralist society was formed in the early twentieth century that had disturbing consequences in later years.

SOUTHERN AFRICA

COMPETITION FOR LAND IN SOUTHERN AFRICA

Dutch colonists began settling in southern Africa in the mid-seventeenth century. The early inhabitants of southern Africa were the San and Khoi; small in number, they lived by hunting and gathering and were easily subdued by white settlers. Bantu-speaking peoples, who engaged in both herding and agriculture, especially the Zulu, had been emigrating from the north in large numbers over a long period. Clashes broke out among the Bantu tribes and between the Bantus and Europeans. Zulu leaders forged their people into a fighting nation that defeated and subjugated other tribes and fought white colonists in several Zulu wars. Although the white settlers eventually defeated the Zulus, they were not able to prevent the movement of Bantu peoples into southern Africa. As a result of both Bantu and European immigration, South Africa became a land with a black majority and a white minority, the basis for race problems in the twentieth century.

The Rise and Fall of the Boer Republics

CONFLICTS BETWEEN THE BRITISH AND BOERS

South Africa attracted large numbers of white colonists because of its benign climate, good soil, and, in the late nineteenth century, the discovery of large gold and diamond deposits. When Great Britain acquired the Dutch colony located at the Cape of Good Hope in 1815, it also inherited the Dutch colonists of the land, who called themselves Boers (farmers). The Boers resented British rule, particularly a law passed in 1833 that ended slavery in the British Empire and forced the Boers to emancipate their slaves. To escape British control, many Boers made a mass migration called the Great Trek into the interior of Africa between 1835 and 1841. There they founded two independent republics, the Orange Free State and the Transvaal. Meanwhile, British settlers moved into the Cape Province and into Natal, a new colony to the east. The relationship between the Boer republics and Great Britain became increasingly tense, especially after gold was discovered in the Transvaal. Non-Boer prospectors, including many British, encountered discrimination at the hands of the Boer government in the Transvaal.

In 1899 war broke out between Great Britain and the two Boer republics. The Boers were ably led by President Paul Kruger of the Transvaal, and for three years Boer commandos (guerrillas), using hit-and-run tactics copied from the Zulus, successfully resisted the might of the British Empire. British forces resorted to the same harsh but effective antiguerrilla measures used in that period by the Spanish in Cuba and the Americans in the Philippines, burning farms and herding women, children, and other noncombatants into concentration camps to deprive the commandos of sanctuary and resources. Hopelessly beaten, the Boers finally surrendered in 1902.

Modern Boer, or Afrikaner, nationalism emerged out of this resistance. In an attempt to conciliate the defeated Boers, Great Britain let them decide whether black and other nonwhite inhabitants should be given the vote; true to their white supremacist tradition, the Boers denied suffrage to all but whites. When the two former Boer states federated with the two British colonies of Natal and the Cape in 1909 to form the Union of South Africa, a self-governing dominion in the British Empire, black people were denied political rights.

BLACK AFRICANS DENIED SUFFRAGE IN UNION OF SOUTH AFRICA

The Rhodesias: One-Man Imperialism

North of the Transvaal and the Orange Free State was an area of high plains and good soil. In earlier centuries it was the site of an African state called Great Zimbabwe. Here, empire-builder Cecil Rhodes, an English adventurer who had made a fortune from diamond mining in South Africa, carved out two new colonies for Great Britain. At his request Britain annexed the territories and called them Northern and Southern Rhodesia, entrusting the South African Company owned by Rhodes to govern them. An unabashed imperialist, he once exclaimed, "I would annex the planets if I could!"

During the 1890s, the company's army was responsible for winning Portuguese acquiescence to the British takeover of that area and for the defeat of the local people, who bitterly resented the company's demands on their land and labor. Fighting did not stop until 1897, after which the company sponsored European immigrants who eventually constituted about 5 percent of the total population.

THE IMPACT OF COLONIAL RULE ON AFRICA

The positive and negative effects of colonial rule on Africans varied greatly and differed from society to society. As always under conditions of change, some groups benefited. They were either lucky or farsighted enough to cooperate with the masters and to take advantage of new circumstances, thereby winning favors, prestige, and sometimes additional land. Among such beneficiaries were the Baganda people of Uganda and the Igbos in Nigeria, who welcomed chances for a British education and cooperated with the British authorities. They were rewarded with positions in the colonial bureaucracy.

EFFECTS OF COLONIALISM ON AFRICANS

On the other hand, large numbers suffered from colonial rule, especially in areas where Europeans sought to settle or to extract minerals. In some instances tribes were split under different European jurisdictions, while in others several traditionally hostile tribes were grouped under a single administration. In parts of Kenya and the Rhodesias, for example, hundreds of thousands of Africans lost their land. Many were forced to live on inferior lands designated as native reserves or became tenants and laborers on the new white-owned farms.

However, many Africans were at first not directly affected when European countries annexed their lands. Large areas, in fact, remained untouched by white rule. Until World War I, colonial officials frequently had little control over the local scene

Western cultural impact on Africa: A drawing of missionary Robert Moffat preaching to the Tswanas.

and had to work within the restraints of local kinship groups, village communities, and tribal ties. In Morocco and Tunisia, European diplomatic entanglements compelled the French to retain native rulers in power.

The indirect effects of imperialism were much more widespread. Europeans investing in Africa demanded laborers to work in mines and on plantations and to build roads and railroads. Whether laborers were paid or not, their service was compulsory. The European attitude toward forced labor was contradictory and tinged with hypocrisy. Europeans abhorred slavery, but they permitted the forced labor of Africans. Yet when facts about King Leopold's methods for exacting labor services in the Congo Free State were made public, adverse European and American public opinion forced the Belgian government to take over responsibility for its administration.

Despite the violence generated by the imposition of colonial rule, some forms of violence in Africa decreased after colonization. Colonial authorities largely suppressed the tribal wars, cattle rustling, and slave raids that had caused much bloodshed before the European takeover. Peace, better public health programs, development of cash crops, and agricultural improvements resulted in large increases in population. In some areas, rural peoples moved into the newly established cities for work, causing new problems of social adjustment.

European control was also accompanied by Christian missionary activity, which had an important impact. In many inaccessible villages, the missionary teacher and preacher was much more likely than the colonial administrator to be the first white

CHRISTIAN MISSIONARIES IN AFRICA

person an African encountered. In the early days, the teachers in the missionary "bush schools" were Europeans, but soon Africans themselves became teachers and missionaries. By the early twentieth century, Western education and Christian religion were expanding hand in hand in many parts of Africa. Christian missionaries and teachers brought with them not only a new religion and education but also medical care and a general acquaintance with the scientific, technological, and intellectual bases of Western civilization; however, they also frequently held the same ethnocentric and racist beliefs of Western societies at the time.

In northern Africa, Islam remained the rallying point of the people and Christianity had little impact. Thus, the majority of Algerians resisted conversion to Christianity, as did the peoples of Morocco, Tunisia, Libya, Egypt, and northern Sudan. At the same time, Muslim missionaries were active in spreading their religion and culture south of the Sahara.

Early in the twentieth century, a new kind of leadership emerged in Africa when many European-educated, black Africans rejected the authority of the traditional chiefs and willingly seized the new opportunities created by colonialism. Some of the new elite received higher education in the West, where they gained new perspectives for judging the colonial administrations of their lands. They found that the colonial practices of the European imperialist states invariably fell short of their professed democratic ideals. Consequently, these modern educated Africans established anticolonial movements. Even before World War I, these new leaders were demanding that African Christian churches be placed under black African leadership and that African independent states be established based on modern democratic concepts.

NEW AFRICAN LEADERS EMERGE

SUMMARY

In the late nineteenth and early twentieth centuries, European imperialism, based on a mixture of economic, strategic, cultural, and nationalistic motives, led to the partition of the African continent. The European preeminence in industrial, technical, and military development enabled Europeans to defeat African societies and seize their territories. Although nationalism created intense rivalries between the imperialist states, diplomacy triumphed and they were able to avoid war against each other as they carved up Africa. Great Britain and France seized the largest amount of African territory, but Germany, Italy, and Belgium also made extensive acquisitions. Spanish and Portuguese holdings dating from an earlier century were enlarged. Africans often resisted European imperialism, but with the exception of the Ethiopians and Liberians, all Africans were eventually subjugated. Many African groups were dislocated or destroyed in the process.

Europeans in Africa extensively exploited the continent's mineral and agricultural products, often by means of forced labor and sometimes with imported outside labor. On the other hand, colonial authorities began to introduce programs for health, education, and social welfare and suppressed intertribal violence. Although Europeans ruled some areas of Africa indirectly and allowed the indigenous cultural patterns to continue, in many cases their colonial administrations eliminated the traditional political leadership and imposed Western systems of government, taxation, and justice. Both Christian and Muslim missionaries worked to win converts from adherents of local African religions.

SUGGESTED SOURCES

Achebe, Chinua. *Things Fall Apart*. 1978. Classic novel on the profound effects of British contact on Igbo society in Nigeria.*

Collins, Robert O. *Problems in African History: Historical Problems of Imperial Africa,* Vol. II. 2004. Updated account of colonial expansion and rule in Africa.*

Farwell, Byron. *The Great Anglo-Boer War*. 1971. This book is acclaimed as the best general history of the war.*

Gilbert, Erik, and Jonathan T. Reynolds. *Africa in World History: From Prehistory to the Present*. 2004. Excellent section on European influences and Africa's place in a global historic context.*

Hochschild, Adam. *King Leopold's Ghost: A Story of Greed, Terror, and Heroism in Colonial Africa*. 1998. Gripping book on the colonization of Africa, with particular attention to the Congo.

The Horizon History of Africa. 1971. A thoughtful text, with lavish illustrations and maps.

Kenyatta, Jomo. *Facing Mount Kenya*. 1962. A collection of studies by the Kenyan nationalist leader that favorably depict the customs of Kenya's Kikuyu tribe before they were altered by the impact of imperialism.*

Nederveen, Jan. *White on Black: Images of Africa and Blacks in Western Popular Culture*. 1992. A thoughtful discussion on how racism toward Africans permeated Western attitudes during the twentieth century.*

Oliver, Roland Anthony, and Anthony Ernest Atmore. *Africa since 1800*. 5th ed. 2005. A standard survey of Africa and European imperialism.*

Pakenham, Thomas. *The Scramble for Africa; White Man's Conquest of the Dark Continent from 1876 to 1912*. 1992. Highly readable book about the colonization of the entire African continent.*

Thompson, Leonard. *A History of South Africa*. Rev. ed. 1995. A well-written and balanced book.*

WEB SOURCES

www.fordham.edu/halsall/africa/africasbook.html

www.bbc.co.uk/worldservice/africa/features/storyofafrica/index.shtml.
Two excellent sites, each offering numerous links to materials dealing with Africa, including a section on European imperialism there.

---

*Paperback available.

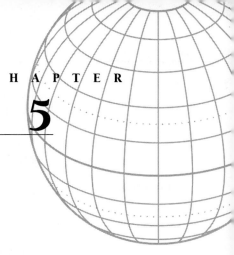

⑥ The Americas

Many of the same processes transforming Europe in the late nineteenth century—industrialization, urbanization, migration, militarism, nationalism, the rise of organized labor, growing demands for constitutional rights—were also transforming the nations and territories of the Western Hemisphere. The United States by 1900 had become one of the world's great powers. As its population soared with massive immigration, mainly from Europe, its economic and military might came to rival that of major European countries. So did its sense of nationalism and imperial reach. Its main interest overseas was the Caribbean, with its cheap labor, tropical export products, strategic location, and stark inequalities of race and class. By the 1920s the Caribbean had become part of the U.S. "backyard," with the United States intervening militarily, politically, and economically in Cuba, Haiti, the Dominican Republic, Nicaragua, Mexico, and elsewhere. Many Latin Americans became outraged at what they saw as heavy-handed U.S. imperialism, inflaming nationalist feelings against the "Colossus of the North." This deepening sense of nationalism, in turn, fostered the spread of radical political ideologies and fueled a growing clamor for the rights of citizenship, processes already well under way. From the 1870s to the 1930s, Latin America's economic dependency on Europe and the United States grew. To the north, Canada, which in the 1860s began a gradual process of gaining independence from Great Britain, also became more economically dependent on the United States while embarking on a democratic political path similar to that of its more powerful southern neighbor. Meanwhile, all of the Americas, north and south, became increasingly interdependent and integrated.

THE UNITED STATES AT THE TURN OF THE CENTURY

General Characteristics

In a little over a century, the United States had grown from a small collection of 13 states hugging North America's eastern seaboard to a continent-wide empire. Free market capitalism, representative democracy for white males, and the prospect of boundless opportunity made the United States the destination of choice for tens of millions of emigrating Europeans. Between 1865 and 1914 the country absorbed more than 25 million immigrants, more than 80 percent from Europe. Most settled

SURGING U.S. POPULATION AND POWER

in cities, providing a vast pool of cheap labor for the country's rapidly expanding industrial and manufacturing sectors. The industrial revolution in steel, textiles, mining, and transportation readily absorbed this massive influx of labor. In 1820 some 90 percent of the population made their living by the soil. A century later more than 50 percent lived in cities.

PROBLEMS AND CHALLENGES

As cities grew, so too did a host of associated problems: sanitation, disease, overcrowding, ethnic strife, political corruption. The urban working class ballooned. So too did the broad middle class, one of the most distinctive features of U.S. society compared to others. And as business grew, huge trusts and monopolies formed, dominating large parts of the economy and posing formidable challenges to a nation founded on the promise of political democracy. After the abolition of slavery in 1865, blacks and other minorities struggled for equal opportunity, as did women, who demanded full rights of citizenship, especially the right to vote. All the while, the United States was becoming a major player on the world stage. The Spanish-Cuban-American War in 1898 marked a significant intensification of U.S. imperialist expansion, which continued through World War I and after.

Populist, Labor, and Progressive Struggles

FARMERS ORGANIZE AGAINST MONOPOLIES

Despite its general affluence and growing economic power, the United States at the turn of the century faced a number of pressing challenges. One of the biggest was the conflict between the rise of big business—personified in robber barons like John D. Rockefeller of Standard Oil, Andrew Carnegie of United States Steel, and J. P. Morgan of the Morgan Bank—and the promise of equal rights for all. If so much economic power was concentrated in so few hands, how could the promise of political equality be realized? Farmers in the South and West felt this conflict with special force. They needed railroads to get their products to market, but too often the railroads were dominated by monopolies and trusts that charged huge sums for transport and storage. Banks often charged higher interest rates to smaller customers, making credit hard to get. And manufactured goods, like threshers and reapers, were often too expensive to buy. Facing high prices for products they needed and low prices for products they sold, farmers organized politically, capturing control of several states in the agricultural belt. These farmer-controlled state legislatures then passed laws regulating the operation of railroads, grain elevators, cotton gins, and stockyards. At the national level, farmers formed the Populist Party in the 1890s and for a time controlled the Democratic Party. Populist politicians allied with small business interests and other reformers to frame national laws curbing the power of monopolies and trusts, establishing the first independent regulatory commission, and securing the first antitrust legislation.

WORKERS ORGANIZE UNIONS

Many wage workers in cities and in railroad, lumbering, and mining enclaves also faced severe problems—low pay, dangerous working conditions, substandard housing, a boom-and-bust business cycle, political bossism. Realizing their lack of individual power, some workers organized into unions, demanding the right to bargain collectively (not enshrined in law until the Wagner Act of 1935), a shorter workday, higher wages, and safer workplaces. The Great Railroad Strike of 1877, which began spontaneously and ended in failure, was the first in a long line of worker protests that mushroomed during this era, most famously in the Homestead (1892) and Pullman (1894) strikes. Federal, state, and local government usually sided with business, which often used police, the courts, and armed strikebreakers to end worker protests and break up unions.

The biggest labor organization of the era was the American Federation of Labor, an association of skilled artisans led by Samuel Gompers that focused on bread-and-butter issues like wages and job security. After 1900 labor organizing spread to the mining towns and lumber camps in the West, where the radical syndicalist Industrial Workers of the World (or Wobblies), led by Big Bill Haywood, envisioned "One Big Union" in which workers would own the means of production. But overall, such radical social doctrines found few adherents. The question of why remains one of the enduring questions of U.S. history, but the fact remains that in contrast to Europe, only about 4 percent of U.S. industrial workers were organized at the turn of the century.

These traditions of struggle among farmers and workers, the concentration of wealth and power in so few hands, widespread poverty, and rapid social change led to a broad-based reform movement among the growing urban middle class, mainly white-collar professionals and small business owners. Beginning in the towns and cities of the East and Midwest in the late 1890s and peaking around 1914, the Progressive reform movement spread through both Democratic and Republican parties, in the 1912 national elections fielding its own slate of candidates. Progressive reformers were a diverse group with many different goals, but the basic ideas inspiring them were (1) to check the growing power of big business, by (2) expanding the role of government, in order to (3) promote social justice, efficiency, and order in a time of increasing social chaos.

Major Progressive era reforms included the graduated (or progressive) federal income tax (16th Amendment); direct election of senators (17th Amendment); the institution of party primaries; reducing corruption in city governments; and new electoral procedures like initiative, referendum, and recall. Progressive reformers also increased the power of state and federal governments to regulate business, limit trusts and monopolies, and expand public services. They passed laws to improve sanitation, education, housing, and working conditions, especially for women and children. The 1893 depression and 1907 financial panic led to monetary reform and establishment of the Federal Reserve Board. Other reforms included pure food and drug laws and creation of the National Park Service. The states, often in tandem with innovative activists like Jane Addams, took a more active role in fighting poverty, while feminists like Margaret Sanger emphasized the importance of birth control in limiting poverty among women.

A related reform movement was the drive to secure the vote (suffrage) for women in national elections, undertaken at the same time as the enfranchisement campaign in Great Britain. The women's suffrage movement, which dated back to the 1848 Seneca Falls Convention, flourished in the reform atmosphere of the Progressive era. The movement became steadily more effective and militant as more women undertook such "unladylike" actions as picketing or chaining themselves to the White House fence. The drive

THE PROGRESSIVE REFORM MOVEMENT

WOMEN'S STRUGGLES FOR RIGHTS OF CITIZENSHIP

for a constitutional amendment, first led by Susan B. Anthony and later by Alice Paul, finally succeeded in August 1920. The 19th Amendment, guaranteeing women the right to vote in all elections, had taken more than seven decades of organized struggle.

Racial and Ethnic Divisions

One issue to which white Progressive reformers paid little attention was racism against blacks, Amerindians, Latinos, and Asians, and associated doctrines of white supremacy. The United States at the turn of the century was beset by racial and ethnic divisions. In 1903 the eminent black activist and scholar W. E. B. DuBois prophesied, "The problem of the twentieth century is the problem of the color line," and in many ways he was proved right. In the United States, the "one drop rule" made a person either black or white, with no in-between racial categories. Latin America also had a long history of racial discrimination, but its racial categories ranged on a spectrum from light-skinned to dark-skinned, and included Amerindians as well as people of European, African, and mixed descent.

BLACK STRUGGLES FOR RIGHTS OF CITIZENSHIP

At the turn of the century, the vast majority of blacks lived in the South. Jim Crow laws, legally mandated segregation of the races, were upheld by the Supreme Court in 1896 in *Plessy v. Ferguson*, a ruling not overturned until *Brown v. Board of Education* in 1954. African Americans and other nonwhites were subjected to discrimination in every sphere of life, from housing and jobs to education and property ownership. Literacy tests, grandfather clauses, and poll taxes effectively disfranchised blacks and other minorities.

Mulberry Street, New York: A neighborhood of new immigrants, a sight that often aroused fears in many Americans at the turn of the century.

Sharecropping trapped former slaves in a semi-servile status, while widespread lynching, as documented by muckraking journalist Ida B. Wells, helped maintain white supremacy. Blacks responded by fighting back through the courts, the press, and organizations like the National Association for the Advancement of Colored People (NAACP), founded by DuBois in 1909. After 1914, seizing on the rising demand for industrial labor generated by World War I, half a million blacks migrated from the South to populate Chicago, Cleveland, Pittsburgh, and many other industrial centers of the North and Midwest. This "Great Migration" sparked dozens of urban race riots, in which white mobs, often in collusion with the police, assaulted and killed blacks and burned their homes and churches, most memorably in East St. Louis in 1917 and Chicago in 1919.

Many U.S. citizens of northern European descent also looked down on immigrants from eastern and southern Europe, like Slavs, Italians, Jews, and Greeks, who flooded U.S. shores from the 1890s. These "nativists" sought to end the policy of open European immigration, succeeding in the mid-1920s.

The Turn toward Overseas Imperialism

Another issue Progressive reformers generally ignored was U.S. imperialism. In fact, the United States had been expansionist since the beginning of its history. Through the nineteenth century most U.S. citizens believed they were a chosen people, their Manifest Destiny to dominate North America and perhaps the whole hemisphere. Viewing the continent's interior as open land, the United States waged aggressive wars of conquest against Native Americans and Mexico, seizing millions of acres. By the 1890s, in an era of rampant European imperialism in Asia and Africa, the United States was poised to follow Europe's lead and expand beyond its borders. Internal pressures compounded the tendency. As one politician put it, "American factories are making more than the American people can use; American soil is producing more than they can consume. Fate has written our policy for us; the trade of the world must and shall be ours." Many in the United States believed they were justified in joining the march to dominate distant lands and to "civilize" these "backward" parts of the world.

In Asia, the United States in effect joined Europe in seizing lands and turning them into colonies. In the Caribbean, instead of acquiring formal colonies, the United States used force and intimidation to establish indirect economic and political controls, while maintaining the formal sovereignty of the nations they dominated.

FORCES PROPELLING U.S. IMPERIALIST EXPANSION

LATIN AMERICA AT THE TURN OF THE CENTURY

General Characteristics

Tremendous diversity characterized the 19 republics and numerous territories and colonies making up Latin America and the Caribbean. Large Amerindian populations retained their ancient languages and cultures in Mexico, Guatemala, the Andean republics, and the Amazon basin. Large African-descended communities populated

Brazil and the Caribbean, the destinations of more than 80 percent of the 10 million African slaves forcibly transported to the New World from the 1500s through the 1800s. European-descended populations predominated in Argentina, Chile, and elsewhere. Everywhere race mixture was the norm, leading to complex racial hierarchies in which lighter skin generally meant more wealth and power, darker skin less. Class divisions were stark, with a tiny elite, a great majority of poor people, and a small middle class.

LATIN AMERICA'S COLONIAL LEGACY

Three hundred years of colonialism (1520s–1820s) had left a profound legacy. In contrast to North America, Amerindians were *included* in society, not excluded. From early on they formed a large servile labor force working in agriculture and mining for the benefit of their Spanish and (in Brazil) Portuguese masters. Another important contrast was that Latin America had no tradition of democracy in the colonial period, even among white propertied men. In theory the Spanish and Portuguese crowns ruled from across the sea, but in practice landowners, bureaucrats, military leaders, and the Roman Catholic Church exercised political power within the colonies. Important consequences followed. After independence in the 1820s, lacking democratic institutions, political-military strongmen or *caudillos* and their allies seized power and were often challenged by other such *caudillos*. One common result was endemic civil war between factions of the elite. Sometimes these faction fights provided an opportunity for lower-class groups to mobilize and challenge their subordinate status, as in the War of the Pacific between Peru and Chile in the 1880s, or in Mexico in the 1910s. But most often poor and subordinate groups had little choice but to grudgingly accept their inferior status.

The Liberal Revolution

ECONOMIC VS. POLITICAL LIBERALISM

In the second half of the nineteenth century, a liberal revolution—economic and political—swept most of Latin America. Economic liberalism essentially meant free market capitalism: privatization of collectively held lands of the Church and Amerindian communities, open markets, foreign investment, and wage labor (as opposed to bound servitude or debt peonage). Political liberalism essentially meant opening up the political system: extension of citizenship rights to groups previously excluded, periodic elections, greater press freedom, and more democratic institutions. Generally, however, economic liberalism far outpaced political liberalism, leading to emergent capitalist economies with only a veneer of democracy.

EXPORT ECONOMIES PREDOMINATE

In this context, capitalist development usually meant production for export. European and North American investors encouraged production of export commodities like sugar, coffee, bananas, beef, rubber, nitrates, guano (piles of bird droppings used as fertilizer), and metals like copper, zinc, and tin, for their own expanding economies. As export production soared, local markets remained stunted, food production stagnated, and industrial development lagged. Foreign interests built modern infrastructure like ports, railways, and processing plants in enclaves separate from the rest of the economy, draining labor and capital and depressing other sectors. Dependency on primary export products and imported manufactures increased vulnerability to the whims of the world market. If world demand for nitrates, for instance, dried up because of a depression in Europe or the United States, the Chilean economy went into a tailspin. The results could be disastrous. To paraphrase an old Mexican adage, when the United States or Europe sneezed, the countries of Latin America caught pneumonia.

As capitalist development took hold, cities grew rapidly, especially along the coasts. Millions of Europeans, mainly from Spain and Italy, poured into Brazil, Argentina, Chile, Cuba, and elsewhere. From 1870 to 1930, some 9 million Europeans migrated to Latin America; in the 1880s Buenos Aires, soon to tout itself as the Paris of South America, received some 640,000 European immigrants. In the same period hundreds of thousands of Asian laborers, from China, the Philippines, and elsewhere, migrated to the Caribbean and elsewhere to work in expanding export enclaves. As in the United States, urbanization and capitalist growth sparked the formation of an organized working class that demanded fair wages, better working conditions, and full rights of citizenship. By the early 1900s labor and civic organizations, protest movements, and strikes mushroomed, often in alliance with professionals and small business owners, who wanted greater political voice but not social revolution. In such an atmosphere nationalist sentiments flourished.

IMMIGRATION AND URBANIZATION

Confronted with organized opposition, dictatorial regimes basically had two choices: to clamp down on the boiling pot of dissent, or to lift the lid and let off steam by giving in to some demands. Institutionalizing the latter approach led to a new style of governance, populism, that incorporated rising urban sectors into electoral coalitions, acceding to some popular demands while dispensing government patronage. Populism became increasingly important as the twentieth century progressed. Ruling groups often combined these tactics using "*pan o palo*" ("bread or stick"). The regime of Porfirio Díaz in Mexico (1876–1910) mastered this strategy, at least for a while, crushing strikes and protests with one hand and buying off opposition groups with the other. But sometimes the contradictions became too great. This was the case in Mexico, where years of capitalist development (economic liberalism) without a corresponding growth in the rights of citizenship (political liberalism) created a tinderbox that needed only a spark to set the whole country ablaze. In 1910, when elites began to squabble over elections, the spark was set flying, and the result was the Mexican Revolution (see Chapter 12).

STRATEGIES OF RULE

UNITED STATES IMPERIALISM IN THE CARIBBEAN

As the liberal revolution transformed the economies and societies of Latin America, the United States increasingly cast its gaze southward. In particular, the United States had long coveted the islands and territories of the Caribbean. In 1823, Secretary of State John Quincy Adams expressed a widely held view when he likened Cuba to a "ripening fruit," destined to fall into the "bosom" of the United States. The Monroe Doctrine of 1823, intended to keep European powers from recolonizing the Americas, was transformed over time into a positive right to intervene. The main U.S. interests were strategic and economic: wanting to keep Europe out, it also wanted to dominate production and trade in fruit, coffee, tobacco, and minerals, and to monopolize the sale of foodstuffs

CREATING THE U.S. BACKYARD

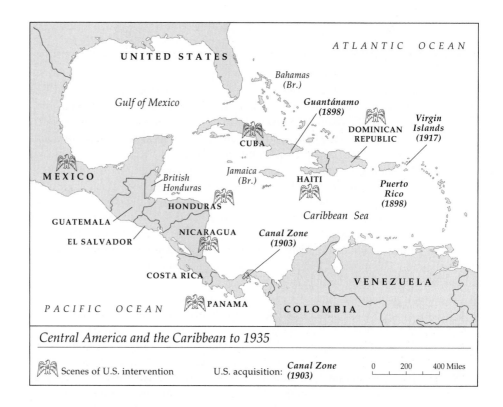

Central America and the Caribbean to 1935

Scenes of U.S. intervention   U.S. acquisition: *Canal Zone (1903)*   0   200   400 Miles

and manufactured goods. In Central America, the principal U.S. interest was a transoceanic canal. For decades merchants and politicians had dreamed of a trans-isthmian waterway, facilitating westward expansion and opening the vast Asian market. After construction of the Panama Canal began in 1904, the cornerstone of U.S. policy was to prevent a rival canal from being built in nearby Nicaragua.

The Spanish-Cuban-American War and Its Aftermath

CUBAN STRUGGLES FOR INDEPENDENCE

Cuba remained one of the few Spanish colonies not to gain independence in the 1820s, mainly because its Cuban-born light-skinned elite feared that fighting the Spanish would spark a massive slave revolt and race war, as had engulfed Haiti in the 1790s. Through the 1800s, a sense of Cuban nationalism and stirrings for independence grew. The Ten Years War (1868–1878), waged mainly in the east, was the first in a series of armed independence struggles. A new generation of leaders, many exiled in New York and Tampa, tirelessly organized for the struggle's final phase. The most prominent was José Martí, poet, essayist, philosopher, and activist, whose antiracist nationalism held enormous promise for *Cuba Libre* (a liberated Cuba), and whose name to this day is revered throughout the island. Spain, meanwhile, had grown weak, its economy backward compared to its European neighbors. Finally, in 1895, conditions were ripe, and Martí and his fellow patriots returned to Cuba to launch the final phase of the struggle.

B I O G R A P H Y

Inside the Monster

Cuba's José Martí

"Every day my life is in danger. I am in danger of giving up my life for my country, for my duty—as I understand it and must execute it—so that Cuba's independence will prevent the expansion of the United States throughout the Antilles, allowing that nation [the United States] to fall, ever more powerfully, upon our American lands. Everything I have done, everything I will do, is toward this end. . . . The same lesser and public duties of these nations—nations like yours and mine—that are most vitally concerned with preventing the opening of Cuba, by annexation by the imperialists [the United States]

and the Spaniards, that road, which must be closed, and which with our blood we are closing, of the annexation of the countries of our America by the brutal and turbulent North [the United States] which despises them—has prevented these nations' apparent adherence and obvious assistance to this sacrifice made for their immediate benefit. I have lived inside the monster and know its entrails—and my weapon is only the slingshot of David."*

. . .

In this unfinished letter, penned on 18 May 1895, the day before his death in combat against the Spanish, the Cuban national hero José Martí (1853–1895) expressed the fears of many Latin Americans about the seemingly insatiable desire for wealth and power impelling the United States overseas. At age 16, Martí founded a newspaper in Havana, Patria Libre (Free Homeland), was arrested and imprisoned by the Spanish, and exiled to Madrid. There he studied law before journeying to Paris, where he earned a wide reputation as an eloquent writer and profound thinker. In 1880 he moved to New York, where he lived for the next 15 years, witnessing firsthand the suffering and discrimination imposed on immigrants and the coldness and grittiness of U.S. urban life. In early 1895 he returned to Cuba to lead the revolution and was killed on the field of battle. Devoting his life to the cause of Cuba Libre, Martí's visionary antiracism and deep humanism continue to resonate among Cubans and throughout the Americas.

*Source: www.cubaminrex.cu/josemarti/marti_testampolitico.htm (the official website of the Cuban Ministry of Foreign Relations). Translated by Michael Schroeder.

Within months Martí was killed, but his compatriots fought on, and for the next three years Cuban patriots waged guerrilla war against the Spanish.

Finally, in early 1898, the Spanish, their treasury empty and soldiers exhausted, were all but defeated. Meanwhile, the U.S. bankers and merchants who dominated the sugar trade and owned much of the island's land grew increasingly anxious about what Cuban independence would mean for their investments. The McKinley administration also feared a rebel victory and its potential for undermining U.S. strategic interests in the Caribbean. Meanwhile, the Hearst newspapers portrayed the Spaniards as inhuman monsters committing horrendous barbarities against the Cubans, whipping up anti-Spanish feelings and paving the way for intervention. In February 1898 came the ideal pretext, when the U.S. battleship *Maine* blew up in Havana harbor, killing 262 men. Blaming the Spanish and demanding justice with the cry, "Remember the *Maine*!" Congress declared war (in fact the *Maine*'s boiler had failed). Within months U.S. forces defeated the Spanish, taking not only Cuba but Puerto Rico, Guam, and the Philippines. A 30-year liberation struggle, on the brink of victory, suddenly became a U.S. war of conquest.

After the war Cuba became neither fully independent nor a formal colony. Instead, the U.S.-imposed Platt Amendment (1901) established a U.S. military government; preserved the U.S. right to intervene in Cuban affairs; provided the United States with military bases (one of which, Guantánamo, they still retain); and required U.S. approval of treaties with foreign powers. Puerto Rico was annexed, becoming a "commonwealth," its inhabitants granted citizenship in 1917. Cuba remained a protectorate until 1934, its economy dominated by U.S. business interests. Before his death José Martí had feared just such an outcome, insisting on full independence and declaring that "to change masters is not to be free." In 1959, 64 years after Martí's death, Fidel Castro would don Martí's mantle to carry on with what he called "the delayed revolution."

Acquiring Panama and Building the Panama Canal

Assuming the presidency in 1901, Theodore Roosevelt, an unabashed imperialist, was determined to wrest Panama from Colombia and realize the vision of a trans-isthmian canal. Years earlier the Colombian government had granted a French company the right to build a canal through its province of Panama. When the company failed, the Roosevelt administration pressured Colombia for canal rights. Irritated by Roosevelt's heavy-handed tactics and holding out for more money, the Colombian Senate rejected a treaty already ratified by the U.S. Senate. Enraged by the actions of those he called "contemptible little creatures . . . the Bogotá lot of jackrabbits," Roosevelt was determined to build and control the canal. In 1903 a group of Panamanians, Europeans, and Colombian soldiers working closely with the State Department revolted and proclaimed Panama an independent country. The Roosevelt administration promptly recognized the new country as a sovereign state, and Panama promptly granted the United States a permanent lease to a canal zone. Panama remained a U.S. protectorate until 1939. Roosevelt later acknowledged, "I took the Canal Zone." Overcoming tremendous technological hurdles and rampant yellow fever, the canal was finally completed in 1914, most of the work undertaken by Jamaican and other West Indian laborers, thousands of whom died building it.

West Indian laborers arriving in Panama.

Intensified U.S. Imperialism in Latin America

With the motto "Speak softly but carry a big stick" and concerned about a recent German and British blockade of Venezuela's ports to force the government to pay its debts (1902), President Roosevelt modified the Monroe Doctrine in 1904 to grant the United States the right to intervene militarily in neighboring countries

CREATING AN IMPERIALIST LEGACY

in cases of "chronic wrong-doing" (such as not paying debts) or failure to maintain "order." This Roosevelt Corollary to the Monroe Doctrine made the United States an "international police power." The doctrine was invoked many times in the coming years, officially sanctioning U.S. imperialist intervention in much of Latin America. U.S. Marines occupied Nicaragua (1912–1925, 1926–1933), Haiti (1915–1934), and the Dominican Republic (1916–1924), in each case establishing National Guards to maintain "order." It intervened repeatedly in Cuba (1898–1902, 1906–1909, 1912, 1917–1922), Guatemala (1906, 1920), and Honduras (seven times between 1907 and 1925), and acquired the Virgin Islands from Denmark (1917). It also occupied the port of Veracruz, Mexico (1914), to help topple the Huerta regime, and spent a year in northern Mexico chasing Pancho Villa (1916–1917).

Roosevelt's successor, William Howard Taft, sought to refine the Roosevelt Corollary by substituting "dollars for bullets." The theory behind "dollar diplomacy" was to promote "order" and "stability" in "backward" countries by fostering commercial and financial relations with the United States. In the commonest pattern, Washington encouraged U.S. banking interests to assume the debts of "disorderly" countries, while U.S. representatives took control of their customhouses. In this way, host countries would pay their debts promptly and European powers were prevented from intervening. U.S.-supervised elections often accompanied these arrangements, as did the marines, increased U.S. investments in export production, dictatorial regimes (despite supposedly free elections), and high-sounding phrases on the virtues of democracy. By such means the Caribbean was transformed into a U.S. lake.

The Impact of U.S. Imperialism

BACKLASH AGAINST U.S. IMPERIALISM

Efforts to dominate other lands and peoples often bring unwanted and unintended consequences. This was especially true in Latin America, where U.S. imperialism provoked a firestorm of protest. Uruguayan José Enrique Rodó's enormously influential essay *Ariel* (1900), for instance, likened the United States to Shakespeare's Caliban—cold, soulless, consumed with vulgar materialism—and Latin America to Ariel—lover of beauty and truth, "the noble and winged part of the spirit." The famed Nicaraguan poet Rubén Darío's "Ode to Roosevelt" (1904) captured the sentiments of many Latin Americans with its images of "men of Saxon eyes and barbaric soul" holding the south captive in their "clutching iron claws," warning that "even though you can count on everything, / You still lack one thing: God." Anti-imperialism, in turn, fueled nationalism and the spread of radical political doctrines like anarchism, syndicalism, socialism, and communism. By the late 1920s the chorus of protest at home and abroad had grown so deafening that the United States was compelled to change course, ushering in the "Good Neighbor Policy" after 1934, which foreswore military intervention in lieu of less visible forms of domination. Still, a century after Darío's warning, the legacy of that anti-Yankee florescence endures.

CANADA

The Western Hemisphere's Northern Nation

For nearly a century after its independence, the United States periodically showed interest in absorbing the British possessions to its north, and during the War of 1812 waged forays into Canada. Frustrating U.S. hopes and embarking on their own experiment in nation-making, in 1867 Canadians established a confederation, the Dominion of Canada, with a parliamentary form of government. Initially the Dominion included only four eastern provinces—Ontario, Quebec, Nova Scotia, and New Brunswick—and was firmly attached to Great Britain. By the early twentieth century the Dominion had expanded westward across the vast Canadian prairies to the Pacific coast to include Manitoba, Saskatchewan, Alberta, and British Columbia. By then Britain had granted Canada substantial control over both external and internal affairs, an important example of an imperial nation allowing growing independence of a former colony. The Dominion, like the United States, was created with little regard for the claims of Native peoples, over the objections of many and the failed armed uprisings of some.

After 1900 the United States sought to dominate Canada economically rather than annex it politically or militarily. By 1914 nearly one-quarter of U.S. foreign investments were concentrated in Canada, initially mostly in agriculture, mining, and transportation, then expanded into manufacturing. In the economic arena the United States thus tried to foster a relationship with Canada somewhat akin to its relations with Latin American nations. Yet in other ways the U.S.-Canada relationship contrasted sharply with U.S. relations with its southern neighbors. Similarly, many aspects of Canada's social, political, and economic development closely resembled that of the United States and set the nation apart from Latin America.

During the years between confederation and the end of World War I, the Dominion became the largest country in the hemisphere. It remains so. Canada's resources of timber, fur, fish, and minerals had boosted its growth while still a British colony and, along with petroleum and natural gas, spurred the Dominion's rapid economic expansion through the period of World War I. In the late nineteenth century, as the western lands of the United States filled with settlers, the Canadian plains declared themselves the "last best west," as lumber camps, cattle ranches, wheat farms, and a Canadian transcontinental railway spread across the prairie provinces.

The Dominion remained primarily a rural nation, diverse in its agricultural products, but the pace of urbanization picked up in the early twentieth century. The mostly French-speaking province of Quebec boasted the port of Montreal on the St. Lawrence River, while the most populous province, Ontario, was home to the city that would become Canada's major economic center, Toronto. Tiny hamlets and smaller commercial, industrial, and agricultural processing centers also grew apace, dotting the nation from the rugged Atlantic coastline to west of the soaring Rocky Mountains. Many settlers to Canada's farms and towns were immigrants, the Dominion luring thousands, mostly eastern European, with the prospect of cheap

THE DOMINION OF CANADA

U.S.-CANADA RELATIONS

CANADA'S GROWING ECONOMY

land and plentiful jobs. As Canadian society became more diverse, it also became more divided culturally, these conflicts often spilling into politics, just as in the United States. Similarly, reform movements emerged to extend the franchise to women, improve schools and housing, and assimilate Natives and foreign-speakers, whether they wished it or not.

CANADA IN WORLD WAR I

World War I was a watershed for Canada. The Dominion entered the war in 1914, its population of 8 million suffering more than 230,000 casualties and the government mobilizing the home front to support the Allies. Many Canadians hailed from the countries fighting the Allies; many other native-born Canadians, including many in Quebec, had grave doubts about the conflict. Increasing its powers, Canada's federal government swept these concerns aside. In the decades to come the Dominion would face the consequences of having poured its energies into a world at war while ignoring significant problems at home. The influenza epidemic of 1919, resulting in more than 50,000 Canadian deaths, seemed a harbinger of hard times.

SUMMARY

Colonized by Europe in the 1500s and 1600s—Spain and Portugal to the south and Britain and France to the north—most of the Americas gained independence from the 1770s to the 1820s, with Canada beginning to gain its independence in the 1860s. In the United States, the combination of torrential immigration, free market capitalism, and political democracy among white men created an enormously creative and aggressive republic that in little more than a century became an empire, spreading across the continent and poised to expand overseas. By 1900 the United States had become the hemisphere's greatest power, relatively affluent and stable despite many internal tensions and on a par, economically and militarily, with the most advanced European nations. Canada emerged as politically liberal, geographically vast, and, mainly because of its much smaller and more dispersed population, far less powerful, economically and militarily, than its southern neighbor. In Latin America, colonial rule had created a very different society. Independence brought civil wars, dictatorships, and continuing inequalities, though by the late 1800s the liberal revolution had brought many changes. As capitalist markets and the idea of political equality spread, the gulf separating the northern and southern parts of the hemisphere shrank. Many of the same trends were transforming both regions: immigration, urbanization, nationalism, militarism, labor organizing, and the growing clamor for equal rights.

Extending its power overseas, the United States rapidly came to dominate the Caribbean and Central America while slamming the door on potential European intervention. This muscular imperialism caused a flowering of anti-imperialism and nationalism across Latin America, facilitating the spread of radical political ideologies. Although denunciations of "Yankee imperialism" grew, so too did the economic and cultural integration of the hemisphere, an integration that intensified as the twentieth century progressed.

SUGGESTED SOURCES

Burns, E. Bradford, and Julie A. Charlip. *Latin America: A Concise Interpretive History*. 7th ed. 2002. An excellent synthetic survey.*

Clayton, Lawrence A., and Michael L. Conniff. *A History of Modern Latin America*. 1999. A readable and informative introduction.*

Dinnerstein, Leonard, et al. *Natives and Strangers: A Multicultural History of Americans*. 1996. A superb introduction to U.S. ethnic and immigration history.*

Gordon, Linda. *The Great Arizona Orphan Abduction*. 1999. Fascinating story of an early twentieth-century event and what it reveals about intersections of race, religion, gender, and immigration.

Jacobson, Matthew Frye. *Barbarian Virtues: The United States Encounters Foreign Peoples at Home and Abroad, 1876–1917*. 2000. An ambitious reinterpretation.*

Kleinberg, S. J. *The Shadow of the Mills: Working Class Families in Pittsburgh, 1870–1907*. 1989. An excellent study of the effects of industrialization on urban workers and their families.

Lewis, David Levering. *W. E. B. DuBois: Biography of a Race*. 1993. *W. E. B. Du Bois: The Fight for Equality and the American Century*. 2000. An outstanding multivolume biography.

Pérez, Louis A. *Cuba: Between Reform and Revolution*. 1988. The best single-volume English-language history of Cuba, with an extraordinary bibliographic essay.*

Sinclair, Upton. *The Jungle*. 1906. A searing novel of the meatpacking industry and immigrant labor in Chicago by a leading socialist of the era.*

Thompson, John Herd, and Stephen J. Randall. *Canada and the United States: Ambivalent Allies*. 1994. A far-ranging discussion of relations between the United States and Canada in the late nineteenth and early twentieth centuries.

Williamson, Edwin. *Penguin History of Latin America*. 1993. A well-written and thorough survey.*

WEB SOURCES

http://lanic.utexas.edu/la/region/history. The Latin American Network Information Center at the University of Texas provides this history site with links to the histories of various countries and the region as a whole.

www.smplanet.com/imperialism/toc.html. A good starting point with links to materials and sites on U.S. imperialism in the pre–World War I period.

---

*Paperback available.

⑥Imperialism in Asia and the Pacific

Western domination of Asia and the main Pacific islands was almost complete by 1900 except that by then Japan had also joined the imperialists. In that year, a futile attempt at resistance in China was crushed by a joint force of eight imperialist nations. With a few exceptions, European nations, the United States, and Japan were primarily interested in raw materials and markets in Asia and not in settlement. Industrialized nations prized Asia's mineral wealth and also needed such agricultural raw materials as rubber, hemp, and sugar. On plantations developed to grow these items, local or imported labor under European supervision produced goods for a world market.

INDUSTRIALIZED NATIONS SEEK RAW MATERIALS AND MARKETS IN ASIA

In addition, industrialized nations coveted the markets for the manufactured goods Asia would supply. The large population of China especially excited the imagination of foreign merchants. As one wishful thinking Englishman said, "If every Chinese would buy a British-made shirt each year, Manchester shirt manufacturers would never suffer economic recession!" By 1900 only Japan, China, Siam (Thailand), Nepal, Afghanistan, Persia, and the Ottoman Empire still retained formal independence. However, with the exception of Japan, they were really no more than "semi-colonies" that Europeans influenced or controlled indirectly.

Western states, later joined by Japan, were able to gain and maintain dominion over Asia for a number of reasons. They possessed overwhelming military power, the product of their advanced technology, and modern industrial bases. Nationalism was another important factor, as highly competitive Western nations vied constantly with one another for real and imagined advantages. Conversely, the people of Asian states, except for the Japanese, lacked a sense of modern nationalism. Because of these factors, as well as local circumstances, notably ineffective governments led by monarchs of declining dynasties, Asian states were unsuccessful in resisting foreign intervention and domination—and sometimes even invited it to resolve local differences.

WESTERN IMPACT ON ASIANS

Eventually, Westerners introduced to Asians the ideas of modern nationalism, which in turn provided the impetus for the dominated peoples to revolt against imperialism. They also exposed Asians to Western science, technology, political philosophy, and cultural norms, much of which could also be turned against the conquerors. Thus, although Western imperialism was at its height, European empires had already sown the seeds of their own destruction. In the twentieth century, first the Japanese and then other Asians would use what they had learned from the West to counter it.

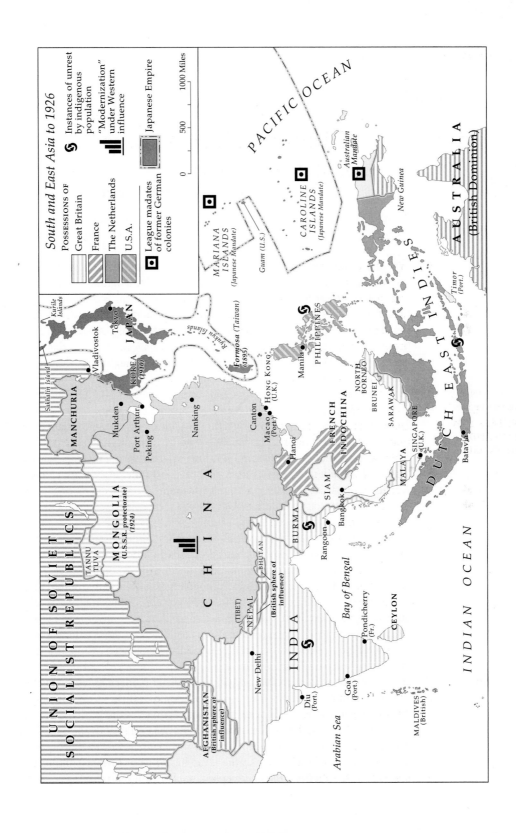

South and East Asia to 1926

Instances of unrest by indigenous population ↻

"Modernization" under Western influence

Japanese Empire

POSSESSIONS OF
Great Britain
France
The Netherlands
U.S.A.

☐ League madates of former German colonies

0   500   1000 Miles

PACIFIC OCEAN

UNION OF SOVIET SOCIALIST REPUBLICS

TANNU TUVA

MONGOLIA (U.S.S.R. protectorate) (1924)

MANCHURIA

Vladivostok

Sakhalin Island

Kurile Islands

Mukden
Port Arthur
Peking

JAPAN

Tokyo

KOREA (1910)

Ryukyu Islands

Formosa (Taiwan) (1895)

CHINA

Nanking

Canton

HONG KONG (U.K.)

Macao (Port.)

Hanoi

FRENCH INDOCHINA

SIAM

Bangkok

BURMA

Rangoon

TIBET

NEPAL

BHUTAN

(British sphere of influence)

AFGHANISTAN (British sphere of influence)

New Delhi

INDIA ↻

Diu (Port.)

Goa (Port.)

Pondicherry (Fr.)

CEYLON

MALDIVES (British)

Arabian Sea

Bay of Bengal

INDIAN OCEAN

MALAYA

SINGAPORE (U.K.)

SARAWAK

BRUNEI

NORTH BORNEO

PHILIPPINES ↻

Manila

DUTCH EAST INDIES ↻

Batavia

Timor (Port.)

MARIANA ISLANDS (Japanese Mandate) ☐

Guam (U.S.)

CAROLINE ISLANDS (Japanese Mandate) ☐

Australian Mandate ☐

New Guinea

AUSTRALIA (British Dominion)

In the Pacific the United States acquired Hawaii and the Philippines by 1900, and its motives and reasons for success were similar in many ways to those of European colonialists on the Asian continent. Strategic naval considerations, however, were also an important motivating factor for U.S. actions.

CHINA

A Tradition-Bound Society

China was geographically isolated from other major cultures and had dominated East Asia for millennia. It boasted a continuous civilization spanning some 4,000 years. In the third century B.C.E., to protect itself from the nomadic peoples on its northern borders, China built the Great Wall, the biggest man-made structure on earth. The Chinese had developed a unique writing system (ideograms and pictograms), local religions (ancestor worship and Taoism), and a political and moral philosophy (Confucianism). Although caravans and sailing boats had carried goods between China and the eastern Mediterranean since ancient times, the only outside culture that had an important influence before the coming of modern Westerners was that of India. Indian Buddhism was accepted enthusiastically by the Chinese in the early centuries of the Christian era.

THE TRADITIONAL CHINESE STATE AND SOCIETY

For more than 2,000 years China had been an empire headed by dynasties that could be overthrown for incompetence. Chinese emperors were assisted by bureaucrats selected on the basis of educational attainments demonstrated in examinations based on Confucian moral philosophy; they ruled a predominantly rural society. There were no hereditary social classes; however, a class system existed that exalted scholars and honored farmers and artisans but denigrated merchants as social parasites. Although most Chinese lived in nuclear families, multigenerational families headed by a senior male or patriarch were admired. Men enjoyed higher status than women, but great respect was paid to the aged.

Since China was the largest, most advanced, and strongest state in East Asia, its civilization, even more than its political power, dominated the area. Korea and Vietnam were under direct or indirect Chinese political control for 2,000 years and absorbed major aspects of Chinese culture. Although Japan was never under China's political sway, it voluntarily adopted much of China's culture. China's traditional role as the giver but not the receiver of cultures contributed to its ethnocentrism and reluctance to learn from other peoples, an attitude that proved disastrous during the era of imperialism.

From its traditional cultural and political perspective, China thought of itself as the "central kingdom" and all foreign nations as tributary vassal states. When the monarchs of the Manchu (or Ch'ing) dynasty received modern seaborne Westerners in the late seventeenth and eighteenth centuries, they, like their predecessors from the Ming dynasty, regarded the foreigners as tribute-bearing vassals.

Westerners came to China to trade: its tea, silks, and porcelains were in great demand in Europe. Until the late eighteenth century, however, Europeans had little to sell in return. This balance of trade in China's favor further reinforced China's self-perception of superiority and indispensability. Westerners, however, rejected China's

Extraterritorial rights and wealth gave Westerners special privileges in China. Two well-dressed gentlemen being carried in sedan chairs as they sightsee.

claims; they believed in legal equality between nations, and by the late nineteenth century looked down on the by-then technologically backward Chinese as inferiors.

The Twilight of the Manchu Dynasty

In the nineteenth century, Chinese traditional culture and Western imperialism met in headlong confrontation. Differences on such issues as diplomatic equality, international relations, laws, and trade made conflict inevitable, but opium precipitated the clash. The Chinese government had banned opium, an ever more popular addictive drug. But it was a lucrative trade item for Western merchants. Great Britain's insistence that its merchants had the right to sell opium to the Chinese triggered war between the two nations in 1839–1842 and again in 1858–1860.

China was defeated both times and had to sign (in the eyes of the Chinese) humiliating "unequal treaties" that forced it to open its ports to opium and other trade, cede territory, and pay an indemnity. The extraterritoriality provisions of these treaties exempted Westerners residing in China from Chinese laws, which were considered harsh and barbarous by Western standards. In addition, China was forced to accept Christian missionaries. Taking advantage of China's defeat by Britain and its internal problems, the

CHINESE AND WESTERN IDEAS IN CONFLICT

expansionist Russian Empire forced China to cede to Russia huge areas in the northwest bordering Russian Central Asia, the northeast, and along the Pacific coast.

CHRISTIAN MISSIONARIES INTRODUCE NEW IDEAS

Although few Chinese converted to Christianity, the missionaries introduced modern medicine and sciences, schools—significantly, also for girls—and other ideas to the Chinese, with revolutionary consequences. In the early twentieth century, modern Western-style schools replaced traditional ones and Western medicine gained acceptance. Above all, missionaries introduced new ideas about social relationships that contributed to the republican revolt against dynastic rule, a social revolt of the individual against the all-powerful family and of women against male dominance.

By 1900 China had been carved up into spheres of influence controlled by Russia, Germany, Great Britain, France, and Japan. In the German sphere of influence, for example, Chinese authority was limited; Germany alone could exploit the resources and sell mainly German goods to the Chinese residents there. Similar conditions applied in the other nations' spheres of influence. China appeared destined for full colonization. In 1899 and again in 1900 the United States proposed an Open Door policy that would allow all nations equal opportunity to trade in China while supporting Chinese independence. It became the cornerstone of U.S. policy toward China up to World War II.

THE MANCHU DYNASTY FAILS TO MEET CHALLENGES

These humiliations weakened and discredited the ruling Manchu dynasty. During the last decades of the nineteenth century, China was plagued internally with rebellions, brigandage, and natural disasters, while externally it struggled unsuccessfully to maintain itself against increasing foreign encroachments. It was China's misfortune that in the most critical years of its contact with the West its destiny was in the hands of an ignorant, corrupt, and unscrupulous woman, Yehonala, better known to the world as the Dowager Empress Tz'u-hsi. She ruled autocratically between 1862, when she became coregent for her young son, and her death in 1908.

THE FUTILE BOXER REBELLION

In the summer of 1900, a group of mostly poor people who practiced magic, hated foreigners, and trained in shadow boxing—hence the name Boxers—inflicted a reign of terror on the capital city Peking and its environs, especially against foreigners and Chinese Christian converts, and besieged the foreign diplomatic quarters in the city. Their patron Tz'u-hsi went so far as to declare war on all the Western nations and to order all foreigners in China killed. Fortunately for China, its diplomats abroad refused to obey her order, and many provincial governors at home also ignored her and succeeded in restricting Boxer violence to Peking and parts of northern China. Eight nations with nationals in China, including the United States, organized an international force to relieve the besieged diplomats and other foreigners in Peking. Just before the relief forces entered Peking in August 1900, Tz'u-hsi fled the capital disguised as a peasant woman. In 1901 China accepted the Boxer Protocol, which provided for punishment of Boxer leaders, a huge indemnity, and an armed and walled legation district to safeguard the foreign diplomatic community in Peking.

The Boxer disaster stripped the Manchus of the last remaining claim to authority. U.S.- and British-educated Sun Yat-sen emerged the foremost revolutionary dedicated to the overthrow of the dynasty. He proposed to replace it with a republic and formulated a program that combined nationalism, democracy, and economic and social reforms. Sun lamented that China had become a semicolony, the prey of all and the responsibility of none. The impotent Manchu dynasty lingered in power until

BIOGRAPHY

A Foe of the Manchus

From 1885, i.e., from the time of our defeat in the war with France, I set before myself the object of the overthrow of the Chi'ng [Manchu] dynasty and the establishment of a Chinese Republic on its ruins. At the very beginning I selected for my propaganda the college at which I was studying, regarding medical science as the kindly aunt who would bring me out onto the high road of politics.

Ten years passed like one day. In Canton Medical School, I made friends with Chen Shih-Liang, who had a very large circle of acquaintances amongst widely traveled people who knew China well. When I began talking of revolution, advocating its ideas, he gladly agreed with me, and declared that he would immediately enter a revolutionary party if I would agree to lead it. . . . [A]ttracted also by the thought that there I should have wider field for my revolutionary propaganda, I went to Hong Kong to continue my education. For four years I gave up all my free time from studies to the cause of revolutionary propaganda, traveling backward and forward between Hong Kong and Amoy.*

. . .

Dr. Sun Yat-sen, 1866–1925, father of the Chinese Republic, wrote here about how he became a revolutionary. Born near Canton of poor parents, Sun was taken by an elder brother to Hawaii as a youth and was educated in a Christian missionary school. He converted to Christianity. While in medical school Sun was drawn to revolutionary politics by the incompetence of the Manchu government. He dedicated his life to overthrowing the Manchus and to modernizing China.

*From *Memoirs of a Chinese Revolutionary* (1918), quoted in *The China Reader*, vol. 2: *Republican China, 1911–1919,* Franz Schurmann and Orville Schell, eds. Copyright 1967 by Random House, Inc. Reprinted by permission of Random House, Inc.

1911, at least partly because the imperialist nations were for the moment satisfied with their gains and did not wish to risk war among one another by demanding additional concessions from China.

THE RISE OF JAPAN AS A GREAT POWER

Although China contained the largest population in Asia, by 1900 Japan had become the most powerful Asian country. Its swift transformation from an isolated feudal state to a respected modern industrial power requires a detailed examination.

In 1853 the United States forced Japan to open its doors to the world. A U.S. naval squadron commanded by Commodore Matthew Perry arrived in Tokyo with an ultimatum that hitherto isolated Japan sign a treaty prepared by the United States. Perry invited Japanese leaders aboard his ships and showed them his formidable cannons, as well as displays of U.S. science and technology, including model steam engines and trains and tracks. The Japanese were suitably impressed. They knew what had happened to China when it resisted British might, and they bowed to the inevitable. Japan signed the treaty as demanded. Great Britain, Russia, France, and

UNITED STATES FORCES JAPAN TO OPEN ITS DOORS

The Meiji emperor proclaiming the constitution in 1889.

the Netherlands followed in the wake of the United States. These treaties opened up Japanese ports for trade with the West, fixed the tariff that the government of Japan could charge on imported goods, and granted extraterritorial rights to the Western signatory states (which exempted their citizens in Japan from obeying Japanese laws).

In 1868 a group of young men, mostly samurai (hereditary nobles and warriors) opposed to the shogunate, overthrew the ineffective feudal government that had bowed to the humiliating Western demands and returned authority to the figurehead emperor and his advisers. The event was called the Meiji Restoration, named after the young emperor who gained power as a result of the revolution. During the early years of the Meiji Restoration, Japan reconciled itself to the limitations that the unequal treaties had placed on its sovereignty. With the same zeal that they had manifested in learning from China over a thousand years earlier, the emperor and his youthful advisers began a program of reforms based on what they perceived to be the best Western models. As the Meiji emperor officially proclaimed in 1868, "Knowledge shall be sought throughout the world so as to strengthen the foundation of imperial rule." Mostly men of military background, his advisers immediately focused on military reform. Their first model for a new army was France because its army was believed to be the best in the world. When France was resoundingly defeated by Germany in the war of 1870–1871, the Japanese quickly switched mentors and patterned their army on that of victorious Germany. Following the same logic, they established a navy based on the British model.

The crowning political achievement of the Meiji Restoration was the promulgation of a constitution in 1889, which made Japan the first Asian nation to commit itself to the daring innovation of constitutional government. The Meiji Constitution, promulgated as a gift of the emperor to the people, pronounced the imperial line as divinely descended, protected many imperial prerogatives, and made the emperor commander in chief of the military forces. However, in a dramatic departure from Japanese tradition, it created a bicameral legislature, known in English as the Diet, which consisted of a largely hereditary House of Peers and a popularly elected lower House of Representatives. Men who paid a certain level of taxes (about 5 percent of adult males) were eligible to vote in the 1890 election. In subsequent years the qualifications for male eligibility to vote went down progressively, but women were denied the vote until after World War II. Political parties were permitted to contest the elections. The Meiji Constitution also provided for government by a prime minister and his cabinet. In time it was accepted that the prime minister and cabinet must receive majority endorsement by the Diet. The constitution also guaranteed many freedoms.

The goal of early Meiji leaders was to promote an emperor-centered nation. They enacted laws to strengthen Japan and safeguard its sovereignty, and later to recover lost sovereign rights.

JAPAN ESTABLISHES A CONSTITUTION

A Modern Economy

Japan's successful transition from an agricultural to an industrial nation was the result of government planning and cooperation between the government and private enterprise. The government took the lead in developing a modern economy by providing transportation and communication networks and by denoting certain key industries and mines as national enterprises. Japan was leery of contracting foreign loans because of the onerous conditions such borrowing entailed, so it financed modernization by squeezing tax revenues out of the farming sector. After defeating China in 1895, Japan exacted a large monetary indemnity from China and used it to finance further industrial expansion.

To plan and ensure steady growth, a ministry of industry coordinated strategic nationalized industries with nonstrategic private enterprises such as the textile industry. After the key industries were firmly established, the government sold them at low prices to private capitalists. Thus, a strong private sector developed, dominated by a few large firms called *zaibatsu,* strictly meaning "financial clique," but in reality conglomerates that worked hand in glove with the government. The two largest *zaibatsu* were Mitsui and Mitsubishi, each with many affiliates that straddled all segments of the economy.

Up to World War I, Japan's heavy industries were mainly designed to meet its strategic and military needs. Since it lacked key raw materials such as iron ore and coal, Japanese military strategists were concerned about the security of the sea lanes and the reliability of foreign sources of raw materials. In light industry, the early emphasis was on building silk and cotton mills, which required little capital, had a traditional base, and mostly employed low-paid, docile young women from the farms. The Japanese government desired not only a rapid industrialization but also a peaceful one. To forestall industrial unrest, it provided legislation that ensured factory safety

JAPAN'S GOVERNMENT PROMOTES INDUSTRIES

and provided workers with some welfare programs. At the same time, the Peace Preservation Law of 1900 outlawed strikes.

Transition from an agrarian to an industrial society produced dislocations and problems, but as latecomers Japanese planners, like those in Germany, benefited from avoiding many of the economic problems that had beset Great Britain and other pioneering nations in the Industrial Revolution.

UNIQUELY JAPANESE EMPLOYER-LABOR RELATIONS

The pattern of Japanese industrialization differed from those of European nations and the United States, partly a result of the uniquely Japanese employment system, whose distinctive and interrelated characteristics persisted throughout the twentieth century. They include a low turnover rate in the labor force; a strong mutual loyalty between employer and employee, where both parties prefer a lifelong commitment to each other; and the prevalence of company-provided welfare and benefits programs for employees. These factors contributed significantly to Japan's successful and rapid industrialization.

Farmers financed Japan's industrialization through payment of high taxes and supplied its labor force. They also produced agricultural goods for export in exchange for foreign machinery and raw materials, and they grew the food for the expanding urban population. Adoption of modern farming techniques and the introduction of chemical fertilizers increased the per acreage yield on the limited arable land. Thus, up to about 1900, Japanese farmers were able to feed a growing population and maintain a tolerable standard of living despite the high burden of taxes they endured.

RAPID POPULATION GROWTH

Whereas Japan's population had been relatively stable in the premodern era, the introduction of modern science and medicine resulted in a rapid increase. Between 1903 and 1919 the population grew from 46 to 56 million people, about a 20 percent increase. Since all arable lands were already under intense cultivation, the land could not support additional people. The surplus was siphoned off to the new commercial and industrial cities such as Tokyo, Yokohama, Nagoya, Osaka, and Kobe. But even in a period of rapid industrial growth, the supply of labor increased faster than demand. Wages, therefore, remained low, and the standard of living for the average person did not improve significantly during the early twentieth century.

After 1900 Japanese farm production could no longer keep up with urban population growth, and food began to make up a significant part of Japanese imports. This growing dependence on imported food, a situation similar to that faced by Great Britain, worried planners, who feared its implications in wartime. Aware that Great Britain's situation was eased by the dominance of its navy and by food produced in its colonies and dominions, Japan, too, turned to colonies that would supply a dependable food source. This was another reason for creating a strong military force: to make possible an expansionist foreign policy.

Modernizing Education, the Bureaucracy, and the Military

JAPAN IMPLEMENTS MODERN SCHOOL SYSTEM

A fundamental reason for Japan's successful modernization was the system of universal education. By 1907 universal compulsory education lasted for six years, and about 5 million boys and girls, 95 percent of children of school age, were attending 27,000 elementary schools. Secondary schools emphasized vocational and technical training and thus provided a firm base for Japan's industrial advance. Flagships of the educational system, the imperial universities trained the sons of the elite for the bureaucracy and the professions, while teachers' and women's colleges trained females for teaching, nursing, and other selected professions. Christian missionary schools also played an important role in giving girls a college and professional education. A highly organized educational bureaucracy monitored the school system and compiled all textbooks. Illiteracy virtually disappeared.

Several themes were stressed for Japanese students: loyalty to the emperor and the state, selfless patriotism, and duty to family. An Imperial Rescript on Education that stated these values was issued in 1890. A copy of the rescript was hung beside the emperor's portrait in every classroom. It became the basis of the moral and ethical instruction of all Japanese children.

The bureaucracy and the military were the twin pillars of Meiji Japan, and Japan's modern education system became the foundation of its efficient bureaucracy. At the heart of the civil service were several thousand graduates of the elite Imperial (later Tokyo) University. Civil servants enjoyed high respect, both because of their rigorous academic training and because they were "officials of the emperor." They drafted legislation for the Diet, had access to cabinet ministers, and generally controlled the administration. As members of a career bureaucracy, they were immune from outside political influences, popular favor, and special interests; therefore, they were a stabilizing factor in society.

THE NEW ARMY AND NAVY

Military education was rigidly specialized and produced an officer corps with a distinctive outlook and experience that emphasized obedience, esprit de corps, and fanatical nationalism. Japanese officers viewed themselves as heirs of the nation's ancient military tradition, and since their education was narrowly limited, they tended to propose simple solutions to complex modern problems. The ordinary citizen, whose ancestors had been accustomed for generations to respecting rulers from the hereditary military class, or samurai, continued to honor the military. Successful in war, the military provided the people with national heroes. Its image was also helped by government propaganda that placed great emphasis on loyalty and devotion to the imperial cause and to its champions, the army and navy. Whereas only samurai could bear arms before 1868, which ensured their privileged status, all males were subject to conscription after the Meiji Restoration. The military and educational reforms contributed to social changes that created a modern society.

The emperor was commander in chief of the armed forces under the Meiji Constitution and was advised in military matters by ministers who were active senior officers of the army and the navy, nominated by their respective services. In time, the military establishment began to control the civilian cabinets and cabinet policy by refusing to nominate men to serve in the army and navy posts in a cabinet not to their liking. Thus, the armed services in effect exercised veto power over the formation and survival of governments. In both absolute and proportional terms, military expenditures increased year by year, from about one-third of the national budget in 1894 to nearly one-half by 1913.

THE DOMINATING INFLUENCE OF THE ARMED FORCES IN GOVERNMENT AND SOCIETY

To strengthen the state's claim of unquestioning obedience and loyalty from its citizens, the Meiji Constitution made Shintoism Japan's official religion. *Shinto* means "The Way of the Gods" and is unique to Japan. Shinto creation myths tell of the divine origin of the imperial house. Until 1945, Shintoism was used to instill patriotism, to impart a sense of Japanese superiority, and to justify aggression.

The Transformation of Japanese Society

Industrialization and modernization depended on new skills, attitudes, and knowledge. Japan's success in these endeavors was due to farsighted leadership as well as to the responsiveness of millions of its citizens, who felt that Westernization was the wave of the future and were willing to make sacrifices to bring it about. Some of the copying was indiscriminate such as the adoption of Western dress and hairstyles, handshaking, and ballroom dancing. Others were fundamental. Legal reform was one. To win acceptance by the West, it was necessary to change Japanese legal institutions, which was accomplished in the 1890s based on the German model. This paved the way for the end of unequal treaties and extraterritorial rights for Westerners. Western legal reforms also introduced Western concepts and the value judgments on which they were based. Although it was easier to understand and accept Western fashion and scientific techniques than morals and ideas, the latter also began to make inroads. Christian missionaries and Westerners hired to work in Japan as experts and teachers, as well as the thousands of young Japanese men and women who went to the West to study, plus Western language books translated into Japanese all contributed to the Westernization of Japan.

In summary, the many rapid changes of the Meiji era were nothing short of revolutionary. Old legal class distinctions were abolished, old laws were replaced, and many old norms were regarded as obsolete. The old static but stable society was replaced by a fluid society where prestige was measured by wealth, education, and political influence. Some social critics nevertheless lamented the passing of the old ways.

WESTERN STYLE LEGAL CODES

Japanese Imperialism Targets China and Korea

Leaders of Meiji Japan turned to imperialism when they saw that their modernization programs were successful, and they continued on that course until 1945. Several reasons account for this quest. Imperialism was the prevailing mood of the late nineteenth century, strengthened by the teachings of social Darwinism, which glorified imperialism as a symbol of international success and racial superiority. Meiji leaders sought international recognition and equality with the great powers by demonstrating military prowess and by conquering colonies. Economic motivation was also important; resource-poor Japan sought security in colonies that would provide secure raw materials and markets.

JAPAN BECOMES IMPERIALISTIC

Japanese foreign policy from the 1890s had the twin goals of self-aggrandizement and the reduction of Western influence in East Asia. Japan defeated China resoundingly in the Sino-Japanese War of 1894–1895 and forced China to cede Taiwan (or Formosa), which became Japan's first overseas colony. Victory against China also brought Japan an indemnity, and Japanese citizens in China obtained the same extraterritorial rights as Westerners. The main issue that had led to the Sino-Japanese War had been control of Korea, a Chinese vassal state that Japan coveted. The war eliminated Chinese political influence from Korea, but the impotent Korean government could ward off neither Japanese nor Russian imperialistic advances. Russia was interested in Korea for its ice-free ports, its resources, and the prestige that would attend Russia's control of that land.

Similar reasons motivated Japan, except that Japanese industries were especially interested in Korean iron ore and coal. Thus, Japan regarded the possibility of Russian control over Korea as "a dagger pointed at her heart," which it must ward off at all costs.

Beyond Korea, both powers also coveted Manchuria, a sparsely populated part of northestern China that was rich in both agricultural and mineral resources. During 1900, with suppression of the Boxer disturbances as pretext, Russia poured 175,000 troops into Manchuria and refused to evacuate them after the Boxer Rebellion had been put down. In 1903, in a blatant gesture of imperialism, the Russian government appointed a viceroy of the Far East and gave him the authority to advance Russian interests in both Manchuria and Korea. This action was a victory for the pro-expansion faction in the Russian court.

Determined to control Korea and Manchuria, Japan began to prepare for war. Between 1893 and 1903 the Japanese military budget increased by more than 300 percent. Japanese leaders also realized the need for allies who could give it support in times of international crisis and found one in Great Britain. In the Anglo-Japanese Alliance of 1902, the two powers agreed to aid each other in their respective imperialist goals in East and South Asia. The treaty was the first modern military pact between a Western and an Asian nation concluded on the basis of equality. It also provided for British neutrality if Japan went to war against one enemy and British assistance if Japan became embroiled in war against two or more nations and vice versa. This last provision, more than any other, strengthened Japan's hand in its rivalry with Russia.

Meanwhile, Japan's constitutional and legal reforms, its successful modernization, and its victory against China convinced Great Britain to end its extraterritorial rights in Japan. This example was followed by other Western nations. By 1911, Japan enjoyed international equality.

The Russo-Japanese War: Japan Electrifies the World

While it was completing its military preparations, Japan negotiated with Russia. Since neither side offered any concessions, the talks bogged down. In 1904 the Japanese navy made a surprise attack and sank the Russian Far Eastern Fleet in its harbor at Port Arthur in southern Manchuria (a Russian sphere of influence in northeastern China). Two days later, Japan declared war.

Most of the battles of the Russo-Japanese War (1904–1905) were fought in Manchuria. It was a measure of China's impotence that it could do nothing to prevent the two antagonists from conducting their campaigns on its territory. The Russians were weakened by social unrest and felt no unity of purpose in waging the war, and the morale of Russian troops was low.

Conversely, the war was popular in Japan and morale was high. Japan's modern military machine won spectacular victories on both land and sea. Russian troops were first expelled from Korea and then surrendered in Port Arthur after suffering a five-month siege. In March 1905 Japan captured Mukden, the chief city of Manchuria, after a major battle in which about 400,000 troops were engaged on each side. In May the Russian Baltic Fleet, which had arrived from Europe via South

Africa, was destroyed in the Korean Straits by the Japanese navy under Admiral Togo Heihachiro. This last feat aroused admiration for the Japanese all over the world, as was evident in President Theodore Roosevelt's exuberant assessment: "This is the greatest phenomenon the world has ever seen. Even the battle of Trafalgar could not match this."

UNITED STATES MEDIATES PEACE BETWEEN RUSSIA AND JAPAN

Defeated on both land and sea, Russia sought peace. Japan, too, was exhausted. When President Roosevelt offered to mediate, both sides accepted eagerly, and the peace conference opened in August 1905 in Portsmouth, New Hampshire. Many of the negotiating sessions were held on a yacht loaned by banking magnate J. P. Morgan. Roosevelt was motivated partly by a desire to achieve a settlement before either side gained a complete victory, which would jeopardize the Open Door policy the United States was trying to uphold in Manchuria. Ability to host a major peace conference would also enhance U.S. international prestige. Roosevelt received the Nobel Peace Prize for his role in brokering the treaty. Although both China and Korea would be vitally affected by the peace terms, neither was invited to the conference.

In the Treaty of Portsmouth, Russia acknowledged Japan's "paramount interests" in Korea and agreed to cede to Japan its railroad rights and sphere of influence in southern Manchuria. Russia also ceded to Japan the southern half of the island of Sakhalin but paid no indemnity. The Japanese people had expected more for their sacrifices, and riots broke out in many Japanese cities when the terms of the treaty were published. The Japanese negotiators had to sneak home to avoid physical harm from demonstrators.

JAPAN ANNEXES KOREA

Japan interpreted its "paramount position" in Korea to mean control of key Korean government agencies, which it proceeded to force on the weak Korean government. Those Koreans who did not wish to be ruled by Japan protested and rioted. In 1907 the king of Korea secretly sent a delegation with an appeal for help against Japanese imperialism to the Hague International Peace Conference, then meeting in the Netherlands, but it failed to gain a hearing. Next, Japan forced the Korean king to abdicate and replaced him with his feebleminded son. In late 1909 a Korean patriot assassinated the Japanese resident-general in Korea. This event gave Japan the pretext it needed to annex Korea, on August 22, 1910. Thus began a harsh colonial rule that lasted until 1945.

The Russo-Japanese War was a landmark conflict for both Japan and the world. There was now little doubt about Japan's great power status. Its victory gave inspiration to people under or threatened by Western imperialism. As Jawaharlal Nehru, later prime minister of independent India, said in his autobiography, it was a "great pick-me-up for Asia." Territorial gains from both wars and the potential for more definitely set Japan on the path of imperialism that ended only with its defeat in World War II.

INDIA

A Fragmented Society

INDIA: LAND OF ANCIENT CULTURE

Like China, India boasted one of the world's oldest continuous major civilizations, begun in approximately 3000 B.C.E. It was the home of many religions and philosophies; one, Hinduism, was the religion of the vast majority of Indians. Another, Buddhism, though almost extinct in its homeland, was nevertheless a major world religion.

Hinduism taught that each person's life was predetermined by his or her actions and behavior in previous lives. Only spiritual perfection, attainable through a combination of devotion, good works, and spiritual learning, released one from the wheel of births and rebirths. Hinduism divided people into hereditary castes, ranging from the exalted Brahman, or priest-scholar caste at the top of society, to the outcastes, or untouchables, at the bottom.

Many peoples had invaded India. After the eighth century C.E., most invaders were Muslims of Arab, Turkish, and Persian ethnic groups, some of whom had settled in India. In time, many Indians, especially those from lower castes, attracted by Islam's promise of equality among believers before Allah, or God, had converted to the conquerors' religion. Muslims were a majority in the northwestern and northeastern parts of the subcontinent and were a minority community in the rest of the land. Many languages from several unrelated linguistic groups further divided the Indian people. While the oldest cities in India dated back over 4,000 years, most Indians lived in villages ruled by village and caste elders.

ISLAM IN INDIA

Europeans seeking trade arrived in India by sea in 1498; soon afterward the Moghul Empire gained control over the subcontinent. Moghuls came from Central Asia and were Muslim in religion, Turkish in ethnicity, and Persian in culture. The first Moghul rulers were great builders who left behind many impressive monuments (one of the seven wonders of the world, the Taj Mahal, is the mausoleum of a famous Moghul empress). However, by the eighteenth century, the Moghul dynasty was in decline, challenged by both its Hindu and Muslim subjects.

British Rule in India

The disintegration of Moghul political power was accompanied by civil wars and foreign intervention. By the middle of the eighteenth century, Great Britain and France were fighting for global colonial supremacy including India, with Britain the winner. In the nineteenth century the British won a series of wars against major princely states and consolidated their grip on the subcontinent. They ruled parts of India directly, while other parts were ruled by Indian princes under British supervision.

To protect India, Great Britain moved to take control over adjacent territories. To the east, it defeated the Burmese in three wars and incorporated Burma into the Indian empire. To the south, it secured the island of Ceylon from the Dutch by treaty. To the west and northwest, Great Britain sought to protect India from both raiding Afghans and Russian expansion in Central Asia by creating a protectorate over Afghanistan and a sphere of influence in eastern Persia (see later section). The Himalaya Mountains protected India from attack by China from the north, and in any case a weak China was in no position to threaten British interests. To secure trade routes between the Indian Ocean and East Asia, Great Britain purchased the tip of the Malay Peninsula from the local ruler and developed it into a free port and a major naval base called Singapore.

GREAT BRITAIN ESTABLISHES CONTROL OVER INDIA

Since the main motive for their control of India was commercial, the British paid close attention to developing the Indian economy. They undertook large irrigation projects to bring new land into cultivation and introduced new crops such as tea and

BRITISH INFLUENCES AND INDIAN REACTIONS

English ladies and gentlemen served afternoon tea by Indian servants. Even minor British officers and officials lived well in India.

coffee. They revitalized old crops such as cotton and jute to supply raw materials to British textile mills. To bring the crops to the seaports and to distribute their manufactured goods to Indian consumers, the British built railroads that linked the coast to the interior. They introduced new processing industries to India and opened coal mines to provide fuel.

While it did not seek to convert Indians to Christianity and allowed each Indian religious community to govern itself by its traditional civil laws, the British administration did introduce measures to correct Indian practices that were considered wrong by Western standards. They abolished *suttee* (or *sati,* burning upper-caste widows alive on their husbands' funeral pyres) and suppressed the *thuggees* ("thugs" in English), members of a Hindu cult that robbed and murdered in the name of religion.

Many Indians accepted the reforms as beneficial and responded to the Western challenge to their traditional values by reexamining and reevaluating their religion and society. As a result, many Indians actively supported such reform measures as the Age of Consent Act of 1891, which raised the marriageable age of girls, and advocated the introduction of further reforms. Hindu traditionalists, however, bitterly resented reform measures as examples of British interference in Indian society and rioted in protest.

Confident of the superiority of its educational system, Great Britain had since the early nineteenth century used public revenues in India to support British-style schools. Private Christian schools, both Catholic and Protestant, had also been established in many cities by British missionaries, including the first school for girls in 1849.

Missionaries did not convert many Indians to Christianity, but their schools for Indian children were crucial in the spread of Western values and knowledge to many Indians.

Gradually, the lines of contact between British and Indians broadened, and new ideas about social reform, popular sovereignty, and modern nationalism took root among the Western-educated Indian elite. Without question, nationalism was the most powerful force in India from 1900 onward. Western liberal ideas and modern nationalistic feelings, either introduced by contact with the British or generated in reaction to British rule, profoundly changed the nature of Indian upper-class society. Hence, most twentieth-century Indian nationalists wanted independence based on Western concepts of nationhood. They sought democracy and representative government, not a return to the authoritarian monarchies of ancient India. British-educated Indians insisted that democracy and self-government were universally applicable ideals; therefore, they argued, Indians should govern themselves and the British should leave India.

In 1885 a group of British-educated Indians and some of their British friends formed an organization called the Indian National Congress, whose goal was to gain for Indians the right of political representation that Britons enjoyed in their homeland. The Congress met in annual sessions to formulate goals and programs. Between sessions, its members lobbied for reforms. All Indians were welcome to join the Congress, which professed no religious biases. However, few Muslims joined, initially because Muslims lagged behind Hindus in political consciousness and later because they feared that majority rule would mean Hindu suppression of the Muslim minority. As a result, most Muslims regarded the Congress as a Hindu organization that did not represent them.

In the face of determined Indian pressure, the British government, which had no clear vision for India's future, slowly and reluctantly made concessions to Indian demands for self-rule. To protect themselves against possible Hindu oppression, Muslim leaders formed the All-India Muslim League in 1906. The League demanded separate electorates for Muslims (Muslims electing their own representatives) in any elected Indian legislature. The Indian National Congress vehemently opposed the idea of separate electorates, but its opposition merely made the Muslims more adamant.

In 1909 Great Britain took the first major step toward Indian self-rule by passing the Indian Councils Act (generally known as the Morley-Minto Reforms, after its authors), which provided for a limited male franchise and for limited powers to the elective councils and assemblies at both the provincial and central government levels. This was far from full self-government because a British-appointed viceroy, governors, and officials still held the reins of power and made most of the important decisions. The reforms did, however, provide a constitutional platform where Indian representatives could voice their opinions, and they introduced Indians to the concept and practice of elections and representative government. They also set the pattern for future constitutional development. Muslims won the right to separate electorates and insisted on being guaranteed separate electorates in the future. They would later demand a separate nation to ensure their identity. (The identification of peoples primarily by their religion is called communalism.) Conversely, Hindus and the Indian National Congress interpreted separate electorates and other concessions to Muslims as a British ploy of "divide and rule" to prolong its dominance of the subcontinent.

MODERN NATIONALISM DEVELOPS IN INDIA

ALL-INDIA MUSLIM LEAGUE FORMED

ELECTIONS IN INDIA UNDER THE MORLEY-MINTO REFORMS

Neither the Indian National Congress nor the All-India Muslim League was satisfied with the concessions of the Morley-Minto Reforms. Both saw self-government as the logical goal of Indian nationalism. They coined a new word, *swaraj,* meaning self-rule, to represent their goal. By 1914 *"swaraj"* was on the lips of every Indian political activist.

A faraway event added to Indian restlessness. It was news of Japanese victories on land and sea over Russia in the Russo-Japanese War of 1904–1905, the first victory by an Asian nation in modern times over a major power of the West. As a foreign traveler in India observed at the time, "Even the remote villages talked over the victories of Japan as they sat in their circles and passed around the pipe at night."

THE PERSIAN AND OTTOMAN EMPIRES

ENDURING ISLAMIC TRADITIONS IN PERSIAN AND OTTOMAN EMPIRES

Two countries bordered India to the west, Afghanistan and Persia, and beyond them, the Ottoman or Turkish Empire, which included not only Turkish areas but most of the Middle East Arab lands, as well as a steadily decreasing amount of European territory in the Balkans. Both empires were part of the Muslim world that could look back on the glorious golden age of Islam from about 800 to 1100 C.E. During this period, Islamic culture, economy, and political power reached their zenith. Islam came out of the same traditions as Judaism and Christianity. Muslims (submitters to Islam) believe in one God (Allah) and in his prophets of the Old and New Testaments, including Jesus, who is considered a great prophet but not God. All people who accept the belief in one God and in Muhammad as his prophet are seen as equal before that God and as equals within the Muslim community. It was largely on the basis of this egalitarian philosophy that Islam spread rapidly to peoples of many diverse cultures.

The Koran (Qur'an), the Muslim holy book, contains instructions for every aspect of a Muslim's life. The leaders in Islam were viewed as both political and religious figures; in its early formation Islamic society did not separate the roles of government and religion. For millions of Muslims, Islam was perceived as a dynamic force for social change, particularly in the treatment of women. Although women were regarded as inferior to men, they nevertheless could inherit property, initiate divorces, and remarry in the event of widowhood or divorce. Largely as a result of its stable and complete nature, Islamic society remained resistant to outside forces. Thus, whereas the political apparatus of the Arab world in North Africa fell to Western colonialism, the culture and religion remained relatively unchanged. As in Africa, Asian and Middle Eastern Muslims rarely, if ever, converted to Christianity, nor did they lose their traditional values of respect for the family and loyalty to one another. Islam would play a major role for many Muslims in their struggle against Western domination.

COMPETING EUROPEAN IMPERIALISMS IN OTTOMAN AND PERSIAN EMPIRES

By 1900 the Persian and Ottoman empires were in decline. They had formerly produced able and vigorous leaders but now were headed by incompetent and sometimes unstable men. These governments had lost much territory and in some cases had to submit to European control in areas that remained in their nominal jurisdiction. They had, however, managed to play off competing foreign forces to retain control in parts of their empires. Great Britain and Russia were rivals with interests and ambitions in both the Persian and Ottoman empires, while Germany had extended its influence into the Ottoman Empire. The German government sent officers to train the Ottoman army and planned to build a Berlin-to-Baghdad railway; German banks loaned money to the Ottoman government and invested in financial enterprises in the Ottoman Empire.

Russia expanded its empire at the expense of the Ottoman Empire around the Black Sea in a series of wars that began in the eighteenth century. In the nineteenth century the Russian empire also advanced southward at the expense of the Persian Empire and more important into Central Asia against the loosely organized tribal states in the region. Russian gains in Central Asia during the nineteenth century equaled half the size of the United States. Thus whereas 2,000 miles divided British- and Russian-controlled lands in Asia in 1800, only 20 miles separated British India from Russian Central Asia in 1900.

Competition in this vast Eurasian region between the British and the Russians (sometimes labeled the "Great Game") came to a head in Persia. Sharing a long border with Persia, Russia was in an advantageous position to infiltrate and penetrate that nation. Russian officers had been sent to Persia to organize the Persian army, Russian banks loaned money to the Persian government, and Russian firms won concessions to build Persian railroads. In return, Russia controlled the Persian customs office and other departments of the Persian government.

Great Britain feared that Russia harbored ambitions in India and believed that the easiest way for Russia to attack India was via the western frontier between Persia and Afghanistan. Based on this assumption, the key to British policy toward Persia was to thwart Russia's southward advance. For this reason, Great Britain was satisfied with the results of the Russo-Japanese War, which forced Russia to turn its attentions to rebuilding its army and navy and to retrench in Persia. It was in this context that Russia and Great Britain began to negotiate their outstanding differences in 1907, which resulted in the Anglo-Russian Convention and Entente. According to the terms of the convention, Russia agreed not to encroach on Afghanistan and conceded it as an exclusive British sphere of influence. Both powers agreed to "respect" Persian "independence," but they then proceeded to divide it into their respective spheres of influence. Russia received the lion's share, or the entire northern half of Persia, including the capital city, Tehran. Great Britain's sphere in the southeast was smaller but was strategically located on the border between Afghanistan and India. What remained of Persia was designated a neutral zone. This settlement eased tension between Russia and Great Britain.

BRITAIN MOVES TO SAFEGUARD ITS INDIAN EMPIRE

Meanwhile, Persians who had traveled and studied in Europe were convinced that Persia needed to reform its antiquated political system if it was to survive. They launched a dual program that involved agitation for Westernization and constitutional reforms as well as the creation of a national consciousness based on deep-rooted traditions and Persia's long history. In the bloodless 1906 revolution, the shah (ruler of Persia) was forced to give up his absolute powers and to convene an elected parliament to draw up a constitution, which was promulgated in December of that year. A civil war broke out in 1908 between conservatives and reformers, complicated by a Russian invasion. In 1909 the Anglo-Persian Oil Company began production in southwestern Persia, and Persia soon became a leading producer of oil. It remained neutral in World War I, during which Western pressures were much reduced.

PERSIA ATTEMPTS REFORMS

INDEPENDENCE MOVEMENTS AMONG SUBJECT PEOPLES OF OTTOMAN EMPIRE

The Ottoman Empire, often called the Sick Man of Europe in the nineteenth century, formed a dangerous power vacuum that tempted major European powers to intervene. The Austro-Hungarian, Russian, and German governments had conflicting imperial ambitions in the Balkan provinces of the Ottoman Empire. They encouraged and sometimes helped the predominantly Christian subject peoples in the region such as the Serbians, Bulgarians, Romanians, and Greeks to rise up against the failing Ottoman Empire. Six independent but unstable states were created as a result of successful uprisings (Serbia, Bulgaria, Romania, Greece, Montenegro, and Albania), that reduced the Ottoman Empire to a foothold in Europe by 1914. However, to prevent Russia from gaining access to the Mediterranean Sea, the British and French encouraged the Ottomans to hang on to this foothold and to retain their hold on the vital Dardanelles Straits.

In Asia, restlessness among the unassimilated Christian Armenian minority caused the Turkish-Ottoman government great alarm and resulted in harsh repression. Its Arab subject population in the Middle East (which outnumbered the ruling Turkish population) had also awakened to the pulls of nationalism and was threatening secession from the empire. North Africa and Egypt, still technically Ottoman provinces, had long since come under French and British control, respectively. Italy annexed the Ottoman Empire's last African possession, Libya, in 1912.

YOUNG TURKS ATTEMPT REFORM IN OTTOMAN EMPIRE

In attempting to hold on to what remained of the crumbling empire, the Ottoman government enlisted German aid. Kaiser Wilhelm II was only too happy to comply because he saw it as an opportunity to expand German influence into the Middle East. German instructors helped to modernize the Ottoman army and, in so doing, helped to awaken a spirit of nationalism among the Turkish officers. Known as the "Young Turks," they formed an organization dedicated to the modernization of the Ottoman Empire. In 1908, the Young Turks staged a successful revolution, and their leader, Enver Bey, became the de facto ruler of the empire. Between 1909 and 1914, the Young Turks attempted a program of "Turkification" of Armenians, Arabs, and other subject nationalities of the empire, which only deepened local nationalistic feelings among the targeted peoples.

From the experience of the Arabs, Armenians, and others, it can be seen that Western nations and Japan were not the only practitioners of imperialism. The Ottoman Empire provided an ironic example of a state, itself the victim of European imperialism, that was in turn imposing a harsh rule on its subject nationalities.

AUSTRALASIA

Like India, Australasia was part of the British Empire. This area included the island continent Australia and the North and South Islands of New Zealand. At the time of Western settlement, Australia was sparsely inhabited by people of the Australoid race, who did not practice agriculture or herding but lived in scattered groups that sustained themselves by hunting and gathering. New Zealand was populated by earlier Polynesian immigrants called Maoris, who lived in tribal societies and were related to the native inhabitants of Hawaii.

Although discovered by Dutch explorers, Australasia was colonized by Great Britain; it therefore became British in population, culture, and institutions. The climate of parts of Australasia resembles that of Europe, and imperialism in this area stressed the settlement of Europeans, a pattern similar to colonizing North America in previous centuries. The first Britons (boatloads of convicts and their guards) arrived in Sydney, Australia, in 1788. It was intended as a dumping ground for convicts when the North American colonies refused to accept them after independence. Most of Australia, however, was not set up as penal colonies, and the entire continent was soon opened up as six colonies for free emigration from Britain; each received self-government as soon as local conditions warranted. In 1901, as in Canada, the six self-governing colonies were federated to form the Commonwealth of Australia, which became a dominion in the British Empire. Until World War II, Australia remained overwhelmingly British in culture and sentiment and enjoyed the protection of the British navy. With the exception of a small number of native aborigines, Australians maintained racial and cultural homogeneity by keeping out Asian immigrants through the White Australia Policy.

GREAT BRITAIN COLONIZES AUSTRALIA AND NEW ZEALAND

New Zealand was also discovered by Dutch explorers in the seventeenth century. British settlers came in the early nineteenth century and subjugated the Maoris in wars. New Zealand was never a penal colony, and Great Britain had no hesitation about granting the settlers self-government. In 1907, the North and South Islands joined to form a dominion within the British Empire. Like Australia, New Zealand passed laws to restrict Asian immigration, which ensured the British heritage of the white New Zealanders.

AUSTRALIA AND NEW ZEALAND BECOME SELF-GOVERNING

The small populations of Australia and New Zealand enjoyed a high standard of living based on economies that emphasized export-oriented farming, animal husbandry, and mining. Both Australia and New Zealand exported wheat, wool, meat, and dairy products, mainly to Great Britain, and depended on Great Britain for manufactured goods. In the early twentieth century, each had only a few industries, most of them processing agricultural and livestock products or minerals.

The labor movement, expressed in unions and in labor parties, was strong in both Australia and New Zealand, with the result that both nations were in the vanguard of social legislation in such areas as old-age pensions, financed by heavy taxes on large properties. New Zealand granted women suffrage in 1893, and the Australian states did so beginning in 1894, leading the world. In 1910, as evidence of growing national maturity, Australia instituted compulsory military training for its young men and began to organize a regular military force. New Zealand followed suit in 1911.

FRENCH INDOCHINA

The Indochina peninsula was the meeting ground of Chinese and Indian cultures in ancient times, hence the name. Steady immigration by settlers from China ensured the predominance of peoples of the Mongolian race. Over 2,000 years ago Chinese conquest and control of northern Vietnam brought in advanced agriculture and irrigation, Chinese writing, social organization, Confucian ideology, and Chinese-style Buddhism.

CHINESE INFLUENCE IN VIETNAM

Since about 900 C.E. Vietnam had had its own government but acknowledged Chinese overlordship. The southward expansion of the Vietnamese people to the tip of the peninsula was completed in the eighteenth century. Indian culture, expressed in Hinduism and Buddhism, came to the region through Indian merchants and missionaries beginning in the early Christian era and prevailed in the western half of Indochina, namely Laos and Cambodia.

FRANCE ESTABLISHES CONTROL OVER INDOCHINA

Although French Catholic missionaries had been active in Indochina since the seventeenth century, French imperial ambitions in the region did not become important until the middle of the nineteenth century. Indochina was important to France because it provided natural resources and became a domain for Catholic missionary work and a back door for expansion into southern China. The advance of French power in Vietnam during the nineteenth century was a good example of "the flag follows the cross" because French annexations were sometimes brought on by attacks on French missionaries and native converts. In 1885 France defeated China in a war fought mainly over Vietnam; China was forced to give up its position as overlord of Vietnam, and it was annexed by France. In 1887 France joined Cochin-China, Tonkin, and Annam (the three components of Vietnam), Laos, and Cambodia to form the Indochina Union. Within the Union, France ruled Cochin-China directly and the others as protectorates. The governor-general, headquartered in Hanoi, controlled overall policy, while the native rulers in the protectorates were allowed to manage routine administration supervised by French resident officials.

FRENCH DOMINATION AND VIETNAMESE REACTIONS

French economic policy in Indochina aimed at exploiting local national resources. The French greatly expanded rice and rubber production and developed the mining of coal and metals, especially in Vietnam. To facilitate economic development, they built roads and railroads, expanded the irrigation system, and introduced modern public health and educational facilities. The average Vietnamese paid dearly for these improvements and benefited little from them. As late as 1939, only 15 percent of school-age children in Indochina were receiving any education.

As in Africa, France pursued a policy of cultural assimilation, a concept aimed at creating a "New France" in Indochina by establishing French schools and promoting French language, culture, and customs. France hoped that eventually a new elite class sympathetic to French rule would emerge among the Indochinese. Major cities in Indochina acquired French-inspired architecture.

However, the new Vietnamese elite became the standard-bearers of modern Vietnamese nationalism. Japan's victory over Russia in 1904–1905 spurred Vietnamese nationalists to organize and publicize their aims and goals. Vietnamese students in Japan organized and openly agitated for throwing out the French. Chinese reform movements that culminated in the successful revolution of 1911 gave additional stimulus to anti-French activities. They were so widespread that the years after 1905 were known as the "era of plots," but all of them were put down by France. An example of the contradiction inherent in France's colonial policy was the closing down of the University of Hanoi because it was a center of revolutionary activities. The university was a creation of the French colonial government, opened to promote its policy of assimilation by imparting French culture and values to the Vietnamese. Yet it was precisely these French-trained Vietnamese who led the nationalist movement to oust the French from Vietnam. Temporarily, the French repression succeeded. Some activists fled to China to continue their work; others, most notably Ho Chi Minh, went to Europe, where they kept up their anti-French activities.

THE DUTCH EAST INDIES (INDONESIA)

The Dutch had been involved in the East Indies since the seventeenth century, after they ousted the Portuguese, but had not extended effective control outside Java to the rest of Indonesia until early in the nineteenth century. From the beginning, the Dutch showed little interest in exporting their culture or religion to their colonies; rather, they regarded them as valuable sources of raw materials and later as a market for the sale of manufactured goods. Plantations, financed by the Netherlands and other Western nations and worked by Javanese and immigrant Chinese laborers, produced tea, coffee, indigo, tobacco, spices, sugar, and palm oil. Petroleum and tin were other valuable raw materials. Like Indians in East Africa, Chinese immigrants gained dominance over commerce in the Dutch East Indies and other areas of Southeast Asia.

THE NETHERLANDS ESTABLISHES COMMERCIAL EMPIRE IN THE EAST INDIES

At the turn of the century, the Dutch introduced reforms called the "ethical policy" to protect Indonesians from the more flagrant forms of economic exploitation. This paternalistic policy established state-supported elementary schools and stressed the moral obligation of the Netherlands to improve the welfare of the local people. Despite this policy, economic prosperity benefited the Dutch rather than the Indonesians.

Dutch rule in Indonesia before World War I was authoritarian. A Dutch-appointed governor-general ruled from Batavia (located on Java, renamed Jakarta after independence), assisted by an all-Dutch advisory council and a cabinet. No popular assemblies of any kind existed beyond the village level. Even though Dutch rulers did not attempt to bring Western ideas and methods to the natives, young Indonesians, like colonials elsewhere, became exposed to them. Indonesians were also impressed by the rising stature of Japan and the respect it received from European powers; for example, in 1899 the Netherlands government granted Japanese residents in Indonesia equal status with Europeans.

INDONESIANS DEVELOP NATIONALIST MOVEMENT

An Indonesian nationalist movement emerged in reaction to Dutch rule. Most notable among the nationalist groups was the Sarekat Islam, formed in 1910. It was a Muslim organization and represented the majority of Indonesians. In 1911 the Sarekat Islam organized anti-Chinese riots, a reflection of native resentment of the strong economic role of the Chinese community in Indonesian life and the fact that the Chinese were Buddhists and Confucians, not Muslims. By World War I the Sarekat Islam had become a mass movement aimed at reviving Islam, attaining independence, and eliminating the economic power of the Chinese.

THE UNITED STATES ACQUIRES HAWAII
AND THE PHILIPPINES

Since independence U.S. merchants had engaged in the famous clipper ship trade for silk, tea, and porcelain from China and spices from the Dutch East Indies. The U.S. government had sent naval squadrons to force the opening of commercial contacts

EXPANDING UNITED STATES INTERESTS IN THE PACIFIC REGION

with Japan and Korea. In 1867 the United States purchased Alaska from Russia and occupied Midway Island in the central Pacific for use as a coaling station for its commercial and naval vessels. U.S. Open Door policy toward China, the participation of its troops to put down the Boxers, and its naval presence in Chinese waters all indicated a continuing U.S. desire to compete with other imperialist powers for influence in China.

In 1887 the United States acquired Pearl Harbor in the Hawaiian Islands for a future naval base. Expanding U.S. economic and strategic interests in the central Pacific culminated in the annexation of Hawaii in 1898. One year later, it annexed Wake Island, thereby filling a gap in its transpacific supply line.

UNITED STATES ANNEXES THE PHILIPPINES

In 1898, after winning the Spanish-Cuban-American War and paying $20 million to Spain, the United States acquired the Philippines and the strategically important Pacific island of Guam. As with Cuba and Puerto Rico, the question of what to do with the populous Philippine Islands became the chief focus of debate between pro- and anti-imperialist politicians. Anti-imperialists argued that the Philippines consisted of many unassimilable peoples and cultures and that the islands were not necessary for the security or economic development of the United States; therefore, their annexation would be a repudiation of U.S. ideals. Those who supported annexation argued that the Philippines were valuable economically as a producer of such tropical items as sugar, coconut oil, and hemp and as consumers of U.S. products. They were also concerned that some powerful European nation or Japan might seize the islands if the United States did not. They saw in Subic Bay an excellent naval base to protect U.S. trade and other interests in Asia. Imperialists further argued that the Filipinos needed a period of U.S. tutelage before they could operate successfully as an independent nation. In annexing the islands, therefore, the United States was only assuming its responsibility, as the British imperialist writer Rudyard Kipling had advocated when he urged Americans to "take up the white man's burden." Protestant ministers also favored annexation as an opportunity to convert Filipinos to Christianity, even though the majority of Filipinos were already Catholics.

The annexationists prevailed both in Congress and in the presidential election of 1900, when anti-expansionist William Jennings Bryan was defeated by William McKinley for the second time. Thus, like Puerto Rico, the Philippines became a U.S. possession.

FILIPINO RESISTANCE TO U.S. RULE IS CRUSHED

Filipino nationalists, who had been fighting the Spanish for independence, had proclaimed a Philippine republic in 1899. Emilio Aguinaldo, a hero of the fight against Spain, was named its first president. However, the United States refused to recognize this government and waged war to suppress it. In 1901 General Arthur MacArthur (father of General Douglas MacArthur) captured Aguinaldo and the independence movement collapsed. The United States sent many more troops to conquer the Philippines than it had sent to pacify Cuba. On occasion, U.S. soldiers committed the same atrocities and pursued the same policies of interning civilians that Americans had condemned when they were used by the Spanish in Cuba and the British in South Africa. About 200,000 Filipinos died from various causes during the fighting, and U.S. dead numbered over 4,000.

U.S. Troops in Philippines. Main Trench of the Outlaws on the Crest of Mount Dajo after the battle.

        This unhappy experience tinged U.S. attitudes toward the Philippines with guilt. While suppressing movements for immediate Philippine independence, the U.S. government also played an active role in preparing for its eventual realization. In 1913 and again in 1919 President Woodrow Wilson formally pledged that the United States would grant independence to the Philippines at an early date. To prepare Filipinos for the responsibility of independence, Governor-General William Howard Taft and his successors launched an ambitious program of public education based on the U.S. model that doubled the literacy rate in just over a generation and introduced English as the second language for a significant minority.

UNITED STATES MAKES REFORMS IN THE PHILIPPINES

        Qualified Filipinos found the doors to civil service jobs open to them. By 1912 half of all ranking judges were Filipinos. In 1907 local elections were held for a national assembly in which two major political parties competed for power. The assembly was the first popularly elected legislative body in Southeast Asia. An upper house in which Filipinos had a majority was added in 1913. However, political reforms were not matched by economic ones. Wealth remained in the hands of U.S. business firms and a few rich Filipinos and Chinese immigrants.

S U M M A R Y

Western imperialism was at its height in Asia and the Pacific at the beginning of the twentieth century. With the exception of Japan, all of Asia was under either direct or indirect control by Western imperial nations. Large areas and ancient civilizations—

the Indian subcontinent, Indochina, the East Indies, and other smaller territories—had become colonies of the imperial powers. Other once-powerful empires were in decay and only nominally independent: Persia and the Ottoman Empire had been reduced in size by successful revolts of subject nationalities and by Western encroachments. China had been stripped of its outlying territories and vassal states and had become a semicolony. In the Pacific, the United States had taken over important territories, especially Hawaii and the Philippines.

Even as Western imperialism stood at its most triumphant, however, movements had been set in motion that would eventually topple it. Victims of imperialism, Asian peoples were among the first non-Westerners to experience modern nationalism. This desire to control their own destinies inspired a new generation of Asian nationalists not only to free their homelands from Western imperialism but also to get rid of their traditional governments and to reform their moribund societies and cultures, partly by borrowing from the West.

Japan was the first Asian nation to succeed in modernizing. Although first opened up by the United States in 1853 and for a while subject to economic imperialism itself, by 1900 Japan had joined the imperialist powers. Its victory in the Russo-Japanese War of 1904–1905 greatly reinforced its new status.

As a result of the technological and scientific innovations introduced by the West, traditional life in Asia changed. Although traditionalists had resisted Western-inspired changes and reforms, modernizers in Japan, Persia, the Ottoman Empire, and other lands sought to adopt Western technology and institutions. In China, the ignominious defeat of the Boxer movement, which sought to counter Western science and technology with superstition and magic, opened the way for forward-looking leaders. They sought to learn from advanced Western nations so that Chinese peoples could throw off the yoke of subjugation.

Australasia had a different historical experience. Australia and New Zealand, sparsely populated by native peoples, had been colonized by people of predominantly British stock who enjoyed a prosperous economy. Great Britain did not repeat the mistake it had made with its North American colonies; by the early twentieth century, Australia and New Zealand had joined Canada as self-governing dominions.

SUGGESTED SOURCES

Cleveland, William L. *A History of the Modern Middle East.* 1994. A cogent, comprehensive, and up-to-date introduction to the whole region. Covers the nineteenth and twentieth centuries.*

Cohen, Paul A. *History in Three Keys: The Boxers as Event, Experience, and Myth.* 1997. This book weaves together historians' accounts, personal narratives, and the myths that developed about the Boxer Rebellion.

Dudden, Arthur Power. *The American Pacific: From the Old China Trade to the Present.* 1992. A highly accessible survey of U.S. interests in the Pacific region.

Duus, Peter. *The Abacus and the Sword: The Japanese Penetration of Korea, 1895–1910.* 1995. A major historical work on Japanese imperialism.

Forster, E. M. *A Passage to India.* 1924. A novel about English men and women in India and their interactions with Indians.* (Also a film.)

Gibson, Arrell Morgan. *Yankees in Paradise: The Pacific Basin Frontier.* 1993. A scholarly examination of the political and economic motivations for U.S. expansion in the Pacific during the nineteenth century.

Griswold, A. Whitney. *The Far Eastern Policy of the United States.* 1966. A well-written and comprehensive overview of U.S. action in the Philippines and China.

Hopkirk, Peter. *The Great Game: The Struggle for Empire in Central Asia.* 1990. This is the exciting story of Anglo-Russian competition for empire in Central Asia in the nineteenth century.*

Jansen, Marius B. *Japan and China: From War to Peace, 1894–1972.* 1975. A survey of Sino-Japanese relations in modern times.

———. *The Making of Modern Japan.* 2000. Sweeping and authoritative account of modern Japan.*

Karnow, Stanley. *In Our Image: America's Empire in the Philippines.* 1989. Lively account of U.S. presence in the Philippines.*

Keene, Donald. *Emperor of Japan, Meiji and His World, 1852–1912.* 2002. Narrative account of the man whose rule saw sweeping changes in Japan.

MacMillan, Margaret. *Women of the Raj.* 1988. Concentrates on the role of English women in India c. 1650–1947; richly illustrated.

Mansfield, Peter. *The Arab World.* 1976. An introduction to the Arab world by a journalist.*

Miller, Stuart. *Benevolent Assimilation: The American Conquest of the Philippines, 1899–1903.* 1982. A colorful account of the Philippine-American War, drawing heavily from contemporary American newspaper materials.

Pleshakov, Constantine. *The Tsar's Last Armada: The Epic Voyage to the Battle of Tsushima.* 2002. Vivid, fascinating story for students of military history and naval warfare.

Preston, Diana. *The Boxer Rebellion.* 1999. A well-researched, lively re-creation of the tragedy in China in 1900.*

Price, Eva Jane. *China Journal, 1889–1900: An American Family during the Boxer Rebellion.* 1989. Poignant account by a missionary woman of her family's life in a remote northern Chinese town.*

Reischauer, Edwin O. *The United States and Japan.* 4th ed. 1978. A brief, interesting survey of the relationship between the two nations by a former U.S. ambassador to Japan.*

Robinson, Donald H. *The Raj.* 1981. An interesting view of British rule in India.* (Also a BBC television production.)

WEB SOURCES

www.fordham.edu/halsall/eastasia/eastasiasbook.html. Excellent site offering numerous links to history of countries in East Asia; includes links to materials on Western imperialism.

www.fordham.edu/halsall/india/indiasbook.html. Excellent site offering numerous links to history of Indian subcontinent; includes links to materials on Western imperialism.

---

*Paperback available.

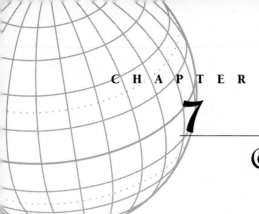

⑥The Origins of World War I

On June 28, 1914, a Serbian nationalist assassinated the Austrian archduke and heir to the throne, Franz Ferdinand, in Sarajevo, Bosnia. While Ferdinand was sitting in the open backseat of a car—it was a beautiful sunny day—a 19-year-old youth stepped out into the street and fired several shots. Before the archduke himself expired, after several times dismissing his wound as "nothing," his wife Sophie had already died from a bullet in the stomach.

The assassin was Gavrilo Princip, a Bosnian of Serbian nationality. Himself stricken with tuberculosis, he was fond of quoting Nietzsche's lines from *Ecce Homo*: "Insatiable as the flame, I glow and consume myself." Princip wished to see Bosnia break away from the Austro-Hungarian Empire and become part of a Greater Serbia. Austria-Hungary soon declared war on Serbia, and by August 4 most of the major European powers were involved in World War I. To understand how a major war could follow from the shooting of an Austrian archduke, it is necessary to investigate the combustible atmosphere that transformed the spark of an assassination into an all-consuming fire that would bring about the deaths of millions.

NATIONALISM

Nationalism was the first element at work. (See Chapter 2 for a more general treatment of nationalism, as well as imperialism and militarism.) This passion was especially strong in the Balkans. Serbia had gained complete independence from the Ottoman Empire in 1878. In that year major European powers at the Congress of Berlin allowed Austria-Hungary to occupy Bosnia and Herzegovina even though these provinces were still legally part of the Ottoman Empire and ethnic Serbians were the largest national group in the occupied province. After King Peter I came to the throne in 1903, Serbia stepped up its efforts to incorporate ethnic Serbian areas still outside its national borders; it was outraged when Austria completely annexed Bosnia and Herzegovina in 1908. Serbia made threats and appealed to Russia for help. Germany promised Austria its backing and sent the Russians a note demanding that the tsarist government recognize the annexation and not support Serbia in the matter. Russia yielded, and without Russian support Serbia had to acknowledge the annexation. As a result of strong Austrian pressure, Serbia also promised to cease activities that were hostile to its northern neighbor.

Sarajevo, 1914: Austrian Archduke Franz Ferdinand and his wife in the rear of the automobile in which they would soon be assassinated.

Despite its promise, Serbia failed to curtail such actions. In fact, within a short period, several new nationalistic societies appeared. One of these was the conspiratorial group Unity or Death, commonly referred to as the Black Hand, which specialized in encouraging ethnic Serbs in areas such as Bosnia to work for unification with Serbia. It helped smuggle men, guns, and propaganda to sympathetic individuals still outside Serbian borders. Led by the chief of intelligence of the Serbian army, the Black Hand organized Princip's bloody deed. Balkan Wars in 1912 and 1913 further increased tensions in the area. Although Serbia greatly expanded its territory at the expense of the Ottoman Turkish Empire, Austria-Hungary prevented the Serbs from gaining land along the Adriatic coast by successfully supporting the creation of an independent Albania. The new Albania, however, did not obtain all the territory it wished; most notably, Kosovo went to Serbia, which the Albanian majority residing there would continue to resent for decades afterward. (See Chapter 33 for a discussion of the conflict there in the 1990s.)

Although the Serbian nationalism of the Black Hand and Princip had precipitated the crisis, the nationalism displayed by other powers widened it. Kaiser Wilhelm II and segments of the German public, including many intellectuals and politicians, believed in the superiority of the German nation and culture. Some Germans dreamed of uniting all Germans in a Pan-German state that would include large areas of Austria-Hungary.

Pan-Germanists were countered by Russian Pan-Slavists, who dreamed of politically uniting with Russia the many Orthodox Slavs who populated the Balkans. As the control of the Ottoman Turkish Empire in the Balkans weakened during the century preceding World War I, the Russians planned to exercise increasing influence in the area but instead suffered a number of disappointments. Russia lost the influence it once had in Bulgaria and, along with Serbia, suffered a diplomatic defeat when Austria-Hungary annexed Bosnia and Herzegovina in 1908. In exchange for this annexation, the Russian government had hoped to gain Austro-Hungarian diplomatic

SERBIAN NATIONALISM

NATIONALISM OF OTHER EUROPEAN NATIONS

support for its goal of pressuring the Turks to allow Russian warships through the Turkish Straits from the Black Sea to the Mediterranean Sea, but Russian efforts were unsuccessful and only heightened the frustrations of Russian nationalists.

A quickening of French nationalism was also apparent. An anti-German disturbance in late 1913 in a French town in the German provinces of Alsace and Lorraine symbolized the painful loss of these provinces to Germany in the Franco-Prussian War. Ten-year-old Raymond Poincaré had watched the Germans march through his hometown in Lorraine in 1870. Elected premier of France in 1912 and president in 1913, he played an active role in leading France into war with Germany in 1914.

Nor were the Serbians, Germans, Russians, and French alone in their nationalism. As Winston Churchill later wrote about this period, "National passions, unduly exalted in the decline of religion, burned beneath the surface of every land with fierce, if shrouded fires." Not even the rival faith of socialism could compete with nationalism. For 25 years, the Second International Workingman's Association had preached the international brotherhood of the working class. It had also often criticized war, attributing it to capitalist forces. Yet the vast majority of its members supported their homelands in the crucial days of early August 1914.

IMPERIALISM

Imperialism was the second combustible element in the prewar atmosphere. The influential German historian Fritz Fischer has written of German imperialistic aims in Europe, Africa, and the Near East and identified them as a chief cause of the war. Although some historians have disputed his charges, what is undeniable is that imperialistic rivalries stimulated hostile feelings between some of the major European powers.

FIRST MOROCCAN CRISIS AND ITS EFFECTS

The first Moroccan crisis of 1905 serves as an excellent illustration. In 1904 Great Britain and France had concluded the Entente Cordiale, an understanding concerning their overseas spheres of influence. As part of the agreement, Great Britain recognized France's desire to control Morocco. Germany disliked the Entente and thought that a stiff challenge to the French position in Morocco might split it apart. In 1905 Kaiser Wilhelm II landed at Tangier and recognized the sultan of Morocco as a ruler independent of French control. Wilhelm also demanded an international conference, which assembled in 1906, to discuss the situation. Meanwhile, the British had become so alarmed at German belligerence over Morocco, as well as at the continuing German naval buildup, that they moved much closer to France. While not going as far as the French would have liked—a promise of British support in case of war with Germany—Great Britain's foreign minister, Sir Edward Grey, did authorize informal military conversations with the French. These conversations continued from time to time over the years and strengthened the impression among some French statesmen that Great Britain would back France in case of a war with Germany.

In addition to bringing Great Britain closer to France, the Moroccan crisis also helped to bring about the Anglo-Russian Entente in 1907. It was not an alliance but primarily a settlement over spheres of influence in Persia, Afghanistan, and Tibet. Nevertheless, it brought Great Britain closer to Russia, France's ally. The Entente increased the Germans' fear of encirclement and to some extent induced them to vigorously back the Dual Monarchy in the annexation crisis of 1908—itself a manifestation of Austro-Hungarian imperialism. Again in 1914, Germany's uncompromising support of Austria-Hungary reflected its fear of losing its only real ally.

MILITARISM

Militarism also contributed to the outbreak of World War I. European nations feverishly expanded their military forces and armaments in the years immediately before 1914. German and Austrian military spending doubled between 1910 and 1914, and other European nations increased their expenditures markedly. By 1914 both Germany and France had assembled standing armies of 800,000 men, with 1 million more in the reserves. About 1.2 million Russians were under arms, although the Russian army was inferior in equipment, training, and leadership. By 1905 the British had begun construction on a new battleship, the *Dreadnought,* designed to be the most powerful ship ever built. Germany responded with increased naval expenditures of its own. From 1900 to 1911, German naval spending nearly tripled. Such contests did little to increase the security of either side; instead, they heightened the hostility and mistrust already existing among nations.

Another manifestation of the militarism of the era was the failure of the peace conferences of 1899 and 1907. Most government and military leaders were more concerned with keeping up in the arms race and maintaining absolute national sovereignty than with achieving disarmament and arbitrating disputes. At the 1907 conference, the delegates quickly postponed the issue of disarmament and passed a resolution calling for further study of the question. The delegates then spent weeks thrashing out the guidelines for the proper conduct of warfare. It was as if they were saying to the world, "Disarmament is a fool's dream, but war will surely come. So let us agree on the rules."

SCHLIEFFEN PLAN

In this militaristic era, the plans and advice of military leaders played an increasingly influential role in government decisions. Germany chose war in 1914 partly because it feared that if it waited, Russia's rearmament program would make Russia a stronger foe. Germany's Schlieffen Plan, which the French and Russian generals knew in broad outline, was a key factor in the peace options and war plans of several nations. In the plan, the German general staff had assumed that in a two-front war with France and Russia, Germany could not defeat both opponents simultaneously. Germany had therefore decided to knock out France first by an invasion through Belgium, while holding off the slowly mobilizing Russians. After defeating France, Germany would then concentrate its forces in the east and crush the Russians. For this plan to work, the German military could not give the Russians a significant head start in mobilizing their forces. Russia, on the other hand, reacting in part to strong French pressure, had to do just what Germany hoped it could not do—divert German troops to the Russian front before France could be defeated. Other nations had their own military plans that demanded lead time for mobilization and deployment of troops.

Thus, in those final hectic days, military considerations afforded diplomacy little time to reach a peaceful settlement. Because it included the military necessity of invading neutral Belgium, the Schlieffen Plan was also likely to bring Great Britain, which wanted nearby Belgium free from either French or German control, into the war.

That troops, weapons, and plans had such influence was partly a result of the continuing belief that war could be more beneficial than harmful. Perhaps the most famous extreme statement of this position came from the German General Friedrich von Bernhardi in his book of 1911, *Germany and the Next War*. It reflected Darwinian influences and contained such statements as "war is a biological necessity" and "the struggle for existence . . . is the basis of all healthy development." Although European political leaders were generally less Darwinian sounding, by mid-1914 most of them still expected a brief and not terribly destructive war—a "short, cleansing thunderstorm," in Winston Churchill's words.

THE ALLIANCE SYSTEM AND WAR PREPARATION

As the events of July and August 1914 clearly indicate, the two European alliance systems were the mechanisms that transformed a local conflict into World War I. After the shooting of Ferdinand, Austria was convinced that the Serbian government was implicated. The government in Vienna believed that, one way or another, it must crush the threat to its empire posed by advocates of Greater Serbia. Before acting, however, Austria sought to keep Russia from mobilizing to aid Serbia, or at least to ensure German backing against Russia should intervention occur. Germany, especially its military leadership, was happy to comply. It believed that sooner or later war with Russia would come, and when it did Germany would need Austrian help. The middle of 1914, after the assassination of Ferdinand and before further Russian modernization and railway development, seemed an appropriate time to deal with Russia. In early July, Germany granted almost unconditional backing—a "blank check"—to her ally, and Austria sent an ultimatum to Serbia on July 23. Austria demanded an end to anti-Austrian organizations and propaganda, the removal of officers and officials accused by Austria of being hostile, Austrian participation in the investigation of the assassination plot, and the suppression of subversive movements directed against Austria-Hungary. The Serbian government was given 48 hours to reply.

THE AUSTRIAN ULTIMATUM AND RUSSIAN MOBILIZATION

Serbia was aware that Russia, its chief supporter, advised caution but would nevertheless ultimately back Serbia in case of hostilities. Russia supported Serbia because after the diplomatic defeat of 1908 it did not wish to lose further influence and power in the Balkans to Austria-Hungary. Serbia was Russia's last bastion of influence in the area. If Austria was allowed to crush Serbia, either diplomatically or militarily, Russia's hopes in the Balkans would be finally smashed. After hearing of Austria's ultimatum, the Russian foreign minister, Sergei Sazonov, declared, "It means a European war!" He accused Austria of "setting fire to Europe," and on July 25 his government approved preliminary military preparations. This was done in the hope that it would frighten Austria into arriving at some sort of compromise. Russia also wished to be prepared in case it was necessary to come to the aid of Serbia.

In addition to its concern about Austria, the tsarist government had also become increasingly troubled about growing German influence in the Ottoman Empire. It is not difficult, therefore, to understand why some Russian officials perceived the demands placed on Serbia as part of a united effort by Austria and Germany to strengthen the Germanic influence in areas long considered of special interest to the Russians.

Serbia, Austria, Russia, Germany, France, and Great Britain in cartoon suggesting how the alliance systems would work.

Partly because of Russian support, Serbia did not accept all the Austrian demands. Nevertheless, its carefully worded reply reflected a conciliatory spirit. Austria, however, despite some belated German qualms, would recognize nothing less than unconditional acceptance. On July 28 Austria declared war on Serbia and bombarded Belgrade, the Serbian capital.

Meanwhile, Russia's ally, France, had been giving strong support to the tsarist government. The French remembered the 1870 war with Prussia (became Germany in 1871) and did not wish to be isolated again in a struggle with Germany. Accordingly, they were prepared to give full backing to their major ally, Russia. In addition, a war against Germany, if won, held out the hope of recovering the lost provinces of Alsace and Lorraine. From July 20 to 23 French President Poincaré and Premier Viviani were in St. Petersburg encouraging the Russians to stand firm.

After some indecisiveness about how to proceed, on July 30 Russia finally decided on a general mobilization of its troops. The French encouraged such an action because France knew of the general thrust of the Schlieffen Plan. If Russia mobilized substantially ahead of Germany, there would be less likelihood that Germany could swiftly defeat France.

Because of Germany's war plan, it was no surprise that after several warnings on previous days, Germany, on July 31, sent an ultimatum with a 12-hour limit demanding that Russia end its war preparations along the German frontier. On the same day, Germany asked the French government what its position would be in case of a Russian-German war. On August 1 the French replied that France would consult

THE REACTIONS OF GERMANY, FRANCE, AND GREAT BRITAIN

BIOGRAPHY

Inflamed with Patriotism

To me those hours seemed like a release from the painful feelings of my youth. . . . Overpowered by stormy enthusiasm, I fell down on my knees and thanked Heaven from an overflowing heart for granting me the good fortune of being permitted to live at this time.

A fight for freedom had begun, mightier than the earth had ever seen; for once Destiny had begun its course, the conviction dawned on even the broad masses that this time not the fate of Serbia or Austria was involved, but whether the German nation was to be or not to be. . . .

As a boy and young man I had so often felt the desire to prove at least once by deeds that for me national enthusiasm was no empty whim. . . . Thus my heart, like that of a million others, overflowed with proud joy that at last I would be able to redeem myself from this paralyzing feeling. I had so often

sung "Deutschland uber Alles" and shouted "Heil" at the top of my lungs, that it seemed to me almost a belated act of grace to be allowed to stand as a witness in the divine court of the eternal judge and proclaim the sincerity of this conviction. . . . [I] was ready at any time to die for my people and for the Reich which embodied it. . . . [D]ays later I was wearing the tunic which I was not to doff until nearly six years later.*

. . .

Adolf Hitler, describing his feelings at the start of World War I, when he was 25 and living an impoverished life in Munich. On August 3, 1914, he volunteered to enlist in the German army. See Chapters 13 and 18 for more on Hitler's youth and his dictatorship in Germany.

*From *Mein Kampf* by Adolf Hitler, translated by Ralph Manheim. Copyright © 1943 by Houghton Mifflin Company. Reprinted by permission.

its own interests. On the same day, the government in Paris ordered mobilization. Germany also mobilized on that day and, having received no reply to its ultimatum, declared war on Russia. Two days later, certain that France was preparing to aid Russia and unwilling to lose any more time, Germany declared war on France and directed its attack through neutral Belgium.

As a result of British-French friendship and military conversations that followed from their entente and the Moroccan crisis of 1905, Great Britain had already been moving toward support of France. A few days before, for example, the British cabinet had voted to give assurance to the French that the British navy would protect the French coast and shipping against any German attack. However, the invasion of Belgium made it much easier to decide on a declaration of war. The neutrality of Belgium, just across the English Channel from Great Britain, was considered essential to British interests. Great Britain, along with France, Germany, Austria, and Russia, had been one of the guarantors of that neutrality since the Treaty of London in 1839. Thus, on August 4 Great Britain declared war on Germany. "All for just a word—'neutrality'—just for a piece of paper," lamented German Chancellor Bethmann-Hollweg, who nevertheless had earlier in the day stated, "Whatever our lot may be, August 4, 1914, will remain for all eternity one of Germany's greatest days."

With the British declaration, almost all the major European powers that would enter the war were committed. Great Britain, France, and Russia opposed Germany and Austria-Hungary. The fear of being left without an ally helped ensure such a widespread war. Italy, the ally of Germany and Austria-Hungary in the Triple Alliance, did not enter the war at this time on the grounds that the alliance was a defensive one and Germany had taken the offensive.

SUMMARY

The assassination of Archduke Franz Ferdinand was the immediate cause of World War I, but four prominent background factors helped to explain how such an event could lead to a war as vast as World War I. As with the Boxer Rebellion of 1900, nationalism, imperialism, and militarism all played a part. So, too, did a fourth factor: the alliance system.

Historians have debated and will continue to debate which nation was most at fault. In recent years, many books, including David Fromkin's *Europe's Last Summer: Who Started the Great War in 1914?* (see Suggested Sources), have followed Fischer's lead in placing the primary blame on Germany. Yet none of the nations that went to war in the summer of 1914 had done all they might have done to prevent the conflict from occurring. Despite some late and relatively weak diplomatic efforts to slow the rapid escalation of events, each nation finally valued security, prestige, influence, and allies more than peace. Only after years of death and destruction did many realize that in 1914 they had undervalued the fruits of peace and vastly underestimated the human and material costs of modern warfare.

SUGGESTED SOURCES

Berghahn, V. R. *Germany and the Approach of War in 1914*. 2nd ed. 1993. An account that balances well the effect of both domestic and international considerations on Germany's foreign policy.

Dedijer, Vladimir. *The Road to Sarajevo*. 1966. A detailed but fascinating account of the events leading up to the assassination of Archduke Franz Ferdinand; sympathetic with the idealism of the conspirators.

Evans, R. J. W., and Hartmut Pogge van Strandmann, eds. *The Coming of the First World War*. 1989. A series of essays that delineates the position of each major country that entered the war in July and August and also looks at the influence of public opinion.*

Ferguson, Niall. *The Pity of War: Explaining World War I*. 2000. A lively revisionist work that challenges many traditional views about the war and its causes; places much blame on Britain for the start and expansion of the war to a global one.*

Fischer, Fritz. *World Power or Decline*. 1975. A summation of the author's controversial case for primarily blaming Germany's imperialist aims for causing World War I.*

Fromkin, David. *Europe's Last Summer: Who Started the Great War in 1914?* 2004. A well-written recent defense of Fritz Fischer's thesis that Germany bore the chief responsibility for starting WWI.*

Hamilton, Richard F., and Holger H. Herwig, eds. *The Origins of World War I*. 2003. The scholarly contributors to this large collection offer many fresh reassessments.

Herrmann, David G. *The Arming of Europe and the Making of the First World War.* 1997. A scholarly work that argues that the changing military capabilities of the powers in the decade before the war strongly affected the diplomacy leading to it.*

Joll, James. *The Origins of the First World War.* 2nd ed. 1992. A concise overview of the causes of the war and a reexamination of differing historical interpretations of them.*

Kennedy, Paul M., ed. *The War Plans of the Great Powers, 1880–1914.* 1985. An excellent and comprehensive collection of essays on the war.*

Lafore, Laurence. *The Long Fuse.* 2nd ed. 1997. A readable work on the origins of the war that while emphasizing Serbian-Austrian tensions also examines the concerns of the other major powers.*

Lieven, D. C. B. *Russia and the Origins of the First World War.* 1983. A clear, well-balanced analysis of why Russia became involved in World War I.*

Remak, Joachim. *The Origin of World War I: 1871–1914.* 2nd ed. 1995. A good, brief, balanced introduction to the subject.*

Strachan, Hew. *The Outbreak of the First World War.* 2005. A concise reexamination by a leading British scholar; especially good on attitudes toward war among socialists, intellectuals, and the general public.*

WEB SOURCES

www.lib.byu.edu/~rdh/wwi/1914m.html. This site contains links to various pre–World War I documents, including many that relate to the causes of the war.

www.worldwar1.com/tlss1914.htm and www.worldwar1.com/tlplot.htm. These two web pages from the same general site contain numerous links to the background and causes of WWI.

www.bbc.co.uk/history/war/wwone/origins_01.shtml. A good essay on the origins of the war with links provided by a British professor on BBC's history site.

---

*Paperback available.

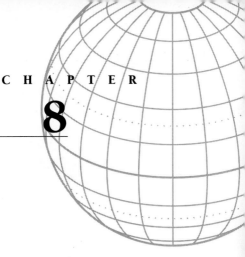

⑥World War I

Those who lived during the conflict that broke out in July 1914 called it the Great War; later it became known as World War I. Both names are appropriate, for 65 million people from 35 nations served in the armed forces, hundreds of millions of civilians were directly involved, and fighting occurred on three continents and on the oceans. The main struggle, however, was in Europe and in the adjacent North Atlantic waters. The war was the ultimate expression of the intense nationalism and militarism of the period. It also taught a grim lesson in how rapidly developing technology can overwhelm its creators; in World War I it sometimes appeared that the submarine, the cannon, and the machine gun were the real commanders.

THE OPENING PHASE OF THE WAR

In the beginning it was a popular war. Many citizens of the participating powers, conditioned by years of nationalist propaganda, greeted the war with enthusiasm. Cheering crowds showered flowers and gifts on the proud troops departing for the front; most thought it would be a short war. There would be an early rout of the enemy and a glorious and profitable peace settlement for their nation. "You will be home before the leaves have fallen from the trees," Kaiser Wilhelm told his departing troops.

Upon declaring war, Germany immediately carried out the Schlieffen Plan. The Germans concentrated the bulk of their forces, seven out of eight armies, against France, while assigning limited forces to hold off the slowly mobilizing Russians. The campaign plan against France called for German forces to carry out a vast encircling movement on the French. German forces would pass west through Belgium, wheel to the south, and then pounce on the unsuspecting French. It worked—almost. All through August the German armies moved forward, driving their French, British, and Belgian opponents ahead of them. A French attempt to launch an attack into southern Germany, known as Plan XVII, failed disastrously. Everywhere, the Germans were advancing and the Allies retreating. It seemed as if the war might be over by autumn, as the Kaiser had predicted.

The Germans were within reach of Paris by early September, but their well-oiled military machine was beginning to develop a number of problems. The forward troops

SCHLIEFFEN PLAN

were finding it difficult to keep up with Schlieffen's demanding march schedules. Supplies, still brought forward by slow-moving horse-drawn wagons, were lagging far behind the front lines. The sheer size of the German forces, some 2 million men, made it difficult for the German commander, General Helmuth von Moltke, to coordinate the movement of his various armies.

At precisely the moment that German momentum was beginning to lag, the Allies were getting their second wind. Under the leadership of General Joseph Joffre, the French and British reorganized the front. Beginning on September 5 at the Marne River, they threw their last reserves, some of them rushed by taxicabs through Paris, into a series of counterattacks. Although the counterattacks made only a limited penetration, the Germans decided to pull back northeastward to the Aisne River. The Schlieffen Plan had failed; subsequently, both sides extended the battle line to the seacoast, digging in along the way. By the middle of October 1914, a heavily fortified trench system, the western front, meandered 450 miles across Belgium and France from the North Sea to the Swiss border.

GERMANS FAIL IN FRANCE—BUT WIN IN PRUSSIA

As the Germans were advancing across France in August, the Russians attacked more quickly than the Germans had expected. Two Russian armies swept into East Prussia and defeated German forces on the Prussian frontier. The German command diverted troops from the western front, but they arrived in East Prussia too late. Meanwhile, German forces already in East Prussia recovered quickly. Maneuvering their outnumbered forces brilliantly, General Paul von Hindenburg and his chief of staff, Erich von Ludendorff, annihilated one Russian army at Tannenberg and routed the other at the Masurian Lakes. Hindenburg became a popular hero, and Ludendorff eventually went on to direct all German army operations. However, the Germans were not yet strong enough to follow up their victories and invade Russia. Meanwhile, the Ottoman Empire and Bulgaria, each for its own reasons, joined Germany and Austria-Hungary. These four nations are traditionally called the Central Powers, and their opponents, the Allies.

THE PERIOD OF STALEMATE

STALEMATE ON BOTH EASTERN AND WESTERN FRONTS

Other battlefronts opened up in Europe during 1915 and 1916, but for the most part the armies there became bogged down like the armies on the western front. Lured by British and French promises of Austrian and Ottoman territory, Italy attacked Austria in 1915. The new battlefront, located in mountainous terrain, soon became deadlocked. In a major strategic move, an Allied expeditionary force attempted to seize the Dardanelles (the passageway between the Mediterranean and the Black Sea) with the object of defeating the Ottoman Empire and opening a water route to supply Russia. Ottoman forces pinned down the attackers at Gallipoli, near the mouth of the Dardanelles, and forced them to withdraw. In the Balkans, where the war had begun, German, Austrian, and Bulgarian troops overran Serbia. The British and French, always sensitive to any potential threat to their Mediterranean supply lines, rushed forces to northern Greece, but no active front developed there.

For almost two years there was considerable movement on the eastern front. In 1915 and 1916 both sides launched major offensives that seized ground and lost it again, but the Germans steadily gained the upper hand and eventually conquered the Russian provinces of Poland and Lithuania. In 1916 German, Austrian, and Bulgarian forces overran Romania, forcing the Russians to enter eastern Romania to prevent an invasion of southern Russia. The eastern front now extended 1,200 miles from the Baltic to the Black Sea. Most of the front consisted of lightly defended sectors interspersed with heavily fortified strong points. Some areas of heavy forests and extensive swamps were not defended at all. Germany did not have sufficient forces to launch a decisive invasion of Russia; in that sense, the eastern front also became a stalemate.

THE WAR OUTSIDE EUROPE

Between 1914 and 1918 fighting spread around the world, although nowhere did it remotely attain the magnitude of the struggle in Europe. In Africa, Allied colonial troops captured German colonies isolated by the blockade. Togo, Cameroon, and German Southwest Africa were quickly overrun, but a small German force held out in part of German East Africa until the end of the war.

JAPAN EXPANDS ITS POWER IN THE PACIFIC AND ASIA

In Asia, the outbreak of war gave Japan an opportunity to improve its position in East Asia and the western Pacific, and Japan lost little time in making the most of it. Following the terms of the Anglo-Japanese Alliance, Japan declared war on Germany. Japanese and British military units cleared German forces from its sphere of influence in China before the end of 1914. While Australian and New Zealand (ANZAC) forces were occupying German colonies south of the equator, units of the Japanese navy seized German-held islands north of it. Japan's other activities in the war consisted of convoy duties to protect Allied shipping.

Japan also took advantage of the war to advance its imperialist designs on China. On January 18, 1915, the Japanese presented to the Chinese government the Twenty-One Demands, which would have turned China into Japan's political and economic protectorate. In effect, Japan insisted on virtually direct control over Manchuria, eastern Inner Mongolia, and the Shantung Peninsula and demanded a monopoly of iron ore and coal mining in the Yangtze valley. Japan also "requested" the right to build railroads in southern China and to share control over Chinese police units and arsenals. China looked for outside support in vain and capitulated on nearly all points on May 15, 1915. Japan subsequently secured pledges from Great Britain, France, Italy, and Russia that they would back its claims in postwar negotiations. After declaring war on Germany, the United States issued a joint statement with Japan in which it agreed that "Japan has special interests in China, particularly in that part to which her possessions are contiguous." Having secured agreement from all the Allies, Japan dropped its opposition to China joining the war against the Central Powers. China's contribution to the Allied cause consisted of sending 200,000 noncombatant laborers who worked in factories and at other tasks in Europe.

THE BRITISH ARE FIRST REPULSED AND THEN TRIUMPHANT IN WEST ASIA

In West Asia the Allies faced a more formidable problem. Unlike Germany, which could not adequately defend its African and Asian colonies, the Ottoman Empire could devote a significant portion of its military forces to defending its West Asian territories. The Ottoman army was on the whole not particularly well trained or led but was initially able to prevent the Russians from advancing deep into Armenia, to repulse a British invasion of Iraq, to monitor the British in Egypt, and to contain an Arab revolt in the Arabian peninsula. By 1917, however, Great Britain had assembled British, ANZAC (Australia and New Zealand), and colonial forces and begun driving into Palestine and Iraq. In addition, the romantic hero Colonel T. E. Lawrence, among others, helped the Arabs to mount a more effective revolt. By 1918, Ottoman control of the Middle East had collapsed and the region was fully in control of Allied and Arab forces.

In a reversal of recent European encroachment on the rest of the world, World War I saw military forces from the outside world appear in Europe. Canadian, Australian, New Zealand, and South African units fought with British troops in Europe and the Middle East. More than a million Indian soldiers and noncombatants, first arriving in France on September 26, 1914, also fought in Europe, the Middle East, and in Egypt, guarding the Suez Canal. French colonial troops from Africa and Vietnam, and token units from Latin American nations saw service on the Allied side on the western front. A Japanese destroyer force patrolled the Mediterranean. After 1917, there was a massive infusion of the United States armed forces on the western front. The presence in Europe of personnel from the other continents was a forewarning of the decline of European global power during the twentieth century.

THE WAR OF ATTRITION BECOMES TOTAL WAR

As the stalemate continued into 1915 and 1916, the struggle evolved into a war of attrition. With the front lines dominated by trenches, machine guns, and powerful artillery, it had become increasingly clear that achieving a breakthrough of the enemy position was impossible. Nevertheless, both sides tried, launching huge offensives that went nowhere but generated massive casualties. Even if an attack did reach and penetrate the enemy position, the attacker then met a second line of trenches, and often a third. No one had ever seen a war like this. In 1915 alone, there were 612,000 German casualties, and over 1,500,000 Allied.

TOTAL WAR

Given these enormous losses, each government had to mobilize all the resources of its nation to win the war. In the process, the difference between the civilian population and the military forces became less distinct. Governments became more authoritarian, increasing their control over the economic, social, political, and cultural lives of their peoples. This process has been referred to by many historians as "total war."

The War on Land

Throughout 1915, 1916, and 1917 the same grim scenario was played and replayed. The attackers would commence with a massive artillery bombardment along a front sometimes 50 miles wide. The bombardment might last for several days and was

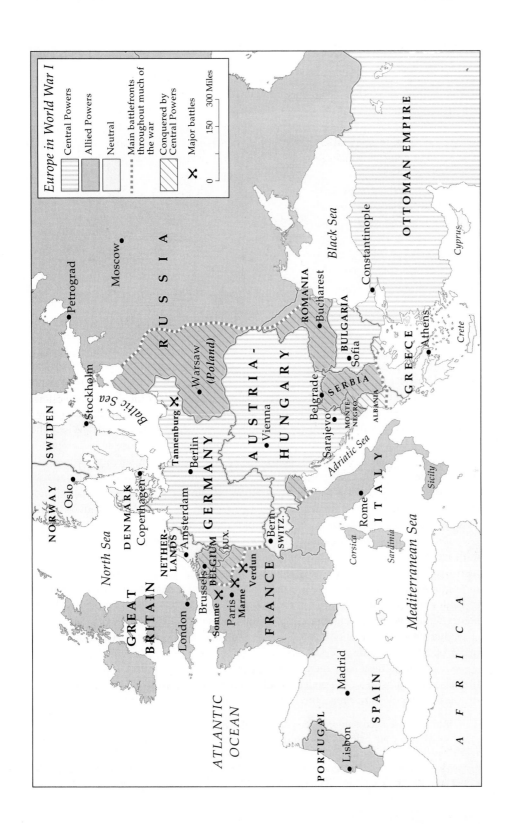

Europe in World War I

Central Powers
Allied Powers
Neutral
Main battlefronts throughout much of the war
Conquered by Central Powers
Major battles

0   150   300 Miles

ATLANTIC OCEAN

GREAT BRITAIN
London

NORWAY
Oslo

SWEDEN
Stockholm

North Sea

Baltic Sea

DENMARK
Copenhagen

NETHER-LANDS
Amsterdam

BELGIUM
Brussels
LUX.

GERMANY
Berlin

RUSSIA
Petrograd
Moscow

Warsaw
(Poland)

Tannenburg

AUSTRIA-HUNGARY
Vienna

FRANCE
Paris
Verdun
Marne
Somme

SWITZ.
Bern

ITALY
Rome

Corsica
Sardinia

Mediterranean Sea

Sicily

ROMANIA
Bucharest

BULGARIA
Sofia

SERBIA
Belgrade
Sarajevo
MONTE-NEGRO
ALBANIA

GREECE
Athens

Black Sea

Constantinople

OTTOMAN EMPIRE

Cyprus

Crete

Adriatic Sea

AFRICA

SPAIN
Madrid

PORTUGAL
Lisbon

109

Death on the western front. A German patrol fires on a
French patrol between the lines.

intended to clear out the mines and barbed wire, smash in the frontline trench system, and kill and wound many of the defenders, while others suffered shell shock
and hysteria. The defenders would take refuge in their underground bunkers while
reinforcements and artillery were rushed up and held ready in the rear. When the
attackers' artillery barrage lifted and the attacking infantry surged forward, the defenders' artillery would rain shells on the attackers, and the defending infantry, reinforced,
would come out of the bunkers, man their machine guns, and mow down the attacking infantry. The attackers would in their turn be reinforced, and occasionally penetrate a few miles or so, but eventually both the attackers and the defenders would
become exhausted and break off the fighting.

BATTLEFIELD MISERY   As the war progressed, commanders would send their men into battle hoping for
a breakthrough but willing to settle for killing and incapacitating more of the enemy's
men than they lost of their own. "I am nibbling them," Joffre explained. Two of the
most gruesome encounters came in 1916, when 2 million men were killed and wounded
in battles at the Somme River and at Verdun. "Humanity . . . must be mad. . . . What
scenes of horror and carnage! . . . Hell cannot be so terrible," wrote a French soldier
at Verdun. Since the casualty rates were approximately equal, neither side "won." Other
major offensives had the same results.

Between battles, men died from sniper fire, frontline patrols, random mortar
fire, disease, exposure, and spoiled or adulterated rations. In Erich Remarque's novel
All Quiet on the Western Front, the hero commented,

> Although we need reinforcement, the recruits give us almost more trouble than they are
> worth. They are helpless in this grim fighting area, they fall like flies. . . . [A] man must
> have a feeling for the contours of the ground, an ear for the sound and character of
> shells, must be able to decide beforehand where they drop, how they burst, and how to
> take shelter.

The young recruits of course know none of these things. They get killed simply because they can hardly tell shrapnel from high-explosive, they are mown down. . . . They flock together like sheep instead of scattering. . . . Some of them in a shell hole took their masks off too soon; they did not know that the gas lies longest in the hollows. . . . Their condition is hopeless, they choke to death with haemorrhages and suffocation.

Survivors endured crowded quarters, trench foot, rats, lice, mud, loss of comrades, and the probability of death during the next offensive. Under such conditions, men became living automatons. "We are not leading the lives of men at all," one British soldier wrote, "but that of animals, living in holes in the ground, and only showing outside to fight and to feed." Some deserted, and on occasions there were mutinies. Most of the troops, however, kept on fighting loyally.

In an attempt to find a way out of the stalemate, each side invented new weapons. They used poison gas and flamethrowers, but, in particular, special hopes were pinned on developing effective airplanes and tanks that might help the infantry to break through entrenchments. Both sides used airplanes and dirigibles (propelled lighter-than-air craft) for observation and for attacks on the front lines and the rear support areas. Airplanes fought each other in spectacular "dogfights," and skillful pilots ("aces") became romantic heroes in an otherwise grim war of impersonal death. Airplanes and dirigibles also attacked cities behind the battlefronts, often for the specific purpose of demoralizing the civilian population. The phenomenon of civilians suffering the same grisly deaths as soldiers and sailors foretold the nature of wars to come. Tanks became a major supporting weapon for infantry attacks in 1917. When used in conjunction with airplanes, they provided the promise of breaking through entrenched positions and thus returning combat to a war of maneuver. However, neither the airplane nor the tank was fully developed during the war, and they were not decisive in bringing victory.

THE ADVENT OF THE AIRPLANE AND THE TANK SUGGESTS A BREAKTHROUGH IN THE STALEMATE

The War at Sea

BRITAIN BLOCKADES GERMANY WITH MINES

While attempting to wear down the enemy on the battlefield, military leaders pursued another goal of the war of attrition—cutting off supplies coming to the enemy by sea. Germany and particularly Great Britain were dependent on overseas sources of raw materials and food, and both nations were thus vulnerable to enemy navies. To protect its own trade and to cut off the commerce of any wartime enemy, Great Britain had built up the world's largest navy. Early in the war, the British mined the North Sea approaches to Germany and cleared German surface raiders from the sea. In addition, the British seized all merchant ships carrying contraband, which Great Britain in effect defined as any product that might help the enemy war effort. The British even seized neutral ships heading for neutral nations if the British suspected their cargoes would be reshipped to Germany. Neutral nations, including the United States, protested, but despite the seizures U.S. merchants sold to any belligerent that could pay. Since little could get through to Germany, U.S. trade benefited the Allies almost exclusively. Although some supplies continued to get through, as time passed it became clear that in the long run the British blockade would strangle Germany.

Germany could also play the blockading game. Great Britain depended on large numbers of ships docking daily at its ports to feed its people and to keep its factories running. If its supplies were cut off, Great Britain would crumble much faster than Germany, and if Great Britain dropped out of the war, France would not last long. To starve out the British, the Germans had developed the submarine, an effective new weapon labeled by a British admiral as "underhanded, unfair, and un-English."

GERMANY BLOCKADES BRITAIN WITH SUBMARINES

Beginning in earnest in 1915, German U-boats fanned out over the western approaches to Great Britain, destroying shipping at a rapid rate. At first, even though their submarines were vulnerable to attacks by airplanes and destroyers when they surfaced, German commanders tried to follow the rules of war by warning British merchant vessels so that their crews could take to the lifeboats. To counter the submarine blockade, the British began to arm merchant ships, have merchant ships ram submarines, send war supplies and soldiers on passenger liners, fly the flags of neutral nations, and register British ships under foreign governments. In response, the Germans began sinking merchant ships without warning, killing many more seamen and passengers. These German actions, exaggerated by Allied propaganda ministries, provoked international outcries. The climax came on May 7, 1915, when a U-boat sank the British passenger liner *Lusitania*, with the loss of 1,198 lives, including 128 Americans. The Germans claimed, possibly correctly, that the ship was carrying munitions and soldiers, and there is some evidence that the vessel was armed as well. By 1916, after repeated incidents, the reaction of the U.S. government became so threatening that the German government restricted the aggressive tactics of its submarines. With the submarine campaign hampered, the German surface fleet steamed out in an attempt to break the blockade at the Battle of Jutland on May 31–June 1, 1916. It was the greatest engagement of surface fleets in history, a confused melee in the rain and fog in which both sides dealt out, and suffered, enormous punishment. In the end, however, it was the vastly outnumbered German High Seas Fleet that fled back to its ports. The Royal Navy had triumphed. British Admiral John Jellicoe, "the man who could have lost the war in a single hour," had held on.

The War at Home

THE HOME FRONT INCORPORATES CIVILIANS INTO THE WAR

If a nation expected to outlast its enemy in a war of attrition, it had to mobilize its civilian population effectively and create a new war front—the "home front." Since the warring governments had believed the conflict would be short, none of them had stockpiled resources or made plans to allocate them in the event of a lengthy struggle. As a war of attrition emerged, the warring governments, whether authoritarian or democratic, took increasing control of broad facets of their society and their national economy. The men who planned the centralization of the home front now became the pivotal figures of the war. Some were technicians, such as Walter Rathenau in Germany and Bernard Baruch in the United States; others

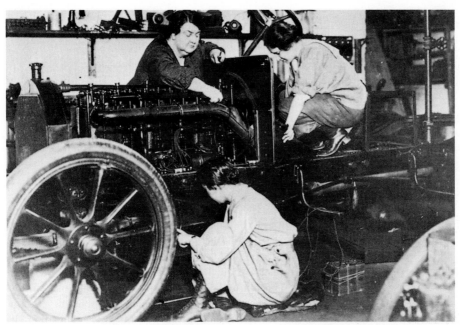

World War I war production needs eased restrictions on what activities were possible for "respectable" women.

were political leaders, such as David Lloyd George in Great Britain and Georges Clemenceau in France.

The managers of the home front had numerous responsibilities, none more crucial than the allocation of manpower. General Kitchener contributed substantially to the Allied war effort when he transformed the small professional army of Great Britain into a force based on mass conscripts, without a notable loss of efficiency. Eventually, all the major belligerents conscripted able-bodied men and in some cases took teenagers, the elderly, and the marginally disabled.

To replace these men in their civilian occupations, cultural tradition was swept aside as women were recruited for labor in the factories and offices and on the farms. In Germany, 702,000 women were employed in the armaments industry in 1917, an increase of 500 percent over 1913. In the German state of Prussia there were 100,000 women railroad employees in 1918, an increase of 1,000 percent over 1914. Also, many more adolescents worked in industry; the number of 14- to 16-year-olds working in German chemical plants increased 225 percent. Many of them were young women.

WOMEN REPLACE MEN IN MANY HITHERTO MALE OCCUPATIONS

Governments seized complete control of the production of industrial raw materials, and when key commodities such as food and natural nitrates were in short supply, governments financed research, development, and production of substitutes. Germany created many *ersatz* (substitute) commodities, such as artificial nitrates, cellulose clothing, bark coffee, and turnip bread. Civilians contributed to the war effort by working overtime, sending packages to service personnel, planting gardens, investing in government bonds, supplementing rationing with fast days and meatless days, and watching for spies and saboteurs.

Because of the tremendous strain on the civilian populations, government propaganda ministries became a crucial aspect of the war effort. These organizations incited citizens to work harder, love their government, and hate the enemy. Vivid propaganda posters portrayed opponents as slavering, inhuman beasts fit only to be exterminated. At the same time, governments suppressed dissent by imposing censorship and jailing critics.

THE BREAK IN THE STALEMATE

GERMANS RESUME SUBMARINE BLOCKADE OF BRITAIN

The decisive point in the war came during the winter of 1916–1917. German morale was weakening under the pressure of the British blockade, and Germany's population was experiencing severe deprivation. German leaders feared that unless something was done to break the impasse, Germany would lose the war. The German naval command pressed for permission to resume unrestricted submarine warfare, sinking all ships heading for the British Isles. The German leaders understood that such a campaign would probably bring the United States into the war, but it was already a virtual ally of Great Britain, providing millions of dollars of war materials to Germany's enemies. They derided the United States as a "disorganized and undisciplined" nation that would not be effective in the war, and some German officers pledged that "not one American will land on the Continent." Even cautious German leaders estimated that it would take a year for the United States to place substantial troops on the western front. Long before the Americans could effectively intervene, they reasoned, Great Britain would be starved out and would surrender, and the other Allies would subsequently collapse. Over the protest of the civilian leaders, the kaiser reluctantly gave his approval.

On February 1, 1917, the restarting of unrestricted submarine warfare marked the beginning of the final phase of the war. For two months the submarine campaign was spectacularly effective, and by April the British found themselves without reserves of industrial raw materials and with only six weeks' supply of food. Meanwhile, on April 6, the United States declared war on Germany. The new submarine campaign not only cost U.S. lives but also, in President Wilson's eyes, demonstrated a malignant militarism that threatened liberal institutions all over the world. This last point had been brought home to Americans when they discovered that Germany had promised to return the southwestern area of the United States to Mexico if Mexico would attack the United States. Congress supported the president, and Americans entered the war believing they were going "over there" to "make the world safe for democracy."

U.S. AND BRITISH NAVIES COMBINE TO CRUSH THE GERMAN SUBMARINE BLOCKADE

Soon after the United States entered the war, it became apparent that the Germans had miscalculated. Although the U.S. Army did take many months to train and transport, the powerful U.S. Navy was immediately ready to deal with the submarines. U.S. and British naval units created a convoy system, and both navies employed new antisubmarine weapons such as depth charges and hydrophone detectors. During the summer and autumn of 1917 the combined navies sank an increasing number of submarines, while more and more merchant ships got through to Great Britain and France. By the autumn of 1917, as U.S. supplies poured in, it was clear the U-boat offensive had failed. If the Germans could not win a quick victory on the battlefield, the Allies, reinforced by the Americans, would win the war.

In fact, the Germans in the autumn of 1917 believed that victory on the western front was still possible, even likely. Russia appeared to be on the verge of collapse; if it did, German troops could be rushed to the western front for a decisive breakthrough before the Americans could make a difference. Russia had held on grimly throughout 1915 and 1916, absorbing millions of casualties, yet saved by the fact that the Germans and Austrians were too committed elsewhere to undertake a decisive offensive across the vast spaces of western Russia. Finally, however, the government of the tsar became the first casualty of the war of attrition. War weariness and privation spurred both civilians and soldiers to take to the streets and drive Tsar Nicholas from power in March 1917. The new provisional government attempted to carry on the war but was crippled by desertion at the front and political dissension at home (see Chapter 12). In November 1917 the Bolsheviks toppled the government, seized power, and immediately began negotiations for peace. On March 3, 1918, at Brest-Litovsk, Russia signed a humiliating peace treaty with Germany and dropped out of the war.

Russia's collapse allowed Germany to send its best troops in the east to the western front during the winter of 1917–1918. Fearing these soldiers might have been infected with Bolshevik propaganda, the German government set up "mental delousing stations" to reindoctrinate them with the correct loyal attitudes. Bolstered by this additional manpower arriving from the eastern front, the Germans prepared to launch a decisive offensive. As Ludendorff put it, "Our general situation requires that we should strike at the earliest possible moment . . . before the Americans throw strong forces into the scale."

Meanwhile, U.S. industry was pouring out an enormous quantity of war material to bolster the French and British armies, and U.S. troops, led by General John "Black Jack" Pershing, began landing in France in numbers that eventually reached 250,000 a month. One of his aides announced, "Lafayette, we are here," in memory of France's contribution to rebel victory in the U.S. War for Independence.

In March 1918 the Germans launched a series of powerful, do-or-die offensives. They employed a new style of infantry tactics, using specially trained "shock troops" to uncover and penetrate weak spots in the enemy line. The Germans broke through the main British and French positions and drove the Allies back, in some cases as much as 50 miles. For Britain and France, it was the most dangerous moment in the war since 1914. By July, the Germans once again stood on the Marne River, just a short distance from Paris. As in 1914, however, they were unable to sustain their momentum. Even with the new tactics, German casualties in these battles had been high. They had lost as many as 1 million men, troops that an increasingly exhausted nation could not replace. The Allies, in contrast,

TSARIST GOVERNMENT COLLAPSES; BOLSHEVIKS SUE FOR PEACE

GERMANS ATTACK; U.S. TROOPS AND SUPPLIES REACH FRANCE; ALLIES COUNTERATTACK

were better able to sustain casualties, especially with the large number of fresh U.S. troops at their disposal.

As the Germans paused in exhaustion, Marshal Ferdinand Foch, the newly created commander in chief of the Allied forces, coordinated a series of counterattacks that drove the Germans back from the gains they had made in their offensives. A spectacular breakthrough by British troops at Amiens on August 8, an attack spearheaded by hordes of tanks, signaled the approaching end of the war. By September 1918 the German army, though not broken, had been pushed out of virtually all of France. On September 29 Ludendorff informed the kaiser that Germany could not win the war and recommended that the German government explore avenues for peace while its military forces were still intact.

THE ENDING OF THE WAR

WILSON PROPOSES FOURTEEN POINTS TO SHAPE THE PEACE

Feverish diplomatic maneuverings punctuated late September and October 1918. Wilson, convinced that demands of unconditional surrender would prolong the war, had brought forth his peace plan, the Fourteen Points, in January 1918. The proposal contained three broad goals. The first goal was to prevent future wars by eliminating practices that had helped to precipitate the current war: trade barriers, interference with freedom of the seas, secret diplomacy, colonial tensions, and arms races. The second goal, aimed at settling particular problems in Europe, was a series of specific proposals concerning territorial integrity, national boundaries, and ethnic nationalism. To Wilson, the third goal was the most important: a League of Nations to preserve peace in the future. In addition to the Fourteen Points, Wilson had another condition for peace—the end of authoritarian government in Germany. He did not call for harsh punishment of the Central Powers. The other Allies, which had suffered much more than the United States, were not particularly happy with Wilson's leniency toward Germany, but they eventually agreed, with some reservations.

As the Germans made overtures for peace on the basis of the Fourteen Points and tinkered with coalition governments that might satisfy Wilson that Germany was no longer an autocracy, the war wound down. Bulgaria surrendered on September 30 and Turkey on October 30. Ethnic minorities in Austria-Hungary began declaring their independence, and on November 3 Austria surrendered, with Kaiser Karl going into exile shortly afterward. On the same day, the German sailors at Kiel mutinied, running up the socialist red flag. Councils of workers and soldiers began springing up in the major German cities in imitation of the Russian Soviets. During the days that followed, socialist leaders encouraged wildcat strikes in many German cities, and the military leaders forced Kaiser Wilhelm II to abdicate and go into exile in the Netherlands.

SOCIAL REVOLUTION AND MILITARY DEFEAT FORCE GERMANY TO THE PEACE TABLE

When representatives of the new German republic arrived in France prepared to sign an armistice (cease-fire) on the basis of the Fourteen Points, they found to their dismay that the Allies had additional terms that would make it impossible for

Germany to renew the fighting if the cease-fire agreement were violated. If Germany wanted to end the fighting, the German army must withdraw to the east bank of the Rhine so that the Allied armies could occupy the west bank and several bridge-heads. Germany was to surrender the bulk of its surface fleet, its submarines, its air force, much of its machine guns and artillery, and its motorized transport. Finally, Germany was to renounce the Treaty of Brest-Litovsk and make reparations for damages sustained by civilians in the occupied territories. The German representatives reluctantly and bitterly signed: "I saw [the German delegation leader] brandish his pen and grind his teeth, . . . the business was settled," Foch recalled. On November 11, 1918, at 11:00 A.M., the guns fell silent on the western front. World War I was over.

It has been estimated that about 10 million fighting men lost their lives in World War I, victims not only of their enemies but also of the advancing technology of warfare. Three-quarters of the dead were from Russia, Germany, France, Austria-Hungary, Great Britain, and Italy. Those wounded in combat numbered about twice the military deaths. One of every 10 men in France was killed, and 3 of every 10 between the ages of 18 and 28. Since the United States had entered the war late, U.S. losses were numerically and proportionally less than those of any of the major European countries. For example, despite a population almost two and one-half times larger than that of France, U.S. combat losses were less than one-tenth of those suffered by the French. An extremely high percentage of well-educated young Europeans, many of them junior officers, lost their lives. The lack of vitality and leadership Great Britain and France displayed in the 1930s was in part a result of the war deaths of many potential leaders.

In addition to the military deaths, countless civilians died between 1914 and 1918 as a result of the war. Some estimates place the figure higher than that of military deaths. The Turks massacred nearly 1 million Armenians in 1915. Some civilians died as a result of shells or bullets, and many others, especially in eastern Europe, were attacked by the maladies that accompanied war: influenza, typhus, cholera, and malnutrition. Even after the war ended, men and women continued to die in the chaos of the Russian civil war and the worldwide influenza epidemic that began in 1918 and eventually killed many more millions than all the war dead of 1914–1918. The ravages of World War I contributed to both disasters.

Accompanying the loss of lives was a great loss of property, especially in Belgium, France, and eastern Europe. German property suffered little in comparison to that of France, where it was estimated that 300,000 homes, 8,000 factories and mines (including steel plants and coal mines, the basis of French heavy industry), 52,000 kilometers of roads, and 6,000 kilometers of railroads had been destroyed. About 7 million acres of arable land in France were also devastated.

The estimated overall direct cost of the war was $180 billion; the indirect cost was approximately another $150 billion. The Carnegie Endowment for International Peace estimated that with the money spent on the war every family in the British Isles,

HUMAN AND ECOMONIC COST OF WORLD WAR I

Belgium, Russia, Germany, the United States, Canada, and Australia could have been provided with a home of its own. In addition, all the property and wealth of Great Britain and France could have been purchased, and a considerable sum would still have remained. From 1870 to 1914 Europe had been the world's banker, with major financial investments on every continent. By 1918, however, many of these investments had been lost or withdrawn to help pay for the war. In addition, Europe was now in debt, principally to the United States, which had now become the great creditor of the world.

SUMMARY

World War I was fought primarily in Europe and the North Atlantic, although some fighting occurred in Asia and Africa and elsewhere on the world's oceans. The French and British halted the Germans at the Battle of the Marne, and both sides dug in. The military weapons on both sides were so equally deadly in effect that neither side could break through their opponent's lines, creating a stalemate on the western front. In the east, German forces routed invading Russian armies, but the eastern front also ended in a stalemate, as did secondary fronts in Italy and northern Greece. Elsewhere, Allied forces conquered German colonies in Asia and Africa and cleared German vessels out of the Indian and Pacific oceans.

As the stalemate persisted, each side attempted to wear down the opponent's armed forces and break the morale of the opponents' civilian population. The war of attrition on the western front entailed rituals of mass slaughter, as assaulting infantry was almost invariably turned back by entrenched defenders. Great Britain conducted a fleet and mine blockade that slowly strangled the German economy and caused great deprivation among German civilians. Germany responded with a submarine blockade of Great Britain but temporarily ceased sinking neutral ships when threatened by the United States. Governments of the warring nations pushed the concept of nationalism to its limits, urging their home front populations to make greater and greater sacrifices for their country and to hate all the people of the opposing nations as the enemy.

In 1917 two major occurrences broke the stalemate. One was the German decision to resume unrestricted warfare, which brought the United States into the war on the side of the Allies. Anglo-American naval cooperation broke the submarine blockade, and U.S. war matériel and U.S. soldiers began to pour into Europe. The second major event was the revolution that knocked Russia out of the war and freed German troops to fight on the western front. In March 1918 the Germans launched their last offensive but were thrown back by Allied troops, who launched a counteroffensive that slowly drove German troops out of France. Unable to stop the Allied offensive, faced with social revolution, and deserted by its allies, Germany agreed to a harsh armistice, which went into effect on November 11, 1918. The death and destruction incurred in this war dwarfed all the conflict that had gone before. Indeed, World War I probably killed more people than all previous wars in the history of the human race, combined.

SUGGESTED SOURCES

Cobb, Humphrey. *Paths of Glory.* 1935. A fictional account of the French army that attacks the high command.* (Also a film.)

Cowley, Robert, ed. *The Great War: Perspectives on the First World War.* 2004. Thirty essays by leading scholars.

Ellis, John. *Eye-Deep in Hell: Trench Warfare in World War I.* Reprinted. 1989. The title tells it all.*

Ferguson, Niall. *The Pity of War: Explaining World War I.* 2000. A lively revisionist work that challenges many traditionalist views about the war and its causes; informative and compelling.

Friedel, Frank. *Over There: The Story of America's First Great Overseas Crusade.* 2nd ed. 1990. A heavily illustrated survey of the U.S. role in World War I. Extensive use of firsthand accounts.*

Gallipoli. An Australian film vividly re-creating the bungled British operation against Turkey. Authentic scenes of trench warfare.

Gilbert, Martin. *The First World War: A Complete History.* 1994. A comprehensive work by a leading English historian and Winston Churchill's official biographer.*

The Great War and the Shaping of the Twentieth Century. 1996. An eight-hour videotape series available from PBS. A companion volume written by Jay Winter and Blaine Baggett is also available.

Gudmundsson, Bruce I. *Stormtroop Tactics: Innovation in the German Army, 1914–1918.* 1989. The best examination of the new German tactics in the 1918 offensives.*

Keegan, John. *The First World War.* 2000. An impressive presentation by a respected scholar.

Lincoln, W. Bruce. *Passage through Armageddon: The Russians in War and Revolution, 1914–1918.* 1986. A spirited presentation of the Russian war effort.*

MacDonald, Lyn. *1915: The Death of Innocence.* 1995. Popular account of the year that shattered the illusion that it would be a short, glorious war.

———. *To the Last Man: Spring 1918.* 1999. The lives of the soldiers in reference to the dramatic close of World War I, with emphasis on firsthand accounts.

Remarque, Erich Maria. *All Quiet on the Western Front.* 1928. A classic novel about the nature of modern war, emphasizing the lives of the soldiers.* (Also a film and a television program.)

Stevenson, David. *Cataclysm: The First World War as Political Tragedy.* 2004. The author of previous books on World War I and its origins, Stevenson here focuses on the political dynamics of the war.

Stokesbury, James L. *A Short History of World War I.* 1981. A well-written general survey of the conflict and a companion to the author's survey of World War II.*

Strachan, Hew. *The First World War.* 2005. The best and most up-to-date short (384 pages) history of the war.*

Strachan, Hew, ed. *World War I: A History.* 1998. A very readable collection of articles by leading scholars.

Winter, Denis. *Death's Men: Soldiers of the Great War.* 1978. Trench warfare in the words of those who fought it.

*Paperback available.

WEB SOURCES

www.worldwar1.com/. The entry site to a vast amount of material connected to World War I.

www.lib.byu.edu/~rdh/wwi/. This archive is international in focus and is an excellent source for primary documents concerning World War I.

www.pitt.edu/~pugachev/greatwar/toc.htm. This site offers links on many aspects of World War I including biographies, art, poetry, pacifism, political history, and women in the war.

PART

II

THE ERA OF REVOLUTION AND WAR

TIME CHART II
1918–1945

Year	South & East Asia	Middle East & Africa	Europe	Western Hemisphere	Trends in Culture, Science, Technology
1918	Chinese Republican Revolution, 1911–1926		Russian Revolution and civil war, 1917–1921	UNITED STATES PREDOMINANT IN LATIN AMERICA Revolution and civil war in Mexico, 1910–1924	
1919		PARIS PEACE CONFERENCE AND FORMATION OF THE LEAGUE OF NATIONS			Popularization of Freudian analysis
		GROWING NATIONALISM Wafd Party in Egypt 1919–1952	Rebellion and civil war in Ireland, 1916–1923		
1920		Ataturk in Turkey			
1921					The Roaring Twenties and modernism in music, art, and architecture
1922	Gandhi leads nonviolent independence movement in India, 1920s–1940s		Mussolini assumes power in Italy		
1923					Decade of the popularization of motion pictures and radio
1924		Reza Shah in Iran	Lenin dies		
1925		Ibn Saud in Saudi Arabia	Locarno treaties	U.S. military withdrawal from Latin America, 1920s–1930s	Advent of surrealism Scopes trial
1926	Chiang leads Northern Expedition in China, 1926–1928				

Year					
1927					
1928			Stalin begins collectivization and first Five-Year Plan, 1928–1929		
				THE GREAT DEPRESSION BEGINS	
1929		Stock market collapses			
1930					
1931	Air travel popularized				Japan occupies Manchuria
1932					
1933	Mexican muralist Diego Rivera	Roosevelt launches New Deal	Hitler assumes power in Germany		
1934	Popularization of jazz music	U.S. Good Neighbor policy, 1930s			Communist Long March in China, 1934–1935
1935			Period of appeasement, 1935–1939	Italy conquers Ethiopia, 1935–1936	
1936			Purges in U.S.S.R., 1936–1939		
1937			Spanish civil war, 1936–1939		Japan invades China
1938			Munich Agreement		
1939			Nazi-Soviet Pact		
			WORLD WAR II		
1940				North African campaigns	
1941	Tank and air warfare	Japan attacks Pearl Harbor	German invasion of U.S.S.R.		Japanese conquest of Southeast Asia
1942			Battle of Stalingrad, 1942–1943		
1943	Amphibious warfare	U.S. war industries buildup			
1944			D-day Normandy invasion		
1945	Mistral first Latin American writer to win Nobel Prize for Literature				Atomic bombs dropped on Hiroshima and Nagasaki

9

⑥General Trends in the Interwar Years

The global trends that characterized the opening of the twentieth century—nationalism, imperialism, political diversity ranging from very conservative to revolutionary, economic disparity, and social and cultural upheaval—continued to dominate events during the interwar years of 1919–1939. After World War I, nationalists intensified their struggles for self-determination, while many Western and Japanese leaders sought to maintain and increase their empires. Some nations escalated the arms race, while at the same time individuals and organizations worked toward disarmament and the formation of meaningful international organizations. Many had fought in World War I believing that victory would lead to more liberal, progressive governments; however, after the war, authoritarian regimes steadily increased in numbers and power. During the interwar years, it was by no means clear which forces would emerge victorious.

PROGRESS IN SCIENCE AND TECHNOLOGY

During the interwar years, scientists and technicians refined and expanded previous achievements in physics, biology, and engineering. Chemists and biologists took major steps toward understanding and explaining the structure and genetic composition of the cell. Medical researchers improved techniques for inoculating against disease, thereby prolonging the span of human life. Ironically, such improvements in health care also contributed to the population explosion in the colonized world at the very time that increased use of birth control methods slowed or stabilized population growth in the industrialized world.

⑥MORE DEADLY WEAPONS

In engineering, structural designers created larger and taller buildings, and propulsion experts developed an infant rocket industry. The armament industries in many nations continued to prosper as their technicians developed bigger and more deadly weapons. Airplanes, submarines, and tanks, introduced during World War I, would play a major role during the coming world conflict.

⑥MORE CONSUMER GOODS

In addition to these developments, during the interwar years more efficient mass production of consumer goods, especially in transportation and communication, profoundly changed how people lived. Henry Ford's mass production techniques and Frederick Taylor's labor efficiency studies dramatically increased the production of consumer goods that could be sold at cheaper prices and still make a good profit.

The sewing machine and many other items became affordable for average Western workers. By 1930 there were more than 5 million automobile owners in Europe. In Great Britain, there were 7 times as many in 1930 as in 1913; in France, there were almost 12 times as many.

In the category of affordable consumer goods, the automobile ushered in a new epoch of mobility that helped break down isolation and parochialism. Driving the family's new Ford Model T (available only in black) on a Sunday afternoon to see what it was like in the next town epitomized the new era. The automobile fostered a number of new industries, especially rubber, asphalt, and concrete. A mass-market tourist industry emerged. The aircraft industry developed more slowly, but by the 1930s commercial air travel catering to wealthy vacationers and enterprising business executives was well established. The transportation revolution took hold quickly in North America, Australia, and, to a lesser extent, western Europe; in Africa, Asia, and Latin America, however, such consumer goods and changes in transport remained luxury items only the very rich could afford.

Widespread use of automotive and air travel created escalating demands for gasoline. To meet this demand, the petroleum industry increased its operations on a global scale. In the process, entrepreneurs created huge international corporations that monopolized petroleum resources. (After World War II, these international corporations would directly clash with petroleum-producing nations in the Middle East, Africa, and Latin America, as these nations sought a more equitable distribution of the profits from this vital industry.)

The radio, another mass-produced consumer item, was a major breakthrough in the field of mass communication, with momentous effects on the culture of the twentieth century. Because of mass production, most Western families could afford a radio, which became the leading form of home entertainment. There were about 3 million radios in Great Britain and Germany by 1930. Such figures were small, however, compared to those for the United States, which far surpassed the rest of the world in the production and ownership of consumer goods.

RADIOS AND FILMS

Motion pictures also became popular: millions flocked to see movies featuring Mary Pickford, Rudolph Valentino, Jean Harlow, Douglas Fairbanks, Edward G. Robinson, and others. These stars were featured everywhere, and the public avidly followed not only their professional careers but also their private lives. Radio, newspapers, films, and magazines fueled public interest in fashion, health, sports, society, and crime. Media coverage popularized personalities from the gangster Al Capone to Charles "Lucky Lindy" Lindbergh, the first person to fly solo nonstop across the Atlantic. In eastern and western Asia, Tokyo, Shanghai, and Cairo became centers of thriving movie industries.

Informational mass communication such as radio news broadcasts and film newsreels had both positive and negative effects. The Western public, as well as a literate urban middle class in much of Asia and Africa, became more informed about national and international affairs and about the politicians and leaders who made decisions. Regional divisions inside nations were often reduced as citizens, especially the young, identified with the practices and ideals displayed in the national media. On the negative side, politicians sought to manipulate the media to present themselves

EFFECTS OF MASS COMMUNICATION

in the most favorable light. As a result, the superficial media image of political lead-ers often became more important than the major issues. Thus, at the very time masses of people throughout the world were becoming better informed, they were also becoming more susceptible to manipulation of the mass media by charismatic indi-viduals. Both Franklin Roosevelt and Adolf Hitler were adept at exploiting radio and motion pictures, although for very different reasons.

ATOMIC ENERGY

Toward the end of the interwar period scientists conducting theoretical research on the nature of the atom unleashed its immense power, with momentous consequences for humanity. After decades of research, scientists succeeded in creating a reliable chain reaction in uranium-235 and plutonium during World War II. By splitting the atom, they were able to release and ultimately to harness the energy that had been locked up inside the atom. In this process, an atom that has been split (atomic fission) shoots out neutrons that strike and split other atoms, releasing incredible power. When encased in a bomb, the chain reaction produces the blast effect of hundreds of conventional bombs, plus radioactive effects that kill and maim over an extended period.

ECONOMIC CRISES

After World War I, economic conditions varied widely from nation to nation. The United States emerged from the war with a huge industrial capacity, no wartime dam-age at home, and enormous amounts of capital owed to it from wartime loans to other Allied nations. U.S. business prospered; despite the unflattering portraits by some nov-elists, the businessperson became the ideal of Americans, compared by one enthusi-ast to Jesus. "The business of this country is business," summed up President Calvin Coolidge. War-generated demands also stimulated industrial growth in Japan and has-tened industrialization in China and India.

In contrast, many businesses and industries in Europe never recovered the dynamism they had displayed before the war. Europe's share of world trade dimin-ished; nations remained deeply in debt, particularly to the United States. In Great Britain and other European nations, unemployment remained almost constantly above 10 percent.

RUNAWAY INFLATION

Except in the United States, surging inflation was another global legacy of the war. By 1919 prices in Great Britain were three times higher than in 1913. By 1926 prices in France were at least seven times higher than in 1913. In Germany, the gov-ernment tried to cope with the inflationary spiral by printing more and more money. Confidence in the German mark fell on the international exchange; however, because of attractive interest rates, U.S. creditors continued to advance money to German bor-rowers. At home, Germans attempted to invest in durable goods that would maintain their value. This only stimulated more price increases. By 1923 the German mark was worth only one-trillionth of its prewar value, and a loaf of bread could cost billions of reichsmarks. People demanded that they be paid every day so that they could rush to the stores to buy anything in sight before their money became even more worth-less. Although the German statesman Gustav Stresemann took energetic steps to end the crisis, social and psychological scars remained, for many Germans had seen their total lifetime savings disappear.

Many parts of the British and French empires also suffered economic difficulties. Western nations had fought the war not only with their own resources but also with those of their vast empires, enlarging the agricultural and industrial sectors of their colonial holdings to support the war effort. Once the war was over, there were surpluses of some goods, but these surpluses were often accompanied by scarcities of vital commodities such as bread and kerosene for cooking and heating. Mounting unemployment in rural areas forced peasants into cities in search of employment. There were few jobs in the cities, which were ill equipped to provide even minimal services for this rapid influx of humanity. Asian, Latin, and African cities were soon plagued with the same kind of social and economic problems that Western cities had endured during the industrialization of the nineteenth century. Many of these problems continued to trouble societies to the end of the twentieth century.

Through expansion of the mass media, even poor peasants became aware of the high standard of living in the West and in urban areas around the world. In poor agricultural areas, where the economy was still at a subsistence level, people demanded improvement in their daily lives. A widening gap existed between societies that enjoyed high living standards and those that remained relatively poor. Although this disparity had existed at the beginning of the twentieth century, in the interwar years many were now aware of these differences and were impatient for change.

STRUGGLES FOR ECONOMIC INDEPENDENCE

Many nationalist leaders in the colonized world believed that their particular economic woes—unemployment, inflation, poverty, scarcities of consumer goods—were caused by imperial domination. As a result, the middle-class elite in India, Egypt, and elsewhere demanded economic as well as political independence. Calls for more local participation in economic spheres often went hand in hand with demands for political autonomy. For example, Egyptian nationalists established an Egyptian bank (Bank Misr) and a locally owned cigarette factory and urged all patriotic Egyptians to boycott British goods and to "buy Egyptian." In India, nationalist leaders urged Indians to adopt *swadeshi*—that is, to buy only Indian-made goods. In China, students and merchants organized boycott campaigns to resist political and economic encroachment of imperialist countries, particularly Japan.

However, total economic self-sufficiency, whether in poor or in rich nations, was an impossible goal in the twentieth century. The economies of nations had become much too interrelated through trade, credit systems, markets, and resource needs to be separated into individual independent entities. International corporations were only one indication of the economic interdependency that surpassed narrow national interests. Like Latin American nations, most African and Asian countries ultimately secured political independence but remained economically tied to the industrialized nations that controlled the majority of the world's industrial might.

THE GREAT DEPRESSION

By 1929 the economic imbalances and problems of the global economic systems resulted in a worldwide economic depression. The Great Depression was a global economic crisis that lasted in many areas until World War II and that vividly demonstrated the interdependency of twentieth-century economies. There were several specific causes. Production far exceeded consumption. Staggering amounts of credit had been extended during the war. Individuals, businesses, and nations had

UNEMPLOYMENT

Unemployment was a problem in Japan through the 1920s and became worse with the Great Depression. Here, priests march through Tokyo soliciting money for victims of an earthquake and for the unemployed.

become obligated to one another in a vast web of indebtedness. In addition, many individuals and nations had estimated their wealth not by tangible goods or resources but by paper assets such as money or stocks. Paper assets printed (as they were in postwar Germany) without real productivity or tangible assets such as gold to support them were in fact worthless. Finally, many gambled recklessly in the stock market.

STOCK MARKET CRASHES

The Great Depression began on October 24, 1929, when the U.S. stock market started to plummet; soon that nation's economy began to crumble. By early 1933 the United States was deeply mired in business cutbacks, unemployment, and bankruptcies. Europe also felt the impact of the economic disaster. In 1930, as the collapse hit Germany, five bankrupt Berlin businessmen committed suicide in one week. Chancellor Heinrich Bruning became known as "the chancellor of hunger." By the early 1930s, 1 million Germans were unemployed, out of a population of 65 million.

As a result of the economic crisis in Germany, the Allies were forced to postpone German reparations payments. The reparations issue had been one of the major sources of economic dispute among the major powers after World War I. In 1924, under the Dawes Plan, an initial foreign loan was promised and Germany's annual reparations payments were reduced. Again in 1929, under the U.S.-devised Young Plan, the reparations were further reduced. Finally, in 1932 the Allies agreed—albeit with great reluctance—that Germany would no longer have to pay reparations.

The economic crisis created by the Great Depression was felt in other European nations as well. By 1932, one man in four in Great Britain was on the dole (welfare), and production fell 28 percent in France and 33 percent in Italy. In early 1930 the depression hit Japan. The Japanese public blamed the politicians, and many argued that the solution to the economic disaster lay in military expansion and the creation of a self-sufficient empire. Many Japanese viewed Germany's turning from democracy to authoritarian policies as a positive object lesson. Although Japan was the first major industrialized nation to recover from the depression, Japanese democracy and parliamentary government never really recovered.

The depression also devastated the largely agricultural economies of Asia, Africa, and Latin America, because most of the nations on these continents were linked to the industrialized world through imperial ties and trade. As industries in Europe and the United States slowed or shut down, demand for raw materials produced elsewhere in the world also plummeted. Because most of the people in these nations were already living at the poverty level, the loss of even a few pennies of income per capita could mean economic ruin. Leaders of poor nations emphasized that when a man's belt was already pulled to the last notch, it was impossible to ask him to tighten it further.

SOCIAL AND POLITICAL TURMOIL

The interwar years also ushered in sweeping social changes. Continuing a movement begun before the war, suffragists mobilized growing support for equal political rights for women. During the 1920s women in most Western nations obtained the vote. In Russia, the new Communist government decreed the political and legal equality of women. In Africa, Asia, and the Middle East, aristocratic and middle-class women were often in the vanguard of nationalist movements. They, too, struggled for political and social rights and joined the international women's movement. Women gathered at international meetings such as the Pan-Pacific Women's Conference to discuss women's concerns; in China new laws promulgated by the Nationalist government gave women legal equality.

As more and more women entered the labor force, old social patterns—already altered by the war and technological developments—changed. In most of the industrialized world, the birth rate continued to drop, and throughout most of the world, the average adult lived longer and the trend toward urbanization accelerated. In Great Britain and elsewhere, upper-class privilege and its monopoly over the political and economic systems began to decline. During World War I many men and women who had been full-time servants in upper- and middle-class homes left their jobs for the battlefronts and wartime industries. Following the war, many never returned to menial jobs. The growing scarcity and rising cost of servants forced the wealthy to change their lifestyles by adopting fashions in housing, dress, and food that required less maintenance, washing and ironing, and cooking.

Superficially, the war ended in a victory for liberal, democratic forces. In reality, the conservatives on the Right and the socialists on the Left were far from

**WOMEN IN
THE WORKPLACE**

destroyed. Struggles between socialist and conservative forces became particularly intense in defeated nations; in Italy and Germany, leftists and conservatives battled openly and violently in the streets of major cities.

THE RISE OF DICTATORIAL REGIMES

Protracted political clashes and economic crises throughout Europe forced more and more people toward the extremes of the political spectrum, leaving fewer and fewer to support the center. Europeans became increasingly unwilling to compromise and grew more fearful of social and political anarchy. By promising easy, quick solutions, authoritarian forces under which individual freedoms were subordinated to the authority of the state, generally dominated by forces from the Right, gained support. One by one, moderate or progressive governments in Italy, Portugal, Spain, Germany, and eastern Europe fell to rightist dictatorial regimes. Through strict control over the media, education, and culture, dictatorial regimes sought to create so-called new men and women who would follow their leaders with unquestioning loyalty. It should be emphasized that these authoritarian regimes differed somewhat from subsequent totalitarian regimes in which all aspects of the society—culture, government, and economics—were dominated by a single party or dictator. (See Chapter 16 for a further discussion of these regimes.)

CHANGING MARXIST GOALS

Faced with defeats in the heartland of Europe, Marxists redefined their immediate goals during the interwar years. In the first fervor of the 1917 revolution, Vladimir Lenin and Leon Trotsky had both argued that the Russian Revolution was merely the first link in a chain of revolutions that would soon sweep the world. Dominated by the Soviet Union, the Third International, or Comintern, aimed to hasten the advent of communism around the world by supporting local Communist parties in their fight against capitalism and imperialism. By the mid-1920s, with continued domestic problems and a new leadership under Stalin, the Soviets began to place less emphasis on international revolution and more emphasis on increasing the strength of the Soviet Union.

Before World War II, Marxist ideology had had little impact on the masses in Africa and Asia. The few Marxist leaders who did emerge generally came from the educated middle class, and they were repressed not only by the ruling classes and religious leaders in their own nations but also by the imperial powers. However, as demands for national autonomy were continually rejected by the colonial powers, some nationalist leaders began to turn to the Soviet Union for support. Some, like Sun Yat-sen in China, did not intend to institute Marxism but looked to secure Soviet assistance in ousting the imperial powers and internal enemies. Two Asian leaders, Mao Tse-tung (Mao Zedong) in China and Ho Chi Minh in French Indochina, did seek to create Marxist states. However, both were faced with the task of converting Marx's ideas, which presumed an industrialized environment, to the needs of peasant societies. (See Chapters 13 and 14 for more on these leaders.)

Ethnic nationalism also continued to be a divisive issue after the war. The delegates at Paris carved out new nations in eastern Europe in an attempt to grant self-determination to peoples living within them. However, many of these new nations still contained minority groups inside their boundaries. The conflicts between these new governments and minority ethnic groups who wanted autonomy contributed to the next global confrontation.

INTERNATIONAL AFFAIRS: CONFLICTS AND THE SEARCH FOR PEACE

The Rise of Anticolonialism

One international trend during the interwar years was the increasing pressure by colonial nationalists for an end to imperialism. World War I had badly weakened the power of the great European nations relative to the rest of the world. As a consequence, the war hastened the day when European colonial empires would collapse. Wartime statements in support of self-determination, particularly by Woodrow Wilson, had stimulated anticolonialism and demands for independence among the subject peoples at the same time that the war had weakened the colonial powers' ability to hold on to their possessions. For example, in China Wilson's statement on national self-determination was widely taken to mean an end to spheres of influence and an end to imperialist concessions. The seeds were thus germinating for the post–World War II breakup of colonial empires.

As described in Chapter 11, none of this had been foreseen at the Paris Peace Conference, where old-fashioned imperialism was business as usual. Western representatives, who controlled the conference, made it clear that self-determination applied to national groups in central and eastern Europe but not to demands from Arabs, Zionists, Chinese, and Indians, among others. In their last major effort to enlarge their empires, Great Britain, France, and Japan used the mandate system created after World War I to take over the colonies of the defeated powers. It was, however, at best a stopgap measure in the face of the mounting drive toward national independence throughout the world.

During the 1930s imperial powers, with varying degrees of reluctance, made concessions to the rising pressures of anti-imperialist nationalism. The British responded by continuing the devolution process that was well under way before World War I in areas that had been settled and controlled by white Europeans, usually of British descent. These dominions—Canada, Newfoundland, Australia, New Zealand, and South Africa—had provided substantial financial and military assistance in the war effort. After the war Great Britain acknowledged this support by agreeing to individual membership in the League of Nations for all of these dominions and for India as well. Later, Great Britain went further along the path of devolution. The Statute of Westminster in 1931 recognized these white-controlled dominions as "autonomous communities." Economic and military links to Great Britain were preserved through the Commonwealth, which was a loosely knit association of the dominions and Great Britain.

However, in the interwar period, Great Britain was willing to grant autonomy only to those parts of the empire with which it retained close ethnic and cultural ties. The more heterogeneous and less Westernized parts of the empire were kept under controls that were as tight as the British—given their weakened world status—could sustain. Similarly, the French fought tenaciously to maintain their far-flung empire. British and French determination to safeguard their empires provoked peoples living under their domination to increase their demands for freedom.

BRITISH DOMINIONS

U.S. AND LATIN AMERICA

In another major example of the decline of imperialism, the United States began to moderate its interventionist approach in Latin America. The United States had interfered repeatedly in the affairs of nations in the Caribbean area, and by 1924 U.S. military and treasury personnel directed fiscal affairs in 10 nations. Many Latin Americans angrily resented this meddling by the "Colossus of the North." Mexican leaders sometimes bitterly complained that being a neighbor of the United States was like being a mouse sleeping next to an elephant. Realizing that a policy of direct interference was often counterproductive, the United States began to withdraw its forces, and after the marines left Haiti in 1934, no U.S. troops remained on Latin American soil.

The more relaxed policy of the United States was sharply tested in Mexico. President Lázaro Cárdenas had moved to nationalize foreign petroleum companies, including U.S. corporation holdings valued by the companies at $500 million. The U.S. business community clamored for action against Mexico, but the Roosevelt administration was determined to pursue a Good Neighbor policy and chose to negotiate. As a result, the U.S. government agreed to lend the Mexican government $24 million to be used to pay off the petroleum companies. In a further retreat from imperialism, the United States recognized the political independence of Cuba in 1932; however, Cuba and many other Caribbean nations remained diplomatic and economic protectorates.

The Search for Collective Security and the Revival of Militarism

During the interwar years, extreme forms of nationalism developed that encouraged the rise of militarism, particularly in Italy, Germany, and Japan. The rise of fascism in Italy and Nazism in Germany stimulated an upsurge of aggressive nationalism that in Nazi Germany was also based on beliefs of ethnic and cultural superiority. In Japan, nationalism coupled with long-held beliefs of cultural superiority resulted in an aggressive, expansionist foreign policy aimed at acquiring an Asian empire.

Recognizing the problems inherent in a world of conflicting nationalisms, Wilson and others urged the formation of effective international organizations that would prevent future great wars. Wilson also spoke about the need for disarmament. There was general agreement that stockpiles of arms had contributed to the martial spirit prevalent before 1914 and had prolonged the war.

INTERNATIONAL ORGANIZATIONS

The League of Nations represented the major postwar attempt to seek peaceful means of settling disputes and sharing responsibility for the protection of its members from aggression. The League consisted of the Assembly (where all members participated); the Council, composed of some of the great powers (Great Britain, France, Italy, and Japan) and four lesser nations elected to serve by rotation; and the Secretariat. The International Court was also established to settle disputes referred to it by member nations.

The League was fairly successful in settling border disputes between Latin American nations and between small European nations such as Sweden, Finland,

Greece, and Albania. It also administered the free city of Danzig and the Saar district, both taken from Germany after the war. In addition, many noted humanists and philanthropists from around the world participated in and lent their energies to League activities.

In matters concerning the interests of major nations, however, the League was a failure. Over and over again, nations refused to work collectively either to settle disputes or to stop aggression. The most powerful nations also refused to commit themselves to joint armed action against aggressors, nor would they act against their own self-interest for the larger good. The League was also hampered by the refusal of the United States to join and, in its early years, by the absence of the Soviet Union and the powers defeated in World War I. In the final analysis, the League's greatest achievements were its efforts in the field of social welfare, its support of agencies for refugees and the poor, and its sponsorship of medical research.

Internationalism on a regional basis, in the form of the Pan-American Association, was well established in the Western Hemisphere. Initiated in 1889 by the United States as a thinly disguised arrangement to facilitate its own goals in the region, the Pan-American Association met at five-year intervals; Pan-American conferences forged a number of agreements on, and created special organizations concerning, copyrights, labor codes, agriculture, child protection, and arbitration procedures. However, these agreements were often ignored in practice.

PAN-AMERICANISM

In the interwar years, several international agreements addressing specific problems appeared to offer some hope for lasting peace. The Locarno treaties (1925) addressed a number of European issues, and the Washington Naval Conference (1922) and the Kellogg-Briand Peace Pact (1928) were concerned with the difficult problems of arms limitation and war. Despite these limited arms agreements, most nations continued to stockpile weapons in order to be prepared for the next war. European and U.S. leaders spoke eloquently of peace and disarmament during the 1920s, but they feared that, except for limitations on naval buildups, their enemies were continuing to race toward armed superiority.

As had happened before World War I, only a few decades earlier, extreme nationalism contributed to military buildups in the 1930s. In Japan, the military exercised substantial power within political circles, stockpiling arms and building up Japan's land and sea forces. As a defeated power, Germany's acquisition of armaments was strictly limited under the terms of the Versailles treaty. However, as it became evident that the Allies would not enforce their own treaty, the Germans moved to rebuild their armed forces. By the mid-1930s it was apparent that the Versailles treaty had failed to prevent Germany from becoming, for a second time in the twentieth century, a major military power. The Soviet Union also expanded its military capabilities, preparing for the looming conflict that would again pit the major powers of the globe against one another.

MILITARY BUILDUPS

After World War I the total arms expenditures of Great Britain, France, and Italy actually increased. France refused to limit its armaments and subsidized arms for Central European nations as a safeguard against Germany. France also built, at great expense and effort, the famous Maginot Line, purported to be an impregnable defense. Only the United States, far removed from the trouble areas of the world, greatly reduced its army. By 1932, 15 nations, including Turkey and Romania, had larger armies than that of the United States. In the final analysis, nationalism far outweighed the opposing movement toward international peace, dooming the League of Nations and other international agreements to failure.

IDEAS AND CULTURE

In the period between the wars, as people continued to search for a deeper meaning to life and the world around them, the works of thinkers such as Marx, Darwin, Freud, and Nietzsche exercised considerable influence. To some, the experiences of World War I made the ideas of these important intellectuals seem more relevant than ever.

The combined impact of these thinkers was particularly evident in the continuing battle between secularism and traditional religious beliefs. The most dramatic struggle took place in the Soviet Union. The new Marxist-Leninist government not only removed the Russian Orthodox Church from its exalted position as the state religion but also encouraged atheistic beliefs and in general persecuted and discriminated against religious believers.

DARWIN AND EVOLUTION

In the United States and western Europe, secularists and proponents of traditional religious teachings generally waged their battles in more democratic arenas, such as in law courts and on the pages of journals. One example was the spectacular Scopes "monkey trial" of 1925, in which a high school biology teacher was found guilty of teaching Darwinian evolution instead of the biblical account of creation. One of the leading and most influential opponents of organized religion in the United States was H. L. Mencken, a writer and editor, who as a young man had been greatly influenced by the ideas of Nietzsche. In colorful, exaggerated language, Mencken railed against theologians, censorship, middle-class values, and Prohibition—to name just a few of his favorite targets.

SECULARISM

Secularists were also active in Latin America and in non-Western areas of the world. In 1917, Mexican revolutionaries pushed through a secular constitution that limited the power of the Catholic Church. In Asia, secularists, often strongly influenced by the West, challenged advocates of Islam, Hinduism, and Buddhism. For example, Mustafa Kemal (Ataturk), head of the Turkish government through most of the 1920s and 1930s, set out to break, with some success, the centuries-old dominance of Islamic tradition over Turkish life.

Technological changes such as the motion picture and the automobile fostered challenges to traditional values in the United States and Europe, especially regarding sex and marriage. People became more familiar with the psychology of Freud, whose analysis of human psychological behavior was often misinterpreted by popularizers to mean that frustrating the sex drive was harmful. Anna Freud and Melanie Klein pioneered the application of Freudian ideas in the psychoanalysis of children.

NEW MUSIC

Advocates of the new lifestyle spoke in the name of increased freedom. An affluent smart set stressed self-indulgent individualism through fast cars, bathtub gin, sex, and hot dance music. New music forms, especially jazz, created fusions of Western

Louie Armstrong with his best small combo, the Hot Five, in the 1920s.

and traditional African and Caribbean music and became widely popular around the world. Conservatives often condemned these new artistic forms as corrupting the morals of the youth; they sometimes even sought to have them banned.

Many women discarded the traditional demure female image to wear short skirts, bob their hair, dance, drink, smoke, and neck. A U.S. college president expressed feelings shared by many conservative Americans when he said, "The low-cut gowns, the rolled hose, and the short skirts were born of the Devil." Despite these new challenges, most people continued to be heavily influenced by traditional religious beliefs. For example, Protestant fundamentalists were largely responsible for prohibiting the manufacture and sale of intoxicating beverages in the United States from 1919 to 1933.

ROARING TWENTIES

Many of the new enthusiasms, often fed by newspapers, radio, and motion pictures, increased appetites for the novel and bizarre, while reflecting a nervous rootlessness and an attempt to escape from the harsh realities of the war years. Thus, people used their leisure time enjoying the abundance of consumer goods and services: automobiles, radios, jazz records, movies, nightclubs, and cabarets. In London, Paris, and Berlin, as in Chicago and New York, the 1920s often roared. A penchant for new pleasures swept over many European cities. The Austrian writer Stefan Zweig wrote that "anything that gave hope of newer and greater thrills . . . anything in the way of narcotics, morphine, cocaine, heroin, found a tremendous market." For a girl "to be sixteen and still under suspicion of virginity," he added, perhaps exaggerating, "would have been considered a disgrace in any school of Berlin."

The rapid change in values and practices frightened traditionalists. A growing number of people throughout the world echoed U.S. president Warren Harding's cry for a return to "normalcy." The cry was echoed in Great Britain, where politicians called for a return to "tranquility" and "honesty." However, in a transformed world in which so much had been destroyed, a return to a pre-1914 existence was impossible.

CHANGING MORAL AND RELIGIOUS VALUES

In the interwar years, people not only challenged traditional religious values and escaped into new pleasures and fads but also questioned a whole range of more traditional beliefs, such as loyalty to one's nation and faith in progress, science, reason, and civilization itself. For some disillusioned intellectuals, the experiences of the war underscored the validity of many of Nietzsche's earlier criticisms. One of the most popular books of 1919 was *The Decline of the West,* by Oswald Spengler, who thought of Nietzsche as Europe's greatest modern prophet. In this book Spengler attempted to build on Nietzsche's pessimistic view of the West and to construct a total survey (past, present, and future) of the rise and fall of Western civilization, comparing the destiny of the West with the fate of previous societies.

Even in the more down-to-earth intellectual atmosphere of the 1930s, the ideas of Nietzsche continued to appeal to some, especially in Germany, where his ideas of a superman were often selectively used to justify the new Nazi order. Hitler himself, although he lacked any sound knowledge of Nietzsche's ideas, was fond of quoting several of his lines and on Mussolini's 60th birthday sent him the philosopher's complete works as a present.

Developments in art and literature paralleled those in philosophy. Frederick Henry, a character in Ernest Hemingway's 1929 novel of World War I, *A Farewell to Arms,* came to the conclusion that "abstract words such as glory, honor, courage or hallow were obscene." (See Chapter 11 for European literature).

Following the Great Depression and the rise of Hitler, writers and artists in the West became more concerned with concrete social and political issues. Writers such as John Steinbeck, author of the novel *The Grapes of Wrath* (1939), expressed sympathy for the poor and stressed the fellowship of humanity.

The depression also led some artists from around the world to embrace Marxist ideas. For example, the Mexican artist Diego Rivera and the Chilean poet Pablo Neruda were influenced by the ideas of Marx and Lenin, who helped to fuel their already critical view of a West that they perceived to be both capitalistic and imperialistic.

Cultural developments and conflicts in the West influenced a generation of largely urban Asians, Africans, and South Americans. The mass media helped to transmit Western cultural ideas to cities Cairo and Shanghai, where the upper and middle classes copied those who roared in New York, Paris, and Berlin. The youth, who were the second generation to have lived under imperial controls and who had received Western educations, began to use the principles of liberalism and democracy to argue for independence for themselves and for their nations—whether in Asia, Africa, Latin America, or the Middle East.

GANDHI AND TRADITIONALISM

On the other hand, despite some Western-oriented secularist leaders such as Jawaharlal Nehru, most Indian Hindus and Muslims regarded religion and religious customs as all-important. The traditional values advocated by Mohandas Gandhi dominated Indian culture. Although Gandhi worked with Nehru to obtain Indian independence and was tolerant of Islam and of some Western ideas, Gandhi's solutions for India's future were largely based on his own understanding of Hinduism, and he remained deeply suspicious of modern secularized Western states.

WESTERN INFLUENCES AND CHINA

In China, as in India, people differed over the relative merits of synthesizing Western ideas with Chinese tradition. The older faiths of Buddhism, Confucianism, and Taoism did not generally exclude one another, and many Chinese practiced teachings from several faiths. Some tried to assimilate beliefs and ideas from the West. For example, Sun Yat-sen, the most outstanding leader of China until his death in 1925, was a Protestant who admired Darwin's teachings and yet respected the Confucian tradition. His successor, Chiang Kai-shek, became a Protestant but also valued traditional Confucian ideas. The Chinese constitution of 1923 stated that a "citizen of the Republic of China shall be free to honor Confucius and to prefer any religion." By the early 1930s, the Chinese Communists were contesting Chiang for power, and their leaders had little respect for either Eastern or Western religious teachings. They agreed with Marx's statement that religion was "the opiate of the people."

Some writers educated in Europe were torn, appreciating aspects of both the new Western culture and the traditions of their homelands. A good example was Léopold Senghor of Senegal, who spent much of the 1930s in France. A poet as well as a future politician, Senghor helped to develop and to popularize the idea of negritude during the 1930s. The concept of negritude was partly based on ideas adopted from Caribbean writers, including Claude McKay, who in the 1920s had become a prominent figure in the Black or Harlem Renaissance in the United States. Senghor defined negritude as "the sum total of the values of the African world." Although a Catholic and admittedly influenced by European writers and thinkers, in his poetry Senghor praised the "Africanness" of his native land and people. Thus, in the interwar years, artists, writers, and intellectuals from around the globe continued to exchange ideas and to be influenced by one another's cultures.

SENGHOR IN SENEGAL

SUGGESTED SOURCES

Galbraith, J. Kenneth. *The Great Crash, 1929.* 1988. Revised edition of a readable work by a leading U.S. liberal economist; includes an introduction comparing the 1929 and 1987 crashes.*

The Great Depression. 1993. Seven-part series on economic crisis and its social impacts. Available on video.

Inherit the Wind. 1960. A remarkable film about the famous Scopes "Monkey Trial," starring Spencer Tracy.

Isherwood, Christopher. *The Berlin Stories.* 1979. A fictionalized reflection of the author's experiences during the depression in Berlin.* The film *Cabaret* was based on Isherwood's Berlin experiences.

Kindleberger, Charles P. *The World in Depression, 1929–1939.* Rev. and enlarged ed. 1986. One of the best books in the series History of the World Economy in the Twentieth Century.*

Koestler, Arthur, et al. *The God That Failed.* 1950. A collection of six autobiographical sketches by U.S. and European writers who relate why they were attracted to communism in the interwar years.

Landes, David S. *The Unbound Prometheus.* 1976. A work containing insights on technological, industrial, and economic developments between the wars.*

Laqueur, Walter. *Weimer: A Cultural History 1918–1933.* 1974. A leading historian deals with a wide variety of topics including Einstein and German education, films, and political thought in an attempt to outline what he calls "the first truly modern culture."*

Lowenstein, Roger. *Origins of the Crash: The Great Bubble and Its Undoing.* 2005. A lively overview of the causes behind the 1929 stock market collapse.*

Marks, Sally. *The Illusion of Peace: International Relations in Europe, 1919–1933.* 2nd ed. 2003. A solid historical overview of European international relations in an era of shifting power alliances.*

The 1920s: From Illusion to Disillusion. Films for the Humanities and Sciences. Eighty-minute video on rapid changes sweeping the world during the 1920s.

Preston, Diana. *Before the Fallout: From Marie Curie to Hiroshima.* 2005. A very readable history of scientific developments leading to the dropping of the atomic bomb.

Solomon, Barbara H. *Ain't We Got Fun.* 1980. A collection of essays, lyrics, and stories that capture the cultural changes occurring in the United States during the 1920s.*

Watson, Peter. *The Modern Mind: An Intellectual History of the 20th Century.* 2001. Pt. 2. A wide-ranging treatment that deals not only with philosophers but also with writers, artists, scientists, social thinkers, theologians, and others.

WEB SOURCES

www.fordham.edu/halsall/mod/modsbook40.html. Links to various developments of the interwar years, especially good for the new states of Europe, European culture, and the League of Nations.

www.fordham.edu/halsall/mod/modsbook41.html. Provides links to materials on the Great Depression in Europe and the United States.

http://econ161.berkeley.edu/TCEH/Slouch_Crash14.html. A good introduction with graphs to the Great Depression in the United States and abroad by a University of California economics professor.

www.indiana.edu/~league/index.htm. Archived printed materials and pictures of the League of Nations and links to other materials regarding the League and interwar international affairs.

*Paperback available.

⑥Russia's Three Revolutions, 1917–1932

In 1917 two major revolutions occurred in Russia. The first overthrew Tsar Nicholas II and established the Provisional Government; the second (eight months later) brought the Marxist Bolsheviks (called Communists after March 1918) to power. Between these two revolutions many groups, including workers, soldiers, peasants, and non-Russian nationalities, sought more freedom and justice for themselves and at times for others. Civil war and Allied intervention followed the Bolshevik takeover, but the Communist government survived and in 1921 instituted the New Economic Policy. This stablizing measure was disrupted in 1928–1929, when the government introduced the first Five-Year plan and the collectivization of agriculture. These two changes were central to what has been referred to as "Stalin's revolution from above," and this third revolution greatly changed the everyday life of Soviet citizens. Although technological, economic, international, and cultural forces all played parts in Soviet life during this period, politics played the most dramatic role.

THE BACKGROUND TO REVOLUTION

In many ways, a Marxist revolution in Russia seemed contrary to the ideas of Marx himself. (See Chapter 2, on Marx and Marxism.) His writings predicted that a socialist or communist—Marx often used the two words interchangeably—revolution would occur first in an advanced Western capitalist country with a large industrial working class, whereas the Russian Empire was dominated by peasants and was still in the early stages of capitalist development. By 1914 factory workers were still less than 2 percent of the population.

By then, with Marx already dead for four decades, western European socialism had become less radical, but radicalism was increasing in Russia. In the year before the beginning of the war, more than 50 percent of the empire's industrial workers engaged in labor protests. Facing working and living conditions inferior to those of their counterparts in western Europe, they became more and more receptive to the ideas and ideologies preached by Russian radicals. Meanwhile, an ineffective Tsar Nicholas II remained determined to maintain as much of his power as possible.

Historians have debated whether revolution could have been avoided if World War I had not occurred. By 1917 it had certainly weakened the tsar's position. When war broke out in 1914, Russia was unprepared to meet the challenge. Once again, as in the Russo-Japanese War of 1904–1905, a combination of industrial and techno-logical backwardness, governmental and military inefficiency, and corruption led to a series of military defeats. At a crucial point in late 1915, Nicholas II left Petrograd (formerly and now again St. Petersburg) to assume personal command of the armies at the front. From the capital his wife, Tsarina Alexandra, sent him a steady stream of advice regarding government actions and personnel. She herself was under the strong influence of the notorious Gregory Rasputin, a self-proclaimed holy man notorious for his lustful appetites. His nearness to the royal family hurt its reputation. The source of Rasputin's power was Alexandra's belief that his ability to alleviate the suffering of her only son, Alexei, from hemophilia indicated Rasputin's closeness to God.

Rasputin's gruesome murder on December 30, 1916, was not enough to restore popular confidence in the government. The tsar remained with the armies at the front, and his ministers in Petrograd seemed incompetent to many Russians and foreign observers. In January 1917, the French ambassador wrote to his government, "I am obliged to report that, at the present moment, the Russian Empire is run by lunatics."[1]

THE REVOLUTIONS OF MARCH AND NOVEMBER 1917

Early in March,[2] sparked by inflation, a decline in real wages, deteriorating working conditions, and food shortages, workers in Petrograd engaged in bread riots, demon-strations, and strikes. Underlying these specific grievances was a seething resentment against the government and society for treating them so shabbily despite their impor-tant contributions to the war effort. On March 8, International Women's Day, women textile workers poured into the streets shouting "Bread!" (By 1917, women made up 43 percent of all Russian industrial workers.) Other Petrograd workers quickly joined them, and within two days over 200,000 strikers brought everyday life to a standstill.

MARCH REVOLUTION AND ABDICATION OF NICHOLAS II

After being informed of the mounting chaos in the capital, Nicholas II tele-graphed back that order should be restored. The city's military commander ordered police and troops to disperse demonstrators, shooting at them if necessary. But after some shooting, the key turning point occurred: Soldiers in one regiment after another refused to comply with orders and instead joined the demonstrators. After realizing he had lost control of Petrograd and the support of key military and political leaders, Nicholas II abdicated the throne on March 15.

Three days earlier leaders from Russia's legislative Duma had formed the Provi-sional Committee in an attempt to restore order. The committee now formed the Pro-visional Government. It was composed primarily of moderates, with only one socialist in its cabinet, the minister of justice, Alexander Kerensky. The power of the new government was challenged throughout its brief existence by a rival organization, the Petrograd Soviet (Council) of Workers' and Soldiers' Deputies. At first this body was

---

[1]Quoted in W. Bruce Lincoln, *Passage through Armageddon: The Russians in War and Revolution, 1914–1918* (New York: Simon & Schuster, 1986), p. 312.

[2]Until 1918, Russia still used the old Julian calendar, which was 13 days behind the Gregorian calendar in use in the West. All dates here, however, are from the Gregorian calendar.

led by the moderate Marxist Mensheviks and the peasant-oriented Socialist Revolutionaries, and it enjoyed the support of many Petrograd soldiers and workers. Encouraged by the Petrograd Soviet, radicals soon formed local Soviets throughout Russia, including some within military units. Despite their distrust of the Provisional Government, which many workers and soldiers thought represented upper-class society, both the Mensheviks and the Socialist Revolutionaries were reluctant to bring it down. For practical and ideological reasons, they were not yet ready to assume the burden of power. Some were influenced by Marx's view of history, which generally held that a country could not initiate a socialist stage until it had first undergone a capitalist one. In their eyes, Russia had just overthrown a feudal order, and a lengthy capitalist period would have to ensue before the capitalist state could be replaced by a socialist state. When the Provisional Government continued the war, in part because of strong Allied pressure, the Soviets gave their support.

Although they had earlier spread their ideas among the Petrograd workers, the Bolsheviks did not play a major role in the opening weeks of the revolution. Their leader was Vladimir Lenin, born Vladimir Ulianov in 1870, the son of a provincial school inspector. Young Lenin had been profoundly affected by the execution of his brother for revolutionary activities and had himself become an opponent of the tsar. By his 20s, Lenin had become a Marxist. He engaged in revolutionary activities that were punished by almost 5 years of prison and Siberian exile. Released in 1900, he spent most of the next 17 years in western Europe. There, in 1903, he played a leading role in splitting the Russian Marxists into two factions: the Mensheviks and his own Bolsheviks. The Mensheviks favored a large, broad-based workers' party, while the Bolsheviks demanded a small, well-disciplined party of dedicated revolutionaries. Lenin distrusted the instincts of the working class, believing it insufficiently revolutionary. His rivals claimed that Lenin's approach was too dictatorial.

On April 16, 1917, Lenin returned by train from Switzerland to Petrograd. **LENIN RETURNS** Knowing of his opposition to Russia's involvement in an "imperialist war," the Germans **TO RUSSIA** allowed him to pass through German territory but quarantined him from contact with any Germans, lest he infect them with his ideas. While Winston Churchill later compared the arrival of this short, balding, goateed, 46-year-old radical to that of a "plague bacillus," Lenin was not an alien infection but a Russian who well understood the volatile mood of the masses. He wanted a Marxist revolution to occur in Russia and to spread quickly from there to some of the more industrialized nations. These nations could in turn help Russia build up the industrial base necessary to construct Marxist socialism.

Following his return, Lenin immediately challenged the dominance of the Mensheviks and Socialist Revolutionaries within the Soviets. At the same time he called for "all power to the Soviets," anticipating that his own Bolshevik party could soon assume a commanding position within them. Lenin strongly criticized the war and called for peasants to seize the landed estates and for workers to take control of the factories. Although at first encountering strong opposition to his radical demands, as 1917 proceeded his party gradually gained support. As early as May, representatives of the Mensheviks and Socialist Revolutionaries had become cabinet members in the

Provisional Government; the Bolsheviks thus had the advantage of being the only major party of the Left not implicated in an increasingly unpopular government. Some peasant soldiers began to desert the front and go home, partly motivated by hopes of seizing property in the countryside. As Lenin later said, they "voted for peace with their feet." By October 1917 Bolshevik strength had substantially increased. They had gained a majority in both the Petrograd and Moscow Soviets; Leon Trotsky, who had returned to Russia in 1917 and decided to become a Bolshevik, was now the chairman of the Petrograd Soviet.

NOVEMBER REVOLUTION BRINGS LENIN TO POWER

Late in October, Lenin returned to the capital after temporarily hiding in Finland and immediately called for a takeover of power. Lenin's urgings and Trotsky's persuasive and dynamic speeches to Soviet deputies, soldiers, and workers moved preparations steadily forward. On the evening of November 6 and the morning of November 7, troops under the control of the Bolshevik-dominated Petrograd Soviet took control of the bridges, railroad and electric stations, state bank, post office, and central telephone station. Finally, after a siege marked more by noise and confusion than by loss of blood, the revolutionaries broke into the Winter Palace during the early morning of November 8. Members of the Provisional Government (except for Prime Minister Alexander Kerensky, who had left the capital to seek out loyal troops) surrendered to representatives of the Petrograd Soviet.

Meanwhile, at a meeting of the Second All-Russian Congress of Soviets, deputies of the Mensheviks and many of the moderate Socialist Revolutionaries strongly objected to the armed takeover that was in progress, but they were outnumbered. Finally, in frustration, they stormed out in protest. Trotsky mocked those who left: "You are bankrupt. Your role is played out. Go where you belong: into the dustbin of history." On November 9, the remaining delegates approved a new government with Lenin as chairman of the Council of People's Commissars and Trotsky as commissar of foreign affairs.

CIVIL WAR AND ALLIED INTERVENTION

Although the Bolsheviks had an extensive following among workers and soldiers, the peasant-oriented Socialist Revolutionaries remained more popular in the nation as a whole. When the previously scheduled elections for the Constituent Assembly took place in late November 1917, the Socialist Revolutionaries won more than twice as many seats as the Bolsheviks. The vote was the most democratic Russia had ever had, with women as well as men participating. When the Assembly met in January 1918, however, Lenin disbanded it after a day, and no major force was able to effectively challenge his action. As the year progressed, the Communists (Bolsheviks) used their newly founded secret police, the Cheka, not only against conservative and liberal parties and groups but also against other radical parties such as the Mensheviks and Socialist Revolutionaries. Nevertheless, Communist control was primarily restricted to the ethnic Russian heartland. In other areas of the empire, many of the non-Russian nationalities refused to accept Soviet rule.

In March 1918, after months of diplomatic maneuvers to prevent it, the militarily prostrate Russians signed the Treaty of Brest-Litovsk with Germany. The treaty

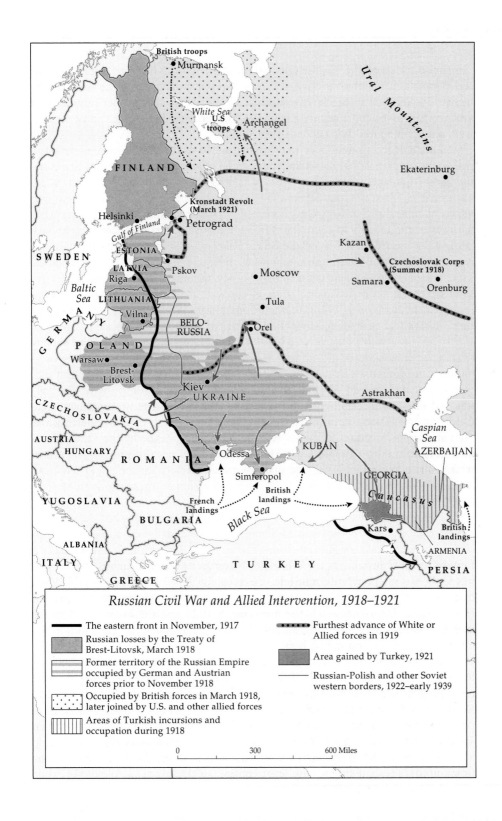

Russian Civil War and Allied Intervention, 1918–1921

▬▬▬	The eastern front in November, 1917	●●●●●	Furthest advance of White or Allied forces in 1919
	Russian losses by the Treaty of Brest-Litovsk, March 1918		Area gained by Turkey, 1921
	Former territory of the Russian Empire occupied by German and Austrian forces prior to November 1918	———	Russian-Polish and other Soviet western borders, 1922–early 1939
	Occupied by British forces in March 1918, later joined by U.S. and other allied forces		
	Areas of Turkish incursions and occupation during 1918		

0   300   600 Miles

recognized the surrender of close to one-third of the Russian Empire's cultivated lands and population, mainly the huge, ethnically non-Russian parts of the tsar's empire west and southwest of the Russian heartland. Already, or soon to be, controlled by Germany, these lands—Finland, Lithuania, Estonia, Latvia, Ukraine, and Poland—were now pronounced independent from Russia.

Although the Communists were willing, however reluctantly, to come to terms with Germany, Russia's former allies were not so inclined. One concern of the Allies was to see that the military supplies they had sent to such ports as Archangel and Murmansk did not fall into German hands. The Allies also wanted to prevent even greater numbers of German troops from being transferred to the western front. They decided to send military forces into Russia, and eventually 14 nations became involved, particularly Great Britain, France, the United States, and Japan. Allied intervention was also motivated by Western anticommunism, the Communists' call for "international socialist revolution," and their cancellation of several billion dollars of tsarist debt to Western creditors. Following the end of the war in November 1918, the Allies remained in Russia, supporting the anti-Communist (White) armies that had organized during that year to challenge the Soviet government in a full-scale civil war.

The conservative officers who led the White armies were supported in varying degrees by other groups, including Cossacks and followers of political parties ranging from the conservative far Right to some Socialist Revolutionaries on the Left. For two years, until the end of 1920, they fought on many fronts against the Communists, or Reds. (Nineteenth-century Europeans used the color red to symbolize radicalism, and the Communists adopted it for their new flag and other symbols such as the red star.) In Siberia, the Whites were supported for a time by the Czechoslovakian Corps, made up of about 40,000 former Czech prisoners of war who had served in the Austro-Hungarian army. The point of greatest danger for the new Soviet government was probably in October 1919, when White forces threatened both Moscow and Petrograd.

In April 1920, with the civil war still under way, Poland attacked Russia. After seesaw campaigning, Poland gained some Ukrainian and Belorussian areas that it claimed by historical right. Despite losing the war with Poland, the Red Army pushed forward on all fronts against the Whites. In November 1920, Red troops in the south forced the last major White contingent to evacuate in Allied ships. Most of the Allied forces also withdrew, leaving only the Japanese in Siberia. Under increasing Soviet and U.S. pressure, the Japanese left the mainland in 1922 and the Russian part of the island of Sakhalin in 1925. All in all, Allied intervention against the Communists was a failure, leaving behind only a legacy of mistrust.

REASONS FOR RED VICTORY

Despite Allied intervention, a war with Poland, and the opposition of powerful forces inside Russia, the Reds defeated the Whites for several reasons. They were more unified than their enemies, who found it almost impossible to work together. Despite differences among themselves—for example, between Trotsky and Stalin—party discipline and the leadership of Lenin kept the Communists working together. Trotsky, as head of the Red Army, displayed impressive organizational and leadership abilities, rushing in his specially equipped train from one front to another. The Communists also had the advantage of controlling the heartland of Russia, while

BIOGRAPHY

A Young Man in Lenin's Russia

I became a Bolshevik and a member of the Communist Party after the Revolution and a short time later joined the Red Army as a political worker and propagandist. As soon as I returned from the Front after the Civil War, the Yuzovka Party organization made me a deputy manager of the Ruchenkov mines. . . .

There was famine in the mines of the Donbass in 1922, and even isolated incidents of cannibalism. The villages were even more ravaged than the mines. My first wife, Galina, died during the famine in 1921. Her death was a great sadness to me. I was left with two children to look after, my son Leonid and my daughter Julia. In 1924 I married again to Nina Petrovna. Those first years of Soviet Power were years of struggle and hardship and self-sacrifice. But the people still believed in the Party; even the most illiterate of our citizens understood the Party's slogans and

rallying cries. The people knew that these hardships were being thrust upon us by the bourgeoisie—both by our own bourgeoisie and by the bourgeoisie of the world at large, which was instigating counterrevolution and intervention against us. We told ourselves that no matter how bad things were, they had been worse in the old days, before the Revolution.*

. . .

From the memoirs of Nikita Khrushchev, leader of the Soviet Union from 1953 until 1964. He was in his middle and late 20s in the period described here. Although assistance from the American Relief Administration helped save many lives, at least 5 million people died in the Soviet famine of the early 1920s.

*From *Khrushchev Remembers*, vol. I, by Nikita Khrushchev, translated and edited by Strobe Talbott. Copyright © 1971 by Little, Brown & Co. Reprinted by permission.

their enemies were scattered around the periphery. Finally, a Red victory held out more hope to the peasants and the minority nationalities than did a White victory. Although both sides forcibly requisitioned food from them, peasants feared that the Whites might also try to restore the rights of landowners. Smaller nationalities feared that the Whites would reestablish the Russian Empire and that they would be dominated once again by the Great Russians. The Soviet leadership at least promised something better.

Yet the hopes of the non-Russian nationalities were almost immediately crushed. In 1920–1921 Bolshevik Russia restored control over most of Ukraine not lost to Poland and over the Caucasian republics of Azerbaijan, Armenia, and Georgia. During the next few years the Bolsheviks also brought most of Central Asia back under Russian rule.

In March 1921 the sailors of the Kronstadt naval base, early supporters of the Communists who had grown tired of their authoritarianism, revolted, but the government crushed the uprising. The anarchist Emma Goldman, then in Petrograd, stated that the brutal slaughter of the sailors severed the last strand that once united her with the Communist cause. Finally, however, Kronstadt and other economic and political unrest (including widespread peasant revolts) helped lead to government concessions encompassed in the New Economic Policy (NEP).

THE NEW ECONOMIC POLICY, 1921–1928

Although the Communists had defeated the Whites and the Kronstadt sailors, they had inherited an exhausted and shrunken country. After heavy losses in World War I, millions more lives had been lost in the strife that followed. (A famine in 1921–1922 took millions of additional lives.) Numerous cities and villages had been destroyed. Many factories sat idle, and the transportation system had almost ceased to function. Crop production had fallen off drastically. Not only had territory been lost to Poland, but in a series of 1920 treaties the Soviet government had also found it necessary to recognize the independence of Finland, Estonia, Latvia, and Lithuania. Parts of the Asiatic portion of the nation were still not firmly under Soviet control.

The Communists had earlier instituted war communism, which had national-ized industry and land, all but abolished private trade, and forced the peasants to turn over most of their crops to the state. Under the NEP, the state continued to main-tain control over major industries, transportation, banking, foreign trade, and most wholesale trade. The new policy now allowed a measure of private enterprise in small industries and retail trade. In addition, the state no longer forcibly requisitioned peas-ant produce. After paying a tax, first mainly in food and later in money, peasants were free to sell what remained on the open market. Economically, the NEP was a notable success. By 1928 the total agricultural and industrial production had roughly reached 1913 levels. Given the devastation of the economy from 1914 through 1920, this was no small accomplishment.

COMMUNIST PARTY AND RISE OF STALIN

From the beginning, the Communist Party had dominated the state, and dur-ing the NEP years, despite easing economic controls, the party tightened its control over all levels of government. Inside the party, the hierarchy strengthened its hold on the rank-and-file membership. The constitution of 1924 proclaimed a federation of republics, the Union of Soviet Socialist Republics (U.S.S.R.). Supreme power sup-posedly resided in the All-Union Congress of Soviets (after 1936, the Supreme Soviet). This body was to elect the Council of People's Commissars (after 1946, the Council of Ministers) and also the Executive Committee and the smaller Presidium that acted for the Congress between sessions. The Communist Party, especially its Central Com-mittee (63 members in 1926), Politburo, and Secretariat, filled the government posts. Important central government figures were members of the party and followed the instructions of the central party leadership. This was true throughout all the republics; claims of any truly autonomous powers for the republics were mere propaganda.

During the NEP years Joseph Stalin replaced Lenin as the most important Com-munist political figure. In 1922 Lenin suffered a stroke, and in January 1924 he died. Although after his death Russian Communists revered him, before his death other leaders maneuvered to fill the power vacuum that resulted from his stroke. The man who seemed to be the front-runner for Lenin's mantle was Leon Trotsky. Unfortunately for Trotsky, others united against him. Trotsky's main opponent was Joseph Stalin, who was 45 years old when Lenin died. Born in Georgia in the Caucasus, Stalin was a longtime Marxist who had been made general secretary of the Communist Party when the office was created in 1922. In 1923 Lenin concluded that Stalin "was too rude" and should be replaced in his position by someone "more patient, more loyal,

Lenin and Stalin, 1922.

more courteous, and more considerate of his comrades." Because of his stroke Lenin could not engineer Stalin's removal. After Lenin's death, Stalin used his position as general secretary to strengthen his control over the party, cleverly playing on the ambitions of others and making useful political allies when he needed them. By 1927 Stalin had Trotsky and a few of his other political opponents expelled from the party. In 1929 Trotsky was forced to leave the Soviet Union, and he eventually settled in Mexico. He watched from afar as "Stalinism," which he referred to as "the syphilis of socialism," was gradually imposed. In 1940 he was axed in the head by a Stalinist agent.

SOCIAL AND CULTURAL DEVELOPMENTS

The NEP years were also ones of social and cultural experimentation. The power of husbands and fathers was curtailed, and the emancipation of women proclaimed. Although sexual equality was not fully achieved, educational and job opportunities for women expanded, and the gap between men's and women's pay decreased. Either spouse could obtain a divorce, and by 1927 the rate had increased to one for every four marriages. The government also mandated maternity leaves and legalized abortions. In the area of religion, it confiscated church land and possessions, and, through the educational system and media, inculcated antireligious and pro-Communist propaganda. The state stressed technical, vocational, and adult education and also briefly experimented with progressive educational techniques. By 1939 about 81 percent of Soviet citizens were literate, compared to 51 percent in 1926.

Benefiting from the presence of some gifted writers and thinkers who remained in the Soviet Union, the NEP period was culturally richer than the Stalinist years that followed. Some "true believers" in the revolution, such as the film director Sergei Eisenstein and, for a time, the poet Vladimir Mayakovsky, shared with their audiences a sense of excitement about the new Communist era. Many others, such as the poet Boris Pasternak, who later wrote *Doctor Zhivago,* were not so enthusiastic, yet created works of merit. Censorship was not yet complete and there was still room for experimentation, but under the increasing power of Stalin and the party vital intellectual forces slowly dissipated.

EARLY SOVIET FOREIGN POLICY

Soviet foreign policy was yet another area of change during the NEP period. In 1919 the Communist International, or Comintern, was created amid hopes of establishing Communist governments elsewhere. The Russian leader of the Comintern predicted that in a year "all of Europe will be Communist," but only in parts of Germany and Hungary did Communist governments briefly exist in 1919 (see Chapter 11). The Comintern eventually consisted of Communist parties of various nations that had, for the most part, split off from larger Socialist parties. Since the Comintern was managed from Moscow, other nations correctly perceived it as a force that encouraged Communist agitation and revolution outside the Soviet Union. In 1923, for example, Comintern agents attempted to take advantage of the unsettled conditions in Germany to encourage Communist takeovers.

While leaving such foreign activities to the nominally independent Comintern, the Soviet government sought to gain diplomatic recognition, trade, and credits from other nations. In 1921 it signed a trade agreement with the British, "One can trade even with cannibals," British prime minister Lloyd George once stated in defense of such trade. The Treaty of Rapallo with Germany in 1922 marked a further breakthrough, as the two nations agreed to restore normal diplomatic and commercial relations. In 1924 Great Britain, France, Italy, China, and a number of other nations also officially recognized the Soviet Union. Although the United States did not extend formal recognition until 1933, it did feed over 10 million famished Russians from 1921 to 1923, primarily through the American Relief Administration. And by 1930 the United States briefly became the chief exporter of goods to Russia.

By the middle of the 1920s the Soviet government appeared to be becoming less revolutionary. In fact, Trotsky and a few others accused Stalin of a lack of enthusiasm for encouraging revolutions abroad. They accurately charged that Stalin's slogan of "socialism in one country" deemphasized the policy of fomenting revolution abroad and stressed instead the construction of a socialist society within the Soviet Union.

In spite of a decline of revolutionary action on the part of the Comintern in the second half of the 1920s, Soviet foreign policy still continued to reflect its origins. In 1927 Great Britain broke off relations with the U.S.S.R. on discovering extensive Soviet espionage and propaganda activities in London.

THE THIRD REVOLUTION: COLLECTIVIZATION AND THE FIRST FIVE-YEAR PLAN

Despite the many changes Russia had experienced in the decade following 1917, the lives of Soviet peasants were not greatly changed from tsarist days. They still made up about 80 percent of the Soviet population; more than half of them were illiterate. Their communal work and leisure habits, social organization, and suspicion of authority had changed little. Many, especially the older peasants, also retained their prerevolutionary religious beliefs and, to the extent possible, their religious ceremonies and customs.

In 1928–1929 Stalin launched a "revolution from above" that compared in significance to the two revolutions of 1917. With help from many party members dissatisfied with the NEP, he cast it overboard, attacked "class enemies," introduced the collectivization of agriculture, and brought forth the Soviet Union's first Five-Year Plan, with its emphasis on rapid industrialization. The economic changes were accompanied by a cultural revolution. It was directed against the NEP's relative cultural tolerance and Lenin's heavy reliance on "bourgeois experts"—the party leadership had used non-Communist professionals and technical experts because of the shortage of well-educated Communists. Now, however, the party removed many of these individuals from their positions while training loyal Communists to obtain professional and technical expertise. From 1927–1928 until 1932–1933, higher education enrollment (often in technical institutes) tripled, with students of working-class origin increasing from one-fourth to one-half the total. Among future Soviet leaders, Khrushchev, Brezhnev, and Kosygin all received varying amounts of advanced technical training in this period. By 1931 the cultural revolution had produced considerable chaos; in June, Stalin criticized excessive harassment of specialists and soon brought this revolution to an end.

The reasons Stalin introduced and continued his more radical economic policies are subject to debate, but five have been frequently mentioned:

REASONS FOR "THIRD REVOLUTION"

1. More grain was needed to help feed the growing urban population, but peasants were not selling enough grain to the state at the low prices the government was willing to pay.

2. More rapid industrialization, especially in heavy industry, was necessary
   if the Soviet Union was to become a stronger military power. "If in
   10 years we do not cover the distance that other countries took 50 or
   100 years to traverse, we will be crushed," Stalin warned.

3. Marxist ideology based socialism on a developed industrial order, and therefore the continued development of a Soviet socialist state was thought by
   many to depend on the expansion of Soviet industry.

4. Both the Five-Year Plan and collectivization would increase the control of
   the party over the economy and over the lives of Soviet citizens.

5. If he now rejected the NEP approach, Stalin would at the same time discredit
   his remaining major political opponents, who had consistently supported it.

EFFECTS OF "THIRD REVOLUTION"

With the inauguration in late 1928 of the first Five-Year Plan, the Soviet economy took on the characteristics that would mark it for the next six decades. Government officials decided what should be produced in the Soviet Union and in what
quantity; consumers' desires had relatively little effect. The government, following
party orders as always, established target figures for the next five years, designed
especially to increase metal and chemical production, electricity and petroleum output, new factory construction, and other industrial growth. The government obtained
capital for expansion in these areas by squeezing high indirect taxes from its population. The purchasing power of Soviet citizens declined, and few consumer goods
were available.

At the end of 1932 the government claimed that it had already met the goals
of the first Five-Year Plan in a little over four years. Although it is impossible to be
sure of the exact figures, and haste in meeting production quotas often caused shoddy
workmanship, production did increase significantly in some areas. Most reliable
estimates agree that iron and steel output went up at least 50 percent during the first
Five-Year Plan. The output of chemicals, machinery, equipment, fertilizers, petroleum,
and electricity increased even more dramatically. New factories, industrial complexes,
and cities sprang up, often located far in the interior, away from vulnerable borders.
Although part of this industrial spurt flowed from genuine enthusiasm by some
workers for Stalin's bold new plans, increased labor discipline and coercion also
helped increase production.

The record in agriculture was not as impressive. Russian peasants in 1933 produced less food than before collectivization, and the amount of livestock markedly
declined. In addition, famine occurred in 1932–1933. The poor record was largely
due to the peasants' resistance to collectivization and the government's use of force.
Stalin was determined to push most peasants into either collective farms or state
farms. In the collectives, peasants worked the land collectively, and, after meeting all
other obligations, they divided what was left of their produce according to the percentage they had earned by their work. On a state farm, on the other hand, workers
received wages directly from the state.

Both collective and state farms were unpopular with the peasants, and few were
willing to give up their old ways. Peasants slaughtered their animals rather than turn
them over to the collective farms. In response to such resistance, the government

Some of the millions of Soviet peasants who were deported from villages during the collectivization process.

killed or sent to Siberia and other parts of the country millions of peasants, often to face premature deaths in forced labor camps. Stalin waged war especially on those designated as "kulaks," who were supposedly prosperous peasants guilty of hoarding. Actually, almost any peasant who was in trouble with the authorities was apt to be included in this category. No group suffered more than the Ukrainian peasants. Stalin's food policies in Ukraine, and to a lesser extent in other regions, led to millions of additional deaths during the famine of 1932–1933.

Despite resistance, however, Stalin succeeded in forcing many peasants onto collective or state farms. He granted only one noteworthy concession, when he allowed collectivized peasants to maintain small private garden plots and a few animals. By the end of the first Five-Year Plan, more than 60 percent of the cultivated land in Russia was under the control of collective farms and about 10 percent under state farms. In subsequent years, the collectivization thrust continued, placing most of the remaining peasants and their produce effectively under the control of the party and state. At a time when Soviet peasants were starving to death, the government forced them to turn over grain to government agencies, which used it to feed the expanding cities, to add to grain reserves, and even to export. (See Chapter 16 for a discussion of the U.S.S.R. in the middle and late 1930s.)

SUMMARY AND THE INTERNATIONAL SIGNIFICANCE OF RUSSIA'S REVOLUTIONS

The years 1917–1932 witnessed cataclysmic changes in Russian life. The three revolutions culminating in Stalin's revolution from above helped to greatly transform Russia. By 1932 it had changed from an overwhelmingly agrarian, religious, and traditional empire with an autocratic government to a rapidly industrializing Marxist society. Its official values were atheistic and revolutionary, and the Communist Party and Soviet government interfered more actively in the lives of the people than had the old tsarist government. Collectivization, in particular, transformed patterns of work. The increased use of education and the media as instruments of propaganda and the use of terror also made it increasingly difficult to ignore or oppose the desires of the authorities. In the immediate postwar years, the revolutionary nature of the government and its aggressive Marxist-Leninist ideas threatened international stability. By 1932, however, the government was more concerned with continuing the internal transformation of the Soviet Union than with causing Communist revolutions in other nations.

Nevertheless, the transformations wrought by the three revolutions remained significant for other countries. Lenin insisted that imperialism was an outgrowth of capitalism and that colonial peoples should rebel and throw off both colonial and capitalist shackles. Soviet leaders also claimed that less advanced countries could copy Soviet methods of rapid industrialization and modernization. Ironically, although Marxism and Marxist socialism began in western Europe, Marxist governments came to power only in less developed regions, first in Russia and then, after World War II, in other countries such as China.

To the colonial powers themselves, the U.S.S.R. was a menace partly because its leaders encouraged colonial peoples, as well as those living in capitalist countries, to rebel. Although Communist parties came into being in western Europe after 1917, they were generally weaker than Socialist parties, also indebted to Marx. The Socialist parties had gradually been moving away from Marxist radicalism, and the loss of some of their more radical members to the new Communist parties just furthered this tendency. Yet, by 1932, with the Great Depression discrediting capitalism in the eyes of many, the appeal of Communist parties and the anticapitalist Soviet Union was on the rise. Thus, even before the beginning of the cold war in the late 1940s, the Soviet Union presented a major challenge to its future cold war enemies.

SUGGESTED SOURCES

Conquest, Robert. *The Harvest of Sorrow: Soviet Collectivization and the Terror-Famine.* 1986. The appalling story of Stalin's policies, which cost millions of Soviet lives.* (A 55-minute documentary on the same subject, called *Harvest of Despair,* is available on video.)

Figes, Orlando. *A People's Tragedy: The Russian Revolution, 1891–1924.* 1996. A long but well-written account.*

Fitzpatrick, Sheila. *The Russian Revolution, 1917–32.* 2nd ed. 1994. A clear, brief, and objective account.*

Foglesong, David S. *America's Secret War against Bolshevism: U.S. Intervention in the Russian Civil War, 1917–1920.* 1995. The author argues that anti-Bolshevik sentiments played a greater role in prompting U.S. intervention than most previous historians have stated.

Goldman, Emma. *My Disillusionment in Russia.* 1970. Recounts the author's experiences in Russia in 1920–1921 after she was deported from the United States.*

Holquist, Peter. *Making War, Forging Revolution: Russia's Continuum of Crisis, 1914–1921.* 2002. This work emphasizes the importance of World War I for understanding the 1917 revolutions and subsequent civil war.

Lincoln, W. Bruce. *Red Victory: A History of the Russian Civil War.* 1989. A comprehensive overview by a scholar who also writes excellent popular history.*

McDermid, Jane, and Anna Hillyar. *Midwives of the Revolution: Female Bolsheviks and Women Workers in 1917.* 1999. A brief work that presents solid information on women Bolsheviks and workers.*

Montefiore, Simon Sebag. *Stalin: The Court of the Red Tsar.* 2003. Chaps. 1–7. These chapters offer a fascinating examination of Stalin's early years, based partly on recently opened archival materials.*

Pasternak, Boris. *Doctor Zhivago.* 1958. A great novel conveying the chaotic conditions of Russia during World War I, the revolution, and the civil war and the reactions of a sensitive man to it all.* (Also a film.)

Patenaude, Bertrand. *The Big Show in Bololand: The American Relief Expedition to Soviet Russia in the Famine of 1921.* 2002. A comprehensive account of U.S. aid to famine victims of the early 1920s.*

Potemkin. 1926. One of Sergei Eisenstein's most famous films, it deals with a mutiny on a battleship during the revolt of 1905.

Raleigh, Donald J. *Experiencing Russia's Civil War: Politics, Society, and Revolutionary Culture in Saratov, 1917–1922.* 2002. An excellent study of the civil war's impact in a Volga River area.*

Reed, John. *Ten Days That Shook the World.* 1919. A firsthand account of the Bolshevik revolt by the famous American Marxist.* (Several films have also appeared with this title. The first, an Eisenstein film, was originally called *October* and is now available on videotape under that title; also available is the 1981 U.S. film *Reds,* which deals with Reed and his Russian experiences.)

Scott, John. *Behind the Urals: An American Worker in Russia's City of Steel.* 1989. A fascinating account of life in the new city of Magnitogorsk during the early days of Stalin's industrialization.*

Service, Robert. *Lenin: A Biography.* 2002. The most comprehensive biography of Lenin available.*

Siegelbaum, Lewis H. *Soviet State and Society between Revolutions, 1918–1929.* 1992. A good brief analysis of the interrelationship between Russia's new Communist government and society and culture.*

Viola, Lynne. *Peasant Rebels under Stalin: Collectivization and the Culture of Peasant Resistance.* 1996. A fascinating and scholarly account of peasant resistance to Stalin's collectivization policies of the late 1920s and early 1930s.*

Volkogonov, Dmitri. *Trotsky: The Eternal Revolutionary.* 1996. A biography by a former Russian general and historian with access to the latest archival material; he also wrote interesting biographies of Lenin and Stalin.

Wade, Rex. *The Russian Revolution, 1917.* 2nd ed. 2005. A well-written, up-to-date treatment of the various forces that transformed Russia in 1917.*

WEB SOURCES

www.soviethistory.org/index.php. A first-rate site, the best for Soviet history. See links to years 1917, 1921, 1924, 1929; the site for each year contains numerous links to other valuable materials in various media forms. For 1917, for example, see "The New Woman," "Bolsheviks Seize Power," and "Constituent Assembly."

www.geocities.com/sheerin104. Provides links for Lenin, Trotsky, Stalin, and other Soviet materials, especially regarding the Russian revolutions of 1917.

---

*Paperback available.

⑥Postwar Settlements and Europe in the 1920s

At the Paris Peace Conference of 1919 the victorious powers dictated terms to the defeated nations. Russia, in the midst of its civil war, did not participate. U.S. president Woodrow Wilson was a major participant and preached idealistic principles including the rather vague idea of self-determination, which suggested that each nationality should have the right to live under a government of its own choice and, where feasible, geographic boundaries should reflect major national or ethnographic boundaries. Wilson also called for a peace without annexations. But the settlements that ensued were at times at odds with Wilson's rhetoric. Although some nationalities were able to create their own states, many ethnic groups remained minorities, and the Western colonial powers rejected self-determination for Africans, Arabs, and others. Germany and its wartime allies considered the peace terms excessively harsh and resented them. The myriad resentments engendered by the peace treaties heightened international tension in the postwar period.

The decade following the Paris Peace Conference was one of economic, social, political, and cultural adjustments to the results of the war and to the Russian revolutions of 1917. From 1919 until 1923–1924, instability pervaded Europe and competing political forces struggled against one another. By the middle of the decade, there were indications that a more stable atmosphere was returning, both among European governments and in domestic affairs. Although many politicians and statesmen expressed newfound confidence in the late 1920s, the postwar foundations remained shaky.

THE PARIS PEACE CONFERENCE

The Paris Peace Conference opened on January 18, 1919, with 27 of the victorious nations represented. It was to be a gathering of only the victors; Germany and other defeated powers were not allowed representation at the conference. Nor was Russia represented; the victors resented the new Bolshevik government, which had made a separate peace with Germany, and a civil war then being waged in Russia provided a pretext for not inviting a Russian delegation to Paris. Originally, the victors made plans to follow the conference with a peace congress that would have included the defeated powers, but this idea was later dropped.

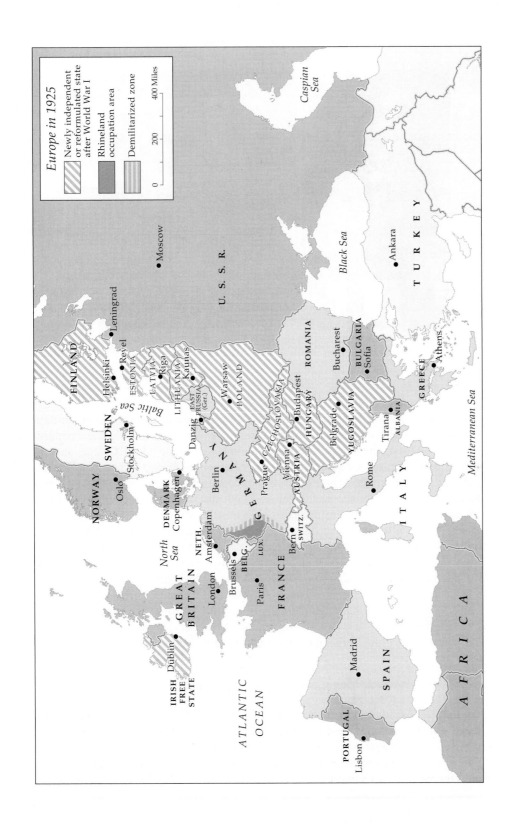

Europe in 1925

Newly independent or reformulated state after World War I

Rhineland occupation area

Demilitarized zone

0   200   400 Miles

Caspian Sea

Moscow

U. S. S. R.

Leningrad

Revel

FINLAND

Helsinki

ESTONIA

LATVIA

Riga

LITHUANIA

Kaunas

EAST PRUSSIA (Ger.)

Danzig

Warsaw

POLAND

Baltic Sea

SWEDEN

Stockholm

NORWAY

Oslo

DENMARK

Copenhagen

North Sea

NETH.

Amsterdam

BELG.

Brussels

LUX.

GREAT BRITAIN

London

IRISH FREE STATE

Dublin

ATLANTIC OCEAN

FRANCE

Paris

SWITZ.

Bern

GERMANY

Berlin

Prague

CZECHOSLOVAKIA

Vienna

AUSTRIA

HUNGARY

Budapest

ROMANIA

Bucharest

YUGOSLAVIA

Belgrade

Rome

ITALY

Tirana

ALBANIA

BULGARIA

Sofia

GREECE

Athens

Black Sea

TURKEY

Ankara

Mediterranean Sea

SPAIN

Madrid

PORTUGAL

Lisbon

AFRICA

At the Paris Peace Conference: Lloyd George, Orlando (of Italy), Clemenceau, and Wilson.

The Supreme Council, which included the heads of state and foreign ministers of the United States, Great Britain, France, Italy, and Japan, made the important decisions at the conference. The dominant figures there were the scholarly U.S. president Woodrow Wilson, the colorful British prime minister David Lloyd George, and the French prime minister Georges Clemenceau, "the tiger of France," who was in his late 70s and still a formidable figure. Since the three men had differing priorities, they had to make concessions to each other to obtain some of their objectives. Wilson was primarily concerned with ensuring that agreement would be reached on a covenant for the League of Nations and that, to the extent possible, the peace would be based on his Fourteen Points. Clemenceau's main preoccupation was to ensure that Germany would never again threaten French security. Lloyd George was not as inclined as Clemenceau to be harsh toward the Germans, but he had just been returned to office after his party had promised to hang the kaiser and to "squeeze the German lemon until the pips [seeds] squeaked." Through the spring and into the summer of 1919, the conference moved at a rapid but often disorderly pace—"a riot in a parrot house," as one member of the British delegation described it.

The Treaty of Versailles

On June 28, exactly five years after the assassination of Archduke Franz Ferdinand, the attending nations signed the Treaty of Versailles with Germany. Germany had protested that the terms were too harsh and not in keeping with Wilson's Fourteen Points, on the basis of which Germany had agreed to lay down its arms. Undoubtedly, the German perception of the treaty was influenced by the fact that almost all the war had been fought on non-German soil, and to many Germans it seemed more a stalemate than a decisive Allied victory. However, Germany had little choice but to sign.

According to the terms of the treaty, Germany lost Alsace-Lorraine to France, several small districts to Belgium, one to Czechoslovakia, and a large portion of eastern Germany to Poland. In addition, plebiscites were to be held in several areas, such as northern Schleswig on the Danish border; Germany eventually lost some of these territories as well. Several German areas, such as the Saar district and the city of Danzig, were to be put under the control of the newly formed League of Nations. The city of Memel was also taken away and eventually ceded to Lithuania. Many of the lost German territories contained only a minority of Germans. In the Saar, Danzig, and Memel, however, Germans predominated. Germany also lost all its overseas colonies, which came under the control of the victors. Despite these losses, Germany's population still outnumbered France's by more than a three-to-two margin and had been growing at a faster rate for some time—both causes of alarm in France.

GERMAN TERRITORIAL LOSSES

According to the treaty, Germany and its allies were guilty of aggression in imposing a war on the Allies. The kaiser was to be tried for offenses against "international morality and the sanctity of treaties," and hundreds of German military officers were charged with war crimes. Although no significant individuals came to trial, Germany was assessed reparations to pay for war damages. The exact figure was not settled at the time of the conference, but the Allies stipulated that Germany would make payments totaling the equivalent of $5 billion by 1921. At that time the final sum, understood to be much higher, would be announced.

REPARATIONS AND OTHER STIPULATIONS

Germany also had to observe various strict limitations on its armed forces and weapons. As an additional safeguard for France, Allied forces were to occupy the Rhineland area west of the Rhine and control three of the river's bridgeheads, in both cases for periods ranging from 5 to 15 years. In addition, the Rhineland and a 30-mile zone east of the river were to be permanently demilitarized.

Although Germany regarded the Treaty of Versailles as severe, the treaty would have been even harsher if French desires had been fully realized. Concerned for its future security, France had proposed, among other points, that the territory west of the Rhine be made into a separate buffer state under French influence. Wilson, however, reduced France's demands on Germany by agreeing, along with Great Britain, to guarantee France against any future German invasion, a guarantee that never became operative because of the U.S. Senate's later refusal to support Wilson's pledge.

Arrangements for the Rest of Europe

The Allies at the conference also dictated terms to the other defeated powers: Austria-Hungary, Bulgaria, and the Ottoman Empire. All had to pay reparations, limit their armies, and acknowledge the loss of some territory. Punishment for Bulgaria was comparatively light in all these categories, though it did lose its former access to the Aegean Sea. To some extent, drafting treaties for the other defeated nations involved sanctioning the reformation of ethnic groupings that had already occurred in central and eastern Europe. By 1919 little was left of the old Austro-Hungarian Empire. Led by the able

CZECHOSLOVAKIA, YUGOSLAVIA, AND POLAND

and respected Thomas Masaryk, the Czechs and Slovaks had appealed to Allied leaders to act on the basis of Wilson's principle of self-determination and recognize the independence of Czechoslovakia. Even before the November 1918 armistice was signed, the Allies had complied, and a separate government was already functioning there. A month before the convening of the Paris Peace Conference, the Kingdom of the Serbs, Croats, and Slovenes (or Yugoslavia, as it would later be officially known) had been proclaimed. It included, or soon would include, formerly independent Serbia and Montenegro, combined with the former Austro-Hungarian areas of Croatia, Slovenia, Bosnia, and Herzegovina. In addition, Romania had seized the Transylvania region from Hungary.

The Poles also gained their independence. Poland had not existed as a nation since it had been divided in the late eighteenth century among Prussia (now part of Germany), Russia, and Austria. Woodrow Wilson's 13th point, proclaimed a full year before the convening of the conference, called for an "independent Poland, to include the territories indisputably Polish, with free and secure access to the sea." By the time Allied diplomats assembled in 1919, a Polish republic had been proclaimed, and the Poles had already taken control of Polish segments of Austria-Hungary, as well as Polish-claimed portions of Germany and Russia. The key territory Poland annexed from Germany was the Polish Corridor, primarily peopled by Poles. The corridor, along with Danzing (under the control of the League of Nations), provided Poland with an outlet to the sea and severed East Prussia from the rest of Germany. The final Polish gains at the expense of Austria-Hungary and Russia were not determined until after Polish success in the Russian-Polish War of 1920.

The Allies ended the union of Austria and Hungary in the Treaty of St. Germain (1919) with Austria and the Treaty of Trianon (1920) with Hungary. Austria and Hungary recognized the losses to Czechoslovakia, Yugoslavia, Poland, and Romania; in addition, Austria recognized the loss of territory to Italy. Fearing the possibility of German dominance over central Europe, the Allies also forbade Austria, now composed of only a German-speaking population, any future union (*Anschluss*) with Germany. Both Austria and Hungary agreed to reparations payments and to limitations on their armies.

SELF-DETERMINATION

In general, the conference delegates claimed to be dividing Austria-Hungary according to the principle of ethnic nationalist self-determination, but this principle was violated in some cases. Earlier bargaining was one reason. The Allies, for example, had made promises to Italy and Romania to bring them into the war. When the boundaries of Italy were drawn through the Alps in accordance with these promises, Italy was given control over several hundred thousand former Austrian German-speaking people in South Tyrol and tens of thousands of Slavs in Istria. (When Italy further demanded the Adriatic port of Fiume, also claimed by the Yugoslavs, Wilson refused and Italy stormed out of the Paris Peace Conference.) Romania, too, was granted control over other ethnic groups. In the Transylvanian territory annexed by Romania there were two Magyars (ethnic Hungarians) for every three Romanians.

Economic or strategic considerations also came into conflict with a strict application of the principle of ethnic self-determination. Both factors helped persuade Allied statesmen to recognize as part of Czechoslovakia a German-speaking area of the former Austro-Hungarian territory that the Nazis later claimed as the Germanic Sudetenland.

In general, the principle of self-determination was much more complex than it first seemed. It was almost impossible to create a new state composed entirely of just one ethnic nationality. Some ethnic groups in the new Kingdom of the Serbs, Croats, and Slovenes were thought to be too closely intermingled or too small to exist as an independent nation. The new Poland contained not only ethnic Poles but also Ukrainians and Jews (together making up about 24 percent of Poland's population), as well as Belorussians, Germans, and other smaller groups. Thus, some ethnic groups, willingly or unwillingly, became part of a larger state.

As already noted, Russia was not invited to the peace conference, and neither the Red Bolsheviks nor the White anti-Bolsheviks were officially recognized by any of the Allied powers as the legitimate government of Russia. The fate of Finland, Estonia, Latvia, and Lithuania, all parts of the former Russian Empire, was not officially dealt with at the conference. Nevertheless, the conference diplomats were concerned by 1919 with the possible spread of communism. Their favorable treatment of Poland and Romania in part reflected a desire to set up strong bulwarks against communism and to create a *cordon sanitaire,* or quarantine zone, to keep communism out of central and western Europe. Hence, between 1918 and 1921, European powers supported independence for the four Baltic nations as part of the *cordon sanitaire.*

RUSSIA

European Imperialism at the Peace Conference

Although President Wilson had called for a peace without annexations, the prewar imperialist drive to acquire new possessions continued at the conference. Great Britain and France, for example, obtained the right to rule as mandates of the League of Nations former German territories in Africa and former Ottoman Turkish lands in the Middle East. (See Chapter 15 and the map in Chapter 4).

The new mandates were divided into A, B, and C categories, and as such give a good indication of the cultural imperialism prevailing early in the twentieth century. Set up by the European and U.S. delegations, the classification was based on Western perceptions of the degree of inferiority of particular non-Western societies—that is, the degree of deviance from Western standards. Type A mandates in the Middle East were considered to be almost ready for independence; Type B mandates, mostly African, were not considered ready for independence for several generations; and Type C, some former German-held islands in the Pacific, were judged unprepared for independence in the foreseeable future. The League of Nations was supposed to safeguard the interests of the peoples in the mandates, but in practice the countries that received the mandates exercised unrestricted authority and treated their mandates like colonies.

EUROPEAN REFUGEES, EMIGRANTS, AND MINORITIES

Faced with new governments and changing boundaries, several million people left their homes and settled elsewhere. Some left their nation behind, as, for example, the Russians who left the new Soviet state to live in such cities as Berlin, Paris, and Shanghai. Some took up a new life in a nation for which they felt kinship, such as the Germans who moved inside the new borders of Germany from areas that had been part of pre-war Germany but were now French or Polish.

However, not all minorities were able to move. Between the wars, minority problems, especially in central and eastern Europe, would continue to cause tension. Of particular significance were the German minorities in Poland and especially Czecho-slovakia, where more than one out of every five individuals was German. Other notable minorities were the Slavic and German minorities in Italy; the Hungarian (Magyar) minorities in Romania, Czechoslovakia, and Yugoslavia; the Ukrainian and Jewish minorities in Poland; the Ukrainians in Romania; and the Great Russians in Estonia, Latvia, and Romania.

Sometimes religious and cultural differences contributed to ethnic tensions. Yugoslavia provides one example. The dominant Serbs were Orthodox, most Croats and Slovenes were Catholic, and many of the people who lived in Bosnia and Herzegovina were Muslim. Hundreds of thousands of Muslim Albanians lived primarily in the Yugoslav area of Kosovo, which bordered Albania.

Between the wars, ethnic minorities and the dominant national groups continued to view each other with hostility. In Yugoslavia such hostility led to the killing of a Croatian political leader in 1928 and the assassination of Alexander I, the Serbian king of Yugoslavia, in 1934. The separation from their home nation of some members of an ethnic group, such as the Germans of Memel and Danzig, provided a convenient grievance and excuse for one nation to interfere in the affairs of another.

ECONOMIC, SOCIAL, AND CULTURAL ADJUSTMENTS

UNEMPLOYMENT AND INFLATION

One of the greatest problems European governments faced after the war was how to reintegrate millions of returning servicemen into their peacetime economies. Some men were unable to find jobs and became part of a severe unemployment problem in Europe during the postwar decade. After years of combat, many also found it difficult to settle down into a civilian routine. They believed that those who had not been through combat were not in a position to hold themselves up as guides and teachers. Some veterans blamed their elders for the folly of the war, and some, especially in Germany and Italy, objected to the peace settlements. Although many servicemen stayed out of politics or supported traditional political leaders, some of the early followers of Benito Mussolini and Adolf Hitler were fellow veterans.

Europeans also found it difficult to adjust to the inflation that had resulted from high government wartime spending, economic disruptions, and some post-war settlements, including the reparations payments imposed on the defeated powers (see Chapter 9). Inflation affected mostly old people on pensions, clerks, civil servants, teachers, and others on fixed incomes. Many of these people had prided themselves on their white-collar, middle-class status and now often saw their wages fall behind those of unionized blue-collar workers, who were in a better position to bargain for salary increases. Many feared that inflation would eat up their savings and that they would be destitute in their old age. Economic insecurities in Italy and Germany, later heightened in Germany by the Great Depression, led white-collar workers increasingly to doubt that moderate governments could find effective solutions. Fearful that the blue-collar parties of the Left would bring social disorder and loss of their status, many white-collar workers turned to the policies of Mussolini and Hitler.

CLASSES AND THE MASSES

The postwar period saw the gap between the aristocracy and the rest of society decrease. Ever since citizens had been encouraged to make sacrifices during the war, flagrant displays of wealth had gone out of style. The 1917 Marxist revolution had destroyed the aristocracy in Russia, and its status was in decline in Germany and Austria-Hungary with the collapse of the monarchies there. The aristocracy elsewhere in Europe often found its real wealth eroded by taxes and inflation.

At the other end of the social scale, the working class and its unions became more respectable. Most wartime governments had realized the need to cooperate with the unions, and this had conferred on the unions a new prestige. Extensive labor unrest immediately followed the war, but by the middle of the 1920s the situation was more stable. In 1924 Great Britain acquired its first Labour government.

The growing power of the masses alarmed some European intellectuals. In *The Revolt of the Masses* (1930), the Spanish philosopher José Ortega y Gasset wrote, "The mass crushes beneath it everything that is different, everything that is excellent, individual, qualified, and select. Anybody who is not like everybody, who does not think like everybody, runs the risk of being eliminated."[1] Ortega and many other European intellectuals perceived this phenomenon in everything from political movements such as communism and fascism to mass culture, influenced by America and new technology. To many European thinkers nothing epitomized mass culture better than Hollywood movies, which inundated postwar Europe. In Berlin and Moscow, despite the presence of films by great directors such as Fritz Lang and Sergei Eisenstein, American films featuring such stars as Charlie Chaplin, Mary Pickford, and Douglas Fairbanks were often more popular.

WOMEN

Another change stimulated by the war related to women. During the war they had been permitted for the first time to engage in some occupations previously reserved for men, and, with so many men at the front, it had become more acceptable for respectable women to be seen in public without male escorts. Although many women gave up their jobs, willingly or unwillingly, when the veterans returned, and there was some reversion to prewar attitudes toward women, the war nevertheless sparked at least some changes that were more lasting. For example, many women who during the war had become office typists remained on the job. Women also secured the right to vote in a number of nations. Great Britain enfranchised most women over 30 in 1918 (reduced to 21 and over in 1928), and German women got the vote in 1919; in France and southern Europe, however, it would take another generation. During the 1920s it became more common to see women smoking and drinking in public. In addition, Soviet Russia's proclamation of the emancipation and equality of women (see Chapter 10), though far from fulfilled, at least helped challenge more traditional views of gender.

---

[1]*The Revolt of the Masses.* 25th ed. (New York: W. W. Norton, 1957), p. 18.

CULTURAL DEVELOPMENTS

The challenge to traditional views was also apparent in the whole realm of culture. While fighting men were still in the trenches, a group known as dadaists founded an artistic and literary movement in Zurich, Switzerland, that for a short time symbolized disenchantment with all the old values. One of the founders wrote, "I loathe fat objectivity and harmony" and "Logic was always false." After the war, the dadaists returned to Paris and Berlin and resorted to displays such as reading poetry while ringing bells. When their actions created disbelief, they replied that their audiences were not the only ones who did not understand their actions—they themselves did not.

Dadaism soon gave way to surrealism, an artistic and literary movement begun in France. Influenced by Freud, surrealists expressed the belief that the unconscious world of dreams and fantasies represented a higher, more real, and more significant world than the external one of everyday life. In their writings, paintings, and films, they attempted to portray this unconscious dream world. Although surrealism as a distinct movement ended at the beginning of World War II, surrealist ideas continued to influence writers, artists, and film directors wishing to go beyond traditional realism.

Two writers who reflected the 1920s spirit of challenging traditional forms and experimenting with new ones were the Irishman James Joyce and Gertrude Stein, who had moved to Paris from America before World War I. Joyce's *Ulysses* (1922) was one of the most significant novels of the interwar period. Its stream-of-consciousness technique reflected the author's interest in the subconscious life of his characters. Stein experimented with language that at times seemed as nonsensical as that of dadaism. She was a patron of many artists and writers who made their way to Paris, and her writings were influenced by psychology, art, the new cinema, and her own unconventional personality.

From the beginning to the end of the 1920s, European literature mirrored the disillusionment of the decade. The most influential poet of these years was T. S. Eliot, who was born in the United States but lived in England after 1914. Although his most celebrated poem of the 1920s, "The Waste Land" (1922), is complex and contains many layers of meaning, its words reflect well the desolate spirit that affected so many of the writers and artists of the time. It is also noteworthy that much of the literature and art of the period was incomprehensible to the average person, a further indication of the contempt of many intellectuals of the 1920s for the tastes of the masses.

CHALLENGES FROM THE LEFT AND RIGHT IN EUROPE

With the collapse of the monarchies in Russia, Germany, and Austria-Hungary, champions of democracy hoped that the postwar period might be a golden age. They had been further encouraged by Woodrow Wilson, who had proclaimed in 1917 that the United States would fight "for the right of those who submit to authority to have a voice in their own government." The hope proved to be utopian. Instead, undemocratic movements of the Left and the Right (see glossary), by challenging and at times overcoming fragile democratic institutions, contributed to the instability of the period.

The Marxist revolution in Russia, by encouraging extreme leftist attempts to overthrow existing governments, contributed to Red scares in other European nations. Fear of extreme leftist elements, in turn, often played into the hands of right-wing leaders, who pledged to maintain or restore order. In Barcelona, Spain, in 1923, for example, General Miguel Primo de Rivera crushed a leftist and Catalan separatist rebellion (the separatists in Catalonia had been encouraged by Wilson's call for self-determination) and established a Spanish dictatorship. Three years later, after years of Left-Right conflicts, a Portuguese military group overthrew the legitimate government in Portugal.

Fascist Italy

The most important and successful right-wing movement of the immediate postwar years was that of the Italian Fascist Benito Mussolini. Before the war, Mussolini had been one of Italy's most prominent socialists and the editor of the official Socialist Party newspaper. In addition to the ideas of Karl Marx, those of Nietzsche also strongly influenced him. "To comprehend Nietzsche," he wrote in 1908, "we must imagine a new race of 'free spirits,' strengthened in war . . . spirits endowed with a sort of sublime perversity, spirits that will free us from the love of our neighbor." Such macho statements were typical of Mussolini, who also thought of himself as a virile man (he reportedly had 169 mistresses during his lifetime). He also said that "war is to man as maternity is to woman" and "the Italians must learn to grow less likeable and to become hard, implacable, and full of hatred."

Shortly after the outbreak of World War I, Mussolini's call for Italian participation on the side of France and Great Britain led the Italian Socialist Party to expel him. He then became the editor of his own newspaper and continued a campaign for Italian intervention. Soon after Italy entered the war in 1915, Mussolini was sent to the front but did not see combat. After the war, he emerged as the leader of a group whose members soon came to be known as Fascists after they had labeled themselves *Fasci di Combattimento,* meaning "combat groups."

A number of factors explain how Mussolini was able to rise from the leader of a small group of malcontents to the legitimate head of the Italian government by late 1922. Although Italy possessed a parliamentary system, it did not have a strong democratic tradition. After the war its prime ministers and the Chamber of Deputies had to deal with a number of serious problems, including an inflation rate that by 1920 had reduced the lira to one-fifth of its prewar value. Like other nations, Italy faced the difficulty of reintegrating veterans into its society and economy and of returning to peacetime norms. In addition, the government had to contend with the anger of those disappointed over the failure of Italy to gain more territory from the postwar settlements.

Mussolini and his black-shirted Fascists helped to magnify these problems and added others of their own. Aided by the alarm created by strikes and land seizures in 1919 and 1920, Mussolini played on the fears of communism and socialism shared by those afraid of losing their property and by those opposed to Marxist atheism. The Fascists attacked and at times killed their leftist opponents. Semilawlessness soon existed as violence countered violence. Many of the rich and powerful were willing to countenance Fascist brutality in the hope that it would destroy leftist forces. In the face of these difficulties, the various parties in the Chamber of Deputies found it increasingly difficult to work together. Finally, confronted with the threat of Fascist

MUSSOLINI BECOMES PRIME MINISTER, 1922

A defiant-looking Mussolini with some of his followers before assuming power in 1922.

bands marching on Rome, Victor Emmanuel III, the constitutional monarch, asked Mussolini to form a new government in 1922.

Since his party still possessed only a small number of representatives in the Chamber of Deputies, Mussolini's first government included only 4 Fascists among the 14 ministers. Undoubtedly, some Italians hoped that, once saddled with the responsibilities of government, Mussolini and his followers would become more moderate. Mussolini did consolidate his power cautiously, but his goal was still authoritarian government. For a short period, other parties continued to criticize the Fascists. In May 1924, for example, the Socialist deputy Giacomo Matteotti stood up in the Chamber of Deputies, amidst flying inkwells and insults, and accused the Fascists of rigging the recent elections and of resorting to murdering their political opponents. When he finished, he said to a colleague, "Now you may write the eulogy for my funeral." Eleven days later, he was stabbed to death by a Fascist gang. The public outrage that followed created the most serious crisis Mussolini had yet faced. Once again, however, the other political parties were unable to effectively move against Mussolini, and by 1925 all political parties except the Fascists were outlawed.

The Weimar Republic and Threats to Its Existence

REASONS FOR INSTABILITY

In February 1919 a Constituent Assembly was convened at Weimar, Germany. By July it had adopted a democratic constitution, which remained in effect until Hitler began circumventing it in 1933. Both before and after adoption of the constitution, political conditions remained in a state of flux. Political instability was partly a result of the Weimar system of representation: Parties in the Reichstag (lower house of parliament) received seats in proportion to the votes each had gained in general elections. This system virtually ensured a multiplicity of parties and made coalition governments almost inevitable. As was often the case in other European nations with similar systems, Weimar coalition governments disintegrated quickly. The moderate Socialist Friedrich Ebert was president from 1919 until 1925, but cabinets under several chancellors changed on the average of once a year.

Stability was also difficult to achieve in Germany because of Germans' resentment of the terms of the Versailles treaty. The Right, as well as many politically moderate Germans, believed their nation had not really been defeated but in fact had been tricked by the Allies or betrayed by their own leaders. Extreme right-wing enemies of the republic insisted that the military had been betrayed in World War I by some of the same politicians who now supported the new form of government, and these extremists insisted that the Versailles treaty could have been resisted by again taking up arms. Partly in an effort to discredit further attacks from the Right, but also because most Germans were indignant regarding the treaty, many German politicians did their best to prevent its full enforcement. This undermining of the treaty fueled continual tensions with the Versailles "winners," which in turn further contributed to the unsettled conditions in Germany, especially before 1924.

Instability also resulted from the lack of any strong tradition of democracy and because parties on the extreme Right and Left opposed both the leadership of various moderate coalitions and the Weimar constitution itself. In January 1919 disturbances involving leftists broke out in Berlin, after which two leading German Communists, Rosa Luxemburg and Karl Liebknecht, were murdered. Later in 1919, Communists briefly established a government in Bavaria until German regular troops and *Freikorps* (free corps) volunteers ended the takeover. In 1920 German leftist forces were put down in the Ruhr mining districts.

The far Right also attempted coups. In March 1920 Berlin was taken over for several days by rightist military forces during the Kapp Putsch. The putsch failed when the Socialist Party and trade unions began a general strike. In 1923 in Munich, the former army corporal Adolf Hitler unsuccessfully attempted to topple both the local Bavarian and the German Republic governments. Although not as clearly on the Right as he would later become, he was certainly strongly opposed to Communists and the far Left. Born in 1889, the son of a minor Austrian customs official, he failed to graduate from high school and went to Vienna hoping to enter art school. He was unsuccessful, but he remained in the Austro-Hungarian capital, living an impoverished life as a creator of advertising cards and small paintings. In 1913 he left Vienna for Munich, Germany. When World War I broke out, he enlisted in the German army and was several times wounded and decorated for bravery.

After the war, Hitler became involved with a small, rather insignificant nationalistic political group in Munich that called itself the German Workers' Party. Within a couple of years he became its Führer, or leader. After leading the unsuccessful "Beer-Hall Putsch" in Munich in 1923, he spent nine months in prison. He used the time to write *Mein Kampf (My Struggle),* a work he originally wished to call *Four and*

HITLER AND THE NAZIS

a Half Years of Struggle against Lies, Stupidity, and Cowardice. In it he spelled out his nationalism, anti-Semitism, and racism. After his release from prison he continued to build up his party, by then called the National Socialist German Workers' (Nazi) Party. In the late 1920s, however, it did not seem to be a major threat because political conditions appeared more stable. In the 1928 Reichstag elections, the Nazis, then a party of some 108,000 paid members, won only about 3 percent of the total vote. But by 1930 the onset of the Great Depression and continued national resentment over the Versailles treaty brought about impressive Nazi gains in the Reichstag elections; the Nazis gained 18 percent of the vote and became the second-largest party in that body.

Eastern Europe

In eastern Europe, with its plethora of new states and ethnic rivalries and grievances, democracy was also on unsettled soil. Two basic economic difficulties further contributed to the region's problems: rural overpopulation and small markets for exports, a problem exacerbated by rising foreign tariffs. In 1919, Communists briefly established a government in Hungary until Romanian troops helped to oust it. A non-democratic right-wing government under Admiral N. Horthy took its place, and right-wing forces remained in power in Hungary throughout the interwar period. In Poland, another military man, Marshal Józef Pilsudski, curtailed his country's experiment in democracy when he took over power in 1926 and ruled, formally or informally, until his death in 1935. In Bulgaria, Romania, and Yugoslavia earlier attempts at more democratic rule were abandoned, and authoritarian monarchical governments were in place by the end of the decade. Among the larger eastern European states, Czechoslovakia, under President Masaryk, adapted best to democracy, but its large German minority would become a major problem when Hitler attempted to unite all Germans in the late 1930s.

THE UNITED KINGDOM AND FRANCE

The biggest problem facing the United Kingdom (Great Britain and Ireland) at the end of World War I was the Irish quest for independence. The Catholic Irish majority on the island had long regarded the Protestant British rulers and Scots-Irish minority as exploiters and religious enemies. The Irish had already been agitating for the right to run their own internal affairs (Home Rule) for about 50 years. A Home Rule bill was enacted in 1914, but because of the outbreak of the war and resistance among Protestants in northern Ireland, the British government decided not to put it into effect until the hostilities ended. After the British government executed 14 ringleaders in 1916 for attempting an uprising, the radical Sinn Fein Party, with Eamon De Valera at its head, became more popular among the Irish.

CONFLICT IN IRELAND

In December 1918 the Sinn Fein Party won a smashing victory in the election of Irish members to the British Parliament. The next month, its leaders organized an Irish parliament of their own and declared their independence from Great

Britain. The British, supported by the Protestants, sent in forces to crush the rebels. A vicious cycle of violent actions, marked by bombs, arson, and torture, followed. In December 1921 the British government and rebel leaders signed a treaty that recognized the Irish Free State, a self-governing dominion comprising most of Ireland. Much of Ulster in the north, where the Protestants were dominant, remained a part of Great Britain.

The trouble was still not over. Some of the Irish nationalists, led by De Valera, were not willing to write off Northern Ireland or accept anything other than complete independence and thus continued to wage an unsuccessful civil war until De Valera's arrest in 1923. De Valera later returned and became the outstanding figure in Irish politics for decades. After World War II, the Republic of Ireland declared its complete independence. Northern Ireland, with its Protestant majority, continued to be united with Great Britain. The Catholic minority in Northern Ireland, however, opposed the union with Great Britain and wanted to be incorporated into the Republic of Ireland. The Irish question remained unanswered.

BRITISH POLITICS AND ECONOMICS

In Great Britain itself Liberals and Conservatives dominated the political process until late 1923, when a split in the Liberal Party enabled the Labour Party to become the second largest in the country. The following year Britain's first Labour government came to power, under Ramsay MacDonald, but it was soundly defeated in a general election later that year. A forged letter, supposedly from the Soviet Comintern leader (G. Zinoviev), that encouraged the British to revolt against their government aided the Conservative victory. The party's leader, Stanley Baldwin, remained in power for the next five years. Baldwin prided himself on being a plain and ordinary man, full of common sense. Under the Conservatives, the British appeared to be returning to happier times; the general standard of living went up, and the state provided even more benefits for the old, widowed, orphaned, and unemployed. But Britain's economic foundation was weak. Basic industries such as iron and steel, coal, cotton, and shipbuilding were declining as a result of a combination of foreign competition, outdated business practices and technology, and legislation that prohibited general strikes and hampered the unionization of civil servants.

FRENCH POLITICS AND ECONOMICS

In France, with its many political parties and coalition governments, politics was less stable. After Edouard Herriot, the leader of the Radical Socialist Party, had governed for 10 months in 1924–1925, six successive governments followed each other in the period from April 1925 to July 1926, most of them brought down when they failed to deal with inflation. Only in July 1926, when Raymond Poincaré became prime minister of a broad-based National Union Coalition, was inflation brought under control. Poincaré's government lasted three years, a long time in French politics, and was instrumental in bringing to France a measure of the calm that characterized the last part of the decade. Unfortunately for France, fundamental problems remained. The temporary equilibrium was largely a result of Poincaré's leadership rather than of change in the basically rickety French political system. In addition, French industry could not successfully compete with German industry, and both its industry and its agriculture remained inefficient compared to those of the United States.

FRANCE'S SEARCH FOR SECURITY
AND EUROPE'S INTERNATIONAL RELATIONS

In international affairs, France's search for security was significant. France had fought two wars with Germany in 50 years and had twice seen German soldiers occupy its lands. The cost in lives and economic damage had been great. Yet Germany, despite its defeat in World War I, remained a potentially stronger nation, with a population considerably larger than that of France. Growing British and French differences over treatment of Germany, as well as other international issues, left the French in an especially difficult position. Great Britain's pledge to support France if Germany attacked in the future had lapsed when the United States had failed to ratify a similar commitment. Great Britain feared German resurgence less than France did and seemed more concerned with restoring prewar trade with Germany. Britain therefore was more willing than France to moderate the level of German reparations payments. Neither the League of Nations, dominated by the Europeans but with no real power, nor subsequent treaties signed with eastern European nations offered much reassurance to French anxieties concerning German revitalization.

FRENCH-GERMAN RELATIONS IN THE EARLY 1920s

Meanwhile, France became increasingly frustrated by German attempts to evade the Versailles treaty. Because of opposition to the treaty at home, and because German statesmen also sensed a lack of Allied unity, Germany had no reservations about trying to subvert it. Germany attempted to evade full compliance with disarmament provisions, failed to comply with some boundary commission decisions, and failed to meet many of its reparations payments on schedule. In 1922, Germany's Rapallo Agreement with Russia, which reduced Germany's diplomatic isolation, caused further French fears.

Against the background of these events, and because of the insistence of the United States that Allied nations repay large wartime loans, France, Belgium, and Italy occupied the Ruhr industrial region in early 1923 when Germany failed to meet a reparations obligation. The Germans in the Ruhr responded with passive resistance, which inadvertently contributed to the already unstable German currency. As the economy faltered and inflation skyrocketed—paying a billion marks for a restaurant meal was not unusual—the Allies held firm, and the German government of Wilhelm Cuno collapsed. The French encouraged separatist movements in the occupied territories, and the Soviet-dominated Comintern helped stir up unrest in central Germany.

WASHINGTON NAVAL CONFERENCE

France's insecurity and Germany's political and economic weakness were a few indications that Europe's global position had weakened during the war. A series of international naval treaties provided further evidence. The major naval powers feared that a new naval shipbuilding race would escalate tensions and increase expenses. In particular, many nations were concerned about the aggressive actions of Japan. The United States invited delegates from eight other nations to attend a conference in Washington, and during 1921 and 1922 several agreements were worked out. One agreement was the Five-Power Naval Treaty, which provided for scrapping 70 ships, a 10-year moratorium on new construction of capital ships, and a global tonnage ratio for capital ships (United States, 5; Great Britain, 5; Japan, 3; France, 1.75; and Italy, 1.75). The treaty also provided for a cessation of further naval fortifications in most of the Pacific area. Another agreement, the Four-Power Treaty, ended the Anglo-Japanese Alliance and replaced it with an agreement among the United States, Great Britain, Japan, and France for mutual consultation in case of threats to the security of any territories belonging to any of them. The Nine-Power Treaty provided for continuation of the Open Door policy and preservation of China's sovereignty but continued the unequal treaties of the imperialist era. In addition, Japan agreed to make a compensated, gradual withdrawal from the Shantung Peninsula in China and also to remove its troops from Siberia.

The agreements made in Washington in effect recognized that World War I had weakened the global power of Europe and augmented the military strength of the United States and Japan. In particular, in return for curbing aggressive tendencies on the Asian mainland, Japan gained de facto recognition as the dominant naval power in Asian waters.

By 1924–1925, however, Europe was at least more stable than in the immediate postwar years. The conflicts in Ireland and Russia were now over, and the Soviet Union, in the midst of its New Economic Policy, seemed less threatening than it had earlier. In 1924 Britain, France, and Italy established official diplomatic relations with it. In Germany, Chancellor Gustav Stresemann not only helped stabilize the currency but also instituted a foreign policy that appeared to be more accommodating than that of his predecessors. After being replaced as chancellor in November 1923—after only 100 days—he remained in various cabinets as foreign minister until his death in 1929. Stresemann helped Germany to improve relations with the former Allies and to scale down reparations payments. The latter accomplishment was aided by the Dawes Plan of 1924, which also provided for U.S. loans, and the Young Plan of 1929.

For many, the Locarno treaties of 1925 represented the greatest sign of hope for a more tranquil era. The most important of these treaties confirmed the existing Franco-German and Belgian-German frontiers and was guaranteed by Great Britain and Italy. Germany, France, Belgium, Poland, and Czechoslovakia also signed a series of agreements promising to submit any conflict to arbitration. Finally, France signed treaties with Poland and Czechoslovakia providing for mutual assistance in case of a German attack.

LOCARNO TREATIES

Although it might appear that the treaties signified no great gain for Germany, the rewards were significant. As the price for apparent German willingness to accept the western frontier imposed on it by the Versailles treaty, France agreed to give way on a number of points that considerably weakened its powers of coercion over Germany. The right of the Allies to ensure Germany's compliance with the disarmament provisions of Versailles now became almost meaningless. The evacuation of part of the Rhineland, which was scheduled to occur in 1925, went forward. Germany was also to join the League of Nations and to be given a permanent seat on its Council. Finally, it was significant that Germany refused at Locarno to confirm its eastern borders, a situation that increased the fears of Czechoslovakia and Poland and helped drive them into the arms of the French.

In 1926 Stresemann and the French and British foreign ministers, Aristide Briand and Austen Chamberlain, were all awarded the Nobel Prize for Peace for their Locarno efforts. Europeans talked of the new spirit of conciliation in the air. This "spirit of Locarno" was further evidenced in 1928 when U.S. Secretary of State Frank Kellogg joined Briand in creating the Kellogg-Briand Pact, in which 64 nations renounced war as an "instrument of national policy." Paradoxically, the same nations reiterated their right to take up arms in self-defense.

ILLUSORY STABILITY

Despite all these agreements, international stability proved illusory. Europe's economic recovery had in general been sluggish. Germany's economy and reparations payments depended partly on U.S. loans. Thus, a serious curtailment of the U.S. loans could have a ripple effect on Germany and the European Allies. Between a Germany bent on revision of the Treaty of Versailles and a France attempting to maintain its security, the potential for serious conflict remained. Germany's unwillingness at Locarno to agree that its eastern frontiers were permanent was also an ill omen.

In addition, the Washington Naval Conference agreements included no guarantee that the signatories would continue to honor them once they no longer felt it was in their interest to do so. The Kellogg-Briand Pact contained no provisions for dealing with aggression. In fact, it was little more than a pious wish, an "international kiss," in the words of one U.S. senator. Attempts in the late 1920s and early 1930s to deal with concrete issues of aggression and disarmament also proved fruitless.

S U M M A R Y

The postwar settlements pleased some nations, angered others, and left still others with decidedly mixed feelings. The new nations of eastern Europe—Finland, Estonia, Latvia, Lithuania, Poland, Czechoslovakia, and Yugoslavia—gained the most from the conflict: their independence. The defeated nations, particularly Germany, which faced various territorial losses, the payment of reparations, and other stipulations such as occupation of the Rhineland, were the most dissatisfied.

The immediate postwar years presented Europe with problems in addition to its weakened global position. It had to deal with refugees, emigrants, minorities, the reintegration of soldiers into a peacetime economy, reparations, the repayment of loans, unemployment, inflation, social and cultural adjustments, armed conflict in Russia and Ireland, and challenges from the Left and the Right to fragile democratic governments. For the time being, some governments were able to withstand the pressure, but others were not; the most notable case was that of Italy, where Mussolini came to power in 1922.

By the middle and latter part of the decade, most of the major powers appeared to be less troubled, as their economies apparently recovered. Agreements such as the Washington Naval Conference treaties, the Locarno treaties, and the Kellogg-Briand Pact all promised greater international equilibrium. Governments also seemed more stable. Stresemann remained Germany's foreign minister from 1923 to 1929, Baldwin was prime minister in Great Britain from 1924 to 1929, and Poincaré was prime minister in France from 1926 to 1929.

Underneath the apparent stabilizing developments of the late 1920s, however, there were problems. The economic underpinnings of many nations remained weak, and in Europe allegiance to democratic political forms was tentative. German resentment toward the Allies also was never far below the surface. All the international agreements in turn depended largely on the domestic stability and prosperity of the signatories, as well as continuing successful diplomacy. Beginning in 1929 and continuing into the 1930s, these problems manifested themselves in depression, aggression, and, finally, total war. The French writer Romain Rolland was more prophetic than he knew when on June 23, 1919, he wrote, "Sad peace! Laughable interlude between the massacres of peoples!"

SUGGESTED SOURCES

Berend, Ivan T. *Decades of Crisis: Central and Eastern Europe before World War II.* 1998. Pts. 1 and 2. Good overview of various aspects of the region up to the Great Depression.*

Bessel, Richard. *Germany after the First World War.* 1995. An excellent work by a leading scholar on the aftereffects of World War I for Weimar Germany.*

Boemeke, Manfred F., Gerald D. Feldman, and Elisabeth Glaser-Schmidt, eds. *The Treaty of Versailles: A Reassessment after 75 Years.* 1998. Twenty-six essays by a group of international scholars provide a comprehensive reexamination of various aspects of the end of the war, the Paris Peace Conference, and the Treaty of Versailles.

Bosworth, R. J. B. *Mussolini.* 2002. The best English-language biography.*

The Conformist. 1970. A Bertolucci film set in Mussolini's Italy. (Also available on video.)

Evans, Richard J. *The Coming of the Third Reich.* 2004. Chaps. 1–3. The first of three projected volumes, this volume covers the period up to and including Hitler's assumption and solidifying of power in 1933.*

Graves, Robert, and Alan Hodge. *The Long Week-End.* 1936. An interesting portrayal of British life and customs in the interwar period.*

Klingaman, William K. *1919: The Year Our World Began.* 1987. A vivid political, social, and cultural narrative of the world's main events and personalities in 1919.*

Kolb, Eberhard. *The Weimar Republic.* 1988. A good overview by a German scholar.*

MacMillan, Margaret. *Paris 1919: Six Months That Changed the World.* 2002. A detailed analysis and overview that actually deals with diplomatic history from 1918 to 1923 and asserts that the peacemakers in Paris did a better job than sometimes acknowledged.*

Marks, Sally. *The Illusion of Peace: International Relations in Europe, 1919–1933.* 2nd ed. 2003. A solid historical overview of European international relations in an era of shifting power alliances.*

Nicolson, Harold. *Peacemaking, 1919.* 1933. The highly personal memoirs of a British participant.*

O'Flaherty, Liam. *The Informer.* 1925. A classic novel dealing with the Irish civil war.* (Also an award-winning film directed by John Ford.)

Passmore, Kevin, ed. *Women, Gender, Fascism in Europe, 1919–45.* 2003. A book of essays dealing with women and fascism in numerous countries.*

Sharp, Alan. *The Versailles Settlement: Peacemaking in Paris, 1919.* 1991. A brief account that takes a multinational approach to the Paris, Peace Conference.*

Shirer, William L. *20th Century Journey.* 1985. More than 300 pages are devoted to the 1920s in this U.S. journalist's account of experiences in the United States and in Paris, London, and other European cities.*

Silone, Ignazio. *Fontamara.* 1934. A leading Italian novelist's depiction of conflict in the 1920s between the village of Fontamara and Mussolini's Fascists.*

Steiner, Zara. *The Lights That Failed: European International History, 1919–1933.* 2005. A comprehensive look at European interwar developments and relations in the pre-Nazi period.

Walworth, Arthur. *Wilson and His Peacemakers.* 1986. A first-rate, comprehensive narrative history of Wilson at the Paris Peace Conference.

Willett, John. *Art and Politics in the Weimar Period: The New Sobriety, 1917–1933.* 1996. An excellent overview of the dynamic world of Weimar arts and politics, with numerous photos and illustrations.*

Wright, Jonathan. *Gustav Stresemann: Weimar's Greatest Statesman.* 2002. An excellent biography of Germany's leading statesman of the 1920s by an English scholar.*

WEB SOURCES

www.yale.edu/lawweb/avalon/imt/menu.htm. This Yale Law School site (The Avalon Project) provides the text of the Treaty of Versailles.

www.fordham.edu/halsall/mod/modsbook42.html. This Fordham site provides links to materials on fascism in Europe.

---

*Paperback available.

⑥Economic and Social Upheaval in the Americas

From the 1910s through the 1930s, the Western Hemisphere was largely spared the horrors of total war—except for Mexico, which became engulfed in the vast social convulsion of the Mexican Revolution, whose shock waves reverberated through the Americas well into the 1920s and after. The United States not only escaped the destruction of World War I but profited immensely from it, emerging from Europe's cataclysm as the world's preeminent economic and military power. "America at the close of the Great War was a Cinderella magically clothed in the most stunning dress at the ball," writes one historian, "a ball to which Cinderella had not even been invited; immense gains with no visible price tag seemed to be the American destiny."[1] But in the Western Hemisphere, such dominance did carry a price. By the late 1920s anti-Yankee sentiment mushroomed throughout Latin America, compelling the United States to retreat from its policy of direct military intervention in the Caribbean basin (see map in Chapter 5).

While the 1920s brought the appearance of permanently rising prosperity, the 1930s shattered the illusion, plunging the hemisphere into the economic nightmare of the Great Depression. As exports plummeted and unemployment soared, many Latin American economies turned inward, becoming more self-sufficient and internally integrated. Populist politics turned more dictatorial, as a new generation of leaders fanned the flames of economic nationalism and gained the support of urban groups with nationalist rhetoric and government patronage. In this age of global economic crisis and the antiliberal, antidemocratic ideologies of fascism and communism, leaders throughout the hemisphere gravitated rightward toward fascism, leftward toward socialism, or borrowed from both, with strong executives directing social welfare states. Most of the Americas came under the rule of dictatorships. The United States and Canada moved slightly left, Mexico even more so, developing far more activist and interventionist governments.

---

[1] Ann Douglass, *Terrible Honesty: Mongrel Manhattan in the 1920s* (New York: Noonday Press, 1996), p. 4.

THE UNITED STATES IN THE INTERWAR YEARS: BUST TO BOOM TO BUST

The U.S. Senate Rejects the Treaty of Versailles

When President Wilson returned from the Paris Peace Conference, he saw the League of Nations as his administration's crowning achievement. But many in the U.S. Senate opposed Article 10 of the Treaty of Versailles, which obliged members of the League of Nations to repel aggression against other League members by means "the Council shall advise." To preserve U.S. freedom of action in world affairs, many senators insisted that reservations be added to the treaty, particularly that Congress must approve any U.S. involvement in League-sponsored actions to curb aggression.

But President Wilson refused to compromise. Feverishly working to mobilize support for the League, in September 1919 he suffered a debilitating stroke. When the treaty came up for a vote in November, its Senate supporters failed to muster the constitutional two-thirds majority. Although in 1921 the United States did sign a separate treaty with Germany that ratified most of the Versailles treaty's provisions, it never joined the League of Nations. Without U.S. membership, that body would prove to be a toothless tiger.

Postwar Labor Unrest, Recession, and Racial Discord

SOCIAL AND POLITICAL UNREST

Even before the Senate rejected the Versailles treaty, raging postwar inflation had wiped out the modest gains workers had made during the war, leading in 1919 to a wave of labor unrest. In January a general strike virtually shut down Seattle. In September, Boston police walked out because the city refused to recognize their union. But the biggest strike, beginning in September, was among 350,000 steelworkers in the Northeast and Midwest, who demanded an 8-hour day (down from 12 hours a day, 7 days a week, the industry standard) and the right to bargain collectively. The strike, which failed, dragged on until early 1920. Altogether some 4 million workers—roughly one-fifth of the nation's labor force, including some 400,000 miners across the coalfields of Appalachia—participated in strikes in 1919. Unrelated to these strikes were a small number of bombings in the spring of 1919, and the Post Office's interception of several dozen bomb-laden packages addressed to leading businessmen and politicians.

THE FIRST RED SCARE

This was only two years after the Bolsheviks had seized power in Russia, and the same year that the Soviet government established the Communist International (or Comintern). The Bolshevik Revolution provided a convenient pretext for the U.S. government's intolerance of workers' demands for collective rights. Beginning in early 1920, U.S. Attorney General A. Mitchell Palmer and his ambitious young assistant J. Edgar Hoover orchestrated a "Red Scare," arresting more than 6,000 suspected communists and anarchists and summarily deporting some 500 non-U.S. citizens. In 1921, two Italian anarchists, Nicola Sacco and Bartolomeo Vanzetti, were convicted of robbery and murder and sentenced to death. Until their execution in Boston in August 1927, their case proved a *cause célèbre* throughout much of the Atlantic world.

In late 1920 the inflationary spiral came to a screeching halt, as consumer demand shriveled and unemployment skyrocketed. In 1920–1921, some 5 million U.S. workers lost their jobs, 100,000 businesses went belly-up, and the national economy shrank by 10 percent. Recovery was slow, but after another smaller recession in 1923, the manufacturing economy picked up steam, led by the steel and automobile industries. The year 1920 also marked a demographic watershed, with urban dwellers outnumbering rural dwellers for the first time in U.S. history.

The postwar economic hard times exacerbated racism against African Americans, half a million of whom had migrated to cities in the North, South, and West during and after the war. During the "red summer" of 1919 (called "red" not for communism but for all the blood that was spilled), more than 250 blacks were killed by white mobs, and more than 70 blacks, some returning war veterans, were lynched in the South. In 1921 in Tulsa, Oklahoma, in the deadliest race riot in U.S. history, rampaging mobs killed 300 blacks and left 10,000 homeless. One response to the relentless assertion of white supremacy was a brand of black nationalism called Garveyism, led by the Jamaican immigrant Marcus Garvey. His Universal Negro Improvement Association called for blacks to reject assimilation into white society and to cultivate racial and cultural pride. In the early 1920s the movement grew rapidly, but declined after its leader was charged with business fraud and deported in 1925, though its legacy endured.

In response to the massive influx of southern and eastern Europeans and the Great Migration of African Americans, nativist U.S. citizens pressured Congress to restrict immigration of "undesirable" populations. They succeeded in 1921 and again in 1924. The National Origins Act of 1924 banned all immigrants from East Asia. It also capped European immigrants at 150,000 per year and imposed annual quotas on European immigrants amounting to 2 percent of each nationality in the United States in 1890—a time when there were far fewer people from southern and eastern Europe and the Mediterranean. The law did not address immigration from the Western Hemisphere, leading to continued large influxes of Latin Americans and Canadians.

This period also saw the meteoric resurgence of the Ku Klux Klan, partly inspired by D. W. Griffith's landmark and blatantly racist film, *The Birth of a Nation* (1915), which hailed the Klan as the savior of the Union and southern white womanhood. The Klan's slogan, "100% Americanism," expressed its antiblack, anti-Mexican, anti-Catholic, anti-Semitic, and antiforeign version of patriotism. At its peak in 1924–1925, with over 4.5 million members nationwide, the Klan vied for control of the Democratic Party and staged a massive march on the nation's capital before collapsing from scandals and internal squabbles. Prohibition, established in 1919 by the 18th Amendment, also reflected the wide cultural divide between immigrants and city dwellers, who tended to be "wet" (opposed Prohibition) and the native-born in small towns and rural areas, who tended to be "dry" (supported Prohibition) and to defend fundamentalist Protestant values.

The role of women in U.S. society was also changing. With the ratification of the 19th Amendment in 1920 granting women the right to vote, women's growing independence became closely linked to their rising participation in the workforce, the

ECONOMIC DOWNTURN

WHITE VIOLENCE AND BLACK RESPONSES

IMMIGRATION RESTRICTIONS

CONSERVATIVE ASCENDENCY

CHANGES FOR WOMEN

emergence of mass consumer culture, and the growing availability of contraception. In 1920 women comprised 20 percent of the labor force and 77 percent of single women worked outside the home, in a labor market that remained heavily segregated by gender. Fertility rates also fell, from an average of 3.6 children in 1900 to 2.5 in 1930.

From the Roaring Twenties to the Great Depression

A MASS CONSUMER SOCIETY

After 1923, the U.S. industrial economy entered a period of sustained growth. Manufacturing output rose by an average of 10 percent per year, inflation dipped to near zero, and the middle class expanded. Automobiles became integral to the U.S. economy and culture, while a vast array of new consumer goods—from washing machines and radios to telephones, vacuum cleaners, and refrigerators, many bought on credit—found their way into millions of homes. Three Republican administrations under Presidents Warren G. Harding, Calvin Coolidge, and Herbert Hoover rejected the Progressive emphasis on activist government to pursue a program of minimal business regulation, low taxes, and high tariffs. As Coolidge remarked, "The chief business of the American people is business." The *Wall Street Journal* aptly noted, "Never before, here or anywhere else, has a government been so completely fused with business," while one stockbroker later recalled, "God, J. P. Morgan, and the Republican Party were going to keep everything going forever."

STRUCTURAL ECONOMIC WEAKNESSES

Despite the apparent prosperity, the U.S. economy exhibited some severe structural weaknesses. Many workers faced wage cuts and layoffs in the depressed railroad, textile, and coal industries. Only workers in skilled trades benefited from unionization, a fraction of the total workforce. In the South, women and children labored in textile mills for up to 60 hours a week for only a few cents per hour. The nation's farmers were in deep trouble, with high mortgages, low crop prices, and increased global competition. Some large landowners mechanized to save money, but many tenants and sharecroppers lost their livelihoods and small farmers their farms.

But the biggest long-term structural problem was that production far exceeded consumption. In a nutshell, companies did not pay workers enough money to buy all the goods the economy produced, leading to huge inventory pileups and an overreliance on credit. For each individual company, keeping workers' wages as low as possible maximized profits and thus made good economic sense. For all companies in general, and the economy as a whole, it was a recipe for disaster. By the late 1920s, most families had no savings, with 4 out of 10 living in poverty. Meanwhile, the wealthiest 1 percent received nearly 20 percent of all income, while the wealthiest 5 percent took home more than the bottom 60 percent—and the gaps were widening.

The overdependence on credit extended to the stock market. No laws controlled the amount of stock—essentially a chunk of a company—that could be bought on credit. Brokers and speculators often bought stock "on the margin," paying 10 percent or less of the stock's market value and putting the remaining 90 percent on credit. If stock prices suddenly dropped, stock owners could easily owe huge sums of money they did not have. The whole structure resembled a house of cards, but few seemed worried. "Stocks have reached a permanently high plateau," commented one distinguished professor of economics on October 17, 1929.

A week later, on Black Thursday, October 24, 1929, the Wall Street stock market began to collapse, sending the United States headlong into a full-fledged crisis. There was a panic to sell, but no one to buy. Within hours most speculators were ruined. Although the stock market crash did not cause the Great Depression in the United States, it was its main short-term trigger. For the next three years, despite repeated assurances from President Hoover, the economy experienced a devastating downward spiral of bankruptcies, bank failures, and mass unemployment—25 percent by the most conservative estimates. The federal government's response under Hoover's leadership was to grant tax cuts to the wealthy and increase tariffs, policies that made a catastrophic situation even worse.

THE GREAT STOCK MARKET CRASH

The New Deal

In the 1932 presidential campaign, Democrat Franklin Delano Roosevelt (FDR) ran on a platform he called "a New Deal for the American people." He was not exactly sure what he meant by the phrase, and neither were the nearly 23 million men and women—nearly 58 percent of voters—who swept him into office. But he had an ebullience of spirit and a willingness to innovate that meshed with the dire situation the nation confronted. Roosevelt was a reformer, not a revolutionary, who wished to tame and restrain capitalism in order to save it. "The only thing we have to fear is fear itself," he boldly announced to an anxious nation on taking office, and it was just what most U.S. citizens wanted and needed to hear.

President Franklin D. Roosevelt projects a cheerful image during the New Deal.

THE FIRST NEW DEAL

Never in U.S. history has the federal government so quickly and so dramatically expanded its role in the everyday lives of ordinary people. "Our greatest primary task is to put people to work," declared Roosevelt, and his administration was willing to run up huge budget deficits to do it. His administration's first 100 days saw the passage of a dizzying array of government programs designed to put money into people's pockets and rekindle their sense of dignity and self-worth. Two days after taking office FDR announced a four-day "bank holiday," assuring his radio listeners that banks would be safe when they reopened. They were. Soon after reforming the banking system and stock market he created the National Recovery Administration (NRA) to improve wages and working conditions and protect consumers. Hastily written and often benefiting big business, the NRA codes were later struck down by the Supreme Court.

Opposed in principle to the dole—handing out money to people in need—Roosevelt instead created a series of public works programs, most prominently the Civilian Conservation Corps (CCC) and the Public Works Administration (PWA), later replaced by the Works Progress Administration (WPA). Thousands of New Deal–era parks, bridges, water towers, and other public works can still be found across the United States. The Agricultural Adjustment Act (AAA) paid farmers not to produce—which made good economic sense, going to the root of the problem of overproduction that had long plagued farmers. But the payments were earmarked for landowners only, encouraging the eviction of thousands of tenants and sharecroppers.

Some programs combined public works with regional planning, most prominently the Tennessee Valley Authority (TVA). Spanning seven of the nation's poorest states, the TVA built a series of flood control and hydroelectric dams along the Tennessee River, providing abundant work and bountiful cheap electricity. Conservatives blocked its more ambitious social development programs and denounced the government's new role as a public utility and regional planner. Environmentalists later decried the ecological damage wrought by the TVA dams. When analyzed closely, virtually all New Deal programs can be seen to have positive and negative outcomes. Roosevelt was a pragmatist, not a theoretician. If a policy or program seemed to work, he built on it. If it did not, he abandoned it and tried something else.

ECONOMIC DEVASTATION

Despite the vast expansion of the federal government's power and spending, the First New Deal barely dented the nation's mass unemployment. Social conditions worsened, as hunger and destitution ravaged the country. Emblematic of the nation's downward spiral was the Dust Bowl in the nation's southern midsection. Poor land management and a severe drought caused massive dust storms and displaced more than a million farmers, an out-migration poignantly captured in John Steinbeck's novel *The Grapes of Wrath* (1939). Meanwhile, opposition to many New Deal programs mounted, as a conservative Supreme Court struck down many provisions and programs as overextensions of executive branch power. By 1934, the First New Deal was sputtering to a halt. At this point a powerful impetus for change emerged from a very different quarter: the millions of U.S. workers in major mass production industries.

RESURGENT LABOR AND THE WAGNER ACT

In what has been called "labor's great upheaval," workers in the automobile, steel, and other industries demanded not only higher wages and safer working conditions, but a fundamentally new relationship with management—one that guaranteed workers' civil rights, a fair slice of the economic pie, and, especially, their right to bargain collectively. Leading the fight were John L. Lewis and the Congress of Industrial Organizations (CIO). Viewing the AFL as too beholden to industry and disinterested in the plight of noncraft workers, the CIO and its offshoots, the United Auto Workers (UAW) and Steel Workers Organizing Committee (SWOC), were given a huge boost by the 1935 Wagner Act, which finally enshrined into federal law the right of workers to form unions and bargain collectively. Autoworkers' 1936 sit-down strike in Flint, Michigan, still ranks among organized labor's most stunning successes. In its wake, hundreds of thousands of other workers, from rubber workers to waitresses, unionized and struck, not only for higher wages and better working conditions, but for dignity.

Emboldened by Democratic victories in the 1934 midterm elections, FDR launched a Second New Deal. Its focus was economic security, its centerpiece the Social Security Act of 1935. A hybrid federal and local program of unemployment insurance, aid to families with dependent children, and old-age pensions, Social Security represented an abrupt departure from traditional views about the proper role of the federal government in society. Many still consider Social Security the most important and successful of all New Deal programs.

THE SECOND NEW DEAL

After his landslide 1936 reelection, FDR tried to pack the Supreme Court with New Deal supporters. He failed, but afterward the Court was much more willing to uphold key New Deal provisions. In 1937, in response to an economic uptick, he slashed spending for many programs, with disastrous results. Unemployment shot up again, compelling Roosevelt to ask for billions more in appropriations. The idea of deficit spending to "prime the pump" and lead an economy out of depression found theoretical support in British economist John Maynard Keynes's landmark 1936 book, *General Theory of Employment, Interest, and Money*. FDR followed this recipe until the outbreak of World War II in Europe, but employment still increased only very gradually. In the end it was not so much the New Deal as the conflagration of world war that pulled the U.S. economy out of the depression.

The Great Depression and New Deal left a lasting legacy. The realignment of the Democratic Party—a coalition of white southerners and northern ethnics, African Americans, union labor, farmers, and urban dwellers—made it the majority party for the next half century. The resulting welfare state, partial and patchwork by European standards, was a far cry from socialism, yet greatly expanded the role of the federal government in the life of the nation. In the larger context, the people of the United States had affirmed their historic democratic experience. Confronted with near-total economic collapse, they worked out their problems inside the traditional democratic system, rejecting the extremist solutions of both the far Right and the far Left.

LEGACY OF THE NEW DEAL

LATIN AMERICA FROM THE 1910s TO THE 1930s

Revolution and Its Aftermath in Mexico

Just as unrestrained capitalist development helped cause the Great Depression, similar developments fueled the twin engines of the Mexican Revolution (1910–1920). As capitalism expanded from the 1850s, a new middle class of professionals and small business owners emerged. Many wanted not only economic prosperity but a political voice and the rights of citizenship. But the dictatorial regime of Porfirio Díaz (1876–1910) essentially shut this emerging middle class out of politics. Díaz and his cronies controlled the government with an iron fist, refusing to share power or grant political freedoms or civil rights. Under the banner "Order and Progress," the regime stifled free speech and either bought off or crushed organized opposition.

TWIN ENGINES OF REVOLUTION

This was one engine of revolution—an emergent middle class that had been shut out of politics for more than a third of a century. But there was a second engine of revolution, also rooted in the previous decades of capitalist development, that gave the Mexican Revolution its genuinely radical, popular character. From the 1870s, large landowners, or *hacendados*, had been gobbling up the land of small farmers, villages, and Indian communities. By the early 1900s, millions of rural Mexicans had lost their land. People were compelled to either migrate to cities, find work in the rapidly expanding U.S.-dominated mining sector, or toil for pennies per day on land that used to be theirs. Hunger and destitution spread throughout the countryside, and the grievances of the landless and poverty-stricken sharpened and grew.

THE REVOLUTION BEGINS

This steep rise in landlessness and poverty among the rural majority was a second engine of revolution. Thus, what began as a middle-class revolt against Díaz soon escalated into a massive social conflagration. The short-term trigger came in 1910, when a wealthy reformer named Francisco Madero ran for president on a platform calling for "no re-election." Díaz jailed him and easily won reelection. After his release, Madero proclaimed a rebellion. Hoping to topple Díaz and install a moderate reformist government, Madero instead ignited a social explosion, as the poor and marginalized exploited the opportunity opened up by squabbles among the elite. Independent revolts began springing up all over Mexico. In the north, Pancho Villa and Pascual Orozco commanded thousands of miners, cowboys, and railroad workers. Far to the south, in the mostly Indian state of Morelos, Emiliano Zapata led an army of thousands of dispossessed dirt farmers under the banner "Land and Liberty." Dozens of lesser-known leaders added to the confusion and tumult, as did two U.S. interventions—one in 1914 in the port city of Veracruz, and the second in 1917 in the northern deserts.

For nearly 10 years Mexico was set ablaze. By the best estimates, in 1910 Mexico's population was 15 million. Ten years later, in 1920, it stood at 14 million—from 1 to 2 million people dead, and at least 250,000 having migrated north into the United States to escape the endless bouts of bloodshed. Mariano Azuela's novel *The Underdogs* powerfully conveys a sense of the era's confusion and chaos. At the end of the story, the protagonist is asked why he keeps fighting. He tosses a stone down a canyon and stares "pensively into the abyss," remarking, "Look at that stone, how it keeps going. . . ." The violence seemed endless.

THE CONSTITUTION OF 1917

The social charter that finally emerged from this chaos was the Constitution of 1917, which still governs Mexico today. A strongly nationalist and remarkably progressive document for the era, it basically represented the victory of the rising middle class, personified in the "Constitutionalist" leader Venustiano Carranza. The Constitution called for major land reform, and forbade foreigners from owning

A brief moment of unity in the Mexican Revolution: Pancho Villa (center) sits in the presidential chair with Emiliano Zapata beside him (right).

Mexican land or subsoil. In the next decades this provision became a major point of contention with the United States, especially regarding oil. The Constitution also established a bill of rights for labor, granting workers the right to bargain collectively and mandating minimum wages and benefits regardless of gender. It established free universal public education, and sought to secularize the government by subordinating the church to the state—requiring all priests to be native-born, and forbidding priests from voting or criticizing the government from the pulpit. Despite a rising feminist movement, the Constitution did not enfranchise women.

The Mexican Revolution left an enduring legacy. Perhaps most important, it instilled a sense of pride and self-worth among Mexico's poor and indigenous population, as captured in the revolutionary murals of Diego Rivera that still grace the walls of prominent public buildings in Mexico City and elsewhere. A new racialist ideology, *indigenismo,* valorized Mexico's Indian past and glorified the mestizo as humanity's most advanced racial mixture—the "Cosmic Race," in one famous formulation—in a radical departure from the previous four centuries of anti-Indian racism. Similar racialist ideologies emerged in Peru, Brazil, Nicaragua, and other nations with a strong Indian presence, influenced by Mexico but developing from local conditions.

LEGACIES OF REVOLUTION

The Revolution symbolized the promise of dignity and rights for the country's downtrodden, but in practice many of those promises went unfulfilled. After 1917, national leaders interpreted the Constitution differently, so that implementation of its provisions waxed and waned. In the mid-1920s the Catholic Church, enraged by the Constitution, promoted a rebellion among the faithful, the Cristero Revolt, that cost upwards of 80,000 lives before it was suppressed. By the late 1920s, the national government coalesced into a single governing party, which went by different names but eventually became the Institutional Revolutionary Party or PRI, which dominated Mexican politics in a "one-party democracy" for the next six decades.

THE CÁRDENAS REFORMS

With the onset of the Great Depression, mass unemployment and disaffection with the government's tepid land reform led to the 1934 election of Mexico's most popular twentieth-century president, Lázaro Cárdenas. During his six years in office Cárdenas distributed 49 million acres to Mexico's land-hungry populace, twice the amount of all his predecessors combined. By 1940, roughly one in three Mexicans had received land under agrarian reform, dramatically curtailing the popular clamor for land. His administration refined the revolutionary government's authoritarian-corporatist structure, bringing state-dominated labor unions more firmly under the umbrella of the national government. Cárdenas was also an economic nationalist, epitomized in his dramatic 1938 nationalization of the Mexican oil industry. The expropriation infuriated U.S. and European oil companies, which claimed they had lost $200 million in property, though it proved immensely popular among Mexicans and Latin Americans.

Anti-Imperialist Groundswell and the Good Neighbor Policy

SANDINO REBELLION IN NICARAGUA

By the late 1920s, three decades of U.S. military intervention in the Caribbean basin had generated a groundswell of anti-imperialist sentiment across Latin America. "Pan-Americanism means submission to the yoke of Wall Street," proclaimed the All-American Anti-Imperialist League in 1928, reflecting a widely held view. Particularly nettlesome was the situation in Nicaragua, where thousands of U.S. Marines were sent to suppress an anti-imperialist rebellion led by the nationalist leader Augusto Sandino. From 1927 until his assassination in 1934, Sandino led an army of peasants and Indians in a fight to restore Nicaraguan national sovereignty. Portrayed throughout much of the Atlantic world as a heroic David fighting the mighty Goliath of U.S. imperialism, Sandino became for many a symbol of defiant resistance against the "Colossus of the North."

THE GOOD NEIGHBOR POLICY

Inside the United States, too, opposition was rising to U.S. military meddling in Latin America. In 1933, with the U.S. economy reeling, President Roosevelt announced a major policy shift. "I would dedicate this nation to the policy of the Good Neighbor," he declared in his inaugural address, a vague formulation that soon solidified into an outright retreat from military intervention. U.S. troops were withdrawn from Nicaragua, Haiti, and elsewhere, but U.S.-supported dictators remained, not coincidentally, in those countries where the United States had most actively intervened: Anastasio Somoza in Nicaragua, Fulgencio Batista in Cuba, and Rafael Trujillo in the Dominican Republic. The Good Neighbor policy did not end U.S. economic

BIOGRAPHY

The Right to Be Free, and to Establish Justice

The official seal of the Defending Army of Nicaraguan National Sovereignty, led by Augusto C. Sandino against the U.S. Marines from 1927 to 1934. Depicting a Sandinista rebel poised to slay a "Yankee" marine invader, the seal conveys the hostility many Latin Americans felt toward the United States for its interventions in Latin American affairs.

To the Nicaraguans, the Central Americans, and the Indo-Hispanic Race: The man who does not ask his country for even a handful of earth for his grave deserves to be heard, and not only to be heard but also believed. I am Nicaraguan and I am proud because in my veins flows above all else the blood of the Indian race, which by some atavism embraces the mystery of being patriotic, loyal, and sincere. . . . I am an artisan, but my idealism is based on a broad horizon of internationalism, which represents the right to be free and to establish justice, even though to accomplish this it may be necessary to establish it upon a foundation of blood. . . . Pessimists will say that we are very small to undertake a task of this magnitude, but. . . our pride and our patriotism are very great. For that reason, before the Homeland and before history, I swear that my sword will defend the nation's honor and redeem the oppressed.

. . .

In this manifesto of July 1927, Augusto Sandino announced his decision to resist by force of arms the U.S. military occupation of his homeland of Nicaragua. For nearly six years, Sandino and his tiny Army in Defense of the National Sovereignty of Nicaragua waged guerrilla war against thousands of U.S. Marines. A year after the final U.S. troop withdrawal of January 1933, the head of the U.S.-created National Guard, Anastasio Somoza, ordered Sandino assassinated. Nationalist movements like Sandino's forced the United States to abandon its policy of direct military intervention in Latin America. The memory of Sandino's struggle endured in Nicaragua and beyond, inspiring a new generation of Nicaraguan revolutionaries who took Sandino's name—calling themselves Sandinistas—and overthrew the Somoza dictatorship in 1979, more than 50 years after Sandino penned these lines.

*From Crítica, Buenos Aires, Argentina, 9 January 1930, in United States Department of State, Records Relating to Internal Affairs of Nicaragua, 817.00/6540. Translated by Michael Schroeder.

or political intervention. In many ways the policy was meant to prolong U.S. domination of the region through more subtle, indirect means. As the fiery Peruvian reformer Victor Raúl Haya de la Torre sardonically quipped, FDR had made the United States "the Good Neighbor of tyrants."

Labor Unrest, Populist Dictatorships, and Economic Nationalism

MOUNTING POPULAR DISCONTENT

By the 1910s, urbanization and capitalist development had dramatically transformed many Latin American nations. As urban working and middle classes grew, so did a host of accompanying social tensions. Just as in the United States and Mexico, workers demanded the right to bargain collectively, while all urban groups demanded a greater political voice. In 1919, hundreds of thousands of workers in Santiago, Buenos Aires, São Paulo, Lima, and elsewhere launched massive demonstrations and general strikes. These movements were not directly linked, but all were rooted in similar processes of capitalist development. As in the United States, government and big business crushed these efforts of workers and middle sectors to wrest greater economic and political rights. For most of the 1920s, organized labor remained weak and its successes few. Still, the dominant classes could not wholly ignore workers' or middle classes' discontent or rely solely on brute force to retain power. Instead, governments developed elaborate mixtures of patronage and coercion to defuse, deflect, and divide opposition.

DEPRESSION AND DICTATORSHIP

With the coming of the Great Depression, unemployment soared and labor unions expanded and radicalized, toppling governments and unintentionally prompting military takeovers. To give a measure of legitimacy to their rule, and to wean their countries from economic dependency on more advanced nations, many dictatorial regimes relied on rhetoric and policies of economic nationalism. State-directed policies of "import substitution" in agriculture and industry aimed to replace long-standing dependence on imported foodstuffs and manufactures, while governments granted workers and middle classes substantially more economic security.

Brazil exemplifies these trends. The largest nation in Latin America, with abundant natural resources and an intricate racial and class structure, Brazil in the first decades of the twentieth century remained overwhelmingly rural. The southeastern coastal cities of São Paulo, Rio de Janeiro, and Pôrto Alegre saw rapid growth, with coffee exports from those cities' hinterlands being the country's main economic strength. Under the Old Republic (1889–1930), the national government was weak and the political system decentralized, with individual states enjoying great autonomy. Corrupt political machines governed states almost as if they were separate countries. As coastal cities grew and new social classes emerged, criticism of the political system mounted. After a bout of postwar labor unrest, in 1922–1924 a series of revolts erupted among young army officers who called for fair elections and honest government. The *Tenente* (Lieutenant) Revolts were violently repressed, with one column of rebels holding out for more than two years in a 15,000-mile trek through the Brazilian backlands.

VARGAS REGIME IN BRAZIL

The Great Depression, which hit Brazil's coffee-dependent economy like a sledgehammer, spelled the demise of the Old Republic. The army under Getúlio Vargas, a former governor, seized power in the Revolution of 1930. Imposing a dictatorship to squelch a revolt in São Paulo and rising labor unrest sparked by mass unemployment, Vargas called for a national assembly to write a new constitution. The

South America
before World War II

0   300   600 Miles

UNITED STATES

ATLANTIC OCEAN

Gulf of Mexico

Caribbean Sea

Caracas
VENEZUELA

BRITISH GUIANA
DUTCH GUIANA
FRENCH GUIANA

Bogotá
COLOMBIA

Quito
ECUADOR

Amazon R.

PERU

BRAZIL

Lima

La Paz
BOLIVIA
Sucre

PACIFIC OCEAN

PARAGUAY

Asuncion

Rio de Janeiro

Santiago

URUGUAY

Buenos Aires
Montevideo

CHILE

ARGENTINA

Falkland Islands (Br.)
Claimed by Argentina as
Islas Malvinas

Constitution of 1934 reduced the political autonomy of states, granted universal suffrage, and granted labor the right to organize and bargain collectively. In 1934–1935 the mass political mobilizations became ferocious, with fascists and communists waging pitched battles in the streets of the major cities. In response to an abortive communist-led revolt in late 1935, Vargas again imposed himself as dictator, and two years later, in 1937, announced a new constitution and, literally, a new state—the Estado Novo.

Brazil under Vargas's Estado Novo pursued an aggressive policy of economic nationalism under an authoritarian, fascist-influenced government, implementing a series of social reforms that by the end of World War II had changed society in important ways. The state became a major player in the national economy, with extensive government investment in steel, oil, chemicals, transport, and other major industries. Its basic strategy of rule was to buy off urban workers through extensive labor reforms, government-dominated unions, and strongly nationalist rhetoric. The Labor Code of 1943, an elaborate social security system, and a powerful national army defused opposition from both the Right and the Left. Like FDR in the United States, Vargas deftly exploited the new communications medium of radio to disseminate his populist message to millions of listeners.

Chile followed a similar trajectory, despite its very different history. Similar to Brazil in its stark inequalities and strong military, Chile was very different in its relatively homogeneous, mostly European-descended population and long history of parliamentary democracy. Like Brazil, Chile also saw economic distress lead to labor unrest, political upheaval, dictatorial populism, and economic nationalism. The Chilean economy, highly dependent on exports of nitrates and copper, declined rapidly after the boom caused by World War I. As the elite and military crushed strikes and protests, the energetic populist reformer Arturo Alessandri reached out to workers and middle sectors. His victory in the 1920 elections marked a transition from traditional elite politicking to mass political mobilizing. His program was progressive, calling for separation of church and state, a uniform labor code, universal suffrage, and a greater role for government in society. Finding his reforms blocked by conservatives and the military, Alessandri was ousted in a 1924 military coup.

ALESSANDRI REGIME IN CHILE

When the Great Depression hit in 1930, the export sector collapsed and the government essentially fell apart. In 1932, a conservative coalition helped reelect Alessandri. By now he had abandoned his reformist edge. Like Vargas an admirer of Italy's Benito Mussolini, Alessandri stifled labor agitation, filled the jails with dissidents, dissolved Congress, and embarked on a program of state-directed industrialization. He could not wholly ignore the demands of workers and middle sectors, however. Like Vargas, his regime expanded public education, social security, and other social programs among a populace polarized between left-wing socialists and communists and right-wing Nazi sympathizers. In the 1930s the bureaucracy expanded dramatically, as a series of governments spearheaded a program of state-directed industrialization. Financing these initiatives through foreign loans and credits, mostly from the U.S. government, the Chilean economy became increasingly dependent on U.S. capital and beholden to U.S. interests, especially in U.S.-dominated copper, nitrate, and oil industries.

In countries with less developed capitalist economies, the Great Depression ushered in U.S.-supported dictatorial regimes that ruled with little regard for the opinions or support of the populace: the Trujillo regime in the Dominican Republic (1930–1961), Batista in Cuba (1933–1959), and the Somoza dynasty in Nicaragua (1936–1979). As brutal as these dictators were, their violence pales in comparison to that of Maximiliano Hernández Martínez, who seized power in El Salvador in 1932. In response to an uprising planned by workers and peasants, the Martínez regime slaughtered upwards of 30,000 people in what has come to be known simply as *La Matanza* (The Massacre). In later years Martínez was dubbed *El Brujo* (The Sorcerer) due to his fascination with the occult. Classic Latin American dictators like Martínez and Trujillo are brilliantly portrayed in the novels of Nobel laureates Miguel Angel Asturias, *The President* (1946), and Gabriel García Márquez, *Autumn of the Patriarch* (1975).

U.S.-SUPPORTED DICTATORSHIPS

CANADA IN THE INTERWAR YEARS

Cars and radios were among the new consumer goods that Canadians rapidly embraced in the years after World War I. In the vast Dominion, these new devices rendered prairie farms, fishing villages, and lumber camps less isolated and fostered a stronger sense of national belonging. Canadians not only bought these goods, they produced them, usually at branch plants U.S. firms had built across its northern border. Canada's proximity to the United States made the Dominion feel a deep tie to its neighbor, a kinship that in many cases was real—by 1940 hundreds of thousands of Canadians had immigrated to the United States, attracted mainly by greater economic opportunities. On the other hand, living next door to the powerful United States helped to foster a sense of Canadian national distinctiveness. This nationalism was expressed through institutions like the Canadian Broadcasting Corporation; through the championing of the Canadian landscape in painting and literature; and in popular culture, from women's magazines like *MacLean's* to the sport of ice hockey.

CANADIAN NATIONALISM GROWS

Hard times also brought many Canadians together, sometimes in opposition to those in power. The depression came early to rural areas, prompting many foreclosures. The wave of prosperity in the late 1920s, an economic bubble based mostly on speculation, passed rapidly. When the crash came in 1929, unemployment lines soon snaked along city streets. Once-thriving agricultural settlements were abandoned, leaving only grain elevators standing next to unused railroad tracks. Mines, mills, and shops closed, while immigration, a boon to businesses in city and countryside, virtually ended. The federal government's response under the Conservative Party came too late for most voters, who in 1935 turned to the Liberals, the other major political party.

By this time leaders of both parties had realized that the New Deal of U.S. president Franklin Delano Roosevelt could be adapted to Canadian conditions, building on homegrown patterns of cooperation and social welfare, and might stem the rising tide of political disaffection. Leftist groups, Communists and especially Socialists, attracted wide followings in their call for an overhaul of a free market capitalism that

DEPRESSION AND REFORM

had left too many Canadians bereft of even a meager livelihood. In addition, varied regionally based political movements—in Quebec (the majority French-speaking province), in Alberta (where drought and financial hardship had ruined farmers' fortunes), and in Nova Scotia (home to farmers, fishing families, and miners, all hard-hit)—put forth platforms to upend the status quo, each making serious political inroads. Many Canadians thought that the national government had failed them, and looked to their hometowns and provinces for solutions to their ills.

CANADA IN WORLD WAR II

The advent of World War II refocused Canadians' vision on the Dominion and their nation's place in the world. Canada joined the war in September 1939, just days after the German invasion of Poland, becoming the first nation in the Western Hemisphere to do so. Canada's economy quickly recovered, supplying manufacturing and agricultural goods to the Allies. Canada also became a source of troops, most for the European theater, with more than 40,000 Canadians losing their lives in the conflict. At war's end, Canada, which unlike the United States had belonged to the League of Nations, became a charter member of a new international body, the United Nations.

SUMMARY

Across the Americas, the interwar years saw profound upheaval and change. Capitalist development deepened, while most governments became far more powerful and more directly involved in national economies and cultures. In the United States, a decade of conservative dominance and apparent economic prosperity in the 1920s was followed by the economic cataclysm of the Great Depression and the reforms of the New Deal. By the late 1930s, the United States had developed a rudimentary welfare state and engineered a partial economic recovery. Similar processes unfolded in Canada. In Mexico, a third of a century of economic liberalism (capitalism) without an expansion of political liberalism (rights of citizenship) led to a social explosion and a decade of violent social revolution and civil war. The tumult generated a new social charter in the Constitution of 1917, a new sense of national identity, and, by the late 1930s, the institutionalization of a stable one-party government.

In response to mounting opposition at home and abroad, in the early 1930s the United States modified its policy of military intervention in the Caribbean basin. Instead of troops it used more indirect ways to dominate Latin American governments and economies. Throughout Latin America, capitalist development sparked the growth of cities, industrial enclaves, and the formation of new social classes that demanded political and economic rights. Movies, radio, and mass circulation newspapers created new cultural communities and brought different parts of the hemisphere into increasing contact with one another. In general, Latin American countries with more developed capitalist economies saw dictatorial regimes combine heavy-handed repression, populist reforms meant to stem revolutionary impulses among workers, and state-directed economic nationalism. In less developed countries, the Great Depression ushered in an era of long-reigning dictators who violently suppressed political opposition and remained in power long after the economic and political crises that had given rise to their regimes had ended.

Everywhere, as states became more powerful, capitalism proved both extremely volatile and virtually unstoppable. As hemispheric integration intensified, people across the Americas absorbed, transformed, and often combined elements of communism, fascism, anarchism, liberalism, nationalism, racialism, and others in creative response to the profound economic, political, and cultural challenges they confronted.

SUGGESTED SOURCES

Dumenil, Lynn. *The Modern Temper: America in the Twenties.* 1995. Readable and insightful.*

Garraty, John A. *The Great Depression.* 1986. An excellent survey.*

Katz, Friedrich. *Pancho Villa.* 1998. Expansive and engrossing.*

Kennedy, David M. *Freedom from Fear: The American People in Depression and War, 1929–1945.* 1999. A Pulitzer Prize–winning work.*

Kessler-Harris, Alice. *In Pursuit of Equity: Men, Women, and the Quest for Economic Citizenship in Twentieth-Century America.* 2001. Brilliant and provocative.*

Klubock, Thomas Miller. *Contested Communities: Class, Gender, and Politics in Chile's El Teniente Copper Mine, 1904–1951.* 1998. First-rate labor history.*

Knight, Alan. *The Mexican Revolution* (2 vols.). 1986. The Revolution as a genuinely radical mass movement; lucid and informed.*

Levine, Robert M., and John J. Crocitti, eds. *The Brazil Reader: History, Culture, Politics.* 1999. A fresh and broad-ranging collection.*

Maclean, Nancy. *Behind the Mask of Chivalry: The Making of the Second Ku Klux Klan.* 1994. A superb and chilling account.*

Nugent, Daniel. *Spent Cartridges of Revolution: An Anthropological History of Namiquipa, Chihuahua.* 1993. Superb study of revolutionary change in an Indian village.*

Strong-Boag, Veronica. *The New Day Recalled: Lives of Girls and Women in English Canada, 1919–1939.* 1988. Excellent description and analysis of cultural change in the interwar years.*

Womack, John, Jr. *Zapata and the Mexican Revolution.* 1972. An outstanding study and read.*

WEB SOURCES

www.memory.loc.gov/ammem/coolhtml/coolhome.html. This Library of Congress site has links to source materials from the 1920s on the U.S. transition to a mass consumer society.

http://econ161.berkeley.edu/TCEH/Slouch_Crash14.html. A good introduction with graphs to the Great Depression in the United States and elsewhere by a University of California economics professor.

www.newdeal.feri.org. Information and links on the New Deal from the Franklin and Eleanor Roosevelt Institute (FERI).

www.historicaltextarchive.com/links.php?op=viewslink&sid=224. Provides many excellent links to materials on the Mexican Revolution.

*Paperback available.

East Asia between the World Wars

China and Japan followed very different paths in the twentieth century. The revolution of 1911 ended the world's longest continuous system of government, and republican China became absorbed in the search for a modern ideology and institutions to replace the discredited and outdated imperial order. As the Chinese made tentative advances toward a new government and society, they had to endure decades of disorder, civil wars, and constraints imposed by foreign imperialism. China's continuing quest for a viable new order throughout the twentieth century would affect every part of that ancient civilization.

Japan, on the other hand, enjoyed continuing success; it had not only shaken off the shackles of inequality but had also emerged from World War I and the peace conferences as an undisputed great power. It continued to move forward in all fields with amazing speed and to close the technological gap between itself and the most advanced Western nations. In the initial postwar era Japanese politics moved toward greater democratization, following the trend that was also characteristic of the Western world. Japan's success in modernization, however, brought in its wake little-understood problems that led it along the path of disaster in the 1930s.

WAR AND REVOLUTION IN CHINA

From Dynasty to Republic

MANCHUS ATTEMPT 11TH HOUR REFORMS

The humiliation of the 1900 Boxer fiasco shattered the remaining moral authority of the Manchu dynasty, and its hold on the people weakened. The imperial government, in a desperate attempt to win popular support, approved all sorts of proposals for change. A constitutional mission sent to Europe and the United States to study their forms of government recommended the gradual introduction of parliamentary institutions. A new educational policy called for Western-style schools and universities and a modern curriculum.

In spite of its 11th-hour reform attempts, however, the dynasty was doomed as new forces emerged to challenge a government that had outlived its usefulness. The merchants and industrialists in the port cities opposed the Manchu dynasty because the unequal treaties it had signed with Western nations gave foreign goods an unfair competitive edge over Chinese goods. Western-educated students who wanted rapid modernization also opposed the reactionary court. Opponents of the dynasty plotted revolution abroad or in the foreign concession areas in Chinese cities, which were outside the jurisdiction of the Chinese government. China was ready for revolution. All it needed was a catalyst.

The antidynastic forces found a leader in Sun Yat-sen. Sun was born in 1866 to a poor farming family near Canton in southern China. Thanks to an elder brother who had established a successful business in Hawaii, he was sent to school there and later studied medicine in Hong Kong, the British colony on China's southern coast. In his studies and travels, Sun was impressed with the progress of the West and correspondingly disgusted with China's backwardness. He gradually turned to revolution and after 1890 devoted himself to traveling, recruiting, and fund-raising toward that end.

Sun's ideology and the ways he proposed to put it into effect clearly showed Western political and social influence. He formulated a program known as the Three People's Principles. They were, first, nationalism, which stressed the overthrow of the Manchus (who were a minority ethnic-cultural group in China) as well as the recovery of China's rights from the imperialists; second, democracy, under a liberal republic in which the people would be sovereign through representative government; and, third, livelihood, a combination of industrial socialism and land reform to ensure that cultivators owned their land.

In 1905 Sun organized a group of men and women students, literati, and military officers into a political party that later adopted the name Kuomintang (the National People's Party or Nationalist Party, hereafter referred to as the KMT). Between 1906 and 1911 Sun and his KMT followers attempted 10 unsuccessful uprisings to overthrow the Manchus. The 11th occurred on October 10, 1911 (hence called the Double Tenth in China), at Wuhan, an important industrial center. The revolt spread quickly across central and southern China. Sun was on a fund-raising tour in the United States and made his way back to China, arriving in Shanghai on December 25. Four days later he was elected provisional president of the Chinese Republic by delegates of a provisional parliament meeting in Nanking. Women units fought in the revolution of 1911, but women failed to obtain equality under the constitutions of the early republic.

Frightened and leaderless, the Manchus were not prepared to fight the revolutionaries. They turned to General Yuan Shih-k'ai, organizer of the largest and best-equipped Manchu army units. Yuan defeated the revolutionaries and then bargained for a settlement that would satisfy his great ambitions. On February 12, 1912, the boy emperor abdicated the throne. On the following day Sun resigned the presidency in favor of Yuan Shih-k'ai in return for Yuan's promise to support the Chinese Republic.

SUN YAT-SEN LEADS ANTIDYNASTIC FORCES

REPUBLIC OF CHINA ESTABLISHED IN 1912

The Era of Warlordism

Ineffectiveness and frustration marked the first years of the republic. Most of Sun's followers were satisfied with the overthrow of the Manchus and did little to fight for his other, little-understood ideals. Yuan Shih-k'ai then outlawed the KMT and proclaimed himself emperor in 1915, but the monarchical concept was now in disrepute and, faced with revolt, Yuan was forced to resign in humiliation three months later.

WARLORDISM BRINGS CHAOS TO CHINA

The death of Yuan in 1916, shortly after his resignation, was the end of an effective central government in China, and chaos set in under local military leaders, or warlords, who ruled parts of China alone or in coalition and fought frequent wars with one another. Warlords came in all descriptions. Manchuria, an area as big as France and Germany combined, was ruled by a former bandit; Szechwan, another huge province, with 60 million people, was for years the battleground of two men surnamed Liu, uncle and nephew; parts of northwestern China were ruled for years by Feng Yu-hsiang, a poorly educated son of a bricklayer who was in succession a Christian, a Communist, and a member of the KMT. Associating cleanliness with godliness, he personally inspected his soldiers' fingernails. Because opium produced more revenue, he also forced farmers to grow poppies rather than grain, causing widespread famine. Peking remained the capital, but obtaining the presidency after Yuan Shih-k'ai's departure became a game of musical chairs won by whatever group temporarily controlled the city and its environs. The central government, unable to collect taxes in most of the country, relied mainly on foreign loans for survival.

Between 1914 and 1918 Western nations were too preoccupied with the war in Europe to meddle further in China. As Great Britain's ally, Japan declared war on Germany in 1914, but the Japanese, for imperialistic reasons, kept China out of the war until 1917. At the end of 1914, a Japanese force landed in Shantung and expelled the German garrison from this province in northern China that Germany had seized as a sphere of influence. China did not participate as a combatant in World War I, but 200,000 Chinese laborers were sent to work in Allied factories and mines in Europe. Although a Chinese delegation participated at the Paris Peace Conference, China had no real voice in the proceedings.

CHINA DURING WORLD WAR I

World War I dealt drastic blows to European industries and trade in China and allowed native industries and trade to develop relatively unhindered by competition. All aspects of the Chinese industrial sector—textiles, iron and steel, coal, and flour mills— and modern banking grew. New industries and enterprises created new merchant and laboring classes in growing urban centers, where the new schools were located and where a new intelligentsia was emerging, all of whom were receptive to the calls of nationalism.

SOCIAL CHANGES IN EARLY TWENTIETH-CENTURY CHINA

The Russian Revolution of 1917 and the U.S. role in World War I also profoundly influenced the Chinese nationalist movement. President Wilson's calls for national self-determination and the abolition of secret diplomacy appealed to many Chinese intellectuals. The new Communist regime in Russia, with its promise of world revolution, its anti-imperialist ideology, and its initial promise to give up tsarist gains, made converts of others. Both stirred intellectual ferment in China, with far-reaching results. Viewed as a period, the years between 1911 and 1928 brought both chaos and hope. Unrestrained by authority, all sorts of new theories were aired and experiments tried. Confucianism, the official ideology of the empire, stressed the Three Bonds, which taught the duty of subjects to the ruler, the young to their elders, and wives to husbands. When the first bond was snapped as a result of the overthrow of the dynasty, the remaining two inevitably loosened. Henceforth, modern educated young men and women would increasingly demand social changes that included the right of individual choice in careers and marriage. Upper-class women revolted against foot binding, and modern educated women demanded equality with men.

Modern educated youths became politically conscious and assertive in national affairs during this period. Increasing numbers of young men and women attended new schools or went to the United States, western Europe, and Japan to study. They formed a new social class of intellectuals who both represented and demanded change. They were nationalistic and were determined to create a strong China that could break free from the shackles of imperialism.

Intellectual Revolution: The May Fourth Movement

The Chinese government and public had hoped that the Treaty of Versailles would restore to Chinese rule Shantung province, a German sphere of influence seized by Japan in 1914. On May 4, 1919, students demonstrated in Peking to protest its awarding to Japan. This became known as the May Fourth Movement, a wide-ranging outburst of social and intellectual protest that had been fermenting for some time. This movement paved the way for the revival of the KMT and the rise of the Chinese Communist Party (hereafter CCP), founded in 1921. The center of the intellectual revolution was National Peking University, where a group of progressive faculty and bright students had set as their task the reexamination of old traditions and systems. To facilitate mass literacy, Hu Shih, a Columbia University–trained professor of philosophy at Peking University, began a movement to replace the difficult archaic classical written form of the Chinese language, used only by scholars, with the vernacular form that closely approximated everyday speech. Hu's language reform was so popular that by the 1920s the vernacular had become mandatory in school textbooks and commonplace in newspapers and popular magazines. The vernacular was key to later mass literacy and universal education movements. A new literature, influenced by Western trends, followed.

STUDENTS SPEARHEAD AN INTELLECTUAL REVOLUTION

Immediately, the May Fourth demonstrations in Peking became a nationwide protest movement as students, merchants, and workers struck throughout China in sympathy with the Peking demonstrators. They forced the government to refrain from signing the Treaty of Versailles and to dismiss blatantly pro-Japanese officials; more significantly, they showed widespread nationalist and anti-imperialist feelings. China however, signed peace treaties with Austria and Hungary and a separate treaty with Germany, all based on equality. It joined the League of Nations.

The May Fourth Movement also inaugurated a new era of political and intellectual activism in China. Many of the young patriots of the movement joined and helped to revitalize the KMT, while others turned to the Soviet Union and Marxism. Female student participants also demanded better educational opportunities and won admission to previously all-male universities.

Nationalist Triumph

Deeply disappointed with warlords, the Western powers, and his loosely organized and ineffective KMT, Sun Yat-sen turned to Soviet Russia for help. In return for aid in the form of Soviet advisers and arms, Sun agreed to admit the 300 members of the newly formed Chinese Communist Party, as individuals, into the KMT and formed a United Front government in Canton with their participation. Sun was

Sun Yat-sen (seated), father of the Chinese republic, with his lieutenant, Chiang Kai-shek, in 1924.

impressed by the quick success of the Communist Revolution in Russia. On their part, disappointed that they had failed to export revolution in Europe, the Soviets hoped to further their cause in Asia by allying with the KMT. In 1921 the Red Army invaded and gained control of Outer Mongolia, which had been a part of the Ch'ing Empire. The Russian Communist government, besides annexing a region of Mongolia called Tannu Tuva, established in 1924 its first satellite, called the Mongolian People's Republic, in the rest of the region.

After 1923 Soviet advisers assisted Sun in reorganizing the KMT and he sent his young ally, Chiang Kai-shek, to Russia for three months to learn new training methods from the Red Army. Chiang also learned to distrust Communist aims in China. On his return from Moscow Chiang established a military academy to train and indoctrinate officers for the KMT army.

CHIANG KAI-SHEK EMERGES AS SUN YAT-SEN'S SUCCESSOR

Sun died of cancer in 1925 and was afterward revered as father of the Republic; Chiang Kai-shek emerged as Sun's successor. Born of a gentry family and trained in military academies in China and Japan as an army officer, he had taken part in the 1911 revolution. As commandant of the Nationalist military academy in Canton, he was responsible for creating the Nationalist army that he later commanded. In 1926 the

BIOGRAPHY

Organizing Peasants for Revolution

During my recent visit to Hunan I conducted an investigation on the spot into the conditions. . . . I called together for fact finding conferences experienced peasants and comrades working for the peasant movement, listened attentively to their reports, and collected a lot of material. . . .

All kinds of arguments against the peasant movement must be speedily set right. The erroneous measures taken by the revolutionary authorities concerning the peasant movement must be speedily changed. Only thus can any good be done for the future of the revolution. For the rise of the present peasant movement is a colossal event. In a very short time, in China's central, southern, and northern provinces, several hundred million peasants will rise like a tornado or tempest, a force so extraordinarily swift and violent that no power, however great, will be able to suppress it. They will break all trammels that now bind them and rush forward along the road to liberation. They will send all imperialists, warlords, corrupt officials, local bullies, and bad gentry to their graves.*

. . .

Mao Tse-tung, a founder of the Chinese Communist Party, contributed to the development of Marxism-Leninism by recognizing peasants as a potentially important revolutionary force in China and, by implication, throughout the non-Western, nonindustrial parts of the world. In 1925 Mao was sent to his native province, Hunan, by the KMT-CCP United Front government to investigate the conditions of the peasants there, and this report, partly reproduced here, was the result. Twenty-five years later he became head of the Communist government in China.

*From "Report on an Investigation of the Hunan Peasant Movement" by Mao Tse-tung (Zedong), quoted in William T. DeBary, ed. *Sources of Chinese Tradition*. Copyright © 1960 by Columbia University Press. Reprinted by permission.

Nationalist government appointed Chiang commander in chief of the National Revolutionary Army, and he began the Northern Expedition to unify China. By harnessing and riding the wave of a popular nationalist movement, Chiang's small army was able within a few months to conquer all the warlords in its path as it marched north to the Yangtze valley in central China. The KMT and the CCP cooperated with each other so long as both were still weak. The Communist strategy was to help the KMT during the Northern Expedition and, in Stalin's phrase, to drop it like so many "squeezed-out lemons" when victory was at hand. In 1927, however, after conquering only the southern half of China, Chiang squeezed first. Supported by the anti-Communist faction of the KMT, Chiang expelled the CCP from the KMT and killed many of its members. He also expelled Soviet advisers from China. In Canton, the Communists started a last-ditch uprising in December 1927. After it failed, Communists were identified by the red dye marks on their necks left by their discarded red scarves, and many were summarily shot. Chiang resumed his march in 1928. In June Peking surrendered, and in December the warlord of Manchuria declared his allegiance to the KMT government. With this act, all of China was nominally unified under the KMT.

THE KMT LAUNCHES SUCCESSFUL NORTHERN EXPEDITION

REFORMS UNDER THE KMT GOVERNMENT

For 10 years, between 1928 and 1937, the Nationalist government ruled China, with Chiang Kai-shek the dominant figure within that government. Between 1928 and 1931 Chiang's enemies, many former warlords who had jumped on the victorious KMT bandwagon during the Northern Expedition, rose either singly or in a coalition to challenge his power. One by one he defeated them, and in the process he slowly expanded the power of the central government, the most modern government China had known. It made significant advances in broadening and enlarging the modern sector during this period, built factories, created new schools and universities for men and women, and improved road and railroad networks. New legal codes based on European models gave women equality for the first time. By 1937 women students accounted for about a quarter of all college students. In cities women entered government service and the professions. However, traditions were still strong in the countryside, where women remained subservient.

A high priority of the KMT was the "rights recovery" movement, an effort to end the unequal treaties and restore sovereignty. In 1928, under pressure from the Nationalist government, all powers except Japan recognized China's tariff autonomy (Japan was compelled to follow later). For the first time since 1842, China was able to set its own tariff rates. Except for those in Shanghai and Tientsin, all foreign concessions were restored to Chinese authority. After promulgating new civil and criminal codes based on Western models, China demanded an end to extraterritorial rights that nationals of some Western nations and Japan still enjoyed. While the Soviet Union and minor Western nations gave up their extraterritorial rights, Great Britain and the United States held on to theirs until 1943.

JAPANESE AND SOVIET AMBITIONS IN CHINA

With its very existence threatened by Japanese aggression after 1931, China deferred pressing Western powers on two remaining items that compromised its sovereignty: the right of Western powers to station troops and naval vessels in certain designated areas of China and the right of Western naval vessels to patrol some Chinese rivers. China reasoned that a Western presence might deter Japan from becoming too blatantly aggressive. It also hoped that Great Britain and the United States might come to China's aid if Japan attempted to close China's open door. Clearly, from the 1920s on the Chinese were much less fearful of western European and U.S. imperialism, which was indeed in retreat, than of Japanese and Soviet imperialism. To non-Marxist Chinese, tsarist Russian imperialism had been replaced by Soviet Marxist imperialism. It is clear from the foregoing that in general terms the KMT government performed well in representing Chinese nationalist aspirations and in recovering lost sovereign rights.

The Nationalist government failed decisively, however, to carry out Sun's principles of democracy and livelihood. Chiang's military training limited his vision of China's needs and his choice of tactics to achieve reforms. The government made no real effort to train the people for the practice of democracy, which was an alien concept to the Chinese, and ruled in an authoritarian manner. Nor did it attempt to implement Sun's principle of livelihood through a redistribution of the land and other policies to revitalize the farm economy. Even when the KMT enacted rent control laws, it made little effort to enforce them. Chiang and his confederates feared the force of social and political change that dramatic economic reform would unleash. Although they enacted reforms such as new marriage and inheritance laws and a law prohibiting foot binding, enforcement was sporadic and confined to urban centers, in part because the government lacked the power and personnel to enforce the laws. Mass movements of the early 1920s such as the trade union movement, which had significantly helped to win popular support for the KMT, were now suppressed. Unwilling to tinker with the social fabric, the KMT let rising demands for reform pass it by.

The Resurgence of the CCP

Intra-KMT civil wars between 1928 and 1931 and major Japanese assaults against China after 1931 (see Chapter 17) gave the CCP remnants a chance to rebuild. Those who had survived the 1927 purges had either gone into hiding in the cities or taken to the hills in southern China, where Mao Tse-tung collected about 10,000 escapees in the winter of 1927–1928. Mao was the son of a prosperous farmer and had a

CCP REGROUPS UNDER MAO'S LEADERSHIP

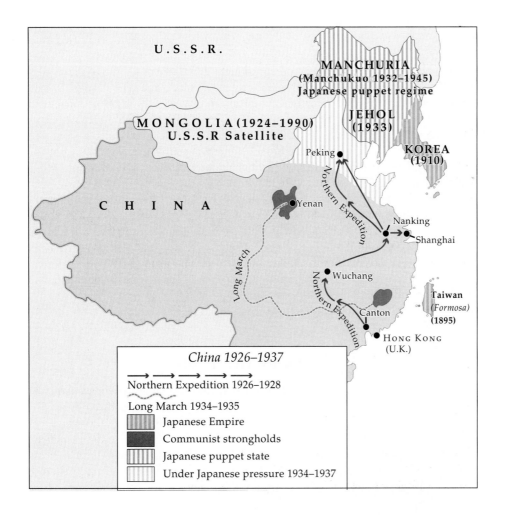

China 1926–1937

→ → → → → Northern Expedition 1926–1928

Long March 1934–1935

Japanese Empire

Communist strongholds

Japanese puppet state

Under Japanese pressure 1934–1937

normal-school education. He was a library assistant at Peking University during the May Fourth Movement, was a founder of the CCP, and organized peasants during the Northern Expedition. Now, with the assistance of Chu Teh, father of the Chinese Red Army, Mao and others developed a guerrilla army and a Soviet-style government.

Since the Communists were hiding out in an economically backward area that contained no industries and therefore had no proletariat, Mao abandoned traditional Marxist concepts of reliance on the urban proletariat as the core of the revolution and turned to the poor peasantry as China's "revolutionary vanguard." During the late 1920s through the 1940s, Mao wrote extensively to reinterpret Marxism and to apply it to the underdeveloped agricultural parts of the world. These writings were the basis of his later claim to be a creative contributor to Marxism-Leninism. Since most of the world was populated by peasants, Mao's modification of Marxist doctrine would eventually give Marxism an enormous impact in nonindustrialized regions of the world.

CCP FLEES TO NORTHWESTERN CHINA IN THE LONG MARCH

In CCP-controlled areas, land was redistributed by force in the name of class warfare. In November 1931 a Chinese Soviet Republic claiming control over 2.5 million people was proclaimed at Juichin, a small town in the mountains of Kiangsi province, with Mao as president. Between 1930 and 1933, KMT armies launched four successive Extermination Campaigns against the Communists. In each case, Mao's guerrilla tactics and peasant support, among other factors, repulsed the better-equipped and numerically superior KMT forces. The tide turned in Chiang's favor in 1934 during the fifth Extermination Campaign, mostly as a result of the strategy of economic blockade carried out in conjunction with economic reforms for the people in the disputed areas. Defeat forced the CCP to flee. About 100,000 men and women of the CCP army and government broke through a poorly defended sector of the blockade and began a 6,000-mile march from southern China to the northwest, while constantly fighting off pursuing KMT forces.

The legendary Long March took 370 days to complete. In 1936 the Communists established their headquarters in Yenan in the poor hinterland area in northern China. Of the 100,000 people who started, about 20,000 made it to Yenan, with Mao Tse-tung in control and his power consolidated. Most of the leaders survived. Mao's headquarters remained in Yenan until after the end of World War II. The main advantage of Yenan was its location, far from Chiang's army and bases and more accessible to the U.S.S.R. Chiang now had to rely on the unreliable troops of his Manchurian warlord ally to continue the fight against the Communists.

JAPAN IN THE 1920s

JAPAN AT THE PARIS PEACE CONFERENCE

Although its participation in World War I had been marginal, Japan went to the Paris Peace Conference as a major power. Its delegates were accorded a special position on the Supreme Council and voiced three specific demands: (1) the transfer of the former German islands in the North Pacific (Marianas, Carolines, and Marshalls) to Japanese control, (2) the confirmation of Japan's claim to former German rights in China's Shantung province, and (3) a declaration of racial equality in the Covenant of the League of Nations. Japan's first demand was essentially met when it received the German islands in the North Pacific to administer as mandates under the League of Nations. Because of U.S. president Wilson's reservations, Japan was persuaded to drop its third demand. Japan considered this a particularly galling defeat, since the race issue was a symbol of discrimination. Defeated on the issue of racial equality, Japan threatened to walk out of the conference unless its second demand was met. Since Wilson feared the collapse of the peace conference, he gave in to Japan's takeover of Shantung, hoping that the League of Nations would right China's wrong in the future. As a result, Japan signed the Treaty of Versailles, whereas China did not.

Liberal Democracy Gains Ground

As Japan's international status grew, its internal developments after World War I reflected the intellectual, social, and economic changes within the nation and worldwide. Within Japan a new generation had come to maturity since the Meiji Restoration. It was better acquainted with the outside world and more confident than its predecessors. The tremendous industrial and commercial expansion that took place in Japan during the war had made the business classes more important in national life. As Japanese businesses expanded in Asia after the war, they offered the prospect of commercial growth unaccompanied by force of arms. The overwhelming victory of democratic Western powers in World War I and the defeat of the less democratic Central powers also convinced many Japanese of the merits of democratic government.

The decade of the 1920s was a period of social transition. Even the physical appearance of Japanese cities was changing, brought about in part by the great earthquake of 1923, which flattened much of Tokyo and Yokohama. Downtown Tokyo, rebuilt with wide boulevards and high-rise buildings, now resembled European and North American cities more than Asian ones. Other cities followed Tokyo's lead. Urban life also changed. Men and women office workers commuted to work by trains and trolley cars. In their leisure hours urban dwellers participated in the new mass culture of restaurants and cafés, movies, and sporting events. Baseball became a national sport, and tennis and golf were popular among the rich. About 17 million records were sold in 1930. These trends led the older and more conservative Japanese to complain that the young were only interested in the "three S's"—sports, screen, and sex. Highly literate, the Japanese public supported several mass circulation daily newspapers, each with a readership in the millions. New Western-language books were almost immediately translated into Japanese.

MODERN CULTURE GAINS IN JAPAN IN THE 1920s

The ascendancy of liberal and democratic tendencies was evident in many ways. In 1926 the Diet enfranchised all men over age 25, increasing the size of the electorate from 3 million to more than 12 million voters. Another bill reduced the hereditary component of the House of Peers in favor of men appointed because of achievement. The Japanese began to accept government by the political party that controlled the majority of votes in the lower house. Two important political parties emerged, providing considerable stability. In addition, many small political parties and

REFORMS IN JAPAN IN THE 1920s

groups were allowed to operate as long as they did not advocate changing the "national polity" or abolishing private property. As a result, a variety of political and social organizations that campaigned for further reforms, including women's rights, mushroomed. The Diet also enacted social legislation favorable to labor. It abolished an earlier law that restricted labor unions and legalized union support of nonrevolutionary socialist movements. Major problems and inequities nonetheless remained. For example, a small group of industrial combines dominated the economy. Big business leaders and their allies among the politicians, bureaucrats, military officers, and landlords also held inordinate power in the government. As a result, many Japanese felt discontented.

In foreign policy, internationalism and international cooperation gained at the expense of militarism. At the Washington Conference in 1921, Japan joined the signing of the Naval Limitation Treaty and agreed to return many of its privileges in Shantung to China. The government reduced the military share of the budget from 42 percent in 1922 to 28 percent in 1928; four divisions were cut out of the army.

Underlying Weaknesses in Japanese Democracy

PROBLEMS IN THE JAPANESE POLITICAL SYSTEM

The progress toward democracy and liberalism in the postwar years was not, however, built on firm foundations. Many deep problems, including those of rural tenancy and a dual economy, consisting of efficient modern industry and agriculture existing alongside inefficient traditional handicrafts, were unresolved. Thus, when the world depression hit Japan in 1930, the post–World War I democratic experiment in government became a victim. Because of its newness, Japanese democratic constitutional government was not firmly rooted. With its firmly entrenched autocratic traditions, its traditional respect for the military, and its veneration of the imperial institution, Japanese society and politics were more akin to those of the German empire than to the more liberal societies of Great Britain and the United States; the Meiji Constitution was closely modeled on that of imperial Germany.

Despite having several very able political leaders, most Japanese, like many in Germany and Italy at this time, had little faith in or respect for elected party governments. The mudslinging and often corrupt election campaigns did nothing to dispel the image of politicians as venal. The *zaibatsu,* or large conglomerates, governed by family law rather than the legal code, contributed heavily to the political parties that they favored. Thus governments came to be called the "Mitsui cabinet" or the "Mitsubishi cabinet," after their respective *zaibatsu* mentors. Mitsui and Mitsubishi were probably the largest conglomates globally at the time. For example, in 1940, Mitsui employed 2 million workers, 1 million each in Japan and in the colonies. Corruption under party governments came under slashing attack from both the Left and the Right after the onset of the depression, when popular suffering made such behavior seem more blatantly immoral.

AUTHORITARIAN AND MILITARISTIC TRENDS IN JAPAN

Even before the Great Depression changed the political and economic climate, and while party governments were in control, antidemocratic forces that would later bring down the shallowly rooted liberal experiment were at work. Even in an era of liberalism, some legislation reflected the strength of traditional authoritarian tendencies. An example of this was the Peace Preservation Law of 1925, amended and strengthened in 1928, which stipulated heavy penalties for membership in the Communist Party and for activities considered subversive. Attacking corruption in the political party system, antidemocratic groups demanded a government that was above parties and other interest groups.

A more important danger signal for Japanese democracy was a renewed tilt toward imperialism, militarism, and militaristic solutions to problems. Both inside and outside the armed forces, ultranationalists willing to use private force to gain political ends became glamorous. For example, in 1921 Prime Minister Hara Kei, a noted believer in constitutional government, was assassinated by an ultranationalist. In 1928, ultranationalist junior officers of the Japanese army in Manchuria blew up a train to assassinate the Chinese warlord of that region for fear that he would not be subservient enough to Japanese interests in the future. In the Manchurian case, the military blocked an inquiry that might have resulted in punishment of the guilty and caused the fall of the government that demanded it. Even when fanatical assassins were brought to justice, ordinary citizens increasingly sympathized with them as pure-hearted patriots opposed to venal politicians.

The Depression

The depression of 1930 marked the watershed between the liberal decade of the 1920s and the militarism of the 1930s. Since a domestic depression in 1926, the Japanese economy had been on shaky ground. When the global depression hit Japan in early 1930, it touched off a major catastrophe. The value of exports fell 50 percent from 1929 to 1931; workers' real income dropped about a third, and unemployment rose to 3 million out of a total population of 64 million. The hardest hit, however, were the farmers, who could not recover production costs despite a bumper crop in 1931. This was followed by widespread crop failures in 1932, which brought conditions of near starvation in several areas.

THE GREAT DEPRESSION'S IMPACT IN JAPAN

The politicians, the party government, and the *zaibatsu,* which composed the parliamentary coalition, were blamed for the depression, even though the party government acted effectively to counter it. Japan went off the gold standard in December 1931, an action that led to a boom in exports. Rising military expenditure brought on by its invasion of Manchuria in 1931 also hastened economic recovery (see Chapter 17). Japan was thus the first major industrial nation to recover from the depression, but the recovery did not benefit the political parties and democratic government. The depression also called into question the validity of the postwar international economic order, which now lay in ruins. As nations erected protectionist tariff walls, the Japanese worried about their raw material and market needs in the future. The failure of the postwar international economy caused the Japanese also to doubt the international political order led by Western democratic nations. The rise of Nazism in Germany further discredited democratic forces in Japan and cast doubts on its parliamentary government because Germany had been Japan's constitutional model and was one of the Western nations the Japanese admired most.

Amid the rough-and-tumble of political life and economic ups and downs, the armed forces alone retained an untarnished image. Antidemocratic forces and advocates of a greater role for the army and navy in government argued that the military best expressed the will of the emperor and the interest of the people. They further argued that military expansion would ensure steady supplies of food, raw materials, and markets for Japanese manufactured products. This was the background that permitted the Japanese army to act independently of civilian authorities in the 1930s and finally to topple them.

SUMMARY

China and Japan during this period were a study in contrasts. The Chinese revolution of 1911 overthrew a discredited dynasty, but the early republican governments were even less capable of preserving Chinese independence than were the Manchus. Warlords struggled against one another and signed away Chinese rights. Japan replaced Europe as the primary imperialist force against China. Sun Yat-sen, father of the Chinese Republic, eventually turned to the Soviet Union to revitalize his political party, the Kuomintang. Shortly after his death, Sun's political heir, Chiang Kai-shek, led a military expedition that defeated the warlords and gave China its first effective, modernizing government. Chiang's Nationalist government strove with success to realize Chinese nationalism and to recover many rights lost to Western imperialists, but it neglected Sun's other principles, livelihood and democracy. Thus the Chinese Communists, who promised a drastic social and economic revolution, gained support that the superior military force of the KMT could not eradicate.

World War I enhanced Japan's international stature and boosted its industries and economy. Japan emerged from the war as the preeminent imperial power in East Asia. World trends that favored democratic and egalitarian political and social forces in the 1920s were also strong in Japan in the same period, evidenced by reforms that resulted in universal male suffrage, greater political freedom, and social betterment. However, the shallowly rooted democratic forces were fatally undermined by the depression, which contributed to the triumph of militarism.

SUGGESTED SOURCES

Duus, Peter. *Party Rivalry and Political Change in Taisho Japan*. 1968. A study of Japan's experiment with democracy.

Duus, Peter, Ramon H. Myers, and Mark R. Peattie. *The Japanese Informal Empire in China, 1895–1937*. 1989. Discusses how Japanese imperialism supplanted Western imperialism in China.*

Greider, Jerome B. *Hu Shih and the Chinese Renaissance, Liberalism in the Chinese Revolution, 1917–1939*. 1970. A sympathetic account of a great twentieth-century Chinese educator and reformer.

Hane, Mikiso. *Modern Japan: A Historical Survey.* 2nd ed. 1992. A concise and evenhanded history of modern Japan.*

Kang, Hildi. *Under the Black Umbrella: Voices from Colonial Korea, 1910–1945.* 2001. The author unravels a complicated story of Japanese rule over Korea.

Large, Stephen S. *Emperors of the Rising Sun.* 1997. Biographies of the three men who ruled Japan from 1868 to 1991.

McKenna, Richard. *The Sand Pebbles.* 1964. A novel set in the mid-1920s that pits American sailors on patrol along the Yangtze River against one another and against Chinese revolutionaries. (Also a film.)

Ono, Kazuko. *Chinese Women in a Century of Revolution, 1850–1950.* Ed. Joshua A. Fogel. 1989. First comprehensive history of women in modern China.*

Pa Chin. *Family.* 1972. A translation of a novel first published in China in 1931 that deals with the conflict between forces of tradition and those of change.*

P'u-i, Henry. *The Last Manchu: The Autobiography of Henry Pu Yi, Last Emperor of China.* Trans. Kuo Ying Paul Tsai, ed. Paul Kramer. 1967. The pathetic story of the last Manchu emperor.* (Also a film, titled *Last Emperor.*)

Salisbury, Harrison. *The Long March, the Untold Story.* 1985. A vibrantly written account of an epic event.

Seidensticker, Edward. *Low City, High City: Tokyo from Edo to the Earthquake, 1867–1923.* 1991. Interesting book on the growth of Tokyo to a great city.*

Sheridan, James E. *China in Disintegration: The Republican Era in Chinese History, 1912–1949.* 1975. A comprehensive study of the republican era.*

Wang, Zheng. *Women in the Chinese Enlightenment: Oral and Textual Histories.* 1999. Studies the development of Chinese feminism through the lives of five women.

Wells, Audrey. *The Political Thought of Sun Yat-sen.* 2001. A good new study.

Wilbur, C. Martin. *Sun Yat-sen: Frustrated Patriot.* 1976. Evenhanded book.

Young, Helen Praeger. *Choosing Revolution: Chinese Women Soldiers on the Long March.* 2001. Story of the more than 2,000 female Communist soldiers who participated in the Long March.

WEB SOURCES

www.fordham.edu/halsall/eastasia/eastasiasbook.html. Contains links to materials on Japan and China including by Sun Yat-Sen and Mao Tse-tung, and about the May Fourth Movement.

www.marxists.org/reference/archive/mao/. This site has many links to materials on and about Mao Tse-tung.

*Paperback available.

14

⑥Nationalist Struggles in India and Southeast Asia

World War I greatly accelerated the movement for self-government in India and Southeast Asia. Before 1914 most nationalist movements of the area merely sought participation in the colonial government; by the late 1920s many would be satisfied only with independence. Because of India's dominance and leadership in Asia's struggle for independence, this chapter focuses on the subcontinent.

INDIA

India during World War I

INDIAN CONTRIBUTIONS TO WORLD WAR I

India was loyal to Great Britain throughout World War I because most Indians realized that the Allies were more liberal and democratic than the Central Powers. The Indian press was nearly unanimous in supporting the British war effort. India contributed substantially to the Allied war cause: 800,000 soldiers went to Europe and the Middle East, 500,000 noncombatant laborers worked in factories and mines in Europe, and many Indians made monetary contributions and war loans. In return, Great Britain appointed more Indians to high government positions, and an Indian delegation participated in postwar peace negotiations.

In August 1917 the British government for the first time proclaimed its goal to be self-government for India within the British Commonwealth, to be implemented in stages. Toward its eventual realization, the British Parliament passed the Government of India Act in 1919. By this act, an electorate of middle-class voters was permitted to elect representatives to provincial assemblies in which the party with a majority formed a government that controlled a number of departments of the provincial administration. However, public security and the provincial budget remained under the control of the British-appointed governor and his nonelected advisers. This system of sharing power in the provinces between appointed officers and the elected Indian representatives was called dyarchy. In the central government, a British-appointed viceroy retained supreme power and appointed a cabinet of Britons and Indians to assist him in the administration. The national assembly of elected Indian representatives could only advise the viceroy. At the insistence of Muslims, separate electorates, whereby Muslims and Hindus elected their separate representatives, were continued. The act of 1919 was intended to remain in effect for 10 years, after which there would be evaluation for changes. Indian moderates welcomed these reforms, but radicals denounced them as inadequate. Because of the worldwide demand for women's suffrage and British women's enfranchisement after World War I, Indian women also won the right to vote on the same terms as men (based on literacy and property qualifications, as in the Morley-Minto Reforms, but liberalized) in 1925.

INDIA'S ELECTED ASSEMBLIES GAIN GREATER POWERS

In 1918 a government commission recommended legislation empowering provincial governments to jail suspected political subversives without trial and to try political cases without a jury. When the recommendations were enacted into law, known as the Rowlatt Act, Indian nationalists were outraged. The Indian National Congress launched public meetings to protest the law. The protests turned violent in Punjab province, where a mob murdered four Europeans in the city Amritsar. Shortly after this incident, about 10,000 people, without official permission, gathered in a large, enclosed square in Amritsar for a meeting. Without warning, the British commanding general in the city ordered troops to fire on the assembled crowd. The official estimate of casualties was 379 killed and over 1,200 wounded. The Amritsar Massacre crystallized anti-British feelings and became a rallying point for the Indian independence movement.

The Rise of Gandhi

Mohandas K. Gandhi was commonly called Mahatma ("Great Soul," or "Holy One") by his followers. He was born in 1869 of prosperous, devout Hindu parents and studied law in Britain. During the four years Gandhi lived in London his mind was opened to Hindu scriptures as well as Christian, Buddhist, and Muslim teachings, and in addition to works of nineteenth-century European writers such as Leo Tolstoy and Henry Thoreau. After a brief, unsuccessful attempt to practice law in India, he took his family to South Africa to represent some Indian clients. He quickly gained a reputation there as a champion of Indian immigrant workers against white South African bigotry and discrimination. He perfected techniques of peaceful protest demonstrations and called his nonviolent movement *Satyagraha* (truth force). He taught his followers the tactic of non-cooperation to protest unjust laws. Gandhi returned to India in 1915 after organizing an ambulance corps of Indian residents in Britain to serve with British troops at the front.

M. K. GANDHI DEVELOPS NONVIOLENT TACTICS

The immediate postwar years were disturbing ones in India. Severe economic problems were associated with demobilization. There was also widespread dissatisfaction with the slow pace of political reform and outrage over the Rowlatt Act, considered humiliating to Indians, and the Amritsar Massacre during which many peaceful protesters were shot down. Many Indian Muslims, already uneasy when the Ottoman Empire joined the Central Powers against Britain in World War I, resented its dismantling at the Paris Peace Conference. They organized a pan-Islamic Khalifat movement to support the authority of the Ottoman emperor as the caliph (leader) of Islam. The movement collapsed when Mustafa Kemal Ataturk ended the Ottoman Empire and created a secular Republic of Turkey (see Chapter 15).

GANDHI LEADS INDIAN NATIONAL CONGRESS

In 1921 the Indian National Congress gave Gandhi sole executive authority. He immediately declared Congress support for the Khalifat movement and launched a campaign of civil disobedience against British rule. His ideas were simple. He argued that since fewer than 200,000 Britons ruled 400 million Indians, the maintenance of

BIOGRAPHY

A New Weapon in the Struggle for Freedom

News was received that the Rowlatt Bill had been published as an Act. That night I fell asleep while thinking over the question. Towards the small hours of the morning I woke up somewhat earlier than usual. I was still in that twilight condition between sleep and consciousness when suddenly the idea broke upon me—it was as if in a dream. Early in the morning I related the whole story to Rajagopalachari [an Indian National Congress leader].

The idea came to me last night in a dream that we should call upon the country to observe a general hartal. Satyagraha is a process of self-purification, and ours is a sacred fight, and it seems to me to be the fitness of things that it should be commenced with an act of self-purification. Let all the people of India, therefore, suspend their business on that day and observe the day as one of fasting and prayer. The Musalmans [Muslims] may not fast for more than one day; so the duration of the fast should be 24 hours. . . .

Rajagopalachari was at once taken up with my suggestion. Other friends too welcomed it. . . . I drafted a brief appeal. The date of the hartal was first fixed on the 30th March 1919, but was subsequently changed to 6th April. . . . The whole of India from one end to the other, towns as well as villages, observed a complete hartal on that day. It was a most wonderful experience.*

. . .

Mohandas K. Gandhi (1869–1948), a British-educated lawyer, became a leader of the Indian National Congress during World War I. He was responsible for changing its direction into a mass movement by such actions as the hartal *described here. A* hartal *is a strike with a moral purpose, accompanied by fasting. Gandhi first employed it as a protest against the British-imposed Rowlatt Act, which cracked down on Indian protests. He won worldwide respect for his saintly lifestyle but was resented by some Indians for his moral scruples. He was assassinated by a Hindu fanatic soon after India won independence.*

*From The Story of My Experiments with Truth by Mohandas K. Gandhi. Copyright © 1927 by Viking Penguin Company. Reprinted by permission of Navajian Trust.

British authority had to be based on Indian cooperation. Consequently, if Indians withdrew their cooperation, British rule could not continue. Despite his upper-middle-class upbringing, Gandhi also realized that the nationalist movement, previously mostly middle class, must be expanded to include the masses, transcend caste lines, and unite Hindus and Muslims. Toward this end, he visited villages throughout India, traveling by foot or riding in fourth-class trains, dressed in simple homespun garb that he made. He preached his message in simple terms and taught the goal of national unity and the tactics of nonviolence to ordinary people. He persuaded the Indian National Congress to lower its membership dues to a nominal sum to attract poor members and to publish its messages in Indian languages as well as in English.

Women became politically active during this period. In 1926 the All-India Women's Conference was established; it later became an unofficial auxiliary of the Congress. Thousands of women came out of the seclusion of their homes to join

A protest march organized by the Indian National Congress against the British in 1928.

Gandhi's demonstrations. The most famous woman activist was Sarojini Naidu, a poet dubbed "India's nightingale." Later she became India's first woman provincial governor.

Gandhi was not only interested in driving out the British. He also crusaded in favor of social reform to rid Hindu society of customs that oppressed and victimized women and certain social classes. He spoke eloquently against child marriage, especially for women, the prohibition against widow remarriage, and, above all, the oppression of the untouchables. He spoke of independence as something one must deserve and implied that Hindus did not deserve self-rule when they oppressed whole categories of their own people. He renamed the untouchables *Harijans*, which means "children of God," to signify their common humanity with other Indians. He founded a journal named *The Harijan*, which published his writings, and often insisted that he be quartered in the untouchable part of a town that he was visiting. In his *ashram*, or retreat, he accepted Harijans and made sure that all castes shared in doing unpleasant menial work, such as sweeping and cleaning toilets, that was the lot of the untouchables throughout Hindu India. He did not believe in legislating social change; rather, he emphasized changing people's hearts and minds.

Gandhi mobilized the masses in repeated *Satyagraha* movements against the British. He organized peaceful demonstrations and strikes and told Indians to confront police brutality by "offering the other cheek." Thus, when Indians rioted and committed violent acts during demonstrations, a disappointed Gandhi would call off his *Satyagraha* and go on a fast to atone for the violence. He also fasted to persuade his British adversaries and his Indian followers to see their error and change their ways as a result of their own moral awakening. Some Indians did not care about the means used so long as they achieved their desired end, and they blamed Gandhi's moral scruples for delaying the attainment of Indian independence.

**GANDHI CHAMPIONS
SOCIAL REFORMS**

Gandhi and J. Nehru in 1938; both had discarded Western clothes in favor of Indian garb, Gandhi for homespuns.

THE SALT MARCH GAINS INTERNATIONAL ATTENTION

Gandhi's Salt March of 1930 exemplified his method of protest. The government had a monopoly on the manufacture and sale of salt and taxed it for revenue. Gandhi chose to protest the salt tax as a burden on the poor and as a symbol of British laws that violated Indian civil rights. In March 1930 Gandhi led 78 followers on the Great Salt March. In a well-publicized media event, they slowly walked 200 miles to the seacoast. Daily, thousands turned out to cheer them on, and some joined the march. When he reached the coast, Gandhi waded into the water and drew out a pitcherful, which he boiled to extract the salt. In so doing, he symbolically defied the salt monopoly and the salt tax law. Indians responded with a general strike and with *Swadeshi*, a movement to boycott British manufactured goods, especially British woven cotton textiles, and to replace them with Indian homespun cotton cloth. The boycott put many British laborers out of work, thus placing additional pressure on the government to make concessions. Gandhi and 60,000 of his supporters were arrested, but the civil disobedience campaign persisted. Finally the government capitulated. Gandhi and his supporters were released from jail, the salt tax was reduced, and some restrictive laws opposed by the Indian National Congress were rescinded.

The campaign showed Gandhi at his most brilliant. A humanitarian, he abhorred violence; a political realist, he understood that his cause would most benefit by winning the sympathy of world public opinion. He further understood that democratic Great Britain was sensitive to public opinion at home and abroad, and that the British government could be forced to make concessions in response to public pressure.

In many ways, Gandhi was a traditionalist—for example, he loved Hindu customs and dreamed of an independent India true to its ancient heritage, one that turned its back on modern technology and industrial society. Gandhi advocated reviving cottage industries not only to support the *Swadeshi* movement but also for their intrinsic economic and social value. For several hours nearly every day, he spun and wove his own cloth, which he wore exclusively after he gave up wearing Western-style clothing. Millions of Indians, of high station and low, also took up the weaving of homespun cloth, so that the spinning wheel came to symbolize the Indian nationalist movement. At his insistence, the Indian National Congress required its members to spend a portion of their day working at a handloom. Yet, even in his lifetime, some of Gandhi's ideas contradicted the modern trends and aspirations of millions of Indians. Demands of World War I had led to massive growth in India's industries, from textiles to iron and steel, and the pattern continued after the war.

GANDHI STRESSES DIGNITY OF LABOR

The Hindu-Muslim Communal Problem

Gandhi advocated a policy of generosity toward Muslims. He welcomed all, especially the Muslims, to join the Indian National Congress, which he sought to make into a body that represented all Indian nationalists. Thus, he disapproved of separate electorates for Muslims or any other minority or special-interest group. Instead, he suggested that Muslims be given a guaranteed number of representatives on the Congress ticket. In this effort Gandhi failed, for several reasons. One was that militant Hindus in the Congress foresaw victory in the elections and refused to set aside a percentage of seats for Muslim representatives. Another was that the Muslims were now largely represented by the All-India Muslim League led by M. A. Jinnah. League leaders, many of whom were also British-trained lawyers, objected to Gandhi's nonconstitutional methods of protest and did not share his rejection of Western values. Moreover, the League relied on separate electorates to protect Muslim rights. Thus, any Muslim who joined the Congress was not recognized by fellow Muslims as a representative of the Muslim community.

HINDUS AND MUSLIMS FAIL TO REACH ACCORD

As a result, in the rancor that surfaced in the post-1919 election campaigns and competition for power, the relative communal peace of the war years quickly evaporated. Congress Hindus sought to capture and hold the power their numbers guaranteed to them. On the other hand, Muslims feared the potential tyranny of Hindu majority rule and demanded safeguards for their rights in any political negotiations.

From the late 1920s on, Great Britain stepped up the timetable for Indian independence in response to Indian demands. However, no proposal the British made was acceptable to both the Indian National Congress and the All-India Muslim League, and neither accepted the other's suggested solutions. Mutual hatred between Hindus and Muslims (Muslim fear of Hindu numbers and Hindu fear of possible new Muslim inroads by conversion) came to outweigh hatred for the foreign ruler. In the final analysis, the inability of Indians to solve their communal problem delayed their attaining self-government.

The India Act of 1935

THE INDIA ACT: LAST STEP BEFORE FULL SELF-GOVERNMENT

After several years of intensive consultations with the representatives of different interests, the British government concluded that India should become a federation of princely states and self-governing provinces. The Government of India Act of 1935 enlarged the electorate to 18 percent of the population, which would elect representatives to both provincial and federal legislatures. Each province was to be entirely self-governing; the party with a majority of elected representatives would form the government. The British-appointed provincial governor became largely a figurehead, except in emergencies, when he could veto actions by the elected government. At the federal level, the British-appointed viceroy was advised by the Executive Council, chosen from the elected members of the federal legislature. He also had the power of veto and emergency powers. At the Muslim League's insistence, separate electorates were retained for Muslims in all elections. In addition, the India Act provided that other minorities and special-interest groups such as Christians, Harijans, women, Europeans, laborers, and landlords would also have their own elected representatives in every assembly, in seats reserved for them according to a quota system. The more than 500 princely states were also given representation in the federal legislature based on their size and population. This act attempted to ensure that all Indians received representation and had a voice in the government. The federal form of government, in which each province had broad rights, was an attempt to satisfy Muslim demands that they should rule themselves in areas where they were a majority.

While the Indian National Congress criticized portions of the act as either insufficient or reactionary, it nevertheless set about to capture as much power as possible in the elections that the act mandated. Although the Muslim League won majorities in the few Muslim-dominated provinces in the provincial elections of 1936, the Indian National Congress captured a majority in all the remaining provinces. Greatly encouraged by its effective organization and vote-getting power, Congress leader Jawaharlal Nehru bragged, "There are only two parties in the country—the Congress and the British." Such statements only aggravated the fears of Muslims over their future in a Hindu-dominated independent India. The India Act also separated Burma from India and provided the Burmese with self-government comparable to that of the Indians.

NATIONALIST MOVEMENTS IN SOUTHEAST ASIA

REFORMS IN DUTCH EAST INDIES

In the Dutch East Indies, a Muslim-rooted nationalist movement had been active since the early twentieth century, but the Dutch government made only slow progress in accommodation to it. The Dutch-created People's Council, which began in 1918, initially had only advisory power. After 1929 half of the Council members were elected Indonesians, and all legislation needed its assent. These reforms did not satisfy either the National Indonesian Party, led by Sukarno, or the Indonesian Communist Party. These two parties vied for leadership in the independence movement.

In Indochina, French tactics of combining direct and indirect rule, cultivation of the native elite, and local ethnic diversity all contributed to retard the nationalist movement. Among all Indochinese, the Vietnamese offered the greatest resistance to French rule. The failure of moderate Vietnamese nationalists to persuade the French to make concessions opened the way for the more extreme elements. Ho Chi Minh emerged during the interwar years as the most prominent nationalist leader. He went to France as a young man. In 1921, after failing to gain concessions for Vietnam at the Paris Peace Conference, Ho helped to organize the French Communist Party. In 1925 he surfaced in Canton, where he worked for Soviet advisers who were then helping the KMT in China. It was not until 1930 that he drew together various dissident Vietnamese groups in Hong Kong and formed the Communist Party of Indochina. Although the French authorities crushed all peasant and nationalist revolts in Vietnam, they failed to eliminate a growing nationalist movement.

FRANCE CRUSHES PROTESTS IN INDOCHINA

In the Philippines, in contrast, a bicameral legislature of elected representatives had taken over lawmaking since 1916. Only the governor-general, the vice governors, and the judges of the supreme court were still appointed from Washington. In 1919 President Wilson promised complete independence, but it took the depression of 1930 to hasten its realization.

Since the Philippines was a U.S. possession, both Filipino products (notably sugar, tobacco, and coconut oil) and Filipino immigrants could freely enter the United States. During the depression, U.S. industry, in particular the sugar industry, and U.S. labor unions agitated in favor of granting independence to the Philippines so that its cheap products and labor could be shut out of the United States. Others supported Philippine independence because of the cost of defending it. Thus, in 1934 the U.S. Congress passed the Tydings-McDuffie Act, which immediately gave full self-government to the Philippines, except for control of its foreign policy by Washington for 10 more years. During that period Washington would also provide protection for the islands. Complete independence was promised for July 4, 1944.

PHILIPPINES MOVES TOWARD INDEPENDENCE

S U M M A R Y

Between the two world wars European imperialism was on the retreat and nationalism was on the rise throughout the colonial world in South and Southeast Asia. As before, India led the way. As a result of Indian contributions in World War I, Britain agreed to grant India self-government, which it proceeded to implement in the acts of 1919 and 1935. Sharp disagreements emerged, however, over the timing and over how Hindus and Muslims would share and divide power in a self-governing India. Led by Mahatma Gandhi, who applied tactics of nonviolent protest that he had earlier developed in South Africa to the Indian independence struggle, the Indian National Congress developed grassroots support but increasingly represented only Hindu aspirations. The prospect of a Hindu-dominated self-governing India led Muslims to cling to separate electorates and to follow the All-India Muslim League and its president, M. A. Jinnah, as their champions. In elections held in accordance with the India Act of 1935, the Congress won majorities in Hindu-populated states, and the League won majorities in Muslim ones.

In comparison, the Dutch East Indies was far behind in its nationalist struggles. In Indochina, likewise, French authoritarian rule continued supreme after successfully suppressing peasant revolts in 1930. In the same year, however, Ho Chi Minh organized the Indochinese Communist Party in exile. The U.S.-ruled Philippines was the only colony in Southeast Asia that made significant progress toward independence, as U.S. policy progressively associated Filipinos in the process of self-government. In 1934 the U.S. Congress passed an act that immediately granted autonomy to the Philippines, with full independence to follow in 10 years.

SUGGESTED SOURCES

Das, Durga. *India from Curzon to Nehru and After.* 1970. Written by India's foremost journalist, who was an eyewitness to many of the events.

Embree, Ainslie T. *India's Search for National Identity.* 1981. A brief, readable, and objective introduction.*

Faswell, Byron. *Armies of the Raj from the Great Indian Mutiny to Independence: 1858–1947.* 1989. A good, colorful book.*

Gandhi. 1982. A sympathetic film portraying the powerful impact of the great Indian leader.

Gandhi, Mohandas K. *The Story of My Experiment with Truth.* Trans. Mahadev Desai. 1945. A frank, personal account.*

Indochine. 1992. A film portraying French rule in Vietnam.

Jalal, Ayesha. *The Sole Spokesman: Jinnah, the Muslim League, and the Demand for Pakistan.* 1985. An authoritative work on the movement for a separate Muslim nation.

James, Lawrence. *Raj, The Making and Unmaking of British India.* 1997. A scholarly survey, well written, enlightening, and entertaining.

Khanh, Huynh Kim. *Vietnamese Communism, 1925–1945.* 1986. A description of the origins and development of Vietnamese communism and the role of the party in the anticolonial struggle.*

Nehru, Jawaharlal. *An Autobiography.* 1989; first published in 1936. A reflective account of his life and times written while in prison in 1934–1935.*

———. *The Discovery of India.* Ed. Robert I. Crane. 1960. India's first postindependence prime minister explains his country's history and heritage.*

Wolpert, Stanley. *Gandhi's Passion: The Life and Legacy of Mahatma Gandhi.* 2002. A balanced, lucid, and thoughtful book.*

———. *Nehru: A Tryst with Destiny.* 1996. An authoritative, analytic biography.

WEB SOURCES

www.fordham.edu/halsall/india/indiasbook.html. Excellent site offering numerous links to history of Indian subcontinent; see, for example, materials under Gandhi and the Muslim League.

www.ibiblio.org/gandhi/gandhi/default.htm. Website with many links to Gandhi materials, including his writings.

---

*Paperback available.

⑥Anticolonialism in the Middle East and Africa

As the anticolonial struggle swept India in the period between the wars, nationalists intensified their efforts in the Middle East and Africa. The strength and extent of these nationalist movements differed widely from area to area. The Middle East was often in a state of turmoil, as Arab nationalists shifted their activity from resisting the Ottomans to opposing British and French control, and Jews attempted to establish a homeland in Palestine. Even states that were nominally independent, such as Iran and Turkey, witnessed the stirring of a new nationalism. In both nations, dynamic leaders emerged who sought modernization and Westernization precisely in order to repel Western domination and to make their nations independent in fact as well as in name. African nationalist movements developed later in the century than their Asian counterparts. Nevertheless, the interwar period witnessed the beginning of anti-Western independence movements throughout Africa.

NATIONALIST UNREST IN THE MIDDLE EAST

Allied political considerations during World War I aided nationalist movements throughout the Middle East. The British were generally willing to assist Arab nationalism, not because they necessarily believed in its aims but because they hoped that an Arab revolt would weaken Ottoman forces and thus help to protect the Suez Canal. Lord Herbert Kitchener of Khartoum, as British high commissioner in Egypt and later secretary of war, discussed the possibility of Arab independence with Abdullah, a son of Sharif Husayn (sharif is a title indicating both a religious and political leader). Sharif Husayn was a leader in the Muslim holy city of Mecca, which was still part of the dying Ottoman Empire in World War I. To aid their war effort and postwar imperial plans, the British made three agreements involving the Middle East that sowed the seeds for a struggle—the Israeli–Palestinian Arab conflict—that has yet to be resolved.

Conflicting Wartime Agreements

The first wartime agreement was the secret correspondence (1915–1916) between Henry McMahon, the British high commissioner in Egypt, and Sharif Husayn, acting in the self-appointed role of champion of Arab independence. The British promised to support an independent Arab state after the war in return for Arab support

213

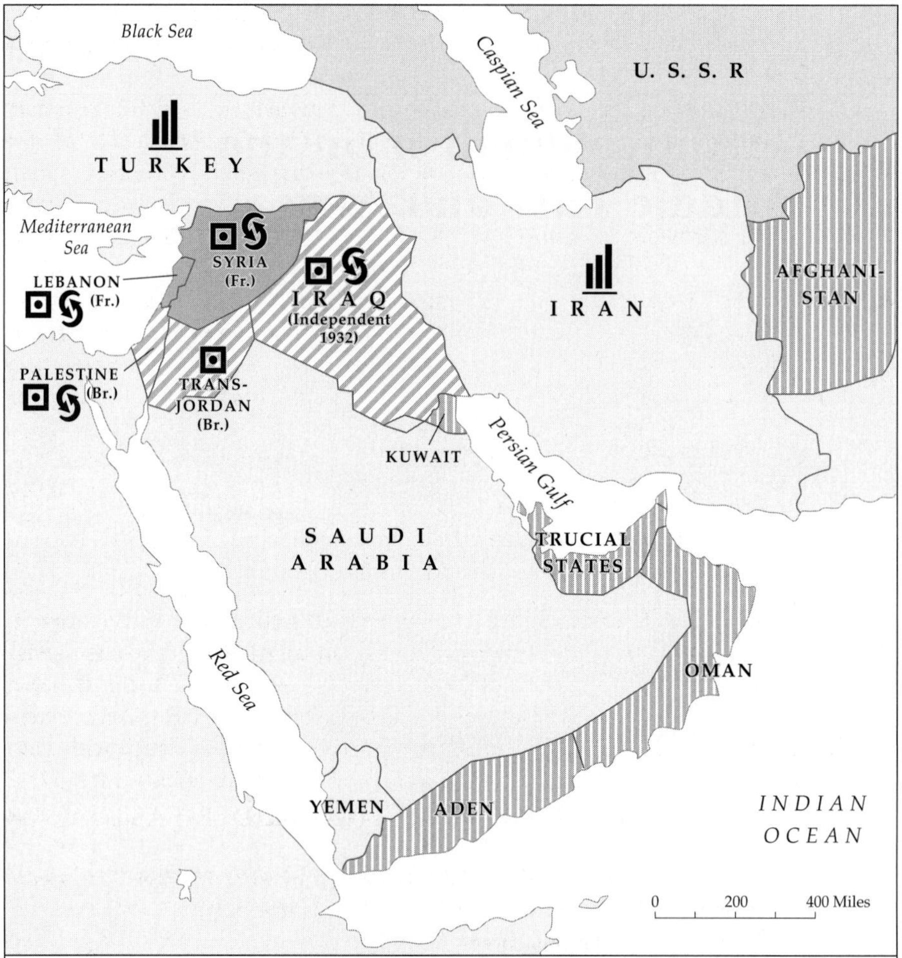

The Middle East in the Interwar Years

League mandates of former Ottoman territory

States undergoing modernization under Western influence

Instances of unrest by indigenous populations

British protectorate

Under British control

Under French control

during the war. The negotiations were protracted because of the conflict over the boundaries for the proposed Arab state. Husayn originally demanded all of the Arab Middle East south of Turkey, including most of the Arabian peninsula. The British countered that they had interests in Iraq and that the French had religious and economic interests in the territory that is today Lebanon. While pointing out that all the territory was clearly Arab, Husayn finally agreed to compromise on Iraq and

Lebanon. As a result, the Arabs raised the standard of revolt against the Ottoman Empire and fought on the Allied side, believing that after the war they would receive independence.

However, the British had made a second secret commitment, which in part contradicted their agreement with Husayn. In the Sykes-Picot Agreement (1916), the British and the French agreed to divide the Ottoman Empire among European nations. The Anatolian peninsula was to be partitioned, and the French were to secure Lebanon and Syria, while the British were to receive Iraq and Palestine and a sphere of influence over the Arabian peninsula. The British probably did not demand direct control over what is today Saudi Arabia because in 1916 the vast petroleum reserves in that nation had not yet been discovered. Because both European terms and Ottoman administrative divisions for these areas were used in both agreements, after the war there was some confusion and argument over the exact terms and borders.

SYKES-PICOT

The Balfour Declaration of November 1917 was the third British statement regarding the Middle East. To understand this pronouncement it is necessary to discuss briefly the Zionist movement, fervently supported by some Jews in Europe and the United States, that sought to establish a Jewish state in Palestine. Theodor Herzl, a Hungarian journalist and Zionist leader, had advocated in his book *Der Judenstaat (The Jewish State)* that Jews have a nation of their own in order to avoid anti-Semitism, which he believed was an evil inherent in Western civilization. The Dreyfus case in France and the pogroms in Poland and Russia had convinced Herzl and other Jewish leaders that Jews needed a state of their own. Herzl favored accepting any territory; parts of Argentina and Uganda were even suggested. However, Chaim Weizmann, a chemist of Polish origin, argued that Palestine, the location of the ancient Jewish state, was the only place in which the Zionists could realize their aspirations. In 1897, at the First Zionist Congress, Zionists pledged to work for the creation of a Jewish state in Palestine.

ZIONISM AND THE BALFOUR DECLARATION

In November 1917 British foreign secretary Arthur Balfour wrote to a prominent British Zionist, Lord Rothschild, publicly stating British support for "the establishment in Palestine of a national home for the Jewish people." Balfour also stated that "nothing shall be done which may prejudice" the rights of the non-Jewish communities (the Arab majority) in Palestine or the rights of Jews in other nations. In such a manner, the British hoped to assuage those Jews, particularly in Great Britain, who opposed the Zionist idea of creating a Jewish state because they feared the existence of such a state would only increase anti-Semitism. Prime Minister David Lloyd George favored the Balfour Declaration because he wanted more support for the war effort. Zionists hailed it as a major step toward the realization of their dream. Although Balfour had not promised that Great Britain would support an independent Jewish state in Palestine, many Jews and non-Jews believed that an independent Jewish state would eventually be established.

Arab leaders promptly condemned the Balfour Declaration and vowed to oppose the creation of a Jewish state in Palestine. About 90 percent of its population was composed of Arabs, many of whom lived in rural villages. Many Westerners, who knew little of the area, concluded—on the basis of the Balfour Declaration, which had referred only to the "non-Jewish population"—that only a few nomads lived in what

PALESTINIAN NATIONALISM

B I O G R A P H Y

A Vision of Zion

In the winter of 1918 the American Jewish Congress held its first convention in Philadelphia. The main purpose was the formulation of a program (to be presented at the Peace Conference in Versailles) for the safeguarding of the civil rights of the Jews in Europe. To my astonishment . . . I was chosen to be one of the delegates from Milwaukee. It was a marvelously stimulating experience; I can still remember how proud I was to have been chosen to represent my own community and what it was like sitting with the rest of the delegation in the overheated train on our way to Philadelphia. I was (as always in that period) the youngest in the group and, in a way, everyone pampered me—except when it came to giving me assignments. Today when journalists ask me when my political career actually began, my mind always flashes back to that convention, to the smoke-filled hall in a Philadelphia hotel where I sat for hours listening, completely absorbed, to the details of the program being thrashed out, to the excitement of the debates and of being able to cast my own vote.*

. . .

In her autobiography, Golda Meir remembers the exciting times in her early 20s when she was just beginning her political career. Born in Ukraine in 1898, Golda Meir and her family immigrated to the United States, where they settled in Milwaukee. While still a student, Meir became an ardent supporter of the Zionist movement for an independent Jewish state and moved to Palestine, where she became a leading figure in the fight to create the independent state of Israel. As a key figure in the Labor Party, Meir twice won in general elections, becoming one of Israel's most famous prime ministers. She died in 1978.

*From *My Life* by Golda Meir. The Putnam Publishing Group. Copyright © 1975 by Golda Meir.

was otherwise a sparsely populated territory. Consequently, many Westerners failed to recognize that if Jewish settlements were supported, another group, the Palestinians, might well lose their homeland. This laid the foundation for the Arab-Israeli conflict.

CONFLICTING CLAIMS   The contradictions inherent in the three agreements became clear at the Paris Peace Conference. Sharif Husayn's son Faysal, Weizmann, and a host of other nationalist leaders appeared in Paris with their documents. Their hopes for national self-determination had been fueled by Wilson's Fourteen Points and declarations favoring self-determination. Although a champion of self-determination, Wilson was willing to back European interests in the Middle East instead of Arab aspirations in order to secure Allied support for the League of Nations and other parts of his program. As a result, the British and the French were able to implement their territorial ambitions in the Middle East. Under the terms agreed on at the San Remo Conference in 1920, the British obtained mandates over Iraq and Palestine, including what is today Jordan, and the French obtained mandates over Syria and Lebanon. When it became clear that the Arabs were not to receive independence, one Iraqi Arab remarked, "Independence is never given, it is taken." In fact, several decades were to pass before Arab national aspirations were realized.

The decisions made at the 1921 Cairo Conference regarding the future government of Iraq and other Arab territories continue to influence events in the region today. British colonial secretary Winston Churchill (front row, center) chaired the conference that included Gertrude Bell (second row, second left), a British expert on Iraq, and T. E. Lawrence (second row, fourth right), who had participated in the Arab Revolt during World War I.

Postwar Developments

Following the Paris conference, France immediately moved troops into Syria and Lebanon, even though a General Syrian Congress had in March 1920 proclaimed Faysal as the constitutional monarch of a united Syria. In the face of superior French military force, Faysal was forced to flee from Syria, but the Syrian Arabs never accepted the French occupation and continued to fight against it. In Lebanon, the French exercised less direct control, relying heavily on the Maronite Christian Lebanese, who were about half the total population. They also enlarged the nation by including within its boundaries several predominantly Muslim areas that had previously been under Syrian domination. By relying on one religious group, the French helped to intensify religious differences in Lebanon that have persisted until the present.

Meanwhile, Great Britain proceeded with its own arrangements. When the Iraqis launched armed rebellions against the British, Britain increased its military presence in the country and launched aerial bombardments of Iraqi towns. To decide what to do with their new imperial holdings in the Middle East, especially oil-rich Iraq, the new colonial secretary, Winston Churchill, held a meeting of key advisers in Cairo in

MONARCHIES IN IRAQ AND JORDAN

1921. In steps that foreshadowed U.S. decisions regarding Iraq in the twenty-first century, the British decided to provide a facade of independence by holding elections in Iraq and crowning Faysal king of a constitutional monarchy that was bound by treaty in a close alliance with Great Britain. British troops remained in Iraq, and the British continued as the major power behind the monarchy.

Great Britain divided the Palestinian mandate into two sections, making Abdullah the emir (prince) of the new state, Transjordan, in the interior, which historically had never been part of Palestine and which had been ruled under the Ottoman Empire from Damascus. (This state was later known as Jordan.) In the coastal area of Palestine proper, the British attempted to balance the conflicting Zionist and Palestinian Arab demands for independence. The 1920s and 1930s were marked by continued political confrontation and sporadic armed conflict between Zionists and Palestinian Arabs.

STRUGGLES IN PALESTINE

Meanwhile, the Zionists worked to translate their goals into reality through Jewish immigration, colonization, and Western support. The Palestinians opposed both Zionist and British activities; by the 1930s, Palestinian opposition was directed largely against the British. The British, responding in the old imperial tradition, sent out a series of commissions to investigate the problems. By 1937 it appeared to the British commission that the conflict was irreconcilable and that Palestine should be partitioned into a Jewish and an Arab state. The Palestinian Arabs, who viewed the territory as theirs, rejected the partition scheme, which allotted about 50 percent of the land to the Jews, who numbered only 30 percent of the population. Many Zionists also opposed the plan because it failed to allot to them all of the territory that had been part of historic Israel.

As a result of continued British controls and the mounting Zionist presence that the British had permitted and sometimes encouraged, from 1936 to 1939 the Palestinians launched a full-scale strike and armed opposition against British troops. The British retaliated with superior weapons and organization and, after inflicting heavy losses, destroyed the Palestinian armed opposition. However, as World War II drew closer, the British sought to placate Arab leaders. The White Paper of 1939 proposed limiting Jewish immigration for five years, after which time immigration quotas were to be subject to Palestinian acquiescence. Further, British control over Palestine was to be discussed after 10 years. The Zionists immediately rejected the 1939 plan, which they dubbed the "Black Paper." Zionists were particularly incensed that the British wanted to limit Jewish immigration into Palestine at the very time that persecutions of Jews were increasing in Nazi-dominated parts of Europe. Thus the British wavered between the Zionists and the Palestinians, while both remained opposed to continued British domination.

MONARCHY IN SAUDI ARABIA

In Mecca, Sharif Husayn, who had proclaimed himself king during World War I, was having troubles of his own. Throughout the war Husayn had fought not only the Central Powers but also local rivals. Ironically, his major rival, Abd al-Aziz Ibn Saud (a follower of the Wahhabi movement, which advocated the establishment of a puritanical Islamic government), had also received British subsidies during the war. Saud had the advantages of religious zeal, better organization, and military strength; by 1925, he succeeded in ousting Husayn. He then established a Saudi Arabian monarchy based on strict adherence to Islamic precepts.

SECULARISM VERSUS SPIRITUALISM

In the Middle East and the Islamic world in general, so-called modernizing leaders wanted to create secular nation-states largely modeled on Western ones. They sought to industrialize the economies of their nations while simultaneously adopting largely Western models in dress, culture, education, and behavior. More traditional or conservative forces in these societies opposed the wholesale adoption of Western institutions and sought to preserve and reinforce traditional spiritual and societal values based on Islam.

MODERNISM IN TURKEY AND IRAN

After World War I, new, Western-looking leaders seemed to predominate, instituting sweeping changes in Turkey and Iran. To a much lesser extent, Afghanistan was affected by similar conflicts between modernizing leaders and a largely conservative, traditional populace. In both Turkey and Iran, largely Muslim and traditional nations, modernizing but authoritarian rulers sought to diminish the importance of religion and religious institutions and to force secularization based on the Western model. In both nations, changes were forced from above rather than from the grassroots level. Perhaps nowhere else in the postwar world were the lines between the conflicting forces of religion and secularism more clearly drawn.

In Turkey, Mustafa Kemal, or Ataturk (father of the Turks), emerged as the leader following the collapse of the old Ottoman government. A professional soldier by training, Ataturk embarked on an ambitious program of Westernization. He eliminated both the old Ottoman sultanate and the caliphate and created a parliamentary state with himself as the president. Using nationalism and his enormous personal popularity, Ataturk attempted to alter the entire structure of Turkish society. He banned the wearing of the veil by women, forced men to wear Western hats rather than the traditional fez, and even had a new alphabet created based on Western models. Ataturk often toured the countryside with a portable blackboard on which he personally taught the new alphabet, thereby turning Turkey into one vast classroom. Turkey also managed to avoid imperial domination or foreign entanglements while steering a careful course of neutrality. Although Ataturk was an authoritarian ruler, he bequeathed to Turkey a relatively effective legislative democracy that survived long after his death. In contrast, many of his reforms regarding religion and the status of women were not as permanent.

In neighboring Iran (formerly Persia), another military officer, Reza Khan, overthrew the Qajar dynasty and also moved to Westernize and secularize the nation. Unlike Ataturk, however, Reza Khan retained the monarchy, with himself at the helm. The Pahlavi dynasty that Reza Khan established lasted until 1979, when it was overthrown in a popular revolution. Reza Khan was able to avoid imperial domination by either the Soviet Union or Great Britain, but his personal ambition and his attempts to undercut the power of the clergy and religion eventually brought down the Pahlavi dynasty.

NATIONALIST STIRRINGS IN AFRICA

As in Asia, people throughout Africa had been swayed by Wilson's persuasive statements regarding self-determination. However, African nationalist movements did not generally reach maturity until after World War II. In general, the first generation of African nationalist leaders represented the educated elite, who often came from old established tribes and who had enjoyed positions of power long before the arrival of the Europeans. These leaders, while well-meaning, often failed to reach the masses of the people who lived in isolated, remote villages. Early African nationalists were often Western educated and argued that they should enjoy equal rights with the Europeans.

Ironically, during World War II, there was a brief rapprochement, as both Africans and European settlers fought against Fascist and Nazi aggression. This cooperation ended after the war when the settlers moved to maintain their superior political and economic status and the black African majority struggled for independence.

Contrasting Imperial Policies

As previously indicated, the imperial policies of the European nations differed widely within Africa, where Germany lost its colonies as a result of World War I (see the map in Chapter 4). For their African empire, the British had developed a system of working through the traditional political institutions, known as indirect rule. However, the application of this policy varied tremendously from colony to colony. It tended to be most successful in areas where there were identifiable tribal authorities, as in Nigeria and the Gold Coast (Ghana), and was less successful in areas where there were conflicting local leaders or where there were white settlers, as in Rhodesia and Kenya.

BRITISH INDIRECT RULE

The British also continuously reaffirmed their intention to grant self-government as soon as they deemed the African peoples ready to assume the responsibilities of national independence. In British eyes, this would not occur, for the most part, for several more generations. During that time, members of the local African elite were to be exposed to and educated in the British system. Once they were educated, the local bureaucracies would be turned over to the African leaders. However, the British still planned to retain overall control for a period of time well into the future. In areas with white settlers, they anticipated turning over the government to them after an unscheduled period had elapsed. Anticipation of eventual self-government intensified African nationalism, causing open breaks between African nationalist movements and the British government.

FRANCE AND ASSIMILATION

In contrast to the British, the French claimed to be dedicated to a policy of maintaining close economic ties with their African colonies and of assimilating Africans into French society. Although the process of assimilation was never realized, it did seem to avoid the implication of African racial inferiority that was sometimes charged to the British approach of maintaining local and British systems in isolation from each other.

Both approaches were, in the final analysis, based on the notion of cultural superiority. British policies seemed to be based on the notion that Africans could never be like the British, and so there was no point in trying to assimilate them. On the other hand, French policies were based on belief in the superiority of French culture and the absolute assurance of the French that, given the opportunity, all people would in fact wish to become French. As a result of these conflicting policies, there tended to be greater nationalist political activity in British-held African territories than in those held by the French, Portuguese, or Belgians.

After the defeat of the Rif rebellion, the French sent the leaders, Abd al Krim (on the far right) and his brother along with their families into exile on Reunion Island. This rather friendly scene obscures the violent fighting in which the opponents had earlier engaged. Although the women of the Krim family were also sent into exile, in keeping with the conservative traditions of the time, they were not included in this posed photograph.

Revolts in North Africa

Keeping firm control over their North African empire of Morocco, Algeria, and Tunisia, the French crushed political movements organized by local nationalists. In the 1920s the Rif rebellion in Morocco, led by the Krim brothers, was brutally crushed by Spanish and French forces. Likewise, the protracted religious and nationalist movement in Libya was attacked and its followers bombed by the Italians. Throughout North Africa, nationalist leaders were closely watched and frequently jailed or sent into exile. In the Western world, nationalist forces and their opponents, such as the French Foreign Legion, were often pictured through the lens of Hollywood cameras. The area became a favorite subject for romanticized tales of adventure such as *The Sheik* and *Beau Geste,* two popular films of the era. These fictionalized accounts created a false impression that the peoples of North Africa were all either desert sheiks, living in exotic desert cities and oases, or poverty-stricken nomads. These stereotyped images continue to distort Western perceptions not only of North Africa but also of Arab and Islamic society in general.

REVOLUTION IN EGYPT

In Egypt, Britain faced a fully developed nationalist movement. Encouraged by the Fourteen Points and Allied declarations, a group of Egyptians led by Saad Zaghlul formed a delegation, or Wafd, to ask for Egyptian independence after the war. However, Egyptian demands were thwarted by British determination to control the vital Suez Canal. When the British rejected the Egyptian demands, a full-scale revolution erupted in 1919. Although Wafdist leaders were exiled, the Wafd Party became the chief political and nationalist organization from 1919 to 1952, and nationalist revolts persisted. The interwar years saw a protracted tricornered conflict for political power among the British, King Fu'ad and his successor King Faruk, and the Wafd. As a means of maintaining their presence in Egypt while undercutting the nationalist movement, the British unilaterally proclaimed Egyptian independence under the constitutional monarchy of King Fu'ad in 1922. Some Egyptian nationalist demands were furthered under the Anglo-Egyptian Treaty of 1936, but the British continued to hold the Suez Canal, to base soldiers on Egyptian territory, and to exercise widespread influence over Egyptian political life. As nationalist demands for complete independence failed, both the monarchy and the Wafd became increasingly corrupt and lost the support of the Egyptian population, which turned to more radical groups on the Left and Right and finally to the army for realization of their nationalist aspirations.

Agitation in West Africa

During the war, African colonies gave loyal support, and thousands of men died in the war effort; however, after the war their efforts were not recognized or rewarded. Many disgruntled former soldiers joined nationalist efforts. Groups from the British-held Gold Coast (Ghana) led the first demands for greater autonomy. Under the leadership of Casely Hayford, educated Africans from the four British colonies in West Africa met in 1920 in Accra, the capital of the Gold Coast, to discuss the implementation of reforms that would lead to independence. This group formed the nucleus of the National Congress of British West Africa, which met periodically for the next decade; after Hayford's death in 1930, however, the Congress withered away, its demands still far from realization.

NATIONALIST STRUGGLES IN NIGERIA

Nigeria, the largest and one of the most important British territories, was one of the focal points for nationalist outbreaks. Women merchants led demonstrations and riots in 1919 and again in 1928 in opposition to British domination. Under the leadership of Herbert Macaulay, Lagos, the capital city, soon became the center of the well-organized and effective nationalist opposition. In 1923 Macaulay organized the Nigerian National Democratic Party, which pushed for more Nigerian participation within the British-dominated political system. Similarly, Blaise Diagne, a customs official who became the first African to be elected to the French Chamber of Deputies, pushed for African national causes in French-held Senegal. However, following the same pattern as the rest of Africa, West African nationalists in both British and French territories faced an uphill battle, and their demands for independence were not met until after World War II.

Here Egyptian women demonstrate against the British occupation and in support of Wafdist demands for independence. In contrast to the absence of women in the earlier photograph of the Krim family, many Egyptian women were taking more public roles as, around the world, women participated in nationalist struggles for freedom.

Nationalists in the Belgian Congo faced even greater difficulties. Although the Belgians had established a local school system, few graduates went on to European universities, and, in general, the Belgians pursued a highly paternalistic policy in the Congo. Not surprisingly, repressive tactics by the Belgians only increased the number of nationalist sympathizers, who in the Congo frequently employed religious messages and beliefs to popularize their programs. The Belgian government responded by reinforcing its authoritarian system.

BELGIAN CONGO

Multiracial Tensions in British East Africa

Nationalist fervor varied greatly in British-dominated East Africa. In Uganda, where British authorities worked through local leaders who exercised local government duties, nationalist demonstrations were rare. In contrast, Kenya was a prime example of the contradictions and failures of British imperial policies. During the interwar years, racial and class divisions among the diverse population led to ongoing conflict. Indians from the subcontinent had been encouraged by the British to settle in fairly large numbers in both Kenya and Uganda and had gradually become the dominant merchants. Owing to their superior social and economic status within the British imperial system, the Indians never assimilated with the indigenous African population. On the other hand, they were never fully accepted by either white European settlers or British officials. Consequently, the issue of Indian citizenship and national participation irrevocably separated the East African population from the Indian immigrants, who generally sought to attain British citizenship.

CONFLICT OVER LAND IN KENYA

British policy in Kenya attempted to balance the rights of the Africans with the goal of furthering white settlement of the rich agricultural land in the Kenyan highlands. The Kikuyu, the largest tribe in the highlands, were particularly alienated by British policies. Not surprisingly, they resented the loss of their traditional landholdings and were also angered by British taxes.

Thus British policies created a racial and class hierarchy with the British, white settlers, and Indians at the top in descending order and the majority African population at the bottom. By the 1920s Kenyan nationalists reacted by establishing several groups, including the Kikuyu Central Association (KCA), formed in 1924. The British responded by arresting Kikuyu leaders, which only increased local hostility. Membership in the KCA grew as younger Kenyans joined the ranks. In 1928 a key Kikuyu leader, Jomo Kenyatta, became secretary of the KCA and presented Kikuyu grievances to the British government in London. Kenyatta remained in Europe until 1946, when he returned to take up the leadership of the Kenyan nationalist movement.

Southern Africa: Nationalism versus White Settler Rule

Nationalist movements in southern Africa faced many of the same problems as those in East Africa. In the Portuguese colonies of Angola and Mozambique, *prazos* (huge feudal estates) held by a very small white minority dominated agricultural and business activities. Like the *colons* in Algeria and the British settlers in Kenya, the *prazeros* clung tenaciously to these colonies and were the major force behind authoritarian Portuguese policies that were similar to those adopted in the Belgian Congo.

EUROPEAN SETTLERS IN SOUTHERN AFRICA

As in Mozambique and Angola, European settlers in British-held Rhodesia controlled economic and political power, placing the black African majority in a subordinate position and depriving them of effective political participation. The relative poverty and economic dependence of the Africans prevented them from forming effective nationalist organizations in the Portuguese colonies and in Rhodesia; the result would be protracted struggles for national independence after World War II.

RACIAL DIVISIONS IN SOUTH AFRICA

The racial and political divisions in the Union of South Africa were complex. After winning a victory over the Boers in South Africa and enjoying considerable support by many European settlers in South Africa during World War I, the British government first incorporated Boer territory and then granted it dominion status within the Commonwealth, a position that implied an equal partnership with the mother country. The British also embarked on a program of economic rehabilitation and assimilation of the Boers. Although the economic programs were fairly successful, attempts to assimilate the Boers failed, and a new brand of Afrikaner (white South Africans of Dutch origin) nationalism emerged.

The Afrikaners, as the Boers called themselves, formed political parties led by the military heroes of the Boer War. The Afrikaners moved to maintain their superior political and economic status through the United Party, which was established in 1934 by Generals Jan Christian Smuts and James Hertzog. By 1934 the segregationist policies that formed the foundation for apartheid ("separate development," a strict government policy of racial segregation) had already become apparent.

With vast natural resources, rich agricultural land, minerals, and water, the Union of South Africa, dominated by the white Afrikaners, prospered. However, the Bantu tribal peoples, who constituted over 80 percent of the population, were kept in subordinate positions as tenant farmers, manual laborers, or workers in the mines and factories. As they became increasingly disenfranchised from the political and economic centers of power, educated black South Africans responded in 1912 by forming the South African Native National Congress, the first political coalition of its type in Africa. The Congress was particularly opposed to the expropriation and removal of African farmers from their ancestral lands. Although the party sought to redress these grievances, its membership, like that of the NAACP in the United States, was rather conservative and still hoped to reach negotiated compromises with the white-led government.

In 1923 the party changed its name to African National Congress of South Africa (ANC) and became the major nationalist organization for black participation and self-determination in South Africa. As in East Africa, Indians formed a small but generally prosperous minority. Here, too, white settlers, particularly the Boers, tended to discriminate against Indians solely on the basis of race. Indeed, it was in South Africa that Gandhi first began his struggle for equality and began to formalize his commitment to nonviolent struggle.

A small group of settlers of British origin attempted to liberalize the society of South Africa but failed, and the Afrikaners kept their dominant positions. To perpetuate their privileged status, the Afrikaners tried a policy of divide and rule and encouraged intertribal differences. As a result of their tribal policies and their vastly superior economic position, the Afrikaners continued to subordinate the majority black African population and to ignore or repress nationalist demands.

THE EMERGENCE OF PAN-AFRICANISM

By the turn of the century, African leaders, who were increasingly alienated by European economic, political, and cultural domination, called for the unity of all Africans, or Pan-Africanism. Called by Henry Sylvester-Williams, the first Pan-African Conference was held in London in 1900. Later conferences, supported by African Americans in Latin America and the United States, were held in various European capitals. E. W. Blyden, a Liberian diplomat born in Trinidad, and W. E. B. DuBois, an African American who was also active in the NAACP, helped to popularize the Pan-African movement in the West.

The noted African American leader Marcus Garvey, who had been born in Jamaica, was another outspoken champion of black nationalism. In the United States, Garvey enjoyed enormous personal popularity among many African Americans. With slogans such as "Africa for the Africans!" "Renaissance of the Negro Race," and "Back to Africa," Garvey attracted widespread support from African Americans in the Western Hemisphere; his Back to Africa movement had over 2 million followers. The Pan-African and Back to Africa movements tended to be dominated by educated Africans and African Americans who advocated an appreciation of African cultures, better education, and racial equality. However, the movement secured few concrete results before World War II.

SUMMARY

During the postwar era, British and French refusals to grant full autonomy assured continued nationalist upheavals in the Middle East. Nationalist leaders, generally from the middle class, persisted in their demands for political and economic power. Their demands, whether presented through diplomatic channels or in revolutions, were consistently rebuffed. The British and French governments were determined to control the Middle Eastern oil fields and the strategic Suez Canal and Persian Gulf. When the middle-class political parties and nationalists failed to secure national independence, as in Egypt and Iraq, masses of people in the region turned to more radical groups and often concluded that only military action would achieve national liberation.

As in India, nationalism in the Arab world was highly developed. Also as in India, nationalism was segmented, both as a result of Arab heritage and of circumstance and because of the division of Arab lands between the British and the French. The progress of Arab nationalism was further complicated by the extension of Jewish nationalism (Zionism) in Palestine.

Nationalist discontent in Africa also continued to mount during the interwar years. The first generation of African nationalists failed to achieve their goals and, in many parts of the continent, as in the areas under the repressive domination of Belgium and Portugal, mobilized only a small fraction of the local populations. Economically and politically, most Africans remained subordinated to the imperial powers and to the European settlers. In South Africa, as the minority Afrikaner population sought to perpetuate its dominant position, the political and economic gaps between the minority white population and the majority black population widened. However, the more repressive the settlers and Western imperial governments became, the more the opposition increased. After 1945 another generation of African leaders emerged to demand and ultimately to achieve national independence.

SUGGESTED SOURCES

Catherwood, Christopher. *Winston's Folly: Imperialism and the Creation of Modern Iraq.* 2004. Lively description of British postwar imperial policies in the Arab world, particularly in Iraq, with far-reaching implications for the present day.

Gelvin, James L. *The Modern Middle East: A History.* 2005. Short, readable text with a useful time line, glossary, and biographical sketches.*

Khalidi, Rashid, Lisa Anderson, Muhammad Muslih, and Reeva S. Simon, eds. *The Origins of Arab Nationalism.* 1993. Historical overview of the development and growth of Arab nationalism in the twentieth century.*

Khapoya, Vincent B. *The African Experience: An Introduction.* 2nd ed. 1998. Short and perceptive overview of African responses and opposition to colonial domination.*

Khater, Akram Fouad. *Sources in the History of the Modern Middle East.* 2004. This collection of primary documents, lectures, essays, and diary excerpts includes short summaries of each selection and makes a good reference point for classroom discussions and writing assignments.*

Lion of the Desert. 1981. An action-packed film depicting the revolt of Libyan Arabs against the Italian invasions during the 1920s and 1930s.

Mahfouz, Naguib. *Midaq Alley*. 1981. A novel by the Nobel Prize–winning Egyptian writer detailing the lives of people living in Cairo during World War II.*

Marcus Garvey: Towards Black Nationhood. Short video of Garvey's life and legacy to the independence struggles in Africa and the civil rights movement in the United States.

Paton, Alan. *Cry, the Beloved Country*. 1961. A compelling novel about the black experience in South Africa under apartheid.* (Also a film.)

Rose, Norman. *Chaim Weizmann: A Biography*. 1986. A sympathetic account of one of Israel's founders and a solid introduction to Zionism.

WEB SOURCES

www.fordham.edu/halsall/islam/islamsbook.html. Has links to various relevant materials under the topic "Islamic Nationalism."

www.fordham.edu/halsall/jewish/jewishsbook.html. Contains some links to the situation of Jews in the Middle East during the interwar years.

www.nmhschool.org/tthornton/mehistorydatabase/mideastindex.htm. A very useful database on the Middle East. See, for example, the two links to the Mandate Period.

www.bbc.co.uk/worldservice/africa/features/storyofafrica/index_section13.shtml. This BBC site provides many excellent links on Africa in the interwar period.

---

*Paperback available.

⑥Dictatorship and Democracy in Europe during the 1930s

During the 1930s right-wing authoritarian governments became increasingly prevalent in Europe. Democratic ideals, which Woodrow Wilson popularized at the end of World War I, had been buffeted during the 1920s by dictators such as Lenin, Stalin, and Mussolini and by authoritarian movements on the Iberian Peninsula and in parts of eastern Europe. After 1929 the devastating economic effects of the Great Depression posed another serious challenge to democracy throughout Europe. By 1932 unemployment was skyrocketing, and people were struggling both in cities and on farms. Such an atmosphere was conducive to the would-be dictators who promised people an end to their misery. Adolf Hitler, who came to power in 1933, was not the only authoritarian politician in the 1930s to benefit from people's misery and a longing for better times, but he became the most infamous. By 1939, after Hitler had dismembered Czechoslovakia and its democratic government, democracy survived only in western and northern Europe.

HITLER AND THE CONSOLIDATION OF NAZI POWER IN GERMANY

Steps to Dictatorship

There is little doubt that the Great Depression aided Hitler in becoming chancellor of Germany, which he did by constitutional means in 1933. In the autumn of 1930, as the 107 brown-uniformed Nazi delegates goose-stepped into the Reichstag building, the depression was still in its early stages. In the summer elections of 1932, by which time economic conditions had worsened considerably—about 30 percent of German workers were unemployed—the Nazis won 230 seats. This was almost 100 more than their nearest rival, but still only 37 percent of the Reichstag seats. As the leader of the largest party in the Reichstag, Hitler was now a major political power. Despite a loss of 34 seats in an autumn election and some internal party differences, the Nazis remained by far the largest party.

Although their most consistent support came from small farmers and the lower-middle-class, by 1932 many young people (including a considerable number of university students), civil servants, and upper-class individuals also supported the Nazis.

After 1930, German governments, unable to command a parliamentary majority, increasingly resorted to ruling by emergency decrees signed by President Paul von Hindenburg. Such decrees were allowed by the Weimar constitution. Nevertheless, parliamentary government ceased to function as originally envisioned, and the situation became more chaotic. Finally, Hindenburg reluctantly bowed to pressure from some conservative politicians and men of property who were impressed by the size of the Nazi following. They convinced the aging president that they could use Hitler for their own purposes. One of the politicians, Franz von Papen, told a friend, "Within two months we"ll have pushed Hitler so far into the corner he'll squeak." Thus Hindenburg, who two years earlier had said contemptuously that the highest office Hitler could ever hope to obtain was head of the postal department, appointed him chancellor of Germany on January 30, 1933.

After assuming the office, Adolf Hitler moved quickly and skillfully to strengthen his control. First, he blamed a fire that had destroyed the Reichstag building on the German Communists. He then convinced Hindenburg to sign an emergency decree that indefinitely suspended basic liberties and the due process of law. Hitler also stepped up his accusations and bullying tactics against the Communists. In Reichstag elections in early March 1933, the Communist vote declined and the Nazi vote increased to 44 percent. Many of the Communist deputies were imprisoned, and none was allowed to take his seat in the new Reichstag. Later that month, using threats and promises, Hitler convinced the Reichstag to agree to the Enabling Act, which transferred legislative power to Hitler and his cabinet and allowed him to suspend parts of the Weimar constitution. The other political parties had thus allowed Hitler to assume dictatorial powers. By the summer of 1933, all political parties except the Nazis were outlawed.

Hitler's next move was to deal with a potential threat within his own Nazi Party. The Storm Troopers (SA), who had been the street fighters of the party, were under the leadership of Ernst Röhm. Röhm and others wanted the Nazi revolution to be a true revolution that would destroy the old aristocratic and conservative elements, including those within the army. Hitler, however, had perceived the desirability of using these groups for his own purposes. On June 30, 1934, the "Night of the Long Knives," he set his elite guard, the *Schutzstaffel* (SS, or black shirts), on the SA and his non-Nazi political opponents, killing Röhm and numerous others.

As a result of Hitler's handling of the more radical elements within his party, the conservative army leaders became more cooperative. After President von Hindenburg died in August 1934, Hitler assumed the presidency. He then ordered the armed forces to swear an oath of personal loyalty to him as Führer (leader). Meanwhile, the Nazi Party took control of state and local governments and the judiciary. The secret police (Gestapo) ferreted out the remnants of political dissent. Arrest, torture, imprisonment, and death were commonplace. Special concentration camps were set up to hold political opponents and others labeled undesirables.

Despite earlier Nazi attacks on capitalism, Hitler's economic program after he came to power was based on supporting big business while making labor happy and controlling both. Once in power, he allowed major industries and large businesses to dominate the economy as long as they supported his regime. Hitler's military rebuilding program, in particular, allowed German industrialists to enjoy favorable contracts and to make

HITLER COMES TO POWER, 1933

HITLER'S CONSOLIDATION OF POWER

large profits. Meanwhile, Hitler put German workers back to work constructing public buildings and autobahns (superhighways) and producing armaments for the German war machine. Already by mid-1935, two-thirds of the number of unemployed in January 1933 were once again working. Forbidding any threats to his authority, Hitler dissolved the old labor unions and prohibited strikes. Workers were enrolled in a powerless national labor organization and were pacified with better wages and working conditions, vacations, pensions, children's camps, and a Nazi ideology that preached overcoming class differences in the process of creating a harmonious racial community.

NAZI IDEOLOGY

Nazism was by now a potent stew of half-cooked ideas of Darwin, Nietzsche, and the nineteenth-century German nationalist composer Richard Wagner, combined with anti-Semitism and anticommunism. Hitler's most important idea, and one that would soon cause much misery in the world, was the theory of the superiority of the Aryans (German race). In 1927 he had said, "Man owes everything that is of any importance to the principle of struggle and to one race which has carried itself forward successfully. Take away the Nordic Germans and nothing remains but the dance of apes." In the mind of Hitler, who had been anti-Semitic since his youth, Jews had polluted the pure Aryan blood and were behind many of the evils confronting Germany: the Versailles treaty, democracy, communism, the depression, and the threat to traditional German values. Although Hitler's ideas were bogus, he believed deeply in them, and their emotional appeal was great, especially when delivered by the master orator himself. At giant rallies, such as the one in Nuremberg in 1934 at which hundreds of thousands participated amidst 130 giant searchlights and 20,000 flags, Hitler stirred crowds to a frenzy by appealing to German romantic nationalism, asking his listeners to pledge themselves to put the *Volk* (the German folk or nation) above all.

To entrench Nazism in Germany in both the present and the future, Hitler and his party created an elaborate program to indoctrinate the German people with loyalty to the Führer and to Nazi ideology. A ministry of culture supervised art, music, drama, literature, architecture, radio, films, and the press to ensure that all media instilled the Nazi program. In public bonfire ceremonies the Nazis burned publications with opposing or "incorrect" views and silenced dissenters.

The Nazis concentrated particularly on indoctrinating young Germans. They attempted to inculcate Nazism and an almost godlike reverence for Hitler in the schools, while Nazi-approved professors taught college youth racial pseudoscience and other "correct" subjects. The party also trained adolescent boys in the Hitler Youth to fight and die for the Führer, while adolescent girls were taught that the home was their rightful place and that they should have many babies to propagate the "superior" German race. Hitler once said "a woman must be a cute, cuddly, naive little thing—tender, sweet, and stupid." In the presence of his mistress, Eva Braun, he would frequently make inconsiderate remarks such as that recorded by Albert Speer: "A highly intelligent man should take a primitive and stupid woman." Despite Hitler's words and sentiments, however, the Nazi desire to expand German industry and military preparation did bring more women into the workforce.

NAZIS AND JEWS

Meanwhile, Hitler began his special campaign to isolate and degrade the Jews of Germany—about 1 percent of the population. In the spring and summer of 1933, they were removed from the civil service and from leading positions in German cultural life. In September 1935 the Nuremberg Laws deprived German Jews of their citizenship and forbade marriages between Jews and those defined as Germans. The Nazis gradually increased the use of terrorist methods against them. On November 9 and 10, 1938, Nazi thugs and others destroyed or ransacked well over 10,000 Jewish shops, homes, and synagogues; killed scores of Jews; and arrested and sent tens of thousands of Jews to concentration camps. Despite Crystal Night (as the Nazis labeled the event, because of all the windows broken that night), until World War II broke out, more Jews emigrated—close to half the total, including such notables as Albert Einstein—than were imprisoned. Only after the beginning of the war did Hitler begin a massive slaughter of Jews who fell under Nazi control.

In addition to persecuting Jews, the Nazis made others submit to compulsory sterilization. From 1934 to 1939 over 300,000 individuals suffered such a fate, including those with various physical and mental handicaps, homosexuals, and prostitutes. A 1937 German textbook on racial science stated, "It is one of the first duties of the community, to see to it, that the increase of those, inferior by heredity, is stopped." And "the law exists for the prevention of hereditarily unsound progeny." For being homosexuals, about 100,000 men were arrested during Hitler's rule, and many ended up in prison or concentration camps.

The Hitler Phenomenon: How and Why?

By 1938 there was little doubt that Hitler was very popular with a majority of the German people, and historians have often asked how a cultured people who produced some of the world's greatest thinkers and composers could so ardently support such a man. This question is linked to another: How was he able to come to power and then consolidate his position so that he was soon a dictator?

As with most historical phenomena, the answer to these questions is complex and multifaceted, but the following reasons (in random order), taken together and not exhaustive, help explain Hitler's success:

- The unhappiness of many Germans with the series of events they had experienced in the two decades before Hitler came to power, especially defeat in World War I, the peace terms imposed on them, the inflation of 1923, and the Great Depression. Germans under age 30, among whom Hitler had many supporters, were especially contemptuous of the failings of the older generation of leaders.

- The failure of a democratic parliamentary system that neither the far Right nor far Left had ever supported and by 1933 was regarded by most Germans as ineffective and at least partly responsible for many of the miseries they suffered.

- The inability of old elites, such as the army command, wealthy industrialists, and large landowners, to generate any mass support, which had become increasingly important since World War I.

- The cooperation with Hitler of some of these elite leaders, impressed by his mass following by 1932. They mistakenly thought they could use him for their purposes.

Two of Europe's leading dictators, Hitler and Mussolini, at a German military review in 1937.

- The failure of other groups to put up a more unified and effective opposition to Hitler. The Left, for example, underestimated him, and German Communists, following Stalin's wishes, refused to join forces with German Socialists against him.
- The natural tendency of people in times of great stress and frustration to blame their problems on others, on scapegoats, and Hitler's provision of a convenient list of them, especially the Allies, Communists, Jews, and most Weimar politicians.
- Hitler's outspoken and utopian nationalism, which appealed strongly to a people humiliated by defeat, reparations, and economic miseries. He appeared to many as a spokesman and symbol of national renewal.
- Hitler's charisma, spellbinding public-speaking ability, and self-assurance. (He once said, and apparently believed, "I go with the certainty of a sleep walker along a path laid out for me by Providence.")
- Hitler's understanding of crowd psychology and the appeal of mass spectacles and his careful orchestration of a personality cult centered on himself.
- Hitler's appeal to both ordinary Germans, who could delight in this former corporal from a lower-class background now commanding German generals born to the aristocracy, and to elites, who supported Hitler partly because they perceived him as the best defense against movements of the far Left that threatened their privileged positions.
- Hitler's many successes after coming to power in 1933, especially his lowering of unemployment and his defiance of the Allies (see Chapter 17).
- Hitler's use of intimidation and force.

Despite Hitler's many successes in a short time, not all Germans approved of his policies. Some leaders of the German Catholic and Protestant churches, for example, resented Hitler's attempt to foster and propagate Nazi ideals contrary to the spirit of Christianity. A papal encyclical of 1937 criticized Nazi racism and paganism. German clergymen and lay leaders who spoke out openly often suffered persecution.

Although Nazi terror helped keep Germans in line, Hitler's popularity lessened the need for it, and bold opposition was scarce. The violations of the rights of Jews and those who opposed Hitler's policies were less important to many Germans than was Hitler's apparent restoration of Germany's economy and international significance, as well as his other successes.

THE CORPORATE STATE IN ITALY

By the time Hitler became chancellor of Germany, Mussolini had already been in power in Italy for a decade, and his Fascist state continued to evolve toward greater authoritarian controls. Until 1929 the Catholic papacy continued to have serious differences with the Italian state, as it had for almost 60 years. In that year, Pope Pius XI and Mussolini came to an agreement, the Lateran Treaty, that recognized papal control over Vatican City and its political independence. At the same time, Catholicism was recognized as the religion of the Italian state. Catholic religious education was allowed in the public schools, and Catholic marriage laws were to become the norm for state law. While this pragmatic agreement by the atheist Mussolini and the Catholic pope proved quite popular among Italy's overwhelmingly Catholic population and greatly increased Mussolini's support, strains between the Italian state and the papacy soon reappeared. In 1930 the pope denounced the government's attempts to train the young in "a pagan worship of the State." Although they did not cause Mussolini serious problems, relations with the papacy were strained for the rest of the decade.

In the 1930s Mussolini's "corporate state" became something of a reality. In theory, such a state would overcome class conflict by bringing representatives of employers, employees, and the government together in corporations to decide on such questions as wages and working hours. By 1934, 22 of these corporations had been established, representing such areas as the clothing trades and mining. Since only Fascist trade unions were allowed to exist and represent the workers in the corporations, the interest of the workers was sacrificed to that of the Fascist Party and the employers. The party, appreciative of the financial and political backing of big business, allowed business to help run an economy more and more dominated by large firms and monopolies. When some businesses found themselves near bankruptcy during the depression, the government invested in them to keep them afloat. As a result, by 1937 the government possessed the controlling interest in shipping, electricity, heavy machinery, steel, and telephones. In 1938 the Chamber of Deputies, a carryover from a more democratic Italy long since dominated by Fascists, was replaced by the Chamber of Fasces and Corporations. Although no real power changed hands, this move symbolized Mussolini's dislike of liberal democracy and his fondness for his type of "corporatism."

AUTHORITARIAN GOVERNMENTS ELSEWHERE IN EUROPE

At the beginning of the 1920s, parliamentary governments, democratic in form, existed almost everywhere in Europe west of the Soviet Union. By 1939 rightist authoritarian governments had taken over most of the nations of Europe, and few republics remained outside western Europe and Scandinavia. However, none of the other governments was as oppressive as Hitler's.

IBERIAN PENINSULA

On the Iberian Peninsula, Spain and Portugal had already witnessed the collapse of democracy in the 1920s. In Spain, General Primo de Rivera took power in 1923 and held it until 1930. In 1931 democratic forces succeeded in restoring democracy until civil war broke out in Spain in 1936 and General Francisco Franco eventually established a dictatorship (see Chapter 17). In Portugal, the military uprising of 1926 led to the eventual dictatorial control of Antonio de Oliveira Salazar, who became prime minister in 1932. Both Franco and Salazar would continue in power for over three decades.

The authoritarianism of Primo de Rivera, Salazar, and Franco had just as much in common with Catholic traditionalist ideas as it did with those of Mussolini, perhaps more. Papal encyclicals such as Leo XIII's *Rerum Novarum* (1891) and Pius XI's *Quadragesimo Anno* (1931) and the writings of Catholic intellectuals such as Gilbert Chesterton and Charles Peguy criticized modern individualism as well as some of the inequities and abuses of both capitalism and Marxism. They emphasized subordinating individual and economic interests and rights to the good of the whole, as understood in the light of Catholic teaching. The Iberian dictators felt they were best qualified to interpret how to implement these beliefs. From 1933 until 1938 Austria pursued a path similar to that followed by the Iberian states: Englebert Dollfuss, sometimes referred to as "Mickey Mouse" because of his small stature, and his successor, Kurt von Schuschnigg, attempted to rule in an authoritarian fashion, which Dollfuss claimed was based on *Quadragesimo Anno.*

EASTERN EUROPE

In eastern Europe, where a variety of authoritarian governments had already appeared by 1930 (see Chapter 11), the trend accelerated following the onset of the depression. So, too, did economic and political nationalism and hostility toward minorities, especially the Jews. The involvement of some Jews in the region's banking, industry, and trade made them convenient scapegoats at a time of economic misery. By 1938 only Czechoslovakia still maintained a viable democratic government in eastern Europe, but its German minority became increasingly troublesome as a result of the depression and Nazi-generated propaganda (see Chapter 17).

✷ STALINISM IN THE SOVIET UNION: 1933–1939

REVOLUTION BETRAYED?

Aware of the rising power of Germany and Japan, Stalin knew that it was more important than ever for the Soviet Union to strengthen its industrial base and its armed forces. As a result, the Second Soviet Five-Year Plan, begun in 1933, continued to emphasize the buildup of heavy industry. At the same time, in a series of actions the exiled Trotsky labeled "the revolution betrayed," Stalin began to downplay some of the ideological innovations introduced after the revolution, especially if they appeared to interfere with industrial productivity. The Communist ideal of egalitarianism, for example, was increasingly ignored. Thus, to get workers and managers to produce more, the party introduced various types of wage incentives and established a variety of incentives on the collective farms. The wages and privileges of technocrats, party and government bureaucrats, and military officers were also increased. A new privileged class of leaders came into existence, but the life of the average agricultural or industrial worker improved little. During the middle and late 1930s, the Soviet people had to cope with cramped housing, food shortages, and a dearth of consumer goods. In the 1930s the regime also retreated from earlier innovations regarding women, family life, and education. In 1930 the Communist Party abolished *Zhenotdel*, the Woman's Department of the Communist Party's Central Committee that had been established in 1919, and Stalin was less sympathetic to women's issues than Lenin had been. The government also made divorce and abortions more difficult to obtain and introduced new incentives for having children. In education, some of the earlier progressive experiments were scrapped, and hard work, discipline, and academic standards were reemphasized.

As the German and Japanese danger became greater, Stalin increasingly appealed to a Russian patriotism that stirred many hearts more than Marxism did. Books, films, and other media now displayed more respect for such figures from the tsarist past as Ivan the Terrible and Peter the Great. Even the Orthodox Church, which was so intricately connected with the tsarist past, began to receive somewhat better treatment. There was, however, no relaxation of the party's attempt to control people's ideas; in fact, Stalin further tightened the party's cultural controls.

As another tool to motivate the Soviet people to work harder for their country, Stalin forced writers and artists to use the techniques of approved "socialist realism" for artistic and literary expression. Basically, this meant that artists and writers were to portray reality as the party wished it portrayed, in a clear, simple form that the average worker could understand. To the party, "reality" during the 1930s often meant the image of pure, courageous workers overcoming all sorts of obstacles and enemies in order to help increase productivity and thereby make the Soviet Union stronger.

Although Stalin was very anxious to strengthen the Soviet Union, he became even more interested in increasing his personal power. He used the assassination of Leningrad Party boss Sergei Kirov as a justification for beginning what Robert Conquest has called "The Great Terror." (Whether Stalin himself helped bring the assassination about continues to be debated.) Arrest followed arrest. Imprisonment, exile to Siberian prison camps, and execution awaited many. Important former political figures were executed after staged trials at which the defendants often confessed to crimes they could not possibly have committed. Despite the need for a strong military, the overwhelming majority of generals and colonels in the army were imprisoned, exiled, or executed. Of the members of the Central Committee of the party in 1934, the most powerful governing group in the Soviet Union, about 70 percent had been shot by 1939. Even the head of the secret police, Nikolai Yezhov, who directed the purge for Stalin during its most intense phase, was removed in 1938 and

THE GREAT TERROR

By the late 1930s, the Stalin cult in the U.S.S.R. extended even into Soviet waters.

eventually executed—only to be replaced by the infamous Lavrentia Beria, who once said, "[Give me someone] for one night, and I'll have him confessing he's the king of England." The flood of arrests did not abate until 1939.

Although the purges of former leaders and party members were the most dramatic events, others also suffered in these years. Prominent among them were intellectuals and those minorities accused of "bourgeois nationalistic tendencies." At times the police arrested ordinary individuals for no apparent reason other than to fill arrest quotas and to terrorize Soviet citizens into becoming more docile. The writer Isaac Babel said, "Today a man talks frankly only with his wife—at night with the blanket pulled over his head." By 1940 about 8 million people had been sent to Soviet labor camps since the late 1920s. Partly because of the high death rate, however, the number in the camps in any one year probably did not exceed 1 million in the early 1930s or 2 million in the late 1930s.

NAZISM AND STALINISM: COMPARISON AND CONTRAST

SIMILARITIES

In practice, German Nazism and Stalin's Soviet Communism had much in common. Despite some recent scholarly studies that indicate that both Hitler and Stalin received much cooperation from others and were not as all-powerful and all-controlling as once thought, both men still exercised great power and can safely be labeled dictators. They both used massive propaganda efforts to convince their subjects that they were almost superhuman and worthy of the greatest adulation. (Earlier, immediately following Lenin's death in 1924, Stalin had begun encouraging the development of a Lenin cult to strengthen the allegiance of Soviet citizens to Communist leadership.)

The respective parties that Hitler and Stalin dominated exercised great control over various phases of life: government, the judiciary, the military, police forces, the economy, ideology, education, the press, and cultural institutions. Both leaders effectively used terror and fear. During their years in power, Hitler and Stalin were each responsible for the deaths of millions, not counting the normal casualties of war. "One death is a tragedy, a million just statistics," Stalin once said.

Despite the similarities between Stalin's Soviet Union and Hitler's Germany, there were some important distinctions. Before and after the Communists came to power in Russia, they preached class warfare and effected a social and cultural revolution that dealt harshly with the prerevolutionary upper and middle classes and with traditional religious beliefs and values. Although Hitler certainly weakened the power of the old German aristocracy, he, as well as men such as Mussolini and Franco, benefited from the fear and support of upper-class individuals who saw the Communists as a much more serious threat to their status, property, and beliefs. Another difference was that although Stalin increasingly appealed in the 1930s to Russian nationalism, he tried to reconcile it, at least in theory, with the internationalist emphasis that had long characterized Communist ideology. Hitler was more openly and aggressively nationalistic. Finally, despite considerable evidence of anti-Semitism on Stalin's part, racist ideas were not part of official Soviet ideology, whereas Hitler's classification of races, with the Aryan Germans on top, was central to his Nazi beliefs.

DIFFERENCES

SOCIAL AND POLITICAL CHANGES IN THE EUROPEAN DEMOCRACIES

The Great Depression and the rise of Nazism greatly affected the European democracies during the 1930s. Unemployment and other hardships experienced by many during the 1930s produced significant social consequences, including a decline in the birth rate in most of the Western democracies and a corresponding proportional increase in the number of older people. Numerous couples were apparently unwilling to have children while they remained in precarious economic circumstances.

Another change was the increasing attraction of workers to more militant unionism and more radical political ideas than those that had appealed to them in the late 1920s. As the depression threw more and more workers out of jobs, they demanded an end to the laissez-faire policies of their governments. Some thought that the depression had proved the failure of capitalism. In Scandinavia, where democratic Socialist parties had alternated in power with more conservative parties during the 1920s, Socialists became dominant in the 1930s.

In France, a leftist coalition Popular Front government was formed in 1936 under France's first Socialist premier, Léon Blum. It was made possible by the temporary cooperation of the French Communist Party, which as a result of elections that year had increased its number of representatives in the Chamber of Deputies from 10 to 73 (out of about 600 deputies in this lower house). The cooperation of the Communists was approved by Stalin and indicated his growing apprehensions

BLUM'S COALITION GOVERNMENT IN FRANCE

about Hitler (see Chapter 17). Blum's Socialist Party received the most votes and 146 seats in the election, in which 85 percent of registered voters participated. The third major party in the coalition, the Radicals, was the least leftist of the three parties, and it obtained 116 seats. Blum's government took a more active role in the economy by increasing public spending and helping workers gain salary increases. Like President Franklin Roosevelt in the United States, Blum hoped to help France out of the lingering depression by stimulating purchasing power. He strengthened the rights of unions and helped workers gain a 40-hour workweek and a two-week paid vacation every year.

Like most earlier French governments, however, Blum's coalition government was unstable, with neither the Communists nor the Radicals giving Blum unqualified support. Moreover, class hatred and fears were strong in France, and Blum's Jewishness seemed to increase the extreme Right's hatred of him. Shortly before the 1936 election he had been seriously beaten and almost killed by young right-wing extremists. Conservatives and many French capitalists did all they could to undermine his government, and the French Senate, less representative and more conservative than the Chamber of Deputies, blocked many of Blum's initiatives. Besides the problems of trying to bring France out of the depression, Blum's task was also complicated by the increasing threat of Hitler and the civil war that broke out in neighboring Spain (see Chapter 17). After about a year in power, Blum resigned, and though he returned as premier for about a month in 1938, the misleadingly named Radical Party provided the two premiers who ruled the longest from mid-1937 until early 1940 . . . by which time World War II had begun.

POLITICS IN GREAT BRITAIN

In Great Britain, the socialist-oriented Labour Party was already in power when the depression hit the nation, and the party did not cope effectively with its early stages. In August 1931 the Labour government under Ramsay MacDonald fell when half the cabinet refused to go along with cuts in government benefits, cuts that U.S. and British bankers insisted were necessary before further U.S. loans could be issued to stabilize the British currency. For the remainder of the decade, though MacDonald served as prime minister of the National Coalition government until 1935, the Conservative Party under Stanley Baldwin and then Neville Chamberlain dominated. Despite being more cautious than the Labour Party, the Conservatives were moved by high unemployment and the public mood to enact some welfare state provisions (e.g., in regard to public housing and expanded social insurance coverage).

SUMMARY

Undermined by the Great Depression, democracy seemed an outdated concept to many in Europe during the 1930s. Right-wing dictatorial and authoritarian personalities such as Hitler, Franco, and many eastern European leaders joined the earlier victorious Mussolini in opposing democracy, individualism, and equality with ideas of national or racial superiority, the superiority of the state over the individual, and various forms of elitism. In Russia Stalin praised democracy and equality, but no less than Hitler he aspired to totalitarian control of his country's actions and thoughts.

Although democratic governments survived in Scandinavia, Great Britain, and France, they had to increase their control over economic life in order to combat the effects of the depression. By 1939 governments that advocated traditional laissez-faire economic policies seemed outmoded. To many, either dictatorships or democratic welfare states represented the future.

SUGGESTED SOURCES

Applebaum, Anne. *Gulag: A History.* 2003. The most up-to-date and readable history of the Soviet prison camp system.*

Berend, Ivan T. *Decades of Crisis: Central and Eastern Europe before World War II.* 1998. Pt. 3. Good overview of various aspects of the region in the 1930s.*

Brandenberger, David. *National Bolshevism: Stalinist Mass Culture and the Formation of Modern Russian National Identity, 1931–1956.* 2002. Chaps. 1–6. A look at how Stalin relied on nationalist as well as Communist elements in molding Stalinist ideology.

Burnt by the Sun. An award-winning 1994 film set in the Soviet Union in 1936. It deals with a family affected by Stalin's purges. (Also available on video.)

Clavin, Patricia. *The Great Depression in Europe, 1929–1939.* 2000. A good brief nontechnical overview of the subject.*

Daniels, Robert V., ed. *The Stalin Revolution: Foundations of the Totalitarian Era.* 4th ed. 1997. A collection of essays in the Heath Problems series.*

Evans, Richard J. *The Coming of the Third Reich.* 2004. Chaps. 4–6. These chapters deal with Hitler and the Nazis in the early 1930s.*

Fischer, Klaus. *Nazi Germany: A New History.* 1996. This best overall history of Nazi Germany also includes several chapters dealing with the 1920s background.*

Fitzpatrick, Sheila. *Everyday Stalinism, Ordinary Life in Extraordinary Times: Soviet Russia in the 1930s.* 1999. A brief examination, primarily focused on people in urban areas; complements the author's *Stalin's Peasants* (1994).

Fritzsche, Peter. *Germans into Nazis.* 1999. A book that attempts to explain Hitler's popularity with the German people, emphasizing the German experiences from 1914 into the 1930s.*

Ginzburg, Evgeniia. *Journey into the Whirlwind.* 1975. The memoirs of a heroic woman caught up in Stalin's purges.*

Kershaw, Ian. *Hitler, 1889–1936: Hubris.* 2000. A long but very insightful biography of Hitler that offers an explanation of how and why he gained control of Germany.*

Koestler, Arthur. *Darkness at Noon.* 1973. A short novel that provides insights into Stalin's purges.*

Mitchell, Allan. *The Nazi Revolution: Hitler's Dictatorship and the German Nation.* 4th ed. 1997. A collection of essays in the Heath Problems series; special attention is devoted to Hitler's personality and to Nazi relations with industry; the churches; the military; and groups such as women, youth, and the Jews.*

Montefiore, Simon Sebag. *Stalin: The Court of the Red Tsar.* 2003. Chaps. 8–29. These chapters offer a fascinating examination of Stalin in the 1930s, based partly on recently opened archival materials.*

Overy, Richard. *The Dictators: Hitler's Germany, Stalin's Russia.* 2004. A thorough comparison and contrast of two dictators and two competing systems.*

Paragraph 175. 2000. A documentary film dealing with the Nazi treatment of homosexuals.

Paxton, Robert O. *The Anatomy of Fascism.* 2004. Chaps. 5–6. These two chapters offer an excellent analysis of the similarities and differences between the regimes of Hitler and Mussolini.*

Service, Robert. *Stalin: A Biography*. 2005. Pts. 1–3. This most recent Stalin biography gives due emphasis to Stalin's abilities and the influence of Marxism-Leninism on him while also dealing with his many brutalities.

Triumph of the Will. The infamous 110-minute propaganda film of the 1934 Nazi Nuremberg rallies. (Also available on video.)

Tucker, Robert C. *Stalin in Power: The Revolution from Above, 1928–1941*. 1990. A comprehensive treatment of Stalin in this period by a leading scholar.*

WEB SOURCES

www.fordham.edu/halsall/mod/modsbook43.html. See this Fordham site for links relating to Hitler and Nazism.

www.fordham.edu/halsall/jewish/jewishsbook.html. Contains links to materials on German anti-Semitism.

www.soviethistory.org/index.php. See links to years 1934, 1936, and 1939 on this excellent source for Soviet history.

---

*Paperback available.

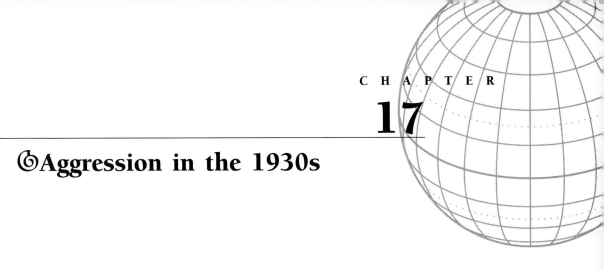

⑥Aggression in the 1930s

During the 1930s the fragile system of international order broke down as several major world powers resorted to force to achieve their national goals and to settle real or imagined grievances. The Global Depression, which the historian Piers Brendon referred to as "the worst peacetime crisis to afflict humanity since the [fourteenth-century] Black Death," was especially significant in sharpening the rivalries that characterized the decade. Although the continuing existence of the vast British and French empires seemed to offer those two imperial powers some economic protection against the worst ravages of the depression, Japan and Germany were not so fortunate when the crisis first struck them. Partly in response to it, powerful Japanese militarists and Hitler came to power and many people in their countries supported their aggressive international policies, which aimed at increasing economic, as well as political, domination over neighboring areas. The depression also contributed to the reluctance of the Western democracies to spend more on military preparedness, thus weakening their ability to oppose aggression. Whereas Japan used military force in expanding its holdings at the expense of China, Hitler made advances by relying on a combination of diplomacy and implicit or explicit threats of force, up until the invasion of Poland on September 1, 1939. Both Japanese aggressions and the actions of Hitler and other European right-wing dictators were met with little more than empty protests and appeasement from Great Britain, France, and the United States.

JAPANESE AGGRESSION AND CHINESE RESPONSE

Japan Seizes Manchuria

The trade barriers erected by many nations following the onset of the depression further convinced many Japanese of the need for a self-sufficient empire. Dependent on importing industrial raw materials and food from mainland Asia, particularly from China, Japanese leaders were now determined to seize those parts of Asia that would give Japan a secure supply of these commodities. In addition, Japanese ultranationalists saw their nation and people as superior to other Asians and therefore believed it was their mission to rule Asia. By either measure, China was Japan's next target. During the same period, China was moving toward modernization and national unity. Japanese militarists could not tolerate Chinese progress, since a strong China would preclude Japanese dominance on the Asian mainland.

COLLISION COURSE
IN MANCHURIA

In the 1930s the Chinese and the Japanese embarked on a collision course in Manchuria, as both intensified their efforts to control the area. Japan had been satisfied to maintain a facade of Chinese sovereignty in Manchuria as long as a disunited China allowed it to control the local warlord. Japan called Manchuria its lifeline and relied on it for such vital resources as iron ore, coal, and grain. The Chinese called Manchuria the "granary of China," where poor Chinese peasants went to pioneer the virgin land. The KMT government had targeted Manchuria as a key area in its movement to recover sovereign rights lost to outside powers. After 1929 the pro-Chiang warlord of Manchuria began a program of economic development that included the building of Chinese-controlled railroad lines and seaports in competition with those already established by Japan.

These KMT initiatives led militant Japanese to fear that unless they acted quickly Chinese authority would be reestablished in Manchuria. Junior officers of the Japanese army in Manchuria, whose goal was to conquer Manchuria and then take over the rest of China, engineered the Manchurian, or Mukden, incident. On September 18, 1931, the Japanese army staged an explosion on the tracks of the Japanese-controlled South Manchurian Railway. Blaming the Chinese, the Japanese forces, aided by the Japanese army in Korea, swung into action and captured all the important cities in the region.

**JAPANESE CONQUEST
OF MANCHURIA**

It was a critical moment for party government in Japan. A strong government might have restrained the army's action and postponed a reckoning with China, but the government in Tokyo was weak and dared not risk a showdown with the army. The army ignored civilian calls for restraint and completed its conquest of Manchuria by early 1932. In March 1932 Manchuria, renamed Manchukuo (land of the Manchus), was proclaimed an independent state headed by the last Manchu emperor, who had abdicated the Chinese throne in 1912 when he was a little boy. In reality, Japan controlled every department of the new government, which it ran as a de facto colony until 1945. These events led to the resignation of the Japanese prime minister and cabinet.

China appealed to the League of Nations and the international community for help. After debates and futile resolutions ordering Japan to cease its aggression—which the Japanese cabinet could not carry out because its army, supported by public opinion, ignored it with contempt—the League appointed an international commission headed by British diplomat Lord Lytton. The Lytton Report condemned Japan for aggression and called on it to restore Manchuria to China. The League Assembly unanimously adopted the Lytton Report but did not attempt to enforce it. Japan withdrew from the League. This was the first major crisis of war and peace to confront the League of Nations, and it had shown itself to be ineffective. U.S. protests also failed to deter the Japanese.

Japan Attacks China

Japanese forces pushed farther into China in the years following the Manchurian incident, brushing aside ineffective Chinese resistance. In 1933 the province of Jehol, which linked Manchuria to northern China, was conquered by Japanese and puppet Manchukuo troops. Japan's next goal was to oust the Chinese central government from

Japanese troops overrunning part of the devastated Shanghai in the war against China.

northern China and form the five provinces in that region into a second puppet state. In response, Chiang Kai-shek clung to the strategy of "unification before resistance." Translated, this meant that Chiang wished to eliminate the Communists and warlords first, to build up the military next, and finally to resist Japan. Meanwhile, he would trade space for time, negotiate, temporize, but not commit his ill-prepared army to battle. In conventional military terms, Chiang's strategy made sense, but he discounted the potential power of nonmilitary and guerrilla forces when mobilized in support of a conventional war.

Above all, Chiang was insensitive to popular opinion, which demanded active resistance to Japan. Chinese students took to the streets calling for an end to civil wars and for all Chinese to form an anti-Japanese united front. The Chinese Communist Party (CCP) was quick to take up the student cause; hard-pressed as it was in Yenan, it wanted a united front, if only to relieve KMT pressure on itself. The Soviet Union also came out for a Chinese united front because a Sino-Japanese war would take Japanese pressure off Soviet Asia and allow the Soviet Union to concentrate on the German menace in Europe. In 1937 Chiang bowed to public pressure and began negotiations for a united front with the CCP.

Given its ambition to dominate China, the last thing Japan wanted was a united front in China, and it decided to strike before a united China could foil its plans. On the night of July 7, 1937, at an important railroad junction near Peking called the Marco Polo Bridge, the Japanese army attacked. Popular feeling in China so strongly favored resistance that no government could have survived unless it complied. In Tokyo the Japanese cabinet vainly attempted to halt the spreading conflict. It failed because it could neither restrain its men at the front nor offer terms the Chinese government could accept. By August serious fighting had spread to several fronts in northern and central China. This was the beginning of World War II in Asia, which in China would last a full eight years.

China during the War

From 1937 to 1941, China fought alone. Until mid-1941 the isolationist United States continued to sell petroleum and iron and other essentials of war to Japan. Great Britain and France were too preoccupied with their own problems in Europe and elsewhere to come to China's aid. The Soviet Union assisted China in the first two years of war, with supplies, a volunteer air force, and loans because it feared that it would be Japan's next target should China fall. Soviet aid ended in 1939, however, because of the threat of war in Europe between the Soviet Union and Germany.

With inadequate aid from abroad, China was no match for Japan. Japan's modern war machine had little trouble conquering major cities along China's coast and rivers. However, Japan's mechanized military became bogged down by China's inadequate roads and railroads. Its occupation of the countryside was ineffective, limited to forays and punitive expeditions. Japan had expected to bring China to its knees within half a year. In spite of, or perhaps because of, the barbarous behavior of Japanese troops, China would not surrender. The worst atrocity was in 1937 during the "Rape of Nanking," where an orgy of rape and the killing of about 250,000 Chinese, almost all civilians, occurred.

CHINESE MIGRATION

In one of humanity's largest migrations, the Chinese government retreated westward to the mountainous interior regions that were out of reach of Japanese tanks, although that area was still within range of Japanese bombers. The retreating Chinese army used the scorched-earth policy, destroying what it could not take. Stage by stage, the Chinese government retreated westward up the gorges of the Yangtze River, impassable to Japan's warships, evacuating whole arsenals, factories, libraries, schools, and universities, until it attained safety in Chungking. Despite enormous hardships, the war hastened modernization in China's interior provinces, bringing new industry and schools to the region. By 1945 free China had twice as many university students as in all China in 1937. On the other hand, education had all but stopped in Japanese-occupied China. Just as World War I brought millions of European women into the workplace, so too did World War II bring Chinese women into the public sphere. Women took part in many aspects of the war effort, including a women's army auxiliary corps and a nursing corps.

WAR OF ATTRITION

After 1939 a war of attrition began. China's wartime capital, Chunking, was firebombed again and again. However, located in the mountainous interior it could not be reached by Japanese armor. In time, a network of caves was excavated around Chunking that sheltered 1.5 million people and many factories in the same way that the subway stations in London provided refuge for Britons during the Nazi bombing of London. The Chinese government continued to fight, convinced that the Japanese would eventually widen the war and thus bring other nations to China's aid. Japan installed puppet governments in the occupied regions of both northern and southern China, but they were unable to attract to them many men or women of stature.

The full-scale war with Japan compelled the KMT and CCP to form a United Front in September 1937. Under its terms, the CCP agreed to abide by Dr. Sun's Three People's Principles, abandon its Marxist policies and Soviet-style government in areas it controlled, and abolish its Red Army. In return, the KMT agreed to reorganize the 40,000-strong Red Army into the national army, in separate units under CCP command, and to recognize CCP control of Yenan and some other areas.

From the beginning, the CCP regarded the Sino-Japanese War as an opportunity to build up its strength while the Japanese destroyed the KMT. While Nationalist armies were preoccupied with the Japanese, the Communists greatly expanded their area of control in the northwest. Shortly after the United Front was formally proclaimed, the Central Committee of the CCP issued the following directive to its cadres: "Our fixed policy should be 70 percent expansion, 20 percent dealing with the Kuomintang, and 10 percent resisting Japan." Besides territorial expansion, the CCP set the target of increasing its army to 1 million men and the party to 1 million members. During the next eight years, Communist units were very successful in northern China in slipping behind Japanese lines and organizing peasant guerrilla bands to harass the Japanese.

KMT AND CCP IN WW II

The United States Moves toward Confronting Japan

From the beginning, the United States strongly opposed Japanese aggression in China. By the late 1930s with Europe moving toward war, the United States became the only nation able to thwart Japanese advances against China. Most Americans regarded Japan not only as a brutal attacker of a nation friendly to the United States but also as a threat to U.S. interests in Asia. For its part, Japan resented the U.S. Exclusion Act of 1924 that prohibited Japanese and other Asians from migrating to the United States. Japan also took offense at high U.S. tariffs against its exports in the aftermath of the Great Depression. When Japan seized Manchuria in 1931, the United States was unwilling to intervene militarily or to deepen the depression by imposing economic sanctions. Secretary of State Henry Stimson announced that the United States would not recognize Japan's seizure of Manchuria because it impaired U.S. rights, violated the Open Door policy, and flouted the Kellogg-Briand Peace Pact. This statement, plus a U.S. threat to build up military strength in the Pacific, failed to deter the Japanese.

When Japan invaded China in 1937, the United States again protested. President Roosevelt stated that aggression was becoming "epidemic" and that a "quarantine" was needed. Thus, the United States arranged limited economic and military aid to the Chinese, placed an embargo on the sale of airplanes to Japan, and abrogated the Commercial Treaty of 1911. In order to increase military preparedness, Congress authorized the construction of aircraft carriers and battleships. None of these actions halted Japanese aggression in China or materially aided the Chinese, and extensive U.S. trade with Japan continued until 1941. Mutual disillusionment, however, led many officials on both sides of the Pacific to believe that a direct confrontation might well occur in the near future.

THE NAZI THREAT TO PEACE
AND THE ALLIED RESPONSE

During the 1930s Great Britain and France failed to deal effectively with the increasing aggressiveness of Nazi Germany and Fascist Italy. In the first half of the decade, before Hitler made his most conspicuous international moves, the major European democratic powers had already been unable to halt aggression. Following Japan's 1931 occupation of Chinese Manchuria, Italy attacked Ethiopia in late 1935. In the second case, as in the first, the British and French delegates to the League of Nations were critical of this aggression but put forward little effective response. Despite a personal appeal by Ethiopian Emperor Haile Selassie, the League imposed only halfhearted, short-lived, and limited economic sanctions on Italy. Nor did Great Britain and France take any meaningful action when, in early 1935, Hitler announced that, in violation of the Treaty of Versailles, he intended to reintroduce military conscription and increase the size of the German armed forces.

German Remilitarization of the Rhineland

In March 1936 Hitler took the most daring gamble of his early years in power when he decided to send troops into the Rhineland, the German territory that according to the Versailles and Locarno treaties was to remain demilitarized. The French had removed their last troops from the area in 1930, but as long as the area was not fortified, a German attack on France was difficult. Many German diplomats, statesmen, and officers considered Hitler's gamble too risky. They believed French soldiers would be sent to turn back the Germans and feared that the German army was not yet ready for war with France. Hitler himself later stated, "If the French had then marched into the Rhineland, we would have had to withdraw with our tails between our legs." But he did not think the French would act. He was right; they did nothing.

REASONS FOR FRENCH AND BRITISH APPEASEMENT

There were various reasons for the failure of France and Great Britain to take more decisive action, both in 1936 and in the years immediately following. Among the most prominent were (1) a genuine hatred of war on the part of many who remembered the horrors of World War I, accompanied by a lack of enthusiasm, amidst the depression, for heavy military spending; (2) a feeling, more common in Great Britain than in France, that perhaps Germany had been dealt with too harshly in the Versailles treaty and that its desire for revision was understandable; (3) Hitler's ability to make some Allied statesmen believe he was a reasonable and peace-loving man with limited goals; (4) fear of further Japanese and Italian aggression, which prevented France and Britain from concentrating exclusively on the dangers presented by Germany; and (5) fear of communism and that if Hitler were overthrown in Germany a worse situation might arise: a Communist government. In 1938 British prime minister Neville Chamberlain, prompted by a discussion of Hitler's possible overthrow, asked, "Who will guarantee that Germany will not become Bolshevik afterwards?" Even if a war against Hitler could be won with Soviet cooperation, some British and French politicians feared that it might mean the spread of communism in eastern and central Europe.

Soviet Response to Japanese and German Aggression

Soviet policies toward Hitler zigzagged. First, Stalin helped Hitler come to power by preventing German Communists from cooperating with other leftists to prevent it. Stalin apparently realized that a Nazi government would be hostile to western European powers, and vice versa, a situation from which the Soviet Union could benefit. Despite Hitler's known hostility to communism, Stalin at first indicated a willingness to do business with him. After Hitler displayed little inclination to reciprocate, however, Stalin began looking for assistance against this potential new threat. Already alarmed by Japan's movements near Soviet borders in Manchuria, the Soviet Union sought and achieved diplomatic recognition in 1933 from the United States. In 1934 it joined the League of Nations, an organization that Lenin had earlier described as "an alliance of world bandits against the proletariat."

After 1934 Soviet delegates frequently attempted to arouse other nations to a realization of the dangers presented by Japan and Germany. In May 1935 the Soviet Union signed the Mutual Assistance Treaty with France, in which each party agreed to come to the assistance of the other in case of an unprovoked attack. The same year, the Soviet government concluded a similar treaty with Czechoslovakia, except in this case neither party was obligated to aid the other unless France first came to the aid of the attacked nation. Both treaties clearly reflected the Soviet Union's growing fear of Germany.

Another important step taken in 1934 and 1935 was that Moscow directed foreign Communist parties to cooperate with other political parties in nations that were willing to take steps to check German aggression. In both Great Britain and France, however, fear and suspicion of Communist aims hindered close cooperation against Germany. In France, conservative distrust delayed ratification of the pact with Moscow until February 1936.

The Soviet Union's apprehensions about Germany and Japan were increased when the two nations signed the Anti-Comintern Pact in 1936. The following year, Italy, which had been moving closer to Germany, also affixed its signature. Although the pact did little more than record the signatories' opposition to international communism, it symbolized the growing affinity of the three powers.

Franco Triumphs in Spain

In the Spanish civil war (1936–1939), dictatorship won a significant victory over democracy. In the summer of 1936 General Francisco Franco invaded Spain from Spanish Morocco, seeking to oust the shaky leftist coalition government of the Spanish Republic. Most of the army, conservative elements in the Spanish Catholic Church, and the middle and upper classes, especially in agrarian areas, supported Franco. The Republican government, on the other hand, relied on support from most urban areas, including the capital, Madrid, and from many of the lower class, especially from the industrial workers. Portions of the Spanish air force and navy also remained loyal to the government. It was a cruel war, with atrocities committed on both sides; an estimated 1 million people died.

Pablo Picasso's modernistic version of the German-bombed market town of Guernica during the Spanish civil war.

FOREIGN INTERVENTION

From the very beginning, however, the Spanish civil war was more than a domestic problem. Ideological forces in Europe seized on the conflict as a symbolic test whose outcome would predict the future direction of European affairs. By 1937 Mussolini was assisting Franco with about 70,000 troops and technicians, plus planes and mechanized equipment. Germany had at least 10,000 military personnel in Spain, including the dreaded Condor Legion, an air force unit that bombed Madrid and other Spanish cities, causing many civilian casualties. On April 26, 1937, the Germans bombed and destroyed the market town and Basque religious center of Guernica, killing and maiming much of the population. "We bombed it, and bombed it, and bombed it, and why not?" one aviator was reputed to have said. The bombings, a preview of World War II terror bombings, outraged many, including the Spaniard Pablo Picasso, who in protest painted *Guernica,* one of the major paintings of the twentieth century.

To counter Fascist and Nazi efforts in Spain, the Soviet Union sent aid and advisers to the Spanish Republic and worked through the Comintern to help drum up volunteers to fight Franco. Even without Soviet promptings, foreigners volunteered to fight on the side of the Spanish government. There were several "international brigades," including the Abraham Lincoln Brigade from the United States and the Canadian McKenzie-Papineau Battalion. The anarchist Emma Goldman also came to Spain to aid in the fight against the Franco forces. For many politically inclined intellectuals, it was a chance, in one way or another, to demonstrate their hatred of fascism and the Nazis. The French novelist and adventurer André Malraux, who organized an air squadron for the Republican side, and the U.S. novelist Ernest Hemingway, who served as correspondent and fund-raiser, were just two of the intellectuals who aided the Popular Front government. Leftist support to the Spanish government, however, was not as effective as that given by Italy and Germany to Franco. The Soviet Union under Stalin was more concerned with using the war as an opportunity to control the Spanish Left and eliminate Trotskyite and anarchist influences in Spain than with helping to win the war. Complex foreign policy considerations also prevented Stalin from doing more to help the anti-Franco forces. Divided internally on the Left-Right political spectrum, Great Britain and France did little to counter outside support to Franco. Fearing that the civil war in Spain might spread, Great Britain and France ineffectually called on outside powers not to intervene in Spain. Thus, Hitler and Mussolini once again witnessed the inability of Great Britain and France to check their actions. In 1939 Franco finally defeated the Spanish Republic and set up a repressive right-wing dictatorship.

German Aggression: March 1938 to March 1939

Hitler had indicated on the first page of his *Mein Kampf* that union with *Anschluss* (German Austria), forbidden in the post–World War I peace treaties signed by Germany and Austria, should be a German goal. He also stated that all German-speaking people should be united in an enlarged German *Reich* (realm or empire). *Lebensraum* (territory or living space) for such an empire could be obtained, conquered if need be, in eastern Europe, then populated by those he thought racially inferior, such as Slavs and Jews. His activities during 1938 and 1939 were in keeping with these long-held beliefs.

In March 1938 Germany moved again. By pressure and bullying tactics, Hitler succeeded in bringing a Nazi to power in Austria and obtaining an invitation for Germany to occupy the nation. German troops marched in without resistance, and the forbidden *Anschluss* took place as Austria became a province of Germany. Once again, the French and British did nothing but protest.

ANSCHLUSS

In late 1938 Hitler demanded that Czechoslovakia cede what Hitler called the Sudetenland to Germany. This Czech territory, which bordered on Germany and the former Austrian Republic, consisted primarily of ethnic Germans. But the area had been a part of the former Austro-Hungarian Empire and not of Germany. On September 15 and again on September 22, the British prime minister, Neville Chamberlain, flew to Germany to see Hitler and try to avert an international crisis. After his first meeting, Chamberlain wrote to his sister, "In spite of the hardness and ruthlessness I thought I saw in his face, I got the impression that here was a man who could be relied upon when he had given his word." On September 29 Chamberlain returned to Germany, where at Munich he and Hitler were joined by Mussolini and the French premier, Edouard Daladier. Czechoslovakia was not invited to participate in the conference; neither was the Soviet Union, which had pledged to come to the aid of Czechoslovakia in case of aggression, providing France did so first.

MUNICH AGREEMENT

France, on the other hand, although it had a defensive alliance with Czechoslovakia, agreed with Britain and Italy that the Sudetenland was to be given to Germany. Neither France nor Great Britain had kept up with the German rearmament, and their intelligence services depicted Germany as even more powerful than it really was. Neither was yet ready to risk war. French military thinking was symbolized by the Maginot Line, a long series of defensive fortifications built on France's eastern front between 1929 and 1934; such defensive-mindedness ill prepared France to come to the aid of its Czechoslovakian ally.

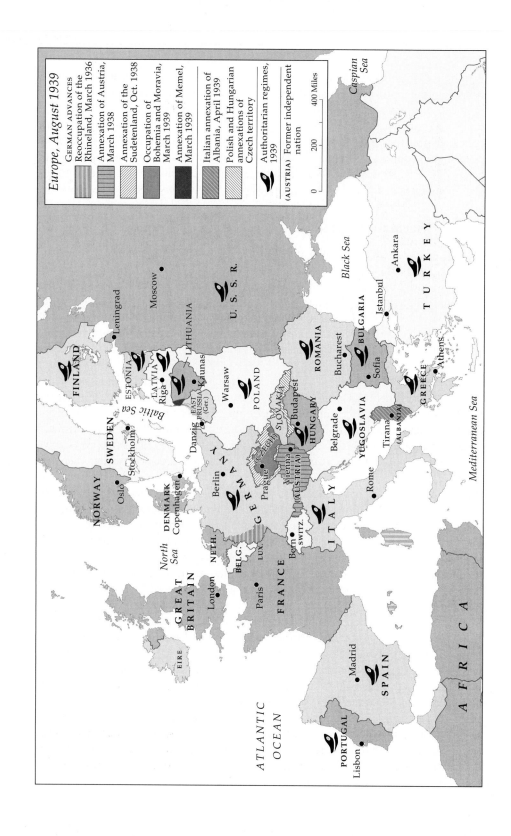

Europe, August 1939

GERMAN ADVANCES
Reoccupation of the Rhineland, March 1936

Annexation of Austria, March 1938

Annexation of the Sudetenland, Oct. 1938

Occupation of Bohemia and Moravia, March 1939

Annexation of Memel, March 1939

Italian annexation of Albania, April 1939

Polish and Hungarian annexations of Czech territory

🔥 Authoritarian regimes, 1939

(AUSTRIA) Former independent nation

0   200   400 Miles

Caspian Sea

Black Sea

TURKEY
• Ankara

• Istanbul

ROMANIA
• Bucharest

BULGARIA
• Sofia

GREECE
• Athens

U. S. S. R.
• Moscow

• Leningrad

FINLAND

ESTONIA
• Riga

LATVIA

LITHUANIA
• Kaunas

EAST PRUSSIA (Ger.)

• Danzig

POLAND
• Warsaw

SWEDEN
• Stockholm

NORWAY
• Oslo

DENMARK
• Copenhagen

Baltic Sea

North Sea

GERMANY
• Berlin

• Prague

CZECH
SLOVAKIA

Vienna
(AUSTRIA)

HUNGARY
• Budapest

YUGOSLAVIA
• Belgrade

Tirana
(ALBANIA)

NETH.

BELG.

LUX.

SWITZ.
• Bern

ITALY
• Rome

GREAT BRITAIN
• London

EIRE

FRANCE
• Paris

Mediterranean Sea

SPAIN
• Madrid

PORTUGAL
• Lisbon

ATLANTIC OCEAN

AFRICA

250

After returning from the Munich Conference, British prime minister Chamberlain displayed a British-German declaration and predicted "peace for our time."

Poland and Hungary also took advantage of the situation and within a few months seized portions of Czechoslovakia. Altogether, Czechoslovakia lost about a third of its population, much of its heavy industry, and important defensive fortifications. When news of the Munich Agreement was received in Prague, people cried openly in the streets. Despite Chamberlain's claim that "peace for our time" had been achieved, the Munich Conference soon became a symbol of the dangers of "appeasement," and Hitler hardly seemed grateful. "If ever that silly old man comes interfering here again with his umbrella," Hitler said about Chamberlain, "I'll kick him downstairs and jump on his stomach in front of photographers."

The signatories of the Munich Agreement had promised to guarantee what remained of Czechoslovakia against aggression. In March 1939, however, Hitler took over most of what was left of that unfortunate nation except for an eastern portion, Ruthenia, that he allowed Hungary to add to its previous gains. A little later that month, Lithuania, faced with an ultimatum, allowed Germany to annex its Germanic city of Memel. Hitler then began putting pressure on Poland for return of the city of Danzig, with its overwhelmingly German population, while also demanding special rail and road rights across the Polish Corridor separating East Prussia from the rest of Germany.

By this time, however, the British and French governments had finally seen the light. Despite continuing doubts about their countries' military readiness, public opinion, especially in Great Britain, had been awakened by the events of March 1939. Appeasement was not working; Hitler always came back for more. On the last day of March, Chamberlain announced that he and the French leaders had agreed to back Poland fully if it was threatened. This awakening, however, came too late for the small nation of Albania, which, already under strong Italian influence, was formally occupied by Mussolini's forces in early April 1939.

HITLER'S ACTIONS OF EARLY 1939

The United States Remains Neutral

Like Great Britain and France, the United States had great difficulty creating an effective response to Hitler's and Mussolini's aggressive actions in Europe. The U.S. public viewed the upheavals in Europe with mixed emotions. On the one hand, there was some concern about the persecution of Jews in Germany and some fear of Hitler's threat to European democracy and to the United States. On the other hand, some Americans, like many Europeans, regarded a strong Germany as a bulwark against Soviet Communism. Many New Deal liberals feared that involvement in European conflicts would distract energy and money from domestic reforms. An even larger number of Americans simply believed that intervention in World War I had been a mistake, and they opposed any actions that would involve the United States in another war.

Americans were thus, on balance, isolationists, and when Congress passed a series of Neutrality Acts, 1935–1937, it reflected public opinion. In this legislation, Congress prohibited U.S. vessels from transporting war matériel to belligerents, prohibited loans to belligerents, declared the United States neutral in the Spanish civil war, and forbade U.S. citizens to travel on belligerent ships. By such actions, Congress hoped to prevent U.S. trade from dragging the United States into war, as had happened in World War I. Roosevelt and his administration went along with Congress reluctantly, although the effect of the Neutrality Acts was to strengthen Hitler, Mussolini, Franco, and Japan.

As aggression in Europe mounted, the United States, distracted by Japanese advances in China and in hopes of preserving peace in Europe, pursued a policy of appeasement similar to that of Great Britain and France. Roosevelt raised little or no objection to Hitler's advances in the Rhineland, Austria, and the Sudetenland. However, Hitler's seizure of the rest of Czechoslovakia and Mussolini's conquest of Albania shocked Americans and began to bring them around to the belief that aggression in Europe should be stopped. Roosevelt appealed to Hitler to refrain from attacking a list of European nations, but Hitler (like the kaiser's advisers in World War I) viewed the United States as degenerate and incompetent and ridiculed Roosevelt's appeal. Despite Roosevelt's change of position, Congress refused to repeal the neutrality legislation, and the United States remained a spectator.

Europe on the Eve of the War

GREAT BRITAIN, FRANCE, AND THE SOVIET UNION

Although the British, and to a somewhat lesser extent the French, were now more determined to oppose any further German advances, Hitler had no way of being sure that his opponents would not again back down. If France and Great Britain did support Poland against German aggression, however, he had to prevent the Soviet Union from becoming involved. If he could obtain a promise of neutrality from Stalin, perhaps Great Britain and France would once again retreat rather than support Poland alone. In any case, he did not want a war on two major fronts.

In 1939 many influential figures in France and Great Britain believed that a strong alliance with the Soviet Union was needed if they hoped to avert a war or defeat Hitler if one should come. However, despite their 1935 Mutual Assistance Treaty, France and the Soviet Union were suspicious of each other. Firm military arrangements in case of war, for example, were never worked out. Nor did France's other potential ally, Great Britain, have much faith in the Soviet Union. Chamberlain, especially, distrusted the Communist giant. Finally, Stalin's purges of the late 1930s, which had devastated the Soviet officer corps, had reduced British and French confidence in the Soviet military—and no doubt encouraged Hitler to become more aggressive.

Stalin, of course, had his own interests in mind, and when Hitler made overtures toward the Soviet Union, Stalin proved willing to improve relations. Stalin had never trusted Great Britain or France and welcomed the possibility of their fighting Germany in a war that might exhaust and weaken all three.

On August 23, 1939, the Soviet government signed a Non-Aggression Pact with Germany. It stipulated that for 10 years both sides would refrain from attacking each other and would remain neutral if the other became "the object of a belligerent action by third power." A secret protocol, as later modified, divided eastern Europe into spheres of influence. Finland, Latvia, Estonia, Lithuania, eastern Poland, and Bessarabia (in Romania) were to be in the Soviet sphere, while Germany's sphere was to be western Poland.

NAZI-SOVIET PACT

With the Soviet Union now neutralized, Germany was ready to attack Poland, and, as a result of the pact, Hitler now had reason to hope that Poland might be deserted by Great Britain and France. He attacked Poland on September 1. Two days later, however, Poland's western allies declared war on Germany. World War II had begun in Europe.

SUMMARY

During the 1930s both Japan and Germany pursued aggressive policies designed to expand their territories. Interested in controlling its sources of supply in East Asia and worried about China's efforts to strengthen itself, Japan moved first in the decade, seizing Manchuria in 1931. Japan's pace of aggression thereafter accelerated; it attacked China in 1937 and subsequently conquered much of it.

In Europe, Nazi Germany and Fascist Italy committed similar aggressions. Between 1936 and 1939 Adolf Hitler tore up the Treaty of Versailles by remilitarizing the Rhineland and annexing Austria and later partitioned Czechoslovakia, all without effective opposition. Mussolini conquered Ethiopia, helped Franco win the civil war in Spain, and annexed Albania. Germany and Italy were aided, as was Japan, by the reluctance of Great Britain, France, and the United States to take stern measures to check aggression. Different ideologies and mutual mistrust on the part of the Soviet Union and the Western democracies prevented them from forming an effective coalition against the aggressors. In August 1939, after years of denouncing Nazi behavior, Stalin signed a pact with Hitler, clearing the way for a division of Poland between the two. Allied appeasement of Germany ended when Hitler attacked Poland, bringing on World War II in Europe.

SUGGESTED SOURCES

Bell, P. M. H. *The Origins of the Second World War in Europe.* 1986. A clear survey suitable for undergraduates.*

Boyce, Robert, and Joseph Maiolo, eds. *The Origins of World War Two: The Debate Continues.* 2003. A good collection of essays reflecting recent scholarly findings.*

Brendon, Piers. *The Dark Valley: A Panorama of the 1930s.* 2002. The best overall global treatment of a tumultuous decade.*

Butow, Robert J. C. *Tojo and the Coming of the War.* 1969. An excellent study of Japanese policy before and during World War II.*

Carley, Michael Jabara. *1939: The Alliance That Never Was and the Coming of World War II.* 1999. A vigorous and very readable book that argues that the anticommunism of leading British and French politicians prevented an alliance with the Soviet Union against Germany in 1939.

Chang, Iris. *The Rape of Nanking: The Forgotten Holocaust of World War II.* 1998. Meticulously researched account of Japanese atrocities that killed 250,000 civilians in the Chinese city of Nanking in 1937.*

Hemingway, Ernest. *For Whom the Bell Tolls.* 1940. A novel depicting the Spanish civil war by a famous American writer who participated in it.* (Also a film.)

Hicks, George. *The Comfort Women: Japan's Brutal Regime of Enforced Prostitution in the Second World War.* 1995. Documentation of this aspect of Japanese imperialism between 1938 and 1945.

Hsiung, James C., and Steven I. Levine, eds. *China's Bitter Victory: The War with Japan, 1937–1945.* 1992. A comprehensive, scholarly analysis of China's epochal war by 12 experts.*

Iriye, Akira. *The Origins of the Second World War in Asia and the Pacific.* 1987. A clear introduction by a leading U.S. historian.*

Large, David Clay. *Between Two Fires: Europe's Path in the 1930s.* 1990. A readable work concentrating on a number of events of the 1930s, including the Spanish civil war, Stalin's purges, and the Munich Conference.*

Overy, Richard, and Andrew Wheatcroft. *The Road to War.* Rev. and updated ed. 2000. A book that takes the opposite view of Carley (see earlier source), stressing the restricted options of France and Great Britain in the late 1930s.*

Payne, Stanley G. *The Spanish Civil War, the Soviet Union, and Communism.* 2004. The best work available on Soviet involvement in the Spanish Civil War.

Watt, Donald Cameron. *How War Came: The Immediate Origins of the Second World War, 1938–1939.* 1989. The best work available on the immediate origins of the war in Europe; well written and comprehensive.*

Young, Louise B. *Japan's Total Empire: Manchuria and the Culture of Wartime Imperialism.* 1999. Innovative study of how Japanese imperialism affected the colonizer and colonized.*

WEB SOURCES

www.yale.edu/lawweb/avalon/wwii/wwiichro.htm. This site contains links to documents reflecting aggression and diplomacy in the 1930s.

dwardmac.pitzer.edu/Anarchist_Archives/spancivwar/Spanishcivilwar.html. A website of anarchist-related materials that contains many materials on the Spanish Civil War.

www.soviethistory.org/index.php. See link to 1939 and then select "Soviet Territorial Agression" for materials on such topics as the Soviet-German Non-Agression Pact.

*Paperback available.

18

⑥World War II

Compared to World War I, World War II was a true global conflict, involving all the world's major powers and stretching from the Arctic Circle to the South Pacific. It lasted six years, killed roughly 60 million people, and ended with the destruction of two cities by atomic bombs, the culmination of centuries of development in weapons technology. As the world began to rebuild after 1945, all concerned had to face the possibility that, in another great war, the human race might destroy itself.

HITLER TRIUMPHANT, 1939–1941

The first two years of the war saw the German army go from victory to victory. To avoid the stalemate that had defeated them in the last war, the Germans relied on a new style of mechanized warfare, featuring close cooperation between *Panzers* (tanks) and aircraft. The world would call it *Blitzkrieg*, or "lightning war."

The invasion of Poland was the first test of this new, highly mobile type of war. Starting on September 1, 1939, great columns of German tanks, closely supported by dive-bombing aircraft, broke through the Polish defensive positions. The tanks drove deep into the interior, linking up far behind the lines and trapping huge concentrations of Polish forces in gigantic battles of encirclement. The Germans took over 500,000 Polish troops as prisoners of war. The German *Luftwaffe* (air force) played a major role throughout the fighting, launching bombing raids in the opening moments of the invasion that destroyed much of the Polish air force. It also carried out nonstop bombing of the Polish capital, Warsaw, reducing much of the great city to rubble and thoroughly demoralizing the civilian population. The Polish campaign was over in just three weeks; the entrenchment nightmare that had characterized World War I would not be repeated. Operating under a prior secret agreement with the Germans, Soviet forces entered eastern Poland, whose ethnic makeup was predominantly Belorussian and Ukrainian. The conquering powers divided Poland, which once again disappeared from the map.

GERMAN AIR AND TANK TACTICS DESTROY POLAND

Hitler offered peace to Great Britain and France if they would recognize his conquest of Poland; when they refused, he made plans to attack and defeat them in the spring and summer of 1940. As German preparations went forward, Great Britain contented itself with driving German surface vessels off the oceans, imposing a blockade, and sending a small army to assist France. The French waited behind the Maginot Line for the German attack, a strategy observers scorned as "sitzkrieg." In April 1940

BRITISH AND FRENCH REFUSE HITLER'S PEACE OFFER

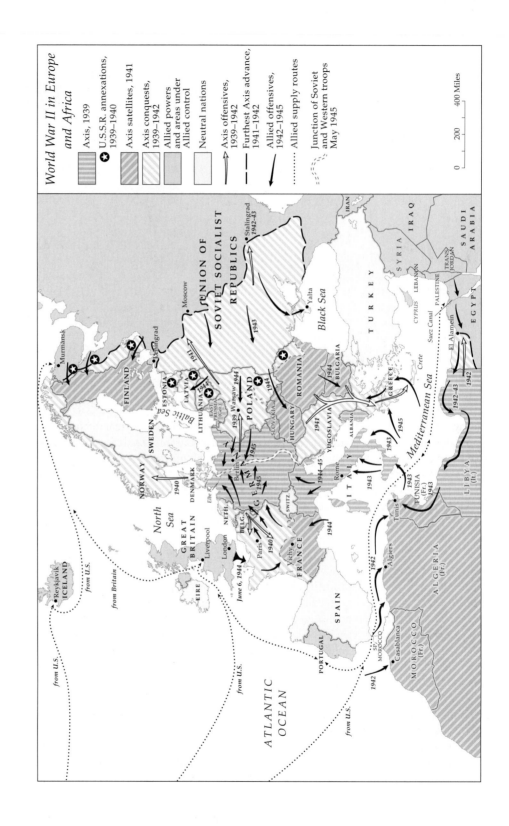

World War II in Europe and Africa

Legend:
- Axis, 1939
- ✪ U.S.S.R. annexations, 1939–1940
- Axis satellites, 1941
- Axis conquests, 1939–1942
- Allied powers and areas under Allied control
- Neutral nations
- → Axis offensives, 1939–1942
- – – – Furthest Axis advance, 1941–1942
- → Allied offensives, 1942–1945
- ·········· Allied supply routes
- Junction of Soviet and Western troops May 1945

0   200   400 Miles

the Germans thrust northward rather than westward. They seized Denmark easily and conquered Norway in two weeks, expelling British forces that had attempted to hold northern Norway. Germany now controlled neutral Sweden's export iron ore and could use the Norwegian coast as a base for air and submarine attacks on British shipping. In Great Britain, the Chamberlain government collapsed and the dynamic Winston Churchill became prime minister.

On May 10, 1940, the Germans launched a great offensive in western Europe. While a diversionary thrust into the Netherlands and Belgium fixed Allied attention, luring French and British forces to the north, the main German attack came in the south. A huge armored force, several thousand tanks in all, passed through the difficult terrain of the Ardennes forest. Catching the Allies completely by surprise, they smashed through weak French defenses at the town of Sedan and then dashed toward the English Channel, cutting across the rear of the main Allied forces lying to the north. The arrival of the German *Panzers* on the coast meant that the entire British army and most of the French army were surrounded in Belgium. The British army found itself fighting in a steadily shrinking perimeter around the coastal port of Dunkirk. Although the British managed to carry out a spectacular rescue operation, evacuating hundreds of thousands of soldiers, they did so only by abandoning virtually all of their weapons and supplies.

In the face of the disaster, Churchill rallied the British people: "We shall fight on the beaches, we shall fight on the landing grounds, we shall fight in the fields and in the streets, we shall fight in the hills; we shall never surrender." In June the Germans drove southward and westward across France, bypassing the Maginot Line. The French army was unable to consolidate a front. With the French near defeat, Italy declared war.

On June 22 France surrendered. For the surrender ceremony, Hitler chose the same spot and the same railroad car where the German representatives had signed the armistice in 1918. Under the terms of surrender, Germany annexed Alsace-Lorraine and occupied northern and western France, enabling Hitler to use the French coastline for submarine and air bases against Great Britain. Unoccupied France, with its capital at Vichy, became an ally of Germany. A small contingent of French troops in Africa and a body of French military refugees in Great Britain, led by General Charles de Gaulle, formed a government in exile and fought on at the side of the British. Whether the French underground resistance significantly harassed the Germans in France is a matter of debate.

While Hitler was overrunning western Europe, the Soviet Union was improving its position in eastern Europe. It annexed the Baltic nations of Lithuania, Latvia, and Estonia and the two border provinces of Romania; after a difficult war with the Finns, it annexed some border sections of Finland and a site for a naval base on the Baltic Sea. These moves, combined with its earlier incorporation of eastern Poland, enabled the Soviet Union to widen the buffer zone between Germany and the heart of the Soviet Union. At the same time, however, these actions, which were followed by the arrest, killing, internment, or deportation of perhaps 10 percent of the local populations, prompted the authoritarian regimes in eastern Europe to strengthen their economic and diplomatic relationships with Hitler.

Meanwhile, Hitler turned his attention to his surviving enemy, Great Britain. He had never really been interested in fighting the British, and he made peace overtures to them based on the status quo. Great Britain rejected the German offers, although

HITLER DEFEATS BRITISH AND FRENCH FORCES IN WESTERN EUROPE

FRANCE SURRENDERS

AIR WAR OVER GREAT BRITAIN

it was too crippled to attack Germany in Europe. Hitler then moved to invade Great Britain. He planned first to use his air force to destroy the British air force. With British planes destroyed, the Germans would be able to bomb or drive off the British fleet; the German army could then invade England. All through the summer and early autumn of 1940 a great air battle, the Battle of Britain, raged, but the Germans failed to destroy the British air force. "Never have so many owed so much to so few," said Churchill of the British airmen. The Germans turned to terror bombing the British cities, hoping to demoralize the British population who would then force the British government to sue for peace.

INSPIRATIONAL LEADERSHIP OF CHURCHILL

Despite extensive damage to some British cities and heavy loss of life, the British persevered. Churchill was an inspirational leader and effectively exhorted the British to fight on: "Hitler knows that he must break us in this island or lose the war. . . . Let us therefore brace ourselves to our duty and so bear ourselves that . . . men will . . . say, 'This was their finest hour.'" By the winter of 1940–1941 it was clear that Great Britain would continue in the war, although essentially on the defensive. Hitler hoped that a more intensive version of the World War I submarine blockade would eventually strangle the British.

Although the British remained unconquered, Hitler turned to his long-standing dream of destroying the Communist government in the Soviet Union, enslaving its people, and colonizing the east with Germanic peoples. He planned to throw his army and air force against the Soviet Union in mid-May 1941 and to destroy Stalin's regime in five months, before winter set in. In preparation for the assault, Hitler forged alliances with Hungary, Romania, and Bulgaria; reached an understanding with Finland; and moved German and allied troops toward the Soviet border.

GERMANS CONQUER BALKANS AND GREECE

Meanwhile Hitler's ally, Mussolini, ran into problems. The British had conquered Italian East Africa, driven into Libya, sunk most of the Italian navy, and supported the Greeks in repelling an Italian invasion. In April 1941, with Yugoslavia on the verge of joining the British and Greeks, Hitler acted. German forces and their allies overwhelmed Yugoslavia, but guerrillas, especially Communist units led by Marshal Tito (Josip Broz), fought the Germans there throughout the war. The British tried to hold Greece and Crete to protect their Mediterranean supply route but were driven out.

Meanwhile, Hitler dispatched the Afrika Corps under General Erwin Rommel to aid the Italians, and Rommel pushed into Egypt toward the Suez Canal. Desperate, the British called on Indian and ANZAC troops to hold Egypt and to protect the Middle Eastern petroleum fields. The Soviets and British deposed the pro-German shah of Iran, Reza Pahlavi, and installed his young son Mohammad as ruler. Turkey, caught between German success in Europe and British and Soviet power in Asia, remained neutral.

GERMANY ATTACKS THE SOVIET UNION

In the meantime, Hitler continued preparations to invade the Soviet Union. On June 22, 1941, Operation Barbarossa began, the largest military campaign of all time. Stalin had refused to believe intelligence information that the attack was imminent, and the German *Blitzkrieg* won its most stunning successes. All through the summer, the Germans advanced deep into the Soviet heartland, surrounding and destroying entire enemy armies. By December, millions of Soviet troops had died or surrendered. "The Russians are finished," Hitler said at one point. "They have nothing left to throw against us." Indeed, by the late fall of 1941 Leningrad was surrounded on three sides;

German armored spearheads were threatening Moscow; and Kiev, the greatest city on the southern front, had already fallen.

A closer look, however, would reveal problems. The Germans were operating over a thousand miles from their supply bases; they were running short of every type of supply; and the vast distances involved meant wear and tear on men and machine alike. Above all, the Soviet army never stopped counterattacking, even as it was being hammered as hard as any army in the entire history of warfare. These were often improvised, clumsy affairs, but they nevertheless took their toll on the Germans. Above all, of course, there was the weather—at first the rain, and then, in November, the snow and staggering cold. By late November, the German *Blitzkrieg* was winding down, and in front of Moscow, in the first week of December, it ground to a halt altogether. Now the Soviets saw their chance. On December 6, 1941, they launched a great counteroffensive. Aided by the signing of a neutrality pact with Japan in the spring of 1941, the gifted and young Soviet chief of staff, General G. K. Zhukov, was able to reinforce his troops with harsh-weather-trained soldiers, horses, and equipment brought from Siberia. Zhukov's troops shattered enemy forces in front of Moscow, inflicting horrendous casualties and driving the Germans back from the capital, permanently, as it turned out. Although a tenacious German defense eventually brought Soviet momentum to a halt, Hitler would have to go back to the drawing board in 1942.

GERMANS FAIL TO CAPTURE MOSCOW

HITLER'S "NEW ORDER" AND THE HOLOCAUST

By the autumn of 1941 Hitler was the master of the continent of Europe and used his control to carry out his demonic vision of a "New Order." At the center of Europe he created the Greater German Nation, consisting of an enlarged Germany, plus much of Poland and Czechoslovakia and parts of Yugoslavia and France. This would be the homeland of the "superior" Aryan race. Germany stripped the nations under its military control for the benefit of the German war effort, often causing severe deprivation and hunger in those countries. Hitler ordered his allies to supply Germany with products on terms favorable to it and to follow its lead in foreign and military affairs. Germany directed commanders in the occupied areas and the governments of the client states to deport "undesirables" to Germany for slave labor; the number eventually reached 9 million. Farther east, Hitler planned to use the Soviet Union for future expansion of the Aryan race. Germans were to be settled there in increasing numbers as a "master class" that would control the vast raw materials in that region. The Slavs and Asiatics there, considered subhumans, would be reduced to serfs.

HITLER PLANS A SLAVE EMPIRE

As a part of the New Order, Hitler's regime decided to implement "The Final Solution," a program now referred to as the Holocaust, to exterminate the Jews and Gypsies of Europe. The Final Solution is an example of genocide, a systematic process to destroy a particular national, ethnic, or racial group. History has recorded many instances of attempted genocide, such as the Turkish massacre of Armenians during World War I. In the east the Nazis and local police forces rounded up Jews, resistance fighters, and Communist Party members; special execution teams shot them and dumped them into mass graves. This method was soon deemed to be too slow and expensive, however, and after 1941 local authorities in nearly every area of Europe

HITLER BEGINS PROGRAM TO EXTERMINATE THE JEWS

The Holocaust: After their uprising in the Warsaw Ghetto was crushed, surviving Jews are marched to the trains that would take them to extermination camps (above). The fate of these Jews, and millions like them, was to be gassed in batches and to have their remains burned in ovens (below).

Hitler's New Order: Millions of slave laborers and political prisoners who were not Jews were beaten, tortured, starved, and worked to death in concentration camps throughout Europe.

BIOGRAPHY

Defying the Holocaust

We have been pointedly reminded that we are in hiding, that we are Jews in chains, chained to one spot, without any rights, but with a thousand duties. We Jews mustn't show our feelings, must be brave and strong, must accept all inconveniences and not grumble, must do what is within our power and trust in God. Sometime this terrible war will be over. Surely the time will come when we are people again, and not just Jews.

Who has inflicted this upon us? Who has made us Jews different from all other people? Who has allowed us to suffer so terribly up till now? It is God that has made us as we are, but it will be God, too who will raise us up again. If we bear all this suffering and if there are still Jews left, when it is over,

then Jews, instead of being doomed, will be held up as an example. . . .

If God lets me live . . . I shall not remain insignificant. I shall work in the world and for mankind!

And now I know that first and foremost I shall require courage and cheerfulness!*

. . .

Anne Frank was a 14-year-old German Jew in hiding in Amsterdam when she wrote this diary entry on April 11, 1944. Four months later she was arrested and sent to Auschwitz and later to the Belsen concentration camp, where she died in 1945.

*Excerpted from Anne Frank: The Diary of a Young Girl by Anne Frank © 1952 by Otto H. Frank. Used by permission of Doubleday, a division of Bantam, Doubleday, Dell Publishing Group, Inc.

under Hitler's control were ordered to send Jews to special extermination camps located primarily in Poland. Arriving packed in railroad boxcars, they were systematically gassed and then cremated, and their remains were processed for soap and blankets.

By one means or another, approximately 6 million Jews, about 75 percent of the European Jewish population, were put to death. Millions of other Europeans perished in slave labor camps from overwork, malnutrition, disease, and abuse. The Allies did little to aid the victims. How much and how soon they knew about the situation, and how much they shared in the guilt for the Holocaust, has been the subject of debate. The horror of the Holocaust convinced many Jews to support the Zionist idea of setting up an independent Jewish state in Palestine. There Jews could control the government instead of being, as elsewhere, a minority group subject to the power and attitudes of the majority.

THE UNITED STATES AND EUROPEAN AFFAIRS

As the power of Hitler spread across Europe, the U.S. government became increasingly concerned. President Roosevelt believed that, unless halted, Nazism and fascism would wipe out democracy in Europe and become a direct threat to the safety of the United States. The general public, however, opposed any action that might lead the United States into war. U.S. neutrality legislation was technically evenhanded, but its effect was to aid Great Britain, since the British could buy and transport U.S. goods to Great Britain while the British naval blockade prevented Germany from getting supplies.

While the U.S. public continued to hope for peace, U.S. leaders began to prepare for a possible war. By 1940 Congress was providing funds for a rapid increase in the armed forces and later in the year created the first peacetime conscription act in U.S. history. Meanwhile, the U.S. economy was booming with orders from the U.S. and British governments for war matériel.

Events in 1940 and 1941 drew the United States ever closer to the war in Europe. In September 1940 the United States agreed to supply Great Britain with 50 old destroyers in exchange for British bases in the Caribbean, Bermuda, and Canada. By 1941, with Hitler's power spreading south and east across Europe, the U.S. government became more assertive. Congress created the massive Lend-Lease Program, which made billions of dollars worth of military equipment available to Great Britain and the Soviet Union. U.S. military forces began to take control of the western Atlantic, sending forces to occupy Greenland and Iceland and escorting convoys to the middle of the Atlantic. By the autumn of 1941, with U.S. destroyers suffering casualties in conflicts with German submarines and with orders to arm merchant ships, the United States was only one step short of war with Germany.

THE UNITED STATES MOVES TOWARD WAR WITH GERMANY

CONFRONTATION BETWEEN JAPAN AND THE UNITED STATES

While Germany was conquering Europe, Japan was continuing to expand its control over Asia. By 1940 it had secured the coal and iron ore of Manchuria and northern China and had seized the major industrial centers and seaports of China. Much of the Japanese army, approximately 1 million men, was bogged down in China, with the Japanese determined to fight on until they finally defeated the Chinese. The Japanese were also determined to move into Southeast Asia to wrest the petroleum, rubber, and tin located there from the Western colonial powers.

The United States and Great Britain began to assist the Chinese by sending supplies by road through Burma and by air from India over the Himalayas to help China to continue the fight against Japan. In addition, U.S. officials warned the Japanese government that the United States was opposed to Japanese expansion into Southeast Asia. From this point on the Japanese government assumed that if Japan attacked Southeast Asia to get the industrial resources there, the United States would intervene in support of the British and the Dutch.

The war in Europe aided Japan in its expansionist plans. In the summer of 1940, with France defeated and Great Britain beleaguered, Japan forced the British to close the Burma Road supply route to China and pressured the Vichy government to agree to Japanese occupation of northern Indochina, thus cutting off another source of supplies to China. The United States responded with an embargo on aviation fuel and scrap metal, although general trade continued. Japan countered by signing the Tripartite Pact with Germany and Italy, in which the three powers pledged to aid each other if any one of them was attacked by a new enemy, which in this case would

THE UNITED STATES OPPOSES JAPANESE EXPANSION IN ASIA

have been the United States. It also recognized Japanese primacy in East and Southeast Asia.

In the summer of 1941 the tension between the United States and Japan heated up. The Japanese moved into southern Indochina and appeared ready to launch a military conquest of Southeast Asia. The United States responded by expanding its embargo and freezing Japanese assets in the United States, while beginning discussions with the Dutch and the British concerning the mutual defense of Southeast Asia. Meanwhile, the Japanese government began a two-pronged program. On the one hand, Japanese diplomats were instructed to try to reach agreements with the United States that would guarantee Japan access to the raw materials of Southeast Asia and a free hand to deal with the Chinese. On the other hand, since the diplomats were likely to fail, the military laid plans for conquering Southeast Asia and eliminating U.S. power in Asia.

JAPAN ATTACKS THE UNITED STATES

By the end of November, faced with the failure of negotiations, the new military-controlled cabinet of General Hideki Tojo decided to proceed with the military plans. Beginning on December 7, 1941, the Japanese attacked the British, Dutch, and Americans throughout Southeast Asia, an onslaught highlighted by a surprise attack on the U.S. Pacific Fleet at Pearl Harbor. The United States declared war on Japan on December 8; Germany and Italy declared war on the United States on December 11, 1941. World War II was now to be intensified in Asia.

JAPANESE CONQUESTS IN ASIA AND THE PACIFIC, 1941–1942

Japan's program for waging war was a mixture of offensive and defensive strategies. Japan intended to seize Southeast Asia and the vital supplies there, defeat Chiang Kai-shek, and drive the U.S. forces from the Philippines and the western Pacific. Japanese leaders believed that once they were in control of East and Southeast Asia and dug in behind a wall of fortified islands in the western Pacific, the Western powers would be unable to fight their way back into Asia and would agree to Japan's having a free hand there.

JAPAN CONQUERS SOUTHEAST ASIA

In the five months following December 7 the Japanese reached most of their goals. The Japanese war machine either destroyed Western military forces or drove them out of East and Southeast Asia. The Japanese bombed the U.S. Pacific Fleet into temporary impotence, although the fleet still had its vital aircraft carriers. Thailand was forced into an alliance with Japan, and the British were driven from Burma and Malaya, surrendering 60,000 men at Singapore. The Dutch East Indies was quickly overrun, and the U.S. Army in the Philippines was forced to surrender. Japan next seized U.S. and British islands in the western Pacific and secured a foothold in the Aleutian Islands and on New Guinea. Australia appeared to be Japan's next target, and Australians prepared for resistance. By April 1942 the Japanese had accumulated a vast land and water domain that geographically dwarfed the conquests of Adolf Hitler.

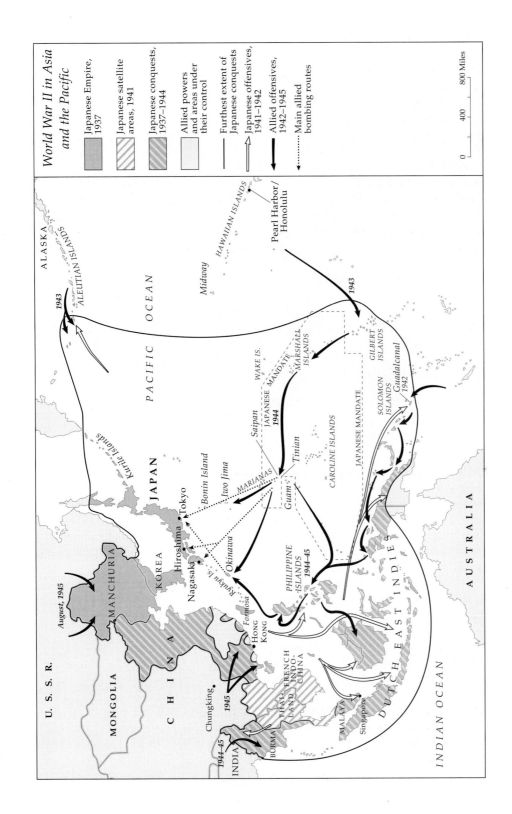

World War II in Asia and the Pacific

Japanese Empire, 1937

Japanese satellite areas, 1941

Japanese conquests, 1937–1944

Allied powers and areas under their control

Furthest extent of Japanese conquests

Japanese offensives, 1941–1942

Allied offensives, 1942–1945

Main allied bombing routes

0   400   800 Miles

ALASKA

ALEUTIAN ISLANDS

1943

PACIFIC OCEAN

Midway

HAWAIIAN ISLANDS

Pearl Harbor / Honolulu

1943

MARSHALL ISLANDS

GILBERT ISLANDS

JAPANESE MANDATE

Guadalcanal 1942

SOLOMON ISLANDS

JAPANESE MANDATE

WAKE IS.

JAPANESE MANDATE
1944

Saipan

Tinian

CAROLINE ISLANDS

Kurile Islands

JAPAN

Bonin Island

Iwo Jima

MARIANAS

Guam

Tokyo

Hiroshima

Nagasaki

Okinawa

Ryukyu Is.

Formosa

PHILIPPINE ISLANDS
1944–45

U. S. S. R.

August, 1945

MANCHURIA

MONGOLIA

KOREA

CHINA

Chungking

Hong Kong

FRENCH INDO-CHINA

THAI-LAND

BURMA

INDIA

1944–45

1945

MALAYA

Singapore

DUTCH EAST INDIES

AUSTRALIA

INDIAN OCEAN

Yalta Summit Conference, 1945: Churchill, Roosevelt, and Stalin plan for the ending of World War II and for the postwar period.

FORGING THE "GRAND ALLIANCE" AGAINST THE AXIS

By 1942 two conflicts of unprecedented magnitude were being waged simultaneously. In the Pacific and East Asia, the United States and China, with limited aid from the British Empire, made war against Japan. In Europe and North Africa, the Soviet Union, Great Britain, the British Empire, and minor allies were locked in combat with Germany and its allies, with the United States about to bring its armed forces into action.

SEPARATE WARS IN ASIA AND EUROPE

Germany, Italy, and Japan (the Axis powers) did not coordinate their side of the two struggles. Their opponents, however, realized it was necessary to come to an agreement on strategic priorities. Before U.S. entry into the war, Roosevelt and Churchill announced in the 1941 Atlantic Charter that opponents of the Axis would fight to halt aggression and not to gain foreign territory, a position similar to Woodrow Wilson's during and after World War I. Stalin gave his qualified approval. From 1942 to 1945 Roosevelt, Churchill, and Stalin met at several conferences around the world, the last at Yalta in the Soviet Crimea, to create a strategy for the defeat of the Axis powers. This was not easy; the Western Allies and the Soviet Union were suspicious of each other, and at times there were intense disagreements between the United States and Great Britain.

Despite their differences, but faced with a common peril, the leaders hammered out a series of broad agreements. The three men agreed that their nations would not make a separate peace but would fight the war through to the unconditional surrender of all the Axis powers. They concurred that Germany should be defeated first for two main reasons: it posed a greater threat to the survival of the Allies, and the Allies could more effectively concentrate against it. They agreed that the Soviet Union would join in the war against Japan after Germany had been defeated. The leaders also decided to place all Allied forces in western Europe under U.S. General Dwight Eisenhower.

By far the greatest point of friction between the Allies was the time and place to attack German forces from the west. The Soviet Union demanded that the United States and Great Britain land in western Europe, presumably France, as soon as possible, creating a second front. This would take some of the pressure off the Soviet Union, whose people were desperately struggling against nine-tenths of Germany's entire frontline forces. With an eye to postwar Europe as well as to the defeat of Germany, the British wanted to attack first what Churchill termed "the soft underbelly of Europe." This involved clearing North Africa, conquering Italy, and liberating the Balkans. This approach would fully open up supply routes to Great Britain and keep the Soviets out of the Mediterranean and eastern Europe, but it involved fighting on difficult terrain in Italy and the Balkans. U.S. leaders vacillated. As the war progressed, the United States supported clearing the Mediterranean but opposed landing in the Balkans. It eventually supported opening a front in France at the earliest opportunity.

ALLIES FIGHT OVER STRATEGIC PRIORITIES

INDUSTRIAL MOBILIZATION FOR TOTAL WAR

The awesome industrial and agricultural output of the United States, which made that nation, in Roosevelt's words, "the Great Arsenal of Democracy," was a crucial factor in the Allied defeat of the Axis powers. U.S. factories not only equipped their own military establishment of 12 million men but also underwrote part of the war effort of Great Britain, the Soviet Union, and other allies. During the war U.S. factories and shipyards produced 300,000 airplanes, 88,000 tanks, 2.5 million trucks, 17.4 million rifles, 315,000 artillery pieces, and 3,000 ships. Some ships were built in as little as 17 days. U.S. military output alone doubled the combined production of the Axis powers.

U.S. INDUSTRIAL OUTPUT SWAMPS THE AXIS

This massive military production, made possible by an ever-increasing alliance among government, industry, and the military, was one aspect of total war. Even more than in World War I, national governments closely regulated the production of raw materials, monitored labor, set production priorities, created manufacturing establishments where needed, and regulated the price and distribution of civilian and military products. Again, even more than in World War I, home front populations were exhorted by government propaganda organizations through pamphlets, radio, and motion pictures to hate the enemy, make sacrifices, and work harder. When World War II was over, the citizens of the Western democracies had become conditioned to function in a national environment in which the government was thoroughly integrated into economic and social life.

UNPRECEDENTED GOVERNMENT CONTROLS OVER ALL ASPECTS OF A WARRING NATION'S ECONOMY AND SOCIETY

World War II, even more than World War I, brought women into roles traditionally dominated by men. Despite some discrimination and harassment, American women, personified by "Rosie the Riveter," took over many assembly-line industrial jobs. In embattled Leningrad, women eventually made up 84 percent of the industrial

ROLE OF WOMEN

workforce. Women in several nations served in auxiliary branches of the armed forces and fought in guerrilla actions in Europe and Asia; some Soviet women experienced combat, including female fighter and bomber pilots.

THE WAR AT SEA

In the new war, navies on both sides attempted to destroy the economy of opponents and to erode the morale of enemy civilians. Early in the war, the British navy mined the approaches to Germany, cutting off all supplies from outside Europe. Unlike in World War I, however, the British were unable to close off a corridor within Norwegian territorial waters, a gap exploited by German submarines and naval surface raiders. In any case, during World War II Germany could draw on the resources of most of Europe and was much less vulnerable to blockade than it had been in World War I.

Great Britain, on the other hand, was just as vulnerable to blockade as ever. After the outbreak of war, Germany embarked on an intensive submarine-building program, and by 1942 it had built a large number of U-boats capable of long-distance travel. U-boats prowled the entire North and South Atlantic, operating from well-defended bases on the coasts of occupied Norway and France. Clusters of submarines, "wolf packs," tore into Allied convoys as far south as Brazil and South Africa, while other U-boats operated along the Atlantic and Gulf coasts of the United States. Land-based aircraft from Norway assisted German submarines in attacking convoys passing around Scandinavia with supplies for the Soviet Union.

ALLIES DESTROY GERMAN SUBMARINE FLEET

The Allies fought the submarines with increasing success, using the convoy system, destroyers, and submarine-hunting escort carriers, and by late 1943 the worst of the submarine threat was over. Submarines failed to sink any of the hundreds of transports that carried more than 1 million soldiers to Europe. Still, the Atlantic was a grim theater of war in which thousands of merchantmen and sailors were blown up, burned in oil fires, or drowned.

WAR IN THE PACIFIC TRANSFORMS NAVAL WARFARE

In the Pacific, the war at sea featured numerous encounters between elements of the surface fleets of the United States and Japan. The largest encounters introduced a new mode of naval combat: carrier warfare. Earlier in the century, naval combat had been decided by large battleships raining heavy shells on the enemy fleet. In the Pacific in World War II, the heart of naval task forces consisted of aircraft carriers, surrounded like queen bees by supporting craft bristling with antiaircraft batteries. Most battles were decided by the number of carriers sunk by the waves of dive-bombers, high-altitude bombers, and torpedo planes launched by opposing naval squadrons hundreds of miles apart. The United States won the largest and most crucial naval battles, in part because it had cracked the Japanese naval code.

Submarine warfare was also extremely important in the Pacific, and here the roles were reversed. Even more than Great Britain, Japan was dependent on shipping to secure food and raw materials and to supply its armies on the Asian mainland and garrisons in the western Pacific. Realizing Japan's vulnerability, the United States mounted a campaign to sink Japan's merchant ships and thus strangle its war effort. By 1945 U.S. submarines and aircraft had succeeded in destroying the bulk of the Japanese merchant marine and had virtually cut Japan off from Asia and the Pacific Islands.

THE AIR WAR

Although there was extensive tactical bombing in support of ground operations, the war in the air was dominated by the strategic bombardment of the enemy's economic and military installations, accompanied by the terror bombing of civilian population centers. These operations, in which helpless civilians were attacked with the same weapons used against military combatants, was another aspect of the total war concept that typified World War II. The Germans had used both strategic and terror bombing in their attacks on Poland, western Europe, and Great Britain. After 1942 the air war began to turn against the Axis; Allied bombers probed deeper and deeper into Germany and central Europe. Allied fighters furnished protection for the bombers and shot down German planes faster than they could be replaced. As German air resistance weakened, Allied bombers became increasingly effective in destroying factories, dams, roads, canals, and railroads, although the Germans rebuilt their factories underground. The Allies also used terror bombing, sending thousands of heavy B-17 and B-24 bombers at a time over German and Japanese cities. The policy culminated in the near-total destruction of the German city of Dresden in February 1945. Here, incendiary bombs—designed explicitly to start fires—triggered a firestorm that killed almost 100,000 people in an especially horrific fashion.

STRATEGIC BOMBING BECOMES TERROR BOMBING

To supplement their rapidly declining regular air force, German engineers developed a series of new weapons. They included the world's first operational jet aircraft, the ME-262; the V-1 buzz bomb, the forerunner of the modern cruise missile; and the V-2 rocket, forerunner of the intercontinental ballistic missile. Although it was an impressive list, all of these weapons came too late and in too few numbers to tip the balance back toward Germany. Nevertheless, they did point toward the future. German rocket designer Dr. Wernher von Braun, for example, would become one of the leading figures in the postwar U.S. space program.

Strategic bombardment came late in the Pacific, but once under way it was devastating. Most of the war in the Pacific was centered on U.S. forces working into positions from which they could bomb the Japanese homeland. The bombardment of Japan was not effective until late 1944, when bombers began to fly over Japan from bases in the Marianas. The Japanese air force was effectively wiped out by 1945, and by the spring and summer of 1945 U.S. bombers flew at will over the cities of Japan once again, using incendiary bombs to create raging firestorms that consumed the wooden buildings of Japanese cities along with hundreds of thousands of Japanese civilians.

THE ALLIES DEFEAT THE AXIS, 1942–1945

Soviet Victories and Nazi Defeat

In 1942 the war in Europe centered on a titanic struggle in the Soviet Union. Here the bulk and the cream of the German armed forces were pitted against the capacity of the U.S.S.R. to fight on virtually alone and endure tremendous suffering while it built up its own massive war machine. Like the Japanese in China, the German army and air force found themselves bogged down on a 1,000-mile front inside an enemy

THE SOVIET UNION BEGINS TO ROLL BACK THE GERMANS ALONG THE VAST EASTERN FRONT

This gigantic statue in Kiev is one of the memorials to the suffering and heroics of Soviet citizens in World War II.

nation of vast geographic dimensions and huge population. Unlike the Japanese, however, Hitler had not taken his primary objectives; Leningrad and Moscow in the north and the Caucasus petroleum fields in the south remained in Soviet hands.

STALINGRAD, A GREAT SOVIET VICTORY

The Germans added to their problems by making a calamitous mistake in dealing with the civilians. Although many non-Russian ethnic groups in the Soviet Union initially greeted the Germans as liberators, and some fought on the German side, the Nazis regarded all Slavs as subhuman. They inflicted so many indiscriminate atrocities on the population that they unified most of the ethnic groups in the Soviet Union against them, stirring up a swarm of guerrillas, who attacked German supply lines and installations.

The turning point of the German-Soviet war came in the winter of 1942–1943. Hitler had launched another great offensive in the summer, aiming at the key southern industrial city of Stalingrad. Slicing through the Soviet defenses and getting to Stalingrad proved to be no problem. Taking the city, however, was another story. The Soviet army fought a last-ditch defense here, turning every building and factory into a miniature fortress that the Germans had no choice but to assault. In November, a huge Soviet counteroffensive north and south of Stalingrad crashed through the Axis defenders in these areas and linked up far behind Stalingrad. The entire German force fighting in the city, the Sixth Army, was encircled. It surrendered in January 1943, and some 91,000 soldiers went into Soviet captivity. Of the 350,000 men in the Sixth Army at the start of the summer offensive, less than 5,000 would return to their homes in postwar Germany. The total German and other Axis troop losses during the Stalingrad campaign numbered in the hundreds of thousands, but the Soviet toll was greater. Overall, there were 1.1 million Soviet casualties, almost 500,000 of these being fatal. Thus, the Soviet victory came at a great price.

By the summer of 1943 the Soviet Union, with some U.S. and British aid, had created an impressive armaments industry that now sustained a huge military machine—over 6 million men, more than double the German army. Soviet forces also outnumbered the Germans three to one in artillery, tanks, and airplanes. With this superiority, the Soviets could now attack along several sectors simultaneously. In July 1943, the Soviets turned back another German offensive near Kursk in what is often labeled the "greatest tank battle in history"; they subsequently made advances all along the front.

By the spring of 1944 Soviet troops had reconquered Ukraine and pushed into Romania and Poland. They also lifted the 900-day siege of Leningrad, but not before 1 million of its citizens had perished—one graphic example of the massive suffering the German invasion inflicted on the Soviet Union, where over 27 million died. The defeat of German forces in the east was now only a matter of time.

D-Day and the Final Phases

With the Germans fully occupied in the Soviet Union, the Western Allies struck in the Mediterranean. In November 1942 the Americans and British used the new technology of amphibious warfare to land on the coasts of Vichy-held Morocco and Algeria, quickly overrunning these areas and pushing eastward. At the same time British and Commonwealth forces pushed westward out of Egypt across Libya. Most of the German and Italian forces in North Africa were caught between the two drives and surrendered in Tunisia in May 1943. In July and August 1943 U.S. and British forces conquered Sicily. In September Allied forces landed on the Italian peninsula, inducing the Italians to overthrow Mussolini and surrender. The Germans pushed troops into Italy and dug in across the peninsula south of Rome, preventing further Allied advance. The armies bogged down in Italy in a scene of fortification and mud resembling the trench warfare of World War I.

EUROPE INVADED FIRST IN ITALY

In the summer and autumn of 1944 the Allies opened the crucial campaigns that were to end the war in Europe. On June 6, 1944—"D-day"—U.S., British, and Canadian forces launched a massive landing on the Normandy coast in France, opening a major second front. For a month German forces held the Allies close to the beaches, but in July the Americans broke out and German resistance collapsed in France. By the autumn German forces had withdrawn to the fortified western border of Germany. In Italy the central part of the peninsula, including Rome, fell to the Allies, but the Germans retained control of the north.

ALLIES OPEN MAJOR SECOND FRONT AT NORMANDY

During 1944 the Soviets continued their relentless drive westward. By December the Soviet army had cleared most of the Balkans and advanced to the outskirts of

ALLIED FORCES MEET IN GERMANY

Budapest and Warsaw. Anti-Communist Poles in Warsaw rose in revolt against the Germans. Soviet troops did not cross the Vistula River to aid the Poles, and the Germans smashed the revolt. Finland, Romania, and Bulgaria surrendered, and Tito's Communist partisans made headway against the Germans in Yugoslavia. British troops entered Greece to finish securing the Mediterranean and to prevent Soviet expansion in that area.

By the spring of 1945 Germany was caught in a massive vise. Western Allied forces crossed the Rhine River and passed eastward, while Soviet forces moved in from the east and surrounded Berlin. Hitler committed suicide in his underground bunker in Berlin on April 30, as Western and Soviet forces met in the middle of Germany. By May 8, 1945, all German units in Europe had surrendered. The war in Europe was over.

Campaigns against Japan, 1942–1945

In mid-1942 the tide began to turn against Japan in the Pacific. A Japanese carrier was smashed at the Battle of Midway, the first important reverse for the Japanese navy. In late 1942 and early 1943, in fighting centered at Guadalcanal, Allied forces gradually pushed the Japanese out of the islands northeast of Australia.

ISLAND-HOPPING TO CREATE AIR BASES WITHIN RANGE OF JAPAN

By 1943 the enormous U.S. war effort was turning out enough war matériel and training enough men to press the war in the Pacific as well as in Europe. In 1943 and early 1944 U.S. forces in the Pacific attacked selected islands in the central Pacific, in a strategy called island-hopping. Once secured, these islands served as bases for attacks on the main objective: the Marianas, which were close enough to Japan to serve as bases for long-range bombing. Meanwhile, General Douglas MacArthur advanced along the coast of New Guinea with the intention of seizing the Philippines and Formosa and using them as bases for invading Japan. The Japanese garrisons on the remaining islands in the perimeter, cut off from supply or reinforcement, were left to starve in isolation or surrender.

In June and July 1944 Admiral Chester Nimitz's forces seized Saipan and Tinian in the Marianas and set up major bases from which the new B-29 bomber could begin the regular bombardment of Japanese cities. Meanwhile, MacArthur began the reconquest of the Philippines. This, plus the destruction of the remainder of the Japanese fleet in a series of naval battles off the Philippines, effectively cut off Japanese forces in Southeast Asia from those in China and Japan.

THE ATOMIC BOMB: THE CLIMAX OF TOTAL WAR

In the spring of 1945, their Axis allies defeated, the Japanese were in full retreat across Asia and the Pacific. The Chinese were pushing forward, while the British and Indians were reconquering Burma. To obtain air bases closer to Japan U.S. forces captured the islands of Iwo Jima and Okinawa, after heavy fighting.

TWO ATOMIC BOMBS END THE WAR WITH JAPAN

The resolute Japanese defense of Iwo Jima and Okinawa, including the extensive use of kamikaze (suicide) air attacks, made it clear that invading the Japanese home islands would lead to a terrible loss of life for both sides. Meanwhile British and American scientists had created two atomic bombs. On July 26, the United States, Britain, and China issued a joint declaration demanding Japan's unconditional surrender. It did

The devastation of the atomic bomb dropped on Nagasaki on August 9, 1945.

not mention the future status of the emperor. Since retaining the emperor was Japan's primary concern, it rejected the Allied demand. Therefore, President Harry Truman, who had succeeded Roosevelt after his death in April 1945, authorized the dropping of an atom bomb on Hiroshima on August 6 and another on Nagasaki on August 9. The bombs created tremendous explosions and killed 200,000 people. Radiation from the bombs continued to kill and maim for years to come. On August 8 the Soviet Union, as earlier agreed, declared war on Japan. Soviet forces, already massed along the Manchurian border, seized control of Manchuria and Korea.

Historians have argued whether Japan would have surrendered without having been hit by the atom bombs. They have also argued whether the bombs were dropped primarily to end the war quickly or to shape the postwar era (see Chapter 20). Without a doubt, the atom bombs ushered in a new era of total war. On August 14 Emperor Hirohito made his first radio address to the people of Japan, to announce Japan's unconditional surrender. On September 2, Allied Supreme Commander General Douglas MacArthur and other Allied commanders accepted Japan's surrender at a ceremony on a U.S. aircraft carrier in Tokyo Bay. World War II was finally over.

JAPAN SURRENDERS

The Human and Economic Costs of World War II

Because of its more lethal technology and the genocidal practices of some of its participants, World War II caused even greater carnage than World War I. Casualty estimates vary, thus the following are approximate figures: 60 million military and civilian dead, 35 million injured, and 3 million missing. In this human disaster, the civilian losses were perhaps the most shocking, as they exceeded military deaths. Civilians died from starvation and disease, perished in air raids and battles, in labor and extermination camps, and in the midst of deportations. For some of the major nations in the war the figures were grim: over 10 million Chinese, over 6 million Germans, 6 million Poles (including Polish Jews), and 2 million Japanese lost their lives. Six million Jews of all nationalities were killed. These losses, dismal as they were, paled in comparison to Soviet casualties: an appalling 27 million Soviets died during the war. In comparison, British and U.S. losses were of a much lower magnitude, in combination numbering no more than 700,000 killed.

In addition to the casualties, war and postwar dislocation uprooted 30 million Europeans from their homes, and the initials DP (displaced person) became familiar. In many nations in postwar Europe, the ethnic majority in an area permanently expelled ethnic minorities; some 17 million Germans were driven out of eastern Europe. In the Soviet Union, millions of people such as Volga Germans, Crimean Tatars, and Chechens were uprooted from their homelands and sent eastward, often to Siberia. Greeks, Turks, Yugoslavs, and Hungarians fled from other nations to their homelands, and about 1 million of the surviving European Jews immigrated to Palestine (later Israel).

Vast stretches of Europe and Asia were physically devastated. Most of the principal cities in central and eastern Europe had been bombed and shelled into rubble. The road, canal, and railroad systems of much of Europe had disappeared, and millions of acres of farmland had been damaged. In Asia, the cities of Japan had been obliterated, and many other Asian cities had been substantially destroyed. Much of China had also been damaged in eight years of war. The total cost of World War II, both in damages and in war expenditures, was estimated at $1.5 trillion.

SUMMARY

When World War II broke out in China in 1937 and in Europe in 1939 Axis powers were far better prepared than their opponents. Using the new military technology of the improved tank and airplane, German forces easily defeated and occupied Poland, Denmark, Norway, the Netherlands, Belgium, Luxembourg, and France. Great Britain held out despite submarine blockades and air bombardment, and the Germans and their Italian and eastern European allies turned their attention southward and eastward in 1941, conquering Yugoslavia and Greece, reinvading Egypt, and smashing into the Soviet Union. Although the Russians suffered immense losses, the Germans bogged down in front of Leningrad and Moscow in December 1941. Meanwhile, the Japanese decided that war was necessary to complete their designs on Southeast Asia. Accordingly, they invaded Southeast Asia and attacked U.S. naval forces in Hawaii in December 1941, quickly overrunning Southeast Asia and the western Pacific. German and Japanese administration of their conquered territories was brutal. In German-controlled Europe, mass enslavement and extermination campaigns led to millions of deaths and suffering for millions more.

To defeat the Axis powers, an effective alliance had to be forged by those nations allied against them, including—insofar as possible—common strategy and unified command. The United States became the economic and military backbone of the war against Germany from the west and of the war against Japan, while the Soviet Union engaged in a massive struggle with the main German forces. Extensive sea and air campaigns strangled the economies of Germany and Japan and inflicted heavy casualties on their civilian populations. The Allies finally defeated Germany by first clearing the Mediterranean and knocking Italy out of the war and then crushing Germany between massive advances from the east and west. The United States defeated Japan by isolating and ignoring the bulk of its armed forces in the Pacific and Asia and seizing selected islands in the Pacific. From these islands, U.S. fliers methodically bombed Japan. Japan surrendered after the United States dropped atomic bombs on Hiroshima and Nagasaki, bombs that significantly increased the already staggering losses of World War II.

SUGGESTED SOURCES

Astor, Gerald. *The Jungle War, Mavericks, Marauders and Madmen in the China-Burma-India Theater of World War II*. 2004. A well-known military historian brings to life a little-written part of the war.

Balkoski, Joseph. *Omaha Beach: D-Day, June 6, 1944*. 2004. A gripping account of the U.S. landing at the central D-day beach.

Barber, John, and Mark Harrison. *The Soviet Home Front, 1941–1945: A Social and Economic History of the USSR in World War II*. 1991. Shows the increasing contribution of women, peasants, and youth to the Soviet war effort.*

Beevor, Antony. *The Fall of Berlin, 1945*. 2002. A very readable work by a British historian who offers some new findings.*

———. *Stalingrad: The Fateful Siege, 1942–1943*. 1998. The best English-language work of the famous battle.*

Bix, Herbert P. *Hirohito and the Making of Modern Japan*. 2000. Authoritative book based on recently released sources that portray the emperor as actively engaged in conducting the war.*

Browning, Christopher. *Ordinary Men*. 1992. A thoughtful, even disturbing, analysis of the otherwise ordinary German citizens who carried out Hitler's murderous racial policies.*

Costello, John. *The Pacific War*. 1981. A comprehensive account of the struggle between the Allies and Japan.*

Dobbs, Michael. *Saboteurs: The Nazi Raid on America*. 2004. A fascinating and highly readable account of the landing of Nazi saboteurs on the U.S. East Coast in 1942.*

Dower, John. *War without Mercy: Race and Power in the Pacific War*. 1986. A history of the Pacific campaign with specific emphasis on the racial qualities of this war.

Glantz, David M. *The Battle for Leningrad, 1941–1944*. 2001. One of many works on World War II by a leading military historian.

Glantz, David M., and Jonathan M. House. *When Titans Clash: How the Red Army Stopped Hitler*. 1995. The best single volume on the war in the East by two leading authorities.*

Iriye, Akira. *Pearl Harbor and the Coming of the Pacific War: A Brief History with Documents and Essays*. 1999. Presents both U.S. and Japanese perspectives on events that led to war.*

Keegan, John. *The Second World War*. 1990. An accurate and dramatic account by one of the world's great military historians.*

Klemperer, Victor. *I Bear Witness, 1941–1945*. 2000. Emotional personal narrative of a Jew in Nazi Germany.

Koistinen, Paul A. C. *Arsenal of World War II: The Political Economy of American Warfare, 1940–1945*. 2004. A detailed scholarly account of U.S. military and economic planning for the war.

Kuznetsov, Anatoli V. *Babi Yar,* uncensored ed. 1970. A well-written, realistic novel about the German occupation of Kiev and the mass killing of Jews at Babi Yar.*

Pennington, Reina. *Wings, Women, and War: Soviet Airwomen in World War II Combat.* 2001. A highly praised treatment based on personal interviews and Soviet archives.

Pyle, Ernie. *Here Is Your War: Story of G.I. Joe.* 2004. A newly reprinted volume of articles by America's most beloved war correspondent.

Reynolds, David, Warren F. Kimball, and A. O. Chubarian, eds. *Allies at War: The Soviet, American, and British Experience, 1939–1945.* 1994. A balanced presentation.

Russia's War. 1999. A 10-part PBS video. (An excellent companion book of the same title by Richard Overy is also available.)

Service, Robert. *Stalin: A Biography.* 2005. Pt. 4. This portion of the most recent Stalin biography deals with Stalin during World War II.

Shaw, Irwin. *The Young Lions.* 1958. A novel depicting the war in Europe and North Africa as experienced by American soldiers and a Nazi.* (Also a film.)

Sheldon, Sayre P., ed. *Her War Story: Twentieth-Century Women Write about War.* 1999. An informative anthology of the disparate roles and reactions of women in World War II.*

Shoah. 1985. A long but gripping film about the Holocaust, based on the testimony of the survivors and their persecutors. (Also available on video.)

Simmons, Cynthia, and Nina Perlina, eds. *Writing the Siege of Leningrad: Women's Diaries, Memoirs, and Documentary Prose.* 2002. One of the editors lived through the siege herself; the collection provides great insight into the suffering and heroism of those involved.*

Terkel, Studs. *The Good War: An Oral History of World War II.* 1997. An unconventional journalist elicits remarkable stories from the World War II era; a classic.*

Weinberg, Gerhard L. *A World at Arms.* 1994. A massive history of World War II by a leading scholar.

The World at War. 1973. A BBC television series that provides an account of the conflict compiled from newsreels and documentaries. Emphasizes the British role. (Also available on video.)

WEB SOURCES

www.ibiblio.org/pha. Contains links to original documents regarding all aspects of World War II, including the prelude to the war.

www.csi.ad.jp/ABOMB/index.html. A Japanese site that contains links to materials, including photographs and oral histories, on the bombing of Hiroshima and Nagisaki.

www.fordham.edu/halsall/mod/modsbook44.html. This Fordham site provides links to many materials on the Holocaust.

www.soviethistory.org/index.php. See links to "Soviet Territorial Agression" (under year 1939) and to "Operation Barborossa," "The Battle of Kursk," "Women at the Front," and the "Deportation of Minorities" (under year 1943).

---

*Paperback available.

THE ERA OF THE COLD WAR
AND THE COLLAPSE OF EMPIRES

TIME CHART III
1945–1991

Year	South & East Asia	Middle East & Africa	Europe	Western Hemisphere	Trends in Culture, Science, Technology
1945		THE UNITED NATIONS ESTABLISHED			The atomic age, 1945–present
1946	ERA OF ASIAN INDEPENDENCE, 1946–1967 First Indochina War, 1946–1954		ORIGINS OF THE COLD WAR	The Peróns in Argentina, 1946–1955	
1947	India and Pakistan independent		Truman Doctrine Marshall Plan		Antibiotic drugs
1948		First Arab-Israeli War	Berlin airlift	Organization of American States established	
1949	Chinese Communist victory		NATO founded		
1950	Korean War, 1950–1953		First Soviet A-bomb tested		
1951		ERA OF INDEPENDENCE IN NORTH, WEST, AND CENTRAL AFRICA, 1951–1964			
1952		Independence struggles in Kenya, 1952–1956			Decade of the popularization of television
1953			Stalin dies		
1954	SEATO Geneva Agreement on Indochina	Algerian revolution, 1954–1962		Arbenz government in Guatemala overthrown	Salk vaccine

Year				
1955		Warsaw Pact		Beginning of the civil rights struggle in United States
1956	Second Arab-Israeli War	Hungarian revolt		
1957	Second Indochina War, 1957–1975	Common Market founded		
1958		DeGaulle becomes president of fifth French Republic		Sputnik launches the space age
1959			Castro assumes power in Cuba	
1960	Sino-Soviet split			
1961		Berlin Wall	Bay of Pigs	
1962			Cuban Missile Crisis	
1963	Organization of African Unity founded			Vatican II convened

ERA OF INTERMITTENT DÉTENTE, 1963–1979

Year				
1963				
1964	Tonkin Gulf Resolution	Khrushchev ousted	Era of rightist coups in Latin America, 1964–1976	Era of green revolution, 1960s–1970s
1965				
1966	Cultural revolution in China, 1966–1976			
1967	Third Arab-Israeli War Civil war in Nigeria, 1967–1970			
1968		Soviet intervention in Czechoslovakia	Decade of political and social turmoil in United States, 1967–1975	

(continued)

Year	South & East Asia	Middle East & Africa	Europe	Western Hemisphere	Trends in Culture, Science, Technology
1969					Moon landing
1970	Bangladesh independent				Growing environmental concerns, 1970s–present
1971					
1972	Nixon visits China	Era of military coups in Africa	Strategic Arms Limitation Treaty (SALT)		
1973		Fourth Arab-Israeli War		Allende government overthrown in Chile	Era of women's activism
1974		**INDEPENDENCE STRUGGLES IN SOUTHERN AFRICA, 1974–1990**			
1975	Vietnam unified		Helsinki Accords		Era of the popularization of computers
1976	Mao dies				
1977					
1978		Iranian revolution, 1978–present		Social revolution and cold war struggles in Central America, 1970s–present	Resurgent Islam
1979	Soviet invasion of Afghanistan, 1979–1989	Egypt-Israel Accords	Thatcher becomes prime minister in Great Britain		Era of rising economic power of Asian Rim
1980	Deng Xiaoping in control of China	Iran-Iraq War, 1980–1988			
1981			Martial law declared in Poland		
1982		Israeli invasion of Lebanon			
1983				Reagan conservatism in United States	
1984		Continued resistance against apartheid in South Africa			Drought and famine in Africa

Year				
1985		Gorbachev comes to power in U.S.S.R.		Chernobyl nuclear accident in Soviet Union
1986	Marcos ousted in the Philippines		Civilian government restored in much of Latin America in 1980s	
1987	Intifada in Israeli-occupied territories, 1987–present	INF ratified		
1988	Benazir Bhutto first woman head of a Muslim state (elected in Pakistan)			
1989	Tiananmen Square massacre Soviet withdrawal from Afghanistan	Collapse of Communist governments in Eastern Europe Waning of the cold war		
1990	U.S. gives up bases in Philippines	Reunification of Germany	Urbanization in Latin America intensifies	World population reaches 5.4 billion
1991	Persian Gulf War Democratization of the Asian Rim	Disintegration of the Soviet Union		

⑥General Trends in the Era of the Cold War and the Collapse of Empires

The chief political developments from the end of World War II until the breakup of the Soviet Union in 1991 were the cold war and the collapse of empires. The cold war, marked by ideological hostilities and a daunting arms race, was chiefly between the United States and the Soviet Union and their respective allies. The collapse of empires, partly caused by nationalist reactions to being dominated by foreign powers, resulted in well over 100 nations receiving their independence. Although it was somewhat different from Western colonial empires, the Soviet empire shared many characteristics with Western empires, and it was the last to collapse.

The policies of Mikhail Gorbachev, who became the leader of the Soviet Union in 1985, were primarily responsible for bringing the cold war to an end. They also, at times inadvertently, helped set off a chain of events that led first to the collapse of Communist rule in Eastern Europe in 1989 and 1990 and then to the breakup of the Soviet Union itself in 1991.

Although political developments captured most of the world's headlines, changes in the spheres of science and technology and economics were also of great significance. They helped produce, for example, increasing life spans, thermonuclear weapons, space travel, and an unprecedented increase in manufacturing and the production of consumer products such as televisions and computers. Unfortunately, this increase also contributed to environmental deterioration.

Although the standard of living of much of the world's population improved dramatically in the first three decades following the war, the gap between the world's richest and poorest nations continued to widen. For decades Communist promises of economic and social justice had a considerable appeal to lower classes and often led to guerrilla warfare. Yet by the late 1980s people in many parts of the world (including those in the Communist countries of Eastern Europe) desired more than Communist promises, and the economic opportunities and the quality of goods produced in capitalist nations seemed increasingly attractive.

Meanwhile, the capitalist states themselves continued the prewar tendency of broadening governmental powers and assuming more responsibilities for the economic well-being of their peoples (see Chapter 12, on Roosevelt and the welfare state). Conversely, in the Communist countries leaders such as Gorbachev and China's Deng Xiaoping took some steps in the direction of capitalism. In general in the postwar era, political leaders displayed an increasingly pragmatic tendency to stress economic considerations over ideology.

Scientific and technological advances and economic growth also supported major changes in the realm of ideas and culture. Communications technology, increased leisure, and the growing purchasing power of youth stimulated ever-changing popular cultural trends, originating primarily in the major Western nations but often spreading around the world. These trends, especially in music, were often irreverent, and advocates of traditional values and upholders of Communist orthodoxy often criticized the new trends as "Western decadence." However, except in some Muslim states such as Iran, traditionalists were generally unsuccessful in preventing the spread of nontraditionalist ideas and values.

SCIENTIFIC AND TECHNOLOGICAL ADVANCES AND ENVIRONMENTAL DECLINE

The postwar years witnessed a stunning display of scientific and technological achievements. One of the most important was the rapid development of atomic technology. By the 1950s scientists had learned how to fuse the atoms in hydrogen isotopes and had created the hydrogen bomb, which was a thousand times more destructive than the original atomic bomb. By the 1970s more than enough thermonuclear weapons existed to destroy all human life on the planet.

Splitting the atom also provided a significant opportunity to create atomic energy for peaceful purposes, thereby supplementing other energy sources. By 1990 over two dozen nations operated a combined total of more than 400 nuclear power plants. However, because of recurring accidents involving radioactive substances, extensive opposition to the development of nuclear energy persisted.

Transportation and communication developments were also significant. In 1947 a piloted jet airplane first flew faster than the speed of sound; jet propulsion eventually became the prime mode of civilian and military air travel. Ballistics technology generated the power to push rockets bearing either space capsules or atomic warheads through the earth's gravitational field into outer space at a rate of thousands of miles in a few moments. In 1957 the Soviet Union launched *Sputnik I,* the first of many artificial satellites. In 1969 U.S. astronauts traveled to the moon—about 240,000 miles—in just four days. At the end of 1989, two Russian astronauts returned to Earth after spending a year on *Mir,* a Russian space station.

TRANSPORTATION AND COMMUNICATION

In the field of communications, television became a major phenomenon of the postwar era—contrary to the prediction of the motion picture producer Darryl Zanuck, who said, "People will soon get tired of staring at a plywood box every night." In 1981 the average primary school child in Mexico City spent 1,460 hours a year watching television and 920 hours attending school. Polls in the United States reflected similar results. Television became an important instrument for entertainment, education, government propaganda, and business advertising. In 1986, for example, U.S. business concerns spent $22.6 billion on television advertising, which was more than the total spent by the national government on education and environmental protection combined.

During the postwar decades global television news coverage, with the United States in the forefront, increasingly influenced governments and citizens around the world. By the late 1980s the U.S.-based Cable News Network (CNN) was being viewed in some 150 nations, providing on-the-spot coverage of important events. In a related development, the invention of the transistor in 1947 eventually revolutionized radio communication, bringing broadcasts into the more remote areas of the world.

COMPUTER ADVANCES

Information processing, as exemplified by the computer, was another dominant postwar development. Computers continually improved the storage, retrieval, and manipulation of enormous amounts of information, especially after the development of small silicon memory chips in the late 1950s. Combined with the most modern means of telecommunication, including communication satellites, computers could transfer data quickly from one part of the world to another. They brought about major changes in business and government practices, research and scholarship, military technology, and intelligence gathering, and in general gradually transformed patterns of thought and behavior.

Despite their many advantages, computers also appeared to threaten privacy. Giant databases available to creditors and advertisers included personal information on more than half of the people in the United States, and government databases increasingly integrated the information they gathered concerning their citizens. The significance of the computer led some to speak of a new computer age or information age.

GENETICS AND MEDICAL DEVELOPMENTS

Some of the most dramatic scientific advances related to the study of genes. Scientists declared that deoxyribonucleic acid (DNA) was the key to heredity, leading scientists and doctors to become increasingly optimistic about the possibility of preventing certain inherited diseases and dealing with defective genes. In 1988 Harvard University was granted the first U.S. patent on an animal: a type of mouse genetically engineered for use in cancer experiments. Genetic engineering also opened up a new realm of possibilities in regard to the breeding of plant and animal food sources, but it simultaneously aroused fears of unforeseen results.

Medical advances improved health care and decreased the world death rate while increasing life expectancy. Partly as a result, the population of the world increased from 1.6 billion in 1900 to 2.4 billion in 1950 and to 5.4 billion by late 1991. Even so, many chronic killers, such as heart disease and cancer, remained to be conquered, and a new incurable contagious disease, acquired immunodeficiency syndrome (AIDS), caused a rapidly increasing number of deaths. By the end of 1991 it was conservatively estimated that in sub-Saharan Africa alone, there were at least 6 million people infected with human immunodeficiency virus (HIV), the virus that causes AIDS. It was also rapidly spreading in other parts of the world. (See Chapter 32 for AIDS at the end of the century.)

ENVIRONMENTAL ISSUES

During the 1960s and 1970s, many people, especially in advanced industrialized nations, became aware of environmental issues for the first time. One area of concern was the depletion of nonrenewable energy resources. Between the end of World War II and the late 1970s, the Western nations and Japan used more petroleum and minerals than had been consumed in all previous history; the United States was the biggest user, alone accounting for approximately 30 percent of world energy consumption during the 1970s. Although the democratic industrialized nations of the world became more energy efficient thereafter and the economically less developed nations of the world increased

Junked cars symbolize the heavy U.S. consumption of energy and world resources.

energy use at a faster rate, by 1991 per capita energy usage in the richer nations of the world was still at least 10 times greater than in the poorer nations.

Just as population growth, industrialization, and urbanization contributed to the need for more energy, they also increased demand for a variety of other resources, such as food, forests, and water. To meet the growing need for food and fodder—also stimulated by an increased world demand for meat and dairy products—scientists and technicians developed new high-yield strains of wheat and rice. Other agricultural techniques, such as using more fertilizers, irrigating lands only marginally fit for agriculture, and reducing the periods in which land was allowed to rest, contributed to increased food supplies. Between 1950 and 1985, as world population doubled, global food production almost tripled.

In certain areas of the world, however, per capita food production decreased in the 1970s and 1980s. Africa's population increased almost twice as fast as its food production. Deforestation on the southern fringes of the Sahara and overgrazing, combined with a series of dry years, caused the desert to spread southward, contributing to famine and countless deaths.

In economically advanced nations, scientific and technological developments and increasing industrialization polluted the air and water. In 1975 alone, more than 10,000 petroleum spills were reported in U.S. navigable waters. In the Communist nations of Eastern Europe and the Soviet Union, pollution and ecological damage, although often unreported, were nevertheless extensive.

Western scientists had earlier discovered, at times belatedly, that many new chemical compounds, such as DDT, PCB, and PBB, had adverse effects on the environment and on people's health. Pesticides such as DDT introduced a special dilemma into a world hungry for food. By killing crop-threatening insects, DDT and a number of other pesticides increased crop yields, yet caused illness and death in humans and animals. In the 1970s in the United States, an estimated 90 percent of residents in the state of Michigan ingested some traces of PBB, a suspected carcinogen, after it had been accidentally fed to cattle.

The development of nuclear power plants in the United States and other nations led to increased concern about radioactive accidents and waste disposal that could damage the environment. In 1957 an unreported explosion in the Ural Mountain area of the Soviet Union spewed tons of radioactive material, killing an unknown number of people and contaminating a large area. The worst accident occurred in 1986 at the Chernobyl nuclear power station in Pripiat, a Ukrainian town about 130 kilometers north of Kiev. A nuclear reactor exploded, spewing at least 50 tons of radioactive particles into the atmosphere. Winds then carried considerable contamination into other nations. In the Soviet Union, hundreds of thousands of people were eventually evacuated from contaminated areas, and millions of people eventually claimed to be adversely affected by the contamination. Recent studies on the total number of premature deaths that have already occurred as a result of the accident, or will in the future as a result of delayed health effects, varies from the thousands to the hundreds of thousands.

Several major fears about the environment grew rapidly during the 1980s, especially in economically advanced nations. As industrial smokestacks continued emitting sulfur dioxide into the atmosphere, more and more nations became alarmed at the destructive ecological effects of acid rain. Scientists also became convinced that heavy emissions of chlorofluorocarbons were depleting atmospheric ozone and consequently increasing solar radiation, skin cancer, and damage to food crops. Another major concern was the greenhouse effect. Many scientists thought that the increased burning of fossil fuels such as coal and petroleum was likely to cause an increase in global temperatures, possibly melting the polar ice caps, changing crop yields, and flooding low-lying parts of the world. Many scientists also attributed the measurable rise in global temperatures in the 1980s to the greenhouse effect.

As a result of increasing environmental concerns, a number of governments took steps to reverse deteriorating conditions. The first clean air act was passed in Great Britain in 1955, and as a result London was less polluted by the end of the 1970s than it had been a quarter century before. During the late 1960s and 1970s, the United States created a series of environmental protection laws, regulating water and air pollution in particular. At Montreal in 1987, 46 nations agreed to reduce chlorofluorocarbon emissions 50 percent by 1999. Poorer nations, however, often perceived concerns about the ozone layer and the greenhouse effect to be a luxury when faced with their need for economic development or with more pressing environmental concerns, such as safe drinking water.

RICH NATIONS AND POOR NATIONS COMPETING IN A GLOBAL ECONOMY

U.S. ECONOMIC DOMINANCE

Following World War II, largely as a result of technological advances, the world's production of manufactured goods increased dramatically. By the early 1970s world manufacturing had increased fourfold in two decades. The leading manufacturer and economic power in these years was the United States, which suffered much less economic damage from the war than other major countries. Toward the end of the war and shortly thereafter, the Allied powers agreed to encourage international economic growth and free trade by formation of the International Monetary Fund (IMF), the International Bank for Reconstruction and Development (World Bank), and the General Agreement on Tariffs and Trade (GATT). The United States played a leading role in the formation of all three institutions, but the Soviet Union declined to participate or to permit its satellite states in Eastern Europe to do so. GATT, which became a permanent organization, was specially created to reduce tariffs and other trade barriers, reductions that were particularly important to the United States, the nation with the greatest productive capacity.

For several years, much of Europe faced unstable economic and political conditions, but in 1947 the U.S.-sponsored Marshall Plan stimulated industrial and agricultural production and trade while also stabilizing postwar inflation and unemployment. By the early 1950s Western Europe was well on the road to economic recovery. In Eastern Europe, which did not participate in the Marshall Plan, recovery was slower. The Soviet Union renewed its Five-Year Plans and once again squeezed economic sacrifices out of its people in order to rebuild heavy industry.

Gradually, the unique postwar economic dominance of the United States gave way to a more balanced world economy. By 1980 the United States produced only 25 percent of the value of the world's goods and services (gross world product), down from its 40 percent share in the early 1950s but roughly equivalent to its 1938 portion. Within the same postwar period, Japan's share went from 2 percent to 10 percent, and Western Europe's also increased, although not nearly as dramatically as Japan's. From 1973 to 1981 members of the Organization of Petroleum Exporting Countries (OPEC) increased the price per barrel of petroleum 10-fold, almost doubling their per capita gross national product (GNP). From 1981 to mid-1990, however, petroleum prices fell by more than 50 percent, and the OPEC share of global wealth declined. Meanwhile, during the 1980s a number of other nations sharply increased their share of the global production of goods and services. From 1973 to 1986 China, Taiwan, South Korea, Singapore, and Hong Kong all saw their economies expand at about triple the U.S. rate. Although the growth of world output declined from 1988 to 1991, these nations along with others in southern and eastern Asia produced the highest economic growth rate of any area in the world. One reason for the region's continuing strong economic growth was abundant Japanese investment. By late 1991 it was estimated that a new Japanese factory opened every three days in Thailand. (See Chapter 34 for a discussion of Japan's economic problems in the 1990s.)

In the United States, foreign imports and investments (especially from Japan), an unfavorable trade balance, and large government budget deficits became major concerns of U.S. citizens. North American business leaders set up an increasing number of factories in poorer nations, where labor was cheaper and environmental restrictions less demanding.

In the first few decades after World War II, the economic status of most people in the world improved as their economies modernized, but the improvements were uneven, and economic modernization had both negative and positive consequences. During the 1970s and 1980s many nations in the poorer areas of the world saw some of their earlier economic gains erode.

THE RISE OF OTHER ECONOMIC CENTERS

THE GROWING DISPARITY OF RICH AND POOR NATIONS

The twentieth-century trend toward disparity of income intensified during the postwar period. In 1960 the average income in the poorest one-fifth of the nations was about 30 times less than that earned in the most prosperous one-fifth. By 1990 it was about 60 times less.

Several developments contributed to this broadening disparity. While richer nations generated more wealth, poorer countries produced faster growing populations. From 1973 to 1981 poor countries found the steep price hikes for petroleum, manufactured goods, and some foods especially burdensome. Because of these increases, they borrowed heavily abroad and incurred excessive debt. When petroleum prices fell in the 1980s, some of the less affluent petroleum-exporting nations were also hard-hit. They had borrowed large amounts of money in the expectation that healthy petroleum revenues would pay off their debts and now were more hard-pressed than ever to meet their obligation to banks, governments, and international lending agencies such as the IMF and the World Bank.

THE DEBTS OF POOR NATIONS

The debt became so staggering for many nations that a few suspended repayments. Most debtor nations, however, worked with the IMF to extend and restructure their repayment schedules. But the IMF frequently demanded domestic financial reforms of debtor nations as the price for restructuring debts or for any new credits. Indebted nations often resented these demands because they included calls for politically unpopular austerity programs, balanced budgets, and more private enterprise. Some charged that the IMF (composed of 151 nations in 1988) was a tool of its major capitalist contributors, particularly the United States. In their view, the IMF was part of an overall system whereby rich nations controlled world finance and trade in order to maintain high prices for their exports to poor nations while paying low prices for basic commodities imported from these nations. For poor nations, the only real answer to the debt problem was for lending agencies to reduce the overall debt.

FOOD AND FAMINE

The most essential need of poor nations after World War II was adequate amounts of food. Although world per capita food production continued to increase, poverty and ineffective world distribution systems combined to deny sufficient amounts of it to poorer peoples. During the early 1980s, for example, half the sugar, banana, and pineapple crops were exported from the Philippines, much of it by U.S. corporations, while most Philippine children were malnourished. Overall, experts contended that producer nations earned only about 15 percent of the final consumer costs of such tropical products.

Famine remained a serious problem. The worst case resulted from Chinese Communist policies begun in 1958 that soon led to millions of famine deaths (see Chapter 22). During the 1970s and 1980s, millions more lives were lost as a result of famines in areas such as Bangladesh, India, Cambodia (under the Communist Khmer Rouge), the Sahel (the area immediately south of the Sahara), and eastern and southern Africa. During 1982, UNICEF estimated that about 40,000 children died each day in the poorer nations of the world as a result of hunger-related diseases, poor health, and deficient sanitation practices.

The gap widened during the final postwar decades not only between a few rich nations and many poor nations but also between the rich and the poor within many nations. Peasants were often forced from land they once farmed, as big producers converted it to the production of export crops. In increasing numbers, these peasants

By the late 1980s over 1.2 million refugees in the southern
Sudan suffered from the effects of drought, famine, civil wars,
and government mismanagement.

migrated to urban centers to swell the size of city slums. In Latin America during the
1980s, 10 percent of rural landowners owned 90 percent of all farmland, while a
majority of rural inhabitants owned none at all.

One of the most evident economic trends of the postwar period was the increasing interdependence of the economies of the world. OPEC petroleum ministers during
the 1970s, for example, greatly influenced the lives of Americans, and drought or bad
harvest conditions in the United States affected the lives of millions of people dependent
on U.S. food exports. The growing power of the multinational corporations also lessened
the control of individual nations over their own economies. Businesses increasingly operated on a global scale. By 1991, for example, there were over 3,600 McDonald's restaurants in almost 60 nations outside the United States; the one in Moscow was the world's
biggest and busiest. The world's largest Kentucky Fried Chicken restaurant was in Beijing.

**GROWING ECONOMIC
INTERDEPENDENCE**

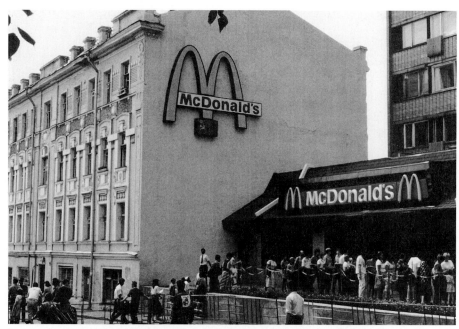

Part of the line of people waiting to get into Moscow's McDonald's, summer 1990.

Expanding fast-food franchises were indicative of still another global economic trend—the growth of the service sector of the world economy, especially in the more affluent nations. Partly stimulated by technological developments in such areas as telecommunications and robotics, an increasing percentage of people worked in providing services, while industry required fewer workers in an increasingly automated world.

SOCIETY AND POLITICS: REBELLIONS AND CONFLICTING IDEOLOGIES

YOUTH

In the social sphere, the years after World War II witnessed a gradual but growing rebellion against the overwhelmingly dominant role that white adult males had held in the interwar years. African Americans in the United States and black Africans demanded equality. In Africa, as well as in Asia, the challenge to the authority of white males was part of a broad anticolonial movement. In addition, by the 1960s youths in many nations were challenging the authority of societies dominated by older men and were becoming more aware of a youth culture of their own. This trend was especially noticeable in some affluent Western nations, where it was stimulated by media, music, and advertising that catered especially to youthful tastes.

WOMEN

Women, particularly in the same affluent Western nations, increasingly demanded equal rights. They gained the right to vote in some additional countries such as Japan (1946) and Portugal (1975). They also gradually increased their political participation

This African woman planting crops typifies the central agricultural role of women in many parts of the world.

in democratic nations both on behalf of issues of special interest to them and in politics generally.

One development of particular importance to women was a scientific breakthrough of the 1950s, the contraceptive pill. Its use by women spread rapidly in the 1960s. Western European and U.S. feminists later became especially active in the struggle for abortion rights, which were generally attained in the 1970s and 1980s. Even in conservative Catholic Spain—where before General Franco's death (1975) a married woman had to have her husband's permission to work outside the home or open a bank account—abortion became legal in 1985.

Although by then Communist governments in Eastern Europe had long allowed abortions and claimed that women enjoyed greater equality than in the West, the lives of women in Communist nations were often difficult. They usually combined full-time work with the major household responsibilities. Women in such nations had fewer appliances and had to expend more time to obtain basic necessities than did women in the industrialized West. Generally, the more economically advanced and democratic a nation, the better off were its women and the greater their political participation. But cultural traditions also played a part in determining their status. In Europe by the 1980s, Scandinavian women were most likely to have high status and hold high public positions. As Japan's economy and world position improved, so too did the position of its women in such areas as access to higher education. Yet, in part because of differing cultural values, Japan's women were still much less likely than U.S. women to hold important business or government positions.

In poorer regions of the world, most women struggled with frequent childbearing, heavy family responsibilities, and hard manual labor. In areas such as Africa and India, they cultivated, gathered, and processed most of the food and cash crops—a Peace Corps workers' toast stated, "Here's to the African farmer and her husband." Women in poor nations were more likely than men to be poor, uneducated, and discriminated against because of cultural and family traditions, labor legislation, and inheritance laws.

Partly because of the increased use of contraceptive devices, families gradually grew smaller and households less traditional and more varied, especially in the industrialized world. Improved health conditions enabled people to live longer, and the percentage of older people in societies increased. Even in poorer nations, where the size of families and the percentage of younger people remained considerably higher than in rich nations, average life expectancy increased by 14 years from 1950 to 1979.

URBANIZATION

Decreasing numbers of peasant farmers and increasing urbanization and literacy were also important postwar phenomena. By 1991 peasants and other people living in rural areas had become a minority in most parts of the world, with the notable exceptions of China, India, and sub-Saharan Africa. In 1950 Latin America had about 6 of 10 people living in rural areas; by 1990 this decreased to 3 of 10. Less rural to begin with, the United States and Europe had only 1 of 4 people living in rural areas in 1991. Literacy trends paralleled urban ones with a sharp overall increase, but a noticeable difference between regions still remained in 1991. Whereas most of the richer industrialized nations reported an adult illiteracy rate of no more than a few percent, more than 25 percent of Chinese adults and almost 40 percent of Indian adults were illiterate.

ETHNIC CONFLICT

Another characteristic of the twentieth century was the persistence of unrest brought about by dissatisfied ethnic and cultural minorities. Although affected by demographic changes, these insurgencies were generally more influenced by long-standing contention between ethnic groups. Some minorities, such as African Americans, sought simple equality. Others, such as the French in the province of Quebec in Canada, agitated for autonomy or separation—primarily through peaceful, legal, and constitutional means. Still others, such as the Basques in Spain and the Tamils in Sri Lanka, with less hope for obtaining autonomy or independence through peaceful means, resorted to sporadic terrorism and sometimes open rebellion. In Great Britain the Irish Republican Army in Northern Ireland carried on intermittent guerrilla warfare against both British troops and armed Protestant paramilitary groups. In Africa ethnic disputes contributed to civil wars, almost splitting Nigeria apart in 1967. Toward the end of the postwar era, conflicts between ethnic nationalities in the Soviet Union and Yugoslavia helped bring about the collapse of both states.

One of the most unfortunate minorities by this time was the Kurdish group, with about 20 million members dispersed over Iraq, Syria, Turkey, Iran, and the Soviet Union. Kurds in Turkey, Iran, and Iraq were often repressed but sometimes gained outside support from regional and superpower nations.

In postwar Europe most right-wing governments were replaced with democracies in Western Europe—with Greece, Spain, and Portugal completing the process in the 1970s—and with Communist governments in the east.

In contrast to the period before World War II, politics in Western Europe were stable and pragmatic, dominated by moderate socialist or moderate conservative parties. As compared to conservatives, socialists favored more sweeping social welfare measures, were less hostile toward the Soviet Union, and were more willing to grant independence to colonies. Both moderate socialists and moderate conservatives in Europe continued to be heirs of the liberal tradition of support for civil rights and individual liberties.

In the United States, politics were primarily pragmatic, socialism was much weaker than in Europe, and the chief ideological split was between conservatives and liberals. The latter sought an expanded government role, especially on behalf of the poor and in protecting the civil rights of minorities, and tended to be more sympathetic than conservatives toward peaceful coexistence with the Soviet Union and China.

COMMUNISM AND ANTICOMMUNISM

By 1948 Communist governments had come to power in Eastern Europe, in most cases as a result of Soviet power, and Communists continued to rule there until 1989. Conversely, after participation in coalition governments from 1945 to 1947 in France and Italy, Communist parties were generally excluded from cabinet participation in Western European governments. Beginning in 1949 Marxist governments came to power in several nations outside Europe, such as China, Vietnam, Cuba, and Ethiopia. Although these and later Communist governments were not carbon copies of the Soviet government and were influenced by their own national traditions, they nevertheless were strongly indebted to the Soviet example and repeated many of its repressive measures.

After Stalin's death in 1953, world communism became less unified. In the early 1960s accumulated disputes between China and the Soviet Union split the Communist world and divided Asian and African Communist parties into pro-Beijing and pro-Moscow factions. In Europe some Communists also desired more independence from Moscow, but on several occasions the USSR used force to suppress what it considered excessive liberalization (see Chapters 20 and 26).

After 1985 the Soviet leadership itself, led by the pragmatic Mikhail Gorbachev, liberalized its own institutions and government and called for more democratization, while at the same time encouraging similar steps in Eastern Europe. The Chinese Communists under Deng Xiaoping sought to prevent significant political reform, but beginning in the late 1970s they pushed through various measures that liberalized the Chinese economy.

For much of the postwar era the chief competing political forces in the Third World (nonaligned African, Asian, and Latin American countries) were Marxism and anti-Communist authoritarianism. Aided by the spread of the transistor radio, proponents of both forces broadened their indoctrination efforts, often reaching peoples living in remote areas. Lenin's linking of capitalism with imperialism and his encouragement of nationalist revolutions against the colonial powers (see Chapter 10) helped build support for communism in areas that were in the grip of Western imperialism. In the Third World, leaders were often struck by the rapid industrialization that occurred in the Soviet Union and the planned economy that helped bring it about. As a revolutionary doctrine directed against the rich and powerful, communism also had an appeal in many nations where the disparity between the rich and poor was great.

Many anti-Communist leaders of Asia, Africa, and Latin America had little in common except their opposition to communism, democracy, and civil liberties. They were generally supporters of the status quo and were opposed to social reforms and the redistribution of property. Some, however, including the shah of Iran, were sympathetic to technological modernization, a force that greatly changed many non-Western societies. Many of these Third World anti-Communist nations were dictatorships or one-party states.

DEMOCRACY AND AUTHORITARIAN GOVERNMENTS

With a few exceptions, such as India and Venezuela, democracy was uncommon in the Third World throughout much of the postwar period. In the 1980s, however, and especially from 1989 to 1991, many authoritarian governments, both of the Left and of the Right, were undermined or overthrown by those wishing a more democratic approach. This was true not only in Latin America, Africa, and Asia but also in Eastern Europe and among some of the 15 republics of the former Soviet Union. Some of the chief reasons for this shift were the increase of educated middle classes, the ever-growing interconnectedness provided by global communication and information technology, and a global economy dominated by the major democratic powers of the world. Thus, people in various regions became more aware of ways of life in democratic countries, and authoritarian rulers became more isolated. Their economic and human rights failures became more apparent. As their subjects increasingly contrasted their lives with the freer and generally more prosperous lives of those living in democracies, pressures from within joined demands from outside for reforms. These factors influenced Mikhail Gorbachev to seek to lessen cold war tensions and support democratization, which in turn helped lead to communism's collapse in Eastern Europe and the Soviet Union. This collapse made communism—and authoritarian anticommunism—less appealing in other parts of the world.

RELIGION AND POLITICS

After 1945 religion continued to play an important role in politics. In the Islamic world, politicians at least paid lip service to Islam, and some nations, such as Saudi Arabia and later Pakistan and Iran, based their laws on interpretations of sharia, the traditional system of Islamic law. The Catholic Church also played a political role in much of Latin America and Europe, where its leadership had been traditionally allied with conservative forces.

In the 1960s, however, Latin American Catholic clergy became increasingly critical of the social injustices perpetuated by right-wing governments. At times, they allied themselves with forces of rebellion. In the 1960s liberal Protestants, Catholics, and Jews in the United States became more active in civil rights and anti–Vietnam War protests and followed the nonviolent resistance tactics of the Baptist minister Martin Luther King Jr. By the early 1980s the momentum in U.S. Protestantism appeared to have swung back to conservative fundamentalists and evangelicals, who stressed the literal interpretation of the Bible and religious rebirth in Christ; they also became more active in politics, generally supporting Republican candidates.

INTERNATIONAL RELATIONS: COLLAPSING EMPIRES AND THE COLD WAR

During the three decades following World War II, the great majority of former colonial territories in Asia and Africa, and some in the Caribbean and the Pacific, became independent. The United States, Belgium, France, Great Britain, Spain, Portugal, and

A Soviet cartoon from the Khrushchev era indicates how independence and anticolonial movements could become involved in cold war politics. The banner calls for freedom for the nations of Africa.

Italy relinquished control over more than one-quarter of the world's population. By 1980 the United Nations had welcomed over 100 new nations since its founding in 1945, and during the 1980s additional colonial areas, especially in the Caribbean and Pacific, gained their independence. Finally, in the 1989–1991 period, the collapse of the Soviet empire brought real national sovereignty to satellite nations and independence to the former Soviet republics.

DECOLONIZATION AND COLD WAR

The decolonization of Western empires came about for many reasons. World War II had weakened Western imperialist control, especially in parts of Asia, where Japan had temporarily taken over. Growing disenchantment with imperialism within the Western nations, the economic cost of maintaining an empire on depleted resources, and increased resistance on the part of colonial peoples also weakened imperialistic controls. This resistance took many forms, including guerrilla warfare and what the colonial powers sometimes referred to as terrorism. But the tactics used by Algerians, Israelis, Vietnamese, and others in their quest for independence bore some similarities to those of resistance fighters in Nazi-occupied areas in World War II. And what one side labeled a "terrorist" the other side often called a "freedom fighter." Whatever term was used, civilians were often killed, but they were also killed in guerrilla or full scale wars. (See the glossary for a definition of terrorism.)

Some powers departed from certain colonies in Asia and Africa only after years of bloody struggle, but in most cases imperial powers granted independence peacefully.

Some Western powers continued to wield influence in their former possessions. France, for example, retained close associations with many of its African colonies, and Great Britain maintained a variety of ties with most of its former empire through the Commonwealth organization.

Developments in the colonies and former colonies were also affected by the cold war between the United States and the Soviet Union that emerged immediately after World War II. At times, both the Soviet Union and the United States used economic and military aid, military advisers, and sometimes troops and covert operations to support friendly, newly independent governments. Many leaders of the new nations, despite vulnerability to superpower imperialism because of their economic poverty, were opposed to joining either camp. These leaders feared being trapped by a form of neoimperialism, under which their nations would become the puppets of the superpowers. They also feared that their nations would become the battleground for superpower struggles. As an African saying goes, "When elephants fight, it is the grass that gets trampled."

To resist this danger, some Third World leaders formed a movement of nonaligned, or neutral, nations that held its first conference in 1961. In 1986, 101 nations took part in this group's eighth summit. The summits often produced calls for a "new economic order" that would lessen the disparity between the rich and the poor nations of the world. Although its members, including such nations as Marxist Cuba and Vietnam, declared themselves to be "against great power and bloc politics," the group was more critical of the United States and its allies, especially Israel, than of the Soviet bloc.

Although the Soviet Union encouraged nationalistic movements against Western imperialism, it enjoyed imperialist successes of its own. The Soviet Union and the Russian Empire that preceded it had already for centuries been an empire of many nationalities. By increasing the size of the Soviet Union with World War II gains and by establishing Communist puppet governments in Eastern Europe in the late 1940s, this empire was greatly expanded, countering the postwar historical trend that witnessed the breakup of empires. The contiguous nature of this empire and the fact that it contained Communist satellite states in Eastern Europe, instead of overseas colonies, distinguished it from other modern empires. Like the others, however, it fostered nationalist resentment and was maintained by force—or the threat of it. Like other modern empires, the Soviet Union collapsed, primarily because its weakened central government was unwilling or unable to use enough force to hold down nationalist forces that sensed the opportunity at hand.

REGIONAL AND INTERNATIONAL ORGANIZATIONS

Partly to counter Soviet influence after World War II, Western leaders encouraged regional and international economic and political cooperation. The Marshall Plan, the North Atlantic Treaty Organization (NATO), the Organization of American States (OAS), and the formation of the European Economic Community (EEC) and its subsequent broadening are examples of regional cooperation.

In Africa and the Middle East, as in the Soviet and Western blocs, some politicians promoted regional unity. Kwame Nkrumah of Ghana wrote a book entitled *Africa Must Unite,* and in 1963 the Organization of African Unity was founded. Islam was still another affiliation that transcended national boundaries. Many militant Muslims were critical of any nationalism that separated Muslims from one another. Secular Arab nationalism also transcended the boundaries of individual Arab states. Both forces competed for popular support in much of the Middle East, but both unifying forces were hampered by regional conflicts exacerbated by outside interference and the involvement of superpowers that had their own strategic, political, and economic interests in the area.

The major international organization of the postwar world, the United Nations (UN), was formed in 1945 by 51 nations to replace the League of Nations. It consisted of six bodies: the General Assembly (159 member states by 1990, with many more added after the former Soviet Union became 15 independent nations), the Security Council, the Secretariat, the Economic and Social Council, the Trusteeship Council, and the International Court of Justice. The Security Council had five permanent members: France, Great Britain, the United States, the Soviet Union, and the People's Republic of China (after taking the place of the Republic of China [Taiwan] in 1971). These permanent members could veto substantive council action. In addition, the council contained 10 nonpermanent members (6 up until 1965) elected for two-year terms by the General Assembly.

The record of the United Nations was mixed. As a forum for international opinion and as an organization that called attention to the economic and social needs of underdeveloped areas, it was often effective. It helped to channel aid to these areas, dependent of course on the willingness of the richer nations of the world to offer assistance.

As a peacekeeping force, the United Nations had a better record than that of the League of Nations. In 1946 it helped pressure the Soviet Union into leaving Iran. In 1950, largely as a result of a temporary Soviet boycott of the United Nations, it condemned North Korea for invading South Korea and sent an international force to aid South Korea. Since the late 1940s, UN peacekeeping forces have served, in some cases for decades, in various parts of the world—for example, in Kashmir (along the India-Pakistan border), Zaire, Cyprus, and the Middle East. In 1988 the UN peacekeeping forces were awarded the Nobel Prize for Peace for their continuing efforts. As a result of heightened cooperation between the Soviet Union and the United States during the last years of the postwar era, the UN became even more effective. For example, in 1990–1991, following the lead of the United States, it condemned the Iraqi occupation of Kuwait and supported a successful military effort to end the occupation.

Despite UN efforts and the absence of another world war, smaller wars and protracted guerrilla warfare became increasingly common in areas of Asia, Africa, and Latin America. By one estimate, 25 million people lost their lives between the end of World War II and 1978 as a result of warfare. Civil war in China, Indo-Pakistani wars, the Korean War, Arab-Israeli wars, and the war in Indochina were just a few of the conflicts in that period. During the 1980s, the Iran-Iraq War and the war in Afghanistan were among the bloodiest conflicts, and civil wars in many African countries, such as Mozambique, spanned the 1970s and 1980s. In addition, there were many crises and near wars. The Berlin crises in 1948–1949 and 1961, the Cuban missile crisis of 1962, the Soviet-Chinese border skirmishes during the 1960s and 1970s, and a variety of Middle East crises throughout the postwar period all contributed to international tensions.

UNITED NATIONS

WARS AND MILITARY SPENDING

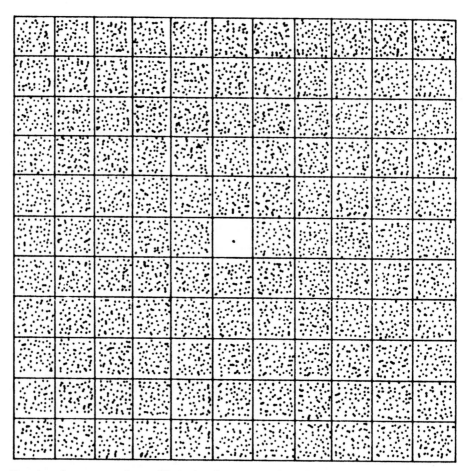

This chart demonstrates the world's nuclear firepower in the early 1980s (represented by all the multi-dot squares) as compared to the firepower of all the bombs dropped in World War II (the single dot in the middle).

Beginning in the late 1940s hostilities and suspicions also fueled a continuing escalation of global military spending and armaments. The United States and the Soviet Union, together with their European allies, easily accounted for the largest percentage of world military spending. From 1975 to 1987, the United States and the Soviet Union alone accounted for about 60 percent of the world total. By 1987 the combined nations of the world were spending an estimated $1.8 million a minute for military purposes. (See Appendix B for data on military expenditures by region for the years 1989, 1994, and 1999.)

The destructive power and proliferation of nuclear weapons increased dramatically after the explosion of the atomic bombs on Hiroshima and Nagasaki. By the mid-1970s the United States and the Soviet Union had developed combined nuclear arsenals with more than a million times the destructive power of the bomb dropped on Hiroshima, enough to kill the population of the earth 12 times over. By that time China, France, Great Britain, and India had also become nuclear powers, and a number of other nations, including Israel, Pakistan, and South Africa, were suspected of possessing nuclear weapons.

Amid the spiraling military spending and developments, some superpower arms limitation treaties were signed, especially in 1972; by 1988 the United States actually possessed fewer, though more sophisticated, nuclear weapons than it had two decades earlier. These developments, however, did not prevent a significant increase in military spending in almost all regions of the world. Most leaders apparently continued to share Theodore Roosevelt's belief that a navy was an "infinitely more potent factor for peace than all the peace societies."

By the late 1980s military spending was becoming an increasingly difficult burden to bear, especially for Soviet citizens, who were much poorer than North Americans. In 1988 the United States and the Soviet Union ratified an intermediate-range nuclear forces (INF) treaty eliminating intermediate land-based missiles from Europe. By 1990–1991, as both sides began destroying some of the newly banned missiles and other disarmament treaties were signed, world military spending had begun to decrease. Especially noticeable were a small U.S. decline and a larger Soviet decrease.

RELIGION AND CULTURE: CHALLENGES TO TRADITIONAL BELIEFS

In the postwar era, the challenge to traditional religious beliefs and values symbolized at the beginning of the century by Nietzsche continued throughout the world. As communism spread to Eastern Europe, China, and Southeast Asia, traditional religions in those areas were usually persecuted or at most grudgingly tolerated. Although in a few cases, especially Poland, the Catholic Church remained strong, in most Catholic nations of Europe the influence of the Church declined. Despite Church opposition, Italians legalized abortion in 1978; many Catholics in various parts of the world rejected papal teachings on birth control.

GROWING SECULARIST INFLUENCE

In the United States, local blue laws regulating Sunday work, amusements, and drinking were gradually eased or revoked. In the early 1960s the U.S. Supreme Court ruled against school-led prayer and devotional reading of the Bible in public schools. In the 1970s it ruled that abortion was a woman's right under certain conditions. In the United States and Western Europe, censorship of pornography also eased, despite religious opposition. In the Third World, as urbanization, education, literacy, and mass media spread, more people became separated from traditional religious beliefs.

Secularism also strongly influenced many intellectuals. Some of them came to accept a view similar to that of the secular French existentialists, who were greatly influenced by Nietzsche. They believed that God did not exist, that the world was "absurd," and that the best one could do was try to live for the present in a responsible and honest manner. Writers such as Jean-Paul Sartre, Albert Camus, and Simone de Beauvoir helped make existentialism one of the most influential of early postwar movements.

Rock music travels around the world: The Rolling Stones came to Prague in the summer of 1990.

Another grouping of writers and artists (sometimes labeled postmodernists) challenged not only traditional religious beliefs but traditions of almost any kind. They rejected any absolute truths, whether religious, scientific, political, or cultural. By the late 1980s this viewpoint was even becoming increasingly evident in the Soviet Union, where previously the government had prevented such radical relativism from having a public voice. Victor Erofeyev, a Russian writer, described the Russian literature that reflected this thinking: "The new Russian literature has called absolutely everything into question: love, children, faith, the Church, culture, beauty, nobility of character, motherhood, and even the wisdom of the common people."[1]

CULTURAL PLURALISM

As the Soviet example illustrated, the ending of Communist rule, which had persecuted traditional religions and restricted cultural freedoms, did not end challenges to traditional religious beliefs. Although Russian Orthodoxy and other religions gained new adherents as belief in communism faded, it was not religion that triumphed as much as it was a tendency to cultural pluralism—the coexistence of many different subcultures and beliefs in a society. This tendency was already evident elsewhere, especially in the democratic countries of the world. Such pluralism ran contrary to adherence to any one set of values, including Christian ones.

---

[1]Victor Eroleyev and Andrew Reynolds, eds., *The Penguin Book of New Russian Writing* (London: Penguin Books, 1995), p. xiv.

In the West, this pluralism was encouraged by numerous trends, but the tremendous expansion of various forms of media was especially important. The media, which often encouraged consumerism and the purchase of a never-ending stream of new products, created instant fads and popularized new trends. The average person in technologically advanced nations was able to select from an ever-increasing array of beliefs, lifestyles, and role models. This was true not only in the West but also in many other parts of the world where Western cultural influences had spread through motion pictures, television, and transistor radios (especially valuable in areas of the world without electricity). Western music attracted people throughout the world, sometimes helping to subvert authoritarian regimes. Pavel Palazchenko, who later became Soviet leader Gorbachev's English interpreter, recalled in his memoirs the Beatles' influence on him and his Soviet friends in the 1960s: "We knew their songs by heart. . . . To the Beatles . . . I owe my accent. . . . The Beatles were our quiet way of rejecting 'the system' while conforming to most of its demands."

Religious and cultural influences that had developed outside the United States and Europe also became part of this cultural pluralism. Zen Buddhism, transcendental meditation, the Hare Krishna sect, and various Muslim movements all had followings in the United States. So, too, did some non-Western and Third World writers and filmmakers who achieved worldwide recognition after 1945, including five Latin American writers awarded the Nobel Prize for Literature between 1945 and 1991.

Despite an overall trend of rising secularism and cultural pluralism, many traditional religions remained vigorous and at times attempted to modernize their religious ideas and practices. At the same time, many people felt threatened or disoriented by the conflicting values being manifested in their societies and continued to stress the importance of traditional values in an increasingly pluralist world. After his elevation in 1958, Pope John XXIII worked toward a revitalization of the Catholic Church and encouraged ecumenical initiatives. The election of the Polish John Paul II as pope in 1978 strengthened the Catholic Church in Poland and, to a lesser extent, in some other Eastern European nations. Protestant fundamentalism also displayed increasing vitality during the late 1970s and the 1980s, especially in the realm of U.S. politics.

Outside the West traditionalism was often connected with anti-Westernism. In Iran, for example, anti-Western Islamic fundamentalism manifested itself strongly in the 1980s. Western, especially U.S., influences were perceived to be corrupting more traditional, cohesive, and religious-based societies. In the words of Iran's Ayatollah Khomeini, the United States was "the great Satan."

Some intellectuals continued to support traditional religions and their teachings. The Anglo-American poet and dramatist T. S. Eliot, who died in 1965, and the acclaimed Russian novelist Alexander Solzhenitsyn were two writers who displayed their traditional religious beliefs in their writing. The exiled Solzhenitsyn lived and wrote in the United States from 1976 to 1994.

Many theologians and writers stood between the traditionalists and those radicals who rejected tradition. For example, the Jewish thinker Martin Buber and the Protestant Paul Tillich (both of whom died in 1965) and the Catholic Hans Küng (b. 1928) attempted to apply theological insights to modern concerns. Most Third

RELIGIOUS RESPONSES TO MODERN LIFE

World intellectuals also rejected any extreme attempts to return to past traditions, especially if they involved intolerance of modern ideas.

Thus, by the beginning of the early 1990s, the world's peoples still displayed many divisions on values. In the 1930s T. S. Eliot wrote in his play *The Rock:*

> Where is the wisdom we have lost in knowledge?
> Where is the knowledge we have lost in information?

More than a half century later, many still doubted whether the new Information Age had led to any significant moral progress or made humans any wiser.

SUGGESTED SOURCES

Al-e Ahmad, Jalal. *Plagued by the West.* Rev. ed. 1982. An influential Iranian critique of Western civilization and its impact on Iran under shahist rule. (Also published in a 1984 edition under the title *Occidentotis.*)

Barnet, Richard J. *The Alliance: America, Europe, Japan, Makers of the Postwar World.* 1983. An insightful account of how the major capitalist nations of the world became and remained allies.*

Blake, David H., and Robert S. Walters. *The Politics of Global Economic Relations.* 4th ed. 1991. A clearly written overview of global economic relations since World War II; presents contrasting points of view concerning major developments.*

Chamberlain, Muriel E. *Decolonization: The Fall of the European Empires.* 2nd ed. 2000. This work surveys the fall of the European empires, including that of the U.S.S.R., in Africa, Asia, the Caribbean, and Eastern Europe, through the 1990s, dealing, for example, with the British return of Hong Kong to China in 1997.*

Charrad, Mounira M. *States and Women's Rights: The Making of Postcolonial Tunisia, Algeria, and Morocco.* 2001. An insightful comparative work on how religion, culture, and politics affected women's rights in three different countries.*

Conrad, Peter. *Modern Times, Modern Places.* 1998. An examination of how "life has changed during the last hundred years," primarily by examining modernist artists, writers, and cultural movements.

Courtois, Stéphane, et al. *The Black Book of Communism: Crimes, Terror, Repression.* 1999. A collection of scholarly essays on Communist regimes around the world, highlighting their crimes and repression.

Feshbach, Murray, and Alfred Friendly Jr. *Ecocide in the USSR: Health and Nature under Siege.* 1993. An in-depth examination of the tremendous damage done to the Soviet environment under Communist rule.*

French, Marilyn. *The War against Women.* 1993. An interesting work that argues that women's global progress has been greatly overestimated.*

Gaddis, John Lewis. *The Cold War: A New History.* 2005. A valuable reassessment by a leading historian of the cold war.

Glover, Jonathan. *Humanity: A Moral History of the Twentieth Century.* 2000. A philosopher examines and reflects on atrocities and other immoral (and moral) behavior during the past century.*

Harrison, Paul. *Inside the Third World.* 3rd ed. 1993. A firsthand account and analysis of the poverty of many modern nations.*

Hobsbawm, Eric. *The Age of Extremes: A History of the World, 1914–1991.* 1994. Part Two of this work by a leading leftist historian offers a challenging interpretation of important global developments.*

Küng, Hans. *Global Responsibility: In Search of a New World Ethic.* 1993. A leading Catholic theologian's attempt to apply Christian values to the world of the 1990s.*

Kurlansky, Mark. *1968: The Year That Rocked the World.* 2004. A very readable account of global events in a year in which antiestablishment sentiments reached their apex.

MacRidis, Roy C., and Mark Hulliung. *Contemporary Political Ideologies: Movements and Regimes.* 6th ed. 1996. A clear overview of the leading ideologies of the twentieth century.*

McNeill, J. R. *Something New under the Sun: An Environmental History of the Twentieth-Century World.* 2000. The work of a scholar who emphasizes how extensive was the damage imposed on the planet during the past century.

Palazchenko, Pavel. *My Years with Gorbachev and Shevardnadze: The Memoirs of a Soviet Interpreter.* 1997. These memoirs throw some light on the crucial changes that occurred under Gorbachev.

Rubin, Barry. *Modern Dictators.* 1987. An interesting examination of postwar Third World dictators in Asia, Africa, Latin America, and the Middle East.*

Sen, Amartya. *Poverty and Famines: An Essay on Entitlement and Deprivation.* 1984. A thoughtful analysis by a Nobel Prize winner in economics.*

Stromberg, Ronald N. *After Everything: Western Intellectual History since 1945.* 5th ed. 1990. A clear overview of Western political, cultural, philosophical, artistic, and scientific trends in the postwar decades.*

Ulam, Adam B. *The Communists: The Story of Power and Lost Illusions, 1948–1991.* 1992. A global overview by a leading expert on communism and the Soviet Union.

Watson, Peter. *The Modern Mind: An Intellectual History of the 20th Century.* 2001. Pts. 3 and 4. A wide-ranging treatment that deals not only with philosophers but also writers, artists, scientists, social thinkers, theologians, and others.

Yergin, Daniel. *The Prize: The Epic Quest for Oil, Money, and Power.* 1991. A long, but very readable, history of the quest for oil and its economic and political implications.*

WEB SOURCES

www.fordham.edu/halsall/mod/modsbook51.html. A Fordham site with links to decolonization materials.

www.fordham.edu/halsall/mod/modsbook46.html. See links to materials on the UN, human rights, the cold war, and literary reflections.

www2.etown.edu/vl/global.html. This site provides a great starting place for finding historical and current materials on global and cross-cultural materials.

www2.etown.edu/vl/globenv.html. Numerous links provided for global environmental issues.

www.fordham.edu/halsall/mod/modsbook57.html

www.fordham.edu/halsall/mod/modsbook58.html

www.fordham.edu/halsall/mod/modsbook59.html

www.fordham.edu/halsall/mod/modsbook60.html.

These four Fordham sites provide links to materials on postwar Western thought, religion, science and technology, and pop culture.

---

*Paperback available.

⑥Postwar Settlements, Europe, and the Early Cold War

World War II was the catalyst for the onset of the cold war, in which rivalry between the United States and the Soviet Union brought on a period of increasingly intense confrontation. When this rivalry was combined with the menace of atomic destruction at supersonic speeds, there emerged the distinct possibility of global holocaust, which in fact came fearsomely close in the Cuban missile crisis of 1962.

THE POSTWAR SETTLEMENT

During World War II the Allies had forged a broad consensus on the terms to be imposed on the defeated, but this agreement broke down quickly after the war as antagonism among the victors intensified. Instead of settling affairs at a formal peace conference as after World War I, the Allies worked out most of the peace terms in military discussions immediately after the war and at a series of foreign ministers' meetings lasting until 1963. Some of these agreements were ratified through bilateral treaties; some de facto arrangements, particularly those dealing with Germany, were not ratified until 1975.

Europe

THE SOVIET UNION EXPANDS WESTWARD

The territorial arrangements in Europe were not as extensive as those made after World War I. The single largest change involved the agreement that the Soviet Union would retain the areas originally acquired in 1939–1940 and again in its possession at the end of the war: Estonia, Latvia, Lithuania, portions of Romania and Finland, and eastern Poland. In addition, the Soviet Union annexed a province of Czechoslovakia and the northern half of East Prussia. These acquisitions moved the Soviet border dramatically westward from its placement in 1939 but left it at about the same place as the border of tsarist Russia in 1914. Although some nations refused to acknowledge the change, Poland received the eastern quarter of Germany in compensation for the loss of eastern Poland.

Boundary changes in the rest of Europe were relatively minor. Hitler's Axis allies—Finland, Hungary, Romania, Bulgaria, and Italy—faced some territorial adjustments, reparations payments, and limitations on their military establishments, but the overall terms were not particularly harsh. The most notable change was Italy's

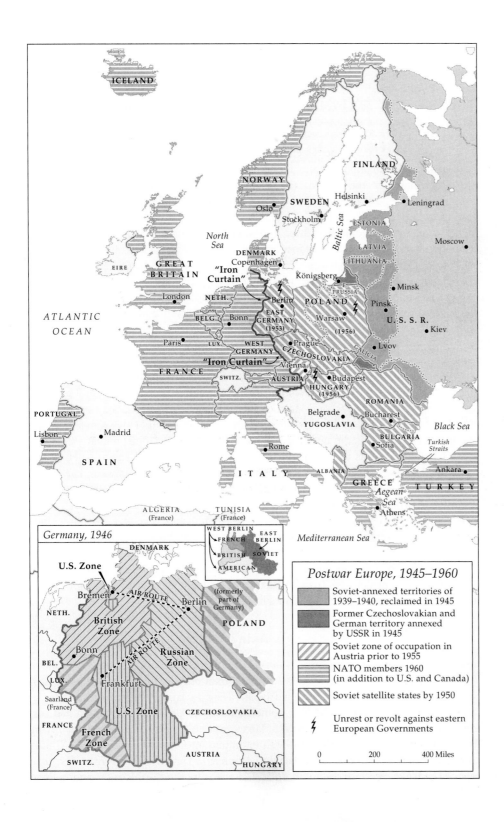

ICELAND

NORWAY

FINLAND

Helsinki

SWEDEN

Oslo

Stockholm

Leningrad

Moscow

North Sea

Baltic Sea

ESTONIA

LATVIA

LITHUANIA

DENMARK

Copenhagen

EIRE

GREAT BRITAIN

"Iron Curtain"

Königsberg

E. PRUSSIA

Minsk

London

NETH.

Berlin

POLAND

Pinsk

U.S.S.R.

BELG.

Bonn

EAST GERMANY (1953)

Warsaw

(1956)

Kiev

ATLANTIC OCEAN

Paris

LUX.

WEST GERMANY

Prague

CZECHOSLOVAKIA

Lvov

GALICIA

"Iron Curtain"

Vienna

FRANCE

SWITZ.

AUSTRIA

Budapest

HUNGARY (1956)

ROMANIA

PORTUGAL

Lisbon

Madrid

Rome

Belgrade

YUGOSLAVIA

Bucharest

BULGARIA

Sofia

Black Sea

Turkish Straits

SPAIN

ITALY

ALBANIA

GREECE

Aegean Sea

Athens

Ankara

TURKEY

ALGERIA (France)

TUNISIA (France)

Mediterranean Sea

WEST BERLIN

FRENCH

EAST BERLIN

BRITISH

SOVIET

AMERICAN

(formerly part of Germany)

POLAND

Germany, 1946

DENMARK

U.S. Zone

Bremen

AIR ROUTE

Berlin

NETH.

British Zone

Russian Zone

Bonn

BEL.

LUX.

Saarland (France)

Frankfurt

AIR ROUTE

U.S. Zone

CZECHOSLOVAKIA

FRANCE

French Zone

AUSTRIA

SWITZ.

HUNGARY

Postwar Europe, 1945–1960

Soviet-annexed territories of 1939–1940, reclaimed in 1945

Former Czechoslovakian and German territory annexed by USSR in 1945

Soviet zone of occupation in Austria prior to 1955

NATO members 1960 (in addition to U.S. and Canada)

Soviet satellite states by 1950

⚡ Unrest or revolt against eastern European Governments

0   200   400 Miles

surrender of the predominantly Slavic province of Istria to Yugoslavia. The western boundary of Germany was set as it had existed in 1937. Austria was detached from Germany and occupied by the United States, Great Britain, France, and the Soviet Union. The occupation forces were withdrawn in 1955, and Austria regained its independence.

GERMANY TO BE OCCUPIED BY ALLIED FORCES

During the war Germany's enemies had considered permanently dismembering it or stripping it of industry and reducing it to a feeble agricultural region. By the war's end, however, the United States believed that a healthy, united Germany was essential to European recovery and to vigorous international trade. But Germany first had to be de-Nazified, and the Allies agreed that it was to be disarmed and temporarily divided into four occupation zones: French, British, U.S., and Soviet. In 1945 most observers believed the occupation would be over in three to five years. Again, as after World War I, the victors were interested in reparations settlements and agreed that the heavily ravaged Soviet Union would receive the largest share. The Allies left the details concerning reparations for later resolution.

FOUR-POWER OCCUPATION OF BERLIN

One feature of the arrangements for the occupation zones became extremely important in postwar years. During the war, the Western forces had agreed to halt west of Berlin while Soviet forces captured the city; this put Berlin in the Soviet occupation zone. After the war, the Western Allies insisted on sharing in the occupation of the city, and an awkward arrangement was worked out. Berlin became a separate occupation authority divided into four zones. The Soviet Union agreed to set aside certain highways, railroads, and air corridors in their occupation zone for the Western powers to use to supply their three sectors in West Berlin. This arrangement left the Western forces in Berlin cut off behind Soviet lines, a precarious military situation.

Finally, there was the matter of war crimes. The Nazis had caused such horror before and during World War II that this time the victorious powers were determined to punish the leaders. An international judicial tribunal assembled at Nuremberg during 1945–1946. The highest-ranking surviving Nazi leaders were put on trial for waging aggressive war and for committing crimes against humanity. Twelve were condemned to death, seven were imprisoned for terms up to life, and three were acquitted. While some attacked the process as "victor's justice," the precedent was set that brutal treatment of prisoners and noncombatants constituted a crime and that "following orders" was not a sufficient defense. Trials of lesser officials followed, and the hunt for uncaptured Nazi war criminals continued in subsequent decades.

Asia

As in Europe, postwar arrangements in Asia devolved from basic agreements made at the midwar conferences. The victors stripped Japan of its empire, divided its possessions among themselves, and occupied Japan. They set Japan's boundaries as those of 1854, which restricted it to the four home islands. The United States, which had carried the great burden of the war with Japan, was to be the sole power occupying Japan and the Ryukyu Island chain, with its important Okinawa air base. The United States also took over the western Pacific Islands as a United Nations Trust Territory. The Soviet Union received the southern half of Sakhalin, the Kuril Islands, and railroad and seaport rights in Manchuria (all lost to Japan in 1905). China regained Taiwan (Formosa), which it had lost to Japan in 1895. Soviet and U.S. forces split Korea into two occupation zones until a mutually suitable government could be installed.

Defeated Japan received much the same treatment as Germany. Japan's armed forces were disbanded, and Japan, in a new constitution, was made to renounce war as an instrument of national policy. Japan was to be governed by a U.S. army of occupation under the direction of General Douglas MacArthur. U.S. forces would stay until the Japanese could demonstrate they were no longer an aggressive people, which they could do by creating a government acceptable to the United States. As at Nuremberg, Japanese leaders were put on trial in Tokyo and Manila for war crimes; seven were executed, and others were imprisoned. Unlike Germany, Japan retained its government, but it was purged of militarists. The emperor was also retained on the condition that he renounce his claim to divinity.

POST-SURRENDER TERMS FOR JAPAN

THE ONSET OF THE COLD WAR

As World War II approached its end, the alliance among the victorious powers began to dissolve. The United States, Great Britain, and the Soviet Union—nations very different in their political, social, and economic characteristics—had been united in a "shotgun marriage" against a fearsome enemy. Even as they were fighting the Axis, however, each of these allies intended to arrange the postwar world along lines that would be most beneficial to itself. Great Britain wished to maintain its empire and retain its closed imperial economic system, the United States wished to retain its spheres of influence in the Western Hemisphere and Asia but also wished to construct a worldwide system of free markets, and the Soviet Union was determined to dominate eastern Europe and to keep Germany militarily impotent in order to prevent another invasion out of the West. In addition, the Soviet Union was willing to exploit opportunities to advance Marxism and Soviet interests around the world if such opportunities did not embroil the Soviet Union in too much difficulty.

Reflecting such a diversity of interests, World War II, a "hot" war, was followed by the cold war, a confrontation featuring primarily the United States and the Soviet Union that persisted to one degree or another throughout much of the postwar period. Historians strongly debate its causes and the responsibility of each power for the outbreak.

CONFLICTING ALLIED GOALS

Phase One: Eastern Europe and Germany

At the last two wartime conferences, Yalta in February 1945 and Potsdam in July and August 1945, it became clear that strong disagreements about the future of eastern Europe and the occupation of Germany were developing between the United States and Great Britain, on the one hand, and the Soviet Union, on the other. Soviet troops already occupied eastern Europe and eastern Germany. The Soviet Union, with approximately 27 million dead, was determined to weld eastern Europe into a buffer zone of friendly nations that would protect it from future invasion. In 1943

U.S.-SOVIET DISAGREEMENTS OVER EASTERN EUROPE

Stalin began to organize Communist governments in exile for Poland and some other eastern European states. These organizations were primed to take over in their countries as Soviet troops moving westward ousted the Germans from eastern Europe. The United States wanted eastern European governments to reflect the will of their people through democratic elections, partly from principle and partly from confidence that such elections would create governments that would be friendly to the United States. It pressed the Soviet Union to permit the creation of governments based on a broad political spectrum, particularly in Poland, but the Soviet Union made only token concessions.

The wartime allies also clashed over German reparations. All the victors believed they were entitled to wring reparations from Germany, and they had talked about setting the figure at $20 billion. Yet the United States was undamaged by the war and its economy had prospered mightily. U.S. leaders also remembered the German experience after World War I and were more interested in rebuilding Germany as a trading partner than in burdening it with reparations. The Soviet Union, on the other hand, had been devastated during the war and wanted to rebuild its economy through either postwar loans from the United States, reparations from defeated Germany, or both. To pressure the Soviets into opening eastern Europe, the United States cut off the Lend-Lease Program and refused to make loans to the Soviet Union. In addition, in 1946, the Western powers ended shipments of industrial materials from their German zones to the Soviet Union, causing great bitterness in the Soviet Union. Meanwhile, the Soviets proceeded to strip their occupation zone in eastern Germany of materials useful to the Soviet economy.

TRUMAN AND STALIN ASSERTIVE LEADERS

The conflict between the United States and the Soviet Union stemmed from more than policy differences. In mid-1945 the two nations were led by Harry Truman and Joseph Stalin, men whose personalities contributed to the tensions. Truman's predecessor, President Roosevelt, a pragmatist, had tried to work in a cooperative spirit with Stalin. Truman was an intelligent, feisty politician who had come to the presidency by accident. He had little training in foreign affairs, but he had always been a critic of Stalinism; now that the war was over, he was temperamentally disposed to "get tough" with the Soviet Union.

Stalin was also a clever, determined political leader, with limited contacts with the outside world. He had displayed an almost paranoid obsession with acquiring and maintaining political power, and he harbored strong suspicions of the nations of the West.

The atomic bomb also harmed postwar relationships. The political fallout in U.S.-Soviet relations echoed the atomic fallout over Japan. Most historians claim that the bomb was used because intense Japanese resistance threatened to prolong the war and greatly increase Allied casualties. On the other hand, some revisionist historians claimed that the bomb was dropped primarily to prevent the Soviet Union from making gains in Asia and to make that country more amenable to U.S. desires concerning Germany and eastern Europe. Whatever the case, U.S. possession of the atomic bomb, while strengthening Truman's resolve, made the Soviet Union fearful and suspicious but did not make it back down on matters concerning eastern Europe or Germany.

After Potsdam, relationships between the two superpowers deteriorated further. The United States blocked Soviet interests in Iran while strengthening its own interests in the area. The Soviet Union continued to suppress anti-Communist elements in Poland, Romania, and Bulgaria and to tighten the grip of Communist parties there. In addition, the Soviet Union began to work for control in Czechoslovakia and Hungary, where free elections had been held and where, in each case, the Communist Party was in a minority.

COLD WAR ESCALATES

Meanwhile, the rhetoric escalated on both sides. In February 1946 Stalin stated that the war had proven the superiority of the Soviet system over "any non-Soviet social order." To prepare for any future military threats, he called for sharp increases in the production of vital strategic materials. The following month, in a speech at Fulton, Missouri, Churchill charged that an "iron curtain" had fallen, dividing a Moscow-controlled Eastern Europe from "free" Western Europe—actually, the situation was still fluid in parts of Eastern Europe. A week after Churchill's speech, Stalin stated that the former British leader was calling for war against the Soviet Union and that any Western aggression in Eastern Europe would be "thrashed." As the year progressed, Stalin also approved of a vigorous campaign against Western cultural influences, which had increased during the wartime cooperation.

Phase Two: The Truman Doctrine and European Developments

Late in 1946 and early in 1947, East-West tensions increased as the Soviet Union began to put pressure on Turkey and Greece. Interested in obtaining secure transit through Turkey's water passage from the Black Sea to the Mediterranean, the Soviet Union demanded joint Soviet-Turkish supervision of the waterway, but the Turkish government refused. Because it was much weaker than the Soviet Union, Turkey looked for help.

In Greece, the end of World War II had brought about a brutal, atrocity-filled civil war between the corrupt, authoritarian Greek government and Communist-dominated guerrillas. British army units backed the government, and Communist regimes in Bulgaria, Albania, and particularly Yugoslavia supported the guerrillas. Churchill had exacted from Stalin a promise not to support the guerrillas there, and Stalin, for reasons of his own, did not help them. In February 1947, unable to bear the cost, the British government announced it was pulling its troops out of Greece.

The Truman administration, faced with what it viewed as a Soviet threat to conquer smaller nations and break out onto the Mediterranean, responded by formulating an assertive policy that continued the intensification of the cold war. Most U.S. diplomats and military leaders, assuming that the Soviet Union was out to destroy the "free" (non-Communist) world, viewed the crisis in the Mediterranean as the crucial test. If aggression against Greece and Turkey could be halted, the Communists would be unlikely to attempt aggression elsewhere. Instead of using atomic bombs, the Truman administration put emphasis on "containing" communism, preventing its advance until the people in the Communist nations tired of Marxism and overthrew their governments. The containment policy, as it came to be called, generally dominated U.S. strategic thought throughout the postwar period. As viewed in 1947, containment meant sending extensive economic and military aid to enable governments

UNITED STATES PURSUES A POLICY TO CONTAIN THE SOVIET UNION

A step into the cold war: President Truman addresses a joint
session of Congress on March 12, 1947, calling for military aid
to Greece and Turkey in order to block Communist expansion
into the Mediterranean.

to defeat external or internal Communist threats through their own efforts. To carry
out this policy, Truman and his advisers had to persuade the U.S. public and Congress
to spend massive amounts of tax dollars for "peacetime" military aid.

**TRUMAN DOCTRINE
OFFERS MILITARY AID
TO BELEAGUERED
ALLIES**

In March 1947 President Truman asked Congress for money for military supplies and military advisers for Greece and Turkey, declaring, "I believe it must be the
policy of the United States to support free peoples who are facing attempted subjugation by armed minorities or by outside pressures." Congress voted $400 million,
and this policy became known as the Truman Doctrine. A naval squadron was already
in the Mediterranean, and military aid and advisers were quickly rushed to Greece.
Bolstered by the U.S. presence, the Turkish government continued to refuse to administer the waterway to the Mediterranean jointly with the Soviet Union. With U.S. aid,
the reorganized and reequipped Greek army drove back the guerrillas, and when
Yugoslavia closed the border with Greece in 1949, cutting off supplies and a place of
refuge, the guerrillas laid down their arms.

Western Europe was another source of cold war tension. Despite several billion dollars in U.S. loans, by 1947 the economy of Western Europe had not revived. France and Italy in particular were plagued with shortages, inflation, unemployment, and inadequate housing. This situation, plus the fact that leftists had played an important role in the wartime resistance movement against Nazism and fascism, induced many French and Italians to vote for Socialist and Communist candidates. The only other major political party in Italy and France that rivaled them in popularity was that of the Christian Democrats, called in France the Popular Republican Movement. Christian democracy developed out of Catholic wartime resistance movements and was at first inclined toward a moderate Catholic leftist position. It had significant support in many European nations and in Latin America as well. However, under both the Italian and French multiparty political systems, no one party was able to obtain a parliamentary majority, and coalition governments were usually necessary. The Socialists and Communists were able to obtain cabinet posts along with the Christian Democrats, but no Communist had yet become prime minister in Italy or France.

The Truman administration concluded that the economic and political situation in Western Europe demanded effective U.S. economic intervention. In June 1947 Secretary of State George Marshall proposed that the nations of Europe consult with one another and with the United States to determine the amount of economic assistance they would need to rebuild their economies. Marshall's offer was technically open to every European nation, including the Soviet Union, although U.S. leaders expected—and hoped—that the Soviet Union would refuse. Western European nations accepted quickly, but the Soviet Union, suspicious that U.S. aid meant U.S. economic penetration, refused and prevented Eastern European nations from participating.

After some reluctance, in 1948 the U.S. Congress created the European Recovery Program, usually referred to as the Marshall Plan, with an initial outlay of $4 billion. By 1951 Marshall Plan aid totaled over $13 billion, most of it going to Great Britain, Germany, France, and Italy. The Marshall Plan has been rated a success; the economy of Western European nations recovered rapidly.

MARSHALL PLAN OFFERS ECONOMIC AID TO EUROPE

Even before the Marshall Plan went into effect, Communist political power in Western Europe was already on the decline. Communists in both Italy and France were excluded from cabinet positions after mid-1947. In the Italian general elections in April 1948, Alcide de Gasperi's Christian Democratic Party attained a near majority and the Communist-Socialist vote dropped to 31 percent. While no single party would again secure an absolute majority in Italy, Christian Democrats would remain the most influential of Italy's numerous parties. Communist-led general strikes in 1947–1948 in both Italy and France caused some disruption, but both were broken by government action. The popularity of the Italian Christian Democrats stemmed in part from the backing of more conservative elements, who saw them as the only major alternative to the Socialists and Communists. During the late 1940s, this phenomenon also occurred in several other European nations, and it moved Christian Democratic parties toward more conservative policies than they had originally espoused.

COMMUNIST PARTIES DEFEATED IN ITALY AND FRANCE

In 1950 the United States extended the concept of foreign aid to the non-Western world in the hope that such aid would prevent new nations from turning to communism. The United States embodied this concept in the Point Four Program, which channeled millions and eventually billions of dollars into the economies of newly emerging nations.

THE SOVIET UNION CREATES SATELLITE STATES IN EASTERN EUROPE

At the same time that the United States was implementing the Truman Doctrine and the Marshall Plan, the Soviet Union was tightening its grip on Moscow-backed Eastern European governments. In 1947–1948 Communist takeovers added Hungary and Czechoslovakia, where democratic postwar coalition governments including Communists had existed, to the Soviet sphere, which already included Poland, Romania, Bulgaria, and Albania. The takeover in Czechoslovakia, the only Eastern European nation with a solid interwar tradition of democratic practice, shocked the West and hastened Congress's approval of the Marshall Plan. To further control Eastern Europe, the Soviet Union created bilateral economic treaties, later followed by the Council for Mutual Economic Assistance (COMECON), a Soviet-controlled economic organization that integrated the economies of Eastern European nations with one another and with the Soviet Union. COMECON assigned some nations (such as Czechoslovakia) industrial goals and other nations (such as Bulgaria) agricultural goals. To reinforce the unity of Communist regimes in Eastern Europe, the Soviet Union created Cominform, a new organization containing most of the European Communist parties.

There was a hole in the Eastern European buffer zone, however: Yugoslavia, although Communist, took an independent, nationalist course under Marshal Tito and, after a bitter confrontation with the Soviet Union, was expelled from Cominform in 1948. Tito cautiously maneuvered his nation into a position of neutrality and eventually became important as one of the leaders of nonaligned nations around the world.

Meanwhile, Stalin orchestrated a purge of those he considered "Titoists" in other Eastern European nations. From 1949 to 1952 many of those so labeled were imprisoned, tried, and, on occasion, executed. Stalin also demanded that each government within the Eastern bloc follow the Soviet example more closely in such matters as centralized party control over the economy, acceleration of collectivized agriculture, persecution of religion, and establishment of a Soviet-style constitution. Nevertheless, these nations never became clones of the Soviet Union. For example, private agriculture and religion continued to be more significant forces in Eastern Europe than in the U.S.S.R., despite Stalin's efforts.

WESTERN ALLIES CREATE WEST GERMANY

To better safeguard Western Europe against the Soviet bloc, the United States and its allies combined the three Western zones of occupation in Germany into a West German state. This was done in stages between 1946 and 1949, and by 1949 the new Federal Republic of Germany featured its own capital (Bonn), constitution, and currency. Its first government was controlled by the Christian Democratic Party, led by the anti-Communist Konrad Adenauer, who was already in his 70s when he came to power. His party held power for two decades. By September 1949 West Germany was operating as a sovereign state, but formal recognition would not come until later. Western troops remained, although they were less visible.

Of all the actions undertaken by the United States and its allies after World War II, the reestablishment of West Germany probably created the most hostility in the Soviet Union. After two devastating twentieth-century experiences, the Soviet Union hated and feared the prospect of a reborn Germany, armed by the West, to be used against the Soviet Union. The Soviets countered by transforming their occupation zone into the Democratic Republic of Germany.

The Soviet Union's main effort to derail the unification of West Germany centered on the spot where the West was most vulnerable: Berlin. In June 1948 the Soviets announced they had closed for repairs the railroads and highways in East Germany set aside to supply Western troops and the civilians in West Berlin. The Western governments immediately gathered all available cargo planes and used the air corridors to supply more than 2 million West Berliners and Western troops with food, clothing, coal, and other supplies. The Berlin Airlift was a triumph of efficiency. At its peak, transport planes touched down at Berlin's Templehof airdrome every few minutes on an around-the-clock schedule. The blockade of Berlin lasted 300 days, until May 1949, when the Soviets conceded defeat and reopened the highways and railroads. The crisis was over, but Berlin remained a trouble spot for the future.

THE SOVIET UNION PUTS PRESSURE ON ALLIES IN BERLIN

Cold war tensions were not confined to international diplomacy; they also affected the people at home. During the war, Americans had been friendly toward "Uncle Joe" Stalin and the Soviet Union. After the war, taking their cues from the government, they began to view the Soviet Union as heading an international conspiracy to overthrow capitalism. It was a short step from antipathy toward the Soviet Union to hostility toward those Americans who were perceived to be, or to have been, friendly to the Soviet Union. Americans were egged on by some leaders to worry about alleged "subversives," "Commie dupes," "parlor pinks," and "fellow travelers." Congress ran several investigations of alleged subversives in the United States and created legislation with such broad power to combat subversive organizations that it posed a threat to civil liberties. The executive branch created a government loyalty program designed to uncover subversives and unreliables in the federal government. Although there were indeed a few pro-Soviet Americans, most of the accused were innocent people, many of whom lost their jobs or saw their reputations tarnished. The climax of anti-Communist hysteria occurred from 1950 to 1954; it was intensified by the Communist takeover of China and the Korean War (see Chapter 24). Senator Joseph McCarthy made the term *McCarthyism* famous because of his unproved charges of subversion directed against a wide variety of Americans, ranging from ordinary citizens to the army command.

FEAR OF COMMUNISM PERVASIVE IN THE UNITED STATES

As the economies of Western European nations recovered with the aid of the Marshall Plan, the influence of Communist parties continued to decline in France and Italy. West Germany under Adenauer recovered its full sovereignty. It also became increasingly prosperous, and in the 1950s there was talk of the German "economic miracle." Adenauer's relationship with a variety of French governments was better than that of any previous German leader of the century. He finally retired as chancellor in late 1963, but his Christian Democratic Party continued in power for six more years. In 1951, aided at least in part by cold war developments, the Conservative Party in Great Britain returned to power after six postwar years of Labour Party control marked by such social welfare policies as the institution of free medical care. The Conservatives, first under Churchill and then under Anthony Eden, Harold Macmillan, and Sir Alec Douglas-Home, remained in power until 1964. The Conservative dominance in

DEVELOPMENTS IN WESTERN EUROPE AND THE U.S.S.R.

Great Britain in the 1950s was symptomatic of a general European trend in that decade toward more conservative governments.

In the Soviet Union, Stalin tightened his hold over the nation. The enormous wartime loss of life and property necessitated massive economic reconstruction, and Stalin also distrusted the more friendly attitude toward the West that the war had generated in the Soviet Union. These factors, plus Stalin's continued concern with his own political power and cold war tensions, led to massive military spending and strict controls over the economic, social, and cultural life of Soviet citizens. One expert has estimated that by 1950 Soviet military and police expenditures used up as much as one-fourth of the U.S.S.R.'s national income. Massive arrests also continued, and prisoners and conscript laborers contributed greatly to the country's economic reconstruction. By the early 1950s, "they produced a third of the country's gold, much of its coal and timber, and a great deal of almost everything else . . . the prisoners worked in almost every industry imaginable—logging, mining, construction, factory work, farming, the designing of airplanes and artillery."[1] Shortly before his death in early 1953, Stalin began accusing various Jews, including many Kremlin doctors, of treasonous behavior, and it is likely that if he had not died soon afterward many Jews would have been deported to remote Soviet areas.

Phase Three: Global Nuclear Confrontation

UNITED STATES CREATES NATO MILITARY ALLIANCE

Reflecting the continuing U.S. alarm at the spread of postwar communism, in 1949 the Truman administration set up the North Atlantic Treaty Organization (NATO). It somewhat resembled the earlier Rio Pact of 1947 between the United States and Latin American nations in being a regional defensive alliance in which the countries agreed to come to the aid of any member nation threatened with aggression. NATO members included the United States, Canada, Iceland, Norway, Denmark, the Netherlands, Belgium, Luxembourg, Great Britain, France, Portugal, and Italy (and soon afterward Greece and Turkey). The new alliance's goal was the eventual integration of the national armed forces of the member nations into a unified military command. In practical terms, NATO was dominated by the U.S. military establishment; a U.S. general (beginning with Eisenhower) was always the supreme commander. The United States Strategic Air Command (SAC) established air bases in Western Europe and the North Atlantic. The United States also began constructing air bases in non-NATO nations such as Spain and Libya, as well as developing bases in U.S.-occupied Japan and Okinawa. From all these bases, U.S. B-29s could drop atomic bombs on the Soviet Union.

Soviet reaction was twofold. First, the Soviet Union increased the size of its army in Europe until it heavily outnumbered the NATO forces opposing it, thus making it likely that the Soviet Union could overrun Western Europe if war broke out with the United States. Their vulnerability often prompted Western European nations to urge restraint during U.S.-Soviet crises. The Soviet Union's second move was to create its own bristling array of atomic weapons. Only five months after NATO was organized, the Soviet Union surprised the world by detonating an atomic bomb.

---

[1]Anne Applebaum, *Gulag: A History* (New York: Doubleday, 2003), p. xvi

In the early 1950s the United States and the Soviet Union found themselves engaged in a fevered arms race, creating weapons of ever more destructive power. In 1952 the United States test exploded a hydrogen bomb; in 1953 the Soviet Union followed suit. The Eisenhower administration decided to base its military policy on "massive retaliation," the concept that in the event of any Soviet attack on the United States or its allies, SAC bombers would destroy the Soviet Union with atomic or thermonuclear bombs. Eisenhower's secretary of state, John Foster Dulles, believed that U.S. military superiority would be an excellent backup for his "brinksmanship" policy of pressing selective issues with the Soviet Union to the limit. By 1955 both superpowers possessed bombers of intercontinental range that could hit the opponent's homeland, but the United States continued to possess many more such aircraft and maintained overall nuclear superiority throughout the 1950s and 1960s.

Meanwhile, the United States continued to tighten its containment noose around the Soviet Union. In Asia (see Chapter 22), the United States organized the Southeast Asia Treaty Organization (SEATO) in 1954. This alliance supported anti-Communist nations in Asia while enlarging the string of SAC air bases surrounding the Soviet Union. In the Middle East, the United States stood behind but was not a member of the Baghdad Pact, allying Great Britain with Iran, Turkey, Iraq, and Pakistan. This alliance system collapsed because of Middle Eastern politics and other factors, but in 1957 President Eisenhower pressured Congress into authorizing him to commit U.S. troops to defend nations in the Middle East against "overt armed aggression from any nation controlled by international communism." Eisenhower used this policy to intervene briefly and unprofitably in Lebanon. The total result of these arrangements was that the United States could bomb the Soviet Union from virtually every direction, but the Soviet Union could bomb the United States only via the North Pole, and even that with difficulty because radar systems in Canada gave early warning of approaching Soviet aircraft.

Despite an extensive U.S. military buildup, the Soviet army, backed by medium-range missiles and bombers, still gave the Soviet Union a distinct advantage in Europe. In an effort to lessen the imbalance there, West Germany was admitted into NATO and permitted to rearm. To accomplish this, the United States had to pressure its reluctant NATO allies, who were caught between fear of the Soviet Union and suspicion of a rearmed Germany.

In 1955 the Soviet Union—with its own fears of a rearmed Germany—formalized a competing military alliance system, the Warsaw Pact, integrating the armed forces of Eastern Europe into a unified force under Soviet command. In addition, the Soviets recognized East Germany as an independent state. Although the hope of unifying Germany still remained in some quarters, as of 1955 Germany had become two separate nations, each integrated into the sphere of influence of a superpower.

Despite their intense integration into the Soviet cold war bloc, Eastern European nations remained restless. Dissatisfaction with living conditions, plus the hopes raised by more liberal Soviet post-Stalinist policies (see later section) led to rebellion in more than 450 towns in East Germany in 1953. The East German disorder was quickly suppressed, but in 1956 the Soviet Union faced a graver crisis in Hungary. Sparked by discontent in Poland that led to the restoration as party head of Wladyslaw

SUPERPOWERS THREATEN EACH OTHER WITH HYDROGEN BOMBS

SOVIET UNION CREATES WARSAW PACT MILITARY ALLIANCE

BIOGRAPHY

Stalin's Corpse

On March 5, 1953, an event took place which shattered Russia—Stalin died. I found it almost impossible to imagine him dead, so much had he been an indispensable part of life.

A sort of general paralysis came over the country. Trained to believe that they were all in Stalin's care, people were lost and bewildered without him. All Russia wept. And so did I. We wept sincerely, tears of grief—and perhaps also tears of fear for the future. . . .

I will never forget going to see Stalin's coffin. . . . The crowd closed tighter and tighter. I was saved by my height. Short people were smothered alive, falling and perishing. We were caught between the walls of houses on one side and a row of army trucks on the other.

"Get those trucks out of the way!" people howled. "Get them out of here!"

"I can't do it! I have no instructions," a very young, towheaded police officer shouted back from one of the trucks, almost crying

with helplessness. And people were being hurtled against the trucks by the crowd, and their heads smashed. The sides of the trucks were splashed with blood. All at once I felt a savage hatred for everything that had given birth to that "I have no instructions," shouted at a moment when people were dying because of someone's stupidity. For the first time in my life I thought with hatred of the man we were burying. He could not be innocent of the disaster. It was the "No instructions" that had caused the chaos and bloodshed at his funeral.*

. . .

The Russian poet Yevgeny Yevtushenko, who was 19 when Stalin died, describes the general sense of grief and shock at Stalin's death and the tragic deaths of an untold number lining up to view his corpse in Moscow on March 6, 1953.

*From *A Precocious Autobiography* by Yevgeny Yevtushenko, translated by Andrew R. McAndrew. Copyright © 1964 by E. P. Dutton. Reprinted by permission.

Gomulka, earlier charged with being a Polish "Titoist," Hungarian demonstrators demanded a restoration of their own: they insisted that Imre Nagy be restored as premier, a post he had held in the years 1953–1955 before being ousted by less reform-minded Hungarian Communists. Demonstrators also demanded the withdrawal of Soviet troops stationed in Hungary. Some police officials were lynched, and some army units went over to the people. Nagy announced that Hungary would cease to be a one-party state or a member of the Warsaw Pact and that it would become a neutral country. But Soviet troops poured in to suppress the rebellion and overthrow the Nagy government.

SOVIET UNION CRUSHES THE HUNGARIAN REBELLION

The United States was caught in a dilemma. It had been the stated policy of the Eisenhower administration to "roll back the iron curtain" and to "liberate Eastern Europe." The Voice of America and Radio Free Europe had been beaming propaganda broadcasts into the region for years in an effort to stir up unrest there. Many Hungarian rebels expected that the United States would now intervene, but the Soviet Union made it plain that intervention meant war. The United States was not prepared to go to war over Eastern Europe; further, it was distracted at that time by a confrontation with its allies, Great Britain and France, over the Suez Canal. The United States did nothing, and the Soviet Union crushed the rebellion. About 25,000 Hungarians, including Nagy, lost their lives, and some 200,000 Hungarians fled to the West. Although the Soviet Union was, and would remain, supreme in Eastern Europe, there was to be no return to the policies of the 1949–1952 period. Conditions gradually improved as living standards rose moderately and repressive policies were slowly relaxed.

A Thaw in the Cold War

Although the cold war intensified at times during the 1950s, the superpowers also made sporadic attempts to negotiate their differences. The death of Stalin in 1953 opened the door to a possible relaxation of tensions. After Stalin died, a scramble for leadership ensued in the Soviet Union, resolved by the accession of Nikita Khrushchev to power. In 1956 Khrushchev made a daring "secret speech" to a closed session of the Twentieth Congress of the Communist Party of the Soviet Union; he criticized Stalin's policies, including his elimination of many innocent people during the 1930s. From then until his removal in 1964 Khrushchev used criticism of Stalin and Stalinist policies to weaken the power of his political rivals within the party hierarchy. While motivated largely by political concerns, Khrushchev's de-Stalinization campaign also led to less censorship. In 1962, for example, Khrushchev personally approved the publication of Alexander Solzhenitsyn's *One Day in the Life of Ivan Denisovich,* the story of a man unjustly sent to a prison camp during Stalin's regime. And that same year the poet Yevtushenko published his anti-Stalinist poem "Stalin's Heirs." By the late 1950s the Communist Party under Khrushchev's leadership had allowed millions of innocent people to be freed from the camps. Khrushchev also desired to improve living standards, including increasing agricultural output. To do so, he limited military spending more than some of his political rivals thought appropriate.

In 1953 there was also a change of leadership in the United States, as the moderate, easygoing Eisenhower ("Ike") succeeded Truman as president. Eisenhower and Khrushchev remained suspicious of each other, each determined to keep his country strong, but both were more willing than their predecessors to negotiate under appropriate circumstances. Concerned with the danger and cost of the escalating cold war, and under pressure from world opinion, Khrushchev and Eisenhower met at a summit conference in Geneva during 1955. Although nothing of substance came from the meeting, enough momentum was established to lead to other meetings. In 1955 the occupying powers agreed to end the occupation of Austria, and the Soviet Union recognized the West German government. Selected groups of Americans and Soviet citizens began visiting each other's nations. At the same time, the U.S. media began to tone down their strident anti-Communist presentations. This thaw in the cold war was limited in both accomplishments and duration, but neither superpower believed that it could bypass the opportunity for discussions. In the future, new discussions would accompany new alarms and distractions.

SUPERPOWER LEADERSHIP BECOMES MORE MODERATE

Phase Four: Missile Races

SPUTNIK INAUGURATES
SPACE AND MISSILE
RACES

On October 4, 1957, the cold war moved into a still more dangerous phase. On that day, the Soviet Union, using a powerful new rocket booster, launched a small satellite, *Sputnik,* into an orbit around the earth. Two months earlier, the Soviet Union had launched an intercontinental ballistic missile (ICBM). The missile age had begun. The Soviets gloried in their achievements. "We will bury you," Khrushchev promised the West. His statement, probably a figurative assertion that Marxist concepts would triumph in the long run, was taken by some in the West to be a threat of imminent nuclear war. Shortly thereafter, in 1958, he pressed his advantage by putting pressure on Berlin. Terming Berlin "a bone in the throat," he warned Western powers that the multiforce occupation of Berlin must end in six months' time or the Soviet Union would turn over the responsibility for Berlin and the supply corridors to East Germany.

Sputnik, the ICBM, and the Berlin threat prompted several reactions in the United States. Americans took pride in leading the world in science and technology and were depressed by Soviet successes. One leading atomic scientist moaned, "[The United States] has lost a battle more important and greater than Pearl Harbor." Some feared attacks by Soviet ICBMs, and a political furor broke out. The Democrats charged the Republicans with having created a "missile gap" and made gains in the 1958 congressional elections. The scientific and educational community was blamed as well, with charges that "Johnny" was not measuring up to "Ivan."

In the face of public outcry, the Eisenhower administration moved quickly. It poured money into scientific research in the universities, tying them more closely to the military-industrial-political complex. The government sent up a satellite in 1958 and created the National Aeronautics and Space Administration (NASA) to advance American space exploration. The administration also spent vast sums of money to launch a major ICBM program and to build submarine-launched ballistic missiles (SLBM) that offered the advantage of a portable missile-firing platform that could not easily be detected. To further strengthen U.S. missile response to the Soviet Union, the United States offered to base intermediate-range and medium-range ballistic missiles in NATO countries, but only Great Britain, Italy, and Turkey agreed to set up missile sites. By 1962–1963 the United States had 450 missiles and 2,000 bombers capable of striking the Soviet Union, compared to 50 to 100 Soviet ICBMs and 200 bombers that could reach the United States. The missile gap had been reversed with a vengeance, and the U.S. margin widened monthly. Despite the U.S. lead, both sides could inflict enormous damage on each other, and a new phrase, "balance of terror," came into use.

Despite the missile race, diplomatic exchanges continued. Khrushchev repeatedly postponed the Berlin "deadline" and pressed for more summit meetings. In 1959, he traveled to the United States. While visiting American farms and high-tech enterprises, Khrushchev took care to present himself as a jovial human being. Sometimes, however, differences in cultural outlook were difficult to bridge. He was upset that security problems prevented his visit to Disneyland. "Is there an epidemic of cholera there or something?" he asked. "Do you have rocket-launching pads there? . . . Or have

The Great Kitchen Debate: Premier Khrushchev and Vice President Nixon argue the merits of Soviet and U.S. ways of life at the U.S. exhibition in Moscow in 1959. Future Soviet leader Leonid Brezhnev is to the right of Nixon.

gangsters taken hold of the place?" He was, however, able to visit Hollywood but was critical of the scantily clad dancers on the set of the movie musical *Can Can*. A meeting with Eisenhower at Camp David went well, and enthusiasts spoke of the "spirit of Camp David" while the Soviet premier explained away his threatening rhetoric. Nuclear disarmament talks were once again in the air, and the United States, the Soviet Union, and Great Britain (which now also had nuclear bombs) stopped testing nuclear weapons in the atmosphere.

Phase Five: To the Brink of Nuclear War

Beginning in 1960 the cold war suddenly heated up into a confrontation in which the two superpowers teetered on the edge of nuclear holocaust. In May 1960, two weeks before a scheduled summit conference in Paris, Soviet forces shot down a U-2, a U.S. high-altitude spy plane that was violating Soviet airspace. Such planes were capable of flying from 12 to 14 miles above the earth and taking photographs that could spot an object as small as a golf ball. The Soviet Union immediately turned that incident and the initial U.S. cover-up into a propaganda coup. In Paris,

DETERIORATION IN INTERNATIONAL RELATIONS

Khrushchev demanded an apology, plus punishment for those involved; when Eisenhower refused, Khrushchev left the conference in a show of anger. The embarrassment of the Eisenhower administration and the missile gap controversy aided the election of John F. Kennedy, who promised new programs to restore U.S. prestige.

President Kennedy displayed many of the characteristics of President Truman. He was a tough political battler and a believer in the containment doctrine; he surrounded himself with advisers who were equally disposed to be tough with the Russians. His administration increased the defense budget and contributed notably to the U.S. surge in missile production. Kennedy was more aware than his predecessors of the necessity for dealing with struggles for independence and social reform in Asia, Africa, and Latin America, which Communists often supported as "wars of liberation." Kennedy therefore coupled the old "massive retaliation" doctrine with the new concept of "flexible response," which entailed building up the "conventional arms"—the army, navy, and marines—to fight in limited wars. As a part of this program, the United States stepped up commitments to train and supply the armed forces of allies in every quarter of the world. On the other hand, the Kennedy administration also created the Peace Corps, in which Americans volunteered to bring educational and technological skills to poorer nations.

Kennedy was soon tested by Khrushchev over the perennial trouble spot, Berlin. Berlin had become a double problem for the Soviet Union. In addition to housing a Western military garrison behind Soviet lines, it spotlighted the weaknesses of East Germany. The Communist regime in East Germany was so unpopular that masses of East Germans were fleeing annually, crossing from East Berlin into West Berlin and then to West Germany and beyond. In 1960, for example, 152,000 East Germans escaped via Berlin; on one day alone, August 6, 1961, 2,305 people arrived in West Berlin from East Germany.

CONFRONTATION OVER BERLIN

The Soviet Union had to do something to stop the outflow of population or East Germany would collapse and communism would be held up to worldwide humiliation. At the June 1961 summit conference in Vienna, Khrushchev once again threatened to turn Berlin over to the East Germans if the city were not demilitarized. Kennedy rejected the solution, but not firmly enough to impress the Soviet premier, who apparently left Vienna with the idea that Kennedy could be pressured. Kennedy apparently also believed that he had left an impression of weakness. To dispel that notion, he announced that Berlin would be defended as a test of "Western courage and will." He called up reservists and asked Congress to institute a "civil defense" bomb shelter program.

Kennedy's clear resolve to remain in Berlin prompted the Soviet Union to authorize East Germany to stop the exodus. The East German government put up the Berlin Wall in August 1961; in the eyes of the West, it became a major symbol of repression and of the failure of communism. Tensions remained high in the months that followed. The U.S.S.R. announced its resumption of atmospheric nuclear testing, and Kennedy sent additional U.S. troops and equipment to Europe. He also went to West Berlin to underscore U.S. determination to protect the city, telling an excited crowd, "Ich bin ein Berliner" (traditionally translated as "I am a Berliner").

U.S. and Soviet tanks confront each other in Berlin at a moment of heightened tension.

Berlin had been a serious confrontation, but it was in Cuba that the world stood at the brink of thermonuclear war. This crisis grew out of the nature of U.S. relationships in Latin America. Traditionally, the United States had not been overly scrupulous about the types of political regimes in postwar Latin America as long as they were "anti-Communist"—that is, anti-Soviet; the United States had previously helped topple a government in Guatemala that it had suspected of becoming Communist (see Chapter 21). In the 1950s Cuba was controlled by the dictator Fulgencio Batista, an ally of the U.S. government and a friend of U.S. businesses ranging from sugar refining to gambling. In return, the United States backed the Batista regime.

In 1959, however, Fidel Castro, after years of guerrilla warfare, overthrew the Batista government. Between 1959 and 1961, defying increasingly hostile U.S. reactions, Castro rapidly moved Cuba toward a new society based on Marxist principles. During this period he consolidated his grip on power, becoming a leftist *caudillo* in tight control of a totalitarian apparatus. Accusing U.S. entrepreneurs and upper-class Cubans of exploiting the Cuban masses, Castro rapidly nationalized both domestic and foreign-owned corporations and instituted egalitarian social reform programs.

CASTRO COMES TO POWER IN CUBA

The Eisenhower administration, seeing Cuba heading out of the U.S. orbit, presumably toward the Soviet Union, reacted with increasing vigor. After its early protests were ignored, the United States organized an economic boycott and stopped buying Cuban sugar, measures designed to disrupt the Cuban economy and to bring Castro down. Faced with U.S. economic warfare, Castro accelerated his nationalization of U.S. business holdings in Cuba and began to build an economic relationship with the Soviet Union.

U.S. LEADERS DECIDE TO OUST CASTRO

By 1960 the Eisenhower administration was convinced that the Castro regime was fast becoming a Soviet ally right in the heart of the U.S. sphere of influence in the Caribbean. The United States broke diplomatic relations with Cuba. In addition, Eisenhower, following the program earlier used successfully to overthrow the government of Guatemala (see Chapter 23), authorized the Central Intelligence Agency (CIA) to recruit and train anti-Castro Cubans living in the United States to invade Cuba and provide a rallying point for the Cuban population to overthrow Castro. This plan was based on the belief that few people wished to live under communism and that now that the Cubans had had a taste of it they would be ready to rebel.

On entering office in 1961, President Kennedy authorized the invasion plans to proceed, with the understanding that the United States was not to be directly involved in the landing itself. In April 1961 the anti-Castro forces bombed Cuban air bases and landed at the Bay of Pigs, but the peasants did not revolt. Kennedy vetoed pleas for air support, Cuban militia moved in, and the invaders surrendered after two days.

CASTRO SMASHES BAY OF PIGS INVASION

The Bay of Pigs provoked a number of reactions that had a major effect on the cold war. Castro, convinced that the United States would try to overthrow him again, quite possibly with a direct invasion, now sought the protection of the Soviet Union. In December 1961 he announced, "I am a Marxist-Leninist and will remain a Marxist-Leninist until the day I die." He also pledged that Cuba would work to spread Marxist revolution throughout Latin America.

More important to the future health of the world were the responses in Washington and Moscow. The fiasco was a sore blow to the prestige of the young new U.S. president. Kennedy, attacked for not supporting the invasion force, apparently decided to move with greater firmness in the future. Combined with Vienna, the Bay of Pigs incident apparently predisposed Khrushchev to consider Kennedy a weak leader; more ominously, it tempted Khrushchev to use Cuba to solve some of his own problems. The Chinese and some of Khrushchev's colleagues in Moscow had been criticizing him for being insufficiently aggressive in cold war confrontations with the United States, and Castro was calling for help. The Americans were clearly passing the Soviet Union in ICBM production and had ringed the U.S.S.R. with missiles and bombers. The 15 U.S. Jupiter missiles in Turkey aimed at the Soviet Union were a particular provocation.

These factors motivated the aging Soviet premier to make a daring, fundamental challenge to the United States by plunging into the heart of the U.S. sphere of influence. Khrushchev secretly began to send medium-range bombers and medium-range missiles to Cuba. These weapons could defend Cuba by hitting the southeastern United States, including Washington, D.C., but they could not hit most American ICBM installations or SAC bases. From Khrushchev's point of view, such a move would demonstrate that he could take a tough line, apply additional pressure to get the Western powers out of Berlin, moderate the imbalance in the arms race, and support Castro, who feared that a U.S. attack was imminent.

In October 1962 American U-2s discovered the missile sites in Cuba, some almost operational and, it was later revealed, protected by tactical nuclear weapons. The Kennedy administration sprang into action and insisted that Soviet missiles and bombers in Cuba must go. The Soviet Union would be given the opportunity to remove them voluntarily. If the Soviet Union refused, the United States would destroy the missiles by air strike or invasion. If such an action meant a collision with the Soviet Union, the United States would go to war. The military command sent some SAC bombers into the air and put others on 15-minute alert, while placing ICBMs in a preliminary state of readiness to fire. The command also moved army units into position in the Southeast and reinforced Guantánamo Bay. Pressuring the Soviet Union to withdraw the missiles and bombers, Kennedy imposed a "quarantine," a peacetime naval blockade of Cuba (by international law an act of war) that prevented additional missiles from reaching Cuba. Latin American nations, at a meeting of the Organization of American States, supported the blockade. On October 22, Kennedy appeared on television to demand that the Soviet Union "halt and eliminate this clandestine and provocative threat to world peace."

The decision now lay with Moscow, and for six days peace or war hung in the balance. President Kennedy privately estimated the chances of war to be "between one out of three and even." Faced with U.S. resolve backed by U.S. nuclear superiority, the Soviet premier retreated. He ordered the Soviet merchant ships carrying missiles to turn back and avoid confrontation with the U.S. Navy. In an exchange of notes, Khrushchev and Kennedy agreed that the Soviet Union would remove the offending missiles and bombers and that the United States would make a public pledge not to invade Cuba. Unofficially, Attorney General Robert Kennedy also informed the Soviet ambassador that the United States would remove its missiles from Turkey at some time in the future. The armed forces of the two nations were ordered to stand down, and the shadow of nuclear war passed over.

UNITED STATES DETECTS SOVIET MISSILES IN CUBA AND ISSUES ULTIMATUM

SUMMARY

The victorious Allies prescribed severe peace terms for both Japan and Germany; both nations lost territory conquered during the course of the twentieth century, and Germany lost one-quarter of its former homeland to Poland. The victors demilitarized and occupied Japan and Germany and imprisoned or executed some of their surviving leaders as war criminals. The Soviet Union was the chief beneficiary of the territorial changes, annexing a large area along its western border and additional territory in Asia.

Near the end of World War II, strains appeared between the Soviet Union and its allies, in part based on differing programs concerning the control and reconstruction of postwar Europe. These differences sharply increased immediately after the war, complicated in particular by U.S. control of the atomic bomb. The Soviet Union was determined to protect itself against any future attack out of the West, and the United

States perceived the Soviet Union to be bent on a program of worldwide conquest. By the late 1940s the Soviet Union had installed friendly Communist governments in Eastern Europe, and the United States dominated Western Europe through the NATO military alliance and the economic ties of the Marshall Plan.

During the 1950s the cold war further intensified. The United States pursued a policy of global containment of the Soviet Union and extended its network of agreements and alliances to Asia. As a consequence, by the late 1950s the United States had surrounded the Soviet Union with a circle of air bases and missile sites from which it could deliver nuclear warheads to the Soviet Union. The Soviet Union could respond by attacking Western Europe. Germany was in effect divided into two nations, with East and West Germany integrated militarily into the European power blocs. Despite the tension between the superpowers, their leaders attempted to moderate their differences by holding discussions to air grievances.

In the early 1960s, the superpowers had a frightening confrontation when the Soviet Union placed missiles in Cuba. The world stood at the brink of nuclear war, but the Soviet Union removed its missiles from Cuba, and the threat passed.

SUGGESTED SOURCES

Beschloss, Michael R. *Mayday: Eisenhower, Khrushchev, and the U-2 Affair.* 1986. A fascinating, dramatic, and well-researched work on the U-2 crisis and its background.*

Craig, Campbell. *Destroying the Village: Eisenhower and Thermonuclear War.* 1998. A well-researched account of Eisenhower's nuclear strategy.*

Frankel, Max. *High Noon in the Cold War: Kennedy, Khrushchev, and the Cuban Missile Crisis.* 2004. A solid and readable account by a former diplomatic journalist.

Gaddis, John. *Strategies of Containment.* 1982. Stresses perception of each superpower that it was taking appropriate defensive measures against the imperialism of the other.

———. *We Now Know: Rethinking Cold War History.* 1998. An excellent work by a major U.S. historian of the cold war; concentrates on the years 1945–1962.*

Gelb, Norman. *The Berlin Wall.* 1986. A complete study of a complex phenomenon, written in a fast-paced, journalistic style.*

Hitchcock, William I. *The Struggle for Europe: The Turbulent History of a Divided Continent 1945 to the Present.* 2004. The best account of Europe in dealing with more than a half-century's history.*

Khrushchev, Nikita. *Khrushchev Remembers.* 1970. The insights of a key player in the cold war struggle.*

LaFeber, Walter. *America, Russia, and the Cold War, 1945–2002.* Updated 9th ed. 2002. A standard readable account that concentrates more on U.S. motives than on those of the Soviet government.*

Leuchtenberg, William E. *A Troubled Feast.* Updated ed. 1983. A concise and lively survey of U.S. history since 1945.*

Mastny, Vojtech. *The Cold War and Soviet Insecurity.* 1996. An excellent analysis of Soviet postwar diplomacy under Stalin.*

McCauley, Martin. *The Khrushchev Era: 1953–1964.* 1995. A leading scholar on Khrushchev briefly reexamines his rule in the light of new scholarship; includes documents.*

McCullough, David. *Truman.* 1992. A well-written, but long, popular biography of a key figure in creating the cold war.*

Schaller, Michael, Virginia Schaff, and Robert D. Schultzinger. *Present Tense: The United States since 1945.* 1992. A solid survey of the period.*

Smith, Bradley F. *Reaching Judgment at Nuremberg.* 1979. A penetrating study of the corrupting effects of Nazism.* (Also a film, *Judgment at Nuremburg.*)

Smoke, Richard. *National Security and the Nuclear Dilemma.* 1993. A trenchant overview of the post–World War II arms race, from a U.S. perspective.

Stern, Sheldon M. *The Week the World Stood Still: Inside the Secret Cuban Missile Crisis.* 2005. A brief and recent book intended for general readers and students by the chief historian at the John F. Kennedy Presidential Library.*

Taubman, William. *Khrushchev: The Man and His Era.* 2003. The best biography of Khrushchev.*

Trachtenberg, Marc. *A Constructed Peace: The Making of the European Settlement, 1945–1963.* 1999. A scholarly analysis of how the superpowers worked out a postwar settlement, this work focuses especially on the German question.*

Zubkova, Elena. *Russia after the War: Hopes, Illusions, and Disappointments.* 1998. One of the best studies of the period by a post-Soviet Russian scholar.*

Zubok, Vladislav, and Constantine Pleshakov. *Inside the Kremlin's Cold War: From Stalin to Khrushchev.* 1996. A scholarly and well-written account by two young historians born in the Soviet Union.*

WEB SOURCES

www.wilsoncenter.org. Go to the Cold War International History Project under "Programs" for links to the latest cold war scholarly findings.

www.soviethistory.org/index.php. See materials for the U.S.S.R. under the years 1947, 1954, 1956, 1961.

www.yale.edu/lawweb/avalon/diplomacy/forrel/cuba/cubamenu.htm. Provides links to documents dealing with the Cuban missile crisis.

www.cnn.com/SPECIALS/cold.war. CNN materials on the cold war; see links to episodes 2–10.

www.fordham.edu/halsall/mod/modsbook50.html. Provides numerous links to materials on Eastern Europe from 1945 into the 1990s.

www.fordham.edu/halsall/mod/modsbook49.html. Provides numerous links to materials on Western Europe from 1945 into the 1990s.

---

* Paperback available.

CHAPTER

21

⑥The Americas after World War II

Beginning in the 1940s, the United States and Canada enjoyed three decades of rapid growth and unprecedented prosperity. Throughout the Americas, World War II catapulted national economies out of depression. In the United States, factories churned out a dizzying array of wartime goods, while the federal government played an increasingly important role in the national economy. After the war, with some minor dips, the economy boomed for nearly a quarter century. Also after the war, confrontation with the Soviet Union led to the cold war and a second "Red Scare" (see Chapter 12 on the first Red Scare in 1919–1920), fueled by the demagogic Senator Joe McCarthy. African Americans, other minorities, and women, emboldened by their participation in World War II, inspired by FDR's "Four Freedoms," and pointing to the contradiction between fighting political tyranny abroad while tolerating injustice at home, demanded equal political and economic rights. By the late 1960s, the civil rights and anti–Vietnam War movements converged with other social movements—including those of black nationalists, Latinos, women, youth, gays, and environmentalists—to radicalize and polarize U.S. society. Meanwhile, the economic golden age was waning in both the United States and Canada. For a complex combination of reasons, including rising foreign competition and a federal government spending beyond its means, the early 1970s marked the end of the postwar boom.

In Latin America, influenced by many of the same forces, postwar demands for economic and political rights grew. Atop pressures for democratic reform by middle sectors and working classes came calls for social revolution by Marxists, inspired by the Chinese Revolution of 1949 and the Cuban Revolution of 1959. In the early 1960s, as demands for reform intensified and guerrilla movements mushroomed, governments and militaries in many countries used the pretext of the cold war to impose dictatorships, often propped up by the United States. By the late 1960s, the Roman Catholic Church had become more concerned with addressing issues of social justice and economic rights, promoting "a preferential option for the poor" under a reformist impulse called "liberation theology." Urbanization surged, as millions of rural poor migrated to cities more closely tied to circuits of international capital. U.S.-based multinational corporations increasingly dominated Latin American economies, standards of living stagnated, and divisions between rich and poor sharpened. In the early 1970s, most of Latin America remained under the rule of military dictatorships.

THE UNITED STATES: AN ECONOMIC GOLDEN AGE AND STRUGGLES OVER FREEDOMS AND RIGHTS

During World War II, the U.S. economy and society underwent profound changes. The economy grew at 10 percent per year, faster than ever before or since. The federal government expanded dramatically, issuing billions of dollars worth of war contracts and guaranteeing profits to corporations supplying war goods. Government-industry collaboration created what Dwight D. Eisenhower later called the "military-industrial complex." Union membership soared, from 10.5 million in 1941 to nearly 15 million in 1945. The huge demand for labor led 750,000 African Americans to migrate from the rural South to major cities, continuing the "Great Migration" sparked by World War I. A series of antiblack urban riots, most prominently in Detroit in 1943, repeated the deadly pattern of the "red summer" of 1919. Women's participation in the labor force also shot up, from less than 15 million in 1941 to nearly 20 million in 1945.

Postwar Economic Boom, Demographic Changes, and the Second Red Scare

FEDERAL SPENDING SURGES

The United States emerged from World War II the most powerful economic and military nation the world had ever known. After a brief postwar recession, pent-up demand for consumer goods led to an explosion of postwar spending. From 1945 to 1960, per capita income nearly doubled. Automobile production soared, from 2 million in 1946 to 8 million in 1955. Instead of encouraging mass transport, the U.S. government subsidized the automobile and oil industries to the tune of $26 billion in the Interstate Highway Act of 1956, the largest public works program in U.S. history. The GI Bill, which granted war veterans subsidized college educations and low-interest mortgages for new homes, represented a long-term investment in the nation's future. Federal government spending skyrocketed, much of it related to the cold war. By the 1950s, federal spending accounted for 20 percent of GNP, dwarfing New Deal expenditures. After a sharp postwar drop, by the mid-1950s the number of women in the workforce exceeded levels reached during World War II, continuing the long-term trend of more women in paid labor.

RISE OF THE SUN BELT

The United States, in short, had become the "affluent society," in the phrase of economist John Kenneth Galbraith. While the fruits of this economic boom were unevenly distributed—the top tenth of the population still took home more than the bottom half, while the income of blacks lagged far behind that of most whites—the middle class expanded dramatically. The economic good times, after a decade of depression and half a decade of war, led to a postwar baby boom, which peaked in 1957. With surging population and prosperity came increasing geographic mobility. Sun-belt cities like Los Angeles, Phoenix, Houston, and Miami saw phenomenal growth. Phoenix went from a sleepy city of 65,000 in 1940 to a sprawling metropolis of 440,000 two decades later. Emblematic of these shifts, in the early 1960s California surpassed New York as the nation's most populous state.

SUBURBAN SPRAWL

Aided by rising wages, affordable cars, extraordinarily cheap gasoline, and taxpayer-funded highways, new suburbs sprouted further from city centers. By 1960, a third of all U.S. citizens, the vast majority white, lived in suburbs. Suburban shopping plazas and malls blossomed, further insulating suburban dwellers from urban dwellers and eroding the economic vitality of inner cities. The environmental consequences of suburban sprawl and industrial growth were far-reaching, with millions of acres of farmland and woodland turned into housing developments and strip malls, wetlands drained, fragile ecosystems disrupted, and billions of tons of industrial pollutants contaminating the nation's skies, lakes, and rivers.

McCARTHYISM AND THE SECOND RED SCARE

Meanwhile, the deterioration of U.S. postwar relations with the Soviet Union (see Chapter 20) had serious domestic consequences. Following the 1947 House Un-American Activities Committee (HUAC) probe of the motion picture industry and apparent Communist successes and threats in Eastern Europe and Asia, the United States experienced a second postwar red scare. Exploiting the nation's fears to advance his political ambitions, in 1950 Senator Joe McCarthy of Wisconsin initiated an anticommunist frenzy, charging that communists had infiltrated the highest levels of government. The anticommunist witch hunt persisted after McCarthy's precipitous fall in the Army-McCarthy hearings of 1954, watched by millions on their television sets—by 1960, more than three-quarters of U.S. families owned at least one television, and by the 1970s this postwar invention had become the nation's most important mass communications medium.

The Civil Rights Movement, the War on Poverty, and the Tumult of the 1960s

The fight to defeat fascism and contain communism abroad inspired many to insist on equal rights at home. Demands for civil rights intensified during World War II. Black labor leader A. Philip Randolph's threat of a massive march on the nation's capital prompted President Roosevelt to issue Executive Order 8802, guaranteeing equal employment opportunities for minorities in firms receiving government contracts. After FDR's death in 1945, President Harry Truman and the Democratic Party recognized the political clout of urban blacks, who now wielded the power of the vote. In 1947 a Truman-appointed Committee on Civil Rights issued a report demonstrating that blacks remained second-class citizens in every sphere of life and charging the federal government with guaranteeing equal civil rights for all.

BROWN V. BOARD OF EDUCATION

Soon the courts played an increasingly important role in the civil rights struggle. Most important was the landmark 1954 Supreme Court decision in *Brown v. Board of Education of Topeka*. The unanimous decision overturned the 1896 *Plessy* decision, which had found racial segregation and Jim Crow laws constitutional. Ruling that "separate facilities are inherently unequal," violating the 14th Amendment's guarantee of equal rights, the Court ordered local school boards to desegregate public schools "with all deliberate speed." Efforts to implement the ruling sparked widespread and militant white resistance. Three years after the decision, President Dwight D. Eisenhower used the Arkansas National Guard and other troops to begin school desegregation in Little Rock, Arkansas.

The *Brown* decision galvanized African Americans to redouble their efforts to gain full civil rights. On December 1, 1955, in Montgomery, Alabama, Rosa Parks, a black seamstress and longtime activist, refused to give up her seat on the bus to a white rider, as local law required. Her arrest sparked a 381-day boycott of the Montgomery bus system, inaugurating the mass movement for civil rights in the South. The boycott catapulted into prominence a charismatic leader, the 26-year-old Baptist minister Dr. Martin Luther King Jr. A gifted orator with a doctorate in divinity, King helped to organize the Southern Christian Leadership Conference (SCLC), which for the next decade played a leading role in the black civil rights movement. In 1964 King received the Nobel Peace Prize for his nonviolent approach to civil rights.

MONTGOMERY BUS BOYCOTT

MARTIN LUTHER KING JR.

In 1960 the Student Non-Violent Coordinating Committee (SNCC) was formed and soon staged sit-ins at lunch counters in violation of local Jim Crow laws. In 1961 the Freedom Rides, organized by the Congress for Racial Equality (CORE), brought whites and blacks together to flout laws mandating racial segregation in public transportation. Hoping to exploit the power of national television to depict the injustices and violence perpetrated on those opposing discrimination, King and the SCLC achieved their aims in Birmingham, Alabama, in 1963. Using water cannons and police dogs to break up a peaceful march by 2,200 demonstrators, city officials played right into the hands of movement activists.

Democratic President John F. Kennedy, elected in 1960, was somewhat sympathetic to the civil rights movement. To appease the "Dixiecrat" wing of the Democratic Party, however, he acted cautiously. Black leaders grew increasingly frustrated with a decade of delay in enforcing the *Brown* decision. The high-water mark of the mass phase of the civil rights movement came in August 1963, in a huge march on Washington. To an audience of hundreds of thousands of demonstrators and millions of television viewers, Dr. King delivered his impassioned "I have a dream" speech. Still, national leaders refused to act.

MARCH ON WASHINGTON

Three months later, on November 22, 1963, Kennedy was assassinated in Dallas, Texas, under circumstances that continue to be debated. His successor, President Lyndon Johnson of Texas, used his powerful political skills to pressure Congress into enacting two major pieces of civil rights legislation. The 1964 Civil Rights Act banned discrimination in public accommodations and employment on the basis of race, color, religion, sex, or national origin. The 1965 Voting Rights Act suspended literacy and other voter tests. After many years of struggle to enforce them, these civil rights laws, supported by Supreme Court decisions, eventually changed the nation by eliminating segregated public accommodations and enabling African Americans and other minorities to vote and hold political office. Yet they did not eliminate racism or illegal discrimination from U.S. society.

CIVIL RIGHTS LAWS

An expansion of individual civil liberties accompanied the civil rights movement. The Supreme Court under Chief Justice Earl Warren expanded the concept of "due process of law" so that the poor and uneducated would have access to fair trials. The Warren Court also broadened rights of free speech and drew a sharper line between church and state, declaring prayers in public schools unconstitutional. The Court also promulgated the "one man, one vote" doctrine in apportioning legislatures, increasing the political clout of cities and suburbs, which previously had been shortchanged by rural interests.

THE WARREN COURT

Civil rights leaders: Martin Luther King Jr., Robert Kennedy, Roy Wilkins of the NAACP, and then vice president Lyndon B. Johnson meet in 1963. All are now dead, two by assasination.

BLACK NATIONALISM

The mainstream civil rights movement, symbolized by King, was only one form of black struggle during these years. Another major movement was led by more radical black nationalist organizations like the Black Panther Party and the Nation of Islam, symbolized by Malcolm X. Such black nationalists rejected nonviolence and integration, focusing instead on cultivating racial pride and creating separate cultural and community institutions. "I don't see any American dream," Malcolm X proclaimed; "I see an American nightmare." Assassinated in 1965, Malcolm X told white citizens they faced a stark choice between peaceful integration and militant black resistance to white supremacy.

THE GREAT SOCIETY

After winning a landslide election in 1964, President Johnson launched a major extension of the New Deal. In his Great Society programs, Johnson hoped to use the spending power of the federal government to lift some 50 million poor citizens out of poverty. New federal programs like Medicare, Medicaid, VISTA, Head Start, and food stamps aimed to improve living conditions and defuse mounting social tensions. They met with some real successes. As a result of the War on Poverty, during the 1960s the number of families living in poverty dropped from 22 percent to 13 percent.

URBAN UPRISINGS

Despite favorable court rulings, government programs, and their own efforts, most African Americans saw little improvement in employment, housing, or public services, and many complained of police brutality and a racist criminal justice system. Black rage boiled over in a series of urban uprisings, beginning in Harlem in 1964. Far larger was the 1965 Watts, Los Angeles, uprising, in which 50,000 angry residents burned and looted for days. Soon the uprisings spread to other cities of the North and West. In April 1968 racial tensions again exploded after a white assassin killed King, with blacks protesting and rioting in scores of cities.

The civil rights and black nationalist movements combined with the growing protest movement against the Vietnam War to inspire women, American Indians, Latinos, gays, and other groups to demand equal rights. In 1960, the mass marketing of an oral contraceptive ("the pill") provided many women with the reproductive self-determination they had long sought. Protected by the 1964 Civil Rights Act, feminists won federal bans against employment and credit bias and founded the National Organization for Women (NOW) to seek full legal equality. A diverse and growing women's movement offered pointed critiques of male domination, traditional gender and sexual roles, family structures, the mass marketing of stereotypical images, and the widespread violence against women that occurred on city streets and in suburban homes. The landmark 1973 Supreme Court decision *Roe v. Wade* extended privacy rights to include women's right to abortion, a ruling that in subsequent decades provoked fierce conflicts between pro-choice and pro-life activists.

THE FEMINIST MOVEMENT

Meanwhile, Mexican American labor leaders Cesar Chavez and Dolores Huerta organized the United Farm Workers to struggle nonviolently for rights among Mexican farmworkers. The American Indian Movement and other Indian organizations demanded greater tribal self-government and recompense for lost lands and resources. The New Left, led by the Students for a Democratic Society (SDS), organized the poor, joined civil rights causes, and led campus protests. Opposition to the Vietnam War mounted among college students and in white and nonwhite working-class neighborhoods, which had the highest rates of conscription, as well as among long-time peace activists and leftists, including the clergy and some union leaders, feminists, and antiwar GI's. By 1967, as draft calls passed 30,000 a month, the antiwar protests mushroomed into a mass movement that dovetailed with civil rights, feminist, and other movements. In the early 1970s, yielding to the argument that if young people were required to fight for their country they should be enfranchised, Congress lowered the voting age in federal elections to 18.

OTHER SOCIAL MOVEMENTS OF THE 1960s

Dissenting young people, mostly white, spearheaded several, often socially divisive, movements during the 1960s, movements tied to more global trends in youth culture. Young men and women, especially in North America and Europe, increasingly questioned the lifestyles and values of their parents. In the United States the hippies waged cultural rebellion, rejecting what they considered their elders' materialism, competition, and inhibitions. Often children of affluence themselves, members of the counterculture glorified nature, leisure, and communal ideals. Their long hair, drug use, rock music, and casual sex shocked and alienated many, but would leave its mark on the dominant culture.

By the early 1970s the reform impulse extended to concern with environmental deterioration. Environmentalists founded Earth Day, worked to ban DDT and other chemical pollutants, and pushed for legislation mandating cleaner air and water. In response, Congress established the Environmental Protection Agency and passed laws protecting endangered species and setting limits on automobile and power plant emissions.

These and other movements seeking social change often provoked a backlash. Environmentalism had broad support, but businesses and some unions decried added costs and lost job opportunities. Many conservatives opposed the women's movement.

BACKLASH AGAINST SOCIAL MOVEMENTS

Groups such as Young Americans for Freedom (YAF) defended racial segregation, opposed women's right to reproductive self-determination, and applauded overseas interventions. The Great Society and Warren Court drew heavy criticism from those believing they were "soft on crime." Complaints mounted that welfare programs gave tax money to undeserving people who refused to work.

Similarly, the civil rights movement's shift from legal to economic issues and from the South to the North produced a white backlash. Many northern whites opposed integration of local public schools, neighborhoods, and workplaces. By the late 1960s opposition to the pace of change coalesced into a strong conservative countermovement, overcoming LBJ's Great Society vision. Appealing to the resentments of what he called the "silent majority," and garnering strong support from growing suburban areas, Republican Richard Nixon captured the presidency in 1968 and 1972. A prominent cold warrior from California, Nixon's terms in office marked the beginning of decades-long conservative Republican ascendancy.

WANING OF THE ECONOMIC GOLDEN AGE

Meanwhile, the escalating costs of the Vietnam War and other cold war commitments, and of the Great Society programs—a small fraction of the former, combined with the rising economic power of foreign competitors to bring an end to the U.S. economic golden age. The years 1972–1974 marked a turning point in U.S. economic history. Real wages reached their peak, declining steeply thereafter. Federal budget deficits, the national debt, and annual trade deficits all rose markedly, while unemployment and inflation edged upward. The oil shock of 1973–1974 and the sharp recession that followed marked the end of the postwar boom (see Chapter 27).

LATIN AMERICA: REFORM AND REVOLUTION, POVERTY AND DICTATORSHIP

Most Latin American nations openly sided with the Allies during World War II. Yielding to strong U.S. pressure, Brazil provided important raw materials and military bases that proved critical in the Battle of the Atlantic. In 1944, one Brazilian combat unit even fought alongside the U.S. Fifth Army in Italy. As in the United States, the war proved a vital stimulus to many Latin American economies. Demand for industrial raw materials soared, leading to a sharp rise in the production of nitrates, copper, rubber, and other export commodities, while manufacture of domestic goods to substitute for imports intensified. After the war, however, U.S. manufactures once again flooded the markets. Meanwhile, the doctrine of national security became the fulcrum of U.S. policy toward Latin America—a doctrine embraced by many Latin American militaries, and aggressively promoted by both the U.S. government and U.S.-dominated transnational bodies like the Organization of American States (OAS), founded in 1948.

POLITICAL CHANGES

In the political sphere, the postwar scene offered a volatile mix of dangers and opportunities for both governments and their opponents. Reformist groups, heartened by FDR's "Four Freedoms" and their own traditions of struggle, pressured governments for greater political and economic rights. Some innovative leaders used these demands to create new forms of political populism, deftly deploying radio and television to spread their message among urban voters, while using government resources to bolster their popularity and defuse opposition. The cold war, however, cast a

UNITED STATES

ATLANTIC OCEAN

Gulf of Mexico

South America since World War II

(1975) Gained independence after World War II

Leftist guerilla warfare

Urban guerilla movement 1960s–1970s

Rightist military coups 1960s–1970s

Scene of U.S. anti-Communist involvement

Representative government or key elements of representative government, as of 2000

✗ Major battle

0   300   600 Miles

Caribbean Sea

GUYANA (1966)
SURINAME (1975)
FRENCH GUIANA

Caracas
VENEZUELA

Bogotá
COLOMBIA

Quito
ECUADOR

Amazon R.

PERU

Lima

B R A Z I L

La Paz
BOLIVIA
Sucre

Brasilia

PACIFIC OCEAN

P
A
R
A
G
U
A
Y

Asuncíon

Santiago
Buenos Aires **URUGUAY**
CHILE
Montevideo

ARGENTINA

✗ 1982
Falkland Islands (Br.)
*Claimed by Argentina as
Islas Malvinas*

shadow over the demands of reformists, as many governments used the fight against international communism to stifle opposition and block reforms.

In the economic arena, nationalists urged state-led industrialization to end poverty and promote economic development. Looking to the historical example of the United States, they argued that only high tariffs on imported manufactures and an activist government would generate sufficient economic growth to lift their countries out of poverty. U.S. economists and policymakers, on the other hand, espoused a more classically liberal view. They pressured Latin American countries to return to the pre-1929 focus on raw materials and primary export products, which, they argued, would more effectively leverage Latin America's "comparative advantage" in world trade. In the early 1950s, the arguments of the economic nationalists coalesced into the policy prescriptions of the Economic Commission on Latin America (ECLA), led by the Argentine economist Raúl Prebisch. The ECLA maintained that Latin American economies needed to industrialize and wean themselves from structural dependency on more advanced industrial economies, particularly the United States. This "dependency thesis" proved extremely influential in the coming decades.

Demographic Explosion and Urbanization

Latin America after 1945 was shaped especially by skyrocketing populations and phenomenally high rates of rural-urban migration. In the half century after 1950, the region's population more than tripled—from 165 to 520 million people. Population growth was highest in the poorest areas—Mexico, Central America, the Caribbean, Brazil, and the Andean republics. The 1950s saw an average fertility rate of 6 births per woman; in the early 1970s the average dropped to 5; and in the 1990s, to less than 3. Most of this burgeoning population came to reside in cities. In 1950 roughly a quarter of Latin Americans lived in cities of over 200,000. In 1980, half did; and in the year 2000, three quarters. Between 1950 and 1980, the region's total population doubled, while its urban population quadrupled.

As a result of both natural population increase and floods of migrants from an impoverished countryside, Mexico City, São Paulo, Rio de Janeiro, Buenos Aires, Bogotá, Lima, and other major urban areas became huge sprawling megacities, ringed by vast shantytowns of millions of people, lacking sewage and sanitation systems, living in makeshift shacks made of bits of tarpaper, metal, and wood. In 1955, a black 42-year-old mother of three named Carolina Maria de Jesus supported her children by collecting scrap paper and glass in the slums of São Paulo. Picking rotting food out of the garbage, living from hand to mouth in a leaky tarpaper shack, with hunger, disease, and violence her constant companions, she used her second-grade education to write a diary on bits of paper plucked from the gutters. "How horrible it is to see your children eat and then ask: 'Is there more?' This word 'more' bounces inside a mother's head as she searches the cooking pot knowing there isn't any more." Excerpts from her diary, later published and translated into more than a dozen languages, provide insight into why reformist and revolutionary impulses proved so powerful in the postwar years.

BIOGRAPHY

Life and Death in the Garbage Dump

May 20, 1958. I opened the window and watched the women passing by with their coats discolored and worn by time. It won't be long until these coats which they got from others, and which should be in a museum, will be replaced by others. The politicians must give us things. That includes me too, because I'm also a *favelado* [slum dweller]. I'm one of the discarded. I'm in the garbage dump and those in the garbage dump either burn themselves or throw themselves into ruin. . . .

When I arrived from the Palace that is the city, my children ran to tell me they had found some macaroni in the garbage. As the food supply was low I cooked some of the macaroni with beans. My son João said to me: "Uh, huh. You told me you weren't going to eat any more things from the garbage." It was the first time I had failed to keep my word. I said, "I had faith in President Kubitschek." "You had faith, and now you don't have it any more?" "No, my son, democracy is losing its followers. In our country everything is weakening. The money is weak. Democracy is weak and the politicians are very weak. Everything that is weak dies one day." . . .

I ate that macaroni from the garbage with fear of death, because in 1953 I sold scrap over there in Zinho. There was a pretty little black boy. . . . Someone had thrown meat into the garbage, and he was picking out the pieces. He told me: "Take some, Carolina. It's still fit to eat." . . . I tried to convince him not to eat that meat, or the hard bread gnawed by the rats. He told me no, because it was two days since he had eaten. . . . The next day I found that little black boy dead. His toes were spread apart. The space must have been eight inches between them. He had blown up as if made out of rubber. His toes looked like a fan. He had no documents. He was buried like any other "Joe." Nobody tried to find out his name. The marginal people don't have names. . . .

The politicians know that I am a poetess. And that a poet will even face death when he sees his people oppressed.*

. . .

Recording her thoughts and dreams on bits of scrap paper she collected and sold for a living, Carolina Maria de Jesus captured the everyday violence and suffering of shantytown life for the tens of millions of Latin Americans who migrated to cities to escape the grinding poverty of rural areas after World War II. In its raw simplicity and unadorned directness, her diary offers a powerful indictment of structural inequalities, illuminating the impulses driving revolutionary movements across Latin America in the postwar years.

*From *Child of the Dark: The Diary of Carolina Maria de Jesus,* translated from the Portuguese by David St. Clair, pp. 40–41. Copyright 1962 by E. P. Dutton, Inc., New York.

Postwar Political Economies: Varieties and Limitations in a Cold War Context

A number of broad themes shaped Latin American politics and economic development in the postwar era. In general, entrenched ruling classes—landowners, the military, the Church hierarchy, and old-guard politicians backed by the U.S. government and corporations—resisted reforms. These groups often used the fight against international communism to justify their defense of the status quo. Challenging

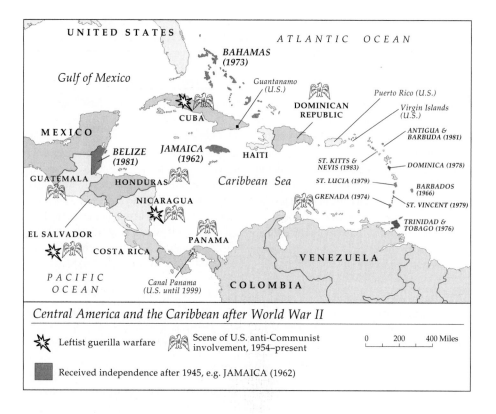

Central America and the Caribbean after World War II

Leftist guerilla warfare   Scene of U.S. anti-Communist involvement, 1954–present

0   200   400 Miles

Received independence after 1945, e.g. JAMAICA (1962)

this old guard and promoting broad-ranging political and economic reforms were workers, middle sectors, students, disgruntled military officers and clergy, the rural and urban poor, and populist politicians. The clash between these contending groups led to diverse outcomes, depending on time, place, and circumstance. Examples from particular countries illustrate these overall themes and demonstrate varied national experiences.

REFORM AND REACTION IN GUATEMALA

In Guatemala, highly dependent on coffee and bananas, the long-running dictatorship (1931–1944) of Jorge Ubico faced mounting challenges in the early 1940s from military officers, students, and workers. Roughly half the country's population was indigenous (or Amerindian), living in villages in the western highlands and laboring seasonally under harsh conditions on large coffee and banana plantations. In 1944 a coalition of reformist groups waged a series of strikes that forced Ubico's resignation and elected a university professor, Juan José Arévalo, as president. In 1945 Arévalo promulgated a liberal constitution that included a progressive labor code, expanded social security, and universal public education. In 1950 Arévalo's successor, Jacobo Arbenz, moved the country further to the left. Especially delicate was the question of land reform. A tiny fraction of Guatemalans owned most arable land, while the U.S.-owned United Fruit Company (UFCo) had vast holdings along the Caribbean coast. When Arbenz launched an agrarian reform program, nationalizing some of UFCo's land with compensation, the U.S. government claimed the regime was acting as a Soviet puppet. Secretary of State John Foster Dulles had close connections with UFCo, as did other U.S. officials. In 1954 a military coup, orchestrated by the CIA, ousted Arevalo and imposed a dictatorship that ruled into the 1990s.

Colombia, also highly dependent on coffee, bananas, and other primary export goods, was sharply split between Liberal and Conservative parties. In 1946 a charismatic Liberal politician, Jorge Gaitán, ran on a populist platform that favored workers and the urban poor over the country's landowning oligarchs. He lost the election but cultivated a huge following among the poor, especially in the capital of Bogotá. Fearing that Gaitán would prevail in the 1950 elections, opponents assassinated him. The killing sparked massive rioting by Gaitán's followers and a military crackdown by the ruling Conservatives. The violence soon spun out of control. For the next two decades, Colombia was engulfed in a massive social conflict known simply as *La Violencia* ("The Violence"). A series of Conservative regimes opposed labor unions, supported state-led industrialization, and welcomed foreign investment. In the 1960s there emerged several leftist guerrilla groups that battled the military and government-supported right-wing paramilitary groups. In the 1970s Colombia became one of the world's leading cocaine producers, feeding the insatiable demand for drugs in the United States and Europe and deepening the country's violence and instability.

VIOLENCE IN COLOMBIA

Bolivia, like Guatemala heavily indigenous, was highly dependent on exports of minerals, especially tin. During World War II a populist political party, the Nationalist Revolutionary Movement (MNR), challenged the country's ruling Conservative oligarchs. In 1952 the MNR ousted the Conservatives and launched a broad-ranging reform program, nationalizing the country's tin mines, subsidizing basic goods and services, and expanding social security. It also launched extensive agrarian reforms, extended the vote to all adults, and raised wages among tin miners and urban dwellers. The revolutionary movement soon sputtered, however, as the oligarchs regrouped and U.S. aid strengthened the MNR's more conservative elements. Still, the country's labor unions, peasant leagues, and indigenous organizations remained strong, in later decades playing an important role in the country's political life.

REVOLUTION IN BOLIVIA

In Brazil, the military ousted the Vargas regime in 1945 (see Chapter 12). Five years later Vargas, portraying himself as the champion of the poor, made a stunning electoral comeback. As opposition from conservative groups mounted, the regime began to unravel, and in 1954 Vargas committed suicide. His successor, Juscelino Kubitschek (1955–1960), continued Vargas's populist and economic nationalist policies. Casting himself as a visionary modernizer, Kubitschek welcomed foreign investment and made major strides in industrialization, especially in automobiles, mining, steel, and petrochemicals. Exemplifying his regime's modernizing outlook and ambition to assert Brazil's continental leadership was the construction of a new capital city, Brasilia, far in the backcountry. But government debt mounted, as did demands for more democratic reforms among rural and urban workers, in part inspired by the 1959 Cuban Revolution. In 1964 the military seized power on the pretext of saving the country from communism. The military ruled until 1985, creating an elaborate national security state that crushed organized opposition and portrayed dissenters as pawns in a vast communist conspiracy.

FROM POPULISM TO DICTATORSHIP IN BRAZIL

PERÓN IN ARGENTINA   Perhaps no country illustrates postwar populism in Latin America better than Argentina under Juan Perón (1946–1955). With its mostly European-descended population, Argentina in 1945 was the wealthiest, most urbanized, industrialized, and literate country in Latin America. Its economy was dependent on exports of meat and grains, with one-fifth of its population of 15 million concentrated in the capital city of Buenos Aires. During the 1930s the military ruled at the behest of the small landowning class, while Buenos Aires' large working class remained mired in poverty. Perón, a military officer and widower, took over the Department of Labor in 1943. Cultivating alliances with union leaders, Perón and his romantic partner, the well-known actress Eva Duarte, carved out a base of popular support among the capital city's working poor. In October 1945, suspicious of his growing power, the army jailed him. Mass demonstrations of *los descamisados* ("the shirtless"), organized by the city's unions, soon forced his release. With his bride Eva ("Evita") campaigning at his side and contributing to his populist mystique, he handily won the 1946 presidential elections.

Once in office, Perón pursued a vigorous program of economic nationalism centered on domestic production of manufactured goods, government-mandated wage increases, and expanded public services. Evita, more popular among working people than her husband, was crucial in crafting the myth of *Peronismo*. Her death from cancer in 1952 at age 33 left a huge gap in the Peronist leadership. Opposition to Perón's populist policies mounted among the military, landowners, the Church, and foreign investors, while rising government debt led to a devastating inflationary spiral. In Argentina as elsewhere, the populist strategy of using government resources to buy popular class support proved unsustainable in the long run. In 1955 the military ousted Perón, establishing a military dictatorship that ruled behind an electoral façade until the early 1980s. Especially brutal was the "dirty war" from the mid-1970s to the early 1980s, in which the military killed and disappeared thousands of alleged subversives.

The Cuban Revolution

PREREVOLUTION CUBA   From the perspective of the cold war, the most significant event in Latin America in the postwar years was the Cuban Revolution of 1959. U.S. intervention in the Cuban War of Independence at the turn of the century had granted Cuba formal independence without effective sovereignty (see Chapter 5). Under the Batista dictatorship (1934–1958), Cuba became a popular vacation spot for wealthy U.S. citizens and a source of cheap sugar for the U.S. market. Meanwhile the vast majority of Cubans owned no land, worked for pennies per day, many in U.S.-owned sugar plantations, and lacked access to clean water, education, and health care. Illiteracy in rural areas stood at nearly 50 percent. By the late 1950s, the capital city of Havana, ringed by a huge slum, had become a center of commercial vice, especially prostitution, pornography, gambling, and narcotics.

A SOCIAL REVOLUTION   In the late 1950s a nationalist guerrilla movement in the eastern mountains, led by Fidel Castro and his 26 July Movement, joined resistance movements led by workers and students in Havana and other cities. On January 1, 1959, this broad-based insurrection, with Castro at its helm, overthrew Batista. Within months the new government launched a social revolution—seizing and redistributing land, raising wages, capping rents, and making racial discrimination illegal. By the end of 1959,

Latin revolutionaries Castro (center left) and Che Guevara (center right) review a parade.

upward of 70 percent of Cubans had benefited materially from the new government's reforms. Since U.S. businesses owned much property in Cuba, a clash with the United States seemed inevitable.

A COLD WAR BATTLEGROUND

The Eisenhower administration, under strong pressure from business interests and anticommunists, interpreted these events through the prism of the cold war. Seeing the new government as a threat to U.S. interests in the Caribbean and beyond, the U.S. administration stepped up its hostile rhetoric, as did Castro. In February 1960, Cuba and the Soviet Union signed a trade agreement in which the Soviets agreed to buy Cuban sugar at a high price and sell Cuba oil at a reduced price. In June, after Standard Oil, Texaco, and Shell refused to refine Soviet oil, Cuba nationalized their refineries. In retaliation, the Eisenhower administration cancelled its commitment to buy its annual Cuban sugar quota of 700,000 tons. The Soviets quickly assumed the quota. In effect, the Castro regime traded one form of dependency for another.

Intending to overthrow Castro and return Cuba to the U.S. sphere, in April 1961 President Kennedy oversaw the disastrous Bay of Pigs invasion, a scheme inherited from his predecessor. The Cubans easily defeated this ill-conceived effort, and a month later, on May Day 1961, Castro proclaimed, "I am a Marxist-Leninist." By this time upward of 85 percent of the Cuban economy was under government control. What began as a nationalist revolution had become, within two years, a cold war battle between superpowers, which reached its most dangerous point in the Cuban Missile Crisis of October 1962 (see Chapter 20).

REVOLUTIONARY SUCCESSES AND FAILURES

Through the 1960s, as Cuban dependence on the Soviet Union grew, thousands of Cubans left their country for the United States. From 1960 to 1962, an annual average of 65,000 mostly wealthy or middle-class Cubans went into exile, making Miami the headquarters of the anti-Castro Cuban exile community. This "brain drain" severely hindered the new regime. Despite early attempts to diversify the economy, in the mid-1960s the revolutionary regime opted to increase its dependence on sugar.

The results were disastrous, as was overreliance on government planning. Intolerant of dissent and squelching civil liberties, the regime jailed thousands of political opponents. However, it made major strides in education, housing, nutrition, and health care. By 1962, basic adult literacy stood at over 90 percent, while malnutrition and homelessness had diminished markedly. By 1970 Cuba had one of the world's most developed and effective national health care systems.

EXPORTING REVOLUTION

Beginning in the mid-1960s, often to the chagrin of his more cautious Soviet patrons, Castro decided to export his revolution to other parts of Latin America and the world. Revolutionary hero Che Guevara went to Bolivia to put into practice his "foco" theory of revolution, which held that a small group of dedicated revolutionaries could ignite a social explosion among the rural poor. The theory proved wrong. In 1967 the small band was captured by the Bolivian military and its leader executed, transforming Che, for some, into a revolutionary martyr and icon. Upset by Castro's support of Che's Bolivian adventure and other Cuban actions, the Soviets retaliated by cutting back on Cuba's oil allotment. Nevertheless, the Cuban revolutionary example inspired dozens of leftist guerrilla movements that mushroomed across the continent in the 1960s and 1970s.

Liberation Theology and a Protestant Reformation

The 1968 Bishop's Conference in Medellín, Colombia, marked the maturation of a reformist impulse in the Roman Catholic Church called liberation theology. Responding to the social and spiritual desperation of the region's millions of poor and marginalized, clergy and laypeople formed Christian base communities, in which people gathered to discuss the Bible in light of their own experiences. Poverty was interpreted as a form of structural violence that could be changed through peaceful collective action. Jesus Christ was reinterpreted as a progressive social reformer, his life and death an inspiration in the struggle for social justice. From the 1960s, liberation theologians helped to mobilize millions of poor people in their struggle to forge better lives for themselves and their families and communities.

Also in the 1960s and continuing through the 1970s and after, Protestantism gained a firm foothold in large parts of Latin America. Pentecostalism in particular, with its individualist ethos and emphasis on a direct relationship between the worshipper and God, spread rapidly in urban and rural areas. By the 1980s, a full-fledged Protestant reformation was reshaping the religious landscape of this once overwhelmingly Roman Catholic land.

CANADA IN THE POSTWAR ERA

CANADA IN THE COLD WAR

In the years after World War II Canada fitfully tried to assert an identity as a "middle power," a nation uninterested in imperialism and a broker in the cause of better international relations. At the same time Canada, now a nation of ten provinces and two massive territories, had its own antipathy toward the Soviet Union. Increasingly, the Dominion's closer ties to its dynamic and stridently anti-Communist southern neighbor drew it into the cold war. In the 1950s the Canadian government, under Conservative leadership, bowed to U.S. pressure by allowing the construction of a series of radar posts near the Arctic Circle and establishing a bilateral air defense system. In the next decade, under Liberal leadership, the Dominion's government distanced itself from the U.S.-led war in Vietnam, garnering the wrath of U.S. President Lyndon Johnson. By the time the Quebec-born, photogenic Liberal Pierre Trudeau was elected Canada's prime minister in 1968, currents of anti-U.S. sentiment coursed through much of the country, heightening nationalist feeling even as economic integration with the United States escalated and divisions within Canadian society and polity widened.

As in the United States and much of the Western industrial world, the quarter century after World War II brought a period of unparalleled economic expansion. As elsewhere, the fruits of this affluent society were not shared equally. U.S. investments expanded, most branch plants built within 100 miles of the long international boundary, the zone where a growing percentage of the Dominion's inhabitants lived. As Canada's rural population declined, its urban population swelled and suburban developments gobbled up acreage once plowed. Public sector employment rose rapidly, as education expanded at all levels, massive construction projects like the Trans-Canada Highway and St. Lawrence Seaway were undertaken, and the provinces and federal government instituted what became a progressively more comprehensive health care system. A vigorous Canadian labor movement encountered increasing resistance from both Canadian capitalists and U.S.-owned firms, but the rise in organized workers in the public sector, many of them women, boosted Canadian union membership.

ECONOMIC AND POLITICAL SHIFTS

Many unions supported the left-leaning New Democratic Party, founded in 1961. Under Canada's parliamentary system, such parties, even if they remained minority bodies, had the potential to affect the course of the national government and were often critical in local and provincial affairs. In 1968, the formation of the Parti Québécois, advocating national sovereignty for Quebec and championing key social democratic policies, pushed to the political forefront issues at the very heart of the nation: the nature of Canadian federalism, relations between minority and majority language groups in an officially bilingual nation, the rights of Aboriginal peoples, relations between church and state, and the meaning of Canada's official policy of multiculturalism.

MAJOR ISSUES

Enactment of this last policy reflected, in part, Canada's expanded efforts to boost its population through immigration. Abandoning a racially discriminatory policy in 1962, Canada thereafter received not only a continued stream of immigrants from across Europe but large numbers from Asia, the Indian subcontinent, and Latin America, especially the Caribbean. The vast majority of immigrants settled in Quebec, Ontario, or British Columbia, remaking these provinces' cities, enriching the nation's cultural, social, and economic life, and further complicating the political landscape.

A MULTICULTURAL CANADA

SUMMARY

In the United States, the quarter century after World War II saw unprecedented levels of prosperity, the spread of mass consumerism, rapid population growth, and a dramatic expansion of civil rights for historically subordinate groups. The cold war both impelled and retarded struggles for rights, as the example of fighting tyranny abroad legitimated such struggles, while the battle against international communism provided a rationale for power-holders to resist change. The 1960s Great Society programs, the height of postwar liberalism, significantly extended the New Deal welfare state. By the late 1960s the confluence of the civil rights movement, black nationalism, the antiwar movement, the women's movement, and Third World liberation struggles had created a revolutionary atmosphere that proved short-lived. Rising foreign competition in a globalizing economy, federal overspending in the cold war, and other factors led to the end of the postwar boom, while a powerful conservative countercurrent marked the beginning of a conservative and Republican ascendancy.

Postwar Canada saw an even broader liberal florescence, as the public sector expanded its role in most arenas. Cultivating an international role as a fair-minded "middle power," Canada also proved a firm U.S. ally in the cold war, even as many Canadians held ambivalent views about their southern superpower neighbor.

In Latin America, a demographic explosion, massive rural-urban migration, rapid urbanization, grinding poverty, continuing stark inequalities, and the cold war provided the overarching context for postwar political and economic developments. As subordinate groups struggled for rights and to escape from poverty, dominant groups resisted social and political change, often using the pretext of the cold war to stifle dissent. Although national experiences varied enormously, in general populist leaders sought to use government resources to pursue nationalist economic policies and to buy off domestic political opposition. The costs usually proved too high. With mounting debt, rising inflation, and a mobilized and expectant populace, militaries intervened to maintain existing relations of power and privilege. The Cuban Revolution, in both its successes and its failures, provided a concrete example of the possibilities of radical social revolution in a poor, Third World country, while bringing the cold war to the United States' historic backyard. By the early 1970s, dictatorships ruled in most of Latin America, while new social movements, often inspired by liberation theology, sought new ways to bring a measure of justice and dignity to the lives of ordinary people.

SUGGESTED SOURCES

Anderson, Terry. *The Movement and the Sixties.* 1995. An overview of protest movements in the United States.*

Baldwin, James. *The Fire Next Time.* 1962. A searing and prophetic indictment of U.S. racism by a towering literary figure.*

Carson, Rachel. *Silent Spring.* 1962. The book that inspired the U.S. environmental movement.*

Evita. 1979. A Broadway musical version of the life and times of the Argentine cult figure Eva Perón. (Also a 1997 film, starring Madonna.)

Handy, Jim. *Gift of the Devil: A History of Guatemala.* 1992. A lively general history with an appeal to nonspecialists.*

Harrington, Michael. *The Other America.* 1962. The book that proved instrumental in impelling the War on Poverty.*

Horowitz, Morton J. *The Warren Court and the Pursuit of Justice.* 1998. Deftly contextualizes the decisions of the Warren Court.*

Isserman, Maurice, and Michael Kazin. *America Divided: The Civil War of the 1960s*. 2000. A balanced and readable account of the tumult of the 1960s.*

Morton, Desmond. *NDP: The Dream of Power*. 1974. A contemporary study of the rise of Canada's New Democratic Party and its challenge to the two major political parties.

Pelletier, Gérard. *The October Crisis*. 1971. Contemporary analysis of a key regional division in Canadian politics.

Rosen, Ruth. *The World Split Open: How the Modern Women's Movement Changed America*. 2000. An excellent study of the modern women's movement.*

Scheper-Hughes, Nancy. *Death without Weeping: The Violence of Everyday Life in Brazil*. 1992. A moving anthropological study of child death and women's suffering in Brazil.*

Winn, Peter. *Americas: The Changing Face of Latin America and the Caribbean*. 1992. A thoughtful and readable overview.*

Yglesias, José. *In the Fist of the Revolution*. 1968. An insightful firsthand account of life in Castro's Cuba.*

WEB SOURCES

scriptorium.lib.duke.edu/wlm. A Duke University site with documents of the 1960s and 1970s from the women's liberation movement.

lists.village.virginia.edu/sixties. Contains documents relating to the radical movements of the 1960s, including several online exhibits.

www.fordham.edu/halsall/mod/modsbook55.html. Contains links to Latin American materials, including Cuba, the Peróns in Argentina, and liberation theology.

lanic.utexas.edu/la/region/history. Provides numerous links to Latin American resources by country and by region.

www.fordham.edu/halsall/mod/modsbook47.html

www.fordham.edu/halsall/mod/modsbook48.html.

These two Fordham University sites provide numerous links to materials on U.S. foreign and domestic policies and developments from 1945 into the 1990s.

---

*Paperback available.

⑥Asia in the Aftermath of World War II

World War II left large parts of Asia devastated and tens of millions of people dead. It also inspired many Asians to demand domestic reforms and national independence. Early in World War II, the triumphant Japanese army and navy had evicted all Western powers from their colonies in Asia east of India. The Japanese were harsh and arrogant rulers, shown in their slogan that Japan was "The leader of Asia, the protector of Asia, the light of Asia." By the end of the war former Asian colonies were nevertheless in no mood for compliant acceptance of their former colonial rulers.

World War II had also dramatically altered the power equation in Asia. Japan was in ruins and under foreign military occupation for the first time in its history. China, Japan's main target and victim, emerged a victor in the war, its international status enhanced. It had gained equality among nations after a century of unequal treaties and now stood as one of the Big Five victorious powers, a founding member of the United Nations and a permanent member of the Security Council. The United States hoped in 1945 that a pro-Western, strong, and united China under a Kuomintang (KMT) government would become the anchor of postwar Asia. However, the war had mortally weakened the Nationalist government, at the same time giving a new lease on life and unprecedented opportunities to the Chinese Communist Party (CCP).

The Soviet Union, which had entered the war against Japan at its very end, reaped many benefits as a victor. With a Communist government installed in North Korea by Soviet occupation troops and its Chinese Communist allies victorious in China in 1949, the Communist movement seemed poised to make new gains, and indigenous Communist parties in several Asian nations took heart. Threatened with the further spread of communism in Asia, a worried United States sought counter-measures. Asia thus became a key theater of the cold war.

THE UNITED STATES REMAKES JAPAN

The Making of a Democratic Japan

The story of postwar Japan was that of the phoenix rising from its ashes, reborn and significantly changed. Wartime agreements between Allied powers stipulated that Japan be stripped of its conquests since 1895, which the emperor's unconditional surrender implicitly accepted. Crushed in war, Japan in September 1945 was open to change to a degree that was unique in history. It had the potential to follow either a democratic or a totalitarian path. By denying the Soviet Union a role in the occupation of Japan, the United States ensured that postwar Japan would follow a Western orientation.

U.S. occupation from 1945 to 1951 provided the catalyst that sent Japan along the road to recovery and prosperity. What happened to Japan after the war differed significantly from what happened to Germany. Unlike Germany, Japan was occupied by the United States rather than by forces from several nations. Although General Douglas MacArthur was Supreme Commander for the Allied Powers (SCAP), in reality he took orders only from the government of the United States. Also, unlike Germany, Japan was not directly governed by the occupation forces; rather, it retained its emperor and its government, which was closely supervised by SCAP.

After their decisive defeat, most Japanese had no wish to return to their imperialist past. With their former sense of national mission shattered, they proved amenable to change and were cooperative with the occupiers, whom they found surprisingly benevolent. With the cold war spreading rapidly from Europe to Asia, the United States had an added impetus to rebuild Japan economically and to restructure its government along parliamentary and democratic lines. It rightly assumed that a prosperous and democratically governed Japanese people would not find communism attractive and would be less likely to disturb world peace again.

The immediate task for the U.S. occupation authorities was to help feed a large population that included 6.5 million repatriated soldiers, colonial personnel, and settlers. U.S. food aid prevented starvation until the Japanese could rebuild their shattered economy. The next task was to create a new political structure based on a new constitution. The emperor was retained as a stabilizing force but was stripped of his formerly divine status, which he renounced in a nationwide radio address, called the Declaration of Humanity, on January 1, 1946. This was the second time the Japanese had heard his voice; the first time was when he announced Japan's surrender. Twenty-five men who were most responsible for the outbreak of the war and were most involved in wartime atrocities were tried and punished at the Tokyo International Court (similar to the Nuremberg trials for Nazi war criminals). Seven, including Tojo, were hanged. Other top Japanese commanders and administrators were punished after trials held in China and the Philippines. About 200,000 former military officers, officials, and industrialists were forbidden to hold office or continue in business. The removal of the old guard allowed older Japanese politicians who had opposed the militarists and eventually a young generation to rise to power.

General MacArthur closely supervised the writing of the new constitution, promulgated in 1947, together with a Bill of Rights. These documents contained elements from the Declaration of Independence, the U.S. Constitution, the Gettysburg Address, and the British parliamentary system. The constitution proclaimed the Japanese people sovereign, enfranchised women, and provided a bicameral legislature (National Diet), with members of both chambers (the former House of Peers was renamed the House of Councillors) elected by universal suffrage. The executive was made directly responsible to the Diet, and the judiciary was independent of the executive. The constitution renounced war and the right of belligerency forever and declared that "land, sea, and

UNITED STATES SUPERVISES THE REMAKING OF JAPAN

A NEW CONSTITUTION AND BILL OF RIGHTS FORM BASIS OF NEW JAPAN

air forces, as well as other war potential, will never be maintained." This provision made the Japanese constitution unique.

These reforms brought about changes in attitudes that altered Japan. On April 11, 1951, the Japanese were greatly shocked when President Truman dismissed General MacArthur in a dispute over the conduct of the Korean War. This event served as an important object lesson in democracy—that a message from a civilian leader could bring down a great and revered military proconsul who had seemed all-powerful, an event that would have been undreamed of in prewar Japan.

JAPAN REGAINS SOVEREIGNTY IN 1951

The United States had always assumed that it would occupy Japan for only a limited time and had in fact turned over many decision-making powers to the Japanese after 1948. A Communist victory in China in 1949 and the outbreak of the Korean War in 1950 emphasized Japan's importance as an anti-Communist bastion and propelled the United States to end the occupation quickly, so that Japan could take its place among the democratic nations of the world. In 1951 Japan and 48 victor nations of World War II signed a peace treaty in San Francisco. The Communist bloc nations refused to sign, and neither of the Chinese governments was included because each claimed to represent all of China. A separate treaty was soon signed between Nationalist China and Japan.

The occupation of Japan formally ended in 1952. Under the terms of a mutual security treaty, the United States retained its bases in Japan and Japan was forbidden to grant military concessions to any other power without U.S. consent. This treaty, which effectively made Japan a U.S. military protectorate, was as much the result of U.S. policy as of Japanese policy under Prime Minister Yoshida Shigeru. Yoshida, like most Japanese, welcomed the security provided by the U.S. nuclear umbrella in the cold war. With U.S. protection, Japan did not need to change its constitution to create a military force; it instead established a self-defense force that lacked the capacity to wage aggressive war. Until the late 1980s Japan never spent over 1 percent of its GNP on defense. It instead concentrated its resources on economic recovery and growth.

LIBERAL DEMOCRATIC PARTY DOMINATES JAPANESE POLITICS

Just as Konrad Adenauer guided West Germany toward recovery and rehabilitation in postwar years, so Yoshida Shigeru guided Japan between 1945 and 1955, called the "Yoshida years." Yoshida served as a diplomat before World War II but opposed the imperialistic policies of the military, for which he suffered brief imprisonment. A staunch anti-Communist and a conservative party leader, he worked well with General MacArthur to rebuild a new Japan, concentrating on economic recovery and efficient government. The conservatively oriented Liberal Democratic Party held uninterrupted power in Japan until the 1990s, relegating the Socialist Party to permanent and ineffective opposition, in what is jokingly called a one-and-a-half-party system.

Laying the Foundations of Economic Recovery

Between 1947 and 1952 the United States gave Japan $2 billion in economic aid. It also instituted economic and social changes designed to promote economic equity among Japanese and to make the Japanese economy sound and viable. The United States pushed Japan to make sweeping land reform, drastically reduced rent, set a limit on land ownership, and sold excess holdings of landlords at a nominal price to

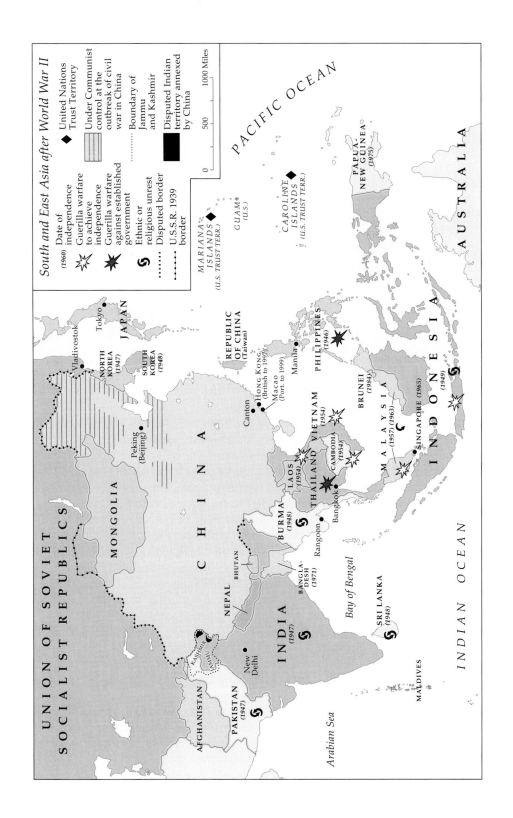

South and East Asia after World War II

Legend:

(1960) Date of independence

☆ Guerilla warfare to achieve independence

✦ Guerilla warfare against established government

↻ Ethnic or religious unrest

······· Disputed border

┄┄┄ U.S.S.R. 1939 border

◆ United Nations Trust Territory

▦ Under Communist control at the outbreak of civil war in China

········ Boundary of Jammu and Kashmir

■ Disputed Indian territory annexed by China

1000 Miles / 500 / 0

PACIFIC OCEAN

UNION OF SOVIET SOCIALIST REPUBLICS

MONGOLIA

CHINA

JAPAN
Tokyo

NORTH KOREA (1947)
Vladivostok

SOUTH KOREA (1948)

Peking (Beijing)

REPUBLIC OF CHINA (Taiwan)

HONG KONG (British to 1997)
Macao (Port. to 1999)
Canton

Manila

PHILIPPINES (1946)

MARIANA ISLANDS (U.S. TRUST TERR.)

GUAM (U.S.)

CAROLINE ISLANDS ◆ (U.S. TRUST TERR.)

PAPUA-NEW GUINEA (1975)

AUSTRALIA

BURMA (1948)
Rangoon

LAOS (1954)
THAILAND
VIETNAM (1954)
CAMBODIA (1954)
Bangkok

BRUNEI (1984)

MALAYSIA
SINGAPORE (1965)
(1957) (1963)

INDONESIA (1949)

NEPAL
BHUTAN
BANGLA-DESH (1971)

INDIA (1947)

SRI LANKA (1948)

Bay of Bengal

INDIAN OCEAN

MALDIVES

AFGHANISTAN
PAKISTAN (1947)

KASHMIR
JAMMU
New Delhi

Arabian Sea

Japanese schools are strict and maintain high academic standards. Students in this class are attentive and well prepared.

existing tenants. Over a million families benefited from the land reform, and 87 percent of farmers became owner-cultivators.

Equally fundamental was the breakup of the *zaibatsu*. Ten family-owned holding companies and dozens of industrial and trading companies were dissolved and their stocks were sold to the public. The Diet passed laws modeled on U.S. antitrust legislation, established the Fair Trade Commission to police business practices, and abolished laws restricting the labor movement and trade unions.

JAPANESE ECONOMY MAKES RAPID ADVANCES

Many factors contributed to Japan's economic miracle. One was its compulsory educational system, extended from 6 to 9 years (later expanded to 12). In addition to a rigorous academic curriculum, schools after 1945 also taught democratic principles. Girls were given more educational and career opportunities than in the past, and all young people were given more chances for higher education.

U.S. military procurement orders during the Korean War also helped Japan's economic recovery. Per capita income rose from $146 in 1951 to $395 in 1960; during the same decade, the GNP increased at an average annual rate of close to 9 percent. By 1968 Japan had risen to third place among the world's industrial powers. Its steady economic growth was helped by new and efficient plants and equipment, a high savings rate, a cooperative attitude between workers and government, government encouragement of business, and a determined work ethic. Since prosperity depended on its ability to export, the Japanese government supported an open and expanding world trading order. Japan agreed to pay reparations to several newly independent nations in Southeast Asia for World War II damages its military had inflicted. These agreements facilitated the resumption and expansion of trade between Japan and some Southeast Asian nations. However, its refusal to apologize for crimes and to compensate surviving women from conquered lands who had been forced to serve as sex slaves prevented the development of good relations.

Japan was the first Asian nation to bring population growth under control. Peace, the return of millions of soldiers, and better medical care brought about a baby boom; between 1945 and 1950, the population increased 15.6 percent, from 72 to 83 million. In 1948, prodded by General MacArthur, the government legalized abortion for economic and medical reasons under the Eugenics Protection Law. As a result of the law and changing social mores, population growth tapered off, in a demographic revolution that took only a decade to accomplish. A low population growth rate enabled the Japanese to enjoy a rapid rise in the standard of living, making it into a mass consumption society.

POPULATION GROWTH SLOWS DRAMATICALLY

THE TRIUMPH OF COMMUNISM IN CHINA

Eight years of war against Japan had devastated China. Estimates of military and civilian deaths were between 7 and 30 million. Economic losses amounted to almost half a trillion U.S. dollars at 1945 value. Chinese authorities in 1945 were faced with a shattered economy, galloping inflation, and over 90 million refugees awaiting resettlement. These conditions overwhelmed the KMT government. War had destroyed its modern base in the coastal areas. Driven inland, it was forced to rely on the local conservative gentry for support; as a result it could not make the needed reforms. Wartime conditions and the urgent needs of the military reinforced existing tendencies toward authoritarianism and militarism, costing the KMT support among the people, especially students and intellectuals.

WORLD WAR II DAMAGES CRIPPLE NATIONALIST CHINA

While the situation for the KMT was deteriorating, the CCP was gaining strength. During the war of 1937–1945, the CCP took advantage of the widespread patriotic movement to expand its guerrilla warfare to organize and control the resistance forces in much of the nominally Japanese-occupied countryside. As Mao Tse-tung said about guerrilla war, "The people are the water, the soldiers are the fish"; that is, a successful war of resistance needs popular support. Whereas the CCP had about 40,000 party members and 30,000 troops in 1937, at the end of the war it claimed 1.2 million party members and control of over 80 million people, mostly in northern China, plus a military force consisting of almost 1 million regulars and 2 million militiamen. These spectacular gains proved Chiang Kai-shek right when he said during the darkest days of the war against Japan that whereas the Japanese were a disease of the skin, the Communists were a disease of the heart, threatening his government.

Communist Victory in the Civil War

The removal of the Japanese from China brought the competition for power between the KMT and the CCP to the forefront once again, and civil war erupted over control of Japanese-occupied areas. The United States, which had become deeply involved in China during the war, was committed to playing a role in shaping postwar

Chinese politics. Initially, it aided the KMT by airlifting its troops from southern and western China to the major population centers in the north to take control before the CCP moved in from the northern countryside.

U.S. ATTEMPTS TO MEDIATE BETWEEN CHINESE WARRING PARTIES

When the U.S. government later recognized how strong the Communists were, it attempted to mediate a solution to the KMT-CCP conflict. Conditioned by its own political tradition, however, it mistakenly visualized the two parties in China as similar to the two political parties in the United States and asked the two sides to give up their independent armies and come together in a coalition government. General George Marshall, with his great prestige as the architect of Allied victory in Europe, was sent to China in December 1945 to mediate a reconciliation between the two Chinese groups. However, neither Chinese faction trusted the other, and neither would give up its hope of eventual total control. Marshall's mission ended in failure, and the United States stopped supporting the Nationalist government.

THE CHINESE CIVIL WAR: COMMUNIST VICTORY

In 1949 the CCP won the civil war, and the KMT government and part of its military forces fled to the island of Taiwan, a Chinese province that had been under Japanese occupation from 1895 to 1945. Many factors—military, economic, political, and psychological—contributed to this outcome. The Japanese invasion was without doubt the key factor. As Mao Zedong[1] admitted to a visiting Japanese delegation in 1964, "We [CCP] should be grateful to Japan, because had the Japanese warlords not invaded China, we [CCP] would still be in our mountain hideouts." Militarily, the KMT army, with about 3 million men in 1946, opposed an approximately equal number of CCP soldiers. But in taking over all areas formerly under Japanese occupation the KMT had become overextended. Its strategic doctrine to hold cities and other strongly fortified positions made it vulnerable to the CCP's guerrilla tactics that destroyed railroads, controlled the countryside, and avoided battle unless on terms favorable to itself. As Mao said, "The enemy advances, we retreat; the enemy camps, we harass; the enemy tires, we attack; the enemy retreats, we pursue." Communist spies also infiltrated the KMT military command, leaking vital information to the CCP. The isolated KMT units, which also often suffered from corruption and poor command, either surrendered or were cut to pieces.

A crumbling KMT government contributed to the collapse of its military. Eight years of war with Japan had taken a heavy toll. The loss or destruction of its economic base and war costs had forced the KMT to print more and more paper money; at the end of the war, the volume of notes issued was 465 times that at the war's outbreak because government revenue covered only one-sixth of its needs. After 1946 the civil war led to continued deficit spending and runaway inflation that especially impoverished the urban middle class and caused economic chaos, corruption, and loss of confidence in the government. When the currency collapsed in late 1948, so did much of the remaining civilian support for the Nationalist cause.

On the other hand, the Communists showed strict military discipline, high morale, and coherent leadership. Although the CCP had carried out only moderate land

---

[1]Hereafter in the text, the spelling of Chinese names will follow the pinyin system, adopted by the People's Republic of China, and the Wade-Giles system for Taiwan, in accordance with each government's convention.

reforms in areas it controlled during the war, it reverted to violent land reform tactics in its areas at the war's end and promised similar drastic programs for all of China. The poor and dispossessed backed the Communists because of this promise, and many students and intellectuals, losing confidence in the KMT, also came to support them.

The international situation, including, ironically, U.S. aid, also helped the CCP. To prevent Mao from taking over China, the United States sent over $2 billion in aid to prop up the KMT government. While U.S. arms equipped the KMT army, the U.S.-style reorganization of the army only furthered confusion and rivalry between units under different commands. When the United States withdrew support in 1948, it contributed to the rapid demoralization of the KMT government and sped its collapse.

The Soviet Union also contributed to the CCP triumph. During World War II, Soviet leader Joseph Stalin, after extracting concessions favorable to the U.S.S.R., recognized the KMT as the only legal government of China and promised to refrain from sending aid to the CCP. Stalin indicated his low regard for the CCP by characterizing them as "margarine" (not the genuine article) or "radish" (red outside, white inside) Communists. Nevertheless, he helped the CCP by timing Soviet withdrawal from Manchuria to ensure that the CCP captured all the huge cache of surrendered Japanese arms, by providing sanctuary to CCP units in North Korea and the U.S.S.R., and by rallying international support to the CCP cause.

On October 1, 1949, standing atop the Gate of Heavenly Peace in Peking, Mao Zedong proclaimed the establishment of the People's Republic of China (hereafter, China). China was immediately recognized by the Soviet Union and other Communist nations. Early in 1950 India and several other nations in Asia and Europe followed suit. Among the major Western powers, only Great Britain, concerned for its huge investments in China and the safety of its Hong Kong colony, extended recognition.

Although minor tame political parties were allowed to exist as window dressing, the People's Republic was a totalitarian state that carried out policies set by the Communist Party. Nationwide mass organizations controlled by the Communist Party, such as the All-China Federation of Trade Unions, paralleled the structure of the party and the government. Because everyone belonged to a union or mass organization, the government was able to reach and control all citizens in their professional or social roles.

PEOPLE'S REPUBLIC OF CHINA ESTABLISHED

China Fails to Modernize

Mao Zedong sought to reshape the thinking and behavior of everyone so that he could create a new society of "collective man." To do this, he initiated campaigns to abolish old loyalties and patterns of thought and to instill new values and obedience to the state. New marriage and divorce laws were enacted to eliminate the old patriarchal family and give women more rights. Citizens were ordered to attend frequent meetings to learn Marxist ideology and the current party lines and to criticize themselves and each other. To keep China on the "correct course" and to emphasize the importance of being "Red" rather than "expert," people were forced to study Mao's thoughts and memorize and repeat his sayings—for example, "All reactionaries are paper tigers." Children sang songs such as "The East Is Red" in praise of Mao, rather than nursery rhymes, and at nursery schools the first words they learned to write were Mao's name.

MARXIST IDEOLOGY TRANSFORMS CHINA

Mao Zedong reviews parade at Square of Heavenly Peace in Peking, celebrating the 14th anniversary of Communist victory in 1963.

As in the Soviet Union, culture and the arts were strictly controlled. For example, the socialist realism style that showed heroic workers and happy collective farmers was approved in painting, while other styles were denounced as decadent. Besides propaganda, force was used to ensure obedience. Whole classes of people were condemned as enemies of the revolution, and "landlords" were killed or jailed and their land was redistributed.

GREAT LEAP FORWARD BRINGS ECONOMIC DISASTER

In economic development, the party emphasized rapid modernization through Soviet-style planning and received massive technological assistance from the Soviet Union. The First Five-Year Plan (1953–1957) stressed building up heavy industry and collectivizing agriculture, but despite rapid progress vast problems remained. This led Mao, who believed that humans were the "decisive force in history" and that China's major asset was its huge population, to ignore objective economic realities. Instead of following the realistic goals set by the Second Five-Year Plan, he initiated in 1958 a crash program called the Great Leap Forward. It involved the mass mobilization of labor, establishment of communes, and building of backyard furnaces to smelt iron, measures pushed forward amid an atmosphere of ideological frenzy. Children were cared for in nurseries, everyone ate in communal dining halls so that men and women alike could devote all their time to work and ideological study.

Instead of instant development, the Great Leap Forward brought total disaster. Most early statistics on initial gains made under the Great Leap were either wildly exaggerated or faked. Figures show that about 600,000 backyard furnaces were built, but the iron they produced, often by melting down tools and implements, was of such low quality that it was almost useless. By 1959 the economy had been crippled by the follies of the Great Leap, the people were exhausted and demoralized, and starvation stalked the land. Economists estimate that the Great Leap caused a loss of $66 billion to the economy; demographers calculate that up to 30 million people died as a result of the Mao-made famine, the worst in Chinese history. When the Central Committee of the CCP met in 1959, even Mao had to admit the magnitude of the catastrophe facing China. His disillusioned senior associates eased him out of direct control of the party and the government, although Mao retained the title of chairman of the Communist Party. Between 1959 and 1966, they pursued a pragmatic approach as they repaired the damage that Mao's policies had inflicted and began to rebuild China (see Chapter 29).

Alliance with the Soviet Union

China's foreign policy was based on several factors. Still weak and barely on its feet in 1949, China needed both economic aid and help from the Soviet Union to forestall possible Western intervention. To secure Soviet aid, Mao went to Moscow in 1950, his first trip abroad, to help celebrate Stalin's 70th birthday. There he paid the following fawning tribute to Stalin:

> Everyone knows that Comrade Stalin had an ardent love for the Chinese people and believed the might of the Chinese revolution to be immeasurable. To the problems of the Chinese revolution he contributed his sublime wisdom. And it was following the theories of Lenin and Stalin and with the support of the Soviet Union . . . that the Chinese Communist Party . . . won its historic victory.

As a result of the trip, the Sino-Soviet Treaty of Friendship and Alliance was signed in 1950, in which Stalin granted Mao a military alliance, provided credit, and promised tens of thousands of Soviet military and civilian experts to help China modernize its armed forces, infrastructure, and industries. During the next decade, at a time when it had barely recovered from the devastations of World War II, the Soviet Union transferred massive amounts of technology to China. It also returned to China the equipment it had looted from Manchuria at the end of World War II. Thousands of Chinese students went to study in the Soviet Union, which replaced Western nations as China's source of modern knowledge. Russian replaced English as the mandatory second language in schools and universities. Mao proclaimed that in international affairs China would "lean to one side"—that is, the Marxist side—in the cold war.

CHINA AND SOVIET UNION FORM ALLIANCE

Understandably, in the light of China's century-long history of humiliation by Western and Japanese imperialism, the new government sought recognition as a great power. The Soviet Union surrendered its remaining privileges in China and accorded it the position of associate leader in the international Communist movement. In 1957 it promised to assist China in its nuclear development. For its part, China orchestrated its foreign policy to aid the international Communist movement and in so doing enhanced its drive for leadership in Asia and for major power status in world affairs. For example, in sending a million "volunteers" to aid North Korea in the Korean War and in assisting North Vietnam's struggles, China not only furthered the Communist cause in Asia but also reasserted its traditional role as the protector of the small states

CHINA'S WORLD STATURE GROWS

on its borders. In 1956 China mediated the disputes between the Soviet Union and its Eastern European satellites, thus helping to maintain Soviet dominance in the Socialist bloc while asserting China's position as associate leader in the international Communist movement.

At the same time that it was strengthening its role in international Communist affairs, China sought to become the leader of all Asia. In 1955, at the Bandung Conference in Indonesia, China was acknowledged as the leader of the Afro-Asian bloc of Third World nations.

SINO-SOVIET RIVALRY FOR LEADERSHIP GROWS

While Mao resented Stalin's interference in China's affairs, he nevertheless respected him as the senior leader of world communism. He had no such regard for Khrushchev, Stalin's successor, whom he labeled a "revisionist." In instituting the communes during the Great Leap Forward, China attempted to put itself on a higher ideological plane than the Soviet Union and even gloated that it was ahead of the U.S.S.R. in its progress toward the Marxist utopia. Khrushchev firmly denied Mao's claims and gloated when the Great Leap Forward failed.

DECOLONIZATION IN ASIA

COLONIAL EMPIRES END IN ASIA

World War II not only ended Japan's empire but led to the end of all empires in Asia. Weakened by two world wars, the European colonial powers found that they could not hold back the rising tide of Asian nationalism, whether peacefully or violently expressed. Between 1946 and 1957 the people of every major colony in southern and Southeast Asia became citizens of new nations. The United States led the way in 1946, granting full independence to the Philippines. Great Britain, however, demonstrated the full magnitude of the collapse of colonialism when it departed from the most valuable possession of any colonial empire, the Indian subcontinent, in 1947, leaving in its wake two new nations, India and Pakistan. One year later, it granted independence to Burma and Sri Lanka (Ceylon). In 1949 the Netherlands, losing a war against Indonesian nationalists and threatened with the loss of U.S. economic aid, reluctantly left Indonesia. France was driven from Indochina in 1954. In 1957 the British granted independence to Malaya, their last major colony in Asia, and combined it with several smaller neighboring British colonies to form the federation of Malaysia. This section concentrates on events in India, Pakistan, and Indochina.

India Wins Its Struggle for Freedom

INDIA DURING WORLD WAR II

Since 1909 Great Britain had reluctantly but steadily granted ever-increasing measures of self-rule to India and Burma; this process led the way for the other nonwhite British possessions in Asia and Africa. Had World War II not occurred, India might have attained final independence before 1947. However, preoccupation with the war and the worsening relations between Hindus and Muslims compelled Great Britain to postpone the final steps toward complete independence until the war was over.

Great Britain declared war against Nazi Germany in 1939 and against Japan in 1941, both on its own behalf and on behalf of India and its other possessions and dominions. Although most Indian National Congress leaders supported British war aims against the Axis, they nevertheless objected to India's automatic entry into the war without prior consultation with Indian leaders. In protest, the eight Congress-controlled provincial governments resigned. The British government, maintaining that World War II was a life-and-death struggle, countered by taking over Congress-controlled provinces and dissolving the India Act of 1935. When the Congress then began a new *Satyagraha* campaign. Britain retaliated by arresting 1,400 Congress leaders, including Gandhi and Nehru.

Muslim League President Mohammed Ali Jinnah, called Great Leader by his followers, declared the closing of Congress ministries in the eight provinces a "Day of Deliverance and Thanksgiving." The Muslim League and League-controlled provinces cooperated with the British administration throughout the war, fostering increased Muslim self-confidence and separate consciousness. Jinnah exemplified Muslim opinion when he said in a speech in 1940 at the annual meeting of the Muslim League,

> Hindus and Muslims belong to two different religious philosophies, social customs, literature. . . . To yoke together two such nations under a single state, one as a numerical minority and the other as a majority, must lead to growing discontent and final destruction of any fabric that may be so built up for the government of such a state. . . . The only course open to us all is to allow the major nations separate homelands for dividing India into "autonomous national states."

Following that speech the League passed the Pakistan Resolution, which called for a separate Muslim state. Pakistan, or the "Land of the Pure," was to consist of those areas of the Indian subcontinent where Muslims formed the majority of the population. Gandhi denounced the resolution as the "vivisection of India."

Most Indians actively aided Great Britain in fighting the Axis. Two million Indian troops fought well in the Middle East, in Africa, and in Southeast Asia while also defending India against a threatened Japanese invasion. India was also a vital link in the transport of U.S. Lend-Lease aid to China. Many Indian prisoners of war (POWs) captured by the Japanese refused to cooperate with their captors and suffered horrible abuse. Sixty thousand POWs were turned over to a pro-Nazi Indian living in Germany named Subhas Bose. Japan installed Bose as head of its puppet state called "Free" India, first on Andaman Island, then in Rangoon, Burma. Bose created the "Indian National Army" from Indian POWs, but it surrendered to the Allies in May 1944 and a fleeing Bose died in a plane crash.

Indian industries grew more rapidly during World War II than in any comparable period, mainly to meet war needs. The Tata iron and steel mills produced more than 1.5 million tons of steel a year, becoming the largest producer in the British Empire. Wartime strains on transportation, demands to feed the armed forces, and loss of Burma's rice surplus resulted in a famine in Bengal with the loss of between 1 and 3 million lives.

A number of British missions came to India during the war years to offer concessions that would mollify the Indian National Congress. They suggested formulas for the transfer of more power to Indians during the war and also promised full independence immediately afterward. However, all British offers failed, either

NEGOTIATIONS BETWEEN BRITISH GOVERNMENT AND INDIANS DURING WORLD WAR II

because of the Congress's intransigence on timing or because of the stumbling block of Muslim-Hindu communal hostility. The Congress now called on Britain immediately to "quit India;" the Muslim League responded by insisting that independence must result in the creation of two successor states, India and Pakistan. This was the deadlocked situation at the war's end.

The Creation of India and Pakistan

INDEPENDENCE AND PARTITION

In July 1945 general elections in Great Britain brought the Labour Party to power. Never sympathetic to imperialism, Prime Minister Clement Attlee declared his government's intention to grant independence to India. He appointed Lord Louis Mountbatten, an able diplomat and war hero who had commanded all Allied forces in Southeast Asia, to accomplish that task. Even then, the final stages of British withdrawal were delayed by Hindu-Muslim antagonism. Communal riots in many parts of India took on the character of full-scale battles, and civil war threatened. Finally Gandhi and other Indian National Congress leaders agreed that it was preferable to let Muslims have a separate state in the northwest and northeast, where they formed a majority, rather than to engulf the whole land in civil war. Mountbatten appointed a Briton to head an impartial commission to draw up the boundaries, assisted by eight Indian high court judges, four each chosen by the Congress and the League parties.

Chaotic flight of refugees at the creation of India and Pakistan. Terrified Muslims cram into a train at the Delhi railroad station, hoping to escape to Pakistan. Similar scenes could be found in Pakistan where Hindus attempted to flee to India. About 14 million refugees attempted to cross the borders to their new countries. Many died from privations and attacks by hostile mobs of the opposing religion.

Approximately 550 Indian princes, who had made separate treaties in the nineteenth century that put them under the protection of the British crown, were told that their states could join either India or Pakistan but could not become independent.

At the stroke of midnight on August 14, 1947, India became a sovereign nation within the British Commonwealth of Nations. At the invitation of the Indian parliament and in gratitude for his efforts, Mountbatten stayed on for a year as governor-general (representative of the British sovereign) of India. At the same time, peoples of the predominantly Muslim northwest and northeast declared their independence as the new nation of Pakistan, which also remained a member of the Commonwealth.

Fearful of their fate in East and West Pakistan, Hindu minorities and Sikhs sought safety by crossing over into India, and many equally frightened Muslims from India fled into Pakistan. More than 14 million people took part in this massive human migration, with 9 million resettling in India and 6 million in Pakistan. An estimated 600,000 people died in the chaos and violence, some in riots and street battles in their towns and villages, others while they were fleeing to their new nation, and still others of starvation or diseases during their grueling journeys. However, 50 million Muslims remained in India, and Prime Minister Nehru labored to ensure that they received protection. Similarly, Jinnah (who became governor-general of Pakistan) worked to protect the remaining 10 million Hindus in Pakistan.

VIOLENCE ACCOMPANIES PARTITION

More heartsick than anyone over the carnage, Gandhi undertook personal missions of peace to the disturbed cities and villages in India. He also began a fast for an end to communal hatred, which had a sobering effect on the violent mobs. On January 30, 1948, at a prayer meeting in India's capital, New Delhi, Gandhi was assassinated by a Hindu extremist who believed that he had been too generous to the Muslims.

Prime Minister Nehru found governing India extremely difficult, as indeed did the leaders of all newly independent nations, partly because most had little prior experience in government and partly because of the many problems of nationhood. One problem was how to feed the inexorably growing population. Over 80 percent of Indians were rural, and most were desperately poor. With a high population density, primitive agricultural methods, and almost total dependence on monsoon rains, the land could not produce enough food for the population. Tragically, every improvement made in food production, sanitary facilities, and public health further boosted the population growth. In 1947 life expectancy for an Indian who survived infancy was 32 years; by 1969, it had reached 52. Increased longevity put such a strain on Indian food resources that Nehru was led to remark, "India must run very fast just to stand still."

MANY PROBLEMS FACE PRIME MINISTER NEHRU

There was also the language problem. The 1950 constitution recognized 16 official languages, and one of them was English. A government plan to make Hindi, a language common to northern India, the national language angered southern Indians who did not speak Hindi, and riots broke out. In retreat, the parliament passed a law, embarrassing to nationalists, to retain English as the national language until the indefinite time when the non-Hindi-speaking peoples would accept Hindi; the matter remained unresolved and English remained the preferred common language of educated Indians.

Politically, Nehru and his Congress Party favored democracy and believed the princely states ruled autocratically by maharajas were anachronisms. After independence, all princely states were integrated, some by force, into 17 states within the Indian federation, each with its own legislature. The national government was modeled after the British parliamentary system, with certain features of the U.S. congressional system added. The prime minister, presiding over the Council of Ministers, or cabinet, came from the majority party in the lower house of parliament. India proudly counted itself the most populous democracy in the world and living proof that democracy could thrive despite high illiteracy and poverty. Because of high illiteracy, symbols such as the cow and plow were used on the ballot to represent the different political parties.

INDIA'S CHECKERED PATH TO ECONOMIC DEVELOPMENT

Economically, the Congress Party governments encouraged industrial development and abandoned the Gandhian ideal of traditional village handicrafts. To maximize development, Nehru and his successors opted for a mixed economy, in which the government owned or controlled the basic industries and regulated private enterprise. To develop industry, modernize agriculture, and stimulate trade, Nehru launched his first Five-Year Plan (1951–1956). Such plans were continued by successive governments. About 10 percent of the capital needed for these five-year plans came from foreign aid by the United States, Britain, Japan, the Soviet Union, other nations, and international agencies. Despite India's poverty, it was the 10th largest industrial power in the world, and because of its importance to both sides in the cold war it became the largest single recipient of foreign aid in the post–World War II era. Between 1947 and 1980 India received over $9 billion in U.S. aid.

The Indian government's main goal in economic development was to raise the pitifully low living standard of its citizens, whose annual per capita income in 1951 was $53. Indians had to spend up to 90 percent of their income on food, in contrast to U.S. citizens, who spent 16 percent. The goal of improving the standard of living and literacy rate was constantly frustrated by the alarmingly fast growth of the population, which was in turn caused in part by illiteracy and poverty that perpetuated traditional values, including early marriages and a desire for many sons. Thus, India needed to import large quantities of grain during the first two postindependence decades. Many new laws were passed in the 1950s that gave women equality in marriage, divorce, and inheritance. These reforms, however, did not apply to Muslim women, whose status continued to be defined by Islamic law.

INDIA SEEKS TO LEAD NEUTRALIST BLOC

India chose a foreign policy of nonalignment with either power bloc in the cold war. Nehru hoped that India could thereby become the leader of a bloc of neutral nations and could mediate in disputes between the major powers. Despite Nehru's professed commitment to peace, he went to war against China and Pakistan and sent troops to evict the Portuguese from Goa, their colony on the Indian coast.

KASHMIR: BITTER SOURCE OF CONFLICT BETWEEN INDIA AND PAKISTAN

Pakistan remained India's primary concern. In addition to the bitterness created by the partition, India and Pakistan had problems over the distribution of water from the Indus River for irrigation. Kashmir, however, was the major bone of contention. Both claimed ownership of this princely state with a population that was 80 percent Muslim, but whose Hindu prince opted to join India. In 1947 India and Pakistan fought over Kashmir until the United Nations imposed a cease-fire that in effect partitioned the state. A UN observer force remained there to monitor the cease-fire. Jinnah and his successors demanded a plebiscite, rejected by all Indian governments due to fear that the Muslim majority would vote to join Kashmir with Pakistan. India and Pakistan fought again in 1965 over Kashmir but agreed to a cease-fire mediated by the Soviet Union, with no boundary changes.

Although Nehru encouraged good relations with Communist nations, he had no tolerance for native Communists and once remarked that India had more Communists in prison than any other nation. Nor was he successful in maintaining friendly relations with China, due to border disputes that led to war between the two nations in 1962. The Chinese soundly defeated the Indian army and occupied sections of disputed territory in the Himalayas. However, the Chinese did not press their advantage, withdrew from certain advanced positions, and called for negotiations. The border disputes remained unsettled, and Sino-Indian relations continued to be strained.

Pakistan after Independence

Most of the problems that plagued India also afflicted Pakistan, a wretchedly poor agricultural nation with little industry, many refugees, and one of the fastest-growing populations in the world. Furthermore, West Pakistan was located along the Indus valley, and East Pakistan was situated on the Ganges delta; the two were separated by almost 1,000 miles, with bitterly hostile India in between. The two halves of this artificial state had little in common except Islam. And among the Muslim population, strong divisions existed between those who embraced modern values and the orthodox Islamic masses. The capital city, Islamabad, was in West Pakistan, and West Pakistanis, who formed less than half of the total population, made up 70 percent of the civil service and 80 percent of the officer corps. Most of the foreign aid and export earnings went to develop industries and services in West Pakistan.

EAST AND WEST PAKISTAN FORM AN UNEASY UNION

A year after independence, Jinnah, the father of Pakistan, died of cancer. In 1951 his successor, Liaquat Ali Khan, was assassinated. The deaths of these two leaders left Pakistan with a heritage of political instability. The military took control in 1958, dissolved the parliament, and instituted a system of modified and indirect elections. The military has controlled Pakistan for most of its life, with brief and generally chaotic interludes of elected civilian governments.

POLITICAL INSTABILITY AND OTHER PROBLEMS BESET PAKISTAN

Pakistan's foreign policy was dictated by fear of its bigger neighbor, India, and it maintained an inordinately large military at a huge cost to ensure its safety. Since India had a neutralist foreign policy with a pro-Soviet leaning, Pakistan allied itself with the U.S.-led Central Treaty Organization (CENTO) and received military and economic aid from the United States. After the war between India and China in 1962, Pakistan maintained friendly relations with China.

The First Indochina War: France Is Forced out of Asia

Unlike Great Britain in India and the United States in the Philippines, France had done little to satisfy nationalistic aspirations in Indochina before World War II. Vichy France surrendered Indochina to Japanese occupation peacefully. During World War II Nationalist China aided and gave sanctuary to a broad spectrum of Indochinese nationalists who resisted Japan, among whom the Communists were the most effective and ruthless. On Japan's surrender, the Communist Vietnamese under Ho Chi Minh established their headquarters in Hanoi and declared all Indochina independent from France. France offered only limited reforms. War between the two sides broke out in late 1945.

HO CHI MINH LEADS INDOCHINA'S WAR OF INDEPENDENCE

The struggle for independence centered in Vietnam, with France controlling South Vietnam and Ho's forces controlling the north. Ho used his considerable influence as Vietnam's foremost nationalist leader to assimilate other Vietnamese nationalist movements, while his subordinate, General Vo Nguyen Giap, led a guerrilla war of attrition, avoiding open battles and resorting to terrorism and sabotage. The French could not distinguish the peaceful citizen from the guerrilla fighter, who often worked at an ordinary job by day and took up arms at night. By 1954 French forces in Vietnam, mostly Foreign Legionnaires, plus 200,000 Vietnamese soldiers, numbered 420,000. They confronted a Vietminh (short for the Vietnamese League for National Independence) army almost as large. For every Frenchman killed, perhaps 10 Vietnamese on the opposing side died.

FRANCE DEPARTS FROM INDOCHINA

The climax of the war came at the siege of Dien Bien Phu in 1954, in which 15,000 of France's best troops were hopelessly trapped in a strongly fortified strategic town in northern Vietnam by Vietnamese troops that were heavily strengthened by arms from the Soviet Union and China. France appealed to the United States, which was already shouldering 80 percent of the cost of the war, to intervene with land and air forces. President Eisenhower, who had just extricated the United States from a deadlocked Korean War, refused to become involved. Without direct U.S. aid, Dien Bien Phu fell. By this time, the war-weary French public was ready to quit Vietnam and pressured its government to comply. France had already agreed to the independence of Laos and Cambodia and now departed from Vietnam, which was partitioned into a Communist north and an anti-Communist south.

THE PROBLEMS OF NEW NATIONHOOD IN SOUTHEAST ASIA

During the first decade of independence, the new nations of Southeast Asia faced similar problems of varying degrees of severity. All their economies had been dislocated and devastated by World War II. The Philippines had suffered most; only Warsaw in Poland was more war damaged than its capital city Manila. Burma and Vietnam had also suffered from military campaigns. All the new nations needed outside economic assistance, but the source and amount of that aid were related to the foreign policies of the newly independent nations and how they lined up in the cold war. For example, the United States gave the Philippines massive aid, from a sense of responsibility for the islands' colonial past and because its government was an ally and accepted U.S. military bases.

Great Britain remained in Malaya until 1960 to clean up the remnants of rebel Communist guerrillas, even though Malaya had become independent in 1957. Great Britain, Australia, and New Zealand also gave aid to Malaya and to other former British colonies in Asia. Only Burma opted out of the Commonwealth at independence and took a strictly neutralist and isolationist stand in international affairs, rejecting all foreign economic aid. North Vietnam, on the other hand, received significant military and economic aid from the Soviet Union and China in its struggle against France.

The task of running a government was difficult for all the newly independent nations. Every one of them had ethnic or religious minorities, many of whom were disaffected from the government, and some revolted in the hope of establishing their own nations. Thus the Muslims of Mindanao Island revolted and waged civil war against the government of the Philippines, as did the non-Burmese hill tribes against the Burmese government.

Many nations persecuted their ethnic minorities—for example, the Indian minority in Burma and the Chinese minority in Indonesia. Even in Malaysia, where relative harmony existed among the three racial groups—Malays, Chinese, and Indians—there were sporadic anti-Chinese riots. Political inexperience, poverty, and traditional attitudes also resulted in rampant corruption, which occurred regardless of the system of government and was as notorious in democratic Philippines as it was in authoritarian Indonesia. While Malaysia and the Philippines continued with the democratic experiment, Burma's elected government was soon replaced by the military, and Indonesia became a "guided democracy" under dictator Sukarno.

Each Southeast Asian nation was also faced with severe social problems closely linked with economic ones. In all nations a wide gulf divided the rich from the poor, but the coming of independence unleashed energies that demanded social reforms, such as greater equality for women, and economic improvements, such as land redistribution, that the new governments could not or would not implement. In Muslim nations the demands for women's rights collided with the Muslim fundamentalists' quest for return to traditional roles for women. Meanwhile, improvements in medicine and public health resulted in an inexorable population increase that wiped out most economic gains.

In North Vietnam, the problem of economic disparity was tackled by forced land reform accompanied by the killing and jailing of former landlords. In non-Communist Asian nations, social and economic inequities made the Communist call for revolution attractive to some. In the Philippines, where no reform took place, the desire of poor peasants for land caused a Communist-led uprising known as the Huk Rebellion. Although largely put down by 1954, the insurgency flared up sporadically because the conditions that caused it were never adequately remedied (see Chapter 28).

THE COLD WAR IN ASIA

After World War II Asia became one of the theaters of the cold war. When the Communists emerged victorious in the Chinese civil war in 1949, President Truman initially did not consider the People's Republic of China a threat to U.S. interests in Asia; he appeared resigned to its conquest of Taiwan and considered recognizing it as the government of China. The outbreak of the Korean War in 1950 and Chinese participation in the war quickly altered U.S. perceptions of the goal of the Communist bloc in Asia. Later, as Communist insurgency movements erupted in the Philippines, Malaya, and Burma and threatened their newly independent and unstable governments, the United States became increasingly concerned over the spread of communism across the Asian continent, as it had over similar Communist expansion in Europe. These fears strengthened U.S. resolve to contain the spread of communism on both continents.

BIOGRAPHY

Inspiration from the West

It must be remembered that the great ambition which led me to the mission school was to learn English, and English only. This ambition I quickly achieved, but I soon discovered I was learning something of far greater importance than the English language. I was imbibing ideas of political equality and liberty. Those who know anything about the political oppression to which the masses of the Korean people were subject can imagine what a revolution took place in the heart of a young Korean Yangban [upper-class person] when he learned for the first time that people in Christian lands were protected against the tyranny of rulers. I said to myself, "It would be a great blessing to my downtrodden fellow men if only we could adopt such a political principle." . . .

Let us gather all our powers and make our nation like the nations of wealthy, powerful, and civilized people. Keep independence in your own hearts. The most important part is to cast out hopelessness. We must become diligent workers. Our own individual dedication is the seed from which will grow the harvest of a sound nation.*

. . .

Syngman Rhee (1875–1965) was born into an aristocratic Korean family. He became a student activist when studying in a missionary school and he founded the Independence Club, which opposed the government's submissive policy toward Japan and advocated modernization; for this he was imprisoned from 1897 to 1904. This passage comes from a book written by Rhee during the years he spent in prison. He became a lifelong crusader against Japanese rule over Korea and was the first president of independent South Korea after World War II. As president, he emphasized nationalism rather than democracy and ruled as a strongman. His government was overthrown as a result of student riots in 1960.

*From Syngman Rhee: The Man behind the Myth by Robert T. Oliver. (Quoted from Syngman Rhee: The Spirit of Independence.) Copyright © 1954 by Dodd, Mead, and Company. Reprinted by permission.

The Korean War and Its Aftermath

Allied leaders had agreed at wartime summit conferences to restore an independent Korea but had worked out no details for implementing their plan. When the Soviet Union declared war on Japan, Soviet troops immediately invaded Korea. As the Soviet Union and the United States had agreed, their representatives accepted the Japanese surrender north and south of the 38th parallel, respectively. As it turned out, they created two nations.

KOREA IS PARTITIONED IN 1945

In the north, the Soviet Union established a Communist state headed by a young Korean Communist named Kim Il Sung. Soviet advisers were important to both the North Korean army and government. One million North Koreans fled to the south. In the south, the United States hoped to help establish a democratic government with popular representative institutions, but it had no definite blueprints to realize its goals. It allowed Koreans exiled in Western countries to return. One

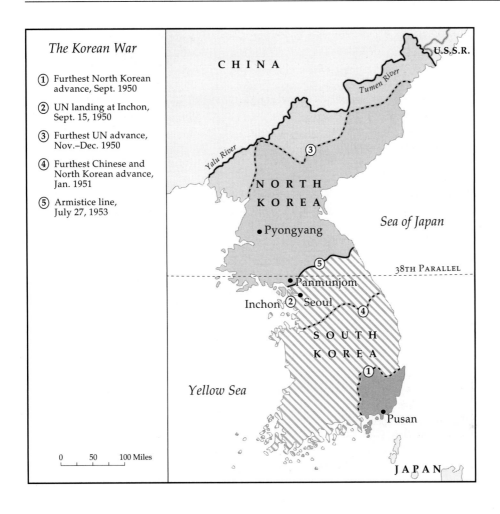

The Korean War

① Furthest North Korean advance, Sept. 1950

② UN landing at Inchon, Sept. 15, 1950

③ Furthest UN advance, Nov.–Dec. 1950

④ Furthest Chinese and North Korean advance, Jan. 1951

⑤ Armistice line, July 27, 1953

CHINA

U.S.S.R.

Tumen River

Yalu River

③

NORTH KOREA

• Pyongyang

Sea of Japan

⑤

• Panmunjom

Inchon ② • Seoul

38TH PARALLEL

④

SOUTH KOREA

①

Yellow Sea

• Pusan

0   50   100 Miles

JAPAN

was 70-year-old Syngman Rhee, a veteran opponent of Japanese imperialism, who organized an authoritarian anti-Communist government in South Korea and became its president.

In 1947 the United States placed the Korean problem before the United Nations, which appointed a commission to supervise elections. Rhee's party won the elections in South Korea in 1948 and declared the establishment of the Republic of Korea, after which the United States withdrew its military forces. Elections held in North Korea without the presence of the UN election commission resulted in the establishment of a Soviet-style Communist state, the Korean Democratic People's Republic. Soviet troops withdrew from North Korea but left in place a well-trained, well-equipped North Korean military force.

Both Korean governments were dedicated to unification, each on its own terms. On June 25, 1950, with the approval of the Soviet Union and China, North Korea launched a surprise attack on South Korea. In the months before the attack, the U.S.

THE KOREAN WAR HEATS UP COLD WAR IN ASIA

UNITED STATES LEADS UN FORCES TO DEFEND SOUTH KOREA

government had sent confusing signals whether it would defend South Korea. Once the North attacked, President Truman, mindful of the lesson of appeasement of the 1930s in China and Europe—that unchecked aggression invited more of the same— decided to commit U.S. troops for the defense of South Korea against North Korean aggression. Truman also termed Korea "the Greece of the Far East," where the United States must contain Communist expansion. In deciding to defend South Korea, Truman also was concerned about the future U.S. role in Asia and the security of Japan, Okinawa, and the Philippines. He secured the support of the United Nations Security Council, which condemned North Korea for aggression against another sovereign state and called on member states to contribute military units to collectively repel the aggressors. The Soviet delegate, who had been boycotting the Security Council for six months to protest the presence of Nationalist China, was not there to cast his veto.

South Korea contributed about one-half of the ground forces of the United Nations command in a war formally termed a "police action." The United States contributed the navy, air force, and two-fifths of the army; the remainder came from 14 nations, including Great Britain, several Commonwealth countries, Turkey, and others.

United Nations Commander in Chief General Douglas MacArthur turned the tide of the Korean War in a brilliant maneuver by landing at Inchon in the rear of the North Korean forces. He then drove the North Koreans out of South Korea and through North Korea toward the Chinese border. As the war changed from one of repelling aggression to one of conquering North Korea, cold war tensions rose high. China became anxious as UN troops approached its border, partly because the remnants of the North Korean air force were still attacking UN troops from Chinese air bases.

CHINA HELPS NORTH KOREA

Stalin had hoped to weaken present U.S. and future Japanese power in Asia by adding South Korea to the Soviet bloc. With the impending collapse of North Korea and fearful that open intervention by Soviet troops would have dangerous consequences, Stalin urged China to save North Korea. It was also in China's interest to have a communist North Korea as a buffer. In October 1950, more than 1 million Chinese troops, called "volunteers," crossed into Korea and by December were driving UN forces back into South Korea. Contingents of the Soviet air force, masquerading as North Korean units, engaged UN forces in the air war. The front stabilized in 1951 close to the 38th parallel, the original boundary between the two Koreas. Armistice talks began in July 1951 but stalled because Stalin wanted to mire the United States in a stalemated war and because a prolonged war would deepen China's dependence on Soviet aid. The armistice was finally signed in 1953 after Stalin's death and the election of Dwight Eisenhower as president of the United States.

STALEMATE IN KOREAN WAR

During the retreat from North Korea, and as the war settled into a stalemate, MacArthur and his military and civilian supporters pressed the military high command to employ Nationalist Chinese troops and to use U.S. air and naval power, including nuclear weapons if necessary, to attack and defeat China. President Truman and his civilian and military advisers, pressured by nervous European allies, rejected these proposals because they risked bogging down the United States in a major war against China that might widen into a conflict with the Soviet Union. When MacArthur began to challenge Truman's decision publicly, the president relieved him of his command for insubordination.

President Syngman Rhee of South Korea thanks General Douglas MacArthur, commander in chief of UN forces, after the liberation of Seoul, capital of South Korea, from North Korean invaders in October 1950.

The stalemated war dragged on until the armistice was signed in 1953. An estimated 4 million people, mostly Korean civilians, died. The United States suffered 142,000 casualties, including over 36,000 in combat dead; South Korean casualties were estimated at 1.3 million, while combined North Korean and Chinese killed and wounded came to an estimated 2 million. Many Americans were indignant over the dismissal of MacArthur and were frustrated that the United States had not clearly won the Korean War. These two issues were added to the already acrimonious political debate in the United States over responsibility for the Communist victory in China.

To clarify its intentions and instill confidence among anti-Communist Asian nations, the United States concluded a mutual defense treaty with South Korea in 1954 and continued to station troops there. The United States also modernized and strengthened the South Korean armed forces and aided in the rebuilding of the terribly devastated land. To President Rhee's government fell the responsibility of postwar reconstruction. Autocratically inclined and still bitter over the brutal Japanese occupation, he put nationalism ahead of democracy in a state threatened by invasion and Communist subversion and used strong-arm tactics to bring dissidents into line. Rhee was toppled in 1960 by student demonstrations, but because the faction-ridden political parties were unable to produce unified leadership, the army seized power in 1961. Although civilian rule was ostensibly restored in 1963, the elections returned a

AN ARMISTICE ENDS HOSTILITIES IN KOREA

SOUTH KOREA PROGRESSES UNDER U.S. PROTECTION

general to the presidency, and the military continued to play a leading role in politics. The generals inaugurated a five-year plan for stimulating capitalist economic development. Successive economic plans, fueled in part by U.S. economic aid and investments, and after 1965 by Japanese investments, put South Korea on the road to prosperity.

COMMUNISM HOLDS TIGHT GRIP OVER NORTH KOREA

Meanwhile, North Korea had developed into one of the purest examples of a monocracy (government by one man); Kim Il Sung concentrated in himself supreme power over the Korean Workers' Party (Communist), the armed forces, and the government and built up a cult of personality that rivaled Stalin's in the Soviet Union and Mao's in China. North Korea received large amounts of Soviet and Chinese aid and, until 1958, the continued protection of Chinese troops. North Korea had a smaller population than South Korea but greater natural resources and more industries built by Japan during its colonial occupation. Its Marxist model economic buildup was accomplished under tight discipline imposed by Kim's government. By the late 1960s, however, South Korea had forged ahead of North Korea.

The truce between the two Koreas was punctuated by incidents of sabotage, infiltration, and armed provocation by North Korea, along one of the most tightly guarded and tense borders in the world. Since provocations from North Korea continued, the UN command in South Korea remained, and the United States continued to maintain over 40,000 military personnel south of the Demilitarized Zone (DMZ). The governments of both Koreas remained committed to eventual reunification of the peninsula, and Kim ruled North Korea until he died in 1994.

U.S. Anti-Communist Policies in Asia during the 1950s

U.S. CONTAINMENT POLICY AGAINST COMMUNISM IN ASIA

By the early 1950s the United States was faced with the rapid spread of communism in Asia. Mao Zedong had come to power in China in 1949. Chinese intervention in the Korean War had helped save North Korea. Communist-led guerrilla insurgents were active in several newly independent nations of Southeast Asia, and Ho Chi Minh's guerrillas were getting the upper hand in Indochina. Some U.S. leaders believed that Stalin had a master scheme to make the world Communist, which he was now putting into effect in Asia with the aid of China. These events led many Americans to feel indignant over "losing" China and "not winning" in Korea.

Under these circumstances, U.S. leaders expanded to Asia the containment doctrine that the United States had first applied to Europe in the late 1940s. It supplied military and economic aid to friendly anti-Communist governments in Asia. However, the United States failed to take into account the force of nationalism and anticolonialism that dominated politics in most newly independent Asian nations, which were beset by social upheavals stemming from peasant demands for land ownership and other reforms. Since communism promised fundamental social and economic reforms, many Asians were attracted to local Communist movements. Thus, in Asia, as in Latin America, the United States often became allied with governments that opposed reform. These alliances would bring trouble in the decades to come.

Another goal of containment was to neutralize China. The Korean War had heightened mutual hostilities between the United States and China. The United States refused to recognize Communist China and used its veto and other means to block

Chinese admission to the United Nations. To prevent a Chinese conquest of Taiwan (seat of the Nationalist government since 1949), it deployed the Seventh Fleet to patrol the Taiwan Strait and concluded a mutual defense treaty with Nationalist China.

To contain the Soviet Union and China, the United States made several alliances with anti-Communist governments in the region. Bilateral mutual defense treaties were concluded with Japan, the Philippines, South Korea, and the Republic of China on Taiwan (hereafter, Taiwan). They were reinforced by multilateral treaties: the South East Asia Treaty Organization (SEATO), established in 1954, which tied Great Britain, France, Australia, New Zealand, Thailand, and the Philippines to a collective defense of the region, and the ANZUS treaty that put Australia and New Zealand under U.S. military protection and gave the United States access to military bases in Australasia. When SEATO and other Asian bases were linked with U.S. bases in Pakistan (under CENTO) and with NATO, U.S.-led alliances had succeeded in ringing the Communist bloc. (The U.S. attempt to halt the spread of communism in Indochina will be taken up in Chapter 28.)

UNITED STATES HEADS MANY ALLIANCES IN ASIA AND THE PACIFIC REGION

Both the Chinese Communist and Nationalist governments maintained that there was only one government of China. The Communists, anxious to complete their victory, sought to destroy the Nationalists on Taiwan. In 1955 and 1958, China bombarded the tiny Nationalist-held offshore islands of Quemoy and Matsu, seemingly as a prelude to an assault on their 100,000 defenders. By treaty the United States was obliged to supply the Nationalist garrisons; thus, conflict between the United States and China became a distinct possibility. The United States stood firm in its commitment to support the Nationalists and threatened to use nuclear weapons if the Communists attempted to invade Taiwan, but it also ordered its supply boats to respect Chinese territorial waters by staying outside the three-mile limit. After the attempt to seize the islands had obviously failed, China ordered its artillery to fire only on alternate days, thus allowing U.S. supply ships to reach the islands. Hostilities were finally reduced to both sides firing propaganda leaflets. The United States also pressured Chiang Kai-shek to renounce any intentions of attacking the mainland. Thus, the tensions over the Taiwan Strait gradually subsided.

CRISIS IN THE TAIWAN STRAIT

SUMMARY

Between 1945 and 1952 the United States occupied and remade Japan. War crime trials punished a small number of Japanese leaders responsible for waging aggressive war and for other crimes. The emperor was retained to facilitate reforms but lost his previous divine status. Thoroughgoing reforms, including political rights for women, a new democratic constitution that forbade waging war, land redistribution, and educational and economic liberalization, affected every aspect of Japanese society. U.S. aid prevented hunger in the difficult immediate postwar years and financed the initial rebuilding of the economy. The Eugenics Protection Law forestalled a population explosion so that the Japanese could enjoy the fruits of their labors with a rising standard of living. These reforms laid the foundations for an economic miracle.

After suffering eight years of Japanese invasion, China was immediately engulfed in civil war after the victory against Japan. The Chinese Communists, despite preventive efforts by the United States, defeated the demoralized Nationalist government, which fled to Taiwan. After 1949 Mao Zedong and other Communist leaders transformed the world's most populous nation into a totalitarian Communist state, the People's Republic of China, and placed it firmly in the socialist camp as an ally of the Soviet Union. It aided North Korea with a million soldiers in the Korean War and gave material and training aid to the Vietnamese Communists, but its economic backwardness and the domestic turmoil that Mao created with the Great Leap Forward prevented it from playing a larger role in the cold war in Asia.

Between 1945 and 1960 most of the colonies in Asia gained independence. Great Britain and the United States led the way and made peaceful and orderly transfers of power. They retained, for the most part, the goodwill of their former colonies. Most former British colonies remained in the Commonwealth, while the Philippines became an ally of the United States. France and the Netherlands were less attuned to a changing world and withdrew from Asia only when they had no other options.

In many nations, independence brought to the forefront ancient regional disputes and internal problems that had been submerged and lain dormant during colonial rule. Thus, Hindus and Muslims in India resurrected ancient rivalries that predated British control. Several countries almost immediately became embroiled in civil wars or insurrections by ethnic or religious minorities. Economic and social problems plagued most of the new nations and often defied both foreign aid and local efforts to find solutions, even when there was a will to do so. Ancient and modern local rivalries and nationalist ambitions became entwined with cold war politics, embroiling the new nations in alliances or leading them to policies of nonalignment.

As the leader of the non-Communist world, the United States became deeply involved in combating the spread of communism in Asia. American forces were dispatched to Korea to prevent the Communist conquest of South Korea. On the other side, China entered the war to prevent the U.S. conquest of North Korea. The armistice that ended the fighting reflected a stalemate that continued unabated into the twenty-first century. The United States also protected the Nationalist government on Taiwan from invasion by China; sent aid to several non-Communist Southeast Asian nations to combat Communist guerrillas; and created formal military alliances, collectively and individually, with nations of the area. When victorious Communist-dominated forces threatened to overrun all Vietnam and wrest it from war-weary France, the United States and other great powers intervened to partition the former colony and restrict the Communists to the northern half. Thus, on two major and several minor occasions, the cold war in Asia erupted into hot wars and left a legacy of three divided lands.

SUGGESTED SOURCES

Ahmed, Akbar. *Jinnah, Pakistan, and Islamic Identity.* 1997. A good evaluation of the father of Pakistan.*

Becker, Jasper. *Hungry Ghosts: Mao's Secret Famine.* 1996. Details the horrendous Mao-inflicted catastrophe, the Great Leap Forward.*

Cheek, Timothy. *Mao Zedong and China's Revolution: A Brief History with Documents.* 2002. A good combination of Mao's biography with a history of China during his time.*

Collins, Larry, and Dominique Lapierre. *Freedom at Midnight*. 1980. A gripping account of the last stages of India's struggle for independence.*

Dower, John W. *Embracing Defeat: Japan in the Wake of World War II*. 1999. Winner of the Pulitzer Prize, this book is acclaimed as the best on postwar Japan.*

Duiker, William J. *Ho Chi Minh*. 2000. Well-researched, informative book on an enigmatic but tremendously important Vietnamese leader.

French, Patrick. *Liberty or Death: India's Journey to Independence and Division*. 1998. A riveting account based on recently declassified material.*

Hinckley, Michael. *The Korean War: The West Confronts Communism*. 2000. Authoritative account by a military historian.*

Li, Zhisui. *The Private Life of Chairman Mao*. 1994. Mao's personal physician of over two decades reveals the intrigues and corruption among China's top leaders.*

Liang, Heng, and Judy Shapiro. *Son of the Revolution*. 1983. A poignant autobiography about growing up in Mao's China.*

Lord Mountbatten: The Last Viceroy. 1984. A TV series that dramatizes the people and events preceding the independence of India and Pakistan.

Mehta, Ved. *A Family Affair: India under Three Prime Ministers*. 1982. A critical study of the politics and personalities of Indian leadership.

Moore, Ray A., and Donald L. Robinson. *Partners for Democracy: Crafting the New Japanese State under MacArthur*. 2002. Study of a successful partnership.*

Reed, Anthony, and David Fisher. *The Proudest Day: India's Long Road to Independence*. 1997. Compelling account of the events that led to the birth of India and Pakistan.*

Russ, Martin. *The Last Parallel*. 1959. A U.S. Marine's firsthand account of fighting in Korea.*

Singh, Anita Inder. *The Origins of the Partition of India, 1936–1947*. 1987. A good book on problems of decolonization and nationalism.

Tharoor, Shashi. *Nehru, the Invention of India*. 2003. An informative biography.

Thornton, Richard C. *Odd Man Out: Truman, Stalin, Mao and the Origins of the Korean War*. 2000. Powerfully written reassessment of a titanic cold war struggle.*

Westad, Odd Arne, ed. *Brothers in Arms: The Rise and Fall of the Sino-Soviet Alliance, 1945–1965*. 1998. Russian, Chinese, and U.S. experts trace the relations between the two Communist powers and the United States.

Wu, Harry, with George Vecsey. *Troublemaker: One Man's Crusade against China's Cruelty*. 1996. The book details the poignant personal experiences of a Chinese dissident.

WEB SOURCES

www.indiana.edu/~japan/Digests/const-2.htm. Site provides a recent scholarly essay on the Japanese Constitution.

www.fordham.edu/halsall/eastasia/eastasiasbook.html. Site provides numerous links to materials on postwar China, Japan, and Korea, including some relating to the Korean War.

www.fordham.edu/halsall/india/indiasbook.html. See links under Gandhi, India since independence, and others.

* Paperback available.

10 pgs

☖African Struggles
for Independence

After World War II Africa moved from a collection of colonies to a diverse group of independent states. As in Asia, most European colonial nations, their strength eroded by two world wars, no longer had the military or economic power or even the will to hold on to their empires in the face of mounting nationalist pressure. In Africa, nationalist struggles for independence were usually impeded or undercut by the complex mosaic of differing ethnic, linguistic, and religious communities, which made unification difficult. Frequently, as in West Africa, differing ethnic and religious groups had been grouped together under one imperial power. The artificial national boundaries drawn by the European powers, often without regard to local populations, became the borders of newly emerging nation-states whose fragile governments then had to deal with the problems of unification and cooperation among heterogeneous populations. For example, in Nigeria and the Sudan, two of the largest African nations, regional differences between the largely Islamic north and Christian or animist south caused resentment, threatened to destroy the federated structure of the republic, and sometimes led to civil wars.

During the years of imperial domination rapid industrialization, urbanization, and increased contact with Western technology and culture caused radical alterations in the traditional patterns of African society; these changes accelerated the various movements toward independence. Members of most African nationalist movements came from diverse social and economic groups, including professionals such as lawyers, doctors, and teachers; urban workers; and peasant farmers. Although these groups had different economic goals, they were unified by their common desire for independence and greater roles in the political and economic sectors of their nations.

AFRICAN NATIONS GAIN INDEPENDENCE

As the peoples of Africa loudly demanded control over their own political and economic destinies, it became evident that the small number of Europeans living in northern and eastern Africa could not hold back the forces favoring national self-determination. By 1963 virtually all of the northern two-thirds of Africa was independent. In southern Africa, however, white minorities still clung to power (see Chapter 30).

The struggle for independence took different forms throughout Africa. In some cases, as in Tunisia, Morocco, and Uganda, the imperial powers granted independence under predetermined conditions. In Libya the United Nations played a key role in establishing an independent political entity. In these instances, Africans secured independence with a minimum of bloodshed. In other areas, where there were well-entrenched European white settlers or where the imperial powers were determined to maintain

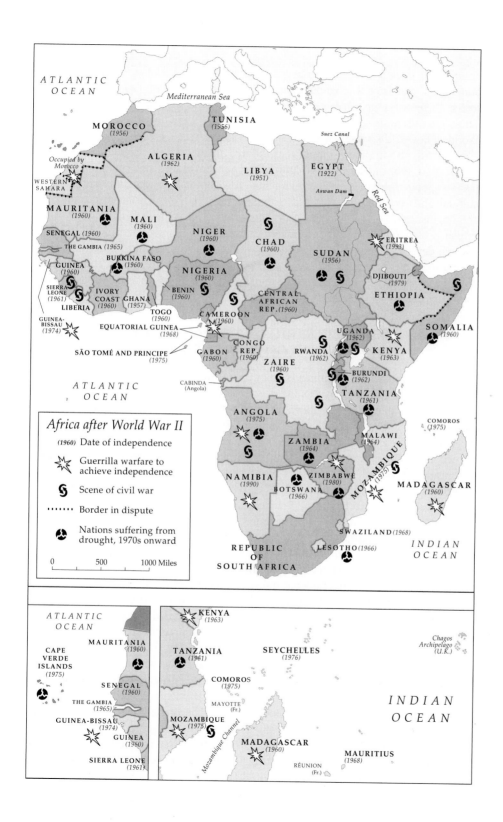

Africa after World War II

(1960) Date of independence

✸ Guerrilla warfare to achieve independence

☢ Scene of civil war

•••••• Border in dispute

☣ Nations suffering from drought, 1970s onward

0   500   1000 Miles

ATLANTIC OCEAN

Mediterranean Sea

MOROCCO *(1956)*

TUNISIA *(1956)*

ALGERIA *(1962)*

LIBYA *(1951)*

EGYPT *(1922)*

Suez Canal

Aswan Dam

Red Sea

Occupied by Morocco

WESTERN SAHARA

MAURITANIA *(1960)*

MALI *(1960)*

NIGER *(1960)*

CHAD *(1960)*

SUDAN *(1956)*

ERITREA *(1993)*

SENEGAL *(1960)*

THE GAMBIA *(1965)*

GUINEA *(1960)*

BURKINA FASO *(1960)*

NIGERIA *(1960)*

BENIN *(1960)*

SIERRA LEONE *(1961)*

IVORY COAST *(1960)*

GHANA *(1957)*

LIBERIA

TOGO *(1960)*

CAMEROON *(1960)*

CENTRAL AFRICAN REP. *(1960)*

DJIBOUTI *(1979)*

ETHIOPIA

SOMALIA *(1960)*

GUINEA-BISSAU *(1974)*

EQUATORIAL GUINEA *(1968)*

SÃO TOMÉ AND PRINCIPE *(1975)*

GABON *(1960)*

CONGO REP. *(1960)*

ZAIRE *(1960)*

UGANDA *(1962)*

RWANDA *(1962)*

KENYA *(1963)*

BURUNDI *(1962)*

TANZANIA *(1961)*

CABINDA *(Angola)*

ATLANTIC OCEAN

ANGOLA *(1975)*

ZAMBIA *(1964)*

MALAWI *(1964)*

MOZAMBIQUE *(1975)*

COMOROS *(1975)*

MADAGASCAR *(1960)*

NAMIBIA *(1990)*

ZIMBABWE *(1980)*

BOTSWANA *(1966)*

SWAZILAND *(1968)*

LESOTHO *(1966)*

REPUBLIC OF SOUTH AFRICA

INDIAN OCEAN

ATLANTIC OCEAN

CAPE VERDE ISLANDS *(1975)*

MAURITANIA *(1960)*

SENEGAL *(1960)*

THE GAMBIA *(1965)*

GUINEA-BISSAU *(1974)*

GUINEA *(1960)*

SIERRA LEONE *(1961)*

KENYA *(1963)*

TANZANIA *(1961)*

COMOROS *(1975)*

MAYOTTE *(Fr.)*

MOZAMBIQUE *(1975)*

Mozambique Channel

MADAGASCAR *(1960)*

SEYCHELLES *(1976)*

Chagos Archipelago *(U.K.)*

INDIAN OCEAN

RÉUNION *(Fr.)*

MAURITIUS *(1968)*

371

control, the struggles for independence were protracted and often violent. In Algeria and Kenya, and later throughout much of southern Africa, African nationalists were forced to resort to guerrilla warfare and armed attacks against the imperial powers. These guerrilla wars, or "wars of liberation," as they were often known in the Third World, followed the same pattern as that in Vietnam (see Chapter 28).

CONTRASTING FRENCH AND BELGIAN POLICIES

Just as the imperial powers had differed in their approaches to their African empires, so, too, did they adopt contrasting policies toward the newly independent nations. Some, in particular France, attempted with notable success to maintain close cultural and economic ties. Indeed, former French colonies remained economically and linguistically tied to France decades after independence had been secured. Former British possessions tended to adopt more independent approaches to economic and cultural development. Others, most notably Belgium in the Congo, abdicated responsibility for their former holdings. A selective look around the African continent will reveal in more detail how most of the colonies finally secured independence and how the various European imperial powers approached their former colonies.

NORTH AFRICA: INDEPENDENCE THROUGH NEGOTIATIONS AND WAR

WAR IN ALGERIA

In North Africa nationalist sentiments had gained enormous popular support by the end of World War II. Libya secured its independence under King Idris through the auspices of the United Nations. The traditional monarchy of King Idris was overthrown by a military coup led by Muammar al-Gadhafi in 1969. By the end of the 1970s, huge petroleum revenues transformed Libya from one of Africa's poorest nations into one of its richest.

Neither Tunisia nor Morocco was considered an integral part of France, and few Europeans had settled in either country; consequently, France was much more willing to grant these colonies independence than neighboring Algeria. In the face of a groundswell for national liberation, France in 1956, after limited struggles, granted independence to Tunisia under Habib Bourguiba and to Morocco under King Mohammad V. Both Bourguiba and Hassan II, Mohammad's son, continued to rule into the 1980s.

In contrast, in order to obtain their independence, the Algerians, led by the National Liberation Front (FLN), fought a bloody war (1954–1962) against the French, who were unwilling to give up what the government had for a century considered an integral part of France. The French *colons,* who were about 10 percent of the Algerian population, were particularly vociferous and determined to keep Algeria as part of France. They even went so far as to establish their own secret army to fight the Algerians and those French who supported independence. The FLN used attacks on urban centers populated by the *colons* and other guerrilla warfare tactics similar to those employed in Vietnam; these included hit-and-run tactics and what has been called the "bombs in a basket" approach, whereby women and children would carry out attacks on the *colons* and the French military. The French retaliated by bombing villages, removing families from the countryside, and in some instances torturing Algerian suspects. General de Gaulle, who came to power in France in 1958, concluded that France could not win the struggle and should negotiate a settlement. After protracted negotiations, continued violence within Algeria, and assassination attempts on de Gaulle, Algeria finally achieved independence in 1962. After independence most of the *colons* left Algeria and settled in France or Spain. The Algerian war cost a million Algerian deaths and thousands of French casualties. In many ways, it divided French society much as the Vietnam War later divided U.S. society.

ECONOMIC PROBLEMS

Following independence, Algeria was in the vanguard of the revolutionary Arab states, but it later established friendlier relations with the United States. Although Algeria had substantial revenues from its petroleum resources, it also faced enormous economic problems. Unemployment was high among its youth, who, as in many of the newly independent nations, formed a large sector of the total population. All of France's former North African imperial holdings retained close economic ties with the former imperial power, with the majority of their imports and exports coming from and going to France. By the 1970s Algeria had become a leader of the Third World, and it often played a key role in mediating disputes between Third World nations and Western powers.

DECOLONIZATION IN WEST AFRICA

As indicated previously, western Africa, particularly the Gold Coast (Ghana), had been in the forefront of African national movements. In 1949 Kwame Nkrumah formed his Convention People's Party (CPP) to demand "self-government now." Strikes and boycotts, accompanied by some violence, were directed against the British administration. As a result, Nkrumah was imprisoned, but internal unrest persisted.

INDEPENDENCE FOR GHANA

Great Britain was willing to give both Ghana and Nigeria independence because (1) there were few or no white settlers in either country and (2) the British hoped that the trained civil elite would retain close economic and political ties with the former imperial power. Thus, in 1957 the British agreed to grant Ghana independence under the leadership of Nkrumah; in the view of many African nationalists, Ghana's independence was the first step toward independence for all of black Africa, but by 1960 the Ghanaian constitution had become authoritarian. Along with seeking further economic and educational development within Ghana, Nkrumah also portrayed himself as the leader of the Pan-African movement. As a result he incurred the enmity of rival African leaders and, more important, alienated other Ghanaians who were more concerned with economic development. Consequently, Nkrumah was overthrown by a military junta in 1966. Attempts to return Ghana to stable civilian government met with varying degrees of success, and as in so many newly independent nations in the twentieth century, the army remained an important force. As a result of poor management and political instability, Ghana was plagued with economic problems, smuggling, and profiteering.

In Nigeria, one of the largest and most populous African nations, the British attempted to solve the problem of ethnic and cultural heterogeneity by forming a federated system that, in theory at least, was to give full local rights to the three main ethnic groupings within the nation. However, riots in 1953 demonstrated the major differences between the predominantly Muslim north and the predominantly Christian Igbos in the southeast. Attempting to reconcile these differences, the British declared

After independence, Ghanaians proudly wore clothes imprinted with pictures of their nationalist leader, Nkrumah.

Nigeria an independent nation in 1960. The carefully prepared constitution called for a federated nation, but the basic ethnic hostilities remained.

BIAFRAN CIVIL WAR   In 1967 the Igbos attempted to secede and to establish their own nation, which they called Biafra. The civil war that followed was characterized by bloody violence and extreme hardship; thousands died of starvation. The war dragged on until 1970, when war-weary and often starving Biafrans surrendered and the military regime of Colonel Yakubu Gowon reunited the nation. The Nigeria case demonstrated that African leaders recognized the difficulties posed by national boundaries that often grouped together under one government different and sometimes antagonistic ethnic, linguistic, or religious communities. However, they also realized that redrawing national borders could create even more complex and potentially violent problems. As a result, the borders generally drawn by the Western imperial powers continued as the borders of the independent nation-states.

In contrast to the British approach, the French tried to retain a close union with their West African empire. As early as 1944, General de Gaulle had promised a French union that would respect indigenous societies while creating a more highly centralized version of the British Commonwealth. However, de Gaulle's attempt to keep some degree of French control over its empire failed to fulfill the national aspirations of West Africans.

B I O G R A P H Y

Nigerian Women and Unions Demand Change

The meetings of the women . . . became galvanized by a new sense of urgency. Leaflets were printed almost every other day on one subject or the other.

Several women had spoken of their experience with the Tax Officers. The women's original resolution had been turned down, it seemed, or simply ignored. At every meeting a report was given about the course of the No More Taxation demand. It was hardly necessary; reality was manifested in their continuing harassment on the roads, in the markets, in their petty businesses. These were recounted in great detail, to cries of indignation. New texts were drafted. New delegations were chosen. The District Officer was bombarded with petitions, demands and threats. Mrs. Kuti had travelled to Lagos countless times and toured the country to gain support for the women's demands. At some point, much later, we heard of the formation of the Nigerian Women's Union. The movement . . . begun over cups of tea and sandwiches to resolve the problem of newlyweds who lacked the necessary social graces, was becoming popular and nation-wide. And it became all tangled up in the move to put an end to the rule of white men in the country. . . .

Some young, radical nationalists were being gaoled for sedition, and sedition had become equivalent to demanding that the white man leave us to rule ourselves. New names came more and more to the fore.

A new grouping was preparing to visit England. . . . They would demand, not just higher institutions for all the colonial countries, but an end to the white man's rule. Their people were going around the whole country to collect money for this purpose. The Women's Union threw its forces behind the efforts. Concerts were held. We surrendered our pocket monies, knowing somehow that even our half-pennies mattered in the great cause.*

. . .

In his account of growing up during the years of mounting nationalist demands for independence, the Nigerian writer Wole Soyinka describes the optimism and nationwide support the independence movement in the 1940s and 1950s enjoyed from all levels of society. In Nigeria women were often traders and merchants, and, as indicated here, they were in the forefront of the struggle for economic and political changes. Nigerian unions and students also played particularly important roles in the nationalist struggle. After independence was achieved in 1960, Soyinka became an outspoken critic of the military officers who took control of the nation (see Chapter 32). Soyinka was awarded the Nobel Prize for Literature in 1986, but in spite of his international renown he was forced into exile during much of the 1990s.

In spite of the considerable financial benefits they received from the French government, nationalists continued to press for independence. After World War II, Felix Houphouet-Boigny played the leading role in forming a political alliance to fight for the independence of the Ivory Coast. Joined by nationalists from other French colonies in West Africa, the move triggered a series of violent confrontations. When de Gaulle

**IVORY COAST
AND FRANCE**

returned to power in 1958, he proposed holding a referendum whereby West African nations could choose either to participate as autonomous units within a French union or to achieve complete independence. In the 1958 referendum only Guinea, led by Ahmed Sékou Touré, voted for complete political and economic separation from France. Sékou Touré ruled Guinea until his death in 1984; subsequently, as in most of West Africa, military officers took over the government but failed to restore civil liberties or to revive the nation's faltering economy.

By 1960, France had granted the rest of its West African colonies full independence. Some, such as Senegal under the noted poet Léopold Senghor, proved remarkably stable. In the Ivory Coast, one of the most prosperous West African nations, a lively artistic heritage, particularly in the fields of ceramics, weaving, and metalsmithing, was continued and expanded. Other West African nations were plagued by a spiral of military coups and countercoups. Indeed, military dictatorships became the predominant political force in most of West Africa and in some ways reflected traditional African respect for the "big man." As Yukubu Gowan, the military president of Nigeria, emphasized, "The trouble with military rule is that every colonel or general is soon full of ambition. The navy takes over today and the army tomorrow." Throughout Africa, military regimes were often able to put down regional disputes and tribal conflicts, but the costs were high. Many smaller ethnic groups were largely decimated by military leaders representing larger or more powerful forces. Military rule also meant that disproportionate amounts of already strained budgets were spent on armaments, high salaries for officers, and perks for the military.

CLOSE TIES WITH FRANCE

Importantly, most former French colonies maintained fairly close economic and cultural ties with France. In contrast, the former British colonies often went their own ways and established economic ties with other outside nations. Through organizations such as the Ghana-Guinea Union, some West African nations attempted to form a nucleus for Pan-African unity on a continental scale. Nkrumah and Sékou Touré were both champions of this ideal.

CHAOS IN ZAIRE

All of the general patterns of African struggles for independence were apparent in the Belgian Congo (later Zaire). There was some violence and bloodshed; the superpowers became involved, and the United Nations attempted to mediate the conflict. Although both the British and the French had tried to prepare and to educate at least an elite to take over the governments of new independent states, the story was quite different in the Congo because Belgian paternalism had kept the Congo under rigid controls. Much as they tried, however, the Belgians could not isolate the Congo from the nationalist fervor of its neighbors. A number of local nationalist movements developed, including one based in Katanga led by Moise Tshombe and another led by Patrice Lumumba.

DIVISIONS IN THE CONGO

In the face of growing nationalist sentiments, the Belgian government abruptly announced Congolese independence in 1960. The new state was immediately threatened by conflicting local rivalries. Tshombe announced the secession of the mineral-rich Katanga province, and Lumumba called for the intervention of the United Nations.

Lumumba's commitment to full political and economic independence alienated many Western businesses and governments (including the United States), all of which opposed his leadership. As a result, the Congo became the arena for some private companies and the superpowers to meddle in African affairs. Hired mercenaries further complicated the situation. Finally, UN police actions in 1963 reunited Katanga with the rest of the Congo, but the fighting continued even after the UN troops left in 1964. After Lumumba's assassination in 1961, the Congolese government was undermined by military threats and political instability.

Following a coup supported by the United States and others, General Joseph Mobutu, who had adopted a staunchly anti-Communist stance, became head of the government in 1965. Mobutu proceeded to change the nation's name to Zaire. He increasingly ruled Zaire as his private fiefdom. Zaire used part of the capital earned from the nation's tremendous mineral wealth to build roads, lines of communication, and educational facilities. However, Mobutu also allocated substantial portions of Zaire's economic wealth to the large army to quell rebellions by groups opposed to his dictatorship. He also amassed a huge personal fortune. Thus Zaire remained more divided and less wealthy than ever before.

MOBUTU TAKES OVER

PEACE AND WAR IN BRITISH EAST AFRICA

As in West Africa, the British moved toward granting *uhuru* (freedom) in East Africa after World War II. Unlike West Africa, however, East African nations came to independence through war as well as through peace. Tanganyika, economically the least developed of the British possessions in East Africa, secured its independence in 1961 after a decade of gradual steps toward autonomy. Unified with neighboring Zanzibar in 1964, it became the Republic of Tanzania. Tanzania emerged as a one-party nation led by Julius Nyerere's Tanganyika African National Union (TANU). Nyerere, one of Africa's leading champions of state socialism, promptly initiated a series of grassroots development projects aimed at increasing agricultural output and providing better social services. China provided much technical and financial assistance for development, but most of the rural population remained poor.

In Kenya the move toward independence was complicated by the presence of a white minority, mostly farmers in the Kenyan highlands. These white settlers, like the *colons* in Algeria, were determined to keep their dominant position. In contrast, the British government had embarked on a gradual program of increased self-determination based on multiracial cooperation that would also include the Indians, Kenya's other minority. These concessions failed to alleviate African grievances, particularly among the Kikuyu, one of the largest of Kenya's ethnic groups. The Kikuyu had been the major victims of European colonizers, who had confiscated large tracts of Kikuyu farmland in the highlands.

As white salaries and standards of living continued to rise, the economic position of blacks deteriorated. The Kenya African Union under Jomo Kenyatta persistently demanded that these inequities be eradicated and that black people be given a larger proportion of the important government positions. When these demands were ignored, the independence movement became more radical.

CONFLICT IN KENYA

In 1952 the Kikuyu organized a national resistance group to fight for "land and freedom." Many of the attacks were directed against African collaborators with the British and white settlers. Popularly known in the West as the Mau Mau, the organization was centered mainly in the countryside. Guerrilla warfare lasted from 1952 to 1956, but the actual number of assassinations and violent acts perpetrated against Europeans by the Mau Mau was widely exaggerated in the Western media.

KENYATTA'S LEADERSHIP

In an effort to destroy the Mau Mau, the British imprisoned Kenyatta. At least 10,000 Kikuyu died in the ensuing struggle. Once the British believed they had militarily defeated the Mau Mau, they then moved to negotiate a political settlement with Kenyatta, and Kenyan independence was proclaimed in 1963.

Kenyatta quickly emerged as the leader of a single-party state. Through a series of political maneuverings, and with the advantages of relative economic prosperity and his own charismatic appeal, he managed to unify the various Kenyan groups into a fairly cohesive nation. While many of the white settlers left Kenya, some remained as new Kenyan citizens. Under Kenyatta's leadership, the Kenyan government remained relatively stable and survived his death in 1978. Although the majority of political power rested in the executive branch, Kenya was unusual in that it managed to retain civilian government and a cohesive national identity even after the demise of its first generation of nationalist leadership.

THE BLACK STRUGGLE FOR FREEDOM IN SOUTHERN AFRICA

Nationalism in Southern Rhodesia and the Portuguese Colonies

In southern Africa, the Portuguese, led by the dictator Salazar, and the white-dominated regimes elsewhere in the area were far more determined to maintain their supremacy than were the colonial powers in the rest of Africa. In Southern Rhodesia (present-day Zimbabwe), for example, the white settlers announced their determination to retain their dominant political and economic position. On the other hand, the British government sought to avoid problems in southern Africa by agreeing to grant independence to Southern Rhodesia along the lines of equal representation. As British prime minister Harold Macmillan noted on a visit to South Africa, "The wind of change is blowing through [Africa], and whether we like it or not this growth of national consciousness is a political fact . . . and our national policies must take account of it." Such an approach meant that the small white population would no longer enjoy the position of privilege it had had under the old regime. The white minority bitterly opposed the British plan and, in open defiance, unilaterally declared its independence as the state of Rhodesia in 1965. With the exception of the white-controlled Republic of South Africa, no nations recognized the new Rhodesian government under Ian Smith, and the United Nations declared an economic boycott of Rhodesia. However, Rhodesian tobacco and minerals continued to be channeled to Western markets, and the economic boycott seemed to have little effect.

WHITE MINORITY REGIME IN RHODESIA

As the pressure mounted, African states surrounding Rhodesia became involved. South Africa assisted the Smith regime, while black African nations supported the growing forces of revolutionary black Rhodesians. Armed insurrections became commonplace throughout the Rhodesian countryside. Great Britain, and later the United States, tried to mediate the dispute and to reach a settlement based on equal black participation in the government, with no success.

At the same time that Rhodesia was falling under siege, blacks in the Portuguese colonies of Mozambique and Angola increased their pressure for independence. The Portuguese dictators Antonio Salazar and Marcello Caetano refused to grant independence or greater autonomy to the last vestiges of Portugal's 400-year-old colonial empire. In 1955 the Salazar regime actually attempted to extend its centralized control by referring to the colonies as "overseas provinces," an approach that was similar to the French concept of Algeria as an integral part of France. Just as the concept of Algeria as French had failed, so, too, did the Portuguese attempts to incorporate its African colonies. Condemnations of Portuguese policies in Africa by the United Nations were ignored. As a result of nationalist sentiments and Portuguese repression, rebellion broke out in Angola and Mozambique in 1961 and 1964, and a decade of war followed.

Racial Repression in the Republic of South Africa

Much of the struggle for independence in the southern third of Africa focused on the Republic of South Africa. One of the richest and most strategically important African nations, its society was still dominated by the conservative Dutch Afrikaners. During World War II, many Afrikaners, who had long chafed under British domination and attempts to liberalize the society, openly favored the Nazi regime. The Dutch Reformed Church reinforced the Afrikaners' philosophy of racial supremacy.

After the war, the Afrikaners in the Republic of South Africa enacted the policy of apartheid, a system of strict racial segregation endorsed and enforced by the government. By the early 1980s the apartheid system had legalized the dominance of 4.5 million white Africans over 800,000 Asians (mostly Indian shopkeepers), 2.8 million "colored" people (those of mixed racial origin), and 22 million black Africans, restricting their civil rights and allowing them no political power. In addition, the apartheid system called for complete segregation of the races in housing, education, religion, and government. It separated black Africans from Asians, both of these from colored Africans, and all three from the white population. In many cases it forced families who lived in areas designated as white, colored, or black to move if they were of the wrong color. Huge largely black townships developed around the outskirts of largely white cities. Black people were permitted into these cities to work in industry or in white homes during the daytime, but they had to leave the cities during the evening hours. They had to carry identification cards at all times; to be caught without a card or after curfew in areas designated as white meant possible imprisonment or the loss of a pass to work in the cities, which meant unemployment and further impoverishment. The Afrikaner government justified these repressive measures on the grounds that they helped to suppress Communist activities.

In the decades after World War II, black society and white society moved further and further apart. Landless black Africans began to seek jobs in the growing industrial

APARTHEID SYSTEM

B I O G R A P H Y

Resisting Apartheid

A short while later [1953] my first ban was served on me in terms of the Riotous Assemblies Act and the Criminal Law Amendment Act. In comparison with my later bans it was a mild affair. I was debarred from entry into all the larger centres of the Union. I was not allowed to attend public gatherings anywhere.

This last provision at once raised the question of attendance at public worship. My church took up the matter with the Department of Justice and told me that while they did not think that the police would interfere with my religious activities, I should apply for permission to be present at public worship.

In the winter of 1954, when the new battery of ruthless laws was freshly in place on the Statute Book, my ban expired. It was not immediately reimposed. I suppose I was being given a chance to go straight. I immediately misbehaved.*

. . .

Albert Luthuli, the grandson of a Zulu chief, describes an episode in his struggle against apartheid in South Africa. He was president of the African National Congress and a leader in the Pan-African movement. He was awarded the Nobel Prize for Peace in 1961.

*From *Let My People Go* by Albert Luthuli. Copyright © 1962 by William Collins Sons & Company, Ltd. Reprinted by permission.

centers, which were profiting from South Africa's great natural wealth in diamonds, uranium, and gold. Here, too, skilled white workers held the highest-paying positions; black workers were given the lowest-paid jobs as manual laborers. Gradually, all white Africans, even in unskilled jobs, were paid a higher wage simply because of skin color.

ANC RESISTS

The apartheid policy and the repressive tactics that accompanied it provoked nonwhite leaders to resist. Initially, they stressed nonviolence after the pattern set by Gandhi, who had spent part of his early life in South Africa. Numerous black leaders, including the Nobel Peace Prize winner Albert Luthuli, were imprisoned. Others, such as the white novelist Alan Paton, who was outspoken in his opposition to the regime, were censored and placed under virtual house arrest. The African National Congress (ANC), under Luthuli's leadership, sought a unified and racially integrated society in South Africa and led the struggle for nonviolent tactics and passive resistance against apartheid.

MANDELA'S LEADERSHIP

Black nationalists also initiated a series of strikes and demonstrations. These culminated in the 1960 Sharpeville incident, in which police opened fire on the unarmed crowd, killing dozens and wounding many. Condemning the ANC as revolutionary, the white South African government declared the organization illegal in 1960. Nelson Mandela, one of the leaders of the ANC, evaded arrest but was ultimately caught and tried under the Suppression of Communism Act. Mandela, who was not a member of any Marxist party, and seven other nationalist leaders were sentenced to life imprisonment. Mandela was finally released from prison in 1990, by which time he had become the symbol of black nationalism in southern Africa. When Great Britain and other members of the Commonwealth criticized apartheid and the repression of black nationalist leaders, the white South African government retaliated by dropping its membership in the Commonwealth in 1961.

To alleviate growing internal and international criticism, the South African government in 1966 announced the creation of Bantustans, or black states, within South African territory. The Bantustans of Bophuthatswana and Transkei were, in fact, large black reservations. Permits were required for black Africans to leave the Bantustans and to go to any area designated as white. White South Africans argued that the Bantustans were created as a logical extension of the apartheid principle of separate development. However, the Bantustans were on only 13 percent of the total land area, generally exceedingly poor, territorially fragmented, and dependent for communication and transport lines on white South Africa. Their foreign affairs were also controlled by the South African government. In 1966, Prime Minister Henrik Verwoerd, a leading proponent of apartheid, was assassinated by a mentally disturbed Greek immigrant, but his successors continued the system of government-sponsored racial segregation. As hopes for concessions faded, black nationalists began to turn to violence (see Chapter 30).

BANTUSTANS

NEW MOVEMENTS TOWARD PAN-AFRICAN UNITY

Many African leaders, from Nkrumah to Nasser, saw Pan-Africanism, a concept born between the wars, both as a means to improve standards of living and as a way to give Africans more political and economic clout in the international arena. African union was encouraged through various Pan-African conferences during the decades of the 1950s and 1960s. The Bandung Conference in 1955 gave enormous impetus to nonaligned movements in many African and Asian nations as they sought to steer a neutral path between the Soviet Union and the United States in the midst of the cold war. Similarly, the First World Congress of Black Writers and Artists, held in Paris in 1956, was an important cultural event in bringing together English- and French-speaking Africans. The next logical step was taken in May 1963, when representatives of the newly independent African states met in Addis Ababa and created the Organization of African Unity (OAU). Much of northern Africa also considered itself part of the Arab world, and leaders such as Nasser in Egypt argued that the predominantly Muslim and Arab nations of Africa belonged to the circles of both Arabism and Africanism.

However, in spite of their broad emotional appeal, both African and Arab unity appeared to be a distant dream. African union was verbally championed by most African leaders, but concrete attempts for unity generally failed, for a variety of political and economic reasons. Personal rivalries for dominant positions among conflicting African leaders also drove wedges between African nations. Most of the educational institutions and economic relations of African states were plugged into Western nations; there was very little, if any, economic interdependence that would facilitate

Black South Africans are massacred at Sharpeville in 1960; in the aftermath, horse-mounted police patrol the carnage.

the movement toward political union. Thus, economic rivalries heightened political differences. The Western powers aggravated the differences among African states by economic and political interference and sometimes by direct or surrogate military interference, as in Zaire.

SUMMARY

With the notable exceptions of Algeria and Kenya, independence came relatively peacefully in northern and central Africa in the 1950s and 1960s. By the 1960s all western and eastern African nations had become independent. Many of these new, struggling nations experienced political upheavals, and military dictatorships often became the norm. In Zaire the particularly bloody conflicts were exacerbated by superpower involvement.

In southern Africa levels of violence rose as colonial and white settler regimes in the Portuguese colonies and Rhodesia clung to power in the face of growing African discontent. The institution of apartheid widened the gulf between the races in South Africa. The white minority remained determined to keep the black majority out of the political system. In reaction to Afrikaner refusals to allow equality, black Africans first used nonviolent methods to force changes, but, as the white minority clung to power, black activists turned to violence.

Independent African nations were troubled with economic crises and persistent political instability, which often led to military interference. Attempts at union, either political or economic, were impeded by cultural differences, outside inter-ference, and political weaknesses.

SUGGESTED SOURCES

Achebe, Chinua. *No Longer at Ease.* 1963. A historical novel, a sequel to *Things Fall Apart*, in which the hero returns to Nigeria after living in Britain.*

Beinart, William. *Twentieth-Century South Africa.* 2nd ed. 2001. Balanced study of the long struggle against apartheid.*

Fage, J. D. *A History of Africa.* 4th ed. 2002. Solid overview of colonial period and independence struggles.*

From Congo to Zaire. A 52-minute video with extensive and rarely seen archival footage on Belgian policies in Congo and the nationalist fights against them.

Gatheru, R. Mugo. *Kenya: From Colonization to Independence, 1888–1970.* 2005. Fulsome historic study of Kenya and its independence movement.*

Horne, Alistair. *A Savage War of Peace: Algeria 1954–1962.* 1970. A moving description of the Algerian Revolution.* Also see the classic Gillo Pontecorno film, *Battle of Algiers,* on DVD.

Spear of the Nation: The Story of the African National Congress. 1986. Films for the Humanities and Sciences. Focuses on the background and policies of the ANC during the liberation struggle.

WEB SOURCES

www.fordham.edu/halsall/africa/africasbook.html

www.bbc.co.uk/worldservice/africa/features/storyofafrica/index.shtml.

Two excellent sites, each offering numerous links to materials dealing with Africa. See especially the sections on both sites dealing with independence.

---

*Paperback available.

24

⑥Economic and Political Developments in the Middle East

As with the rest of Asia and most of Africa, Middle Eastern nations achieved independence after World War II, but the region's vital petroleum fields and its strategic importance in terms of the cold war meant that the superpowers constantly sought to secure allies in the area. While the petroleum-rich nations were able to finance vast and far-reaching development programs, the poor nations without petroleum revenues continued to suffer the problems of underdevelopment. In addition, the ongoing Arab-Israeli conflict contributed to tensions and intermittent warfare; however, even if this conflict had been resolved, the region would have experienced major changes and upheavals. Consequently, the developments and changes in the region are dealt with in this chapter, and the Israeli–Palestinian Arab conflict is described in Chapter 25.

Finally, various Islamist parties in nations as diverse as Iran and Jordan, among others, gained popularity. Many people who supported these militant Islamic groups were disaffected with the spread of Western culture in their formerly traditional societies. When authoritarian regimes failed to solve the economic or social problems in the region and systematically suppressed all forms of political dissent, many people turned to Islamic religious movements as a means of expressing their opposition to their governments. Tension between secular forces and religious, traditional forces reflected similar trends throughout the world during the late twentieth century.

INDEPENDENT NATIONS AFTER WORLD WAR II

As war clouds gathered in Europe, Great Britain took steps to quell the growing nationalist storms in the Middle East. Great Britain wanted to ensure loyalty, or at least quiet, in the Arab world because of the area's vital strategic location. Consequently, the British tried to placate Arab nationalists, many of whom were prone to favor the Axis powers. Arab support for the Axis powers did not generally stem from ideological agreements with them but was based on the old expression "An enemy of my enemy is my friend." Encouraged by Nazi propaganda and hating the British presence in the area, Arab nationalists were encouraged to believe that if the Germans won the war, they would grant the Arabs complete independence.

INDEPENDENCE IN SYRIA AND LEBANON

In much of the Arab world, Great Britain attempted to secure its interests through censorship, military control, repression of Arab nationalists, and pro-Allied propaganda campaigns. After the fall of France and the creation of the pro-Nazi Vichy regime, Allied forces gradually occupied French-held Syria and Lebanon. In spite of French protests, the

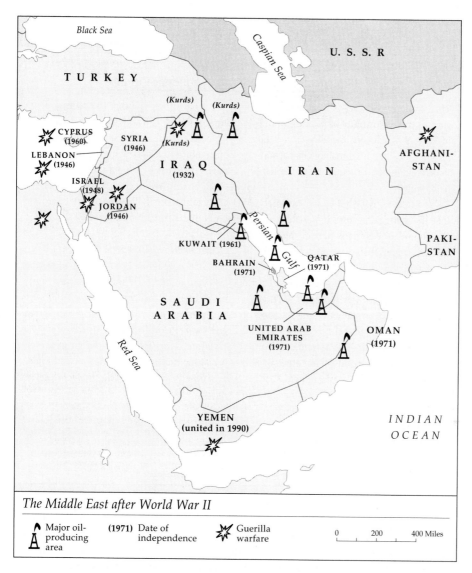

The Middle East after World War II

| ⚒ | Major oil-producing area | **(1971)** | Date of independence | ✳ | Guerilla warfare |

0   200   400 Miles

U.S. and British governments encouraged nationalist sentiments, particularly in Syria and Lebanon. By the end of the war, most Middle Eastern nations had achieved national autonomy; however, the Western powers were still anxious to maintain their military and petroleum interests in the region. The problems involving the future of the British mandate in Palestine were particularly intractable and led directly to the ongoing Arab-Israeli conflict. Although this conflict was intrinsically intertwined with political, economic, and social developments in the region, it will be discussed at length in the following chapter.

To protect their vital interests in the Middle East, the British encouraged the creation of the Arab League in 1945. The league was designed to foster interstate cooperation; however, it was weakened by feuds among the various independent

ARAB LEAGUE

BIOGRAPHY

Nasser on Imperialism and Development

This conference [Casablanca Summit] also gave us the opportunity of meeting a number of leaders of African liberation . . . such as President Kwame Nkrumah of Ghana, and . . . President Ahmed Sekou Touré of the Republic of Guinea.

First: . . . it should not be forgotten that the struggle against Imperialism in the Congo and in Algeria is part of the struggle against Imperialism in the whole African Continent.

Second: . . . the problems of Africa are part of the cause of world peace. . . . Thus the problems of disarmament and the use of atomic energy for peaceful purposes, should be no less in our consideration than the problems of the liquidation of Imperialism and the abolition of racial segregation.

Third: We were also of the opinion that the economic and social development of the African peoples constitutes the pivot on which the whole of the Africa struggle turns.

Fourth: We were of the opinion that the United Nations is a major factor.

Fifth: We saw that the success of the aims of the African struggle can be achieved if Africa is turned into a constructive meeting-place not into a destructive battleground between the blocs.

Sixth: We realized that one of our gravest responsibilities is to safeguard the unity of the African march.*

. . .

Gamal Abdel Nasser was the dominant political power in Egypt from the 1952 revolution until his death in 1970. He was a powerful, charismatic force not only throughout the Arab world but in Africa and Asia as well. In this speech, given after he attended an African summit in Casablanca in 1961, Nasser highlights a number of the problems facing African and Middle Eastern nations; many of these remain relevant today.

*From speech delivered by President Gamal Abdel Nasser at the National Assembly on the Result of the Casablanca Summit Conference on January 23, 1961, in *President Gamal Abdel Nasser's Speeches and Press-Interviews,* January–December 1961, Cairo, United Arab Republic, Information Department.

Arab nations. After the war, interdynastic disputes among the Hashimites in Jordan and Iraq, the Saudi monarchy in Saudi Arabia, and King Faruk in Egypt were major stumbling blocks to Arab unification. After 1952 the Arab world was divided by rivalries between the conservative, generally promonarchy forces (Saudi Arabia and Jordan) and the so-called revolutionary forces in Egypt (under Nasser), Syria, and Iraq.

1952 REVOLUTION IN EGYPT

Mounting nationalist demands and the humiliating loss of the first Arab-Israeli war in 1948 led to sweeping changes in much of the Arab world. In Egypt the people blamed the corrupt monarchy of King Faruk for the loss of Palestine and the Israeli military victory in 1948. In 1952 a determined group of army officers ousted King Faruk in an almost bloodless coup d'état. The officers, led by Gamal Abdel Nasser, announced plans for the eradication of imperialism and for massive economic and social reforms. The Aswan Dam, a huge development project to increase agricultural land and to provide hydroelectric power for villages and a new industrial

Egyptian president Nasser chats with Chinese premier Zhou
Enlai in Cairo in 1965.

base, was the cornerstone of the economic program. The largest project of its kind in
the world at the time, the Aswan project was originally supported by the West.

However, during the 1950s Nasser moved toward a stance of positive neutralism
and improved relations with the Eastern bloc and China; as a result, the United States
and its Western allies became increasingly hostile to his regime. Thus, as in Asia and
Latin America, the Middle East became a field for cold war competitions. A highly
charismatic personality and a brilliant public speaker in colloquial Arabic, Nasser was
extremely popular throughout the Arab world. His support among Arab nationalists also
caused Israelis to fear that he might be able to unify the Arab world and launch a successful military attack against Israel. As Nasser's popularity skyrocketed in the Arab
world, he became increasingly unpopular in the West, and the United States ultimately
decided to withdraw its support for the Aswan Dam, thereby setting in process a chain
of events that led directly to the second Arab-Israeli war in 1956 (see Chapter 25).

THE ARAB COLD WAR AND DOMESTIC DEVELOPMENT

The second Arab-Israeli war (1956) resulted in another Israeli military victory but again
failed to achieve a peace settlement. The war also led to a wave of anti-Western and
pro-Nasser sentiments in the Middle East. Indeed, every Arab-Israeli war resulted in

major political upheavals in the Arab world. After 1956, pro-Western Arab governments, particularly the conservative monarchies, were severely threatened by pro-Nasser forces. This conflict between prorevolutionary forces and conservative regimes was dubbed the Arab cold war. After some delay, the Soviets agreed to lend financial and technical assistance to build the Aswan Dam. In 1958 revolutionary activity in the region reached its peak. The conservative Hashimite monarchy in Iraq (see Chapter 15) was overthrown by a military junta, which was in turn ousted in 1963 by an officer group from the Ba'ath Party, which espoused Arab unity and socialism. In the following two decades, Ba'athists continued to rule in Iraq, while a more conservative Ba'athist group ruled in Syria under Hafiz al-Asad. The precarious throne of King Hussein, the Hashimite monarch of Jordan, was saved only by British military intervention.

In 1958 the U.S. Marines intervened in a civil war in Lebanon, acting under the proviso of the Eisenhower Doctrine that the United States would intervene in support of governments fighting communism. Actually, the Lebanese civil war was largely a conflict between conservatives and the leftist pro-Nasser forces; the war was temporarily settled by reestablishing another coalition government of Christian and Muslim Lebanese. However, the coalition perpetuated the problem of religious communalism in Lebanon.

ATATURK'S LEGACY

Within the Arab world, Middle Eastern nations after World War II generally sought to create secular nationalist states similar to those found in the West; in non-Arab Turkey and Iran this continued a process begun under Ataturk and Reza Shah. Modernizing regimes often copied plans for agricultural and industrial development from the West and placed great emphasis on advanced technologies. In Turkey both democratic and sporadic military governments continued the process of modernization. The Turkish military considered itself the guardian of Ataturk's Westernizing legacy and intervened to protect it whenever the military believed the legacy was threatened by forces either on the Left or by religious groups on the Right. The continued conflict between Israel and the Arab states, however, forced Middle Eastern nations to apportion increasing amounts of their gross national products to large armies and arms purchases from both the West and the Soviet bloc.

PETROLEUM AND MODERNIZATION

In spite of political problems and continued warfare, the Arab governments attempted, with varying degrees of success, to improve the standard of living of their people. They improved education—for girls as well as boys—and initiated other social welfare projects. By the 1960s and 1970s, when petroleum revenues increased, economic development surged dramatically, particularly in the petroleum-rich nations of Saudi Arabia and Libya and the sheikdoms of the Arab Persian Gulf. These areas, which previously had been among the poorest in the Middle East, were able with petrodollars to embark on ambitious programs to build new hospitals, homes, schools, airports, and roads. Often, as in Kuwait, the government provided its citizens free education through the university level, low-cost or free housing, free medical care (including dental and eye services), and even low-interest loans for starting new businesses. The Middle East tended to be divided between rich, relatively sparsely populated nations with conservative regimes and heavily populated, poor states often with socialist governments. Thus, nations with little or no petroleum, such as Egypt, which had the largest Arab population, remained desperately poor and constantly had to struggle to provide even minimum services for their peoples.

SUPERPOWER RIVALRY IN THE MIDDLE EAST

To complicate matters further, the Middle East, with its vast petroleum reserves and strategic location, was of major importance to both the United States and the Soviet Union. After World War II, as already noted, both nations periodically became directly and indirectly involved in various regional disputes.

The United States moved to establish closer relations with Middle Eastern nations. During the cold war, Turkey had become one of the cornerstones of U.S. military strategy against the Soviet Union. The United States built large military bases in Turkey and supported Turkish entry into NATO (see Chapter 20).

DIVISION OF CYPRUS

However, the status of the strategic island of Cyprus off the Turkish coast remained a major area of disagreement among Turkey, Greece (another U.S. NATO ally), and the United States. The population of Cyprus comprised a majority of people who were of Greek heritage and a minority who were of Turkish ancestry. Some Cypriots wanted an independent nation, and others wanted to merge with Greece. Following an attempted Greek coup d'état and a Turkish armed invasion in 1974, the so-called Green Line manned by UN forces divided Cyprus into Greek and Turkish sectors. The U.S. government tended to favor Turkish claims because of the close military alliance, but public opinion in the United States was overwhelmingly pro-Greek. Consequently, Turkey gradually moved further away from the U.S. orbit, and Cyprus remained an area of heightened tension in the eastern Mediterranean. Even after the cold war ended, the island remained divided, and protracted UN mediation failed to resolve the differences among the Greek, Turkish, and Cypriot governments.

U.S. ALLIES

During the 1970s and 1980s the United States relied on the Arab states of Egypt and Saudi Arabia, on Israel, and on U.S. military strength in the Red Sea and the Persian Gulf to counter possible Soviet expansion into the Arab world. Following Anwar Sadat's assassination in 1981 (see Chapter 25), U.S. reliance on Israel and Saudi Arabia increased. The main thrust of U.S. military power in the region was through the Rapid Deployment Force, whereby armed units could be moved into the area. However, although the Saudis pressured for increased armaments (including sophisticated reconnaissance planes such as AWACS), most nations, both Arab and non-Arab, in the Middle East were reluctant to accept the permanent stationing of U.S. forces on their territories. Nonetheless, the United States created a substantial informal military presence in Egypt and Saudi Arabia.

U.S.S.R. IN AFGHANISTAN

Then, in December 1979, the Soviet Union moved into Afghanistan. The collapse of the pro-U.S. Iranian regime and the unstable nature of the revolutionary Iranian government caused both the Soviet Union and the United States to reassess their positions in the region.

Since World War II, Afghanistan had remained one of the poorest and least-developed nations in the area, one in which numerous political factions constantly attempted to gain power. Following a cycle of coups and countercoups, Babrak Karmal, backed by the Soviet Union, emerged as the leader of Afghanistan. To protect the dependent regime, the Soviet Union moved over 80,000 troops into Afghanistan. Political hostility to the Karmal regime and the presence of foreign troops led to an armed resistance movement dominated by militant Muslims, or Mujahedin. Many Mujahedin emulated the Iranian revolution and received military aid and training from the United States or its allies. As fighting in Afghanistan escalated, over a million refugees fled into Pakistan, which already had severe population problems.

Soviet involvement in Afghanistan largely isolated the Soviet Union from the Islamic world. The traditional governments in the Middle East, particularly in Saudi Arabia and the petroleum-rich sheikdoms of the Persian Gulf, fearing both the spread of the Iranian revolution—with its particular brand of Islamic radicalism—and the Soviet influence in the region, condemned the Soviet actions in Afghanistan and sent volunteers to fight with the Mujahedin. Because the mountainous terrain was ideal for guerrilla warfare, Soviet forces, even with superior military equipment, found it impossible to eradicate the Afghan opposition. In 1988 and 1989 the Soviets withdrew from Afghanistan, leaving the pro-Soviet Afghan government and the Mujahedin in a protracted struggle for control over the nation. The war in Afghanistan further debilitated the fragile Soviet economy and contributed to the collapse of the Soviet Union (see Chapter 31). In the 1990s many of the trained Arab fighters returned to Saudi Arabia and other Arab nations determined to institute their brand of Islamic governments in their home countries (see Chapter 34).

The United States also concentrated on extending its military links with nations around the Persian Gulf. For the first time in its history, it established a permanent naval force in the Indian Ocean, with a new naval base at Diego Garcia; the United States also developed facilities in Somalia. Although the Soviets built up bases in South Yemen, in Ethiopia, and on the Indian Ocean, on balance, the United States, Great Britain, and France maintained military superiority in the region. Regional disputes, particularly over access to and control of the vital Persian Gulf, constantly threatened to upset the precarious military balance devised by the Soviets and the United States.

U.S. IN PERSIAN GULF

CIVIL WAR IN LEBANON

Meanwhile, Lebanon became a battleground for both domestic and regional disputes. After 1970, Palestinian border raids from Lebanon into Israel increased, and the Israelis retaliated with ground and air strikes, including the bombing of Lebanese villages. The ongoing domestic tensions and border violence resulted in a protracted and bloody civil war that in effect divided Lebanon into several distinct sections. The Lebanese civil war, which continued intermittently, after 1975, for over 14 years, was partially caused by communal differences between Muslims and Christians. Political splits between the Left and the Right and the presence of many armed and politically active Palestinians also contributed to upsetting the fragile governmental balance. In addition, outside interference by Israel, Syria, and other Arab nations and interventions by Western powers made compromises to reunite the nation almost impossible. Indeed, Lebanon became a surrogate battleground for wider conflicts. The war resulted in the Syrian occupation of parts of Lebanon, while the United Nations stationed troops along the border with Israel. Armed confrontations continued in southern Lebanon as Palestinian and leftist Lebanese forces fought with the Israelis and the Israeli-supported enclave in southern Lebanon. Clashes among the various forces also continued in Beirut. Mediation efforts by the United States, Saudi Arabia, and other nations from 1975 to 1981 failed to remedy the cycle of violence that turned Beirut, once one of the loveliest cities in the Middle East, into a scene of bombings, random assassinations, and extensive destruction. When Israel launched a massive invasion of Lebanon in 1982, the conflict exploded into the fifth Arab-Israeli war (see Chapter 25).

Israel won another military victory in 1982, but the conflict failed to resolve either the Arab-Israeli conflict or the problems in Lebanon. In the aftermath of years of war, it appeared that Lebanon was moving increasingly toward a de facto partition, with separate Muslim and Christian governments. Although Israeli and Syrian forces continued to occupy large parts of the fractured nation, a fragile peace was achieved by 1991.

DIVISIONS IN LEBANON

THE IRANIAN REVOLUTION:
TRIUMPH FOR ISLAMIST MILITANTS

By the 1970s continued economic, political, and social problems had caused many people in the region to question and ultimately to reject the Western-based secular nationalist programs that their governments had instituted. As the governments, often military dictatorships, failed to satisfy the demands of the people, to solve the Arab-Israeli conflict, and to avoid entanglements with or dependency on the superpowers, many in the Middle East—as elsewhere in the world—began to turn toward religion. Increasingly, militant Muslims argued that the Western-based models, whether from the United States or the Soviet Union, were foreign, artificial imports that did not reflect the realities of Middle Eastern societies. They advocated the institution of Islamic governments ruled not by secular, essentially Western, legal codes (as in Turkey or Tunisia) but by the sharia, the Islamic law.

SECULAR VERSUS RELIGIOUS FORCES

The move away from secularism was not limited to Muslims. The Maronite Christians in Lebanon and some Jewish Israelis, particularly many new emigrants from the United States, pushed for increased religious participation in government and in society in general. Thus, the ongoing trend of tension between the secular and the spiritual was brought into clear focus. This conflict would later break out into open warfare in Lebanon and would form the basis of sweeping revolutionary changes in Iran.

SHAH AND "WHITE REVOLUTION"

The modernizing state of Iran had become one of the cornerstones of U.S. foreign policy after World War II. The pro–United States ruler Mohammad Reza Shah built up a huge military complex using U.S. foreign aid and petroleum revenues. He also implemented the "White Revolution" to develop Iran agriculturally and industrially while improving living standards for all Iranians. Economic development seemed rapid, but it was accompanied by growing inflation, corruption in the highest levels of government, an actual decline in some agricultural sectors, and increased political repression. In addition, the shah kept a tight rein on all facets of political life through SAVAK, his often brutal and much-feared secret police.

ISLAMIC REVOLUTION

In reaction, disaffected Iranians from the political Left and from the strongly entrenched Shi'i clergy on the Right joined forces to launch a protracted and often bloody struggle that led to the overthrow of the shah in 1979. The shah and his family went into exile, and an Islamic republic based on strict application of Islamic law was instituted, with the Imam (referred to in the West as the Ayatollah) Ruhollah Khomeini acting as the final voice of authority.

The new revolutionary government of Iran vowed to eradicate the abuses of the old regime, to champion traditional Islamic values, and to improve living conditions. Iranian leaders denounced the United States as "the Great Satan" for its support of the old regime and demanded that the shah be returned to stand trial for his alleged crimes. After the United States refused, the U.S. embassy in Iran was occupied in November 1979 and the staff taken hostage. For over a year there ensued threats, negotiations, and denunciations. The United States froze Iranian assets and attempted a rescue mission that had to be aborted. Finally, in January 1981, a complex agreement was reached and the hostages were released.

The furor over the hostages often obscured the severe domestic problems faced by the new regime. Within Iran, there were open clashes as a number of different

In 1978 demonstrations, boycotts, and strikes by thousands of Iranians helped overthrow the Pahlavi dynasty. Many revolutionary women, as seen above, adopted Islamic dress as a symbol of their opposition to the shah. In much of the Muslim world, men and women wear Islamic garb to demonstrate their hostility to Westernization, particularly in cultural and social fields.

parties, particularly from the Left and the Right, sought to gain power. The religious Right emerged victorious, with the mullahs (clergy) becoming the dominant political force in Iran. They championed the creation of Islamic governments not only in Iran but throughout the vast Islamic world. The religious forces also pushed for the implementation of strict, traditional values in all aspects of society, including traditional dress and codes of behavior for women. The victory of the Islamist forces in Iran gave moral support to other Islamist movements in the Arab world and in much of Asia. By the 1990s Islamist parties had become enormously popular. In nations as widespread and diverse as Algeria, Egypt, the Sudan (where an Islamic regime already held power), and Jordan, militant Islamist movements demanded more conservative social legislation, particularly regarding women and the family. In many of these nations it was likely that if open and free elections were held, the Islamist forces would easily win (see Chapter 34).

THE IRAN-IRAQ AND GULF WARS

The Islamist fervor of Iran threatened not only the secular Arab governments but also the Saudi monarchy, which, although it based its legitimacy on Islam, maintained close relations with the United States. Islamist groups in Egypt, Tunisia, Lebanon, and elsewhere in the Muslim world were encouraged by the successes of the Iranian revolution and occasionally (as in Lebanon) even received direct support from Iran.

HIGH COSTS OF WAR

After Iran called for an Islamic revolution in neighboring Iraq, the Ba'athist government under Saddam Hussein moved to defuse the Islamic revolution and to settle old grievances by attacking Iran in September 1980. In a brutal power struggle, the war dragged on as Iran refused to compromise with the Iraqi regime, or what Iranians called the "Great Satan's Puppet Ba'ath party." By 1988, the eighth year of the war, there had been over a million casualties and the two nations had spent more than $450 billion—more than the United States had expended in all the years of fighting in Vietnam. Attempting to win the war, Iran used waves of men, some as young as 14, to clear mine fields, while Iraq used poison gas; the capital cities of both nations were periodically attacked by missiles. To continue this war of attrition, Iraq obtained military supplies from the Soviet Union, other Arab nations, and the United States, while Iran secured supplies from North Korea, China, and Israel, among others.

FOREIGN INVOLVEMENT

Owing to its opposition to the Iranian revolutionary regime, the United States tended to support Iraq during this long war. It increased its military presence in the Gulf and agreed to arms shipments to Iraq. However, after the war it became common knowledge that despite its public stance against the Iranian regime, which had been accused of supporting terrorism throughout the world, the United States had quietly continued negotiations with Iran. Through its ally Israel, the United States had also sold or approved arms shipments to Iran, thereby enabling it to continue the struggle. The Israeli government held that continued division within the Arab world and diversions such as the Iran-Iraq War prevented the Arabs from directing hostilities against Israel. As one Israeli official said, "We don't want this war ever to end." Henry Kissinger also noted that the United States did not want either side to win. Thus, as in previous instances, a local dispute became entangled with larger regional and international issues and with the unresolved Arab-Israeli conflict.

By the summer of 1988 the Iranian regime, which was finding it increasingly difficult to secure young volunteers to fight the war and was suffering under continued Iraqi attacks, began negotiations through the offices of the United Nations and an uneasy armistice was arranged. Following Khomeini's death in 1989, the mullahs (clergy) retained power; although the new leaders tended to be more pragmatic in their relations with the West, they continued the conservative social policies initiated after the revolution.

FINANCIAL PROBLEMS IN IRAQ

Iraq emerged from the war with a large, battle-trained, well-equipped military, but its economy had been severely weakened; it also owed vast amounts of money borrowed during the war to Arab nations, particularly to Saudi Arabia and Kuwait. When these nations began pressing for the return of loans, Saddam Hussein angrily countered that Iraqis had fought and died in the war in part to protect the Gulf states from possible overthrow by the revolutionary Islamic government in Iran. Consequently, Iraq considered the money provided to buy arms during the war as payment by the Gulf states for having borne the burden of the war. In addition, Saddam Hussein was angry over what he perceived to be attempts to strangle Iraq economically. Western and petroleum-rich nations refused to grant loans for the rebuilding of Iraq, and Kuwait was allegedly slant drilling into Iraqi petroleum fields, a practice that deprived Iraq of much-needed petroleum revenues. Although Iraq had diplomatic relations with Kuwait, it had long-standing grievances with its neighbor and considered Kuwait an integral part of the historic borders of Iraq. Determined to maintain his total control over the Iraqi government and military, Saddam Hussein also sought to garner popular support by adopting an aggressive stance against the United States and Israel.

When negotiations among Arab regimes failed to resolve the differences, and relying on what appeared to be a lack of U.S. interest in the problem, Iraq invaded Kuwait in August 1990. The international community, including most Arab states, promptly condemned the aggression and demanded an immediate withdrawal by Iraq and the return of the Kuwaiti monarchy. With the Soviet Union in economic shambles, the United States had emerged as the sole superpower, and it was determined to maintain its petroleum and political interests in the region. Indeed, some experts believed that had the superpowers still been caught up in the cold war they would have restrained both their allies, thereby avoiding the war altogether. However, as the sole superpower, the United States was able to fashion an international coalition and, under the auspices of the United Nations, began a colossal military buildup in Saudi Arabia and the Persian Gulf. When Saddam Hussein refused to withdraw Iraqi troops from Kuwait, the coalition forces, led by the United States, began a huge monthlong aerial bombardment in January 1991. A short ground war in Kuwait followed in February, with massive coalition victories on all fronts. The war ended in a clear-cut military victory for the coalition forces and the United States and the return of the pro-Western monarchy to Kuwait.

However, the Gulf War had mixed political results. Although there were uprisings among Kurds in northern Iraq and Shi'i in the south, Saddam Hussein's oppressive regime stayed in power. In addition, with the weakening of Iraq as the major Arab military power, Iran increasingly emerged as the regional force in the Persian Gulf; hence, the gulf remained an area of high tension and uncertainty. The Gulf War was the first major war of the post–cold war era.

INVASION OF KUWAIT

S U M M A R Y

Regional differences, territorial disputes, and domestic problems made the Middle East a hot spot. Like most of the Third World, it was an area of rapid change and uncertainty. The political fights between leftists and conservative forces within Middle Eastern nations and among the various governments of the region led to upheavals. The Arab-Israeli conflict also contributed to violence in the region. The emergence of various militant religious groups radically altered the nature of many Middle Eastern governments, particularly in Iran. Lebanon also became the surrogate battleground for many of these disputes. In addition, both superpowers had problems dealing with the new independent and dynamic nations and sought to establish alliances and military bases in the region.

During the cold war, regional problems were further complicated by the geopolitical interests of the United States and the Soviet Union. Because of their strategic locations and their regional position as the world's largest producers of petroleum, Middle Eastern nations were of vital concern not only to the superpowers but also to the rest of the industrialized world. The Soviets suffered a defeat in Afghanistan, while the United States had continued problems in maintaining its petroleum and military interests in the area. The Persian Gulf became a flash point for many of these conflicting interests and was the battleground in the long Iran-Iraq conflict and the far shorter Gulf War of 1991.

SUGGESTED SOURCES

Bowen, Donna Lee, and Evelyn A. Early, eds. *Everyday Life in the Muslim Middle East.* 1993. Anthology of poems, photographs, and essays focusing on a wide range of experiences in the region.*

Fisk, Robert. *Pity the Nation: The Abduction of Lebanon.* 1990. Well-written account of Lebanon's civil war by a noted wartime correspondent who lived through the long years of violence.*

Gelvin, James L. *The Modern Middle East: A History.* 2005. A short readable text with a useful time line, glossary, and biographical sketches.*

Gerner, Deborah J. *Understanding the Contemporary Middle East.* 1999. Broad coverage, including chapters on literature, women, ethnicity, and population growth.*

Halliday, Fred. *Nation and Religion in the Middle East.* 2000. Incisive discussion of tensions between secular political and religious forces with sections on Turkey, Saudi Arabia, and Iran.*

Korany, Bahgat, and Ali E. Hillal Dessouki. *The Foreign Policy of Arab States: The Challenge of Change.* 1991. Scholarly study of complex political policies adopted by Arab governments during the cold war.*

Makdisi, Jean Said. *Beirut Fragments.* 1990/1999. Moving firsthand narrative of survival during the Lebanese war.*

Richards, Alan, and John Waterbury, eds. *A Political Economy of the Middle East.* 2nd ed. 1996. A comprehensive account of economic developments and problems, with emphasis on the impact of U.S. power and the end of the cold war.*

Shaaban, Bouthaina. *Both Right and Left Handed: Arab Women Talk about Their Lives.* 1988/1991. Arab women tell their personal stories and the tensions between secular and religious forces.*

Woodward, Peter. *Nasser.* 1992. Short biography of key Arab nationalist leader.*

WEB SOURCES

www.fordham.edu/halsall/mod/modsbook54.html. A valuable site on the Middle East since 1914 with most links dealing with the decades after World War II.

www.fordham.edu/halsall/islam/islamsbook.html. See links under the "Islamic World since 1945."

www.nmhschool.org/tthornton/mehistorydatabase/mideastindex.htm. A very useful database on the Middle East. See, for example, the link "Civil War (Lebanon), Revolution (Iran), Uprising (Palestine), 1974–1989."

*Paperback available.

⑤The Israeli–Palestinian Arab Conflict

9/95

The Middle East after World War II was swept by waves of nationalist fervor and became a region of enormous upheaval and conflict (see Chapter 24). Palestine was one of the major focal points of those changes. Before the war, Great Britain, in its Palestine mandate, had tried to pacify Palestinian Arab opposition by limiting Jewish immigration and by promising independence in the future. Because of the anti-Semitic basis of the Nazi regime, Great Britain knew that world Jewry would support the Allied war efforts. Thus assured of Jewish support, Great Britain felt safe in making friendly gestures toward the Arabs. This policy angered the Zionists, who believed all Jews in the diaspora (Jews scattered throughout the world) had the right to settle in Palestine.

THE CREATION OF ISRAEL AND THE 1948 WAR

When World War II ended, the Arab-Israeli conflict became the major political and military problem in the Middle East. After 1945, both the Zionists and the Palestinian Arabs pushed for the creation of their own individual nations; the problem was that each of these nationalist groups sought to establish its independence within the same geographic territory. The Palestinians, who in 1945 were about two-thirds of the local population and owned about 80 percent of the land, believed the territory was theirs. On the other hand, the Zionists believed that through historical and religious involvement, the territory was theirs. In addition, Jewish national claims had enormous emotional support in the West and among Jewish survivors of the Holocaust, as a result of the tremendous suffering of the Jewish communities within Nazi-controlled Europe. The Holocaust, with its untold horrors, had caused many Westerners to conclude that the Zionists were correct in advocating a Jewish national state that would protect the religious and political rights of the Jewish people. In opposition, the Palestinians and other Arabs generally viewed anti-Semitism and the Holocaust as Western problems for which they were not responsible and for which they should not be forced to pay.

In this situation, the British, who had played Palestinian and Zionist nationalisms against each other, were caught on the horns of a dilemma. If the British continued to support the creation of a Jewish state and the further immigration of survivors of the Holocaust to Palestine, Great Britain risked losing support in the Arab world, with its petroleum resources and strategic locations. On the other hand,

BRITISH WITHDRAWAL

by attempting to limit Jewish immigration into Palestine, the British were placed in the untenable moral position of opposing and often imprisoning Jewish immigrants coming directly from the concentration camps in Europe. The British administration in Palestine also faced increased armed opposition by both the resident Zionists and the Palestinian Arabs. Furthermore, the British had severe domestic economic problems and were forced to cope with mounting nationalist demands throughout the empire.

UNSCOP

The British solved their dilemma by washing their hands of it. In 1947, the year of Indian independence, Great Britain turned the problem over to the United Nations, which promptly formed a committee to investigate the problem. The United Nations Special Committee on Palestine (UNSCOP) recommended in its majority report that Palestine be divided into a Jewish state and an Arab state. Partition had been suggested on previous occasions but was not overwhelmingly popular. The Palestinians immediately opposed the UNSCOP plan, which allocated approximately 50 percent of the territory, including the more fertile coastal areas, to the Jewish state. The Zionists reluctantly accepted the idea of partition but were dissatisfied because the plan did not allot to them all the area of Palestine.

Despite the mounting violence in Palestine, in November 1947 the United Nations voted for the partition plan that was to be implemented when the British withdrew in May 1948. In the interim, violence spread throughout Palestine as both sides began to prepare for battle. On May 14, 1948, as the British hastily withdrew, David Ben-Gurion, who was fairly confident of U.S. and Soviet support, announced the creation of the state of Israel.

1948 WAR

The surrounding Arab states and the Palestinian Arabs refused to recognize the new state, and the first Arab-Israeli war promptly began. The Arab forces, saddled with corrupt leadership, divided chains of command, faulty weapons, and no clear-cut military strategy, were no match for the well-organized, trained, and spirited Israelis. The Israelis won the 1948 war, expanding Israeli territory by approximately one-third more than that granted under the original UN partition plan. The West Bank, which had been apportioned to the Arab state under the UN plan, was incorporated into Jordan. Jerusalem was divided between Israeli and Jordanian control, and the Gaza Strip was administered by Egypt.

PALESTINIAN REFUGEES

One way or another, all Palestinian Arabs found themselves under the control of others. Before and during the war, thousands of Palestinians, particularly peasants, fled their farms and homes. The Arabs maintained that the refugees, who clustered in southern Lebanon, the West Bank, and the Gaza Strip, had been forced to leave because of Zionist terrorism and violence. The Israelis argued that they were not responsible for the refugees, who, according to Israel, had left as a result of Arab pressures or of their own free will; however, there is no doubt that the 1948 war left almost 1 million Palestinians homeless. Receiving meager support from the UN, these refugees numbered over 2 million by the 1990s, but they remained determined to return to their homeland. The guerrillas of the Palestinian liberation organizations that were active from 1967 onward came predominantly from the refugee camps.

With enormous domestic economic and political problems of their own, the Arab governments did little to solve the refugee problem and indeed often used the

Golda Meir and the first Israeli prime minister, David Ben-Gurion. He proclaimed her "one of the two most important statesmen of the Jewish people."

Palestinians for their own political aims. As the former Algerian leader Ahmed Ben Bella once remarked, "The Arabs in power bargain on the backs of the Palestinians." On the other hand, the Israelis denied responsibility and refused to accept the return of most of the refugees, who they maintained would become a subversive presence within Israel. In addition, the Israelis stressed that the return of the Palestinians would alter the basic ethnic and religious structure of Israel and would thereby change its Zionist basis. Thus, although Israel won the 1948 war, no peace treaties were concluded, and the borders of Israel and the surrounding Arab nations remained tense.

DOMESTIC DEVELOPMENTS IN ISRAEL

On the domestic front, the newly created state of Israel concentrated on building new economic, political, and military structures while moving to assimilate large numbers of Jewish immigrants. By the 1970s Israel's multiparty system would lead to increased political divisions and infighting. Golda Meir, a leading Labor politician and prime minister, joked that if four Israelis met in a room they would create five political parties.

Economically, the kibbutzim, collective agricultural settlements created by the early Zionist immigrants, became less important as the nation's economy was increasingly geared toward a capitalist system based on manufacturing in the form of small factories, particularly those producing armaments and small cut diamonds. With huge expenditures devoted to the military, Israel remained heavily dependent on foreign assistance from Western nations, particularly France and later the United States, and donations from Jewish communities around the world.

THE 1956 WAR:
THE COLD WAR SPREADS TO THE MIDDLE EAST

Events in Egypt soon led to a second Arab-Israeli war. A new regime under Nasser had come to power in Egypt in 1952 (see Chapter 24). The new Egyptian government had announced a far-reaching development program with the Aswan (High) Dam, described as "more magnificent and 17 times greater than the Pyramids," as its cornerstone. Nasser hoped to secure assistance from the West and the World Bank in order to build this massive project. When Nasser moved to improve Egyptian relations with the Soviet Union, China, and neutral Third World nations, Western support waned. In particular, U.S. Secretary of State John Foster Dulles was opposed to neutralism, which he believed was thinly disguised communism. After Nasser failed to receive military arms from the United States, he concluded an arms deal with Czechoslovakia. In light of these developments, Dulles announced the withdrawal of U.S. assistance for the Aswan Dam.

NATIONALIZATION OF THE SUEZ CANAL

In Cairo, the refusal was correctly interpreted as an insult to Egypt and as a direct slap in the face to Nasser. In retaliation, on July 26, 1956, to the astonishment of many Western officials, Nasser nationalized the Suez Canal, which had previously been administered by the Suez Canal Company, whose stockholders were predominantly European. Furious, the British and French decided to take back the canal by force and to topple Nasser. The French government was also anxious to overthrow Nasser in order to end his support for the Algerians, who were fighting for independence. For political and military reasons, the Israelis were also willing to join in military actions with the French and British. The Israelis were being harassed by commando raids along their borders and feared Nasser's success in mobilizing Arabs throughout the region. An agreement was reached whereby Israel would launch an attack across the Sinai Peninsula but would stop short of the Suez Canal. The British and French were then to intervene between the Israeli and Egyptian forces and occupy the canal. The scenario anticipated the immediate downfall of Nasser, followed by a more malleable or pro-Western Egyptian government.

1956 ATTACK

In late October 1956 the Israelis successfully launched their attack and occupied the Sinai peninsula. After some delay, the British and French bombed Egyptian airfields and parachuted troops into positions along the Suez Canal. The tripartite collusion, which the British, French, and Israelis publicly denied for many years, was a military success but a political fiasco. Contrary to Western expectations, Nasser did not fall. In fact, the war strengthened his argument that the Western powers and Israel had imperial designs in the Middle East. The United States had opposed the use of military force and was placed in the awkward position of having to confront its closest allies, Great Britain and France; meanwhile, the Soviets played up the confrontation

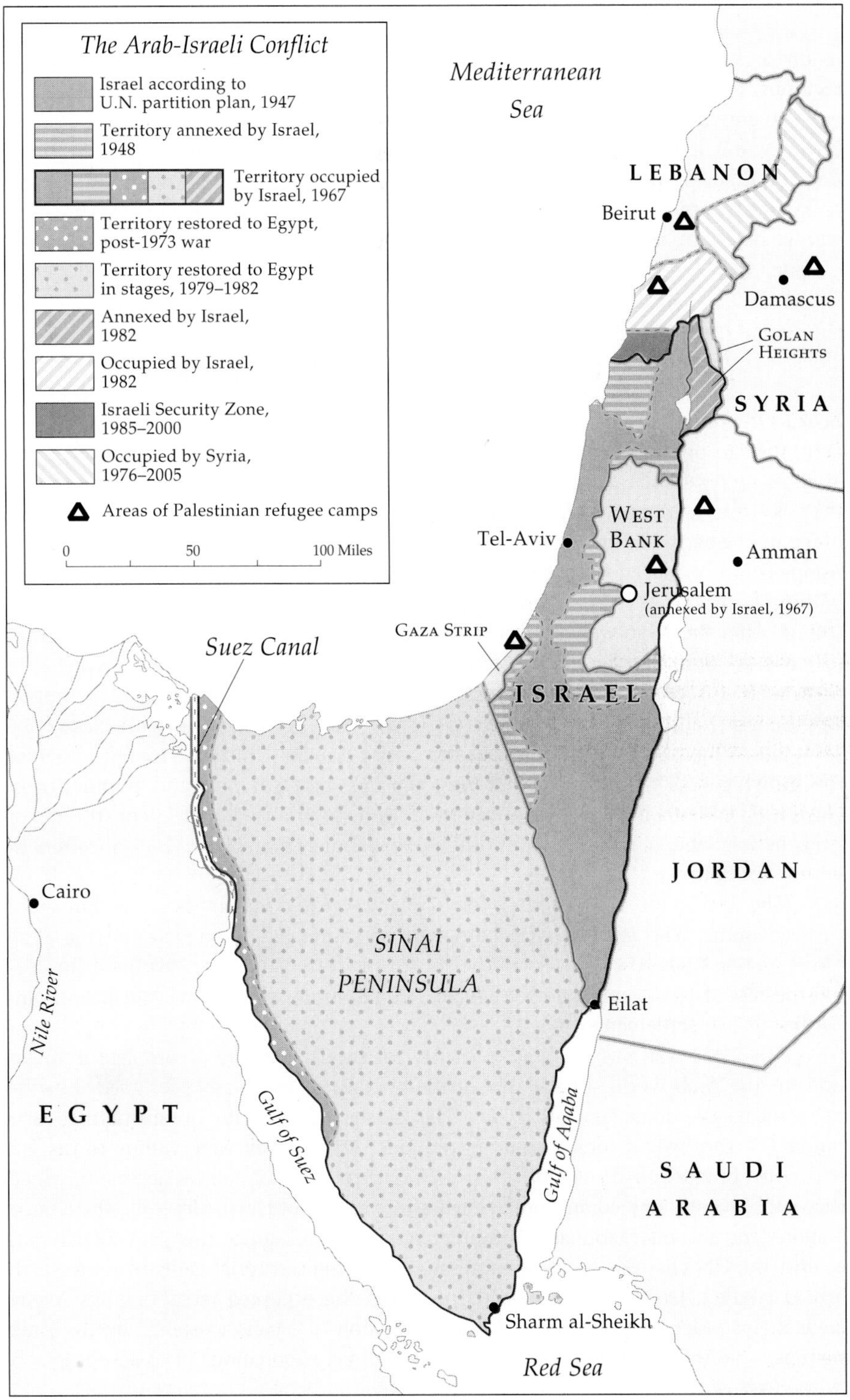

The Arab-Israeli Conflict

- Israel according to U.N. partition plan, 1947
- Territory annexed by Israel, 1948
- Territory occupied by Israel, 1967
- Territory restored to Egypt, post-1973 war
- Territory restored to Egypt in stages, 1979–1982
- Annexed by Israel, 1982
- Occupied by Israel, 1982
- Israeli Security Zone, 1985–2000
- Occupied by Syria, 1976–2005
- △ Areas of Palestinian refugee camps

0   50   100 Miles

Mediterranean Sea

LEBANON

Beirut

Damascus

GOLAN HEIGHTS

SYRIA

WEST BANK

Tel-Aviv

Amman

Jerusalem
(annexed by Israel, 1967)

Gaza Strip

ISRAEL

Suez Canal

JORDAN

Cairo

SINAI PENINSULA

Nile River

EGYPT

Gulf of Suez

Eilat

Gulf of Aqaba

SAUDI ARABIA

Sharm al-Sheikh

Red Sea

to divert attention from their invasion of Hungary. This divergence led to strained relations among the NATO allies.

Eventually, the British, French, and Israeli forces withdrew from Egyptian territory, but Israel secured free access through the Straits of Tiran to its southern port of Eilat. This acquisition, which the Egyptians and the Arab world never recognized, was to be the immediate cause of the 1967 Arab-Israeli war. The 1956 war also led to widespread political changes in much of the Arab world (see Chapter 24).

THE 1967 SIX-DAY WAR AND AFTER

Because there had been no peace settlement following the 1956 war, both sides had continued to prepare for the next violent confrontation. In May 1967 Nasser, in an attempt to regain his preeminent position as leader of the Arab world, asked that the UN forces stationed in Egyptian territory, particularly those along the vital Straits of Tiran at Sharm al-Sheikh, be withdrawn. Acting according to UN mandates that troops could be placed in sovereign territory only with the consent of the concerned nation, U Thant, the UN secretary-general, reluctantly agreed to withdraw the troops. After the 1956 war Israel had announced that it would consider any attempt to close the Straits of Tiran a cause for war. Quickly, both Israel and Egypt began to prepare for yet another confrontation. Syria and Egypt already had a mutual defense pact; although King Hussein of Jordan had been feuding with Nasser, he soon joined Egypt. Both the United States and the Soviet Union attempted to defuse the growing tensions. However, fearing the apparent strength and popularity of Nasser, Israel launched a preemptive strike against the airfields of Egypt, the major Arab nation, and of other surrounding Arab nations, destroying Arab air strength within six hours.

ISRAELI MILITARY VICTORY

The 1967 June war lasted six days but was really won by Israel within those first six hours. The Israelis, with complete air supremacy, soon defeated the Arab forces and occupied the Gaza Strip, the entire Sinai Peninsula, the West Bank (including the rest of Jerusalem), and the Golan Heights, from which Syria had been bombarding Israeli settlements.

The 1967 war was a dramatic victory for the Israelis and a complete humiliation for the Arab world. In the face of the massive defeat, Nasser resigned, but the Egyptian masses demanded his return. The Israelis were initially optimistic that their military victory would force peace negotiations. At first they were willing to discuss the return of most of the occupied territories, with the exception of Jerusalem, which they subsequently unified and proclaimed as the capital of Israel. However, the United Nations and the international community refused to recognize this gain, which was against the UN charter provision expressly forbidding territorial gains made through armed conflict. Israel refused to withdraw from the occupied territories until there were direct peace negotiations and full recognition of Israel's existence by the Arab nations. The Arab nations refused to enter into direct negotiations or to accept Israel's

Israeli soldiers pray at the Wailing Wall after taking east Jerusalem in the 1967 war.

right to any of the territory secured in the war. They also continued to demand the recognition of Palestinian rights to a homeland of their own.

The 1967 war also increased the refugee problem, since over 200,000 Palestinians crossed from the West Bank to the East Bank in Jordan. Only a small fraction of this number were permitted to return to the occupied territories after the war. Thus the stalemate was complete—no war, no peace. Various attempts were made to mediate the dispute, particularly by the United States, but all failed.

In the interim, the Palestinians concluded that no outside powers, including the Arab governments, would secure an independent Palestinian state. Consequently, a number of Palestinian guerrilla groups emerged from the disasters of the 1967 war and formed loose alliances under the umbrella of the Palestine Liberation Organization (PLO). The largest and best known of these groups was al-Fatah, led by Yasir Arafat. The PLO began a series of raids and attacks into Israeli territory; when these tactics failed to secure the objective of a Palestinian state, some Palestinians expanded the struggle to targets outside the Middle East and to those powers or individuals who supported Israel. These tactics included skyjackings, assassinations, and bombings. Some Arab leaders, including al-Asad in Syria and al-Gadhafi in Libya, also

PALESTINIANS ORGANIZE

supported these tactics. Israel retaliated with raids and attacks into surrounding Arab nations and ultimately with assassinations of Palestinian leaders. Thus the cycle of mounting terrorism spread around the globe.

WAR IN JORDAN

The PLO was particularly strong in Jordan, where about half the population was Palestinian. As it became clear to King Hussein that he was close to losing control of his government to the PLO, he launched an armed attack against Palestinian units in Jordan in September 1970. In the ensuing bloody war the Jordanian forces inflicted heavy casualties on the Palestinians. Nasser, in one of his last accomplishments before his death in September 1970, effected a settlement between the warring factions. Following the Jordanian civil war, the PLO moved its main base of operations to Lebanon, which then became the stage for armed clashes between Palestinians and Israelis.

EGYPT AND ISRAEL: WAR, THEN PEACE

Anwar Sadat, a fellow army officer with Nasser, succeeded as Egyptian president following Nasser's death. Most observers predicted that Sadat would not survive long, but their analyses were proved wrong as he revealed far more political acumen than had been anticipated. With strong fortifications along the Suez Canal, the Israelis were confident that the Egyptians could never cross. In October 1973, after several years of preparation, each of which he had termed his "year of decision" and which some Egyptians had dubbed his "years of indecision," Sadat launched a successful attack across the canal to take back Egyptian territory and force negotiations to settle the long-term conflict. Several weeks of tank and air battles in the Sinai followed and culminated in the Israelis making a countercrossing onto the western bank of the canal; Israeli and Syrian troops also clashed along the Golan Heights. The war caused a major confrontation between the Soviets, who backed Syria, and the United States, which was the main supplier of arms to Israel. Following tense negotiations between the Soviets and Secretary of State Henry Kissinger, a cease-fire was implemented. Militarily, both sides claimed a victory.

SADAT NEGOTIATES

Following the war, Sadat was hailed as the Arab leader who had taken the resolution of the Arab-Israeli conflict off the back burner and placed it at the forefront of international attention. Sadat also hoped to secure substantial economic aid from the United States in order to bolster the weak Egyptian economy. With the limited 1973 victory, Sadat moved to enter into negotiations with Israel, with the United States as an arbitrator. The United States was anxious to secure a settlement of the conflict in order to maintain a balance with the Soviet Union in the region. The United States was also eager to ensure the continued free flow of petroleum, which Arab oil producers, led by Saudi Arabia, had threatened to restrict for all nations that supported Israel. The United States feared a total Arab boycott of petroleum, but, although supplies diminished, the cutoff never materialized.

Several years of negotiations followed, characterized by Henry Kissinger's shuttle diplomacy from Tel Aviv to Cairo to Damascus, and back again. The outgrowth of these protracted negotiations was the reopening of the Suez Canal and partial withdrawal of Israeli troops from the Sinai and the Golan Heights. Although further direct negotiations were held briefly in Geneva, the issue of Palestinian participation

In March 1979 President Sadat of Egypt, President Carter of the United States, and Prime Minister Begin of Israel signed a peace treaty ending the war between Egypt and Israel, but the treaty failed to settle the ongoing conflict between the Israelis and the Palestinians.

prevented a settlement. The Arabs demanded that the Palestinians, represented by the PLO, be participants in negotiations that were to deal with their vital national interests, but the Israelis refused to include them.

As discussions dragged on with no resolution in sight, Sadat, who was anxious for a settlement so that Egypt could spend substantial amounts of money on domestic development projects in Egypt rather than on arms, decided to take matters into his own hands. In November 1977 he made a dramatic personal visit to Israel. During his speech to the Knesset, the Israeli parliament, he urged direct peace settlements. Sadat's visit, the first public visit by an Arab leader to Israel, altered the psychological atmosphere of distrust and led to direct negotiations between Egyptian and Israeli leaders. With Sadat as leader of Egypt, Israel also saw a possible opportunity to reach a peace settlement with the major and most populous Arab nation. Egyptian-Israeli negotiations intensified during the Camp David meetings in the United States in the fall of 1978, when President Jimmy Carter directly mediated between Sadat and Israeli Prime Minister Menachem Begin.

The Camp David talks culminated with the signing of a peace treaty between Egypt and Israel in the spring of 1979. The settlement provided for a full peace between Israel and Egypt and a gradual return of the Sinai peninsula to Egypt, but it did not address the issue of Palestinian self-determination or the continued Israeli occupation of the West Bank and the Gaza Strip. Likewise, the treaty contained no agreement on the status of Jerusalem, a city with sacred meaning for Jews, Christians, and Muslims.

CAMP DAVID TALKS

The rest of the Arab world, particularly the Palestinians, opposed the peace treaty. Arab nations refused to recognize Israel until Palestinian demands for a homeland were fulfilled, and Israel refused to negotiate with the PLO, which Israelis considered a terrorist organization.

Following the separate peace treaty with Israel, Egypt was ostracized from the Arab world. Many Arabs, particularly militant Muslims, held Sadat personally responsible for the treaty and the failures to secure Palestinian national rights. As he instituted repressive political controls and ignored or failed to address growing corruption in both government and economic arenas, Sadat became increasingly unpopular in Egypt.

SADAT'S ASSASSINATION

To demonstrate their hatred of Sadat's national and foreign policies and in hopes of fomenting an Islamic revolution, Egyptian Muslim radicals assassinated Sadat in October 1981 during the anniversary celebration of the 1973 war. Although the assassination indicated the widespread support of Muslim militants in Egypt, the expected revolution did not occur and Sadat's successor, Hosni Mubarak, managed to steer a middle-of-the-road course between secular nationalist and Islamist forces. President Mubarak's subsequent attempts to resume good relations with the Arab nations and the Soviet Union turned the settlement between Egypt and Israel into what has been called a "cold peace."

THE 1982 WAR IN LEBANON

Lebanon had become a battleground for both domestic and regional disputes (see Chapter 24). During the 1970s, the PLO had used southern Lebanon as a base from which to launch attacks on Israel. Israel retaliated by raiding southern Lebanon in an attempt to eradicate Palestinian organizations. Hundreds of Lebanese and Palestinians died in the raids and counterattacks. By the 1980s Israel made it clear that it would not tolerate the continued presence of the PLO in Lebanon, where the disintegration of a unified Lebanese government had allowed the Palestinians to establish something of a state within a state. In June 1982 Israel launched a full-scale invasion of Lebanon with the primary intention of destroying the PLO military and political presence there. In the ensuing war, Israel bombarded Lebanese cities by land, sea, and air. Thousands of people, mostly civilians, were killed, injured, and made homeless. After bloody combat with the Palestinians and their Lebanese allies, the Israelis and their Lebanese Christian allies besieged West Beirut.

BLOODSHED IN LEBANON

Following weeks of protracted Israeli bombings of the city, the PLO fighters and leaders were evacuated under the auspices of international peacekeeping forces. Bashir Gemayel, son of one of the leading rightist Lebanese Christians and leader of the largest private militia, was elected president of the war-torn nation. His assassination in September led Christian militiamen to massacre hundreds of Palestinians and others in Sabra and Shatila, the large Palestinian refugee camps in West Beirut under Israeli control. After 1982, as Israeli and Syrian forces remained in occupation of the southern and eastern sections of the small nation, Lebanese religious and political militias continued to fight among themselves. When international peacekeeping forces, including U.S. Marines, failed to keep the peace and attacks against Israeli occupying forces by Lebanese Shi'i groups intensified, Israel withdrew from much of southern Lebanon in 1985. However, Israel continued its occupation of the so-called security zone in Lebanon; likewise, the Syrians continued to maintain a large military force in Lebanon. Thus, it was evident that until solutions for the problem of Palestinian self-determination and a settlement of the wider Arab-Israeli conflict were devised, there was little likelihood of a resolution to either the conflict or the Israeli and Syrian military occupations in much of Lebanon.

ISRAELIS AND PALESTINIANS

The 1982 war was a severe blow to the Palestinian liberation movement, but it also caused serious political divisions within Israel. The ultimate status of the West Bank and the Gaza Strip, which had been under Israeli occupation since the 1967 war, became the focal point of the controversy. Israelis were widely divided on the issue. The Likud, the conservative party of the Right, generally wanted to keep all of the occupied territories, while the Labor Party generally advocated a "land for peace" solution in which some of the territories would be traded for a settlement of the ongoing conflict with the Palestinians.

However, the Palestinians insisted that the PLO was their sole representative, and the Israeli government absolutely refused to deal with the PLO. Meanwhile, the number of Israeli settlements in the occupied territories continued to increase, and the 1.4 million Palestinians in the occupied territories became increasingly hostile to Israeli military control.

PALESTINIAN UPRISING

After intermittent confrontations, the conflict broke out in a full-scale *Intifada* (uprising) in December 1987. Palestinians, particularly the young people, demonstrated, went out on strike, boycotted Israeli goods and services, and threw stones. The Israeli army retaliated with an Iron Fist policy in an attempt to smash the uprising. By 1991 more than 1,000 Palestinians and dozens of Israelis had been killed; although there were fewer massive demonstrations, the conflict and Palestinian opposition to continued Israeli occupation showed few signs of ending.

SHIFTS IN ISRAELI POLITICS

The uprising caused political debates within Israel and among Jewish Americans over possible solutions. The Israeli elections in the 1980s failed to give either the conservative Likud Party or the Labor Party a clear-cut majority, and they were therefore forced to create a kind of dual government in which both shared power. By 1988 it was clear that the Israeli population was fairly evenly divided between those who wished to keep the occupied territories and those who wished to reach a settlement with the Palestinians and return at least portions of the territory.

FACE-TO-FACE NEGOTIATIONS

In a sweeping move, the PLO in 1988 declared the independence of Palestine (the West Bank and Gaza), recognized the existence of Israel, and called for a negotiated settlement. Dozens of nations recognized the new Palestinian state and lauded the move toward peace. As the Soviet Union grew weaker (see Chapter 31), and following U.S. victory in the Gulf War (see Chapter 24), the United States felt confident enough to play the role of mediator in this long-standing conflict. In 1991, in a precedent-breaking move, all the parties involved agreed to public, face-to-face meetings in Madrid under the auspices of the United States and other nations.

Young Palestinians waving a Palestinian flag face Israeli troops during protests over Israeli occupation of the West Bank and Gaza Strip.

These negotiations centered on the withdrawal of Israel from the occupied territories, self-determination for the Palestinians, and security for Israel. However, Israel continued to build new settlements and to maintain its military control over the Palestinians in the occupied territories. These policies guaranteed the continuation of Palestinian opposition. As will be described in Chapter 32, it was clear that the conflict would continue until the two major parties—the Israelis and the Palestinians—were able to reach a face-to-face negotiated settlement.

SUMMARY

The creation of Israel in 1948 resulted in the first Arab-Israeli war, the displacement and loss of self-government for the Palestinians, and the opposition of the Arab nations to Israel. The 1948 war and the subsequent four wars were military victories for the Israelis, but all failed to resolve the conflict. In the 1967 war Israel expanded the territory under its control, ultimately annexing East Jerusalem and parts of the Syrian Golan Heights. Following the 1973 war the Egyptians and Israelis, with substantial involvement of the United States, negotiated a territorial disengagement and peace treaty in 1979; however, this treaty did not resolve the root causes of the conflict. The continued Israeli occupation of the West Bank and the Gaza Strip, the status of Jerusalem, and the creation of an independent Palestinian state remained points of conflict between the Israelis and the Palestinians.

SUGGESTED SOURCES

Ashrawi, Hanan. *This Side of Peace: A Personal Account.* 1995. An autobiography by a well-known spokesperson for Palestinian rights.

Bregman, Ahron. *Israel's Wars: A History since 1947.* 2nd ed. 2002. An updated overview of the conflict with an emphasis on the military aspects.*

Eisenberg, Laura Zittrain, and Neil Caplan. *Negotiating Arab-Israeli Peace: Patterns, Problems, Possibilities.* 1998. Insightful analysis of the difficulties facing the peace process; includes primary documentary material.*

Hiltermann, Joost R. *Behind the Intifada.* 1991. A study of the causes and motivations behind the Palestinian uprising in the occupied territories.*

Neff, Donald. *Warriors at Suez.* 1981; *Warriors for Jerusalem.* 1984. Highly entertaining yet informative descriptions of the personalities behind the 1956 and 1967 wars.*

Sadat, Anwar. *In Search of Identity: An Autobiography.* 1979. The Egyptian leader's personal account of his political life and negotiations with Israel.*

Smith, Charles D. *Palestine and the Arab-Israeli Conflict.* 5th ed. 2004. Solid text with useful inclusion of primary documents.*

Sprinzak, Ehud, and Larry Diamond, eds. *Israeli Democracy under Stress.* 1993. Anthology of political, religious, and ethnic complexities in Israeli society.*

Young, Elise G. *Keepers of the History: Women and the Arab-Israeli Conflict.* 1992. A provocative account focusing on Israeli and Palestinian women.

WEB SOURCES

www.fordham.edu/halsall/islam/islamsbook.html. See links under "The Palestine/Israel Conflict."

www.fordham.edu/halsall/jewish/jewishsbook.html. See links under "The State of Israel."

www.fordham.edu/halsall/mod/modsbook54.html. See especially links under "Israel and Palestine."

www.nmhschool.org/tthornton/mehistorydatabase/mideastindex.htm. A useful database on the Middle East. See, for example, the link to "The Arab-Israeli Wars, 1948–1973."

---

*Paperback available.

26

⑥Détente and Europe, 1963–1984

Following the Berlin crisis of 1961 and the Cuban missile crisis of 1962 the super-powers pulled back from confrontation and there was a movement toward détente (a lessening of tensions) in the cold war. Beginning in the 1960s, Western European nations, especially France, became less dependent on the United States. Eastern European nations, thanks in part to the Sino-Soviet split, were able to achieve more autonomy than the Soviet Union had previously allowed. During the 1970s U.S. diplomatic initiatives toward Communist China further contributed to transforming the bipolar U.S.-Soviet global rivalry into a multipolar global balance of power. Events in Czechoslovakia in 1968 and in Poland in 1981, however, seemed to indicate that the Soviet Union was still determined to keep Eastern European countries firmly within its orbit. In the late 1970s and early 1980s, tensions between the superpowers again intensified.

THE DAWN OF DÉTENTE

The Cuban missile crisis had been frightening, and in its aftermath many world leaders became interested in lessening tensions and thus reducing the chances of nuclear war. In 1963 the major atomic powers, joined by over 100 nations, signed the Nuclear Test Ban Treaty, which prohibited testing in outer space, in the atmosphere, and underwater. France and the People's Republic of China refused to sign; the French wished to do more testing to catch up with the advanced nuclear powers, and the Chinese needed tests to complete the development of their first atomic bomb. In 1964 the People's Republic exploded a bomb and became a new and potentially powerful member of the atomic club.

The Chinese bomb spurred international action to deal with the growing threat of nuclear proliferation. The established atomic powers took the position that the world would be safer if no more nations created their own atomic bombs. The United States, the Soviet Union, and Great Britain prepared a draft treaty for the United Nations in which the signatories agreed not to develop atomic weapons. Eventually, 98 nations signed the Nuclear Non-Proliferation Treaty. Again, France and China refused to sign; India, Pakistan, Israel, and other nations undertaking nuclear weapons research also refused.

Meanwhile, the United States and the Soviet Union proceeded with a number of bilateral agreements. Taking a lesson from the Cuban missile crisis, in June 1963

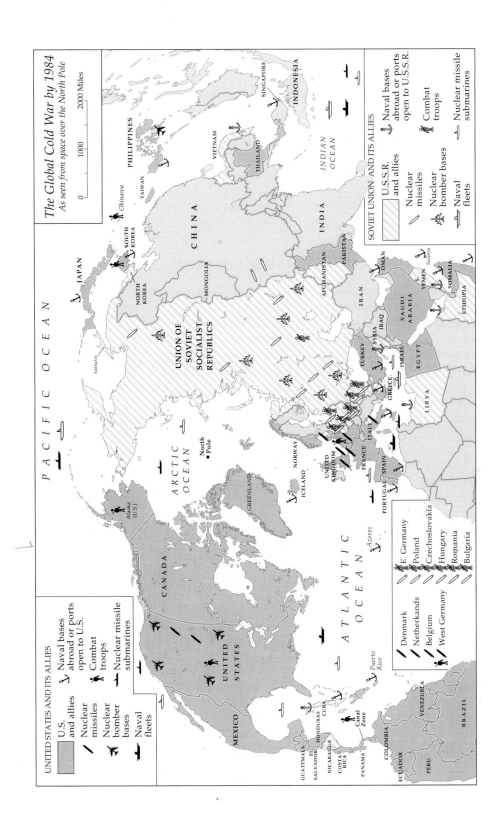

The Global Cold War by 1984
As seen from space over the North Pole

0   1000   2000 Miles

UNITED STATES AND ITS ALLIES

	U.S. and allies		Naval bases abroad or ports open to U.S.
	Nuclear missiles		Combat troops
	Nuclear bomber bases		Nuclear missile submarines
	Naval fleets		

SOVIET UNION AND ITS ALLIES

	U.S.S.R. and allies		Naval bases abroad or ports open to U.S.S.R.
	Nuclear missiles		Combat troops
	Nuclear bomber bases		Nuclear missile submarines
	Naval fleets		

Denmark
Netherlands
Belgium
West Germany

E. Germany
Poland
Czechoslovakia
Hungary
Romania
Bulgaria

PACIFIC OCEAN

JAPAN
SOUTH KOREA
NORTH KOREA
Okinawa
TAIWAN
Sakhalin
MONGOLIA
CHINA
PHILIPPINES
SINGAPORE
INDONESIA
VIETNAM
THAILAND
INDIAN OCEAN
INDIA
PAKISTAN
AFGHANISTAN
IRAN
OMAN
P.S. YEMEN
Socotra
SOMALIA
ETHIOPIA
SAUDI ARABIA
IRAQ
SYRIA
ISRAEL
EGYPT
TURKEY
GREECE
LIBYA
ITALY
FRANCE
SPAIN
PORTUGAL
UNITED KINGDOM
ICELAND
NORWAY
GREENLAND

UNION OF SOVIET SOCIALIST REPUBLICS

ARCTIC OCEAN
North Pole
Azores
ATLANTIC OCEAN

Alaska (U.S.)
CANADA
UNITED STATES
MEXICO
GUATEMALA
EL SALVADOR
HONDURAS
NICARAGUA
COSTA RICA
PANAMA
Canal Zone
CUBA
Puerto Rico
COLOMBIA
VENEZUELA
ECUADOR
PERU
BRAZIL

411

the two countries agreed to install a hotline, a direct personal telephone connection between the U.S. president and the Soviet premier that might be used to defuse a developing crisis.[1] A new trading era between the two countries began when the United States agreed in 1963 to sell large quantities of wheat to the Soviet Union at a time of shortage. Soon the United States was regularly selling a wide variety of products to the Soviet Union. Tourism was encouraged, and ordinary U.S. citizens found themselves looking at Lenin's tomb in Moscow or visiting the Hermitage Museum in Leningrad, while Soviet officials viewed New York from the Empire State Building or visited the Lincoln Memorial. There were also cultural exchanges, as the Bolshoi Ballet and Louis Armstrong crossed the Atlantic to perform.

THE COMMON MARKET AND DE GAULLE

FORMATION AND DEVELOPMENT OF THE COMMON MARKET

In 1967 the European Economic Community (EEC, or Common Market), founded in 1957, joined with the European Coal and Steel Community and the European Atomic Energy Community to form the European Communities (EC), later the European Community. In 1968 the EEC, which continued to exist within the EC, attained its goal of ending tariffs between member nations (France, West Germany, Italy, Belgium, the Netherlands, and Luxembourg). A completely free flow of trade, however, remained elusive because of factors such as differing product standards and government contracts. In 1973 Great Britain, Ireland, and Denmark became members of the EC, and in 1981 Greece joined. As the organization grew, its departments, including the Council of Ministers and the European Parliament, also increased in significance.

Members of the EC and other European nations continued their postwar economic recovery. West Germany, especially, impressed the world with its strong postwar economic performance. The U.S. government bargained strenuously to reduce EC tariffs on U.S. goods, fearing that they would not be competitive in Europe with comparable goods from EC nations. At the same time, U.S. families purchased an increasing number of European automobiles, television sets, and other products. Coupled with U.S. military expenditures in Europe, such spending helped to bring about a U.S. balance-of-payments deficit that increased throughout the 1960s. The devaluation of U.S. currency in 1971 and 1973 against European currencies clearly indicated that the U.S. dollar no longer dominated Europe as it once had.

DE GAULLE IN POWER, 1958–1969

If the EC symbolized growing economic Western European independence, General Charles de Gaulle personified another trend: the area's attempt to end its political dependence on the United States. He came to power in 1958, after the French Fourth Republic had produced 27 governments in 13 years. In the midst of a governmental

---

[1]During the tense days of October 1962, with the avoidance of nuclear war seeming to hinge on successful negotiations, Soviet Ambassador Anatoly Dobrynin had used Western Union to send coded cables to Moscow. He later stated that he could only hope that the bicycle messenger delivering his cables would take them directly to the Western Union office "and not stop to chat on the way with some girl!" See Dobrynin's *In Confidence: Moscow's Ambassador to America's Six Cold War Presidents (1962–1986)* (New York: Time Books, 1995), p. 96.

General Charles de Gaulle in French Africa shortly before being elected president of France in 1958.

crisis revolving around Algeria, de Gaulle was invited by the French Assembly to rule while a new constitution was drawn up. The new constitution provided for much stronger executive powers than in the past. It created a president, elected for a seven-year term, who appointed the prime minister; the president was given other powers that clearly made him the dominant figure in the government. De Gaulle was elected to the post in 1958 and remained the president of France until he resigned in 1969.

De Gaulle was an aloof and haughty figure—he once said, "When I want to know what France thinks, I ask myself." Roosevelt had stated that de Gaulle imagined himself another Joan of Arc. A nationalist in every inch of his imposing frame, he was continually concerned with the greatness and prestige of France. One of his first priorities was resolving the costly Algerian war, and by 1962 he had finally persuaded the French to acquiesce to Algerian independence. From the beginning of his presidency, de Gaulle encouraged France to develop its own atomic capability, and in 1960 France tested its first atomic bomb.

Another major goal for de Gaulle was to extricate France from the grip of the United States. He began to remove French troops from the U.S.-dominated North Atlantic Treaty Organization (NATO) as early as 1959, and by 1967 he had withdrawn all French forces from NATO. Since the United States would not allow the French to control U.S. nuclear weapons, de Gaulle no longer allowed such weapons in France and had all NATO forces leave French soil.

De Gaulle envisioned France as the head of the Third Force, which would stand between the United States and the Soviet Union. He hoped that most Western European nations would follow his lead; in part, that meant a leading role for France in the Common Market. During the 1960s de Gaulle blocked British entry into the organization because he feared the rivalry of Great Britain and its close ties with the United States. He also tried to improve relations with the Soviet Union and the Eastern European nations, recognized the People's Republic of China, and traveled to such areas as Latin America and Canada in an effort to exercise global statesmanship. Although France did not gain the leading role he envisioned, de Gaulle did make a major contribution to the growing sense of independence in Europe.

DOMESTIC UNREST IN FRANCE, 1968

In May 1968 students at several campuses of the University of Paris openly revolted against authorities, the police, and the French government. The student revolt in Paris was matched by student demonstrations in the United States, Great Britain, Italy, West Germany, and other nations during the late 1960s. Causes for Western student unrest varied: the boredom bred by an affluent, technological civilization; the impact of New Left ideologies influenced by Mao Zedong and Castro; the opposition to the Vietnam War; local student grievances; and a host of other causes. In Paris, the students were soon joined by leftist political leaders and by a large number of workers who went on strike. De Gaulle's regime was at first threatened with chaos, but wage concessions to workers, promises of university reforms, and support from French citizens opposed to the unrest helped him restore order. Nevertheless, the events were a blow to his prestige, and when the nation refused to approve an administrative reorganization referendum in 1969, de Gaulle resigned.

THE SOVIET UNION: BREZHNEV TO CHERNENKO

KHRUSHCHEV OUSTED FROM POWER, 1964

In October 1964 Nikita Khrushchev's colleagues ousted him from power, sent him into retirement, and kept him under close supervision until he died in 1971. He was forced out for a number of reasons: a poor harvest in 1963, along with a sluggish economy; foreign policy failures, including the Cuban missile crisis and a growing split with China; an increasingly abrasive, authoritarian, and incautious political style; and a backlash against his attack on Stalinism and attempts to reform the Communist system and bureaucracy. In addition, he was accused of "hair-brained schemes" and creating a new "personality cult." Leonid Brezhnev, the chief instigator of the coup, replaced Khrushchev in the key position of first secretary of the Communist Party, while Alexei Kosygin took over as premier. After 1964 Brezhnev was the dominant figure in Soviet politics. Like Khrushchev, he was not a dictator but the most prominent of a small group of political leaders in a one-party state. Like most of them, Brezhnev had a technical background and a long history of party work. The oligarchic nature of rule did not, however, prevent Brezhnev from eventually acquiring numerous titles and honors. He received so many medals that some Russians joked he would require "chest-expansion surgery" to fit them all on.

THE BREZHNEV ERA, 1964–1982

During the Brezhnev era, the Soviet Union in some areas continued to follow the path marked out by Khrushchev. Throughout most of the late 1960s and the 1970s military spending remained the top priority, but the government also gradually improved the living standard of the average Soviet citizen. The government continued to develop the nation's rich resources of petroleum, gas, and minerals at a slow but steady pace. By 1974 the U.S.S.R. had become the world's largest petroleum producer. On the other hand, agriculture remained the most troubled area of the Soviet economy. Crop failures in 1972 and 1975 forced the Soviet government to make large grain purchases from the United States. From 1979 through 1982 the U.S.S.R. experienced four poor harvests in succession, the Soviet economy stagnated, and the standard of living declined. Despite some experiments in economic liberalization, the party and government kept tight control over the economy.

A major difference between the two eras was that Brezhnev put an end to Khrushchev's "de-Stalinization" campaign. Khrushchev's overall record on literature and intellectual life was considerably more liberal than Stalin's had been, and once writers experienced this thaw, the party discovered it was difficult to contain them. Nevertheless, in 1966, Brezhnev and his colleagues apparently decided matters had gone far enough: Andrei Siniavsky and Yuli Daniel were put on trial for "anti-Soviet propaganda," although their only crime had been to send literature to the West for publication. They were sentenced, respectively, to seven and five years in Soviet labor camps. But their trial and sentences sparked even greater opposition from Soviet intellectuals and helped launch a full-blown dissident movement that continued into the 1970s.

Other trials and the realistic fears of increased official sympathy for the Stalinist past continued to fuel opposition to the government. Underground literature and the number of manuscripts sent abroad increased. The underground *Chronicle of Current Events,* published regularly from 1968 to 1972 and sporadically thereafter, reflected the opposition of scattered intellectuals, religious groups, and ethnic minorities. While the party continued to sentence dissidents to prison, labor camps, and mental institutions, it also allowed or forced some of the more prominent ones to leave the U.S.S.R., as Alexander Solzhenitsyn did in 1974. In January 1980 one of the country's few remaining free dissident leaders, the prominent physicist Andrei Sakharov, was exiled to the city of Gorky.

INCREASING DISSIDENT OPPOSITION

Meanwhile, the vitality of the aging Soviet leadership was also declining. Brezhnev suffered a stroke in 1976 and, in the words of the Russian historian Roy Medvedev, "He gradually found it more and more difficult to carry out the most simple protocol functions and could no longer understand what was going on around him." When he died in 1982, the Soviet people also seemed less vital and optimistic. Economic and political decline had taken their toll. Corruption, favoritism, and alcoholism were on their way up; life expectancy and belief in communism were moving in the other direction. Between late 1982 and early 1985 the party had two more leaders whose health was poor and who soon died in office: Yuri Andropov and Konstantin Chernenko.

EASTERN EUROPE IN THE 1960s: THE PURSUIT AND LIMITS OF AUTONOMY

If de Gaulle and some other Europeans resented early postwar U.S. domination of Western Europe, Eastern Europeans were even more hostile toward Soviet hegemony over them and sought ways to reduce it. Khrushchev's de-Stalinization campaign inside

**IMPACT OF
SINO-SOVIET SPLIT**

the U.S.S.R. continued to encourage some Eastern Europeans to hope that they could lessen the Soviet dominance of their region imposed by Stalin. Yet the use of Soviet troops to put down the Hungarian rebellion of 1956 (see Chapter 20) was proof enough that Khrushchev intended to allow only so much latitude to any Eastern European deviations from Soviet communism. In the early 1960s, the Sino-Soviet split further encouraged Eastern Europeans to develop their own brands of communism. If there could be a Chinese communism different from Soviet communism, then why not a Polish or Hungarian communism? But only small Albania, which sided with China, succeeded in leaving the Soviet orbit. Yet while Romania remained a politically oppressive Soviet ally, its government insisted on a measure of independence in economic and foreign policies. In 1963, when COMECON (the Soviet bloc economic organization) attempted to hamper Romanian industrial advancement, Romania refused to cooperate. In its foreign relations, Romania was on better terms with China and Israel than was the Soviet Union; on occasion it also voted differently at the United Nations.

Some Eastern European nations also pursued policies that were more liberal than those in the U.S.S.R. In Hungary, the János Kádár regime improved economic conditions by relaxing centralized economic planning and allowing more local initiative. The government also permitted more personal freedom; in 1964, for example, more than 100,000 Hungarians were allowed to visit Western nations. In Poland most of the farmland, unlike that in the Soviet Union, remained in private hands. Poland and Romania, as well as Hungary, also allowed more religious freedom.

There were, however, limits to how much autonomy the Soviet Union would allow its satellites, and in 1968 Czechoslovakia passed those limits. During the mid-1960s, discontent spread in Czechoslovakia under the Stalinist Antonin Novotny. In December 1967–January 1968, he was replaced by Alexander Dubček as first secretary of the Czechoslovak Communist Party. Soon afterward, encouraged by public opinion, Dubček and his colleagues began to carry out a policy of liberalization. They greatly reduced censorship, recognized civil liberties, rehabilitated victims of past party injustices, and allowed autonomous political groupings to emerge. Relations with Western nations grew warmer, and Dubček displayed a desire to place Soviet-Czechoslovakian ties on a more equal footing.

**SOVIET INVASION OF
CZECHOSLOVAKIA, 1968**

Soviet leaders became increasingly alarmed about the liberalization policies and feared that they might spread like a virus to other Eastern European nations. Dissent in the Soviet Union, already a problem for the regime, might also be encouraged if the Czechoslovakians were allowed such freedoms. In addition, Czechoslovakia's strategic position between the U.S.S.R. and West Germany undoubtedly magnified Soviet fears; although, unlike the Hungarian government in 1956, the Czechoslovakian leadership never announced any intention to withdraw from the Warsaw Pact. The Soviet Union began to pressure the Czechoslovakian leaders to rescind their reforms, but they refused to give way. On August 21, 1968, Soviet, East German, Polish, Hungarian, and Bulgarian troops invaded Czechoslovakia. Believing it would be suicidal to offer armed resistance, the nation's leaders and people simply offered a sullen and passive noncooperation. In April 1969 Dubček was forced out of office, and Gustav Husák became head of the party. The "Prague Spring" of 1968 and the accompanying hopes for a more humane socialism were dead.

Prague, Czechoslovakia, 1968: Soviet tanks and troops suppress the liberal Communist regime of Alexander Dubček.

Following the invasion, Husák restored Czechoslovakia to the status of a police state on which the Soviet Union could rely, and Soviet leaders elaborated their justification for interference—Western observers would label it the Brezhnev Doctrine. It stated that "every Communist party is responsible not only to its own people but also to all the socialist countries" and that "the sovereignty of individual socialist countries cannot be counterposed to the interests of world socialism."

THE FLOWERING OF DÉTENTE

Despite the strained feelings stimulated by the Vietnam War and the 1968 invasion of Czechoslovakia, the "spirit of détente" was well under way when Richard Nixon became president of the United States in 1969. Both de Gaulle and Willy Brandt, German foreign minister (1966–1969) and then chancellor (1969–1974), pursued a policy of détente before the term became linked with the efforts of Nixon and the Soviet leader Leonid Brezhnev in the early 1970s. Brandt, a former mayor of West Berlin and a Social Democrat (moderate socialist), urged the creation of an *Ostpolitik*, "a hand offered to the East." In 1972, by which time Nixon was also pushing détente, the two German nations formally recognized each other. The United States recognized East Germany, and the Soviet Union pledged not to block access to Berlin. That year, both Germanies were admitted to the United Nations.

Nixon had been a hard-line anti-Communist cold warrior in the 1940s and 1950s, but, partly to demonstrate U.S. leadership among its allies, he shifted his position after becoming president and intended to make his mark in history by easing cold war tensions. In particular, he expected to improve relationships with both the

EUROPEAN ORIGINS OF DÉTENTE

Soviet Union and China. These two nations had become antagonists (see Chapter 29), and Nixon hoped to take advantage of the distrust between the two powers to improve relations with both. To carry out his initiatives, Nixon relied on the diplomatic skills of Henry Kissinger, who sought to replace the cold war with a more complex multipolar balance of power.

NUCLEAR WEAPONS DEVELOPMENTS

The core of the cold war lay in the nuclear arms race, and both the United States and the Soviet Union were ready to consider means to slow it down. The Soviet Union had, at great cost to its economy, achieved a rough parity with the United States in tonnage of deliverable atomic destruction but was increasingly distracted by its split with China. The United States was staggering under the economic burden of the Vietnam War, and its society was distracted by social unrest. In addition, both nations were faced with the costs of implementing two new major weapons systems now deemed necessary to keep abreast or ahead in the arms race. One was the antiballistic missile (ABM), a defensive missile designed to destroy incoming missiles. The special attraction and also danger of this weapon was that the first nation that believed itself fully protected by its ABMs would be tempted to launch a successful attack on its less-well-defended adversary. To increase the sophistication of the offense against the ABM, military technicians had created another weapons system, the multiple independently targeted reentry vehicle (MIRV). The MIRV consisted of several warheads, each programmed to hit a different target, all mounted on a single rocket. The cost of fully implementing these systems promised to be a crushing burden on both nations.

SOVIET UNION AND UNITED STATES SIGN ARMS AGREEMENTS

In 1969 Nixon and Brezhnev agreed to arms limitation talks. By 1972 the basic agreement had been hammered out, and Nixon traveled to Moscow to sign the Strategic Arms Limitation Talks (SALT) Treaty. The treaty suspended the building of ICBMs, capped the number of missile-firing submarines that could be employed, and limited the deployment of ABMs. Even with these limitations, both nations remained capable of overkill—that is, destroying their opponent many times over. The spirit of accord was enhanced in 1973 when Brezhnev visited Washington. Meanwhile, a number of bilateral and multilateral agreements were hammered out, including one pact to not deploy nuclear weapons on the ocean floor and another to not manufacture bacteriological weapons. In 1974, at Vladivostok in the Soviet Far East, President Gerald Ford and party leader Brezhnev signed a preliminary agreement designed to extend strategic arms limitations into the 1980s. The same year, the two nations also agreed to not conduct underground nuclear tests of more than 150 kilotons.

UNITED STATES AND CHINA IMPROVE RELATIONS

The series of agreements between the United States and the Soviet Union were important for world peace, but it was the sudden rapprochement between the United States and China in 1971–1972 that startled and excited the world. Since 1950, there had been a bamboo curtain between the United States and China; they had no diplomatic, economic, or cultural relations, and the two governments constantly attacked each other in public statements. The Chinese had conducted a relentless propaganda campaign against "the paper tiger of American imperialism," while the U.S. government encouraged anti–"Red China" attitudes among Americans.

Both nations, however, had reasons to change their policies. China feared the Soviet Union and also feared that improved U.S.-Soviet relations would isolate China and reduce its influence. China was also worried that if the United States lessened its involvement in Asia, the vacuum would be filled by Japan and the Soviet Union. All these factors crystallized at a time when China was emerging from the turmoil of the Cultural Revolution (see Chapter 29). At the same time, the United States was extricating itself from a disastrous war in Indochina, attempting to negotiate a settlement on some basic issues with the Soviet Union, and rethinking some of its belief that an expansionist China must be contained.

Late in 1969 secret negotiations began toward the normalization of Sino-U.S. relations. In 1971 the United States refrained from employing its veto when the United Nations expelled Taiwan and seated the People's Republic in the General Assembly and in China's permanent seat in the Security Council. In 1972, amid mixed feelings both at home and around the world, Nixon traveled to Beijing, where he received a polite but restrained welcome. Nixon met briefly with Mao and participated in discussions with other Chinese leaders. At the Great Hall of the People, Nixon and his hosts banqueted, toasted one another with potent mao-tai cocktails, and before departing exchanged gifts—Nixon received two giant pandas, Hsing-Hsing and Ling-Ling.

The Americans and Chinese did not come to any major agreements but were satisfied at that time to air their differences. The final communiqué ambiguously noted that "the United States acknowledges that all Chinese on either side of the Taiwan Straits maintain there is but one China and that Taiwan is part of China." Shortly thereafter, the two nations agreed to establish cultural and economic contacts to open China to U.S. tourists and to open liaison offices (embassies, in all but name) in each other's capitals. The momentum established by the Sino-U.S. rapprochement quickly extended to China's relations with Japan, and later that same year Japan recognized the Communist government of China and established normal diplomatic relations.

After 1972 the main obstacle to complete normalization of relations between the United States and China continued to be China's insistence that the United States withdraw its recognition of Taiwan and abrogate its mutual defense pact with that island's government. The United States feared that China would attack Taiwan if the United States withdrew its pledge of military support. In 1978 the administration of President Carter, apparently receiving tacit assurances that China would not attack Taiwan, agreed to China's two principal conditions. On January 1, 1979, the two nations opened embassies in Beijing and Washington. Normalization was now complete, although the United States and China remained wary of each other. The United States continued to retain economic and cultural ties with Taiwan. In 1984 President Reagan visited China, and the United States subsequently increased its technical aid and agreed to sell China certain weapons.

At Helsinki, Finland, in 1975, a the process of détente expanded to Europe as a whole. In addition to affirming respect for human rights, 33 European nations plus the United States and Canada agreed in effect that the existing boundaries in Europe, including the German-Polish border, were "inviolable." The results of World War II had finally been ratified. (Helsinki watch groups, established to monitor their countries' compliance with human rights standards, became part of the dissident movement in some of the Communist countries.)

HELSINKI AGREEMENTS, 1975

During the 1970s the arms race expanded, despite the easing of political tensions and despite a series of agreements on nuclear testing and proliferation and on strategic

Parodox: During the 1970s the superpowers pursued a policy of détente while at the same time continuing their post–World War II arms race. Above, Soviet President Brezhnev plants one of his trademark kisses on the cheek of U.S. President Carter at the 1979 SALT II conference in Vienna; below, Soviet missiles on parade through Moscow.

arms limitations. Nuclear powers continued to test under ground frequently, and China still tested above ground. Even though the 1972 SALT Treaty limited the number of nuclear weapons, the Soviet Union and the United States continued to improve their nuclear weapons in speed, range, accuracy, and, above all, power. By 1978 the two nations were in a state of approximate nuclear parity. They possessed over 40,000 strategic nuclear warheads with a total destructive force equal to 1.5 million bombs of the magnitude that fell on Hiroshima. Experts pronounced the arms race at the stage of mutual assured destruction (MAD).

In addition to the potential for nuclear devastation from the "limited" bombs and missiles, military scientists had developed or were developing weapons not limited by treaty. Such weapons included low-flying cruise missiles and stealth bombers that could escape radar detection; the neutron bomb, which killed people with little damage to property; laser beams, the "ray gun" of science fiction now become reality; and space satellites and platforms that could fire missiles and lasers.

WESTERN EUROPE, 1970–1984: ECONOMICS AND POLITICS

Western Europe entered the 1970s after several decades of economic growth. Of the major powers, only Great Britain continued to have serious economic problems; a sluggish economic growth rate, balance-of-payments deficits, labor unrest, and inflation all troubled the Labour Party government that had taken over from the Conservatives in 1964 and continued in power until 1970. Nevertheless, even in Great Britain, the standard of living of most individuals continued to improve.

RECESSION AND INFLATION

In 1974 and 1975, however, increased food and petroleum prices and an economic recession temporarily shook Western European nations that had become used to prosperity. West Germany's inflation rate had been under 2 percent in 1969 but by 1974 had risen to 7 percent. Great Britain's was a little under 6 percent in 1969, but by 1975 it was close to 25 percent. Italy's inflation and unemployment rates in 1974 were among Europe's highest. It was perhaps no accident that the men chosen to head the French and West German governments in 1974, Valéry Giscard d'Estaing and Helmut Schmidt, had both been finance or economics ministers in previous governments. Schmidt took over from his party's leader, Willy Brandt, who had resigned after it was discovered that a member of his staff was an East German spy. In Great Britain, after four years out of power, Labour Party chief Harold Wilson, an economist by training, was also voted back into office in 1974.

By the late 1970s Western European nations gradually had begun to recover from the economic shock of the earlier part of the decade. By 1978 the inflation rate in Great Britain had fallen to about 9 percent and in West Germany to 2 percent. Although the British continued to be plagued by long-standing economic problems, they increased production of North Sea petroleum, reducing dependence on foreign sources. By 1981 several Western European nations were listed among the wealthiest in the world. Switzerland, Sweden, Denmark, West Germany, Norway, and Belgium all had a higher per capita GNP than the United States; the Netherlands and France were not far behind. During the early 1980s, however, the global recession brought to Western Europe its highest unemployment rates since World War II.

Despite economic ups and downs, Western European politics remained fairly stable, with moderately conservative and moderately socialist parties dominating. Italy's frequent changes of government—averaging slightly over one a year in the postwar decades—became so common that they seemed almost routine. In Portugal and Spain, where right-wing governments had long ruled, the people restored democracy in 1975–1977 and maintained it with less difficulty than many had predicted. By

1984 both countries had moderate socialist governments, as did France, Greece, and Sweden.

MITTERRAND, KOHL, AND THATCHER

The most important Western socialist leader of the 1980s was French president François Mitterrand, elected in 1981 and reelected to another seven-year term in 1988. Two other important political figures were the Christian Democrat (moderately conservative) Helmut Kohl, who replaced the Social Democrat (moderately socialist) Helmut Schmidt as West Germany's chancellor in 1982, and the British prime minister Margaret Thatcher, elected in 1979. Sometimes compared with President Reagan because of her conservatism, she pursued a policy aimed at reducing Great Britain's welfare state and turning more and more of its functions over to free enterprise (privatization). Her supporters claimed that she revived the British economy, and her opponents charged that she benefited the rich at the expense of the poor. (See Chapter 31 for more on Thatcher and her policies.) Regardless of differing political views, however, conservatives such as Kohl and Thatcher and socialists such as Mitterrand all worked in the 1980s to augment European prosperity.

TERRORISM

Although most Western Europeans were content with their governments, not all was calm in the political waters. Radical terrorists plagued Germany and Italy in particular with sporadic bombings, kidnappings, and assassinations. In Germany it was primarily the anticapitalists of the Baader-Meinhof group and of the *Rote Armee Fraktion* who engaged in bomb attacks, bank robberies, murdering industrialists, and hostage taking, including passengers on a Lufthansa jet in 1977. By this time, some Germans were greatly alarmed and seemed willing to countenance the curtailment of civil liberties in the fight against terrorism. The Schmidt government, however, generally resisted any extreme reaction. Although leftist Red Brigades were involved in some Italian terrorist attacks, right-wing elements were involved in others. In 1981 Pope John Paul II was wounded by a Turkish terrorist with apparent connections to the Bulgarian secret police. Basque separatists in Spain committed acts of violence in their campaigns for independence, as did members of the radical Irish Republican Army (IRA), which struggled to separate Northern Ireland from the United Kingdom and join it to the Irish Republic. In 1981 several IRA prisoners gained wide attention as they starved themselves to death as a protest against British policy in Northern Ireland. For the deadliest attack, exploding a bomb at a Bologna railway station in 1984, killing 85 people, right-wing terrorists were convicted before a higher court overturned the convictions on appeal.

EASTERN EUROPE, 1970–1984: COMMUNIST REGIMES AND ECONOMICS

ECONOMIC AND SOCIAL CHANGES

In the 1970s and early 1980s Eastern European nations continued efforts to become something more than mere puppets of the U.S.S.R. Some, such as Hungary, experimented with economic reorganization. Lacking popular legitimacy and kept in power by Soviet willingness to prevent their overthrow, Eastern European governments made greater attempts to gain more popular support. While adequate housing remained scarce, personal incomes rose, and television sets, washing machines, and refrigerators became much more common. By the beginning of the 1980s one family out of four in Hungary and two out of five in East Germany owned an automobile. Travel to other nations, primarily within the Eastern bloc, continued to increase significantly. The process of urbanization and industrialization also proceeded at a rapid pace. By 1980 only Albania and Yugoslavia were more rural than urban. East Germany and Czechoslovakia had a higher percentage of urban population than did the Soviet Union. Improved living standards, however, were in large part dependent on stable prices, large loans from the West, and favorable trade relations with the U.S.S.R., which furnished energy and raw materials below world prices. Better short-term conditions also came at the expense of more long-term environmental damage. The increased prosperity of the 1970s—growth was especially strong in the first half of the decade—was thus based on an unstable foundation.

The fragile economic and political status of Eastern Europe became especially evident in the early 1980s during the development of an extended crisis in Poland. In 1980 the Polish government attempted to increase meat prices, and disturbances broke out. Earlier, in 1970 and 1976, price increases had also led to strikes and riots, the 1970 turbulence even driving Wladyslaw Gomulka from power. This time, however, the unrest was more widespread and coordinated, and the government was forced to recognize Solidarity, a powerful new independent labor union. This was an unprecedented step in the Communist world, where trade unions were heretofore kept under close party control. The government agreed to salary increases and made concessions regarding political prisoners, censorship, additional religious access to the mass media, and a number of other worker demands. Communist Party leader Edward Gierek was replaced by Stanislaw Kania, and for the next year liberalization proceeded at a rapid pace, as Solidarity, under the leadership of Lech Walesa, prodded the government. The Catholic Church, headed by the Polish Pope John Paul II, was sympathetic to the union and supported the push for liberalization.

THE POLISH CRISIS OF 1981–1982

As the Poles gained more freedom, Soviet leaders became increasingly alarmed and resorted to a variety of measures to express their displeasure. In an effort to appease Soviet leaders and to bolster the declining prestige of the party, in October 1981 the Central Committee of the Polish Communist Party replaced Kania as first secretary and put in his place General Wojciech Jaruzelski. In December 1981 Jaruzelski, without warning, declared a state of national emergency, established martial law, and set up the Military Council of National Salvation to run the nation. Armored units appeared in the streets of Warsaw and other cities. Solidarity leaders were arrested and the union declared illegal. A few months later, the Polish government increased food prices.

Alarmed by Poland's precarious economic position and upset by the crackdown on Solidarity, Western governments became either hostile to or cautious about providing further credit. Already worried about rising worldwide indebtedness, Western governments became increasingly concerned about the large debts of Eastern European nations. By early 1982 the six Soviet satellites owed over $50 billion to Western governments and banks. At about the same time, the Soviet Union, beset by its own economic problems and debts to the West, began to reduce its energy deliveries to Eastern Europe and to charge prices more in line with world prices. As a result of these factors, as well as a global recession, the rate of increase in living standards leveled off sharply in the early 1980s. In some cases, living standards declined. While the Soviet Union encouraged its satellites to meet the situation by becoming less dependent on the West, some Eastern bloc leaders believed that the best solution was more economic reform and better relations with the West. By late 1982 the Polish government had freed most of those who had been arrested in December 1981 and had lifted many of the restrictions imposed at that time. Partly as a consequence of these actions, Western governments and banks agreed to the rescheduling of Polish debts.

THE COLLAPSE OF DÉTENTE

U.S. PRESIDENT CARTER AND THE SOVIET UNION

By the late 1970s earlier optimism that the cold war had virtually ended had begun to fade. President Carter's emphasis on human rights—he once called it "the soul of our foreign policy"—and his sympathy for Soviet dissidents irritated the Soviet leadership. The continued Soviet military buildup of the 1970s alarmed some U.S. political leaders, and the movement toward international accords lost momentum rapidly as cold war discord flared in the Middle East, Africa, and Latin America. The movement of Soviet troops into Afghanistan in late 1979 especially soured relations. The U.S.S.R.'s leaders took the action mainly because of fears of growing Muslim strength in a country bordering on portions of its own Central Asian Muslims and to replace what they considered an unreliable and ineffective Marxist government with one more to their liking. Fearing, however, that the invasion was part of some larger design in a troubled area, near a still unsettled Iran and the Persian Gulf, U.S. President Carter called the Soviet action "the greatest threat to peace since the Second World War." As a result of increased U.S. hostility and suspicion flowing from the invasion, the U.S. government failed to ratify the 1979 SALT II Treaty, and in the summer of 1980 the United States boycotted the Olympic Games in Moscow and placed an embargo on U.S. grain shipments to the Soviet Union.

THE WORSENING OF U.S.–SOVIET RELATIONS IN THE EARLY 1980s

During the presidency of Ronald Reagan in the early 1980s, a number of events contributed further to the worsening of U.S.-Soviet relations. Soviet fears were nourished by Reagan's determination to increase U.S. military spending and by Reagan's harsh words, such as his calling the Soviet Union an "evil empire." In the face of recent Soviet deployment of SS-20s and other missiles threatening Western Europe, the United States proceeded with the previously scheduled deployment of Pershing II and cruise missiles in Western Europe. In reaction to the new missile deployments, the Soviets broke off arms talks in Geneva in late 1983. At the same time, Soviet leader Andropov had angry words for President Reagan's newest weapons plan: the Strategic Defense Initiative (SDI), often referred to as Star Wars. Andropov charged that by advocating a space-based defense system that would destroy Soviet missiles before they could reach U.S. territory, Reagan hoped to prevent the Soviets from launching any type of retaliatory strike if the United States decided to attack the U.S.S.R. first.

The United States, on the other hand, was angered by the major role that the Soviet Union had played in turning back the Solidarity movement in Poland. It responded with limited sanctions not only against Poland but also against the Soviet Union, which the United States charged bore a "heavy and direct responsibility for the repression in Poland." Although most observers believed that Soviet troops would have invaded Poland if the Polish government had not repressed the growing freedom led by Solidarity, recent evidence has cast serious doubts about this assumption. In 1983 over Soviet territory, the Soviet air force shot down a Korean civilian jetliner, which the Soviet military apparently believed was a spy plane. Although later U.S. intelligence information appeared to contradict him, President Reagan declared that "there is no way a pilot could mistake this for anything other than a civilian airliner." He condemned the act and cited it as evidence of the barbaric nature of the Soviet system.

Other areas of interaction and cooperation fostered by détente suffered as relations deteriorated. U.S.-Soviet trade and Jewish emigration from the Soviet Union, both of which had increased during the 1970s, declined in the early 1980s. Partly in retaliation for the U.S. boycott of the 1980 Olympics, the Soviet Union and many Communist nations friendly to the Soviet Union refused to take part in the 1984 Summer Olympics in Los Angeles.

S U M M A R Y

From the Nuclear Test Ban Treaty of 1963 through most of the 1970s, superpower relations were generally characterized by a spirit of détente. Both the United States and the Soviet Union attempted to find points of agreement and succeeded in expanding trade and cultural contacts and agreeing on a strategic arms limitation treaty. In the 1970s the United States and China ended a long period of hostility and established diplomatic, cultural, and economic relations with each other. Most of the international community, which displayed an increasing tendency toward multipolarity, joined in signing a number of treaties designed to limit the testing and proliferation of nuclear weapons. Meanwhile, however, the uninterrupted postwar arms race produced ever more destructive weapons. From time to time, international events, such as the war in Indochina and the Soviet invasion of Czechoslovakia in 1968, stalled progress toward improved relations. The appearance of Soviet troops in Afghanistan in December 1979 and events of the early 1980s signaled that the spirit of détente had faded and that the arms race was accelerating.

From the 1960s into the 1980s some of the European allies of the two superpowers made attempts to lessen their dependence on the United States or on the U.S.S.R. The Common Market, Western European economic prosperity, and de Gaulle all encouraged this trend in the West, while the Prague Spring of 1968, certain Romanian and Hungarian policies, and the activities of Poland's Solidarity union reflected the desire for more independence in Eastern Europe.

Although Europe remained, in general, economically and politically stable, there were some serious problems. The economic problems of 1974–1975 and 1981–1982 shook Western European nations. Unstable governments, youth unrest, and outbursts of terrorism also plagued some of these nations for various periods during the 1960s and following decades. In Eastern Europe, the early 1980s displayed a number of economic shortcomings, including heavy indebtedness to Western governments and banks.

SUGGESTED SOURCES

Bacon, Edwin, and Mark Sandle, eds. *Brezhnev Reconsidered.* 2002. An excellent selection of short essays by leading scholars.

Binyon, Michael. *Life in Russia.* 1983. A brief look at everyday life in Russia in the late 1970s and early 1980s by a British journalist.*

Boll, Heinrich. *The Safety Net.* 1977. This satirical novel by a Nobel Prize recipient is about a German tycoon whose fear of terrorists radically alters his everyday life and that of his family.*

Craig, Gordon A. *The Germans.* 1991. An examination of the German people in the 1980s from a historical perspective; contains an afterword on the German events of 1989–1990.*

Garthoff, Raymond L. *Détente and Confrontation: American-Soviet Relations from Nixon to Reagan.* Rev. ed. 1994. The best overall work on the rise and fall of détente.

Jenkins, Peter. *Mrs. Thatcher's Revolution: The Ending of the Socialist Era.* 1988. A distinguished British journalist offers his insights into a decade of "Thatcherism."*

Konwicki, Tadeusz. *A Minor Apocalypse.* 1979. A novel by one of Poland's leading writers that captures well the anguished condition of the nation under communism.*

Kubik, Jan. *The Power of Symbols against the Symbols of Power: The Rise of Solidarity and the Fall of State Socialism in Poland.* 1994. A scholarly work stressing the significance of the Polish trade union.*

Lacouture, Jean. *De Gaulle: The Ruler, 1945–1970.* 1991. The second volume of a comprehensive and distinguished biography.*

Laqueur, Walter. *Europe in Our Time: A History, 1945–1992.* 1992. A description of economic, social, political, and cultural developments in the postwar era by one of the most prolific historians of modern times.*

Marwick, Arthur. *The Sixties: Cultural Revolution in Britain, France, Italy and the United States, 1958–1974.* 1999. A British historian emphasizes the importance of the changes of the 1960s in this long but interesting work.*

Ouimet, Matthew J. *The Rise and Fall of the Brezhnev Doctrine in Soviet Foreign Policy.* 2003. Revisionist history regarding Soviet foreign policy toward Eastern Europe, especially in the early 1980s.*

Pinder, John. *The European Union: A Very Short Introduction.* 2001. A clear, concise overview of the development of the European Common Market.*

Tompsom, William. *The Soviet Union under Brezhnev.* 2003. A solid brief work on the Soviet leader of almost two decades.*

Williams, Kieran. *The Prague Spring and Its Aftermath: Czechoslovak Politics, 1968–1970.* 1997. A good summary based on archival sources from several countries.*

Young, Hugo. *This Blessed Plot: Britain and Europe from Churchill to Blair.* 1999. An interesting and controversial work by a leading British journalist that surveys the attitudes of British politicians toward closer ties with the rest of Europe during the last half of the twentieth century.

WEB SOURCES

www.soviethistory.org/index.php. See materials under the years 1968, 1973, and 1980.

www.cnn.com/SPECIALS/cold.war. CNN materials on the cold war; see links to episodes 11–19.

www.wilsoncenter.org. Go to the Cold War International History Project under "Programs" for links to the latest cold war scholarly findings.

www.fordham.edu/halsall/mod/modsbook50.html. Provides numerous links to materials on Eastern Europe from 1945 into the 1990s.

www.fordham.edu/halsall/mod/modsbook49.html. Provides numerous links to materials on Western Europe from 1945 into the 1990s.

*Paperback available.

27

⑥The Americas in the Late Cold War Era

In the 1970s and 1980s, several broad patterns emerged in the United States, Canada, and Latin America. In the United States, economic turmoil, disenchantment with big government, and the growing political clout of religious fundamentalism fueled mounting conservatism and the rise of the New Right, epitomized in the presidency of Ronald Reagan. Canada saw a similar conservative ascendancy, for many of the same reasons. In Latin America, military dictatorships tightened their grips on power during the 1970s, waging dirty wars against their own citizens in Argentina, Chile, Brazil, and elsewhere—suspending constitutional guarantees, filling the jails with alleged subversives, and killing (or disappearing) thousands. Meanwhile, economic conditions for the impoverished majority continued to deteriorate. In the 1980s a resurgent civil society led to a broad democratic transition in many countries. In Central America, civil wars between left-wing revolutionary movements and U.S.-backed right-wing military governments killed hundreds of thousands, while the triumph, then demise, of the Sandinista Revolution in Nicaragua was the last major cold war battle in the Western Hemisphere.

THE UNITED STATES: ECONOMIC TROUBLES AND RISING CONSERVATISM

The early and mid-1970s marked a significant turning point in postwar U.S. history. Final defeat in Vietnam combined with soaring government debt, stagnating wages and productivity, rising overseas competition, Watergate and other government scandals, and a major oil shock marking the end of the era of cheap gasoline. The OPEC oil embargo of 1973–1974 and tripling of gasoline and home fuel prices triggered a devastating inflationary spiral. By the late 1970s an era of "stagflation" had set in, combining high inflation and high unemployment with stagnant growth. The "misery index" (the rate of inflation plus the rate of unemployment) stood at 11 percent in 1970. By 1980 it had nearly doubled. In the 20 years after 1972, real wages (adjusted for inflation) declined by nearly 20 percent. Measured in 1982 dollars, the average worker took home $316 a week but only $255 20 years later.

Especially hard-hit was the manufacturing sector. With rising fuel prices and increased foreign competition, the automobile and steel industries, long the mainstays of the U.S. economy, declined precipitously. The 1970s and 1980s saw widespread deindustrialization and the rise of the Rust Belt, with cities like Detroit, Pittsburgh, Cleveland, and other manufacturing centers experiencing steep declines. The deindustrialization of Flint, Michigan—a city long dominated by General Motors and touted by its boosters as "Autotown"—was dramatized in Michael Moore's 1989 film *Roger & Me*.

From Nixon to Carter

The federal government struggled unsuccessfully with these economic problems. President Nixon, attempting to control inflation, shelved his conservatism to adopt a planned budget deficit and wage-price freeze. Gerald Ford, Nixon's successor, tightened spending and credit in the midst of the oil embargo. The resulting recession, along with his unpopular pardon of former President Nixon a year earlier, probably cost him the 1976 election, won by Democrat Jimmy Carter. Carter was no more successful in overcoming the structural problems of high inflation and sagging economic growth.

Public cynicism toward government surged after the 1968 Tet Offensive by the Viet Cong made clear that the U.S. military was bogged down in Vietnam, contrary to persistent government claims. Final U.S. withdrawal from Vietnam in early 1973—the first major war the United States had lost—coincided with the onset of

WATERGATE

Watergate: Senators Howard Baker and Sam Ervin examine a witness during congressional hearings pertaining to the break-in of the national headquarters of the Democratic Party. The investigation led to the resignation of President Nixon and the jailing of several Republican administration leaders.

the Watergate scandal. Beginning in May 1973, lengthy congressional hearings uncovered an elaborate criminal conspiracy by Nixon and his chief aides to obstruct justice by attempting to cover up a 1972 break-in of Democratic Party headquarters by Republican operatives. New disclosures emerged weekly, as millions watched the drama unfold on television. In August 1974, a few weeks after the House of Representatives Judiciary Committee voted bills of impeachment, Nixon became the first U.S. president to resign his office. Within the year, the U.S.-supported South Vietnamese government fell. Meanwhile, a Senate investigative committee uncovered a history of abuse of power and lawbreaking by the FBI and CIA stretching back to the beginnings of the cold war, further fueling growing popular disillusionment with government.

THE CARTER ADMINISTRATION

Promising "I'll never lie to you," Democratic presidential candidate Jimmy Carter, a former governor of Georgia, capitalized on the electorate's disenchantment. Domestically, Carter and Congress tried unsuccessfully to lower inflation by cutting spending on social programs and eliminating government regulations. To address the nation's energy crisis, his administration lowered the speed limit to 55 miles per hour, encouraged people to lower their home thermostats, and promoted nuclear and other alternative forms of energy. Yet dependence on imported oil reached record levels. By the late 1970s the United States imported more than 40 percent of the oil it consumed. The 1979 accident at Three Mile Island nuclear power plant in Pennsylvania galvanized opponents of nuclear energy and effectively halted further nuclear expansion.

In foreign policy, Carter departed from the traditional postwar focus on containing communism to stress peace initiatives and human rights. The 1979 U.S.-brokered Camp David accord between Israel and Egypt and an agreement to return the Panama Canal Zone to Panama by the year 2000 were among his administration's significant foreign policy achievements. To the chagrin of cold warriors, Carter refused to intercede against the Sandinista Revolution in Nicaragua, which ousted the Somoza dictatorship in July 1979. Meanwhile, events in Southwest Asia would prove his administration's undoing. Soon after an Islamic revolution in early 1979 toppled the shah of Iran—whom the United States had supported since a CIA-sponsored coup in 1953—revolutionaries invaded the U.S. embassy in Tehran and seized 53 hostages. For the remainder of Carter's term, the Iranian hostage crisis dominated the news—spawning the nightly TV program *Nightline,* for instance, which began each broadcast with a headline of the number of days the hostages had been held—and fueled a perception that Carter was weak and indecisive. The 1979 Soviet invasion of Afghanistan to suppress an Islamic rebellion reinforced this view.

RISE OF THE NEW RIGHT

The late 1970s also saw substantial cultural shifts at home, which together can be characterized as the rise of the New Right. Stagflation led many to question the liberal emphasis on government-based solutions to nagging social problems, with many citizens viewing taxes as unnecessarily high. In 1978 California's Proposition 13, which banned further property tax increases, heralded the onset of a tax revolt in many other states. The sexual revolution, begun in the 1960s, sparked a backlash by proponents of "family values," who saw nonmarital sex, abortion, and homosexuality as abominations. The failure of the equal rights amendment (ERA) to gain passage in the requisite number of states—an amendment first proposed in the 1920s and revived in the 1960s—was largely the consequence of a well-funded campaign by those who proclaimed that it was contrary to fundamental religious precepts and would undermine women's "natural" roles as homemakers, wives, and mothers. The rise of Christian and Jewish fundamentalism, occurring at the same time as the rise of Islamic fundamentalism in the Middle East, was epitomized in the growing political clout of the Moral Majority, led by the conservative Virginia minister Jerry Falwell and dedicated to electing "pro-life, pro-family, pro-America" candidates.

The combination of events caused Carter's popularity to plummet on the eve of the 1980 elections, a trend exacerbated by his penchant for candor. Describing what he saw as the "crisis of confidence" and "malaise" that had beset the nation, Carter played into the hands of his Republican adversary, the former Hollywood movie actor and ex-governor of California Ronald Reagan. With his sunny, affable disposition and formidable acting skills, Reagan capitalized on the electorate's growing conservatism and desire for more optimistic, less analytical leadership. Emphasizing "states' rights," condemning "welfare cheats" and affirmative action, and proclaiming that "it's morning in America," Reagan triumphed in the 1980 elections, winning 44 states and 51 percent of the popular vote.

The Reagan Era

Over the next eight years, the Reagan Revolution transformed the United States in important ways. In a frontal assault on the core tenets of the New Deal, Reagan insisted that "government is not the solution, government is the problem." The central pillars of Reagan's economic policies, or Reaganomics, were to cut federal taxes, especially for the wealthy; jettison government regulations; and emphasize the economy's "supply side" rather than its "demand side." This meant shifting from the New Deal's emphasis on public sector expenditures and entitlement programs to policies favoring business. According to proponents of supply-side economics, because the owners of capital and businesses created jobs—especially big capital and big business—the proper role of government was to free these groups from burdensome taxes and regulations, thus permitting the free market to operate under optimal conditions. Critics denounced the policy as trickle-down economics, because only gradually, if ever, would the poor and middle class reap any benefits.

REAGANOMICS

On taking office, Reagan convinced the Republican-dominated Congress to pass tax cuts for the wealthy and slash spending on social programs. Combined with a tightening of the money supply, the result was a severe recession in 1981–1982, which brought down inflation and interest rates. After 1982 the economy gradually picked up steam, though by this time the conflict with the Soviet Union had intensified, leading to huge increases in defense spending. Billions were poured into Reagan's Strategic Defense Initiative (or "Star Wars"), which conceived of a space-based shield of laser-equipped satellites protecting North America from possible missile attack. With tax revenues down and military spending up, budget deficits and the national debt skyrocketed. Having pledged to balance the budget, Reagan oversaw a series of record deficits, which exceeded $100 billion a year through the 1980s. By the end of Reagan's second term the national debt had tripled to $2.7 trillion. Although some analysts

RECORD BUDGET DEFICITS

argue that this massive defense spending caused the Soviet Union's collapse, most scholars believe that long-term internal weaknesses led to its demise.

ASSAULT ON LABOR UNIONS

A related outgrowth of supply-side economics was an assault on labor unions. When air traffic controllers struck in 1981, Reagan fired all the strikers and replaced them with nonunion workers, encouraging businesses to take a hard line against organized labor. By 1990 only 16 percent of nonagricultural workers were unionized, compared to more than 26 percent in 1960. The erosion of manufacturing jobs and shrinkage of organized labor was accompanied by a ballooning in the number of nonunion and service sector jobs, most part-time and without health or retirement benefits—in retail, fast food, telemarketing, computer programming, and the like— what some have called the "Wal-Martization of America." To make ends meet most families needed two full-time breadwinners.

RISING POVERTY

The number of families living in poverty rose, by 1990 nearly matching the percentage before the War on Poverty. Economic inequality also increased markedly. During the 1980s, the poorest 20 percent saw their incomes decline by one-tenth, while the wealthiest 20 percent saw their incomes rise by more than one-sixth. The wealthiest 1 percent of the population came to own more than 40 percent of the nation's wealth, the highest level since the Great Depression. The term "yuppie"— young urban professional—entered the vocabulary as a mild epithet, connoting hyper-consumption among the well-to-do and the growing gap in wealth and income that accompanied the shift from manufacturing to service jobs.

DEREGULATION

The emphasis on business deregulation and loosening of antitrust laws led to a frenzy of mergers and acquisitions. As larger businesses absorbed smaller firms, the resulting huge concentrations of capital became reminiscent of the trusts and monopolies of the Gilded Age a century earlier. From the taxpayer's perspective, especially significant was the deregulation of the savings and loan industry. Freeing up such companies to make risky investments, the federal government continued to guarantee savings deposits under Federal Deposit Insurance Corporation, created in the New Deal. A string of failures among savings and loan institutions ensued, with the federal government bailing out the industry to the tune of $250 billion.

CIVIL RIGHTS AND THE ENVIRONMENT

As it curtailed its role in society and the market, the federal government also cut back on its enforcement of civil rights and environmental and workplace safety laws and regulations. Although racial discrimination was now illegal, by virtually every social index—income, employment, education, life expectancy—blacks, Latinos, and other minorities lagged increasingly behind whites. On the environmental front, the Reagan administration loosened or declined to enforce many laws and regulations regarding air and water quality, wetlands, endangered species, and wilderness preservation, while opening up vast tracts of federal lands, especially in the West, for logging, mining, ranching, and oil exploration and drilling.

THE WAR ON DRUGS

Meanwhile, in the deteriorating city centers of the Rust Belt, an epidemic of crack—a particularly addictive form of cocaine—spurred growing crime and incarceration rates, especially among poor, young, minority males. In contrast to its hands-off approach toward civil rights, the environment, and markets generally, the federal government responded to illicit drug use and abuse with a "War on Drugs." This activist approach emphasized eradication overseas (especially in the Andean republics of Latin America), interdiction, and stiffer penalties on users, abusers, and traffickers. New federal drug laws imposed much stiffer mandatory sentences on users and dealers of crack cocaine—most of whom were minorities—than on those of powdered cocaine, who tended to be white. As a result, the number of black men enmeshed in the criminal justice system reached record levels.

PUBLIC HEALTH

Public health also suffered during the 1980s due to government cutbacks, skyrocketing health care costs, the erosion of jobs with medical benefits, the reduction in reproductive rights, and the outbreak of a hitherto unknown and fatal disease, acquired immunodeficiency syndrome, or AIDS. Spread by sexual contact, needle sharing, and blood transfusions, in the early and mid-1980s AIDS ravaged the male homosexual community, prompting gay organizations to mobilize for "safe sex" and to pressure the federal government for more resources for prevention and treatment. By the 1990s the spread of AIDS in North America declined markedly, a result of these campaigns and new drugs that sharply lowered mortality rates from a disease that still has no cure.

IMMIGRATION

The U.S. nonwhite immigrant population grew substantially during the 1970s and 1980s, mainly the result of changing immigration laws after 1965 and the flood of illegal immigrants across the nation's southern border. Nearly 12 million people entered the country legally from 1970 to 1990, with 80 percent from Asia and Latin America. Most undocumented immigrants hailed from Mexico and Central America, with hundreds of thousands entering the country annually. Most new immigrants, documented and not, settled in the Sunbelt states. The 1986 Immigration Reform and Control Act put tighter controls on immigration while granting amnesty to longtime residents. More significant was the 1990 Immigration Act, which raised annual quotas by 40 percent. By the 1990s, a language other than English was spoken in roughly one household in seven, a figure comparable to a century earlier. Founded as a nation of immigrants, the United States continued to be rejuvenated by a rich diversity of peoples, languages, and cultures.

IRAN-CONTRA

In Reagan's second term a major scandal erupted—the Iran-Contra affair—reminiscent in some ways of Watergate. Determined to circumvent a congressional ban on military aid to the counterrevolutionaries (or Contras) fighting the Sandinista government in Nicaragua, top Reagan administration officials illegally arranged a secret deal with Iran. For nearly two years, the Iranians, at war with Iraq, shipped arms to the Contras in exchange for covert U.S. military aid. Eleven U.S. officials later were convicted of trying to cover up the scheme. While Reagan denied any complicity, the scandal cast a shadow over his administration and sowed doubt about who was really in charge at the White House.

The changes launched under Reagan continued under his vice president and successor, former CIA director George H. W. Bush, elected in 1988. Less charismatic and more hands-on than his predecessor, Bush clashed with a Democrat-controlled Congress over fiscal, environmental, and other policies, leading to gridlock over many issues. The major events during his presidency occurred overseas, especially the fall of the Berlin Wall and of communism in Eastern Europe, the collapse of the Soviet Union, and the Persian Gulf War (see Chapters 24 and 31 for more on these events). At home Bush continued his party's courting of the religious right and the so-called Reagan Democrats.

Poverty and wealth in Latin America: shantytown suburbs and downtown office buildings in Caracas, Venezuela.

LATIN AMERICA: DICTATORSHIP, DEMOCRACY, AND DEBT

Several broad trends marked Latin America and the Caribbean in the 1970s and 1980s. Military coups in Brazil (1964), Argentina (1966), and Chile (1973) were followed by nearly two decades of right-wing military dictatorships. The dirty wars waged by these countries' military regimes against their own citizens in the 1970s and 1980s—which included mass arrests, systematic use of torture, and mass killings and disappearances—left an enduring collective memory of state repression and violence. In Central America, the 1979 triumph of the Sandinista Revolution in Nicaragua galvanized leftists throughout the Caribbean. The Sandinista victory also steeled the resolve of traditional elites in other Central American countries to maintain their power and of the Reagan administration to maintain U.S. dominance over its historic backyard. The result was a series of brutal civil wars in Guatemala, El Salvador, Honduras, and Nicaragua that in the 1980s killed hundreds of thousands. In many of the more advanced economies of South America, rule by hard-line military dictatorships succumbed in the 1980s to a resurgent civil society demanding more democratic forms of governance.

Throughout the continent, widespread poverty, yawning inequalities, and persistent underdevelopment remained major issues. Cities continued to grow rapidly, further swelling the vast slums (see Chapter 21). As populations ballooned, domestic industrialization schemes faltered and world prices for traditional export products declined. By the early 1970s many countries found themselves in increasingly dire economic straits. Borrowing money for national development seemed one answer. After 1973–1974, with the world flush with OPEC petrodollars and with the encouragement of U.S., European, and international financial institutions (such as the World Bank and the Inter-American Development Bank), Latin America's debt load increased dramatically. Genuine economic development continued to lag, however, and by the early 1980s the debtors' bills came due. Printing more money to pay these bills inevitably led to hyperinflation (all inflation rates cited below are annual).

The developed world's response to Latin America's crushing debt and hyperinflation was a new model of economic liberalism, or "neoliberalism." The basic idea behind neoliberalism was to shrink state expenditures as much as possible and thereby minimize governments' interference in the free play of market forces. This meant slashing public funding for education, health care, public transport, and other areas, while permitting the unimpeded flow of foreign capital. Blaming a failed populism for Latin America's economic woes, the world's leading financial institutions required governments to enact "austerity measures" as a precondition for further loans. Chief among these institutions were the International Monetary Fund (IMF) and World Bank, established after World War II (see Chapter 19). The IMF's neoliberal worldview was cut of the same cloth as the Reagan-Thatcher model of shrinking the state's social role, privatizing state-run enterprises, and deregulating production and markets.

As Latin Americans grappled with growing debt, populations, and poverty, hemispheric integration intensified. Millions migrated north to the United States, creating a powerful engine for change in U.S. culture, while a host of U.S. influences—especially big businesses, the War on Drugs, technology, and popular cultural products such as movies, music, and consumerism—increasingly transformed the peoples and countries of Latin America.

NEOLIBERALISM

Mexico: Ossification of the PRI, Democratic Insurgencies, and Economic Crises

The "Mexican miracle" was how some observers described the nation's strides toward industrialization and economic modernization in the two decades following World War II. The economy grew at a rapid clip, with massive public sector investments in oil, chemicals, transport, electricity, and mining. Despite its rhetoric, however, the ruling Institutional Revolutionary Party (PRI) had grown less revolutionary and more conservative, authoritarian, and corrupt in the years following the Cárdenas reforms (1934–1940). Unlike most Latin American countries, Mexico's military remained firmly under civilian control, while oil revenues provided the ruling regime with the resources necessary to maintain social peace despite widespread poverty, surging population growth, and rapid urbanization. By the late 1960s demands for democracy intensified, particularly among students and insurgent labor unions.

A pivotal moment came in 1968, when Mexico City was slated to host the Olympics. Taking advantage of the international spotlight, a coalition of students and middle-class dissenters staged protests and demonstrations at the National University and in Tlatelolco Square, in the heart of Mexico City, demanding an opening of the

ECONOMIC GROWTH AND POLITICAL CORRUPTION

THE MASSACRE OF 1968

political system. The PRI government responded with a brutal crackdown, the infamous Tlatelolco massacre of October 1968. Firing automatic weapons, the military killed hundreds of students and imprisoned thousands more. In subsequent years the government maintained that the police had slain a handful of terrorists who had begun the gun battle. Most Mexicans knew better, and the episode cast a pall of illegitimacy over PRI rule.

ECONOMIC IMPLOSION

By the 1970s, the weaknesses of Mexico's path toward economic development became increasingly apparent. Even with the surge in oil prices after 1974, oil revenues could not cover the costs of huge government expenditures and massive amounts of food imported for the burgeoning urban population. The abundance of cheap credit in world markets and the expectation of continually rising oil prices led the government to borrow billions of dollars from international lenders, quadrupling Mexico's debt to $80 billion. Instead oil prices stagnated, inflation surged, and in 1982, following a worldwide economic downturn, the government essentially went bankrupt.

The economic crisis of 1982 and the pressures exerted by international creditors forced the PRI to refashion its economic development strategy. Following the neoliberal model, the government began privatizing by selling off large portions of state-owned banks, mines, and factories to private interests. For the next five years the economy stagnated, inflation topped 100 percent, and government debt increased. The number of people living in poverty rose to nearly 60 percent, real wages plummeted, and unemployment soared. In 1985, the year a devastating earthquake killed more than 8,000 people in Mexico City, the capital's unemployment rate stood at more than 33 percent. Meanwhile Mexico earned the dubious distinction of having more millionaires per capita than any country in Latin America.

CRISIS OF LEGITIMACY

During the 1980s, many Mexicans became fed up with the PRI's economic failures and transparent corruption and sought viable political alternatives. In the 1988 presidential elections, the PRI candidate Carlos Salinas de Gortari barely eked out a victory, an outcome many attributed to massive electoral fraud. After six decades, the days of the PRI's untrammeled political dominance seemed to be coming to an end.

Brazil, Argentina, and Chile: From Military Dictatorships to Emergent Democracies

A similar dynamic between entrenched ruling groups, insurgent democratic movements, and global economic trends shaped Brazil, Argentina, and Chile from the 1960s through the 1980s. In Brazil, the reformist regime of João Goulart (1961–1964) faced rampaging inflation, massive poverty, and a huge debt load. The military, feeling increasingly threatened by the growing power of Goulart's supporters, who included urban and rural workers demanding higher wages and greater political rights, in 1964 ousted Goulart and seized power. A series of authoritarian military regimes governed Brazil until 1985.

Demonstrating its commitment to maintaining power at any cost, in 1967–1968 the military cracked down hard on mass mobilizations and strikes. In 1969 militant resisters to the regime began waging guerrilla war in major cities by kidnapping foreign diplomats and demanding ransoms and the release of political prisoners. State repression intensified. By the early 1970s the military had quashed the urban guerrilla movement by mass imprisonment, torture, and crushing of organized dissent.

Favoring foreign investment, export production, and national industrialization, the economic technocrats under the military regimes succeeded in fostering sustained economic growth. By the early 1970s, reflecting Brazil's transformation, manufactured goods displaced coffee as the country's principal export product. Mirroring the situation in Mexico, some foreign observers spoke of the "Brazilian miracle." Yet, as in Mexico, major structural weaknesses underlay the government's development strategy, with the economic boom benefiting only a tiny minority. The vast majority of Brazilians could not afford to buy shoes or decent clothing, even as their country emerged as a major exporter of footwear and textiles. Roughly half the adult population were infected with tuberculosis (active and inactive), a third had from parasitic diseases, and two-thirds of the children were malnourished. The desperate economic straits that had confronted Carolina Maria de Jesus in the 1950s had only sharpened (see Chapter 21).

By the early 1980s, Brazil had accumulated the world's largest foreign debt—nearly $100 billion—while inflation surged at more than 100 percent. The economic crisis, combined with growing demands for greater political and economic equality, compelled the military gradually to transfer power to elected civilians. In 1990, Fernando Collor de Mello became the first civilian elected president in nearly three decades, his government inheriting the same severe economic and social problems that plagued his predecessors.

Similar trends unfolded in Argentina. After the military overthrew President Juan Perón in 1955, the country's economic problems remained: huge debt, high inflation and unemployment, foreign domination of the economy, and highly skewed landownership. The civilian and military governments that followed Perón's ouster failed to resolve these structural problems. In 1966 a military coup overthrew the elected government, suspended the constitution, and dissolved Congress and the Supreme Court. Freezing wages, devaluing the peso, and welcoming foreign investment, the regime oversaw the growing domination of the economy by U.S. and European capital.

As unemployment and poverty mounted, workers and students in Buenos Aires and the industrial cities of the interior rose up in protests and revolts. An urban guerrilla movement, the Montoneros, staged a series of audacious robberies, kidnappings, and assassinations. As in Brazil, the military cracked down hard. Seeing the aged Perón as a bulwark of conservatism, in 1973 the ruling junta permitted his return from exile to run for president. He won handily but died a year later, leaving in power his vice president and second wife, Isabel. The urban guerrilla campaign intensified, and in 1976 the generals overthrew Isabel Perón.

From 1976 to 1983 the military and paramilitary death squads waged a dirty war against the guerrillas, imprisoning and torturing thousands and murdering (or disappearing) upward of 20,000 alleged subversives. Crushing the guerrilla movement and terrorizing the populace, the regime failed to address the country's economic and social ills. By the early 1980s, inflation raged at more than 100 percent, unemployment surged, banks failed at an alarming rate, and real income was lower than a decade earlier.

DICTATORSHIP AND POVERTY IN BRAZIL

DICTATORSHIP AND THE DIRTY WAR IN ARGENTINA

THE FALKLANDS WAR

Hoping to shore up their flagging popularity, the generals embarked on a military adventure that backfired and destroyed their regime. Since 1820 Argentina had claimed the Islas Malvinas in the South Atlantic, but Great Britain had taken these islands in 1833 and held them as the Falkland Islands dependency. In 1982, in a surprise attack, Argentine forces took the islands, occupied by a small military garrison and 1,800 British subjects, plus 600,000 sheep. The nationalist fervor that swept the country evaporated when Britain's Thatcher government organized a major task force, smashed the Argentine navy and air force, and retook the islands.

A FRAGILE DEMOCRACY

Thoroughly discredited, the military junta arranged for free elections in 1983. In an upset, Radical Party leader Raúl Alfonsín defeated the Peronist candidate. Despite the demands of human rights activists and families of the disappeared, the Alfonsín government tried and convicted only a handful of the highest-ranking military officers who had instigated the dirty war. Meanwhile inflation spun out of control, reaching 1,200 percent in 1989, while the foreign debt approached $60 billion. The Peronists under Carlos Saúl Menem, victorious in the 1989 presidential elections, imposed harsh austerity measures recommended by the IMF, bringing inflation and debt service under partial control. Still, Argentina's economic woes remained, and the collective memory of state-directed violence and terror created by the dirty war would endure well into the twenty-first century.

Chile, with its long history of parliamentary democracy, followed a similar path. Attempting to placate the military and the Right, and to defuse mounting pressures for reform from the Left, the popular leader of the Christian Democrats Eduardo Frei (1964–1970) enacted wide-ranging land, health, and educational reforms and increased the government's share in the pivotal copper industry. Frei's reforms served mainly to raise expectations among the country's huge urban working class.

OVERTHROW OF ALLENDE IN CHILE

In 1970 a plurality of Chilean voters elected the Marxist Salvador Allende as president. His election galvanized his right-wing opponents in industry and the military, who launched a concerted campaign to undermine his administration. They were joined by the U.S. State Department and CIA, which also saw Allende's socialism as a direct threat to long-term U.S. hemispheric interests. In a major tragedy of Chile's postwar history—and the first military intervention in Chilean politics since the 1920s—in September 1973 the military under General Augusto Pinochet stormed the presidential palace, killed Allende, and seized state power.

THE PINOCHET DICTATORSHIP

After a brief transitional period, Pinochet ruled Chile with an iron fist from 1974 to 1989. Forging tight alliances with the Catholic Church, big business, and the U.S. government, his regime imprisoned and killed thousands of opponents in a brutal dirty war similar to those waged by the Brazilian and Argentine militaries during the same period. The eradication of civil rights and political freedoms under Pinochet was dramatized for North American audiences in the movie *Missing* (1982), a theme treated more broadly in the screen adaptation of Argentine author Manuel Puig's *Kiss of the Spider Woman* (1985).

THE CHICAGO BOYS

Following a hemispheric neoliberal trend, Pinochet set about privatizing major industries and slashing public subsidies and services. Charged with engineering these reforms were the "Chicago Boys," free market economists trained mainly at the University of Chicago. The results of their radical laissez-faire restructurings were mixed, with sharply curtailed inflation combined with a severe economic contraction in the mid-1970s, robust growth in the late 1970s, a deep recession in the early 1980s, and strong growth in the mid- and late 1980s. Yielding to popular discontent, in 1990 Pinochet stepped down after a plebiscite showed a solid majority opposed to him. The collective memory of Chile's descent into dictatorship remained strong well into the twenty-first century, and the military continued to closely monitor civilian affairs.

The experiences of these three Southern Cone countries highlight broader patterns in Latin America from the early 1960s to the late 1980s. As in Mexico under the Porfiriato (1876–1910; see Chapter 12), political liberalism—the rights of citizenship—was sacrificed to economic liberalism. The political repression and free market reforms mainly benefited elites and foreign investors, while for Latin America's impoverished urban and rural majority, the 1970s, much like the 1980s, would be remembered as a "lost decade."

Central America: Revolutionary Movements, Military Dictatorships, and Civil Wars

In Central America, meanwhile, right-wing military dictatorships used the pretext of the cold war to suppress trade unionists, community organizers, and Cuba-inspired left-wing revolutionary movements. The Somoza dictatorship in Nicaragua (1936–1979), and its fight against the leftist Sandinista movement from the early 1960s, were emblematic of broader trends in Central America during these years. The unbridled avarice and corruption of Somoza and his cronies became especially apparent in the wake of the December 1972 Managua earthquake, which killed tens of thousands and destroyed much of the capital city, as the ruling clique pocketed millions of dollars in foreign aid that poured into the country.

NICARAGUA UNDER SOMOZA

Named after the nationalist guerrilla chieftain who fought the U.S. Marines to a stalemate in the 1920s and 1930s, and led by the charismatic Carlos Fonseca, the Sandinistas (the Frente Sandinista de Liberación Nacional, or FSLN) articulated a coherent political program that emphasized opposition to the Somoza dictatorship, grassroots democracy, political nonalignment (neither pro-U.S. nor pro-Soviet), a mixed economy, and social justice for the impoverished majority. After 1972, emboldened by middle- and upper-class alienation from the Somoza regime, the Sandinistas stepped up their organizing efforts in city and countryside, as captured in Omar Cabezas's colorful memoir *Fire From the Mountain* (1985). A divided elite, Somocista intransigence, and the human rights policies of the Carter administration provided the FSLN with a strategic political opening. In July 1979, with widespread popular support and after a long and bloody struggle, the Sandinistas ousted Somoza and seized power.

THE SANDINISTA REVOLUTION

Some 18 months after the Sandinista triumph, Ronald Reagan became president of the United States. Shoehorning events in Nicaragua into a cold war context, the Reagan administration portrayed the Sandinista regime as a direct extension of the Soviet "Evil Empire" and an abiding threat to democracy and freedom throughout the hemisphere. Matching its rhetoric with deeds, the U.S. administration funded, organized, and trained counterrevolutionary, or Contra, forces in Honduras, composed mainly of former Somocista National Guardsmen; mined Nicaraguan harbors; imposed

THE CONTRA WAR

B I O G R A P H Y

Struggling for the Dignity of Guatemala's Indigenous Peoples

So I said, "I'm going away." I went because they hadn't kidnapped anyone, or raped anyone, in our village. . . . I was ashamed to stay safely in my village and not think about the others. . . . My father knew and he said: "Where you are going you may not have control over your life. You can be killed at any time." . . . But I knew that teaching others how to defend themselves against the enemy was a commitment to my people and my commitment as a Christian. I have faith and I believe that happiness belongs to everyone, but that happiness has been stolen by the few. I had to go and teach others. That's why I went to the villages most in need, the ones most threatened.*

. . .

In her autobiography, Rigoberta Menchú, a Quiché Indian, recalls her decision as an 18-year-old to take an active role in defending Guatemala's Indians against the repression of the Guatemalan government. Menchú gives a harrowing account of the violence committed against her homeland's indigenous peoples. Two

of Menchú's brothers died young of malnutrition; her father, an antigovernment organizer, died in a takeover incident in Guatemala City; her 12-year-old brother was tortured and then burned alive; and her mother was slowly tortured to death. Menchú went into self-imposed exile in Mexico, where she publicized the plight of Guatemala's indigenous peoples and championed Indian cultures throughout the Western Hemisphere. Working to organize the Indians so they could defend themselves and their culture from attack, demanding human rights and social and economic improvement, Menchú advocated negotiation with the government to bring peaceful reforms. In 1992 she was awarded the Nobel Peace Prize. In subsequent years heated debates erupted on the accuracy of specific passages in her testimony, but not on the genocidal government policies she so vividly describes.

*From I, Rigoberta Menchú: An Indian Woman in Guatemala by Rigoberta Menchú. Edited and introduced by Elisabeth Burgos-Debray and translated by Ann Wright. © 1984 by Verso, London.

a devastating trade embargo; and launched an extensive perception management program at home. As in Cuba in 1959–1960, what began as a homegrown national liberation movement quickly became a major cold war battleground.

As the Contra war and U.S. trade embargo destroyed much of the economy, the Sandinista regime grew increasingly centralized and authoritarian, while its initiatives in health care, education, housing, social security, and related arenas became bogged down by hyperinflation and the growing share of the national budget devoted to defense. Especially from the mid-1980s, the regime's policy of universal military conscription became widely unpopular among ordinary Nicaraguans. By the late 1980s, with the country having suffered more than a decade of war and progressive impoverishment, the revolution was running out of steam. Internal and external pressures compelled the Sandinistas to hold internationally supervised elections, and in 1990 a coalition of anti-Sandinista political parties defeated the beleaguered ruling regime, effectively ending the revolutionary experiment.

Elsewhere in Central America, the 1970s and 1980s saw mounting popular opposition to gaping social inequalities and long-lived dictatorships, which in turn sparked brutal military crackdowns against virtually all organized dissent. In El Salvador, the army, police, and paramilitary death squads organized by the country's most powerful landowning families killed tens of thousands of community and labor organizers and activists, while the country's principal leftist revolutionary movement proved unable to topple the regime. In Guatemala, the military and elite-sponsored paramilitaries worked to root out several guerrilla insurgencies by a genocidal scorched-earth policy against the country's indigenous peoples. Reaching its height in the early 1980s and continuing until a peace accord in the mid-1990s, the offensive killed over 200,000 people. In Honduras, state-sponsored violence never approached the level reached in neighboring countries, though right-wing death squads linked to the military did kill and disappear thousands.

The scale of the carnage in Guatemala, El Salvador, Nicaragua, and Honduras, and the U.S. government's complicity in it, fostered the formation of an increasingly active and vocal peace and justice movement within the United States. The bloodshed and violence also prompted hundreds of thousands of Central Americans to migrate north. Miami, Los Angeles, Houston, Atlanta, Washington, D.C., New York, and other U.S. cities emerged as centers of Central American exile communities—alongside the *barrios* of Mexicans, Haitians, Dominicans, Cubans, and others from south of the border—further intensifying the integration of the United States with the countries, peoples, and cultures of its historic backyard.

CIVIL WARS IN CENTRAL AMERICA

CANADA IN THE LATE COLD WAR ERA

The oil crisis of the mid-1970s hit Canada hard. Most of its rich reserves of petroleum were owned by foreign (often U.S.) firms. The oil fields were located in western Canada, while consumption was highest in central Canada, especially Ontario, so provinces were at odds both with each other and the federal government over shortages. Meanwhile, high inflation socked all Canadians. The result was widespread disgruntlement expressed at many targets: OPEC, U.S. foreign policy and the U.S. government, and Canadian politicians at all levels. As in the United States, the oil crisis marked the end of the postwar boom. The next two decades witnessed difficult economic times, the unraveling of postwar liberal consensus, and the ascent of social and economic conservatism.

Symbolizing this shift was the 1984 election of Conservative Brian Mulroney as prime minister. Reelected in 1988, Mulroney, like U.S. President Reagan, oversaw the dismantling of some aspects of his nation's systems of social welfare. Organized labor, still stronger than in the United States, declined, bringing down real wages for many Canadians. Bouts of double-digit unemployment hit in the mid-1970s and again in the mid-1980s, while inflation, housing costs, and interest rates stayed stubbornly high, as did the tax burden and the cost of health care. Meanwhile, spending dipped only slightly and episodically. The result was steadily mounting personal consumer debt matched by growing government deficits.

THE MULRONEY ADMINISTRATION

The Canada Act of 1982 effectively ended Great Britain's involvement in Canada's legislative and constitutional affairs, though Queen Elizabeth II remained

CANADIAN NATIONALISM AND CULTURE

Queen of Canada and Head of State. Meanwhile, as economic integration with the United States continued—and often in counterpoint to that integration—Canadian nationalism flourished, especially in the arts, the communications industry, and higher education, with Canadian universities favoring the hiring of their own rather than academics from "below the 49th parallel." Increasingly the concept of "Canadian" culture and society became more inclusive, as recognition grew that Canada was home to immigrants from around the world, to long-neglected Native peoples, to many other people of color, and, as feminists pointed out, to women as well as men. For many Canadians, environmental concerns also lay at the center of national consciousness, even as they recognized that they needed the cooperation of other countries, especially the United States, to address many ecological concerns, from the depletion of fish stocks in the Atlantic provinces to the acid rain denuding trees in central Canada to the toxic pesticides sprayed on prairie crops.

SUMMARY

During the late cold war era, questions regarding the proper role of government in society lay at the center of wide-ranging debates spanning the hemisphere, leading to different outcomes depending on a host of factors. In the United States, disillusionment with big government had multiple causes, including the Vietnam debacle, Watergate and other government scandals, the failings of New Deal liberalism, the erosion of U.S. economic and military power overseas, the backlash against civil rights, gay, and feminist movements, and the rise of religious fundamentalism. The overall result was the rise of the New Right, the Reagan Revolution, and a redefinition of the federal government's role in the economy and society.

Paradoxically, however, this redefinition did not shrink big government. In fact, the reverse was true. Despite the rhetorical assault on federal power, the overall trends in these years—a sharp rise in defense spending and the national debt, growing integration of big government and big business, a hemispheric "War on Drugs," and related government initiatives—were toward an increasingly powerful and interventionist national government. Denouncing tax-and-spend liberals as proponents of a failed paradigm out of step with the times, the Reagan and Bush administrations continued to tax and continued to spend, but with different priorities, a different agenda, and different groups of winners and losers.

Canada saw a comparable move to the right, as ballooning budget deficits and stagnant growth sparked growing disenchantment with the free-spending liberalism of the 1950s and 1960s. Meanwhile Canadian nationalism and regionalism flourished, fueled by antipathy toward the superpower to the south, minorities' demands for autonomy and rights, and a torrent of immigrants from around the world.

In Latin America, regimes headed by conservatives, militaries, and traditional elites, and supported by the United States, tended to dominate from the mid-1960s to the mid-1980s. Thereafter and continuing beyond the 1990s, the political playing field shifted, sometimes dramatically. Facing dire economic circumstances and intense government repression, organizations of small business owners, workers, students, youth, women, faith-based communities, and others demanded an end to military impunity, an opening of the political system, and constitutional guarantees of civil liberties. Dominant groups responded to these mounting democratic challenges from below by ceding some power in order to retain what power they could. The 1990s and first five years of the twenty-first century saw a widening political divergence, with the Latin American political landscape shifting more decisively leftward (see Chapter 33), Canada retaining its socially activist state, and the United States—especially after the terrorist attacks of September 11, 2001—witnessing the broadened dominion of the conservative vision propounded by Ronald Reagan nearly a quarter century earlier.

SUGGESTED SOURCES

Adler, William M. *Mollie's Job: A Story of Life and Work on the Global Assembly Line.* 2000. Creative and readable examination of transformations in work and the global economy.*

Argueto, Manilo. *One Day of Life.* Trans. Bill Brow. 1983. Powerful novel set in El Salvador that captures the dynamics of political violence and civil war.*

Busch, Andrew E. *Ronald Reagan and the Politics of Freedom.* 2001. Trenchant treatment of the Reagan presidency.*

Fitzgerald, Frances. *Way Out There in the Blue: Reagan, Star Wars, and the End of the Cold War.* 2000. Excellent survey and analysis of the Reagan years by a Pulitzer Prize–winning author.*

Gratton, Michael. *So What Are the Boys Saying? An Inside Look at Brian Mulroney in Power.* 1987. Fine description and analysis of the Mulroney years in Canada.*

Guatemala: Never Again! The Official Report of the Human Rights Office, Archdiocese of Guatemala. 1999. Detailed examination of the human rights violations in Guatemala, especially in the paroxysm of the early 1980s.*

Lernoux, Penny. *Cry of the People.* 1982. Groundbreaking and influential analysis by a prizewinning journalist of struggles for human rights in Latin America.*

McGirr, Lisa. *Suburban Warriors: The Origins of the New American Right.* 2001. Incisive grassroots study of the rise of the New Right.*

Nunca Más: The Report of the Argentine National Commission on the Disappeared. 1986. The official Argentine Truth Commission report. Chilling and essential.*

Poniatowska, Elena. *Massacre in Mexico.* Trans. Helen R. Lane. 1975. Compilation of eyewitness testimonies of the 1968 Tlatelolco massacre.*

Schulman, Bruce J. *The Seventies: The Great Shift in American Culture, Society, and Politics.* 2001. Lively and informed analysis of the "me decade."*

Timerman, Jacobo. *Prisoner Without a Name, Cell Without a Number.* Trans. Toby Talbot. 1981. Searing testimonial account of the Argentine dirty war.*

Wills, Garry. *Reagan's America.* 1987. Superb treatment of the Reagan years.*

Zimmermann, Matilde. *Sandinista: Carlos Fonseca and the Nicaraguan Revolution.* 2000. First-rate historical biography of the Sandinistas' intellectual guiding light.*

WEB SOURCES

www.gwu.edu/~nsarchiv/NSAEBB. This site contains numerous links to "critical declassified records on issues including U.S. national security, foreign policy, diplomatic and military history, intelligence policy, and more," and many links to Latin American materials. See also the sites listed at the end of Chapter 21.

*Paperback available.

28

⑥South and Southeast Asia in the Late Cold War Era

The large, diverse region of South and Southeast Asia continued to suffer from civil and international wars. Conflicts that remained unsettled after France left Indochina in 1954 and cold war rivalries brought on renewed wars there. After U.S. withdrawal from Vietnam, two additional wars, one caused by Vietnam's invasion of Cambodia and the other by a Chinese invasion of Vietnam, reflected regional antagonisms and power struggles among Communist nations. Short wars between India and China and between India and Pakistan were the results of regional rivalries and did not directly draw in the superpowers. Many governments in the region also battled insurgency movements caused by ethnic, religious, or economic discontent.

Newly independent nations in the region also struggled against problems associated with economic development, population explosion, unfulfilled and conflicting social aspirations, and political instability. While some nations maintained democratic political systems, others became battlegrounds between democratic and authoritarian forces.

THE CONTINUING COLD WAR IN SOUTHEAST ASIA

The Great Powers Partition Vietnam

The economic, political, and international relations of all nations of Asia were profoundly affected by the cold war. In Indochina after 1954, Communist and nationalist ambitions also embroiled the United States and the U.S.S.R. in local conflicts.

Where communism was not an issue, the United States supported independence for Asian peoples. Thus it had pressured the Netherlands to relinquish control over Indonesia. On the other hand, it supported France against the Communist-led independence movement in Indochina. After France's defeat in 1954 an international conference was convened at Geneva, Switzerland, where representatives of the United States, Great Britain, and France met with those of the Soviet Union and China and with Communist and non-Communist Vietnamese leaders.

The Geneva Agreement ended French rule. It temporarily partitioned Vietnam at the 17th parallel, the north to remain under Ho Chi Minh's control and the south under a non-Communist government that France had installed. In both parts of Vietnam the International Control Commission, consisting of India, Canada, and

Poland, was to hold elections in 1956 to determine the political future of a united Vietnam. Laos and Cambodia became independent neutral nations. The United States and South Vietnam did not sign the Geneva Agreement because Ho Chi Minh's Communist government was allowed to control the north.

The two halves of Vietnam quickly polarized into a Communist and an anti-Communist nation. In the north, Ho Chi Minh established the Democratic Republic of Vietnam with Hanoi as the capital. With economic and military aid from the Soviet Union and China, Ho built an effective totalitarian regime based on the Chinese model. His brutal land reform and religious persecution drove a million northern-born Vietnamese, many Catholics and ethnic Chinese, to flee to the south and triggered a peasant revolt that was put down by the army.

South of the 17th parallel the Republic of Vietnam was ruled by President Ngo Dinh Diem, a Catholic in a predominantly Buddhist land. About 90,000 supporters of Ho fled from South to North Vietnam. Supported by a French-trained army, Diem suppressed various armed religious sects and in 1956 promulgated a constitution that gave him extensive powers. Although a nationalist, Diem became increasingly unpopular because his government was corrupt and authoritarian and because he blatantly favored the Catholic minority. The government arrested and executed Communists and other opponents, while Communists who infiltrated from the north assassinated officials of the South Vietnamese government. The United States supplied economic aid to South Vietnam and, fearing a Communist victory, encouraged the South Vietnamese government, which readily agreed, not to hold elections mandated by the Geneva Agreement.

The Second Indochina War

Several religious and political groups, most notably the South Vietnamese Communists (Viet Cong), revolted against the South Vietnamese government in 1958. They were strengthened by southerners who had gone north in 1954 and now infiltrated back into their homeland as well-trained Communist cadres. In 1960 they formed the National Liberation Front (NLF) of South Vietnam. Laotian and Cambodian Communist guerrillas also revolted against their governments.

The superpowers soon turned these local and civil wars, especially the one in South Vietnam, into a cold war conflict. The Soviet Union and China hailed their ally's goal as a "war of national liberation" but initially gave it little more than moral support. Viewing the NLF-led revolt as a Communist bid to topple a friendly government, President Eisenhower invoked the Truman Doctrine and sent U.S. military aid and advisers to strengthen the South Vietnamese army (ARVN). President Kennedy continued this policy, expanding aid to South Vietnam and also giving aid to anti-Communist forces in neighboring Laos.

The Soviet Union, China, and other Communist bloc nations countered by supplying North Vietnam with weapons, economic aid, and technical advisers. China also sent labor battalions to replace North Vietnamese who had been drafted into the army. To help the Viet Cong fight a guerilla war of ambush and assassinations, North Vietnam sent supplies and troops through Laos and Cambodia into South Vietnam

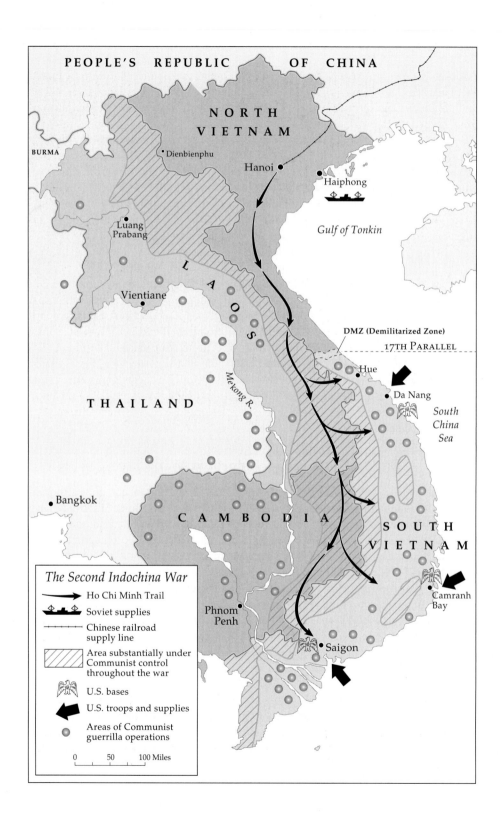

The Second Indochina War

- → Ho Chi Minh Trail
- Soviet supplies
- Chinese railroad supply line
- ▨ Area substantially under Communist control throughout the war
- U.S. bases
- ⬅ U.S. troops and supplies
- Areas of Communist guerrilla operations

0   50   100 Miles

A Buddhist monk burns himself to death in Saigon in 1963 in protest against the Diem regime.

along the Ho Chi Minh Trail, which was a network of roads and paths in the mountain spine of Indochina. The Viet Cong controlled peasants in the countryside by intimidation and won their support through land reforms.

Diem's anti-Buddhist policies led to popular protests headed by the Buddhist clergy; several monks shocked the world by publicly setting themselves afire. Late in 1963 the United States gave tacit approval to a coup by South Vietnamese generals that killed both Diem and his hated brother, the security chief. Political instability followed as a succession of generals tried and failed to organize stable governments.

Lyndon Johnson, who succeeded Kennedy as president in 1963, sharply escalated U.S. involvement in Indochina. He maneuvered Congress into passing the August 7, 1964, Tonkin Gulf Resolution, which empowered him to "take all necessary measures to repel any armed attack against the forces of the United States in order to prevent further aggression." Johnson increased U.S. combat troops until they reached 500,000 men in 1968. He also authorized air strikes against military targets in North Vietnam and along the Ho Chi Minh Trail. Australia, Thailand, South Korea, the Philippines, and several other U.S. allies sent small military contingents to aid South Vietnam.

**INSTABILITY IN
SOUTH VIETNAM**

U.S. FORCES BOGGED DOWN IN VIETNAMESE CONFLICT

It was extremely difficult for U.S. forces, despite superior arms, equipment, and supplies, to fight disciplined guerrillas in an oppressively hot climate among peasants of an alien culture. The poorly led South Vietnamese army and the inexperienced and unstable South Vietnamese government made weak partners. By 1968 the United States and North Vietnamese forces were doing most of the fighting in South Vietnam. Fortunately, the major powers had tacitly agreed that the conflict should not be enlarged into a nuclear war.

The Tet (lunar new year) offensive of 1968 was the turning point in the war. Taking advantage of a traditional holiday when their adversaries were off guard, the Communists launched heavy simultaneous assaults on all important towns in South Vietnam and inflicted heavy casualties. Although the Communists were eventually driven back with severe losses, the Tet offensive dashed hopes of a quick, victorious end to the war and forced war-weary American leaders to negotiate an end to the war with North Vietnam.

Unpopular because he intensified U.S. commitment to the war in Vietnam, Johnson did not seek reelection. Richard Nixon, the Republican candidate and winner of the 1968 election, took steps designed to hasten the end of U.S. involvement in the conflict. He improved relations with the Soviet Union and China, heavily bombed North Vietnam to pressure it to negotiate seriously, and strengthened the ARVN, while slowly withdrawing U.S. troops.

On January 27, 1973, the United States and North Vietnam signed the Paris Agreement, which provided for a cease-fire and the complete withdrawal of U.S. troops from South Vietnam in 60 days. The United States also promised economic aid to both North and South Vietnam. Chief negotiators Henry Kissinger (United States) and Le Duc Tho (North Vietnam) were awarded the Nobel Prize for Peace in 1973.

NORTH VIETNAM VICTORIOUS AT CONFLICT'S END

Fighting ended in South Vietnam in 1975, when North Vietnam crushed the South Vietnamese government. The Communist victory ended the 30-year nationalist struggle for a united, independent Vietnam at an estimated cost of 3.2 million lives, mostly civilian Vietnamese. Over 57,000 U.S. troops died. A unified Socialist Republic of Vietnam came into being in 1976; Saigon was renamed Ho Chi Minh City (Ho had died in 1969).

MANY REFUGEES ESCAPE COMMUNIST VIETNAM

U.S. withdrawal also led to victory for Communists in Laos and Cambodia. North Vietnamese Communists dominated the newly unified Vietnamese government. Remarkably resilient and capable in war, their peacetime Marxist economic policies, harshly implemented, brought hardship and stagnation to the country. Vietnam's economy was further weakened by a costly war to control Cambodia and by a U.S. embargo. Millions of Vietnamese fled their country in leaky boats and risked the elements and pirates for haven anywhere else. Some fled for political reasons, but many later refugees fled to escape economic deprivation. Many were ethnic Chinese. Unable to feed its fast-growing population, in 1987 Vietnam began to return to some private enterprise to revive its moribund economy and attract foreign investment. It agreed to accept the return of some of its people who had fled to Hong Kong and other nearby lands and received a monetary payment for each returnee.

In Cambodia, Communists were murderously intolerant of each other after assuming power. The fanatical Communist leader Pol Pot and his supporters butchered

Vietnam opened its economy to foreign investment in 1987. This Export Processing Zone was run by an investment group from Taiwan.

over 1 million their urban middle-class compatriots with genocidal fury, destroying much of Cambodia's culture and ruining its economy.

Communist Quarrels after The War

Contrary to fears engendered by the domino theory, communism spread no further in Asia after 1975. Instead, the Communist nations of Asia began to fight one another, demonstrating that nationalism and imperialism were often stronger impulses than common political and economic ideology. Historical Vietnamese imperialism, temporarily halted by French colonialism and U.S. intervention, now triumphed across Indochina. In 1978 Vietnam invaded Cambodia, ousted China's client Pol Pot, and put its puppets in power. Pol Pot's supporters and other Cambodians opposed to the Vietnamese then fought a guerrilla war against the Vietnamese-installed government and tied down a large portion of the Vietnamese military for a decade, in a replay of what had happened in Vietnam during the Second Indochina War, but with the roles reversed. Vietnam also established control over Laos. The Vietnamese army, fifth largest in the world, battle-tried and well armed with Soviet and Chinese weapons and captured U.S. armor, became widely feared by the militarily weak non-Communist nations of Southeast Asia. Many Southeast Asian nations, once afraid of the presence of the United States, came to regret the day the United States withdrew.

VIETNAM INVADES LAOS AND CAMBODIA

HOSTILITIES BETWEEN CHINA AND VIETNAM

Vietnam's ambitions were checked by its former mentor, China. Sino-Vietnamese enmity was a historic fact of long standing, acutely felt by the Vietnamese, who feared the long shadow cast by the much larger and historically dominant China. (China had ruled northern Vietnam for 1,000 years until circa 900 C.E. and was Vietnam's overlord state until 1885.) To counter China, Vietnam cultivated close ties with China's arch rival, the Soviet Union, that culminated in a Friendship and Mutual Defense Treaty between the two nations. China feared the expansion of Vietnam and being bordered to the south, as well as to the north, by an unfriendly power. It also deeply resented Vietnam's ingratitude for the 300,000 Chinese sent to help North Vietnam in its wars against France and the United States and between $15 and $20 billion in economic aid from China. Charging Vietnam with mistreating ethnic Chinese in Vietnam and accusing Vietnam of imperialism in Cambodia, China launched a punitive campaign against Vietnam in 1979 with 250,000 troops. The inexperienced Chinese army performed poorly against the battle-hardened Vietnamese. After a limited invasion, China declared that it had punished Vietnam and withdrew, but threatened to return if Vietnamese behavior required it in the future.

SOVIET UNION GAINS INCREASING INFLUENCE IN VIETNAM

The Chinese incursion put Vietnam squarely in the Soviet camp. Numerous Soviet technicians were sent to Vietnam, and large amounts of Soviet aid poured in to keep the inefficient and war-damaged Vietnamese economy afloat. In return, the Soviet navy obtained Camranh Bay, with its excellent natural harbor and U.S.-built installations, as a base from which it could challenge the U.S. Navy at Subic Bay in the Philippines and exert power in Asian and western Pacific waters. U.S.-Vietnamese relations remained strained because Vietnam would not cooperate in accounting for U.S. military personnel missing in action since the 1960s. As a result, the United States refused to give aid to Vietnam and embargoed trade with it.

Throughout the 1980s Chinese-supported Cambodian guerrillas battled Vietnamese soldiers and their Cambodian allies in persistent warfare that sometimes spilled over the Thai border. Vietnamese troops finally withdrew from Cambodia in 1989, followed by the formation of a coalition government that included several former guerrilla factions in 1991. Indonesia and Japan played major roles in the negotiations, and Japanese troops assumed their first post–World War II overseas mission as peacekeepers. Peace, however, remained elusive as former adversaries continued sporadic hostilities.

RACIAL, ETHNIC, AND RELIGIOUS CONFLICTS IN SOUTH ASIA

Every country in South Asia was affected by legacies of hatreds that long preceded independence. Every nation suffered from sporadic outbreaks of ethnic or religious violence. They ranged from the breakup of Pakistan to prolonged and intractable civil war in Sri Lanka to persistent communal outbreaks among Hindus, Muslims, Sikhs, and ethnic groups in India.

ETHNIC-RELIGIOUS CONFLICTS IN INDIA

Communal problems in India between Hindus and Muslims had delayed its independence and resulted in the partition of the subcontinent into India and Pakistan (see Chapter 14). In postindependence India, communal antagonisms persisted and occasionally flared into rioting, most recently in Kashmir. Other minority groups, such as the Gurkas, who lived near Nepal, and the tribal people in Assam, agitated or revolted for special treatment or autonomy. In the 1980s serious troubles with the Sikhs, a religious minority of about 16 million people who lived in the northern state of Punjab, erupted into violence. The Sikhs had done well in the government and the military, and their state was one of the richest in the land. However, when the Indian government refused Sikh demands for special religious recognition and greater autonomy for Punjab, extremists resorted to armed terrorism and began to store arms in their holy shrine, the Golden Temple in Amritsar. In 1984 Prime Minister Indira Gandhi ordered the Indian army to oust Sikh terrorists from the Golden Temple, which resulted in hundreds killed and damages to the temple. After her assassination by her disgruntled Sikh bodyguards, Indira Gandhi's son and successor, Prime Minister Rajiv Gandhi, negotiated an accord with moderate Sikh leaders that included greater autonomy for Punjab and other concessions. The extremists, however, who would have been satisfied only with an independent Sikh state, were not mollified, and sporadic acts of terrorism continued. A multiethnic secular nation, India's many religious and linguistic groups continued to live in uneasy peace.

Despite ethnic problems, India enjoyed elected governments except between 1975 and 1977, when Prime Minister Indira Gandhi (daughter of Nehru and no relation to Mahatma Gandhi) suspended the constitution and ruled under emergency laws. When she allowed free elections in 1977, the Indian electorate demonstrated its political savvy and commitment to democratic principles by throwing Gandhi and her Congress Party out of office. The Janata Party that replaced her was ineffective and unstable, however, and Gandhi was swept back to power in the 1980 election. When she was assassinated in 1984, leaders of the Congress Party quickly elevated her son Rajiv to the prime ministership. Rajiv Gandhi, an airline pilot with little background in politics, was at first popular because he was young, because he supported modernization, and above all because of the circumstances of his succession, but he was handicapped by political inexperience.

INDIAN DEMOCRACY TRIUMPHS OVER PROBLEMS AND SETBACKS

Rajiv Gandhi's elevation to prime minister by the majority Congress Party despite his almost total political inexperience reflected the strong family-dynastic tradition in India and much of Asia. He resigned as prime minister in 1989 because of electoral losses suffered by the Congress Party. While campaigning for the 1990 general election Gandhi was assassinated by a Tamil extremist group from Sri Lanka, whose secessionist fight he had initially supported and then abandoned. V. P. Singh of the National Front became prime minister of India. Subsequent elections have ended the Congress Party's domination in politics and weakened the Nehru-Gandhi family's leadership.

Throughout Nehru and Indira Gandhi's tenure of power India's economy combined state planning and private enterprise. This was due to the Congress Party's socialist professions and India's close ties with the Soviet Union. State planning mired the Indian economy in corruption and red tape. Doctrinaire economic theories stymied progress. The economy began to grow faster after Rajiv Gandhi became prime minister because he favored private enterprise, deregulation, and high technology. As a result, India's middle class grew to become larger than the total population of the United States. The fall of communism in the former Soviet Union and Eastern Europe,

INDIA'S TROUBLED ECONOMY

their economic bankruptcy, and their turn to capitalism discredited the planned economic system and drove the last nail into India's socialist coffin. Deregulation, the market economy, and foreign investments since 1990 have propelled India to unprecedented growth.

ETHNIC-RELIGIOUS CONFLICTS IN SRI LANKA

India, the dominant regional power, intervened in the ethnic conflict in neighboring Sri Lanka. Because the Buddhist Sinhalese majority controlled the island's government, the disgruntled Hindu Tamil minority then resorted to terrorism to gain autonomy or to secede. In 1987 the Indian government forced a mediated settlement between the two sides and landed troops to enforce its terms, but it became mired in Sri Lanka. India withdrew its troops without having achieved its goals. Rajiv Gandhi paid for the involvement with his life: he was assassinated by a Sri Lankan Tamil, who blamed him for betraying them.

EAST PAKISTAN BECOMES BANGLADESH

Ethnic divisions split Pakistan apart and ended the myth of Muslim unity. In the 1970 Pakistani elections, the more populous East Pakistan won a majority, whereupon the generals, who came from West Pakistan, postponed convening the National Assembly. This was the last straw for the East Pakistanis, who had long resented their inferior status. Led by Sheikh Mujibur Rahman of the winning political party, called the Awami League, East Pakistan declared its independence and renamed itself Bangladesh in 1971. West Pakistan sent an army to crush the rebellion. A bloody war ensued in which more than 1 million people lost their lives and 10 million fled to neighboring India. India seized the opportunity to humble its enemy Pakistan and sent troops to help Bangladesh. Indian intervention forced Pakistan to give up its attempt to reconquer the east. The military ruled Bangladesh for most of its early years, but elections were held in 1989 that brought Kaleda Zia to power as prime minister. The first three women leaders in Muslim countries, two in Bangladesh and Benazir Bhutto in Pakistan, came from the Indian subcontinent.

POLITICAL INSTABILITY IN PAKISTAN

Pakistan was ruled by parliamentary governments in its first years of independence but after 1964 was for long periods under either direct or veiled military control. In 1977 General Mohammad Zia ul-Haq seized power from the elected prime minister Zufilkar Ali Bhutto. After ruling for 12 years, General Zia was killed in an airplane crash in 1988. In elections held in late 1988 the People's Party, headed by Benazir Bhutto (daughter of the former prime minister), won a handy victory. As a result she was named prime minister, the first woman head of government in a Muslim country. She has twice been elected and dismissed from office. Politics remained frequently violent, and social and ethnic unrest persisted.

UNSTABLE POLITICS IN NON-COMMUNIST SOUTHEAST ASIA

COUP BRINGS MILITARY TO POWER IN INDONESIA

Indonesia, the largest nation in Southeast Asia and the most populous Muslim nation in the world, has been ruled by authoritarian governments since independence. Sukarno ruled Indonesia in an eccentric fashion as president for life under the guise of a guided democracy. In the face of deteriorating health and impending economic disaster, he held on to power by playing off the army against the Communist Party of Indonesia (PKI) and its front organizations, which he increasingly favored. In a sequence of events that remain unclear, the PKI staged a coup against the army in

A spellbinding speaker, President Sukarno of Indonesia addresses a giant rally.

1965 and killed a number of senior officers. However, it failed to capture several key leaders, one of whom, General Suharto, seized leadership and crushed the rebellion, killing between 150,000 and 500,000 people in the process. Sukarno was stripped of power and died in 1970. Suharto remained in power for 32 years, heading an authoritarian and military-dominated regime and winning elections that were generally considered to have been unfair.

Burma changed its name to Myanmar in 1989. It was a parliamentary democracy at independence but has been ruled by military men since 1962. Its economy stagnated and the people's standard of living deteriorated. Widespread demonstrations led by students and the Buddhist clergy forced the ruling junta to call elections in 1990. Aung San Suu Kyi, daughter of Burma's foremost independence fighter and then under house arrest, organized an opposition party that handily won the elections. However, she remained under house arrest, and the generals continued to rule.

Neighboring Thailand also had a checkered course for democracy and was frequently under corrupt military rule. Unlike isolationist Burma, Thailand actively participated in international alliances and organizations, and its economy has prospered since the 1980s. A rising standard of living and openness to the world led to the growth of a middle class, a civil society, and reverence for a long-reigning king who exercised his political influence in favor of reforms and the development of democratic government.

POLITICAL INSTABILITY PREVAILS IN MYANMAR, THAILAND, AND THE PHILIPPINES

BIOGRAPHY

Continuing Her Father's Legacy

Many people ask me how I came to be involved in this nationwide movement for democracy. As the daughter of the man regarded as the father of modern Burma it was inevitable that I should have been closely attuned to political currents in the country. From childhood I was deeply interested in the history of the independence movement and in the social and political development of the Union of Burma. . . . [My father had been] an upright man who put the welfare of his country above his own interests. . . . [Studying his life I too] came to feel such a deep sense of responsibility for the welfare of my country. . . . My years abroad provided me with the opportunity to assess Burma's problems from the broad perspective of the international scene, while my frequent visits home kept me in touch with developments within the country. It was not difficult to recognize that the nation was inexorably deteriorating under the government of the BSPP [Burma Socialist Programme Party— the ruling party dominated by military men]. But I could not see any signs of a popular opposition movement which I could support whole-heartedly until I came to Burma last April [1988]. Then I found that the mood of the people had changed and that the time for a popular anti-government movement was fast approaching. The massacre of peaceful demonstrators last August

precipitated such a movement and decided me to come out in support of the people's aspirations. This decision was prompted partly by the belief that as my father's daughter I have a responsibility towards my country.*

. . .

Aung San Suu Kyi is the daughter of Aung San, leader of Burma's independence movement who was assassinated by political opponents in 1947, just before Burma achieved independence from Britain. On a continent where family rule often resulted in massive corruption and abuse of power, Aung San Suu Kyi represented the tradition where a parent's fame left an obligation on the children to give further service to their country. She married an Englishman and lived in Great Britain until her mother's serious illness called her home in 1988. There she found a budding democracy movement against Burma's oppressive military rulers and plunged into organizing the National Coalition, which swept the elections in 1990. The generals placed her under house arrest and would not allow the elected representatives to form a government. Aung San Suu Kyi won the Nobel Peace Prize in 1991 for her courage in defending democracy and human rights. She continued to struggle for democracy in her country.

*From "In the Eye of the Revolution" by Aung San Suu Kyi, in Michael Aris (Ed.), *Freedom from Fear*, New York: Penguin Books, 1991, pp. 211–212.

The Philippine constitution established a U.S.-style democratic government that worked turbulently under a two-party system through the 1960s. Ferdinand Marcos was elected president in 1965 and reelected in 1969. In 1972, Marcos suspended the constitution and declared martial law. During the 1980s, an ailing Marcos shared power with the military and with his wife, Imelda, in what came to be called a conjugal dictatorship. Under mounting U.S. and domestic pressure, Marcos held presidential elections in

1986. He was opposed by Corazon Aquino, widow of an opponent who had been assassinated. Massive fraud allowed Marcos to declare himself the winner, but by then the United States had switched its support to Aquino. A military coup led by reform-minded officers finally toppled Marcos; Aquino was inaugurated president, and democracy was restored to the Philippines. Although personally upright, Aquino was politically inexperienced, she made no economic reforms, and her government was plagued by many coup attempts. Subsequent free elections resulted in smooth transfers of power.

Despite ethnic problems, Malaysia and Singapore have maintained uninterrupted democratic parliamentary governments since independence. Singapore briefly joined with Malaysia but seceded to form a separate ministate in 1965. Its almost 80 percent ethnic Chinese population was guided by the elected prime minister Lee Kuan Yu, who oversaw his orderly and prosperous nation in the manner of a family patriarch. After Lee retired, his political party continued to rule Singapore through electoral victory. Since Singapore's secession Malaysia has been ruled by its slight Malay ethnic majority with unabashed bias in favor of that group.

Ethnic and religious minorities were a problem throughout Southeast Asia because they were numerically small but economically powerful. The success of the Chinese minorities in several countries excited envy and often brought retaliation and victimization. For example, it was customary for Filipino politicians to shake down Chinese Filipinos, and, during the army countercoup in Indonesia in 1965, many of the victims were local Chinese who were killed because of their wealth. Ethnic Indians were similarly victimized in Myanmar. The recent rise of militant Islam among the Malays in Malaysia added to the disquiet of the Chinese and Hindu Indians in that area.

ETHNIC PROBLEMS IN SOUTHEAST ASIA

THE QUEST FOR ECONOMIC DEVELOPMENT

Economic development followed an unsteady course in both south and Southeast Asia. As a result, the region on the one hand boasted the economic resurgence of Singapore, while on the other Bangladesh and Burma remained among the poorest nations of the world. The reasons for the disparity were complex, ranging from the quality and quantity of natural resources to ideology and religion, political leadership and stability, and cold war alignments. Due to corruption and mismanagement, abundant natural resources were no guarantee for economic development, Indonesia being a prime example.

Overpopulation was a key factor that hindered development in most nations. The government of Singapore carried out a highly successful policy of family planning and population control. By the late 1980s it had achieved almost zero population growth, and by 2000 the government was taking measures to arrest the declining birthrate by offering incentives to couples for having children and accepting highly qualified immigrants.

CORRELATION BETWEEN POPULATION AND ECONOMIC GROWTH

Bangladesh was at the other end of the spectrum, where the birthrate stood at 4.3 percent and the natural population increase was a high 2.8 percent per year. This Wisconsin-sized nation, which had few industries and depended almost solely on farming in perilously flood-prone delta land, had 118 million people in

Indian Prime Minister Indira Gandhi meets the leader of Bangladesh, a nation that owed its independence to India.

1990. Only 29 percent of them were literate, and 75 percent lived in abject poverty by United Nations standards. Per capita GNP stood at a desperate $70 per year. Pakistan had 32 million people in 1947 in what was then West Pakistan; by 1990 the population had increased to 118 million. India had 350 million people in 1947 and 844 million in 1990. Similar rates of increase held true for Indonesia and the Philippines.

Several factors explained this unprecedented and catastrophic population explosion. One was improved public health and medicine that eliminated epidemics and vastly decreased infant mortality, allowing those who survived infancy to live longer. While life expectancy in India was just over 30 years at independence in 1947, the average life span had increased to 57 years for men and 58 years for women by 1990. Pakistan and Bangladesh had similar but slightly lower life expectancies.

FEW NATIONS HAVE SUCCESS IN POPULATION CONTROL

Outside Singapore, nations of the region had only limited success with population control; some had not seriously tried. Reasons for population explosions were generally interrelated. One was lack of resources to set up family-planning clinics and train personnel; another was the low educational level of the people, especially women. For example, in India, one-third of school-age girls were not in school, and the minimum legal age for marriage for women was 15. Uneducated people were generally ignorant about birth control and supported traditional values of early marriages and large families, in which a woman gained respect by bearing many children, especially sons.

Even those governments that had the will still had a most difficult task in convincing very traditional people to desire small families. Prime Minister Indira Gandhi tried in India in 1975 with the slogan "Stop at two [children]." (Indian upper- and middle-class families needed no such reminders.) Her government also forced sterilization for some men during 1975–1977 when the constitution and legal due process were suspended. Her tactics outraged tradition-minded Indians, especially the Muslim minority, and they contributed to her electoral defeat in 1977. Her successor governments have soft-pedaled this issue ever since.

Despite the huge population increases there had been no famine in postindependence Asia. However, most of the people on the Indian subcontinent and in the Philippines were desperately poor and subsisted on only two-thirds of the calorie intake of Westerners. A key factor in preventing starvation was effective international relief and humanitarian efforts, particularly in crisis-ridden Bangladesh. Another was the green revolution, begun in the 1960s, which introduced high-yielding "miracle" rice and wheat that doubled the world rice and wheat harvest between 1967 and 1992. It averted famine in countries such as India and allowed it to produce enough food to feed its huge population. Other factors were the clearing of virgin lands to increase the acreage under cultivation and large new irrigation projects that made possible double- and triple-cropping. However, progress brought pollution and erosion. There was also a widening gap between the rich and poor, as many small farmers who could not afford the necessary capital to invest in farm machinery, chemical fertilizers, and pesticides were squeezed out.

GREEN REVOLUTION PROVIDES MORE FOOD

Burgeoning populations have stymied efforts to improve education and standard of living. Per capita GNP remained low at $330 per year in India in 1988 and $350 in Pakistan; even resource-rich Indonesia's per capita GNP remained low at $430 because of the rapid population increase to 191 million by 1990. Compared with Singapore's more than $10,000, the contrast is startling.

All nations in the region have benefited from foreign aid. Cold war rivalries helped neutralist India to obtain aid from both the Eastern and Western blocs; it received over $9 billion from the United States between 1947 and 1980 and billions from the Soviet Union. The Philippines and Thailand received huge amounts of aid from the United States. Great Britain, Canada, and Australia gave aid to Asian Commonwealth nations. Since the 1980s Japan has supplanted the United States as the chief aid giver and investor in Southeast Asia. In addition, international agencies such as the World Bank and the Asian Development Bank have provided aid.

MANY NATIONS IN REGION RECEIVE FOREIGN AID

Inept and corrupt governments throughout the region crippled development. For example, the Philippines, despite massive and continuing U.S. aid, remained on the verge of economic ruin partly because of mismanagement and corruption during the Marcos decades, which continued after his ouster. In Indonesia, corruption by the Suharto family and cronies siphoned billions from public funds. Burma was yet another nation of rich natural resources ruined by an inept and corrupt military government that professed to follow a "Burmese road to socialism."

Economic inequities also partly explain continuing insurgencies in several countries in the region.

HUGE MILITARY SPENDING THROUGHOUT SOUTH AND SOUTHEAST ASIA

Large military expenditures also slowed economic development. Nearly all nations in the region either had grandiose imperialistic dreams or feared real or imagined enemies. All allocated large amounts of scarce resources to arms and military forces. India, for example, committed a large part of its resources to its military in order to guard against China, watch Pakistan, and sustain its pretensions as the regional power of south Asia. Thus, India became a nuclear power, maintained an aircraft carrier in its naval fleet, and sent troops to intervene in Sri Lanka's civil war. Fearful of the much larger India, Pakistan also maintained a strong military and secretly developed nuclear weapons.

The Association of South East Asian Nations (ASEAN), formed in 1967 by Thailand, the Philippines, Indonesia, Malaysia, Singapore, and (later) Brunei, Vietnam, Laos, Cambodia, and Myanmar, set a positive trend. Member nations held regular consultations on economic and other issues of mutual concern and worked to coordinate economic and trade policies and to foster cooperation. Starting in the 1980s Malaysia, Thailand, and Indonesia began to chart significant economic progress and rapid growth rate, hoping to become the "little Japans" of the future. Inspired by the European Union, ASEAN later set a goal of establishing a free trade area by the year 2020.

SOCIETIES IN FLUX

UNEVEN PROGRESS AND WIDE GAPS

By the end of the cold war era, a wide chasm separated the rich from the poor, the modern from the traditional, the educated from the illiterate, and the secular from the religious, reflecting an uneven pace of progress. On the one hand, there had been regionwide improvements in life expectancy, medical care, and the literacy rate. Mass communication had reached even remote villages. On the other hand, television had shown impoverished villagers the lifestyles of the rich in their own nations and overseas, stirring up hopes and expectations for a better life that were too often unrealizable or that were met too slowly.

WOMEN MAKE GAINS, BUT ALSO SUFFER DISABILITIES

Women had made tangible gains. In nations where elections were held, women won the right to vote and voted in numbers equal to men. India, Pakistan, Bangladesh, Sri Lanka, and the Philippines had elected women heads of government, an achievement unmatched in most Western nations. Women also held numerous high diplomatic and government positions. As the urban middle class increased in size, more women asserted their rights. The Indian parliament passed laws soon after independence that made women politically equal to men, enforced monogamy (except among Muslims), and granted Hindu widows the right to remarry, wives the right to obtain a divorce, and daughters equal rights in inheritance with sons. However, except for those in the urban middle class, few women either understood their rights or felt confident enough to exercise them. Thus, laws that protected women tended to be unfulfilled, and girls continued to marry early (sometimes younger than the legal age of 15), and those without sufficient dowries were treated harshly by their in-laws. In all countries there were more illiterate women than men, and women were often left on the farm while men went to the cities to seek higher-paying work. In a reverse pattern from developed countries, women had a shorter life expectancy than men.

In Pakistan, Bangladesh, and Malaysia, a resurgent Islamic fundamentalist movement sought, and sometimes succeeded, to rescind civil and criminal codes introduced by Britain in favor of traditional Islamic law. Fundamentalist vigilantes became emboldened to insist on the veiling of women and to intimidate modernized Muslims, especially women, to give up freer lifestyles. So as not to alienate Muslims, the Indian constitution allowed the Muslim community to remain under the rule of their religious laws, and Muslim men were allowed more than one wife. In the Philippines the Catholic Church contributed to the ethos of the homebound woman by encouraging traditional ideals and large families. Only in economically prosperous Singapore did women win economic independence. In other nations, real equality either did not exist or remained only partially realized.

COLD WAR ALLIANCES AND NEUTRALISM

The foreign policy of every nation in the region was affected by the cold war, and each nation's place and policy in the cold war was in turn the result of its domestic politics, ideology, colonial experience, and relationships with its neighbors. Some nations chose alignment with one of the superpowers, while others chose neutrality or nonalignment.

Despite India's professed neutrality, it in fact tilted toward the Soviet Union. When India's initially friendly relations with China were replaced by rivalry and deteriorated into war in 1962, the Soviet Union rewarded India with weapons and diplomatic support and continued to give India military and financial aid until its dissolution. In return, India refused to criticize the Soviet Union for invading Afghanistan in 1978, even when the U.S.S.R. conceded its disastrous intervention there a failure and withdrew.

SUPERPOWER RIVALRIES, ALLIANCES, AND NEUTRALISM

In 1961 India, Egypt, and Yugoslavia sponsored the Nonaligned Movement, whose Asian members included Bangladesh, Indonesia, Malaysia, and Singapore. Whereas India could not have aspired to primacy in either camp of the cold war, its leadership was assured among the neutralist nations; thus, it suited India's national interest to be neutralist. Meanwhile, India and Pakistan, the latter a U.S. ally in the cold war, continued to be each other's worst enemies, intermittently threatening each other with war.

Confronted with neutralist but pro-Soviet India, Pakistan chose a pro-Western stance, and also developed close relations with China after 1962. In 1974 India became a nuclear power to intimidate Pakistan, which propelled Pakistan to also develop a nuclear capability. The United States opposed nuclear proliferation but gave aid to Pakistan because of its leading role in supporting the anti-Soviet guerrilla fighters in Afghanistan. Pakistan gave refuge to over 3.5 million Afghans who had fled their homeland, allowed its territory to be used as a staging ground for the Afghan guerrillas fighting against the Marxist government in Afghanistan, and became a conduit for U.S. military and economic aid to the insurgents.

Non-Communist states of Southeast Asia (except for neutralist Burma, renamed Myanmar) tilted toward the West in the cold war. After the United States withdrew from the Indochina war, however, weak countries were afraid of antagonizing their powerful Communist neighbors. They also feared Japan's economic and potential military clout.

An uneasy relationship developed between the United States and the Philippines, where the two largest U.S. overseas bases, Clark Air Force Base and Subic Bay Naval Station, were located. The United States paid the Philippine government a handsome, ever-increasing rent for the bases, plus additional economic aid, which generated much-needed income for the Filipino economy. Nevertheless, many Filipinos resented the massive U.S. presence in their nation as a symbol of its residual colonial status and agitated for its termination. In the middle of negotiations for lease renewal in 1990, Mount Pinotubo burst into violent volcanic eruption. Ashes poured onto nearby Clark Air Force Base and destroyed the facility. With the disintegration of the Soviet Union, the strategic value of the bases had declined. With an economic recession in the United States, paying high rent for the bases seemed wasteful, and with the host nation resenting continued U.S. presence, the United States decided not to renew its leases and withdrew from both bases.

SUMMARY

The cold war once again became a hot war in former French Indochina, where the United States failed to stem the advancing tide of communism. After 1975 Indochina was ruled by Communist governments and dominated by Vietnam. However, the domino theory did not apply beyond Indochina. In Communist-ruled nations regional imperialism resurfaced, as Vietnam attempted to dominate Laos and Cambodia and China sought to check Vietnam.

Political stability was another regionwide problem as newly independent nations that often lacked experienced leaders tackled the problems of nationhood. Some remained democratic, but others succumbed to military or strongman rule. Everywhere people sought democratic rights. Internally, each nation also faced conflicts between dominant majorities and ethnic and religious minorities. Old ethnic and religious hostilities submerged under imperialism resurfaced, frequently defying solutions. New enmities created additional bitter feelings between states. Different value systems also battled for preeminence.

The newly independent nations found themselves beset by common problems, especially population explosion, poverty, and economic backwardness. Economic progress was uneven. Most received foreign aid, and some, such as India, received aid from both superpowers. Burma rejected foreign aid in favor of isolation, while the Philippines received massive aid from the United States; both had mismanaged themselves into near bankruptcy. Economists also worried that Bangladesh would never progress beyond its desperate poverty. Tiny Singapore alone developed a strong economy, although Thailand, Malaysia, and Indonesia began to follow.

Women in all nations struggled for equality and scored some spectacular successes. Most nations enacted laws to protect and advance the status of women, although in all countries poor women remained second-class citizens. In Muslim countries Islamic fundamentalism clashed with secular lifestyles and women's liberation.

Almost all nations, even those that professed neutrality, played some role in or were affected by the cold war. India led the neutralist nations but tilted toward the Soviet Union while Pakistan joined a U.S.-headed alliance, in part motivated by fear of and enmity toward India. Emphasizing economic advancement, ASEAN is an example of regional cooperation in Southeast Asia.

SUGGESTED SOURCES

Bhutto, Benazir. *Daughter of Destiny: An Autobiography.* 1989. A moving book by a courageous woman.

Brass, Paul B. *The Politics of India since Independence.* 2nd ed. 1994. Significant to understanding present-day India.*

Das, Gurcharan. *India Unbound: The Social and Economic Revolution from Independence to the Global Information Age.* 2002. Explains how changes in Indian policies after 1991 paved the way for later explosive growth.*

Duiker, William J. *The Communist Road to Power in Vietnam.* 1996. Objective and comprehensive history from 1900 to 1975.*

Forbes, Geraldine. *Women in Modern India, The Cambridge History of Modern India,* IV.2. 1996. Compelling study of Indian women from the nineteenth century to the present.*

Friend, Theodore. *Indonesian Destinies.* 2003. An engrossing account about the world's most populous Muslim nation during the past half century.*

Goodno, James B. *The Philippines: Land of Broken Promise.* 1991. This book deals with many subjects; it is partly based on interviews and partly on the author's firsthand knowledge.

Gupta, Pranay. *Mother India: A Political Biography of Indira Gandhi.* 1992. A candid, sweeping biography.

Harrison, Selig S., Paul H. Kreisberg, and Dennis Kux, eds. *India and Pakistan: The First Fifty Years.* 1999. Many experts discuss a wide range of topics.*

Him, Chantrithy. *When Broken Glass Floats: Growing Up under the Khmer Rouge: A Memoir.* 1999. A Cambodian woman recalls the death of all members of her family under the brutal Pol Pot regime.

Karnow, Stanley. *Vietnam: A History.* 1983. A balanced account of the war. (Also a 13-part television series.)

Lapierre, Dominique. *The City of Joy.* 1985. About Mother Theresa's Calcutta.*

Lind, Michael. *Vietnam, the Necessary War: A Reinterpretation of America's Most Disastrous Military Conflict.* 1999. A challenging review of shifting American public opinion and military miscalculations that resulted in U.S. failure in Vietnam.*

Romilos, Beth Day. *Inside the Palace: The Rise and Fall of Ferdinand and Imelda Marcos.* 1987. An insider's look at the Marcos regime by an American journalist and wife of a prominent Filipino.

Tarling, Nicholas, ed. *The Cambridge History of Southeast Asia,* Vol. 4, *From World War II to the Present.* 1999. Definitive general history of the postcolonial period.*

Victor, Barbara. *The Lady: Aung San Suu Kyi, Nobel Laureate and Burma's Prisoner.* 1998, updated 2002. A short account of the activist's life in politics.*

*Paperback available.

WEB SOURCES

www.mtholyoke.edu/acad/intrel/vietnam.htm. Provides numerous links to documents relating to U.S. involvement in Vietnam from 1941 to the fall of Saigon.

www.historyplace.com/unitedstates/vietnam/index.html. Presents detailed time lines for U.S. involvement in Vietnam from 1945 to 1975.

www.sscnet.ucla.edu/southasia/History/Independent/indep.html. A university site on India with links to materials on Indira Gandhi and others.

home.iae.nl/users/arcengel/Indonesia/1965.htm. This site offers a detailed time line for the history of Indonesia from 1965 to 1998.

⑥Competing Systems in East Asia in the Late Cold War Era

Throughout the cold war era, East Asia continued to be divided politically, economically, and socially. Wars and near-wars caused nations in the region to maintain large armed forces and join alliances. The Korean War and the Indochina War involved one superpower (the United States) directly, while the other, the Soviet Union, was represented by its proxies (North Korea and North Vietnam) and a sometime ally, China. North and South Korea remained intensely hostile after the ceasefire that ended formal hostilities in 1953. The Chinese civil war was never resolved because the governments of both China and Taiwan professed to represent the entire nation, and China continually threatened to use force to compel Taiwan into its fold.

Two quite different political systems coexisted uneasily. China and North Korea were ruled by Communist governments. The once authoritarian governments of South Korea and Taiwan remained staunchly anti-Communist and began moving rapidly toward pluralistic and democratic political systems in the late 1980s, joining firmly democratic Japan.

While Japan, South Korea, and Taiwan became industrialized and wealthy nations, a command economic system dictated by Marxist theories and by centralized planning failed to bring prosperity to the Communist nations. After 1978 China resurrected the private sector to revive its moribund economy, but North Korea did not budge its economy from Marxist orthodoxy. Improvements brought about by privatization, and the restoration of incentives, inevitably led Chinese citizens to demand political and social reforms, which were forcibly suppressed.

COMPETING POLITICAL SYSTEMS

A great ideological divide separated the Communist from the non-Communist nations of East Asia into the 1990s. The seven-year U.S. occupation had transformed Japan into a democratic and plural society. The parliamentary democracy established in the 1947 constitution continued to function. The Liberal Democratic Party retained power through 1992, with the Socialist Party relegated to ineffective opposition. During the 1980s democracy progressed impressively in South Korea and Taiwan. In contrast, Communist parties clung to power in China and North Korea. While North Korea remained stable under one-man Communist rule, China was repeatedly rocked by massive disturbances in power struggles within the Communist Party and by prodemocracy movements.

Political Evolution in Taiwan and South Korea

TAIWAN AND SOUTH KOREA BECOME DEMOCRATIC

Deeply scarred by defeat on the mainland and fearful of invasion by China, Chiang Kai-shek promulgated emergency laws and maintained an authoritarian government on Taiwan until his death in 1975. His son Chiang Ching-kuo assumed the presidency of Taiwan in 1978, following a pattern of family rule characteristic of much of Asia. Chiang Ching-kuo continued and accelerated the economic development begun by his father, and he also inaugurated political reforms. He declared that none in his family would succeed him and picked Taiwan-born and U.S.-educated Lee T'eng-hui as vice president. Chiang died in 1989, but the reforms he had begun transformed Taiwan's political system into an open and democratic one. As an observer said about Taiwan, "Other countries ranging from Albania to Paraguay have also cast off their repressive governments, but one would be hard-pressed to find any place on earth that has so successfully combined an economic with a political miracle." By 1991 all repressive laws that abridged civil and political rights had been rescinded. Nationwide elections were held in 1991 and 1992 that international observers pronounced fair. Although the Kuomintang (KMT) won strong majorities in both elections, a democratic opposition was clearly emerging in Taiwan.

South Korea's military-dominated government also began to make democratic reforms and hold free elections after 1988, propelled by powerful student demonstrations. It, too, joined the ranks of democratic nations with a multiparty political system.

China's Continuing Political Tumult

MAO LAUNCHES CULTURAL REVOLUTION IN CHINA

Pragmatic Communist Party leaders Liu Shaoqi and Deng Xiaoping ruled China between 1960 and 1966 and repaired the deep economic damage wreaked by Mao's discredited Great Leap Forward. Seething with resentment at his ouster from power, Mao plotted to end his forced retirement. Mao, his wife Jiang Qing (a former actress who until then had played only a minor public role), and some allies went to the campuses of universities and secondary schools, enrolled millions of young people in the Red Guards, and used them to oust the party cadres and bureaucrats from power. Mao called his campaign to seize power the Great Proletarian Cultural Revolution. He dreamed of a China in which material incentives played no part and ideological purity, as he interpreted it, counted for more than expertise. An old man, he had little time left in which to attempt to realize his dream.

CULTURAL REVOLUTION PLUNGES CHINA INTO CHAOS

Between 1966 and 1968 China was thrown into a frenzy of turmoil as Red Guards shut down schools, government offices ceased to function, collective farms were thrown into chaos, and factories stopped producing. Mao especially hated intellectuals, whom he derided as "swollen in head, weak in legs, sharp in tongue but empty in belly." His supporters humiliated, tortured, and jailed millions of party officials, bureaucrats, teachers, and managers, including chief of state Liu Shaoqi and party general-secretary Deng Xiaoping. Many of his victims were killed, others committed suicide in despair, and millions were sent to labor camps. Mao's followers also destroyed countless works of art and ancient monuments. Mao returned to power, elevated in a personality cult that even Stalin might have envied. By 1969 China was in utter chaos, as rival Red Guard units battled one another in power struggles. Mao then called in the army to put down the Red Guards, after which many young people were sent to the countryside to work on farms. Although normality began to return slowly after 1970, power struggles within the top ranks of the Communist Party continued unabated.

Frail and senile, Mao died in September 1976. His death was followed shortly by the downfall of his widow, Jiang Qing, and her radical supporters who had risen to power during the Cultural Revolution. Deng Xiaoping and other surviving pragmatists (Liu Shaoqi had died in jail), now rehabilitated, returned to power. In 1981 China's new rulers held a show trial that condemned Jiang and her three top supporters, called the "Gang of Four," for persecuting millions of people, executing 34,375, and committing other crimes. Although Mao was not on trial, the convictions of his protégés made him guilty by implication. Later in 1981 a special meeting of the Central Committee of the Chinese Communist Party passed a resolution that said: "The 'Great Cultural Revolution' from May 1966 to October 1976 caused the most devastating setback and heavy losses to the party, the state, and the people in the history of the Peoples' Republic, and this 'Great Cultural Revolution' was initiated and led by Comrade Mao Zedong." One of Mao's colleagues added,

> Had Chairman Mao died in 1956, there would have been no doubt that he was a great leader of the Chinese people. . . . Had he died in 1966, his meritorious achievements would have been somewhat tarnished. However, his achievements were still very good. Since he actually died in 1976, there was nothing we can [sic] do about it.

Without doubt Mao was a hugely successful revolutionary, but he lived too long for his own, his party's, or China's good. With these assessments of Mao's final years, the Maoist era finally came to an end.

Deng Xiaoping placed his allies in top positions in the government and the party. A tough Marxist, Deng had headed an earlier purge of intellectuals. A pragmatist on economic policy, he had been denounced during the Cultural Revolution for saying that it did not matter what a cat's colors were so long as it caught mice. Thus, he was willing to make far-ranging economic reforms to improve the people's standard of living, but he adamantly opposed political reforms that would abridge the Communist Party's monopoly of power.

CHINESE ECONOMY RECOVERS UNDER DENG XIAOPING'S REFORMS

Mao had closed China's doors, condemning it to economic stagnation while the rest of the world had forged ahead. Economic improvements necessitated the opening of China to outside contacts. During the 1980s China sent ever-larger contingents of scholars and graduate students to universities in the United States, Canada, Japan, and Western Europe. By 1989 there were about 40,000 Chinese studying in the United States alone. China needed the knowledge and skills its students acquired in the West to sustain progress and modernization, yet the Communist Party sought to suppress their yearning for political reform and democratization. Many intellectuals believed that the economic modernization Deng sought could not be fully realized without political modernization through the introduction of democracy and the rule of law. The pace, scope, and direction of the reforms heightened

DENG REFUSES TO MAKE POLITICAL REFORMS

Students led peaceful demonstrations in Beijing and other Chinese cities in 1989 to protest Communist rule and to demand democratic reforms. They were violently put down by troops.

The "Goddess of Democracy" became the symbol of Chinese student defiance against Communist rule and demand for reform before the deadly crackdown at Tiananmen Square in 1989.

For a moment in Bejing in 1989 this young man slowed down the column of army tanks that bloodily put down a peaceful student-led demonstration for reform against Communist rule.

public expectations and exposed the Communist Party's shortcomings and corruption. Herein lay Deng's dilemma: while he wanted Western science and technology, he labeled Western values "spiritual pollution," which he sought to exclude lest they corrode his power base.

Before 1989 several episodes already showed that the Communist Party under Deng would not tolerate popular demands for liberalization. During 1978 and 1979 the government allowed the erection of a "Democracy Wall" in a park in Beijing where citizens could post their views. Because the posters often denounced the party and the government's wrongdoings, the authorities abruptly closed down the wall in 1980. Several dissidents who had posted their views on the wall were tried and given harsh sentences in labor camps. After the Communist Party's partial denunciation of Mao in 1981, no further criticisms were allowed. In 1986 students became frustrated with the gap between reality and promise and took to the streets in demonstrations. They were sternly put down, and some educators and journalists who had spoken out for greater freedom were disciplined. Deng became disillusioned with his protégé Hu Yaobang for advocating a freer political climate and a faster pace of economic reforms and engineered his ouster as party general-secretary at the Thirteenth Communist Party Congress in the fall of 1987. Hu was replaced by Zhao Ziyang, whom Deng seemed to be grooming as his successor.

In the spring of 1989 Beijing students marched to protest pervasive corruption by Communist bureaucrats and to petition the government to crack down on corrupt officials and to grant reforms such as freedom of speech. Like Mao, Deng was contemptuous of intellectuals, and, like Mao, he believed that power emanated from the barrel of a gun. He refused to discuss student demands and issued an ultimatum for the unarmed students and their sympathizers to disperse. Before the deadline, the government ordered tanks and soldiers to mow down peaceful protestors in Beijing's Tiananmen Square and in many cities across China. Heavy censorship was imposed, and a widespread crackdown took place that brought a reign of terror for the students, intellectuals, and leaders of an infant independent trade union movement. Communist officials who supported lenient treatment of students, most notably Zhao Ziyang, were purged and jailed and replaced with hard-liners willing to implement Deng's repressive policies.

Deng and his supporters were willing to ignore world censure for their bloody repression of peaceful protesters that resulted in thousands of casualties. They felt vindicated by events in the Soviet Union that led to the unraveling of that Communist superpower in the wake of Mikhail Gorbachev's political reforms (see Chapter 31). With the toppling of communism in the former Soviet Union and Eastern Europe, they felt sure their crackdown had saved them from a similar fate. Although ostensibly retired, Deng actually continued to rule through proxies until he died in 1997.

BLOODY CRACKDOWN OF STUDENT PROTEST IN 1989

CONTRASTING ECONOMIC SYSTEMS

Ideology determined East Asian economic systems. Japan's economy continued to expand on the firm foundations built during the U.S. occupation. Similarly, the capitalist economies of South Korea, Taiwan, and Hong Kong forged ahead. Conversely, the doctrinaire application of Communist economic theories and centralized economic planning based on the Soviet model held back progress in China and North Korea. The magnitude of China's economic distress forced Deng to embrace limited free enterprise after 1978, in a successful attempt to revive the nation's stagnant economy. Only North Korea retained its straitjacket Communist economic practices and was left behind, even by Communist standards. Thus the ideological division of East Asian nations along economic lines has blurred, with capitalism in the ascendant.

RAPID GAINS UNDER CAPITALIST ECONOMIES, WHILE COMMUNIST STATES STAGNATE

Japan's Continuing Economic Miracle

JAPAN BECOMES ECONOMIC SUPERPOWER

Politically stable and secure under U.S. protection from foreign enemies, an increasingly confident Japan scored one economic success after another. All the things that contributed to Japan's initial economic recovery continued after 1960. A German industrialist who visited Japan in the late 1960s remarked that the Japanese worked the way Germans used to work. Even in the 1990s Japanese company managers frequently had to force their workers to take the annual vacations that were their due.

Since exports were key to Japan's prosperity, it attempted to follow a "no enemies" foreign policy in furtherance of trade. It maintained diplomatic relations with most nations and gave loans, credit, and economic aid to many. By the 1980s Japan had become a world economic power, second only to the United States and the largest investor and supplier of foreign aid throughout Asia. As labor costs soared in Japan, Japanese manufacturers built plants in Southeast Asian nations, where workers were paid less.

RESOURCES AND MARKETS DRIVE JAPAN'S FOREIGN POLICY

Japan's economy suffered several severe shocks in the early 1970s. Two, which the Japanese dubbed the "Nixon shocks," came from the United States in 1971. To counter an adverse balance of trade, mainly against West Germany and Japan, the United States placed a 10 percent surcharge on all imports and devalued the dollar, which hurt Japanese exports to the United States. Later that year, without prior notice to Japan, President Nixon announced that he was planning to visit China to mend Sino-American relations, which had been marked by hostility since the Korean War. Following the lead of the United States, Japan had maintained diplomatic relations with Nationalist China on Taiwan until 1972 and the two had become important trading partners. Following the new U.S. initiative, Japan quickly switched formal diplomatic relations from Taiwan to China, establishing an opening for profitable trade with that giant nation.

The "petroleum shock" occurred in 1973 as OPEC raised oil prices by 450 percent and some members refused to sell petroleum to Japan because of its friendly relations with Israel. Since Japan imported all its oil, 80 percent of which came from the Middle East, the shock was considerable. Although the problem of supply was solved quickly, Japan suffered from double-digit inflation in 1973 and 1974. Moreover, OPEC action raised the possibility that other producer nations might form similar cartels, a frightening prospect for resource-poor Japan, which imported 100 percent of its iron ore, bauxite, wool, rubber, and phosphates and high percentages of other industrial raw materials.

Japan responded in several ways. One was to establish diplomatic relations with China because China produced petroleum and other valuable raw materials Japan needed, and in turn desperately needed Japan's machinery and technology. It also developed a "raw materials diplomacy" of befriending potential trading partners, negotiating long-term agreements with them, and supporting global free trade.

JAPAN FOCUSES ON HIGH-TECHNOLOGY INDUSTRIES

The crises of the 1970s also led to a larger debate in Japan over long-term national policies and goals. The Japanese decided to favor a slower growth rate than they had pursued in the preceding decades and to shift from smokestack industries such as steel and chemicals to clean industries such as computers, opticals, and high technology. After debating how to distribute the fruits of future growth, the Japanese agreed increasingly to divert profits and revenues to higher wages, better living conditions, and environmental protection.

Differing priorities and perceptions have resulted in clashes between Japan on the one hand and the United States and other countries over environmental, ecological, and other issues. While fuel-efficient Japanese-made cars consumed less petroleum, a nonrenewable resource, and caused less pollution than larger and more wasteful U.S.-made cars, Japan supported whaling and drift-net fishing that threatened marine life, which the United States and Western European nations were anxious to protect. Lacking coal and petroleum, Japan committed itself to nuclear plants for energy generation and stockpiled plutonium for that purpose, which the United States opposed because of the danger of nuclear accidents and because plutonium can be used to build nuclear weapons.

Japan weathered the economic crises of the 1970s, and during the 1980s it continued to sustain an impressive growth rate. By the time it attained the second-largest GNP (surpassing the by then floundering Soviet economy in 1987), Japan had become an industrial superpower and a global trading and investing nation. The Liberal Democratic Party (LDP) continued to win every election, so that although the premiership rotated among LDP factions and leaders, Japan experienced political stability and a continuity of policy.

Japan's economic strength provoked international problems. It chalked up enormous trade surpluses against most nations, especially its largest trading partner, the United States. Both governments worked to redress the imbalance by such measures as a sharp upward revaluation of the yen and the removal of many import restrictions; Japan significantly lowered tariffs. The United States also prodded Japan to play a larger role in international monetary institutions and international peacekeeping. Japan paid the United States for the upkeep of American military installations in Japan. In 1987 the Diet overcame a great psychological block and voted to increase defense spending over the previous limit of 1 percent of the GNP.

JAPAN ENJOYS LARGE SURPLUSES AGAINST MOST TRADING PARTNERS

However, as Japan continued to enjoy a huge trade surplus, mostly against the United States, it became worried about rising protectionist sentiments in much of the world. It also became concerned about the adverse effect of the expansion of the European Community and the North American Free Trade Agreement on Japan.

To maintain its competitive edge, especially against the United States, Japan encouraged research that placed it well in the forefront of advanced technology, especially information technology. With an average per capita GNP of over $23,000 in 1989, Japan was a high-income and high-labor-cost nation that had to rely on robots in domestic and overseas manufacturing plants to maintain its products' competitiveness.

Booming Economies of Taiwan, South Korea, and Hong Kong

From the 1960s on, Taiwan, South Korea, Singapore, and Hong Kong followed Japan's path in economic advancement and became global trading nations. They were variously dubbed "the Little Japans," "the Four Dragons," or "the Four Tigers" (see the discussion of Singapore in Chapter 28).

TAIWAN MAKES RAPID ECONOMIC ADVANCES

Taiwan had within a generation been transformed from a poor agricultural nation to an industrial power. After 1949 the Nationalist government initiated peaceful land reforms and introduced technological innovations that increased farm production and built up the physical and social infrastructure. Resource-poor, it had to rely on trade, first developing labor-intensive and export-oriented light industries in the 1960s, followed by heavy industries in the 1970s and sophisticated high-technology industries in the 1980s.

Modernization required capital, qualified personnel, and scientific management. U.S. economic aid provided much-needed capital, totalling $1.5 billion, until 1964. Taiwan's authoritarian government provided political stability and favorable investment conditions that attracted foreign capital. Taiwan created an excellent educational system, with nine years of free, compulsory education, although most students went on to finish 12 grades. Over 25 percent of postsecondary school young people were in colleges and universities, which produced a highly qualified workforce. Many of the brightest youths went on to graduate schools on the island and abroad, providing the necessary personnel for research and management.

Taiwan enjoyed an unemployment rate of less than 2 percent, low inflation, and fast growth. Its economy grew at a 9 percent annual rate, to become 40 times as large in 1987 as it had been in 1969, and its foreign trade grew from 21st in the world in 1978 to 13th in 1990. In 1992 it was first in the world in foreign currency reserve holdings, with about $84 billion. It was rare in its simultaneous achievement of rapid economic growth and equitable distribution of wealth (the ratio of the highest and the lowest 20 percent of wage earners in 1991 was 4.88:1, a smaller gap than in the United States). Per capita GNP for its 20 million people surpassed $10,000 in 1992 (from less than $145 in 1951). By all criteria, Taiwan was almost a fully developed nation. Economists referred to its rapid development as a miracle.

SOUTH KOREA BECOMES AN ECONOMIC POWERHOUSE

Like Taiwan, South Korea progressed from a poor agricultural nation, ravaged by war and flooded with refugees, to an economic power, despite heavy defense expenditures (5.8 percent of GNP in 1987). Its development pattern was similar to Taiwan's. It also received economic aid from the United States until the economy reached a takeoff point. Despite a lack of petroleum and many mineral resources, South Korea's economy grew by leaps and bounds, and in the 1980s some of its products (e.g., Hyundai automobiles) competed with those of Japan in international markets. Shipbuilding skyrocketed from almost nothing to third in the world. As time went on, the prospect of impending reunification of the more populous South Korea (44 million in 1990) with the impoverished North Korea (24 million) became less attractive. After 1990 many South Korean experts went to Germany to study the problems it faced with reunification. (Based on Germany's expenditure in integrating former East Germany, they estimated that South Korea would need to spend $800 billion to bring North Korea up to its standard of living.) In the early 1990s South Korea and Taiwan ran neck and neck in their GNP, their export share, and the upward revaluation of their currencies. Both had opened their markets to imports. Unlike Taiwan, however, South Korea had a substantial foreign debt.

Hyundai Heavy Industries in South Korea. Japan, South Korea, and China are the largest shipbuilding nations in the world; Hyundai is the world's largest shipbuilder.

HONG KONG THRIVES UNDER BRITISH RULE

Hong Kong, Great Britain's last imperial outpost in Asia, built up a bustling and thriving capitalist economy after World War II, and it replaced Shanghai as the premier trading city along the China coast. Most of Hong Kong's 6 million people were refugees who had fled from Chinese communism, and British rule of law and free trade policy made it a showcase of capitalism. Its financial capital, know-how, and infrastructure were essential to the success of the free enterprise zones established by China after Mao's death to attract foreign capital and thus lift and revitalize China's lagging economy. The bright lights and free lifestyle of Hong Kong were the envy of millions of Chinese across the colony's border and the destination of tens of thousands of refugees from China and Vietnam every year.

In 1984 Great Britain signed an agreement with China to return the colony composed of Hong Kong and its environs in 1997. China promised Hong Kong a separate administration and respect for its economic and social systems for 50 years after 1997. However, in light of repressions in China after the Tiananmen Square massacre, Hong Kong citizens, already jittery, became even more fearful of what would happen to them after 1997, and emigration from Hong Kong accelerated.

China's Search for Prosperity

In contrast to the rapid progress that marked Japan, Taiwan, South Korea, and Hong Kong, China's politics caused chaos in its economy throughout the Maoist decades. Just after the pragmatists repaired the damages inflicted by the failed Great Leap Forward, Mao Zedong unleashed his teenage Red Guards to disrupt the economy. By Mao's death in 1976, China was in shambles because industries were outdated and collective farmers had no incentive to produce, and millions were near starvation. China's Soviet-derived system of centralized planning was marked by institutionalized corruption, irrational prices, disjunction between supplier and consumer, and low-quality goods.

When Deng Xiaoping came to power in 1978 the Communist Party changed emphasis from ideology to "economics in command." Because China was near bankruptcy and compared unfavorably with the economic miracle that was Taiwan, there was enormous pressure for reform along the lines of Communist Hungary and Yugoslavia, which had made economic strides with decentralization and capitalist incentives.

Deng's attempt to revive the socialist economic system was called *gaige,* which means "restructure." It began tentatively in 1978 with rural reform in Deng's home province Sichuan, a rich agricultural region whose 100 million people were close to starvation because of mismanagement. Individual plots of land were offered to Sichuan farmers, who were still obliged to deliver stipulated amounts of grain to the state but could sell the rest on a free market. The results were so good that by 1984 all of China's 54,000 communes had been abolished. Farmers were offered land-use contracts of up to 50 years and were allowed to pass their houses on to their heirs. As a result, farmers made long-term improvements, agricultural output soared, and rural income almost tripled. Surplus farm laborers were absorbed into small rural industries that sprang up. Although prosperity was uneven, new, better farmhouses mushroomed throughout China, testifying to the overall success of the program.

Deng's strategy of reforming the farm sector first was a sound one, for he thereby enlisted 800 million supporters before he began to tackle the more complex problem of restructuring other sectors of the economy. *Gaige* in industry was more complicated than privatizing agriculture. In 1980 an estimated 60 percent of China's industry and technology was completely obsolete. Although Deng encouraged some private enterprise and foreign investment in joint enterprises (by 1984, 128 U.S. firms had offices in Beijing), most large industries continued to be state-run and unprofitable. They continued to limp along because firing their large workforce would produce social and economic unrest. The government still allocated key resources and determined who received foreign capital and technologies. It was also difficult to adjust prices to reflect production costs and consumer demand in a society accustomed to government price setting and subsidies for basic commodities. Many found the inflation and unemployment that resulted from the reforms unsettling and potentially dangerous.

Some senior party leaders opposed reforms because they believed in a Soviet-style centrally planned economy. Generals faced with a reduced share of the pie for the military, middle-ranking party bureaucrats at risk of losing their perks, and ordinary workers accustomed to the "iron rice bowl," or lifetime jobs that were low paying but that expected little of them in return and gave them subsidized housing and food, also opposed reforms.

Moving cautiously, Deng nudged many senior colleagues who opposed him to retire and placed his supporters in key positions. He persuaded military leaders to demobilize 20 percent of their forces (1 million troops) and cut their share of the GNP from 11.7 percent in 1978 to 6.7 percent by 1985, using the argument that a revitalized industrial sector would make possible more sophisticated military technology later. This trend was reversed after 1989 to reward the military for its loyalty in suppressing the students.

RESTRUCTURING THE MILITARY

A decade and a half after Mao's death, most Chinese were undoubtedly better fed, clothed, and housed than they had been during his lifetime. Improvements had also brought about greater inequality; coastal areas adjacent to Hong Kong and across the strait from Taiwan forged ahead as a result of investments from their capitalist neighbors. There was a great dichotomy among China's people. Most of the 80 percent who lived in the countryside were poorly educated compared to urban dwellers. Deng hoped that in the long run the wealth of the prosperous southeast coast would trickle down to the other regions. In the short run he hoped that continued material improvements and a rising standard of living would be a sufficient sop to offset the political repression. He also hoped that in time the lure of trade with China would overcome international anger toward his regime's human rights violations. Deng's strategy worked because while the students, intellectuals, and factory workers who demonstrated for political and other reforms in major cities in 1989 were bloodily put down, the countryside remained quiet and generally apathetic.

UNEVEN PACE OF ECONOMIC REFORM

In contrast, China's ally North Korea remained a monocracy under Kim Il Sung's (1912–1994) Stalinist-style rule, and its economy was mired in Marxist controls. Conditions deteriorated badly after 1991, when the former Soviet Union stopped giving aid and China reduced its share because it no longer needed to compete with the U.S.S.R for North Korea's loyalty.

The contrasts between the prosperous capitalist economies of Japan, Taiwan, South Korea, and Hong Kong and the drab poverty of the Communist nations were very stark. While significant improvements occurred in China under Deng, even faster progress was made in Taiwan. For example, while the per capita GNP ratio between Taiwan and China was 10:1 in 1976, it had widened to about 25:1 by 1990 (over $8,000 for Taiwan and $330 for China). Similar contrasts divided North from South Korea.

CONDITIONS DETERIORATE IN NORTH KOREA

SOCIAL CHANGES AND CONTRASTS

Social changes in Japan, Taiwan, and South Korea resulted from rising living standards and educational levels and assimilation of Western ideas and trends. A large, confident middle class in all three nations needed little government prodding to limit family size, seek advanced education, or advocate environmental protection. After Mao Zedong's death the Chinese showed the same longing for material well-being and social progress as citizens in non-Communist countries, but a wide, although narrowing, gap remained between China and its neighbor. Only North Korea remained totally isolated.

Japan, Taiwan, South Korea, and Hong Kong

JAPAN UNDERGOES WIDE-RANGING SOCIAL CHANGES

During the cold war era sweeping changes affected every aspect of Japanese life. Significantly, Japan was the first Asian nation to bring population growth under control, although (at an estimated 124 million in 1991) it remained one of the most densely populated countries on earth. Education reforms and legal equality gave new opportunities to Japanese women. The booming economy provided jobs and economic independence to women, although real equality between men and women in employment still lagged behind that in the United States by about 10 years. Because of educational and career demands and opportunities, both Japanese men and Japanese women married late; a man's average age at marriage was 27 years, and a woman's was 25. Many women resisted marriage and postponed having children, and they disregarded government propaganda and subsidies that encouraged larger families. Farmers had the most difficult time finding wives because of the rigors and isolation of farm life; some advertised as far as Sri Lanka for wives. These tendencies worried many Japanese planners, for not only did Japan have one of the lowest birthrates (at 1.1 percent per year) and population growth rates (at 0.5 percent per year, attributable to increasing longevity), but it also had the world's highest life expectancy—82 years for women and 76 years for men. The cost of a dwindling working-age population supporting a growing aging population loomed large. In a culture that traditionally revered the elderly, older Japanese now complained about the decline in respect.

STRESSES OF MODERN LIFE

The Japanese were literate (99 percent) and predominantly urban. By 1972 one in four lived in the Tokyo-Osaka industrial belt. Although they were among the most affluent people in the world, many Japanese lived in cramped apartments, worked long hours, and commuted great distances in crowded public transportation. Stressful lives, heavy smoking, and the newly acquired preference for red meat, fast foods, and fatty foods took their toll in a high incidence of strokes and heart attacks. Pollution was also a major problem. Still, although the Japanese had social problems caused by rapid change, up to the early 1990s their society lacked many of the ills that afflicted the West. There was virtually no drug problem, and juvenile delinquency and adult crime rates were low.

Since the mid-1960s Japan's humiliation stemming from its military defeat had been replaced by a growing national self-confidence sustained by its economic success; however, this new nationalism was diffuse, like that of other modern states, and not accompanied by a reemergence of militarism or an emperor-based ideology. The involvement of Emperor Hirohito in World War II and Japan's defeat had lessened the emperor's significance. After his death in 1989 he was succeeded by his son Akihito, who was a child during the war.

JAPAN FAILS TO OWN UP TO CRIMES OF IMPERIALIST PAST

Unlike Germany, Japan's government did not make full reckoning with the crimes committed by the nation's leaders before and during World War II; in fact, it continually attempted to cover them up. For example, it repeatedly introduced school history textbooks that ignored or soft-pedaled its brutal imperialist past. Japan only reluctantly admitted the kidnapping of over 200,000 young women from Korea, Taiwan, China, and other conquered lands to be the sex slaves of Japanese soldiers during World War II. Countless numbers of these women died of abuse. Men from conquered lands had been drafted and sent into combat or forced labor. Japan refused to compensate the survivors or the families of the dead. Such behavior kept alive hatred of Japan in Asia, most notably in China, Taiwan, and Korea. The failure to acknowledge and make amends for past wrongs also prevented Japan from gaining full international acceptance and playing the significant world role that its enormous economic success otherwise warranted.

In Taiwan, Hong Kong, and South Korea rapid economic progress had also resulted in major social changes. Each had over 90 percent literacy rates and educational systems that were among the world's best. Taiwan's average life span was 77 years for women and 72 years for men. All three countries had within a generation changed from high to low birthrates, and the natural increase to just over 1 percent per year in Taiwan was similar to that for advanced Western nations. As a result, Taiwan developed a labor shortage in the late 1980s and had to deal with the problem of illegal immigrant workers as well as contracting legal foreign workers. Fearful of the consequences of an aging population and labor shortages, Taiwan's government changed its planned parenthood slogan from "Two [children] are good, but one is enough" to "Two are good; three are not too many," but, as in Singapore, to no effect.

All three nations were confronted with problems associated with rapid progress, such as environmental degradation, pollution, urban congestion, and snarled traffic. Social patterns had also changed rapidly. Labor shortages encouraged women to enter the workplace in growing numbers. Two-salary nuclear families were becoming the norm, and retirement centers and nursing homes for the old were replacing the traditional multigenerational household. The increasingly prosperous, sophisticated, and well-educated peoples of Taiwan, Hong Kong, and South Korea had within a generation transformed their traditional societies into modern civil societies. It was this social transformation that propelled Taiwan and South Korea toward political democracy. Fear that the Communist rulers of China did not understand these social and political forces clouded Hong Kong's future.

RAPID PROGRESS AND ATTENDANT PROBLEMS FOR TAIWAN, SOUTH KOREA, AND HONG KONG

China

Convinced that China would not advance unless it could slow the population explosion, Deng Xiaoping enacted severe birth control measures. Couples were ordered to have only one child, and drastic sanctions were placed on those who disobeyed, from forced abortions to fines, loss of housing, and reduced educational opportunities for children with siblings.

While the government was relatively successful in cities, where controls were easy to enforce and where people tended to be more modern in attitude, enforcing the single-child policy proved very difficult in the countryside, where there was little education and few opportunities. This difficulty was partly due to the conservative attitudes of the country people, who valued children, especially sons, but ironically

CHINA INSTITUTES ONE-CHILD POLICY

was also due to Deng's successful policy of privatizing farming. The hand-tool-using Chinese farmer needed children to help with chores, and boys were valued because of their strength and because rural young couples lived with the husband's parents. The severe measures were successful in reducing annual population growth to 1.5 percent in the 1980s and just over 1 percent in the 1990s. In 1990 the estimated population stood at 1.13 billion. China's large population remained its major handicap in moving toward modernization and higher living standards; rising expectations that could not be fulfilled threatened stability in the nation.

INTERNATIONAL AND INTRAREGIONAL RELATIONS

International relations in East Asia were very complex. They were dictated by superpower struggles, regional antagonisms, and unresolved internal conflicts. Sino-Soviet and U.S.-Soviet relations were pivotal in dictating major shifts in Sino-American and Sino-Japanese relations.

STRAINS DEVELOP BETWEEN CHINA AND SOVIET UNION

The 1960s witnessed the steady deterioration of Sino-Soviet relations, which Mao had earlier characterized as "lasting, unbreakable, and invincible." Ideology was one reason. Mao Zedong claimed that his ideas advanced Marxism-Leninism and made it applicable to revolutionary movements in the agrarian non-Western world. The Soviet Union firmly rejected Mao's claims. Mao also asserted that he was the senior worldwide Communist leader after Stalin's death in 1953, another claim that the Soviet Union denied. There were also territorial disputes between the two nations that went back to the nineteenth century. Khrushchev's de-Stalinization campaign, which he launched without prior consultation with Mao, and his dismantling of Stalin's personality cult further upset Mao, who was busily creating his own.

The two Communist giants were clearly on a collision course. In 1960 the Soviet Union abruptly ended all technical aid to China and recalled its experts, together with the blueprints of their unfinished aid projects, leaving Chinese planners in the lurch. The split widened in 1962 when Khrushchev bowed to U.S. pressure and withdrew nuclear missiles from Cuba without consulting the Chinese, who called him a coward for doing so. When China and India went to war over a disputed boundary in 1962, the Soviet Union sided with India. Relations had deteriorated to such a low point by 1964 that when China detonated a nuclear device, the Soviet Union considered launching a preemptive strike to destroy its nuclear industry. In 1969 high-tension border skirmishes occurred in disputed territories. China's fear that the Soviet Union might apply the Brezhnev Doctrine to China (i.e., as the senior Communist state, the U.S.S.R. had the right to use military force to enforce the correct practice of communism in other Communist states) led Mao to repair relations with the United States and to rejoin the international community.

CHANGING RELATIONS BETWEEN SUPER-POWERS AND REGIONAL IMPLICATIONS

Also fearful of the Soviet Union and anxious to disengage itself from the Vietnam War, the United States moved toward rapprochement with China. In 1971 the United States dropped its opposition to China taking its seat in the United Nations in the place of Taiwan. President Richard Nixon visited China in 1972, and the United States established diplomatic relations with China in 1979 and severed formal ties with Taiwan.

Chinese foreign policy under Deng Xiaoping was characterized by pragmatism and flexibility. China steadily increased its trade with the West and its participation in international organizations. Politically it abandoned providing even moral support for revolutionary movements in the Third World. It also softened its denunciations of both the Soviet Union and the United States. However, it never stopped professing its goal of reunification with Taiwan, by force if necessary.

Even before the crackdown on the 1989 prodemocracy demonstrations, the Chinese leadership had taken steps to lessen outside influences on its citizens. It required all Chinese to obtain special passes before they could enter the four special economic zones along the southern coast. It increased ideological indoctrination in the schools and stringently screened applicants who wished to study abroad. The disintegration of the Soviet Union and the end of the Soviet empire in Eastern Europe and (Outer) Mongolia heightened the siege mentality of China's Communist leaders as they clung to power. China's relations with the West were strained by the Tiananmen Square killings, but the United States, the European Community, and Japan, all major trading partners, were unwilling to place economic sanctions on China in retaliation for its human rights violations.

Japan's foreign policy remained anchored to its alliance with the United States, although trade issues, mainly Japan's surplus trade balance with the United States, strained relations, and racial overtones sometimes threatened to poison them. Japan was the largest contributor of international aid to other Asian nations and the largest investor in the region.

JAPAN INCREASES ROLE IN WORLD AFFAIRS

Although Japan played an important part in ending the civil war in Cambodia and sent a peacekeeping force to that nation (after the Japanese Diet reluctantly passed the necessary enabling bill), it generally pursued a low-profile foreign policy in Asia. This approach was due in part to the legacy of World War II and a lingering hatred of Japan's ignoble conduct toward conquered people and in part to Japan's unwillingness to own up to the past and thereby lay it to rest. Thus, Japan had few friends in Asia despite its pursuit of a no-enemies foreign policy. Similarly, while Japan desired the raw materials of the Soviet Union and the latter sorely needed Japanese technology and know-how, unresolved territorial claims to the Kurile Islands (taken by the Soviet Union at the end of World War II and now part of Russia) prevented the development of a mutually beneficial relationship between Japan and Russia.

TENSIONS CONTINUE IN EASTERN ASIA

The divisions between the two Koreas and the two Chinas were the region's most intractable problems. Neither Korea gave up its goal of unification on its own terms. North Korea repeatedly tried destabilizing South Korea by infiltration, sabotage, assassinations, and threats to disrupt the 1988 Olympic Games held in Seoul, which it boycotted after failing to obtain cosponsorship. The DMZ between the two Koreas remained one of the most tightly guarded in the world, and the United States continued to maintain a 40,000-strong military force in South Korea. The North Korean government, considered an unpredictable rogue regime by the international community, was suspected of developing nuclear weapons. North Korea lost a former mentor after the disintegration of the Soviet Union; only China remained as an ally of sorts. Several developments in 1991–1992 portended greater stability on the Korean peninsula. They were the establishment of formal relations between South Korea and China with the intention of isolating North Korea, the admission of both Koreas to the United Nations, and the opening of contacts between the two Koreas through the International Red Cross.

Since the 1970s Taiwan had been forced out of most international organizations at the insistence of China. Its economic success, however, gave it considerable clout internationally. After Japan, Taiwan was the largest investor nation in Southeast Asia; it also became a worldwide giver of loans and aid. In 1989 it reopened commercial and cultural relations with some Soviet republics and Eastern European nations and began giving economic aid to some of the former Communist nations. In the late 1980s Taiwan relaxed restrictions against contacts and trade with China; as a result millions from Taiwan visited China, and Taiwanese enterprises invested billions in China, where labor costs were low. No political solutions were found acceptable to both sides, and the prosperous citizens of Taiwan feared and disliked the Communist system.

As several world regions moved to greater economic integration in the 1990s (the European Community, the North American Free Trade Agreement, and ASEAN), all the nations of East Asia feared future closing of economic doors to them. Political and historical problems, however, precluded their creating an economic union.

SUMMARY

Resource-poor Japan continued its economic miracle, becoming the nation with the second-largest GNP globally. Japan remained a democratic, pluralistic society; it benefited from U.S. military protection and remained a firm member of the Western community of nations. In the final decades of the twentieth century, Japan played a constructive role as trading partner, loan supplier, and aid provider to other nations in Asia.

U.S. military protection and economic aid helped war-torn South Korea and Taiwan build up strong economies that continued to prosper after aid ended. In recent decades Taiwan, South Korea, and British Hong Kong emerged as "Little Japans," becoming fully developed. The highly educated and economically secure citizens of Taiwan and South Korea demanded and realized political participation in their governments. Hong Kong's political future was clouded by its projected return to China in 1997.

Chinese politics were mired in Communist political and ideological struggles. Mao Zedong all but destroyed China's political and social infrastructure in the tumult of the Cultural Revolution that returned him to power for the last decade of his life. Deng Xiaoping's rise and tenure of power after 1978 brought economic prosperity to Chinese farmers through the dismantling of Marxist communal farming. Industries were more difficult to privatize and modernize. Because it had lost so much ground during the Maoist decades, China faced a Herculean task in catching up. In politics Deng and his supporters were orthodox Marxists and refused to give up their totalitarian power, as the Tiananmen Square massacre of reform-minded students in 1989 conclusively demonstrated. When communism crumbled in Eastern Europe and the former Soviet Union, China, North Korea, and Vietnam were the only Communist states remaining on the Eurasian continent.

The crimes of the past imperialist Japanese government prevented Japan from playing the major role in Asia that its economic power warranted. The unresolved unification questions of China and Korea continued to make East Asia politically unstable along the fracture lines.

SUGGESTED SOURCES

Bailey, Paul J. *Post War Japan: 1945 to the Present*. 1996. Sound scholarship and smooth reading.*

Cheng, Nien. *Life and Death in Shanghai*. 1987. An autobiography by a survivor of the Cultural Revolution detailing the excesses of the Maoist movement.*

Clough, Ralph N. *Cooperation or Conflict in the Taiwan Strait?* 1999. Timely book that ties in U.S. interest in the continuing conflict between China and Taiwan.*

Crump, Thomas. *The Death of an Emperor: Japan at the Crossroads*. 1991. On the legacy of Hirohito and a changing Japan.*

Hirohito: The Chrysanthemum Throne. 1980. Leaders of the 20th Century Series (Coronet). A video depicting the Japanese economic miracle.

Iwao, Sumiko. *The Japanese Woman: Traditional Images and Changing Reality*. 1992. A leading authority on Japanese women debunks many stereotypes.*

Kingston, Jeffrey. *Japan in Transformation, 1952–2000*. 2001. A short, insightful look at the massive changes that transformed Japan.*

Lee, Chae-jin. *China and Korea: Dynamic Relations*. 1996. A comprehensive review of relations from the Korean War to the mid-1990s.*

Lilley, James. *China Hand: Nine Decades of Adventure, Espionage and Diplomacy in Asia*. 2004. Firsthand account that takes the reader into the White House, the CIA, and all over Asia.

MacDonald, Donald Stone. *The Koreans: Contemporary Politics and Society*. 2nd ed. 1992. The best introductory book on Korea.*

Marti, Michael E. *China and the Legacy of Deng Xiaoping: From Communist Revolution to Capitalist Evolution*. 2002. A short, succinct account of how Deng set China on a new course.

Mitter, Rana. *A Bitter Revolution: China's Struggle in the Modern World*. 2004. A thoughtful analysis of China's quest for modernity.

Oberdorfer, Don. *The Two Koreas, A Contemporary History*. New ed. 2001. An engrossing and informative account.*

Salisbury, Harrison E. *The New Emperors: China in the Era of Mao and Deng*. 1992. Details how power has corrupted China's leaders.*

Schaller, Michael. *The United States and China into the Twenty-first Century*. 3rd ed. 2002. A study of U.S.-China relations from both countries' perspectives.

Taylor, Jay. *The Generalissimo's Son: Chiang Ching-kuo and the Revolution in China and Taiwan*. 2000. A well-written biography of an important player in several decades of East Asian history.

Terrill, Ross. *Madame Mao, the White Boned Devil*. Rev. ed. 1999. Well-written biography of the woman who sought to rule China.

Thurston, Ann. *The Ordeal of the Intellectuals in China's Great Cultural Revolution*. 1988. The Communist persecution of the educated is chillingly depicted.

Ying, Hong. *Daughter of the River*. Trans. Howard Goldblatt. 1997. Poignant account of a Chinese girl growing up in a poor and repressive society.

WEB SOURCES

www.fordham.edu/halsall/eastasia/eastasiasbook.html. See links to materials on China, Japan, and other parts of East Asia for the late cold war era, for example, in regard to China on the Cultural Revolution, Deng Xiaoping, and Tiananmen Square, 1989.

vlib.iue.it/history/asia/China/index.html. This World-Wide Web Virtual Library History site for China provides numerous links to all periods of Chinese history and other fields of study. See the History section under "People's Republic of China 1949."

www.gwu.edu/~nsarchiv/NSAEBB/NSAEBB16. Contains National Security Archive materials on Tiananmen Square, 1989.

www.uni-erfurt.de/ostasiatische_geschichte/index_en.htm. A German university site that has some valuable links in English to materials on the history of East and Southeast Asia. See, for example, several of the links dealing with the cold war in Asia.

---

*Paperback available.

⑥Africa in the Later Years of the Cold War

In the 1970s and 1980s Africa, like the rest of the developing world, endured a multitude of problems but also showed clear signs of promise for economic, social, and political improvement. The chief spot that attracted international concern was southern Africa, dominated in the early 1970s by European imperial powers and white minority governments.

As superpowers and their surrogates began to play a significant role, the cold war, already a major factor over much of the world, affected eastern and southern Africa. The independent nations of Africa also faced common problems of political factionalism, military takeovers, and conflict between the industrial and rural sectors. Some of these problems were typical of those faced by Third World nations around the globe, but others were unique to Africa. The following narrative highlights political and economic developments in selected postindependence African nations and concludes with an overview of the common problems facing all African peoples.

TURMOIL IN INDEPENDENT AFRICAN NATIONS

Rivalries in North Africa

North African nations struggled with a variety of regional rivalries while playing a substantial role in Arab, African, and international politics. Libya, under Muammar al-Gadhafi, used petroleum revenues not only to launch massive development and agricultural programs but also to champion Islamic revolutions throughout the Middle East and much of Africa. Al-Gadhafi's particular brand of Islamic-based social revolution, which was explained in his Green Books (similar to Mao's more famous Red Book), was often opposed by both the United States and the Soviet Union as a threat to their own aims in the region. In contrast, Algeria steered a neutral path between the two superpowers and became a successful negotiator between the West and the Third World. Because of its reputation as "an honest broker," Algeria helped to mediate the release of the U.S. hostages from Iran in 1980–1981.

In addition, rivalries among North African nations for the dominant role in the region contributed to increased military expenditures that channeled scarce moneys away from much-needed programs such as education, housing, and public services. For example, as early as the 1960s Algeria and Morocco clashed over control of parts of the Sahara, which is rich in natural resources. The dispute over control of the

CONFLICT IN SAHARA

Islam is a major and growing force in much of Africa and by the 1980s became a major political force as well. Here Muslims gather outside the Mopti mosque in Mali. Constructed of mud brick, the mosque is repaired annually.

western Sahara turned into a protracted war throughout the 1970s and 1980s between the Polisario, armed revolutionaries seeking an independent Sahara Arab Democratic Republic, and Morocco. Determined to exercise sovereignty over the area, Morocco constructed a wall of earth over 1,000 miles long, created to enclose the most valuable part of the western Sahara and to impede guerrilla activity. In 1988 all the involved parties reluctantly agreed to hold a referendum, under the auspices of the United Nations, to decide their political future; over 17 years later the vote has yet to occur. Regional wars in Africa, as elsewhere in the world, also undermined programs for economic development.

DICTATORS IN WEST AFRICA

The political and economic development of Ghana and Nigeria during the 1970s and 1980s is typical of most West African nations. When it became independent Ghana was the world's leading cocoa-exporting nation and its economic future seemed bright. It also had a thriving private market economy, largely dominated by women. The market women of Ghana sold and traded goods in city and town markets and were a well-established force.

However, whenever world demand and prices for cocoa dropped, Ghana, like all nations dependent on one-crop economies, suffered severe economic reverses. Many Third World nations in Africa and elsewhere experienced a decline of agricultural productivity while becoming deeply indebted to Western nations and banks. Grandiose development schemes for the construction of stadiums and buildings in the capital city, coupled with huge expenditures on the military and corruption within the government, further undermined economic development. Following the advice of international lending institutions during the 1960s and 1970s to invest in the urban, industrial sector, Ghana also borrowed heavily and largely ignored the agricultural sector.

In Ghana—and elsewhere throughout the African continent—government failures led to military coups d'état. Having seized power while the leader Kwame Nkrumah was visiting China in 1966, the military promised economic reforms and a speedy return to democracy. However, the elections in 1979 were commonly believed to have been rigged and the military again stepped in, accusing, with some justification, the elected government of corruption and inefficiency. Although all political parties were abolished, the military failed to solve either the economic or social problems of the nation. Following a cycle of military coups and countercoups and a worsening economic situation, many of Ghana's most highly educated and dedicated citizens left the country to seek better lives elsewhere. The brain drain of educated Africans to Europe and the United States further undermined the potential for a speedy political and economic recovery. Pressured by the Western nations and economic institutions, Jerry Rawlings, who had emerged as the military strongman, promised a return to democracy. He permitted a return of political parties and promised elections by 1992. However, when Rawlings resigned his military commission so that he could run for president, few Ghanaians believed that the military was actually relinquishing power or that the elections would be free and open.

MILITARY TAKEOVERS

The situation in Nigeria was similar. With an estimated population of over 100 million, Nigeria was Africa's most populous nation, with enormous economic potential. Although the Biafran civil war had been socially and economically costly, most believed that increased revenues from Nigeria's petroleum exports would ensure a speedy economic recovery. The military regime that had come to power during the long civil war made the usual promises to eradicate corruption and inefficiency and to return to democracy as soon as possible. However, most petroleum revenues never reached the poor in rural areas but were expended on the military and in Lagos, the capital city. A few people became enormously wealthy, while the agricultural sectors languished. Peasants reacted by pouring into the cities in search of jobs and a better life. City services were totally inadequate for the burgeoning population, and there were not nearly enough jobs to meet the demand. Consequently, huge slums sprang up around Lagos and other cities. This became a pattern across the Third World.

URBAN AREAS EXPAND

Plagued by internal corruption and power struggles, the military was ill prepared to implement meaningful reforms, and, as in Ghana, a series of coups and countercoups ensued. Elections were finally held in 1979, and Shehu Shagari became president. Shagari's tenure in office occurred during the period of peak prices for petroleum, and hopes were high. Although Shagari was believed to have been personally honest, he failed to eradicate corruption at the highest levels; this corruption, coupled with falling oil prices in the 1980s, led to yet another military takeover. The new regime extended its power over the civilian judicial institutions and announced plans for reform. To alleviate pressure on Lagos, which had become one of the most expensive cities in the world, with massive crime and traffic problems, the government announced that the capital would be moved to a new city, Abuja, by 1992. But the building of the new city was riddled with corruption and substandard construction.

Facing pressure from the West, the military reluctantly agreed to move toward democracy. After political parties were legalized in 1990–1991, a multitude of parties representing ethnic, personal, and regional interests emerged with over two dozen candidates for president. As in Ghana, the fragility of democratic institutions and the lack of national consensus made many pessimistic about the survival of democracy.

Dictatorial Convulsions and Cold War Intrusions in East Africa

Uganda, one of Great Britain's most prosperous colonies, went down a calamitous road of death and devastation after it received its independence in 1962. Lacking a broad base of support, the government fell to the military leadership of Milton Obote. Subsequently, while he was attending the 1971 Commonwealth conference outside Uganda, Obote was ousted by Idi Amin. Obote finally took up residence in neighboring Tanzania.

IDI AMIN AND UGANDA

Idi Amin was a Muslim in a nation where 80 percent of the population was Christian. His rule was characterized by a bizarre combination of flamboyance, cruelty, and personal eccentricity. He delighted in sending long, rambling telegrams to Queen Elizabeth and Richard Nixon, and he offered public advice on how they should govern. At the same time, he instituted a reign of terror in Uganda, massacring his political and tribal opponents by the thousands. In 1972 Amin gave the Asian population, which was mostly engaged in business, 90 days to leave Uganda. Using his Islamic allegiance, he established close ties with many Arab nations and was vociferous in his antipathy for Israel, South Africa, and Western imperialism.

The mounting violence in Uganda made its neighbors uneasy. After Amin's ill-considered attempt to invade Tanzania, Tanzanian President Julius Nyerere moved Tanzanian forces into Uganda in January 1979. Libya, under al-Gadhafi openly supported Amin. In the ensuing chaos, Amin escaped, eventually moving to Saudi Arabia. The new Ugandan compromise government was plagued with internal divisions, violence, economic ruin, refugees, and uncertainty. Only large amounts of foreign aid, mostly from Arab nations, saved the nation from total economic collapse. Rebuilding and developing this formerly prosperous area was an enormous task.

UPHEAVAL IN HORN OF AFRICA

Owing to its strategic geographic location, the Horn of Africa (a collective name for the eastern sector of the continent projecting into the Indian Ocean) became one of the major areas of U.S.-Soviet competition. Ethiopia, a centuries-old Coptic Christian kingdom, regained its independence in 1941 when British forces defeated the Italians and returned Emperor Haile Selassie to power. In 1952 Eritrea, with its predominantly Muslim population, was federated within Ethiopia in spite of Eritrean preference for independence and a closer association with Arab states. Eritreans and other ethnic groups within Ethiopia, particularly the Somali minority in eastern

Ethiopia, viewed themselves as victims of both Ethiopian and European imperialism, and they continued armed opposition to all Ethiopian regimes.

Haile Selassie was extremely pro-Western, and Ethiopia soon became a major pivot in U.S. policies for Africa. The United States built a radar tracking station and a major military base in Ethiopia and provided large sums of foreign aid. In addition, Israelis were brought in to train army officers and to provide technical skills. Israeli involvement in Ethiopia typified a pattern whereby each superpower encouraged its allies to further its interests in a region.

In spite of substantial foreign aid, Ethiopia remained a desperately impoverished nation. The peasants, who constituted over 90 percent of the population, were among the poorest in the world. The Coptic Church and the emperor's family kept tight control over a largely feudal system. With minimal natural resources and a terrain of high plateaus separated by deep valleys, Ethiopia faced major obstacles to economic development. The emperor's regime was further weakened by its disregard of the widespread starvation brought on by several years of drought and famine.

In 1974, as a consequence of these problems, a group of army officers led by Mengistu Haile Mariam rebelled, ousted the emperor, and created a military government. The new Ethiopian government adopted a pro-Soviet stance and became a major center for Soviet influence, especially a naval presence, in Africa.

Neighboring Somalia, formerly an Italian colony, became independent in 1960. In 1969 the conservative Somali government was replaced by a military-led socialist regime that was originally friendly to the Soviet Union. Somalia claimed the Somali-populated Ogaden region in Ethiopia and in 1977 began aiding guerrillas in that area. Thousands fled from the war zone to gather in huge refugee camps. By the 1980s, war, drought, and famine had made living conditions in Somalia among the worst on earth. Political rivalries, corruption, and red tape prevented massive foreign aid programs and food shipments from stopping the human suffering and starvation.

As Ethiopia moved closer to the Soviet Union, Somalia moved closer to the United States. Both superpowers were anxious to control the vital shipping routes through the Red Sea and the Suez Canal. Furthermore, the Horn was a strategic area from which both the United States and the Soviet Union serviced naval units watching the petroleum-rich Arabian peninsula. With its enormous economic problems and regional rivalries, the Horn of Africa was a focal point of cold war tensions in Africa.

DROUGHT AND FAMINE

FREEDOM STRUGGLES IN SOUTHERN AFRICA

Independence in Mozambique, Angola, and Zimbabwe

As the Portuguese in Angola and Mozambique and the white minorities in Rhodesia (later called Zimbabwe) and South Africa fought to keep control of those areas in the 1970s and 1980s, the black majority populations intensified their struggles for independence, increasingly resorting to guerrilla warfare. Both sides sought and received outside support. From the first, independent black African nations assisted the liberation movements of southern Africa; later, the Soviet Union, China, and Cuba also gave support. Nations along the borders of South Africa, such as Mozambique, became known as "frontline states." These nations provided training bases, often run by foreign Marxist advisers, for guerrillas operating in the target areas.

On the other side, Great Britain and the United States, both of which had substantial economic investments in mining and raw materials in South Africa, continued to maintain economic ties with the white minority regime. The South African and Western governments also argued that the sale of arms to South Africa was necessary because of its strategic location on the southern Cape and because of its steadfast opposition to the Soviet Union.

INDEPENDENCE MOVEMENTS

The Portuguese colonies of Angola and Mozambique were the chief scenes of nationalist guerrilla warfare in the early 1970s. Both the Popular Liberation Movement of Angola (MPLA) and the National Front for the Liberation of Mozambique (FRELIMO) rebels escalated guerrilla attacks against the Portuguese army and landowners in a classic example of wars of national liberation. Both MPLA and FRELIMO received aid from the Soviet bloc and sympathetic African nations. Although Portugal received some military assistance from European NATO nations, the colonial wars severely drained its already weak economy. Finally, following a coup in 1974, the new Portuguese leaders moved to settle the conflicts. In a relatively peaceful transition, Mozambique declared its independence. The new regime, dominated by Marxist leaders from FRELIMO, launched programs for improving health care facilities and other social welfare institutions and subsequently inaugurated a massive campaign to increase literacy. In addition, the regime was openly friendly to other African liberation movements, particularly in Rhodesia.

WARFARE IN ANGOLA

As in Mozambique, nationalist guerrillas in Angola forced the Portuguese to leave, but a second Angolan war broke out before a stable government could be created. In 1975 competing nationalist organizations, each supported by various ethnic and linguistic groups and by different superpowers, vied for power. South Africa, which opposed the Soviet-backed MPLA, occupied parts of southern Angola, while the United States and private mercenaries assisted rival nationalist groups. Finally, Cuban troops moved in to bolster the MPLA, which took control of the government and declared independence in 1975.

By 1978 the situation had temporarily stabilized, and the Marxist Angolan government turned its attention to rebuilding the nation's economic base, which had been largely destroyed by over a decade of warfare. On the other hand, continual internal rivalries impeded development. The revenues from Angola's petroleum resources helped in the reconstruction, but, in part because of its petroleum, Angola remained a nation of interest to the industrialized West (see Chapter 32).

With black independence marching south toward its very border, the South African government moved to reinforce its apartheid system. It employed a broad range of economic, political, and military efforts to cripple the support that neighboring black nations were giving to independence movements in Rhodesia and Southwest Africa and to black people in South Africa. From 1981 on, Angola was attacked by South African armed forces. However, by the time of the 1988 negotiations among the rival parties, Angolan and Cuban forces had largely defeated the South African Defense Forces and the Western-backed movements of the National Union for the

Total Independence of Angola (UNITA) and the National Front for the Liberation of Angola (FLNA), and the leftist government remained in power.

South Africa also conducted raids into Mozambique and gave support to a rebel insurgency group that was so cruel that the whole world condemned it. South Africa also used its economic power, particularly its control over much of the railroad system of the region, to intimidate Rhodesia and Botswana. In a very real way both the "enclave states" of Botswana, Lesotho, and Swaziland and the frontline states of Rhodesia and Angola were victims of the continuation of apartheid in South Africa.

Besides Mozambique and Angola, the liberation movement focused on Rhodesia. South Africa supported the Ian Smith regime, but the rest of Africa and the international community refused to recognize his white minority government. In the face of increasing violence on the domestic front and mounting international opposition, Smith finally granted token black representation in 1978, but it was a far cry from true participation. The move failed to satisfy the demands of black nationalists, who tended to become more radical as their aspirations for self-determination were continually rejected by the small white minority. Escalating tensions induced many white Rhodesian farmers to leave, while others clung to their political power and their estates. Fearing the growing Cuban and Soviet presence in the region, Great Britain and the United States launched another series of negotiations; these led to relatively free elections in the spring of 1979 and independence in 1980.

ZIMBABWE GAINS FULL INDEPENDENCE

The new nation, named Zimbabwe (for an ancient African culture in that area) and led by Robert Mugabe, moved to deal with the continuing problems of superpower involvement, political opponents, and internal development. Although the infant nation faced massive domestic problems involving economic development and political divisions, coupled with continued hostility from South Africa, Zimbabwe was initially relatively successful. Negotiations succeeded in preventing the worst excesses of total civil war, the parliamentary system remained intact, and the white minority continued to participate in the political system. Ian Smith even became a member of parliament. Unfortunately, protracted droughts in the late 1980s and early 1990s threatened to cripple Zimbabwe's economic progress and seemed likely to turn the formerly fertile southeastern part of the African continent into a vast dust bowl. Although Mugabe initially spoke in favor of democracy and openness, he responded to economic and political crises by becoming increasingly dictatorial and repressive.

Meanwhile, South Africa took the offensive in southwestern Africa. It denied independence to the projected new black state of Namibia and retained the area as a buffer against black African and Marxist governments to the north. In the sense of being a region of Africa ruled by an outside white government, Namibia was the last African colony. South Africa had held Namibia as a League of Nations mandate since 1919 and in spite of UN opposition annexed the territory in 1949. In retaliation, the United Nations censured South Africa for its racist policies. In 1966 the black independence South West Africa People's Organization (SWAPO) launched an armed struggle against South African domination. Although South Africa responded quickly with armed force, the struggle continued. As the Namibian forces escalated their attacks, the South African regime arrested and imprisoned SWAPO leaders, and by

UN INVOLVEMENT IN NAMIBIA

1972 armed confrontations were commonplace. The United Nations declared 1975 the deadline for South African withdrawal; however, the deadline came and went with no appreciable changes in South African policy.

At the same time, SWAPO continued its attacks. SWAPO had the public support of its African neighbors and the Communist bloc, but political divisions among various nationalist groups in Namibia also became apparent as the situation polarized leftist and more conservative forces. Finally, UN-backed negotiations led to the independence of Namibia in 1989. The first national elections resulted in a huge voter turnout and a resounding victory for SWAPO, but rival political forces, particularly those formerly supported by the United States and South Africa, launched armed attacks against the elected government.

Apartheid versus Equality in South Africa

Despite objections from around the world, successive Afrikaner leaders continued the segregation policies of apartheid. Black African nationalist leaders were imprisoned or forced underground or escaped into exile. After the African National Congress (ANC) was outlawed in 1960, the leaders, including Nelson Mandela and Oliver Tambo, reluctantly concluded that only the force of arms would end apartheid. Following the Rivonia Trials from 1963 to 1964, Mandela was sentenced to life imprisonment; Tambo escaped into exile. Many of the armed ANC members continued to operate from the frontline states of Zambia, Tanzania, and Angola. Sabotage bombings and attacks increased within South Africa, and in 1973 there were massive strikes.

VIOLENCE IN SOWETO

The most serious violence occurred in Soweto in 1976, when schoolchildren demonstrated against the use of Afrikaans as the major language of instruction. The students were also protesting the Bantu Education Act, which institutionalized inferior education programs for the majority black population. The violence soon spread from Soweto to the rest of the country and indicated that many black Africans had become radicalized. The South African government responded with a new series of repressive tactics, typified by the death of Steven Biko, a well-known student nationalist spokesperson. Biko died of brain injuries inflicted by police beatings in 1977.

INTERNATIONAL OPPOSITION TO APARTHEID

International organizations widely condemned South Africa for its racial policies, and in 1984 a major critic of apartheid, Bishop Desmond Tutu, was awarded the Nobel Prize for Peace. Both Tutu and the Reverend Allan Boesak called for economic boycotts of white businesses and divestment by Western interests as a means of undercutting the apartheid regime and forcing changes. While the boycott helped to call international attention to the situation, outsiders continued to purchase South African goods, to operate industries there, and to sell armaments to the regime.

The United Nations annually condemned the South African system of apartheid and its continued domination of Namibia. In addition, many church leaders, including the pope, and activist organizations around the world voiced their opposition to apartheid. In attempts to lessen its growing isolation in international forums, South Africa modified racial barriers to allow multiracial memberships on sports teams. By means of largely cosmetic changes, South Africans, who were keen sports enthusiasts, hoped to be readmitted to international competitions. Strict censorship regulations had prohibited

In Althone, South African police use rhinocerous-hide whips to beat antigovernment demonstrators in 1985.

many publications and mass media productions from depicting black Africans in roles of equality, but by the mid-1970s the government was pressured into allowing less restricted television broadcasts. Some job restrictions among the races and other racially based laws were modified, but the limitations on citizenship were augmented. (For comparison with the U.S. civil rights movement against segregation see Chapter 21.)

Although a new constitution implemented by Prime Minister P. W. Botha in 1984 permitted Asians and colored minorities technically to became junior partners in the political system, its main result was to reinforce the complete exclusion of the black majority. During the 1987 "White Only" elections, a political button stating "If voting could change the system, it would be illegal" encapsulated the problem. Black activists and sympathetic white citizens joined in large-scale demonstrations against apartheid, both in South Africa and in other nations, but the South African regime showed few signs of changing its racial policies and in 1986 adopted Emergency Powers to crush black opposition. It forced more and more black Africans into the Bantustans, renamed "homelands" to appease world opinion. Identity cards were gradually replaced with travel documents (passports). South Africa thereby became the first African nation with no black African citizens.

The black liberation movement was impeded by the poverty of its people and by the overwhelming military power of the government. Old ethnic divisions, which the white South African government continually sought to intensify, broke out increasingly in widespread violence as rival black African groups clashed with supporters of the ANC.

BLACK LIBERATION STRUGGLES

BIOGRAPHY

Life and Death under Apartheid

The last thing I ever dreamed of when I was daily battling for survival and for an identity other than that of inferiority and fourth-class citizen, which apartheid foisted on me, was that someday I would attend an American college, edit its newspaper, graduate with honors, practise journalism and write a book. How could I have dreamed of all this when I was born of illiterate parents who could not afford to pay my way through school, let alone pay the rent for our shack and put enough food on the table; when black people in Alexandra lived under constant police terror and the threat of deportation to impoverished tribal reserves; when at ten I contemplated suicide because I found the burden of living in a ghetto, poverty-stricken and without hope, too heavy to shoulder; when in 1976 I got deeply involved in the Soweto protests, in which hundreds of black students were killed by the police and thousands fled the country to escape imprisonment and torture? . . .

Much has been written and spoken about the politics of apartheid: the forced removals of black communities from their ancestral lands, the Influx Control and Pass laws that mandate where blacks can live, work, raise families, be buried; the migrant labour system that forces black men to live away from their families eleven months out of a year. . . .

When I was growing up in Alexandra it meant hate, bitterness, hunger, pain, terror, violence, fear, dashed hopes and dreams. Today it still means the same for millions of black children who are trapped in the ghettos of South Africa, in a lingering nightmare of a racial system. . . .

At thirteen I stumbled across tennis, a sport so "white" most blacks thought I was mad for thinking I could excel in it; others mistook me for an Uncle Tom. Through tennis I learned the important lesson that South Africa's 4.5 million whites are not all racists. As I grew older, and got to understand them more—their fears, longings, hopes, ignorance and mistaken beliefs, and they mine—this lesson became the conviction that whites are in some ways victims of apartheid, too, and that it is the system, not they, that has to be destroyed.*

. . .

In his moving autobiography Mark Mathabane describes growing up in Alexandra, a black ghetto outside Johannesburg, South Africa. Through intelligence, extraordinary hard work, love from his family, and some luck, Mathabane managed to secure an education and obtain a tennis scholarship to an American college. Mathabane now lives in the United States, where he frequently lectures on apartheid and the struggle against it. Mathabane's sister has also written about her life in South Africa under apartheid, with emphasis on the problems faced by women. See Miriam's Song, *by Miriam Mathabane as told to Mark Mathabane (New York: Simon & Schuster, 2000).*

*From Kaffir Boy: The True Story of a Black Youth's Coming of Age in Apartheid South Africa by Mark Mathabane, pp. ix–xi. Copyright © 1986 by New American Library, New York.

In particular, the ANC faced opposition from the Inkatha Freedom Party led by the "chief" of the KwaZulu, Gatsha Buthelezi, who had received support from the Afrikaner government. Mandela accused factions within the Afrikaner community and South African military of inspiring violence and financing opposition to the ANC. Although the movement had the sympathy of the rest of Africa, most African nations were too weak and poor to offer much direct assistance.

Hoping to avoid a bloody confrontation, President F. W. de Klerk further modified some apartheid regulations, released Mandela from prison in 1990, removed the ban on political groups, and opened negotiations with the ANC. Mandela and de Klerk struggled to find some acceptable compromise but were limited by political considerations. De Klerk was particularly vulnerable to opposition from segments of the Afrikaner population that rejected all changes to the apartheid system. Mandela, too, faced criticism from more radical elements within the ANC for negotiating directly with the white regime.

MANDELA AND DE KLERK NEGOTIATE

COMMON PROBLEMS FACING AFRICAN NATIONS

Several major problems confronted African nations after their independence. First, all African leaders had to deal with widespread poverty and often with starvation. Economic problems exacerbated preexisting religious, ethnic, and regional divisions that made it difficult and often impossible to forge national unity. As previously noted, the national boundaries drawn by European colonial powers frequently did not reflect the cultural, ethnic, or linguistic patterns of the peoples living within them. Consequently, newly independent African nations often had to deal with a multitude of different and sometimes hostile ethnic groups within one nation. Border disputes among neighboring nations also deflected energy and money away from internal development to armaments and the military. These problems, and the failures of the civilian governments to solve them, frequently led to open interference by the military. Togo experienced the first military coup d'état in independent black Africa in 1963. The leader of that coup, Lt. General Gnassingbe Eyadema, remained in power into the twenty-first century.

In the two decades after 1963 there were about 80 military coups in African nations. Thus, as in many other parts of the world, particularly in Latin America in earlier decades, military coups and countercoups became the rule rather than the exception. The preeminence of the military in government also meant that large portions of national revenues were expended on the military sector. Military leaders often lacked the expertise to formulate and implement much-needed development projects. This was particularly true in the agricultural sector, in which the overwhelming majority of Africans worked. Hence, the tasks of nation building and economic development often proved more difficult than the struggles for independence had been.

HIGH MILITARY EXPENDITURES

AGRICULTURE: CRISIS AND POTENTIAL

Africa has particular environmental problems. The highest rainfalls occur around the equator, but the majority of the continent is either semiarid or desert. Rains tend to be unpredictable and often fall in such torrents that soil erosion is a major problem.

REFUGEE PROBLEMS

The problem of droughts and the resultant famines was particularly acute along the Sahel, a hot, dry stretch of land running from Mauritania, south of the Sahara in the west, to Somalia in the east. From 1977 onward this region had one of the worst refugee problems in the world. Many people moved from their homes to escape the devastation caused by prolonged droughts (in some areas 90 percent of the livestock perished) and to avoid continuing regional conflicts.

By the late 1980s droughts had also created huge dust bowls in Botswana and southern Africa, areas that had previously been highly productive agricultural centers. In Chad, the Sudan, Ethiopia, and Mozambique (nations also plagued by civil war), over 600,000 persons died of starvation, and the lives of 19 million starving people were threatened throughout the Sahel and East Africa. An estimated 150 million others were rapidly running out of food.

Even with increased rains by the mid-1980s, famines continued because there was no seed to plant; massive numbers of people had left their traditional farm holdings, livestock had long since been killed or had died, and deforestation was widespread. Affluent nations were slow to recognize the problem, and relief agencies and the governments of the afflicted nations were sometimes inefficient in distributing food.

SUCCESSFUL DEVELOPMENT PROJECTS

On the positive side, individual projects, such as Burkina Faso's public health blitz that inoculated three-quarters of its children against measles, meningitis, and yellow fever and Ethiopia's well-digging project in Bale province, were remarkably successful. Other grassroots and self-help projects that required minimal outside money or support systems often worked out well.

Despite their plethora of troubles, many Africans saw promise of improvement. Several African nations attacked their agricultural problems by introducing agroforestry (tree farms), making more efficient use of animal and human resources, pursuing land reclamation through water harvesting in microbasins, and practicing water conservation. The best procedure for these projects appeared to be a combination of market and government projects, mainly for urban areas, and locally run projects in rural areas. In 1980 African nations elaborated such a program under the Lagos Plan of Action, but its implementation was impeded by political and military divisions. Only decades before, India had faced similar agricultural shortages, yet had become self-sufficient in food. There was a similar potential for Africa.

POPULATION GROWTH

In addition to these environmental issues, newly independent African nations faced a number of political, social, and economic troubles. One African child in every seven died before his or her fifth birthday. Many African nations remained desperately poor. For example, in 1991 the average life expectancy in Malawi was only 47 years and the per capita income was still less than $200 per year.

Uncertainty about children surviving, as well as religious and social traditions, made most parents want large families, thus contributing to the high population growth in many nations. As a consequence of these environmental conditions, many African nations were not able to increase agricultural output fast enough to keep pace with the growing population. During the 1980s food output in Africa as a whole actually declined. Ironically, advanced Western technological "solutions" such as gigantic dams often exacerbated the problems and contributed to increased soil depletion and declining production.

SUMMARY

North African nations were plagued by border disputes and internal problems of development. However, Libya, with vast petroleum revenues, launched massive and largely successful development projects. Algeria, which also had petroleum, devoted considerable resources to domestic development; but, with a much larger and generally young population to feed and provide services for, economic growth was not as rapid or extensive. By the 1970s and 1980s military dictators had become the rule in much of sub-Saharan Africa. Ghana and Nigeria were representative of nations that experienced a cycle of military coups and economic crises. Some military dictators, such as Idi Amin in Uganda, were particularly repressive and were eventually overthrown.

African nations, particularly in the Horn of Africa and the southern sector, had also experienced outside intervention from neighboring nations and the superpowers. In the process, a number of African nations became battlegrounds for cold war rivalries. In southern Africa levels of violence rose as the South African government clung to the apartheid system, which excluded the majority black population from all political activity and equal rights in the workplace. By the beginning of the 1990s political equality for all people, particularly the black majority in South Africa, had yet to be achieved; thus, the Horn of Africa and South Africa remained crisis points.

Mounting economic troubles also exacerbated religious, ethnic, and regional divisions that made it difficult and often impossible to forge national unity. Regional disputes also directed much-needed resources toward armed conflicts and away from economic development programs. There were some success stories in agriculture, but drought, underproduction, and famines continued to ravage much of Africa. In spite of these daunting problems, the vast natural resources, agricultural potential, and labor force in Africa made the continent important to the industrialized world and provided the potential for future improvements in the quality of life for all African peoples.

SUGGESTED SOURCES

Adjibolosoo, Senyo B.-S.K., and Benjamin Ofori-Amoah, eds. *Addressing Misconceptions about Africa's Development: Seeing beyond the Veil.* 1998. Provocative reassessments regarding economic systems in Africa.

Bayart, Jean-Francois. *The State of Africa: The Politics of the Belly.* 1992. An interdisciplinary analysis of contemporary society and politics in Africa.*

Fighting on Both Sides of the Law: Mandela and His Early Crusade. Films for the Humanities. A 51-minute video on the ANC and Mandela's political struggle against apartheid prior to his conviction and imprisonment for treason.

In Danku the Soup Is Sweeter. Filmakers Library. A 30-minute video that highlights successful women entrepreneurs in Ghana.

Last Year's Rain Fell on Monday. Filmakers Library. A visual overview in a 58-minute video of Namibia, one of the driest places on earth; it brings to the forefront the vital issue of water as a scarce resource.

Le Sueur, James. *The Decolonization Reader.* 2003. Useful chapters on cold war politics in North Africa, nationalist movements in West Africa and Kenya, and the crises in Zaire, as well as chapters on Asia.*

Meredith, Martin. *Our Votes, Our Guns: Robert Mugabe and the Tragedy of Zimbabwe.* 2003. Describes Mugabe's increasingly repressive regime.* See also *Dying to Be Free: Zimbabwe's Struggle for Change.* Films for the Humanities. A 51-minute video featuring firsthand footage of Zimbabwe's struggle for independence and Mugabe's policies.

Nzongola-Ntalaja, George. *The Congo from Leopold to Kabila: A People's History.* 2002. Incisive study of Congolese democratic movement and political oppression in colonial and post-colonial Congo.*

Zartman, I. William. *Ripe for Resolution: Conflict and Intervention in Africa.* 1989. A scholarly analysis of the key crises, with useful maps.*

WEB SOURCES

www.fordham.edu/halsall/africa/africasbook.html and

www.bbc.co.uk/worldservice/africa/features/storyofafrica/index.shtml. Two excellent sites, each offering numerous links to materials dealing with Africa.

www.fordham.edu/halsall/mod/modsbook53.html. Fordham site containing links to materials from Bishop Demond Tutu, Nelson Mandela, and other sources.

www-sul.stanford.edu/depts/ssrg/africa. A very useful Stanford University site providing links to individual African countries and topics, including history.

www2.etown.edu/vl/africa.html. This World Wide Web Virtual Library source for Africa provides numerous links.

www.columbia.edu/cu/lweb/indiv/africa/cuvl/cult.html. A Columbia University site with hundreds of links on the history and cultures of Africa.

---

*Paperback available.

⑥Gorbachev, Europe, and the End of the Cold War, 1985–1991

The years 1985–1991 brought profound changes to Europe and to the Soviet Union. By the end of 1991 the Soviet empire had collapsed: Communist governments had fallen in Eastern Europe, the U.S.S.R. itself had disintegrated, and Boris Yeltsin, the leader of Russia, the largest and most powerful republic in the U.S.S.R., was no longer a Communist. Nor was Europe any longer divided into western and eastern cold war blocs—even the term *Eastern Europe* seemed outdated. The Berlin Wall, which for three decades had symbolized this partition, had been smashed down and the Democratic and Federal republics (East and West Germany) reunited into a new Germany of about 78 million people. Although there were many complex reasons for this transformation, including the heroic efforts of dissidents, the chief catalyst was the activity of Soviet leader Mikhail Gorbachev.

In Western Europe there were other important developments—aside from changes (like arms reductions) motivated by Gorbachev's policies and communism's collapse. One was the growing tendency, following the example of Great Britain's Margaret Thatcher, to cut back on state subsidies and turn government holdings over to private interests. (After the collapse of communism in east-central Europe, where such holdings had long predominated, a larger-scale privatization began in that region.) There were also new steps taken to move toward a more unified European Community (EC).

GORBACHEV, REFORM, CRISES, AND THE END OF THE COLD WAR

After coming to power as general secretary of the Soviet Union's Communist Party in March 1985, Mikhail Gorbachev began a process of reforming the Communist system at home and modifying its dealings with foreign powers. Once begun, the reforms assumed a momentum of their own, sometimes exceeding Gorbachev's intentions. By Christmas Day 1991, the 15 republics of the Soviet Union had all declared their independence, and Gorbachev, without a nation to lead, resigned as president.

Domestic Reforms, 1985–1989

Soon after he came to power Gorbachev began pressing for a whole series of changes in Soviet society, despite the difficulties such changes might bring with them.

His domestic program was soon characterized by three words: *glasnost* (openness), *perestroika* (restructuring), and *demokratizatsiia* (democratization).

GLASNOST

Glasnost encompassed the ideas of more freedom of expression and less censorship and government secrecy. Writers became free to criticize without fearing punishment, and many dissidents were released from detention. Permission to emigrate and travel abroad increased significantly, and many Soviet intellectuals supported Gorbachev's policies. Films, plays, and books that had long been forbidden suddenly appeared, including Boris Pasternak's long-suppressed *Doctor Zhivago.* New historical interpretations, especially ones critical of the Stalin and Brezhnev eras, were published. According to the Soviet newspaper *Izvestia,* the old history books were full of "lies," and the government canceled all final history examinations for primary and secondary school students at the end of the 1987–1988 school year. The government tolerated some demonstrations and strikes, and Gorbachev initiated a more liberal attitude toward religious believers and broadened the legal rights of Soviet citizens. In December 1988 the government suspended the jamming of foreign radio broadcasts, including the Russian-language programs of U.S.-financed Radio Liberty.

PERESTROIKA

Perestroika, although a term eventually used to symbolize all of Gorbachev's reforms, originally referred primarily to economic restructuring, for economic improvement was Gorbachev's first priority and led to many of his other reforms, including those associated with *glasnost.* During the decade before 1985 the growth of the Soviet economy had slowed considerably compared to earlier periods. It grew at less than half the rate of the 1960s; some economic supporters of Gorbachev asserted that there had been no real growth in national income during the early 1980s. Moreover, the economy was plagued with various structural defects, poor worker productivity, and shortages of both housing and consumer goods.

One persistent problem that Gorbachev and his supporters faced was deficient agricultural production. Despite having more farmers than all of the industrialized West and Japan put together, the Soviet Union was forced year after year to spend precious hard currency to import Western grain. Not only did Soviet farmers produce much less than Western farmers—roughly one-seventh per capita—but as much as one-third of the vegetable crop spoiled each year before it could reach consumers.

High defense expenditures presented another major problem. Although roughly equivalent to that of the United States, Soviet military spending represented a much greater burden because the per capita GNP of the U.S.S.R. was less than half that of its superpower rival.

Another important factor stimulating change was the challenge of the information age. At a time when computers and telecommunications were becoming increasingly important in business and economic affairs, the Soviet Union was falling further behind the United States and many other nations in Europe and Asia. As late as 1988 personal computers in the Soviet Union numbered in the tens of thousands, while there were about 20 million in the United States. The director of Moscow's Institute for Space Research even admitted that to find adequate computers for his institute he had to buy U.S.-made ones on Moscow's black market.

Earlier Soviet leaders, especially Khrushchev, had experimented with piecemeal economic reforms, but Gorbachev and his backers realized that more radical measures

Under Gorbachev, joint ventures with foreign businesses increased, exemplified by Moscow's Pizza Hut getting ready to open in the summer of 1990.

were needed. In an effort to stem alcoholism and its retardant effects on worker productivity, he instituted a "vodka reform" that increased alcohol prices and made it more difficult to obtain. In 1986 and 1987 the government began permitting individuals and cooperatives to offer some lawful private alternatives to state enterprises, especially in the long-neglected area of services, such as restaurants and repairs. It also established joint ventures with foreign businesses that signed agreements to provide for a variety of enterprises, from fast foods to dental fillings and hotel construction. As of January 1988, state enterprises began switching to a system of self-financing.

Gorbachev's long-range economic plans called for reducing centralized control of the economy and allowing more local initiatives to factories, farms, and peasants, as well as limited private enterprise. Further, Gorbachev and his supporters wanted to increase both worker productivity and quality control and to restructure prices and salaries to more adequately reflect real market values. Finally, he increasingly called for *perestroika* to be applied to various other areas of Soviet life, such as the government, society, and culture.

Gorbachev's third watchword, *demokratizatsiia,* meant increased participation of Soviet citizens in the political process. In 1988 he brought forth a series of changes designed to reduce the role of the Communist Party in the everyday political and economic life of the nation. These changes mandated secret-ballot, multiple-candidate (although not multiparty) elections to Soviet bodies at all levels and limited the term of elected government officials to a maximum of 10 years in any position.

In the spring of 1989, after elections that were for the most part contested, a new Soviet congress of 2,250 deputies met in a spirited two-week televised session that presented to Soviet citizens the most open political debates they had witnessed in seven decades of Soviet rule. Before adjourning, the congress elected by secret ballot a new and more powerful 542-member Supreme Soviet, with Gorbachev as its president. Pronouncements and resolutions of this period made clear the interconnection of Gorbachev's three political watchwords. He believed that all three reforms, reinforcing each other, were necessary to revitalize the Soviet Union.

By 1989 it was clear that Gorbachev wished to create a far more humane system than any of his Soviet predecessors had done and one that was neither totalitarian nor terroristic. Yet up to this point he also showed no intention of working to achieve a Western-style multiparty government with a capitalist economy. He believed he could reform the Soviet system without destroying it.

Gorbachev's Three Crises, 1988–1991

Partly as a result of the persistence of long-standing Soviet problems—some of which Gorbachev's reforms were attempting to correct—and partly as a result of hopes, fears, and confusion sown by the reforms themselves, Gorbachev faced three crises by the early 1990s.

One was a federal or nationalities crisis that by the end of 1991 led to the dismantling of the Soviet Union. Soviet harmony among the more than 100 Soviet ethnic nationalities was always somewhat of a myth, but state repression had maintained order and kept the Russians, by far the single most populous nationality, dominant. As Communist controls eased under Gorbachev, old grievances against other ethnic groups and against the Russian-dominated Soviet state quickly resurfaced among the subordinated nationalities.

Conflict between Armenians and Azerbaijanis in the Caucasus Mountains occurred sporadically in 1988, leading to deaths, massive demonstrations, strikes, and the flight of about 180,000 people from their homes before a devastating earthquake hit the region and temporarily diverted attention from nationalistic rivalries.

In the three Soviet Baltic republics of Estonia, Latvia, and Lithuania, nationalism took another form. "Popular front" organizations, created in all three republics in 1988, increasingly pushed for more national autonomy. By 1991, influenced by the collapse of Soviet controls in east-central Europe (see below), all three Baltic republics were insisting on complete independence. In January 1991 Soviet army troops stormed a government press building in Vilnius, Lithuania, killing 13 civilians. Gorbachev claimed that he had not authorized the attack, but it occurred amid other signs that he was not willing to allow his reforms to develop to the point of permitting Baltic independence.

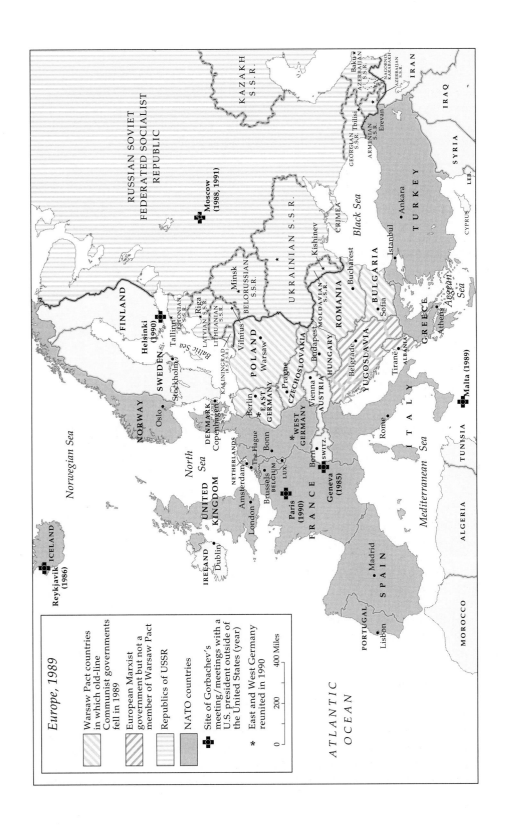

Europe, 1989

Warsaw Pact countries in which old-line Communist governments fell in 1989

European Marxist government but not a member of Warsaw Pact

Republics of USSR

NATO countries

Site of Gorbachev's meeting/meetings with a U.S. president outside of the United States (year)

* East and West Germany reunited in 1990

0   200   400 Miles

ATLANTIC OCEAN

ICELAND
Reykjavik (1986)

Norwegian Sea

IRELAND
Dublin

UNITED KINGDOM
London

North Sea

NETHERLANDS
Amsterdam
The Hague
BELGIUM
Brussels
LUX.

FRANCE
Paris (1990)

NORWAY
Oslo

DENMARK
Copenhagen

SWEDEN
Stockholm

FINLAND
Helsinki (1990)

Baltic Sea

ESTONIAN S.S.R.
Tallinn
LATVIAN S.S.R.
Riga
LITHUANIAN S.S.R.
Vilnius
KALININGRAD (R.S.F.S.R.)

BELORUSSIAN S.S.R.
Minsk

POLAND
Warsaw

EAST GERMANY
Berlin

WEST GERMANY
Bonn
Bern
SWITZ.
Geneva (1985)

CZECHOSLOVAKIA
Prague

AUSTRIA
Vienna

HUNGARY
Budapest

ITALY
Rome

SPAIN
Madrid

PORTUGAL
Lisbon

MOROCCO

ALGERIA

TUNISIA

Mediterranean Sea

Malta (1989)

RUSSIAN SOVIET FEDERATED SOCIALIST REPUBLIC

KAZAKH S.S.R.

Moscow (1988, 1991)

UKRAINIAN S.S.R.
Kishinev
MOLDAVIAN S.S.R.

CRIMEA

Black Sea

ROMANIA
Bucharest

BULGARIA
Sofia

YUGOSLAVIA
Belgrade

ALBANIA
Tiranë

GREECE
Athens

Aegean Sea

TURKEY
Ankara
Istanbul

GEORGIAN S.S.R.
Tbilisi
ARMENIAN S.S.R.
Erevan
AZERBAIJAN S.S.R.
Baku
NAGORNO-KARABAKH
AZERBAIJAN S.S.R.

IRAN

IRAQ

SYRIA

LEB.

CYPRUS

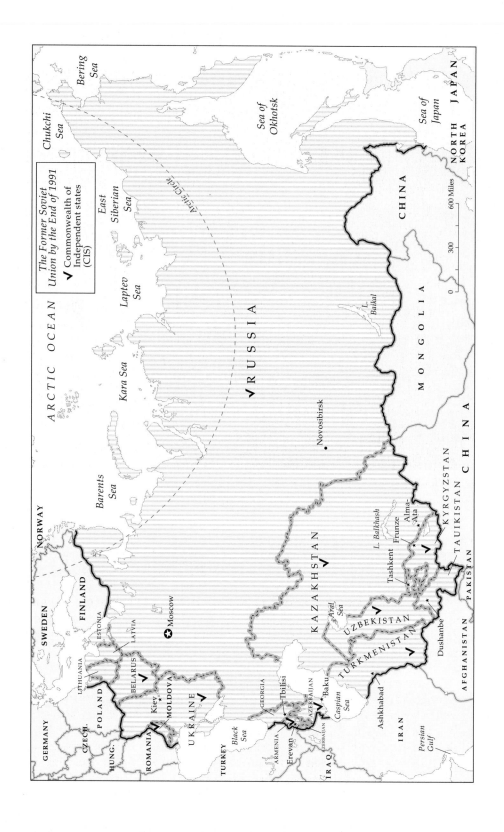

The Former Soviet
Union by the End of 1991

✔ Commonwealth of
Independent states
(CIS)

ARCTIC OCEAN

Chukchi
Sea

Bering
Sea

Barents
Sea

Kara Sea

Laptev
Sea

East
Siberian
Sea

Sea of
Okhotsk

Sea of
Japan

NORTH
KOREA

JAPAN

NORWAY

SWEDEN

FINLAND

ESTONIA

LATVIA

LITHUANIA

✔ Moscow

✔ RUSSIA

Novosibirsk

L. Baikal

CHINA

MONGOLIA

600 Miles

300

0

GERMANY

CZECH.

HUNG.

POLAND

BELARUS ✔

Kiev

MOLDOVA ★

UKRAINE ✔

ROMANIA

TURKEY

Black
Sea

GEORGIA

Tbilisi ★

ARMENIA.

Erevan ★

IRAQ

AZERBAIJAN ★ Baku

AZERBAIJAN

Caspian
Sea

KAZAKHSTAN ✔

Aral
Sea

UZBEKISTAN ✔

Tashkent

L. Balkhash

Frunze ★

Alma-
Ata

KYRGYZSTAN ✔

TAJIKISTAN

Dushanbe ★

TURKMENISTAN ✔

Ashkhabad ★

IRAN

Persian
Gulf

AFGHANISTAN

PAKISTAN

CHINA

Arctic Circle

500

Estonian demonstrators in Tallinn demanding independence, summer 1990.

Not only the Baltic republics but also the other republics declared their sovereignty, especially after the huge Russian Republic (RSFSR) declared its sovereignty from the federal government in June 1990. By early 1991 the federal crisis had become inextricably intertwined with the other two crises, the political and the economic.

From 1985 to early 1990 Gorbachev battled mainly against entrenched bureaucrats and conservative Communist Party personnel who feared his changes might threaten their many privileges and established routines. These individuals, many among the long-privileged elite, often stalled, delayed, and, at times, weakened reforms.

Yet by the end of the 1980s Gorbachev also faced criticism from those who thought that he was not enough of a reformer, that he was too timid. Although most deputies to the new Supreme Soviet that met in mid-1989 were opposed to sweeping reforms, a more liberal minority within the Soviet formed the Inter-Regional Group. For a while its chief spokesman was longtime dissident Andrei Sakharov, freed by Gorbachev from his Gorky exile in December 1986. But ill health led to his death at the end of 1989. Boris Yeltsin, who had served as head of the party in Moscow for two years until denounced by Gorbachev and replaced in late 1987, then emerged as the group's leading voice.

POLITICAL CRISIS

By the end of 1989 other voices were also speaking out for an acceleration of reform. Gorbachev's policies had made possible the emergence of tens of thousands of informal, voluntary groups. Some of them, like the popular fronts in the Baltic republics, were large and primarily political. They existed on every level from city to all-union. In the years 1987–1989 about 20 substantial independent political organizations composed of either Moscow or St. Petersburg residents sprang up, and many times that number appeared in other cities or on higher levels. Although not all of them pressed for faster reform, they represented a broadening of democracy.

In early February 1990, on the eve of an important meeting of the Communist Party's Central Committee, the voices of the people were heard in a massive prodemocracy demonstration in Moscow. The next day Gorbachev proposed to his fellow Communists that they agree to allow a multiparty system, and a few days later, following a bitter debate, they voted to accept his proposal.

Subsequent elections to local and republican parliaments further strengthened the hand of those desiring faster reforms, and in May 1990 Yeltsin was elected chairman of the Russian Republic's Supreme Soviet. He quickly became Gorbachev's first serious reformist competitor and continued to criticize him for being too timid in pushing reforms. The rivalry between the two men helped push Gorbachev temporarily toward the secret police and the military forces.

By early 1991 Yeltsin had become increasingly successful in portraying Gorbachev as someone more in tune with the old Communist authoritarian system than with the new, more democratic politics that by then had gone beyond Gorbachev's initial intentions. With Yeltsin and reformist mayors in cities such as Moscow and Leningrad frequently challenging Gorbachev's authority within the Russian Republic itself, people on the local Russian level were often confused about whose orders they should follow. Undoubtedly, one of the causes of the blossoming political crisis was the inexperience of the leaders in the give-and-take of a liberalized democratic process.

ECONOMIC CRISIS

Gorbachev's third crisis, the economic one, grew yearly more acute from 1988 to 1991. By the late 1980s declining world petroleum prices were already contributing to large budget deficits for the U.S.S.R., the world's largest petroleum producer. The wrenching difficulties of transforming the old command (planned) economy also brought to the fore new problems, as did the ethnic and political crises. To make matters worse, Gorbachev seemed to lack a clear vision of exactly what type of economy he wanted. If he had one, he certainly was not able to effectively explain it to Soviet citizens.

In any case, many of Gorbachev's economic "reforms" had produced more opposition than support. By late 1988, when he eased back on his unpopular antialcohol measures, there was increased grumbling about the high prices that some of the new cooperatives and private entrepreneurs were charging for other goods and services. Declining food supplies and consumer goods and increasing inflation and unemployment brought about further unpopular measures in early 1991: currency reform and price increases. Gorbachev's popularity fell to an all-time low.

Gorbachev's "New-Thinking" Foreign Policy and the End of the Cold War

While Gorbachev and other Soviet leaders used the term *perestroika* to symbolize his domestic reforms, they often chose the phrase "new thinking" to characterize his foreign policy. It was indeed new in many ways. Soviet détente policies of the 1970s had aimed at decreasing superpower tensions but without abandoning "ideological struggle." Gorbachev was also now willing to jettison such struggle. While there were numerous reasons for this change in policy, Soviet economic difficulties were perhaps the greatest factor. The cold war and the arms race were just too expensive for the stagnant Soviet economy to continue. Gorbachev admitted that the Soviet Union bore some responsibility for the past arms race, and a 1988 party conference declared that "foreign policy activity should contribute ever more to releasing the nation's resources for peaceful construction, for *perestroika*." At about the same time, the Soviet government admitted it had been wrong not to give its full support to the United Nations because the world needed a stable structure for international affairs. In the sphere of regional conflicts, it renounced exporting revolution or counterrevolution and expressed its desire to help find solutions to conflicts in such places as Angola, Cambodia, and the Middle East.

GORBACHEV'S SUMMIT MEETINGS WITH REAGAN AND BUSH

Soviet foreign policy demonstrated its new orientation in deeds as well as in words. By the end of 1988 Gorbachev had met with U.S. President Reagan on five occasions in three years, producing agreements that reversed the deteriorating relations of the early 1980s. The most important was the Intermediate Nuclear Forces (INF) Treaty, ratified in 1988, which mandated the destruction of all (about 2,800) Soviet and U.S. land-based nuclear missiles in the 300- to 3,400-mile range. Other agreements provided for increased exchanges of students, cultural programs, scientific research, and nuclear testing information. Despite Gorbachev's strong objections to President Reagan's SDI— "What we need is Star Peace and not Star Wars," he quipped on one occasion—Soviet negotiators continued strategic arms reduction talks (START) with U.S. representatives in order to cut the number of long-range nuclear weapons on each side.

After the election of George Bush, Gorbachev continued his summit diplomacy and disarmament talks. In November 1990 Gorbachev, Bush, and 20 other NATO and Warsaw Pact leaders met in Paris to sign the most sweeping arms control treaty in history. It committed the signatories to destroy tens of thousands of howitzers, tanks, and other conventional weapons. In July 1991 the two leaders signed the START Treaty, which promised approximately a 30 percent cut in long-range nuclear weapons over the next seven years. In late September Bush announced several additional unilateral disarmament steps, and a week later Gorbachev went even further, promising among other steps to observe a one-year moratorium on nuclear testing. By the end of 1991 it almost appeared as if the two leaders were involved in a "disarmament race." Only fears about who would become responsible for the 27,000 Soviet nuclear warheads in the disintegrating Soviet Union restrained the euphoric feeling that the arms race between the two former cold war rivals was over.

Gorbachev and Reagan at their first summit (Geneva, November 1985).

SOVIET RELATIONS WITH EUROPE

An equally significant Soviet foreign policy turnaround came in 1989 and 1990 when one Communist government after another was toppled in Eastern Europe—and the Soviet Union did not intervene. As will be revealed shortly, Gorbachev had much to do with the collapse of these governments and did not intervene for many reasons, including the devastating impact such intervention would have had on both reforms at home and relations abroad, especially with the West.

Gorbachev stressed Soviet links with Western Europe, advocating "the end of the schism of Europe" and referring to it as our "common home." In the fall of 1988 he met with the heads of the governments of Italy, West Germany, and France and had numerous subsequent meetings with European leaders. Both the Western European nations and the United States granted some economic assistance to the disintegrating U.S.S.R. or directly to the increasingly independent republics.

SOVIET TROOPS WITHDRAW FROM AFGHANISTAN

Improving U.S.-Soviet relations also helped solve regional conflicts such as the one in Afghanistan. Already in 1985, Gorbachev had told other Soviet leaders that Soviet troops should leave that neighboring country. The occupation was a drain on the Soviet economy, a "bleeding wound" in Gorbachev's words, and by 1989 resulted in the deaths of more than 14,000 Soviet troops. In addition, more than 50,000 were wounded, and even more contracted infectious diseases. He wished, however, to trade a pullout for a U.S. pledge of mutual noninterference in Afghanistan (the United States was aiding the Muslim rebels). In 1988 a UN-sponsored accord was reached, and in early 1989 the U.S.S.R. withdrew its final troops from Afghanistan.

The Soviet invasion of Afghanistan in 1979 had been a major source of Sino-Soviet friction, and by withdrawing the Soviet Union improved its relations with China. The Soviet government also eased tensions with China by reducing Soviet forces stationed along the Chinese border and encouraging Vietnam to withdraw its troops from Cambodia. In May 1989 Gorbachev visited China, and relations between the two Communist giants were normalized after almost 30 years of strain.

SOVIET-CHINESE RELATIONS

Gorbachev's efforts to improve Soviet-Chinese relations were symptomatic of his efforts to better Soviet relations in Asia as well as in Europe. He sought increased trade on both continents and help from Asian capitalist nations for Siberian development. Despite Japan's unhappiness over Soviet unwillingness to return the Kurile Islands taken after World War II, Japan did become a major source of loans.

COMMUNISM IN EASTERN EUROPE, 1985–1988: ECONOMIC AND POLITICAL CHALLENGES

By early 1985 Eastern Europe, like the Soviet Union, faced growing economic and political difficulties. Although living standards varied considerably from East Germany to Romania, Eastern European consumers were noticeably worse off than Western Europeans in regard to the availability of both goods and services. The economic growth rate from 1980 to 1984 was approximately one-fourth that of the early 1970s. There was a growing technological gap between the two parts of Europe, especially in regard to computers and telecommunications. This gap was broadened in the late 1970s and early 1980s as Western Europe invested much more heavily in a whole range of modernized and energy-efficient machinery. Foreign debt also promised continuing hardships, as in another way did Eastern Europe's severe industrial pollution.

ECONOMIC PROBLEMS

The governments of Eastern Europe found their economic problems compounded by lack of popular support. This difficulty was seen most clearly in Poland, where the Communist government seemed unable to reverse a significant decline in the standard of living compared to the 1970s. The government refused to deal with the outlawed Solidarity union, and most Polish workers refused to cooperate with a government in which they had little faith. Similar conditions of popular unrest made many of the other governments of Eastern Europe reluctant to risk introducing measures of economic austerity, even though some of the funds subsidizing living standards were badly needed to pay off debts and to invest in industrial research and modernization.

The Soviets' insistence that they would not allow change in Communist Eastern Europe to undermine Soviet security had always been a major limitation on political and economic reform movements, as Hungary, Czechoslovakia, and Poland had learned. The appearance of Gorbachev on the Soviet scene opened up a whole new range of possibilities, however, because he actively encouraged reform. His thinking appeared to be more akin to Alexander Dubček's than to that of Brezhnev, who had intervened to overturn the Czechoslovakian leader in 1968.

GORBACHEV'S NEW
APPROACH TO
EASTERN EUROPE

Gorbachev did not ignore Soviet security interests, but he defined them differently than his predecessors had. Economic stagnation in the Soviet bloc and a costly arms race appeared to him more threatening to Soviet security than Eastern European political reforms. He encouraged economic restructuring throughout the bloc and signed the INF agreement, which removed a whole class of Soviet missiles from Europe. He promised unilateral reductions of Soviet European forces and pushed for more European cooperative efforts and reductions in both nuclear and conventional forces throughout Europe. The new Soviet foreign policy was popular with most Eastern European political leaders, who for various reasons desired better relations, especially increased trade, with the West.

The attitude of political leaders toward Soviet economic reforms, however, was more varied. Polish and Hungarian leaders were generally supportive. The East German leader Erich Honecker was reluctant to move in the direction Gorbachev advocated for the Soviet Union. In Romania the independent-minded party chief Nicolae Ceausescu was more concerned with personal power and with reducing his foreign debt than with restructuring Romania's economy, the most miserable in the Soviet bloc. For his part, despite his enthusiasm for economic *perestroika,* Gorbachev displayed a willingness to tolerate different economic approaches among the nations of Eastern Europe.

The Communist parties of Eastern Europe also reacted in varying ways to Gorbachev's political reforms. Again, there was less enthusiasm among East German and Romanian leaders and more support among Poland's and Hungary's party bosses, who had already allowed more freedom in their nations than had existed in the U.S.S.R. In Poland General Jaruzelski praised Gorbachev's policies and declared that the Soviet Union and Poland were now moving in the same direction: "Poland has not experienced such a happy convergence for the whole of the past millennium."

THE COLLAPSE OF COMMUNISM IN EASTERN EUROPE AND THE REUNIFICATION OF GERMANY, 1988–1991

THE FALL OF
COMMUNIST
GOVERNMENTS IN
EASTERN EUROPE

Between 1988 and 1991 two momentous developments—the virtually bloodless collapse of the Communist governments in Eastern Europe and the swift reunification of Germany—brought an end to an era that had dominated eastern and central Europe for over 40 years. There were primarily two reasons that these events occurred when they did: (1) the people of Eastern Europe strongly demonstrated their displeasure with their Communist governments and (2) unlike the situtations in Hungary in 1956 and Czechoslovakia in 1968, it became increasingly clear that Soviet troops would not be used to prop up Communist governments, a realization that in turn encouraged and fueled popular dissatisfaction. If Gorbachev had not taken the stance he had, it is unlikely that Eastern European citizens would have demonstrated their displeasure so forcefully and that governments would have collapsed and Germany been reunified so soon.

The immediate events leading to the collapse began in Poland in the spring and summer of 1988, when a number of strikes and continuing economic misery (e.g., high inflation that reduced real wages by about 20 percent compared to 1980) nudged

---

B I O G R A P H Y

A Czech Student in the Velvet Revolution

Jana Markvartova is the daughter of a doctor and a lawyer, a privileged child of Czechoslovakia's elite. Before this week, she had never really talked to any of the hundreds of thousands of people who are this country's manual laborers.

Today, Miss Markvartova stood before nearly 200 workers at the Domaci Potreby household appliance factory in the polluted industrial outskirts of the city and told them how the police here had violently broken up a peaceful demonstration by students last Friday night. Then tearfully, she asked the workers to support a two-hour general strike that the students have called for Monday to demand wholesale changes in the country's leadership.

"We need your help," Miss Markvartova told the workers. "It is your work that allows us to study and to develop our minds and our ideas. But alone our ideas are nothing. We need you. We need you to join our strike."

Her efforts paid off. The workers voted overwhelmingly to support the strike.

In the last week, Miss Markvartova and students like her at Prague's universities have realized that they must reach out to workers at factories, farms and industries if their demonstrations and strikes are to succeed in forcing change on their resistant Communist government.*

. . .

Although Gorbachev played the chief individual role in the changes that swept Eastern Europe and the Soviet Union from 1989 to 1991, countless other individuals including the 21-year-old philosophy student described here helped bring about the collapse of Communist governments.

*From "Students Ask Workers' Aid in Czech Rally" by Esther B. Fein in the *New York Times*, November 24, 1989.

Polish leaders further along the road to reform. The government opened roundtable talks with Solidarity leader Lech Walesa and other supporters of change in Poland. In early 1989 it agreed to once again legalize Solidarity, to revamp Poland's parliament, and to allow Solidarity to run candidates for all 100 seats of a new upper house and for 35 percent of those of the lower house.

In elections in June 1989, Solidarity candidates won over 99 percent of the seats they were allowed to contest. A few months later, for the first time in a Soviet bloc nation, a coalition government was formed with a non-Communist head—Prime Minister Tadeusz Mazowiecki. After it became clear that the Soviet Union had no intention of intervening to maintain Communist dominance, other Communist governments, lacking popular support, began collapsing like dominoes in Eastern Europe.

By the end of 1989 old-line Communist leaders had been replaced throughout the former Eastern European bloc nations. In some countries reformist Communists or coalition governments took over, as in Romania and Bulgaria, but in others, such as Czechoslovakia, power fell to people the Communists had once persecuted. When Vaclav Havel, a playwright and often-imprisoned human rights advocate, became president of Czechoslovakia in December 1989, it became clear that the voice of the

As East German border guards look on, a man pounds away at the Berlin Wall, November 1989.

people in Eastern Europe could no longer be stifled. As was generally the case in the region, the changeover in Czechoslovakia (the "Velvet Revolution") was surprisingly bloodless.

In 1990 and 1991 democratic forces continued to develop in the region. In December 1990 Lech Walesa was elected Poland's president, and in the October 1991 elections the Bulgarian Socialist Party (the former Communist Party) was narrowly defeated and ousted from political dominance.

The internal political changes sweeping Eastern Europe affected foreign policy developments. The region's nations improved Western ties, and in 1991 the Warsaw Pact military alliance came to an end and Soviet troops began leaving Eastern European nations.

Although Albania and Yugoslavia were not part of the Soviet bloc, they were Eastern European Communist nations that experienced some of the same problems and challenges faced by bloc nations. Albania, the poorest nation in Europe, was slow to change but by the end of 1991 had a coalition government with a reforming former head of the Communist Party as its president. By late 1989 Yugoslavia's foreign debt, inflation, and unemployment combined to make it one of the most economically troubled nations of Europe. But as in the Soviet Union, its economic problems were intertwined with federal-ethnic and political problems that soon reached crisis proportions. As central Communist control weakened, this state of Serbs, Croats, Bosnian Muslims, Slovenes, Macedonians, Albanians, and other ethnic groups began to disintegrate. Besides ethnic rivalries, often sharpened by past grievances, differing levels of economic well-being and clashing attitudes toward political and economic reforms also contributed to divisiveness. Another factor sowing discord was the aggressive Serbian nationalism of Serb Republic President Slobodan Milošević who took various actions to ensure Serbian dominance in Yugoslav territories. (See Chapter 3 for information on this region in the 1990s.)

One result of the collapsing communism in Eastern Europe was the reunification of Germany. For almost three decades the Berlin Wall had stood as a symbol of the cold war. But in early November 1989 it was opened by a reformist East German Communist government that, because of demonstrations, had recently replaced the hard-line government of Erich Honecker. Over a million East Germans visited West Berlin and West Germany in the first few days after the opening of the wall. After elections in March 1990 brought a non-Communist coalition to power in East Germany, it agreed to reunification with West Germany, whose chancellor, Helmut Kohl, became head of a reunified Germany in October 1990.

THE REUNIFICATION OF GERMANY

THE COLLAPSE OF THE SOVIET UNION IN 1991: HOW AND WHY

By 1991 Gorbachev was admired far more abroad than at home. His role in ending the cold war and Soviet control over east-central Europe earned him the gratitude of people in numerous countries. In the Western democracies he was perceived as a Westernizer, attempting to make the U.S.S.R. more like the West. While many Soviet citizens also appreciated these accomplishments and efforts, others were embittered by the collapse of the Soviet empire and too much Westernization. While Soviet society generally welcomed Gorbachev's policies of *glasnost* and democratization, it was less enthusiastic about government economic policies, which only worsened conditions. Finally, Gorbachev's retreat to a temporary alliance with more reactionary forces in late 1990 alienated many of the democratic elements he had earlier encouraged.

After months of political retreat, Gorbachev moved back toward the reformers in the spring of 1991. In doing so, he was partly motivated by huge reform demonstrations and strikes, especially a widespread miners' strike in March. In late July, he spoke on behalf of a free market economy and called for the Communist Party to abandon many of its Marxist-Leninist ideas.

Meanwhile, however, his powers were declining as each of his three intertwined crises (federal/nationalities, political, and economic) continued to worsen. In June, his chief political opponent, Boris Yeltsin, further strengthened his position by trouncing his rivals in a popular election for the office of president of the Russian Republic; Gorbachev, in contrast, had never participated in a direct democratic election. Yeltsin now became even more insistent on diverting powers from the federal government to the national republics, a process already proceeding at breakneck speed.

With his powers diminishing, Gorbachev gave ground and agreed to a new compromise union treaty, officially transferring many powers to the republics. It was to be signed on August 20 with Yeltsin and four of the five Central Asian leaders. By then, Gorbachev was willing to concede that the three Baltic and three Caucasian republics would not sign the treaty but would follow their own independent paths, but he hoped that Ukraine and the remaining republics would sign later in the year.

A FAILED COUP, AUGUST 1991

Two days before the August 20 signing could occur, however, conservative leaders, including the head of the KGB and the defense minister, attempted a coup. Fearing loss of their powers and the disintegration of the Soviet Union, they put Gorbachev under house arrest while he was vacationing in the Crimea. The next morning the plotters announced that Gorbachev was sick and that an eight-member Emergency Committee had assumed power. However, neither it nor the tanks and troops it mobilized were resolute enough to fire on resisters led by Boris Yeltsin in Moscow. By August 22, the coup had failed, and Gorbachev returned to Moscow that same morning. Coup leaders were arrested, and Yeltsin became the hero of the day.

The events that followed the failed coup were almost as dramatic as the coup itself. It created an immediate backlash against the Communist Party. After first defending his party, Gorbachev backtracked. A few days after his return, he resigned as its general secretary. He also followed Yeltsin's example as president of the Russian Republic and suspended the party's political activities throughout the Soviet Union.

THE COLLAPSE OF THE U.S.S.R.

While the Communist or Soviet aspect of the Soviet Union was rapidly disintegrating, so, too, was the union aspect. Within a few weeks the Soviet government officially recognized the independence of the three Baltic republics. Other republics also rushed to declare their independence. On December 8 the presidents of the three founding members of the U.S.S.R. in 1922—Russia, Ukraine, and Belorussia (now Belarus)—agreed to disband the union and instead to form the Commonwealth of Independent States (CIS). On December 21 eight other former Soviet republics joined them in the CIS. Besides the three Baltic republics, Georgia also remained outside the new commonwealth. Even within the CIS, however, its members soon made it clear that they valued their independence more than any commonwealth ties. Now a president without a country, Gorbachev resigned his office on December 25, 1991.

REASONS FOR THE COLLAPSE

Although Gorbachev's three crises and his own failures helped lead to the fall of the Soviet Union, other causes also contributed to this twofold collapse of more than seven decades of Communist power and of a union of nationalities, most of which had been unified for a much longer period. Like tensions between Soviet nationalities, many of these causes had been developing before Gorbachev came to power, slowly eroding the foundations of the U.S.S.R. and Communist power. Among the most important were the following (in no particular order of importance): (1) economic and social decline, including rising alcoholism, death rates, and corruption; (2) growing disillusionment and anger with the Soviet system and its privileged elite; (3) the ideological erosion of Marxism-Leninism-Stalinism; (4) the gradual weakening in the post-Stalin decades of party controls over Soviet citizens; (5) social developments, such as the growth of a more urbanized and better-educated population; and (6) foreign influences, including developments in other Communist-governed countries and the policies of Western nations.

Even before Gorbachev came to power, the better-educated Soviet population of the 1970s and early 1980s traveled abroad more, even if only to other Communist countries. They came into contact more with foreigners and foreign ways and ideas. Through such channels as tourists, movies, and music, they became more familiar with the popular culture and consumerism of Western countries such as the United States. Inevitably, comparisons with countries better able to provide for their people increased discontent with the Soviet government and system. After Gorbachev came to power, the collapse of Communist regimes in Eastern Europe contributed in several ways to the Soviet Union's twofold disintegration.

Yet in the final analysis, the main reason that the breakups of both the Soviet bloc and the U.S.S.R. itself occurred when and how they did was Gorbachev and his policies, although Boris Yeltsin was also an important catalyst for the collapse of the U.S.S.R. In contrast to Khrushchev or Brezhnev, Gorbachev was unwilling to hold the Soviet empire together by force, and within the U.S.S.R. he presided over a transformation that by 1991 had eliminated many characteristics of the earlier Soviet system.

By means of his *perestroika* policies, assisted by *glasnost* and democratization, Gorbachev attempted to transform the U.S.S.R. into an efficient and humane socialist society. But despite his intelligence and many political talents, he was unable to hold his country together—partly because of his own failings. After a year or two in power, he became increasingly impatient to institute changes in both domestic and foreign policy, and he sometimes failed to think through the consequences of policies before he enacted them. His organizational skills also left something to be desired.

Compared to someone like Yeltsin, Gorbachev was never as comfortable among the common people, and he failed to realize how deeply feelings such as nationalism and resentment toward Communist privileges ran among Soviet citizens. Despite "Gorbimania" and his charismatic appeal in the West, he increasingly was unable to inspire the Soviet peoples with his vision of the future, partly because it was somewhat murky, always changing and evolving. Although by 1991 Gorbachev's own political values had evolved far from Leninism, Gorbachev remained reluctant to renounce Lenin and communism openly, and he did not resign as Communist Party head until August 24, 1991. This reluctance helped Yeltsin and others to depict Gorbachev as someone not sufficiently converted to new democratic principles.

Yet, given the difficulties he faced (including reactionary resistance and ambitious politicians such as Yeltsin, decades of Communist rule and misrule, and the natural aspirations of many non-Russians for national independence), it is hardly surprising that he failed to hold the Soviet Union together. In many other ways, however, he did not fail. In addition to being mainly responsible for ending the cold war, he set in motion changes that helped bring much greater freedom to many peoples in the world, peoples in east-central Europe as well as in most of the former U.S.S.R.

WESTERN EUROPE, 1985–1991: ECONOMICS, POLITICS, AND THE COMMON MARKET

The general prosperity that characterized Europe before 1985 continued after that date, especially in Germany, Scandinavia, and Switzerland. Economic growth increased from 1984 through 1988, with 1988 registering the most growth in over a decade. Unemployment remained high, however, hovering around 11 percent in the Common Market nations during the same five-year period. From 1989 to 1991 economic growth slowed, with Great Britain's economy actually in recession in 1990 and 1991.

Many Western European nations faced economic problems similar to those in the United States. One concern was how to maintain high wages and extensive social services while remaining globally competitive and not increasing taxes. Throughout the postwar era, the trend was for governments to grow and to provide more and more services. By the late 1980s about one out of every five Western European workers was a government employee. Big government was especially the trend in the Scandinavian nations, where the welfare state was the most developed. As Western European populations aged and birthrates declined, however, the proportion of the population working, and thus taxable, diminished. Many governments found it increasingly difficult to raise sufficient revenues to fund services without raising taxes, and this in turn led to voter discontent.

THATCHER'S CONSERVATIVE POLICIES IN GREAT BRITAIN

Faced with increased public hostility, Western European governments, like the United States in the 1980s, began to reverse, or at least to slow down, the growth of the welfare state. This approach was most strongly pursued by Great Britain's prime minister Margaret Thatcher, who in the early 1980s had said that what irritated her most about politics in the postwar era was its drift toward collectivism. In the years 1985 to 1990, this daughter of a prosperous grocer continued her privatization policies, selling government-owned enterprises such as utilities to private stockholders and deregulating areas such as private housing. She weakened Great Britain's once powerful unions and tightened controls over health services, unemployment, and welfare benefits. And she made many enemies in Great Britain's universities by refusing to allocate more funding and by enacting legislation restricting faculty tenure. But economic growth and relatively low inflation and unemployment helped keep the "iron lady," as she was called, in power.

During 1989, however, inflation and the government's budget deficit rose, as did the perception that the prime minister was too arrogant, inflexible, and out of touch with the common people. In 1990 her government replaced local property taxes with an extremely unpopular poll (head) tax, in which each individual paid the same amount regardless of income. As one objector put it, "A millionaire will pay half as much as a pensioner couple." Thatcher's resistance to faster European Common Market integration also weakened her. In November 1990, after being in office longer than any other twentieth-century British prime minister, she resigned under pressure. She was replaced as Conservative Party leader and prime minister by John Major, former chancellor of the exchequer. At age 47, this son of a circus performer was just the sort of self-made man that Thatcher liked to champion. After dropping out of school at 16, he made his way in the world of banking and politics.

If Thatcher represented the most noted case of chipping away at big government, she was not alone. In the late 1980s, Spain, Portugal, and France, despite having socialist heads of state, also sold some public enterprises to private owners. Prime Minister Felipe Gonzalez of Spain was accused by many of his former political allies of betraying the poor in his quest to stimulate economic growth. Presidents Mário Soares in Portugal and François Mitterrand in France were forced by political necessity to cooperate with prime ministers from other political parties who strongly pushed privatization. Even Sweden signaled its readiness to cut back on big government. In late 1991 it rejected the Social Democratic Party that had governed for 53 of the previous 59 years and had championed the welfare state. Sweden's new conservative government promised to privatize much state-owned industry and reduce Swedes' tax burdens, which in the 1980s had been the highest in Western Europe.

CHIPPING AWAY AT "BIG GOVERNMENT"

Despite this movement to slow and even reverse the growth of some aspects of government, a broad consensus continued to exist in Western Europe that prevented any wholesale dismantling of the welfare state. Most European governments continued to provide more cradle-to-grave services than did the U.S. government.

Even before the collapse of communism in Eastern Europe, Western European Communist political parties were on the decline. Some Europeans thought communism less relevant in a Europe of high technology, consumerism, and a smaller percentage of blue-collar workers. After the fall of Eastern European communism, the Italian Communist Party, Western Europe's strongest, tried harder than ever to distance itself from the failed communism of Eastern Europe and changed its name to the Democratic Party of the Left.

While moderate socialist and conservative parties dominated Western European politics, there were some notable groups on the edges. Two issues especially seemed to mobilize votes for fringe parties—the environment and foreign workers and immigrants.

Environmental concerns attracted voters to Green parties. In 1987–1988 the Greens won 42 seats in the 520-member West German Federal Assembly (Bundestag) and 20 in the 349-member Swedish Parliament. Smaller Green parties also existed in many other Western European nations. Although environmental concerns were most prominent, Green parties also spoke out on other topics, such as women's rights and fairer treatment for foreign workers.

GREEN PARTIES

At the same time, right-wing nationalist parties in West Germany, France, and other nations played on increasing hostility toward foreign workers and immigrants. Low population growth, expanding economies, and a willingness to turn undesirable jobs over to foreign workers had all brought many such laborers to Western Europe. Nations had also allowed other types of immigration. Although the presence of many "illegals" made it difficult to guess how many foreign workers lived in Western Europe,

FOREIGN WORKERS AND IMMIGRANTS

there were probably over 15 million in the 1980s. By 1988 almost a million blacks and Asians lived in London, and incidents of racial conflict became more common. In German cities there were many Turkish and other foreign workers. In Frankfurt, Munich, and Stuttgart combined, about one in five residents was foreign. In France there were many Africans and Asians. By the end of 1991 over 10 percent of the population had been born outside France. All these immigrants put additional pressure on government social services and the taxes that paid for them.

In the 1988 presidential contest in France, right-wing candidate Jean-Marie Le Pen blamed many of his nation's problems, such as crime and unemployment, on foreign-born minorities. In West Germany the Republican Party, a new right-wing organization, played a similar tune and in local elections sometimes did better than the Greens.

THE EUROPEAN COMMUNITY

Concerns about immigrants were heightened from 1989 to 1991 by two pressing fears. The first was that Eastern European governments would ease restrictions on emigration, unleashing a new wave of immigrants into Western Europe. The second was that the end of frontier barriers among the nations of the European Community (EC), anticipated to take place by the beginning of 1993, would also make it easier for non-EC citizens to move about, legally or illegally, within the 12-nation community. (Portugal and Spain joined the previous 10 members in 1986.)

The breakdown of frontier barriers was just one of the plans and actions that EC members had made by 1991 to bring about the integration of Europe. In 1987 member nations ratified a treaty, the Single European Act, pledging to go beyond eliminating tariffs between them and to try by 1992 to remove a variety of other financial, commercial, and customs barriers that hampered the free flow of goods within the EC. The act also pointed to highly integrative goals such as a common currency and more unified social, foreign, and defense policies. In December 1991, at Maastricht in the Netherlands, EC nations reiterated these commitments and agreed on new specifics, including a timetable for monetary union—not later than 1999, although some community nations might not immediately join. German chancellor Helmut Kohl stated, "Maastricht stands as a decisive breakthrough for Europe." Mitterrand of France declared, "We have created a European union."

Before leaving office in late 1990, Britain's Thatcher had been the main roadblock to further unity. In 1988 she warned of efforts to "suppress nationhood and consolidate power at the center of a European conglomerate." She spoke out against a common currency and expressed fears that EC economic and social policies would once again encourage the type of governmental paternalism that her anti–welfare state policies had aimed at curbing. Although a less vocal critic of the EC, John Major obtained an agreement at Maastricht that Great Britain could decide later if it wished to adopt a common EC currency and would be exempted from the agreement signed by the other 11 nations to expand EC authority over economic and social issues such as minimum wages.

Although the Maastricht meeting occurred after communism's collapse in east-central Europe, the question of EC policy toward newly non-Communist European nations received little attention at the meeting. After the fall of communism several nations in eastern Europe expressed an interest in joining the organization. Broadening European unity by opening up the EC to former Communist countries—which were "alarmingly dilapidated" in Mitterrand's words—promised to be much more difficult than embracing more prosperous nations such as Austria and Sweden, which also wanted to join. EC nations disagreed on how strongly to encourage eastern European aspirations.

SUMMARY

From 1985 until the end of 1991, Europe changed in a way that few would have dared to believe possible in the mid-1980s. When Mikhail Gorbachev came to power as the Soviet leader in 1985, the Soviet economy was stagnating and pressures for reform were building. Gorbachev recognized the need for reforms and began pushing a whole series of domestic and foreign policies that soon gathered a momentum of their own. In less than seven years these policies and numerous other forces, especially popular political movements, led to the collapse of Communist governments in Soviet bloc states in Eastern Europe, the end of the cold war, the reunification of Germany, and the collapse of the Soviet Union itself. Along the way, the Soviet Union signed numerous important arms control treaties with Western powers.

While the collapse of the forced unity of the Soviet empire was widely hailed by proponents of democracy, a difficult transition, often complicated by strong ethnic rivalries and by occasionally armed conflict, was still under way by the end of 1991. Although not a part of the former Soviet bloc, Yugoslavia, split by civil war in late 1991, was an extreme example of where such rivalries could lead.

Although much more prosperous and stable than their fellow Europeans to the east, Western Europeans grappled with their own problems. Following the example of Britain's Margaret Thatcher, many of their government leaders attempted to curtail the growth of big government. Leaders also sought methods to deal with rising hostility toward foreign workers and immigrants, and most Western European heads of state, especially within the 12-member European Community, worked toward creating greater European economic and political unity.

By the end of 1991, the very terms *Western Europe* and *Eastern Europe* were losing their validity. A new, less divided, Europe had come into existence, and a major task for the remainder of the century would be dealing with the legacy of the transforming events of 1985–1991.

SUGGESTED SOURCES

Ardagh, John. *Germany and the Germans: The United Germany in the Mid-1990s.* 1996. A description of German life in the 1980s and 1990s, including the reunification of East and West Germany.*

Brown, Archie. *The Gorbachev Factor.* 1995. The best analysis and interpretation of Gorbachev's role in the dramatic events of 1985–1991.*

Chernyaev, Anatoly S. *My Six Years with Gorbachev.* 2000. Insightful work by a former Gorbachev adviser.

English, Robert D. *Russia and the Idea of the West: Gorbachev, Intellectuals, and the End of the Cold War.* 2000. A readable and scholarly examination of the origins and impact of new ideas, especially Western-influenced ideas, on the Gorbachev revolution.

Evans, Eric. *Thatcher and Thatcherism*. 2nd ed. 1997. A good brief overview.*

Garthoff, Raymond L. *The Great Transition: American-Soviet Relations and the End of the Cold War*. 1994. An insightful account and examination of U.S-Soviet relations during the 1980s and early 1990s.

Glenny, Misha. *The Fall of Yugoslavia: The Third Balkan War*. 3rd rev. ed. 1996. A fascinating account by a BBC correspondent, with a 1996 epilogue.*

Gorbachev, Mikhail. *Memoirs*. 1996. A long work that reveals much about the former Soviet leader and his perspectives.

Kenney, Padaric. *A Carnival of Revolution: Central Europe 1989*. 2004. The author relies on oral histories, as well as his own experiences and more traditional sources, in creating a very readable account of the grassroots movements that brought about the collapse of communism in central Europe.*

Little Vera. 1988. A Soviet film depicting alienated and sexually active youth, urban ugliness, crowded housing, alcoholism, and stressful family relations.

Matlock, Jack F., Jr. *Autopsy of an Empire: The American Ambassador's Account of the Collapse of the Soviet Union*. 1995. Unlike some ambassadors to the Soviet Union, Matlock was an expert on the country and was fluent in Russian even before his appointment there; his account reflects his many insights.

————.*Reagan and Gorbachev: How the Cold War Ended*. 2004. The former ambassador relies on his own experiences, as well as other valuable sources, to sort out the roles of both leaders.

Remnick, David. *Lenin's Tomb: The Last Days of the Soviet Empire*. 1993. A most readable narrative and analysis by a former correspondent in Moscow.*

Rothschild, Joseph, and Nancy M. Wingfield. *Return to Diversity: A Political History of East Central Europe since World War II*. 3rd ed. 2000. The best overall treatment of the rise and fall of communism and the post-Communist decade in the former Soviet bloc.*

Stent, Angela E. *Russia and Germany Reborn: Unification, the Soviet Collapse, and the New Europe*. 2000. An excellent and readable work by a first-rate scholar.*

Swann, Dennis. *The Economics of the Common Market: Integration in the European Union*. 8th ed. 1995. An excellent brief history of the Common Market.*

Yeltsin, Boris. *Against the Grain: An Autobiography*. 1990. A book that offers some revealing insights into one of Gorbachev's chief political rivals, the hero of the anticoup forces of August 1991 and independent Russia's first president.

Young, Hugo. *The Iron Lady: A Biography of Margaret Thatcher*. 1990. A long and insightful work that relates the life and policies of one of Europe's most important postwar politicians.*

WEB SOURCES

www.soviethistory.org/index.php. See materials under the years 1986 and 1991.

www.fordham.edu/halsall/mod/modsbook50.html. See especially the links under "1989: What Happened and Why?"

---

*Paperback available.

PART

IV

THE POST–COLD WAR PERIOD

TIME CHART IV
1991–2005

Year	South & East Asia	Middle East & Africa	Europe	Western Hemisphere	Trends in Culture, Science, Technology
1991			Civil war breaks out in Yugoslavia		
1992			Russian inflation exceeds 2,000 percent	Clinton elected U.S. president	"Earth summit" on environmental concerns at Rio de Janeiro, Brazil
1993	Socialist Party wins election in Japan (first time since 1948)	Israeli-Palestinian peace agreement; UN forces sent to Somalia	Czechoslovakia divides into two countries; Yeltsin troops fire on Russian parliamentary building	U.S.-Russian START II Treaty signed but not ratified	
1994	Liberal Democratic Party returns to power in Japan; Kim Il Sung of North Korea dies, succeeded by his son Kim Jong Il (officially in 1997)	Nelson Mandela elected president of South Africa; civil war breaks out in Rwanda	Russian invasion of Chechnia	Zapatistas launch rebellion against Mexican government	Islam continues as a strong political and cultural force
1995			Jacques Chirac elected French president; Dayton Accord signed on Bosnia-Herzegovina		Electronic information highway continues rapid expansion
1996	Congress Party in India defeated		Yeltsin elected president of Russia	Clinton reelected U.S. president	Microfossils discovered on Mars
1997	Hong Kong reverts to China; Deng Xiaoping dies, Jiang Zemin in control of Chinese Communist Party	Fall of Mobutu government in Zaire	Tony Blair becomes British prime minister		Kyoto Protocol signed with goal of reducing emissions that harm environment, but did not go into effect until enough countries ratified it in 2005; United States does not ratify it believing it would harm U.S. economy
1998	Asian financial crisis Pakistan conducts nuclear weapons tests	Civil wars in western Africa	G. Schröder becomes German chancellor	U.S. President Clinton impeached by House of Representatives but acquitted (in 1999) by Senate.	

Year	East/South Asia	Middle East & Wars	Europe/Russia	Americas	World/Science
1999	General Pervez Musharraf takes power from civilian leaders in Pakistan		Poland, Hungary, and the Czech Republic admitted into NATO; NATO bombing of Serbia		World population reaches 6 billion
2000	Opposition candidates in South Korea and Taiwan win presidential elections	Israeli-Palestinian clashes	Russians capture Chechen capital of Grozny; V. Putin elected president of Russia	PRI candiate loses first presidential election in Mexico in seven decades; George W. Bush wins most disputed presidential election in U.S. history	Human genome deciphered
2001		Ongoing violence between Israelis and Palestinians		Latinos surpass African Americans to become U.S. largest minority group; Terrorist attacks on New York and Washington (September 11)	
2002	North Korea admits to having nuclear weapons program	War in Afghanistan	Euro replaces the national currencies in many EU countries		
2003	Jiang Zemin retires; Hu Jingtao succeeds him as general secretary of the Chinese Communist party	War in Iraq			
2004			Putin reelected for another four-year term in Russia; 10 new countries join EU; 7 new countries join NATO; Coordinated bombings on trains in Madrid kill 191 people	Bush reelected U.S. president	Biggest natural disaster in contemporary history, a tsunami, kills more than 200,000 people and completely destroys many coastal towns in southern Asia (December)
2005		Ongoing violence in Iraq and Afghanistan	Islamic suicide bombers attack London's transportation system, killing themselves and 52 others; IRA announces it was going to abandon armed struggle	Hurricane Katrina devastates New Orleans and Gulf Coast (August)	

CHAPTER

32

⑥The Post–Cold War World

SCIENCE AND TECHNOLOGY

As the twenty-first century dawned, the five interrelated issues crucial in 1900 (see Chapter 1) were still major factors around the world. During the 1990s scientists probed deep into space in search of the possibility of life in other galaxies. By 1996 scientists at NASA announced the discovery of microfossils on Mars and by 2004 were speculating that water and life might once have existed on that planet. Although these odysseys are far cries from the 30-minute flights of the Wright brothers' experiments, they indicate humanity's continuing quest to explore space and time.

Despite these achievements, contemporary societies continue to face the paradox that while technology offers the possibility of incredible advances, there is a growing threat to the continued existence of life on earth. At the same time that scientists such as Professor Stephen Hawking at Cambridge University in England might be close to explaining the creation of the universe, major human-induced environmental crises such as global warming (the greenhouse effect, largely caused by carbon dioxide released through the burning of fossil fuels) and the depletion of the ozone layer (largely caused by chlorofluorocarbons [CFSs]) defy easy solutions. One U.S. senator summed up the feeling of many when he remarked, "We only have one planet. If we screw it up we have no place to go."

AIDS EPIDEMIC

Developments in public health and medicine demonstrate another facet of this ambiguity. Although scientific and technological achievements in medicine have benefited millions, they still have not conquered a host of old and new problems. For example, although smallpox, an age-old scourge of humanity, was eradicated in the twentieth century and polio was almost eliminated, a virulent new plague, AIDS, spread around the world, with over 40 million people worldwide being infected with HIV/AIDS by 2005. AIDS has been particularly devastating in many African nations where some 11 million children have been orphaned because of the disease and over 20 million people have died from it. Similarly, the successful mapping of the human genome by scientists in 2000 made it possible to identify and possibly cure a host of genetic diseases, but it also raised complex ethical questions regarding its use and potential for abuse.

ENVIRONMENTAL CRISES

By the twenty-first century, population increase, lack of fresh water, environmental problems such as global warming, the destruction of forest and agricultural lands, and the overuse of natural resources all threatened life on earth. By 2005, world population was about four times greater than it had been in 1900—urban population was about 13 times greater—and all reliable projections predicted continued dramatic increases, heightening the chances of widespread famines in poor countries. (See Appendix A: World Geography for more on population figures.)

During the twentieth century fresh-water use increased 9-fold, and in 2004 was already far more costly in poor nations than in the rich ones. For example, in the poor African nation of Uganda water costs 5.7 percent of an individual's daily wage as compared to 0.0006 percent of the daily wage for an American. The problem is exacerbated by the huge amount of water used to raise cattle for meat that is mostly consumed in the rich northern nations as compared to the amount needed to grow maize or rice that are the major food sources for the world's poor. One flush of an American toilet uses more water than the average African has available for a day's cleaning, cooking, washing, and drinking combined. Overall, it was estimated that about one-fifth of the earth's population lacks safe drinking water and more than two-fifths have inadequate sanitation. And the use of unsafe water continues to be a major cause of deaths in poorer nations.

Global warming remained a particularly intractable environmental problem, as from 1900 to 1999 world energy use increased 16-fold and carbon dioxide emissions 13-fold. By 2000 increases in motor vehicle exhaust and other emissions had heightened the greenhouse effect (see Chapter 19) to the extent that the UN Intergovernmental Panel on Climate Change (IPCC), relying on more than 2,000 scientists from around the world, concluded in 2001 that "analyses for the last 1,000 years over the Northern Hemisphere indicate that the magnitude of 20th century warming is likely to have been the largest of any century during this period. In addition, the 1990s are likely to have been the warmest decade of the millennium." And from 2000 to 2005, average yearly temperatures were higher than the 1990s average, with 2005 being the hottest year recorded since scientists established adequate records. By that year more evidence than ever was available regarding global temperature increases and the effects they were having—the melting of glaciers; rising waters threatening islands, coastlands, and flood-prone cities; vanishing species; an increase of some diseases; and more unstable weather, including hurricanes and tornadoes. In 2006 former U.S. vice president Al Gore's book and documentary film *An Inconvenient Truth* highlighted the global warming dangers that were increasingly alarming the overwhelming number of scientists who had studied the problem, including those in the national academies of science of the major countries of the world.

During the 1990s hopes had been high for the mobilization of a consensus on how to deal with the problem, but meetings at much-publicized "earth summits" in Rio de Janeiro and Buenos Aires highlighted the sharp disagreements concerning solutions to environmental crises. Although many European and small, poor nations wanted to enact stringent and far-reaching environmental protection regulations, the United States (with about 5 percent of the world population but accounting for 25 percent of the world's GNP, 25 percent consumption of the world's energy units, and 32 percent production of carbon dioxide emissions) and some other nations opposed regulations that might threaten their citizens' lifestyles or hinder economic growth. The 1997 Kyoto Protocol called for a reduction in use of the six gases mainly

GLOBAL WARMING

responsible for global warming with the first phase calling for the largest users of fossil fuels, namely the United States and Japan, to take steps to reduce their use. Although many nations signed the Kyoto Protocol, the United States refused—the protocol nevertheless went into effect for signatories in early 2005. China and India, two future economic powerhouses, have also been reluctant to enact or enforce much-needed environmental regulations. Partly as a result, seven of the ten most polluted cities on earth are in China.

Although the end of the cold war altered military and economic realities around the world, governments have been ill prepared to coordinate responses to ecological challenges and many scientists and environmentalists continue to warn that time may be running out.

INCREASED ARMAMENTS

Increased technological sophistication has also contributed to the increased development of deadly weapons. Although the end of the cold war meant that the United States and the former Soviet Union no longer threatened one another with mutual destruction, regional conflicts continued to pose dangers for nuclear confrontations. In 2004 global arms sales and weapons transfers reached almost $37 billion dollars, with the United States by far the leading supplier of weapons. A number of international leaders and Nobel Prize winners have called for an international code of conduct on the arms trade. Oscar Arias, a Nobel Peace Prize recipient and former president of Costa Rica, argued that if it had the will, the international community could eradicate poverty and guarantee health care for all while curtailing the sale of arms.

NUCLEAR PROLIFERATION

Nuclear proliferation poses yet another major danger. Nation after nation from France to China to India to Israel developed nuclear capabilities in the twentieth century, and in the twenty-first century North Korea and Iran seemed poised to join the ranks of nations with nuclear capabilities. Many nations, particularly the United States, opposed the spread of nuclear weapons to nations such as Iran and North Korea and issued a wide range of threats to halt further proliferation of nuclear weapons or other weapons of mass destruction (WMD). However, at the same time, nations with nuclear capabilities including the United States continued to develop more sophisticated means of delivery of nuclear weapons against potential enemies.

TERRORISM

Developments in science and technology also meant that the early twentieth-century problem of terrorism (see Chapter 1) had assumed much more deadly proportions a century later. Decades before the lethal attacks of September 11, 2001 (see subsequent chapters for such terrorist activities since 1991), security experts, scholars, and writers, among others, had envisioned the possibility of a terrorist attack with consequences far exceeding any earlier terrorist actions. In a 1980 novel, *The Fifth Horseman,* Larry Collins and Dominique LaPierre depicted terrorists smuggling a nuclear bomb into New York City. Nevertheless, in the 1990s terrorists' actions in the United States remained small scale compared to the damage a terrorist nuclear bomb could inflict. A bomb at the World Trade Center in 1993 killed only a small percentage of those whom terrorists intended to kill, and a more deadly bombing of a federal building in Oklahoma City in 1995 killed less than 200 people. But for the most part, U.S. citizens still associated terrorist attacks with foreign occurrences. And indeed the U.S. State Department estimated that of more than 2,000 international terrorist attacks between 1995 and 2000, only 15 of them occurred in North America.

The crashing of three of the four hijacked planes into the twin towers of the World Trade Center and the Pentagon on September 11, 2001, followed soon afterward by the apparently unrelated sending of anthrax spore–laden letters through the mail to different areas causing five deaths and additional infections, acted as a rude wake-up call signaling that terrorism was now a major U.S. problem. It also meant that most people in the only remaining superpower would probably never feel as secure as they had previously. *Newsweek*, for example, in its November 5, 2001, edition listed on its cover all sorts of vulnerable terrorist targets. The list included airports, chemical plants, dams, food supplies, the Internet, malls, mass transit, nuclear power plants, post offices, seaports, skyscrapers, stadiums, and water supplies. The list reflected not only the widespread possibilities for terrorist attacks, but also the greatly increased potential damage due to twentieth-century scientific and technological developments. Besides the news media devoting a great deal of coverage to the terrorist threat, one of the most popular U.S. post-9/11 television dramas was *24*, whose hero Jack Bauer was constantly fighting horrific terrorist threats. Although the U.S. invasion of Iraq in 2003 did not diminish global terrorism, other parts of the world (e.g., the Middle East, Indonesia, Spain, England, and Russia), not the United States, suffered major terrorist incidents from 2002 until mid-2005.

In the twentieth century, humans developed skills and knowledge in the scientific and technological fields so rapidly that political and social institutions have been unable to absorb or to understand their impact. The global reaction to the use of genetically modified (GM) seeds is an example of the complex interaction of societies and science. The GM revolution has the potential to increase food production and improve living conditions for millions of people in impoverished countries. On the other hand, wealthy, Western multinational corporations largely monopolize the development and marketing of GM seeds. In addition, because the potential environmental impacts of GM seeds are unknown, many rich European nations have strongly opposed GM crops and have banned their sale in domestic markets. Conversely, some poor, predominantly agricultural nations as well as the United States have had less negative reactions to the GM revolution.

GENETIC DEVELOPMENTS

Other nations have increased productivity by the simple and inexpensive method of planting different varieties of seeds (e.g., rice); by 2000, using this method, many rice farmers in China had doubled their yields. Thus, the highly sophisticated technology of the industrial world may be inappropriate to many nations' social and economic needs, which can be met by far simpler approaches. Early in the twentieth century, Mohandas Gandhi had advocated using labor-intensive pragmatic approaches in rural areas. Faced with hard economic and ecological choices, many poor nations are recognizing the validity of Gandhi's approach. Traditional irrigation systems are being revitalized, and labor, a surplus commodity in much of the global south or Third World, is being used instead of machinery. Architects such as the late Hasan Fathi from Egypt advocated the revival of age-old earthen and mud architecture to provide inexpensive yet artistically pleasing housing for the poor around much of the world. Some homeowners in the United States and Europe have also adopted this method of architecture.

APPROPRIATE TECHNOLOGY

Technological advances including computers, cell phones, and satellite television have swept the world and appear in even the remotest and poorest nations. Here a group of children in India gather around an outdoor computer Kiosk to play a computerized game of cricket.

Although modern science and technology can control and solve some pressing problems, many societies lack the resources, will, and determination to finance or to implement the solutions. An older but related challenge also continues to exist, and that is how to more effectively use science and technology to prevent natural disasters. In late 2004 the world was reminded of this by the biggest natural disaster in contemporary history, a tsunami caused by an underwater earthquake. It killed more than 200,000 people in a few hours and completely destroyed many coastal towns across a large stretch of southern Asia. In the late summer of 2005, a deadly hurricane that hit U.S. southeastern states, especially Louisiana and Mississippi (see Chapter 33), served as another reminder that science and technology alone were not yet sufficient to prevent natural disasters.

ECONOMIC TRENDS

The famine in India at the beginning of the twentieth century was caused by problems in food production and distribution, politics, and economics. So, too, at the end of the century in the 1990s famines devastated Somalia and much of the Sudan, Mozambique, and other African nations. These famines were also the result of a complex web of interrelated issues that continued into the twenty-first century.

After the end of the cold war, three major developments—the technological revolution, growing free trade within Europe and the Western Hemisphere, and the emergence of newly industrialized nations in Asia—caused revolutionary economic changes around the globe. Differences over economic and environmental policies between the rich "north" (Europe, North America, and Japan) and the poor "south" (Africa, Latin America, most of the Middle East, and much of Asia) widened with the globalization of economies. Because of rapid economic and technical growth in the developed world, the gap between the rich north, with access to and control of modern technology, and the poor south, with outdated and poorly developed agricultural and industrial systems, grew. High indebtedness to rich nations and tariffs imposed on agricultural products in the industrialized West caused most poor countries, particularly in Africa, to become even poorer. As one African government official commented about the effects of globalization, "We have opened our economy. That's why we are flat on our back."

GAP BETWEEN RICH AND POOR NATIONS

However, the notable economic growth in some parts of Asia seemed to indicate that massive investments in education for all might be the key to overcoming the worsening cycle of poverty. By the beginning of the twenty-first century, China and India were emerging as new economic powerhouses and it was estimated that by 2050 they might rank ahead of the United States in total gross domestic product (GDP). Their massive populations were one reason, but so too was their increased emphasis on education, especially of a scientific and technological nature. This emphasis and their large populations help explain why by 2001 China and India were each graduating many more college students than the United States—China twice as many, and six times as many with engineering degrees. Already by 2003, illustrating its increasing role in the global economy, China was making about 40 percent of all U.S.-sold furniture, and about 5,000 Chinese suppliers made up about five-sixths of all suppliers to Wal-Mart, the world's largest corporation. By early 2005, China was also producing a majority of the world's shoes, copiers, DVD players, and microwave ovens and was the world's largest importer of both iron and steel and the third largest importer of oil and manufactured goods.

CHINA AND INDIA

The growth of the Chinese and Indian economies touched on another global economic issue—the disparity in global labor costs and the pressure it placed on workers in well-paid countries. Many U.S. union workers, for example, lost jobs or were asked to renegotiate contracts because employers claimed they could not remain competitive if they continued paying the higher wages and job benefits that U.S. union workers received. Higher health care benefits, partly because the United States lacked the type of national health insurance that many other industrialized nations possessed, contributed significantly to the problem. Although union members often resented the fact that corporation executives seemed less willing to cut their own salaries and benefits, they sometimes agreed to concessions, fearing that otherwise their company might declare bankruptcy or close down their plant or other business dealings and instead ship operations to a foreign country with cheaper labor costs.

GLOBAL LABOR COSTS

Although rich nations have talked extensively about relieving at least some of the crippling burden of debt carried by many poor nations, by the beginning of the twenty-first century little had actually been done to lessen those debts. While some

DEBT RELIEF

rich northern nations such as Norway and Denmark supported major foreign aid to poor nations, giving close to 1 percent of their gross national incomes (GNI), the United States ranked close to the bottom in percentage given in foreign aid with 0.15 percent of its GNP going to foreign aid in 2005.

POPULATION GROWTH

Ever-increasing populations have also eaten up the economic gains made by many poor nations. Although by the 1990s fertility rates in China, India, and a dozen other developing nations had declined by nearly two-thirds, the fact that their large populations were mostly young indicates considerable population growth in the future, even with stringent birth control policies. Education for women and widespread use of contraception seemed the best hope for limiting family size around the world. But some conservative forces, including such diverse institutions as the government of Saudi Arabia and the Vatican, objected to some measures for limiting family size.

The basic problem of unequal distribution of wealth remains unsolved, and many nations remain trapped in a cycle of poverty while a few industrialized and technologically advanced nations continue to prosper. The problems of hunger, poverty, population growth, environmental degradation, high military expenditures, and unequal distribution of wealth are all related. How and whether national governments and multinational organizations can be mobilized to solve these problems remain uncertain.

SOCIAL AND POLITICAL TRENDS

RIGHTS OF MINORITIES AND WOMEN

Just as Emma Goldman and Jane Addams in the early twentieth century had visions of the kinds of societies they wished to create, so too do women, racial and ethnic minorities, indigenous peoples, homosexuals, and other activist groups and individuals continue to seek sweeping political and social changes that will bring a full measure of citizens' rights in the twenty-first century. The 1992 recipient of the Nobel Peace Prize is a prime example. Given on the 500th anniversary of the landing of Christopher Columbus, the award to Rigoberta Menchu, a human rights activist, indicated the growing awareness of the plight of indigenous peoples in the Western Hemisphere. Menchu's struggle for the rights of indigenous people, for women, and for better economic and political conditions for the poor echoes those of Goldman and Addams at the beginning of the twentieth century. The 2003 Nobel Peace Prize recipient, Shirin Ebadi, an Iranian activist, stressed that the struggle for equal rights continues to the present day.

Although women have attained the highest political offices in many nations, the percentage of women in parliaments has not changed appreciably over the past 30 years. Estimates in the 1990s showed that women did about two-thirds of the work of the world and produced about 45 percent of the world's food, but women's work was often undervalued, underpaid, or unpaid. Women also made up 70 percent of the over 2 billion people living in poverty.

CHILD LABOR

Like women, children are also considered a source of free or cheap labor, and they too often lacked basic legal or social protections. In many Western nations, working mothers have become the norm; many families rely on two incomes to survive.

As democratic movements spread around the
world during the past 20 years, people from
nations as diverse as Ghana and South Africa,
Afghanistan and Iraq have flocked to exercise
their voting rights in free and open elections.
In Soweto, as depicted here, people stood for
hours in the hot sun to vote in South Africa's
third democratic election.

Many other women are the sole providers for one-parent households. The constantly
changing structure of family life remains a major political and social issue.

The end of the cold war and the collapse of the Soviet Union seemed to unleash
a drive for democracy. In the 1990s open elections were held in many eastern European nations for the first time since the 1930s. Many African nations also liberalized
their political systems, and, although barring women from voting, even conservative and
authoritarian Saudi Arabia held limited elections in 2005. In Latin America free elections in Argentina, Brazil, and Chile reinforced the move against military dictatorships
and toward the creation of workable, albeit fragile, democracies. In the post-9/11 era,
the United States became particularly vocal about the need for democracy around the
world. On the other hand, dictatorial regimes remained in power in China and much
of the Middle East, and considerable backsliding toward authoritarianism occurred in
other areas. Freedom House, an organization that monitors democracy, estimated that
in 2004 there were only 117 electoral democracies as compared to 118 in 1996.

Just as unsatisfied national aspirations of ethnic groups destabilized the world
in the early twentieth century, into the twenty-first century they continued to threaten
the cohesion of existing nation-states and cause armed conflicts from the Balkans in

**DEMOCRACY
MOVEMENTS**

ETHNIC CONFLICTS

Europe to Sudan in Africa. With the collapse of the U.S.S.R. and Soviet hegemony over eastern Europe, new or resurrected nations such as Estonia, Latvia, and Lithuania appeared, just as some had earlier emerged from the ashes of the Russian, Austro-Hungarian, and German empires. Democratic ideals were endorsed but not everywhere implemented in the former Soviet republics and eastern Europe.

At the same time that the Soviet Union split into many separate nations, Czechoslovakia and Yugoslavia also fell apart. Similarly, unrealized ethnic aspirations of the Kurds in Iran, Iraq, and Turkey, of ethnic groups in the Sudan, and among the Tamils in Sri Lanka and the Amerindians in Mexico and Guatemala, threatened the cohesion of those nations. In the Middle East, Palestinians continued to struggle for self-determination. By 2005 dozens of ethnic conflicts threatened the existence of many nations, and it seemed likely that in the future new nations would emerge out of violent confrontations. Bishop Desmond Tutu, a Nobel Peace Prize winner and human rights activist in South Africa, sounded a more positive note when he wrote in *No Future without Forgiveness:* "At the end of their conflicts, the warring groups in Northern Ireland, the Balkans, the Middle East, Sri Lanka, Burma, Afghanistan, Angola, the Sudan . . . and elsewhere are going to have to sit down together to determine . . . how they might have a shared future devoid of strife. . . . They see more than just a glimmer of hope in what we have attempted in South Africa."

INTERNATIONAL RELATIONS

At the beginning of the twentieth century, the Boxer Rebellion demonstrated both the complexities of international relations and the desire of powerful nations to dominate or dictate to small or weak states. During the twentieth century, the complex forces of nationalism and economics sometimes fostered international cooperation while at other times the same forces contributed to political strife and armed intervention to protect economic and national self-interests. The 1991 Gulf War, the war in Afghanistan in 2002, and the 2003 U.S. and coalition invasion of Iraq all demonstrated that members of the international community, led by the United States, would protect their own economic (in the later case, petroleum) interests by armed intervention.

WAR IN IRAQ

The creation of an international military coalition of many nations in 1991 during the Gulf War contrasted with the 2003 attack on Iraq, when the United States, as the sole superpower in the twenty-first century, demonstrated that it was willing if it deemed it to be in its self-interest to wage war against perceived threats and opponents without much international support. However, the collapse of the Soviet Union, the growing power of multinational corporations, the economic might of Japan, and the growing strength of China and India have all diminished any one nation's ability to control global affairs.

NEED FOR INTERNATIONAL COOPERATION

Increasingly, national leaders have come to realize that the scope of many of the problems facing their societies necessitates international cooperation. No one nation can solve the environmental crises caused by industrialization and overpopulation. No one nation can institute effective legislation to regulate multinational corporations, or eradicate terrorism. And no one nation can resolve the complex problems of inflation, indebtedness, and scarcity. Ironically, many of these problems—abuse by multinational corporations, pollution, militarism, terrorism—are so huge and complex that individuals often despair of understanding or solving them and find solace in alliances with nationalistic loyalties. Thus, at the very time that strong international relationships are more vital than ever, there is an opposing tendency in much of the world toward commitment to nationalist loyalties based on narrow ethnic or regional identities. Or, as the Nigerian writer Wole Soyinka warned, "Man resorts to his cultural affiliations when politics appear to have failed him."

As Dag Hammarskjold, a former UN secretary-general, once observed, "The United Nations was created not to bring mankind to heaven, but to save him from hell." Since the end of the cold war, the United Nations has been called on to shoulder increasing burdens in stopping, controlling, and policing disputes among ethnic and political enemies in places as far apart as Somalia, Bosnia, Cambodia, western Africa, and Cyprus. UN secretary Kofi Annan (from Ghana in West Africa) urged the nations of the world to form regional peacekeeping forces, to create an "early warning" system for threats to peace, and to increase financial support for the overburdened United Nations, but by 2005 little concrete progress on these fronts had been made. After the 9/11 terrorist attacks and faced with continued violence and warfare in Afghanistan and Iraq, the United States was particularly reluctant to grant the United Nations political or economic independence.

CULTURAL TRENDS

In 1988 the grand old man of Egyptian literature, Naguib Mahfouz, received the Nobel Prize for Literature. Like Nietzsche nearly a century before, Mahfouz had often been criticized by conservatives for his harsh depictions of modern life and his secular approaches to sex and family life; he barely escaped an assassination attempt by Islamist groups for his political views. Similarly, but generally nonviolently, some Christian fundamentalists in the West have urged the banning of some rock and rap videos and the censorship of some films, records, and art exhibitions.

SECULAR VERSUS TRADITIONAL RELIGIOUS VALUES

By the twenty-first century, disillusionment and fear about the uncertainties created by modern technology and the collapse of Marxism as a secular replacement for religious beliefs caused many to turn toward spiritual goals. Muslim, Christian, Hindu, and Jewish communities have all experienced a resurgence of religious fervor and sometimes of religious fanaticism. To some extent, the growth of militant, sometimes violent, religion has been precipitated by the failure of secular societies to solve human problems. Thus, on the one hand, there has been a movement toward continued change and experimentation; on the other hand, there has been a growing trend toward the return of conservative, traditional ways. The resurgence of militant Islam throughout the Middle East and parts of Africa and Asia is just one indication of this trend. Many organized religious movements also experienced an increase in adherents throughout the world, and many openly questioned the value of the cultural and societal changes that had occurred in the twentieth century.

During the twentieth century, scientific and political changes occurred at a dizzying pace. As a result, all societies experienced some form of culture shock. These

CULTURE SHOCK

Within the skybridge between these twin towers in Kuala Lumpur, Malaysia, is the world's highest mosque; by 2005 even-higher skyscrapers were being built in Shanghai and India.

changes, first apparent in the industrialized Western nations, spread throughout the world. Initially Western societies eagerly embraced the changes, which seemed to offer an opportunity for unlimited progress. Western artists explored revolutionary dramatic, literary, and artistic styles, and many people experimented with new and unconventional lifestyles. But by the end of the twentieth century, some conservative forces in the Western world reacted against many of these experimental expressions and advocated stricter legal and governmental regulations of the arts and unconventional lifestyles.

The effects of technology and Western modes of life have been particularly traumatic in traditional societies. Although most societies have embraced the use of manufactured goods that offer immediate improvements in daily life (e.g., refrigerators, radios, trucks, computers), modernization has often meant Westernization, which has entailed the loss of long-held cultural values and beliefs. Television, computers, and the Internet have all acted to spread Westernization. Some traditional societies have refused to give up their own institutions and beliefs for Western ways or secularism that seem both foreign and undesirable. Everywhere, some people continue to try to balance the uncertainties of modern existence by returning to traditional values and religion.

In the social, cultural, and economic arenas, many traditional methods are being revitalized. Artists in various countries are infusing their work with old cultural designs, music, and themes to produce new artistic expressions. Musicians, in particular, have led the way in incorporating traditional musical forms and expressions from around the world in new ways.

Despite some attempts to restrict foreign influences, globalization and the intermingling of cultures continue. The first five winners of the Nobel Prize for Literature in the twenty-first century illustrate this well. The plays and novels of Gao Xingjian, born in 1940 in China, reflect Western modernist influences and were eventually banned in his homeland. Toward the end of the 1980s he left China and settled in Paris, where he continued his writings. The next Nobel Prize winner (in 2001) was V. S. Naipaul, who was born on the island of Trinidad in 1932, but whose ancestors came from India. He later studied in England and eventually settled there. His novels and travel writings have settings in various parts of the globe including Latin America, Africa, and Asia and deal with topics as varied as religion and guerilla warfare. The 2002 prize recipient was the Jewish Hungarian novelist Imre Kertész, who as a teenager survived Auschwitz and Buchenwald. In addition to his original writings, he has translated many German-language authors including Nietzsche and Freud. The 2003 recipient was the novelist J. M. Coetzee, who was born in South Africa but worked and pursued graduate studies in England and the United States. Subsequently, he taught at U.S. universities, as well as at the University of Cape Town in the land of his birth. In 2002 he emigrated to Australia. In addition to his fiction, Coetzee has translated Dutch and Afrikaans literature. The 2004 prizewinner, the Austrian Elfriede Jelinek, is the daughter of a Czech-Jewish father. Although primarily a novelist and playwright, Jelinek has also translated works of English, French, and U.S. writers. One of her favorite themes is the oppression of women.

GLOBALIZATION

SUGGESTED SOURCES

Badey, Thomas J., ed. *Violence and Terrorism 05/06.* 8th ed. 2005. Thirty-eight articles on various aspects of the subject.*

Bayer, Ronald, and Gerald M. Oppenheimer. *AIDS Doctors: Voices from the Epidemic.* 2000. Moving narrative of the history and human costs of a contemporary health crisis.

A Brief History of Time. 1992. A film version of Stephen Hawking's best-selling book on the origin of the universe; the film traces Hawking's remarkable scientific investigations and long struggle with amyotrophic lateral sclerosis (Lou Gehrig's disease).

Bulliet, Richard W. *The Case for Islamo-Christian Civilization.* 2004. Bulliet challenges and refutes much conventional wisdom about the so-called clash of civilizations between Islam and Christianity and focuses on the commonalities of these two major religions.

Darwin's Nightmare. 2004. A powerful documentary film depicting Lake Victoria fisherman and others in Tanzania adversely affected by globalization, ecology, AIDS, and the arms trade.

Frank, Thomas. *One Market under God: Extreme Capitalism, Market Populism, and the End of Economic Democracy.* 2000. A critical view of many new economic trends.*

French, Marilyn. *The War against Women.* 1992. A sober analysis of the economic and cultural status of women in the contemporary world.

Friedman, Thomas L. *The World Is Flat: A Brief History of the Twenty-first Century.* 2005. As with his earlier *The Lexus and the Olive Tree: Understanding Globalization* (2000), this new book by a *New York Times* foreign-affairs columnist is a very readable mix of globalization analysis and recounting personal experiences, at home and abroad.

God in Government. 2005. A documentary exploration of the rise of religious conservative movements among Muslims, Christians, Jews, and Hindus.

Gore, Al. *An Inconvenient Truth.* 2006. A book and documentary film on global warming.*

Great Decisions. 1993. A PBS eight-part television series on the post–cold war role of the United States, the United Nations, Russia and the Central Asian republics, as well as India and Pakistan.

Harriss, John. *The Family: A Social History of the Twentieth Century.* 1991. Part of the Oxford series on social, cultural, and scientific developments, with lavish illustrations.

Hertsgaard, Mark. *Earth Odyssey: Around the World in Search of Our Environmental Future.* 1999. A very readable combination of travel writing and environmental observations and analysis.*

Jackson, Robert M., ed. *Global Issues 05/06.* 21st ed. 2005. Forty-three articles on important global issues.*

McNeill, J. R., *Something New under the Sun: An Environmental History of the Twentieth-Century World.* 2000. The work of a scholar who emphasizes how extensive was the damage imposed on the planet during the twentieth century.

Parrenas, Rhacel Salazar. *Servants of Globalization: Women, Migration, and Domestic Work.* 2001. A study of migrant Filipina domestic workers in cities such as Rome and Los Angeles.*

Sen, Amartya. *Development as Freedom.* 2000. This Indian-born British economist who won the 1998 Nobel Prize for Economics deals with economic development from wide-ranging global, social, political, and ethical perspectives.*

Tenner, Edward. *Why Things Bite Back: Technology and the Revenge of the Unintended Consequences.* 1997. An argument to apply caution in adopting and using new technologies.*

Tutu, Desmond Mpilo, *No Future without Forgiveness.* 1999. Personal account by the recipient of the Nobel Peace Prize about the Truth and Reconciliation Commission in South Africa and its importance as a model for mediating similar conflicts around the world.

WEB SOURCES

www.esuhistoryprof.com/cybrary.htm. An excellent gateway to various materials on modern terrorism.

www2.etown.edu/vl/globenv.html. Numerous links for global environmental issues.

www2.etown.edu/vl/peace.html. Numerous links for issues related to peace, conflict resolution, and international security.

www2.etown.edu/vl/global.html. This site provides a great starting place for finding historical and current materials on global and cross-cultural issues.

www.mtholyoke.edu/acad/intrel/poverty.htm. Links to numerous materials on world poverty.

www.mtholyoke.edu/acad/intrel/globecon.htm. Links to numerous materials on global economic developments.

nobelprize.org/literature/laureates. This website provides a great deal of material by and about Noble laureates for literature from 1901 to the present.

---

*Paperback available.

⑥Europe and the Americas in a New Era

The collapse of Communist governments in eastern Europe and the Soviet Union and the end of the cold war brought sweeping changes in those regions and also strongly affected policies of major Western powers. In Europe both the European Union (EU) and NATO added new members from among the former Communist countries, and in the Americas forces of integration also advanced between the United States, Latin America, and Canada. Resistance to certain aspects of integration, however, were also evident, and the U.S. decision to invade Iraq in 2003 introduced tensions between the United States and some of Europe's major powers. With the end of the cold war, other security threats or perceived threats became more prominent. After the destruction of New York's World Trade Center by terrorists on September 11, 2001, U.S. President George W. Bush declared "war on terror" and proclaimed that the invasion of Iraq was part of that war. Meanwhile, it was in other countries such as Russia, Spain, and Great Britain that those labeled terrorists subsequently struck.

EUROPE

As Europe struggled to adjust to the post–cold war world, the transition was especially difficult for Russia (partly European and partly Asian) and other former Communist countries, which simultaneously attempted to establish more democratic governments and market economies. They also had to contend with long-neglected environmental problems and ethnic and nationality differences. The Western world often under-estimated the difficulty and complexity of such a transition.

Western European democratic states also had to adjust to the new reality in central and eastern Europe. The 15 member countries (from 1995 to 2004, after Austria, Finland, and Sweden joined in 1995) of the EU not only had to deal with maintaining their global economic competitiveness and deciding whether to pursue policies of closer integration among themselves, which they generally did, but also had to address the desire of many former European Communist countries to join the EU. Most EU countries were also part of NATO, which faced a similar challenge, made even more difficult by Russia's strong opposition to the continued eastward expansion of NATO. Despite hesitations and opposition, however, both the EU and NATO expanded considerably. In 2004, 10 new countries joined the EU—Cyprus, the Czech Republic, Estonia, Hungary, Latvia, Lithuania, Malta, Poland, Slovakia, and Slovenia—thus expanding it to 25 members. Earlier that same year, Bulgaria, Estonia, Latvia, Lithuania, Romania, Slovakia, and Slovenia joined NATO, which had earlier (in 1999) added Poland, Hungary, and the Czech Republic to its membership. But negative votes on a new EU constitution by voters in France and the Netherlands and failure to agree on a new EU budget, both occurring in mid-2005, impeded, at least temporarily, the continuing integration of Europe.

Russia and Other Former Communist States: Economic Challenges

PRIVATIZATION

The transition from a communist-socialist economy to a market economy necessitated privatization—the sale of many government-owned enterprises and assets to private owners, including corporations. Although privatization occurred very slowly in some countries—such as Bulgaria, Romania, Slovakia, and Ukraine—in others it moved more rapidly. By 1996 most of the gross domestic product (GDP) of the Czech Republic (in early 1993 the former Czechoslovakia split into the Czech Republic and Slovakia), Poland, and Russia came from an expanded private sector.

ECONOMIC DIFFICULTIES OF EARLY 1990s

At first, economic transition was usually accompanied by increased inflation and unemployment and decreased production, but the economic situation generally improved by 1996. In early 1990, inflation in Poland was close to 1,200 percent, but by 1995 it was about 28 percent. Poland was also the first of the former satellite states to increase its post-Communist economic growth. The Czech Republic was one of the most successful eastern European nations in transforming its economy. In 1995 its inflation rate was 10 percent and its unemployment rate only 3.5 percent. Even countries such as Russia and Ukraine, whose economies continued to decline, seemed better off by 1995. For example, Russian inflation was more than 2,000 percent in 1992 but only about 130 percent in 1995.

FINANCIAL CRISIS OF 1998 AND ITS AFTERMATH

In August 1998, however, a financial crisis struck Russia. Its causes were many, including unsound government banking and monetary policies, an Asian financial crisis that led many Asians to sell Russian treasury bills, and decreased demand for crude oil, Russia's primary hard-currency export. Russia devalued its currency (from 6 to 27 rubles per U.S. dollar), defaulted on some of its obligations, and suspended payment on its international debts. By the beginning of 1999, average real personal income was considerably lower than it had been in 1995. The Russian crisis also adversely affected the economies of some of the other former Soviet states, as well as other countries in eastern and central Europe.

Yet the devaluation of the Russian ruble had some benefits. Although it greatly increased the prices of imports, it also gave a boost to Russian businesses, which found it easier to compete with higher-priced imports. Several other factors aided a Russian economic recovery that by the end of 2004 had led to six years of economic growth averaging 6.5 percent annually. Increased world oil and natural gas prices helped boost Russian energy profits, and more responsible fiscal policies and increased tax revenues helped lessen inflation and spur economic growth. Most of the growth occurred under a new president, Vladimir Putin, who replaced Boris Yeltsin after he resigned on the last day of the twentieth century (see below).

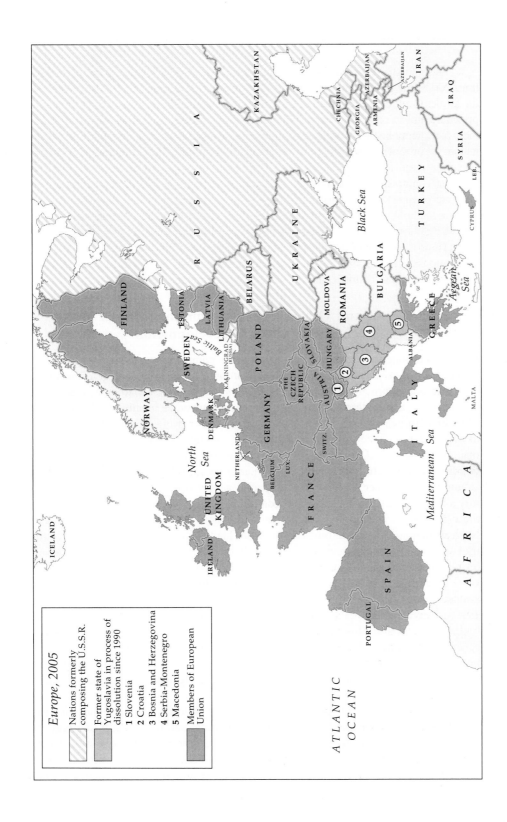

Europe, 2005

Nations formerly composing the U.S.S.R.

Former state of Yugoslavia in process of dissolution since 1990

1 Slovenia
2 Croatia
3 Bosnia and Herzegovina
4 Serbia-Montenegro
5 Macedonia

Members of European Union

ATLANTIC OCEAN

ICELAND

North Sea

IRELAND

UNITED KINGDOM

NORWAY

SWEDEN

FINLAND

DENMARK

NETHERLANDS

BELGIUM

LUX.

FRANCE

SWITZ.

GERMANY

THE CZECH REPUBLIC

Baltic Sea

KALININGRAD (RUSSIA)

ESTONIA

LATVIA

LITHUANIA

POLAND

SLOVAKIA

AUSTRIA

HUNGARY

SPAIN

PORTUGAL

ITALY

Mediterranean Sea

MALTA

AFRICA

BELARUS

UKRAINE

RUSSIA

MOLDOVA

ROMANIA

BULGARIA

GREECE

ALBANIA

Aegean Sea

Black Sea

KAZAKHSTAN

CHECHNIA

GEORGIA

ARMENIA

AZERBAIJAN

TURKEY

CYPRUS

SYRIA

LEB.

IRAQ

IRAN

1 2 3 4 5

535

**ECONOMIC GROWTH,
2000–2004**

As in Russia, economic growth in eastern Europe as a whole was also stronger from 2000 through 2004 than in any comparable period during the 1990s. In general, the former Communist countries of eastern Europe continued to adopt market economic principles and to expand the availability of consumer goods. Countries such as Poland, the Czech Republic, and Hungary continued to advance most rapidly while the Balkan nations were much slower in bringing about the transition from Communist systems. The enthusiasm for obtaining the type of material goods that those in more advanced capitalist countries had taken for granted was so strong that *The Economist,* a staunch advocate of capitalism, editorialized in 1999 that it would be sad if the slogan of the 1989 revolutions overthrowing communism turned out to be "Dialectical materialism [the Marxist interpretation of reality] is dead. Long live materialism."

The cost of economic transformation was often painful, however, as the EU and international agencies such as the International Monetary Fund (IMF) pressured the former Communist countries to cut back on government spending.

Russia and Other Former Communist States: Social and Cultural Developments

In eastern Europe and Russia the transition from communism to a market economy widened differences in income and wealth. Although a small percentage of people— including many former members of the Communist elite—grew wealthy, many others suffered, especially as former government subsidies declined. A European Children's Trust report in 2000 estimated that the number of citizens living in poverty in the countries of the former Soviet Union and eastern Europe had increased more than 10-fold in the decade following the collapse of communism. In Russia an elite of financially powerful oligarchs emerged, partly because Yeltsin enabled them to buy large stakes in former state-owned companies at low prices. By the end of the century a majority of Russians still had incomes below the official poverty line. Although those still below the poverty line declined to about 18 percent by 2004, the gap between rich and poor continued to increase. Many other former Communist countries witnessed a similar phenomenon—for example, in Poland in early 2005 about 33 percent of the population still lived on less than $25 a week.

**CHANGING WOMEN'S
CONDITIONS**

Whereas Communist countries often prided themselves on not discriminating against women—although in subtle ways they often did—in the post-Communist 1990s many reverted to a more traditional view of women's roles, especially in Catholic Poland and Muslim Albania. Women's representation in government bodies generally declined, and women often suffered more than men from government cutbacks in social services. In Russia at least 90 percent of the single-parent families of the early 1990s were headed by women who generally received no financial help from the fathers of their children.

**DECLINING SOCIAL
SERVICES**

Government and defense workers, military personnel, educators, and scientists also suffered from decreasing government expenditures. Although health care budgets decreased in many of the former Communist countries, the deterioration was especially notable in Russia. In 1995 the government budgeted about 1 percent of government spending for health, much less than a decade before and below that spent by other

As Communist countries moved from communism to a market economy, younger people
adapted more quickly to the new world of capitalist advertisements and products. This
billboard seen on a St. Petersburg street in 1995 says, "GSM in Petersburg: Mobile
communication of a new generation."

industrial nations. Along with other causes such as high rates of alcoholism, smoking, and environmental pollution, the low expenditure helped to explain Russia's high
death rate: by 2004 average male life expectancy was only about 60 years, slightly up
from the rate at the end of the twentieth century. Furthermore, the Russian death rate
continued its post-Communist trend of exceeding the birth rate, and its population
continued to decline. Men in the more Westernized former Communist countries of
Poland, Hungary, and the Czech Republic could expect to live about 10 years longer
than those in Russia; as in the West, women could expect to live longer than men in
all of these countries.

Increasing crime and corruption were other serious social concerns. In many
countries the number of major crimes committed at least doubled between 1989 and
1995. By 1994 about 80 percent of Russia's banks and businesses paid protection
money to Russian organized crime syndicates (mafias); by 1999 such mafias were
sending massive amounts of money abroad for safekeeping. In some former Communist countries the term "mafia capitalism" was used to indicate the strong influence of organized crime and corruption on the economic system.

INCREASING CRIME

Yet, despite charges that Marxism had been replaced by materialism, consumerism,
mafias, and corruption, the collapse of communism did provide new opportunities for
individuals, churches, and other institutions to more freely express diverse views and to
exercise more individual choices in their lives. The popular culture of the former

MORE FREEDOMS

Communist countries also became more similar to Western popular culture, although not all citizens were delighted to see such phenomena as advertising, soap operas, and pornography become more prevalent.

Russia and Other Former Communist States: Political Developments

In moving toward increased democracy, the former Communist nations faced several major obstacles. They had to develop a stable system of political parties and to learn the art of compromise, not only between parties but also between branches of government. They also had to enact laws applicable for democratic societies. Finally, some of them had to deal with severe ethnic divisions.

Serious conflicts between executive and legislative branches of government occurred in several countries, most notably in Russia. In October 1993 President Yeltsin ordered Russian troops to fire on the parliamentary building. He then proclaimed a new constitution, approved by a majority of voters, which, at least on paper, strengthened presidential powers. In reality, Yelstin and his government were never able to exercise the amount of power the constitution suggested; Duma members, regional governors, wealthy oligarchs, and even less-wealthy tax-evading citizens resisted the Yeltsin administration's efforts to strengthen its authority. Relations between the president and Duma (Russia's lower and more powerful house in its bicameral system), where the Communist Party was one of the strongest parties, continued to be uneasy throughout most of Yeltsin's years in power. But after Yeltsin resigned on December 31, 1999, and Vladimir Putin replaced him as acting president, the more vigorous Putin, elected and reelected to four-year terms of his own, was able to considerably strengthen his authority over governors, oligarchs, and others. As he strengthened his powers and reduced media independence, Western charges that he was being too authoritarian increased.

TRANSFORMED POLITICAL SYSTEMS

In Bulgaria, Hungary, Poland, Romania, Serbia, and Slovakia, transformed Communist parties with new names (often called socialist) and more market-friendly and democratic platforms gained power for varying periods, especially in the mid-1990s. Their success often stemmed from voters' unhappiness with the performance of inexperienced less-leftist governments and with these governments' reduced social spending. Even after being admitted into NATO in 1999, Poland, Hungary, and the Czech Republic generally operated with leftist coalition governments, containing numerous ex-Communists.

The extent to which democratic practices and the rule of law were established varied from country to country. By 2004, the European Union believed sufficient progress had been made in the Czech Republic, Estonia, Hungary, Latvia, Lithuania, Poland, Slovakia, and Slovenia to admit them into its organization. In 2003 and 2004 public pressures and democratic elections brought about the election of Western-oriented reformers as presidents, first in Georgia and then in Ukraine (a country about the size of France), and both leaders expressed a desire to eventually join the EU. In Russia, almost a decade and a half after the collapse of communism, the results were still mixed. On the one hand, democratic elections, however imperfect and tarnished

Boris Yeltsin and his successor, Vladimir Putin.

with charges of fraud, had become the norm, and there was little doubt that Vladimir Putin was the choice of the majority of the Russian people when he was elected to a second presidential term in 2004. On the other hand, Putin's moves to strengthen his own authority had weakened media independence, local government authority, and the influence of parliament. Putin also weakened the clout of wealthy oligarchs, most dramatically by having the richest oligarch of all, Mikhail Khodorkovsky, arrested in 2003 on charges of fraud and tax evasion. Many observers believed that his arrest and conviction (in 2005) were politically motivated.

Ethnic and nationality differences, long a problem in eastern Europe but earlier contained by the Communists, caused serious difficulties in some countries. They led to the breakup of Czechoslovakia in early 1993, to rising anti-Semitic and anti-Romani (incorrectly labeled Gypsies) sentiments in some countries, and to discrimination against Hungarians in Slovakia and Romania. In Yugoslavia's Bosnia-Herzegovina and Kosovo and in Russia's Chechnia province, conflicts led to tens of thousands of deaths.

In mid-1991 Slovenia and Croatia declared their independence from a Yugoslavia they believed was dominated by Serbs under their nationalist leader Slobodan Milŏsević. A full-scale civil war broke out as federal troops, overwhelmingly led by Serbian officers,

ETHNIC CONFLICTS

invaded Slovenia and Croatia. Assisted by Serb guerrilla forces in Croatia, the federal forces captured some Croatian territory, and, despite outside diplomatic pressures and frequent cease-fires, the war continued, resulting in more than 10,000 casualties by 1992.

SERBS, CROATIANS, AND BOSNIANS

Although the United Nations helped to end the conflicts in Croatia and Slovenia in 1992, major warfare then erupted in Bosnia-Herzegovina, another republic seeking independence from Yugoslavia. In this republic, Muslim Slavs and Serbs (mainly Orthodox Christian) were the largest nationalities, and the Croats (mainly Catholic) were the third-largest group. Aided by Serbs serving in the Yugoslavian army, the Serbs of Bosnia-Herzegovina rose up against the republic's predominantly Muslim government. Brutal warfare raged, taking a heavy toll on combatants and civilians alike until a fragile peace accord was signed in Dayton, Ohio, in December 1995. In areas where the Serbs took over, they often practiced ethnic cleansing, killing unarmed Bosnian Muslims or driving them from their homes. In addition, many Muslim women were raped.

The Dayton Accord stipulated the preservation of Bosnia-Herzegovina as a single political entity, but with two administrative divisions almost equal in size, the Muslim-Croat Federation and the Serb Republic of Bosnia. To prevent further fighting and to lay the groundwork for stability, a NATO-led Peace Implementation Force (IFOR) of about 60,000 troops, one-third of which were U.S. soldiers, was stationed in Bosnia-Herzegovina. Although the troops were originally scheduled to remain only one year, they stayed longer because of continuing tensions between the ethnic communities. By 1996, however, Bosnia-Herzegovina had clearly separated itself from Yugoslavia, as had Croatia, Macedonia, and Slovenia.

VIOLENCE IN KOSOVO

The last major Yugoslav conflict of the 1990s occurred in Kosovo, where Muslim Albanians outnumbered Serbs and where strong ethnic, religious, and political differences had a long history. According to the 1974 constitution Kosovo was an autonomous province of the Serbian republic's portion of Yugoslavia. But in 1989, under Milŏsević's leadership, Serbia ended the autonomy of Kosovo, and Kosovar Albanian hostility toward Serbia and Serbians in Kosovo increased. After years of escalating tensions, Serb forces in early 1998 launched a major offensive against a recently formed independence-seeking guerrilla force, the Kosovo Liberation Army (KLA), and its supporters. Another goal of the offensive was to reduce the proportion of Kosovar Albanians, who now numbered close to 90 percent of the population of Kosovo. In March 1999, after major powers failed to bring about a peace settlement, NATO began bombing Serbia and continued to do so into June, when Serbia finally agreed to a UN peace plan. During those few months, Serb forces intensified the killing and the uprooting and expulsion of Kosovar Albanians from their homes in a systematic program of ethnic cleansing. More than 1 million Kosovars became refugees, mostly in Macedonia and Albania, creating the biggest refugee crisis since World War II. Serbian forces also engaged in mass murders and rapes, burned villages, and looted and destroyed homes.

After the end of the war, NATO forces, UN officials, and a small Russian contingent attempted to maintain the peace, facilitate the return of refugees, and restore Kosovar autonomy, but tensions remained. Following the popular election of Vojislav Kostunica as president of Yugoslavia in September 2000, Milŏsević stepped down only after massive street demonstrations and political pressure, and the following year he was turned over for trial to the Hague War Crimes Tribunal. Many in Serbia, however, believed that the tribunal was biased against their nationality, and the handover of Milŏsević and other Serbians charged with war crimes contributed to a right-wing nationalist anti-Western reaction that prevented major reforms from gaining more traction. In 2003, the last two parts of Yugoslavia abandoned the old name and became simply Serbia-Montenegro, but the agreement was only a temporary remedy and contained a provision that within three years the issue of separation between the two would again be examined.

Russia was also threatened with separatist movements by some of the many nationalities remaining within its borders, especially by the Chechens, a Muslim people in the North Caucasus. Although Chechnia proclaimed its independence in 1991, a full-scale Russian invasion of Chechnia did not begin until December 1994. Fighting between Russian troops and Chechen rebels continued for almost two years, except for some brief armistices and cease-fires. In late 1999 Russia launched another major air and ground offensive in Chechnia after it blamed some Moscow bombings and attacks by Islamic militants in Dagestan, which bordered Chechnia, on Chechen "terrorists." In the war that followed, the major Western powers criticized Russia for causing unnecessary and excessive civilian suffering, including turning hundreds of thousands of civilians into refugees. In February 2000 the Russians captured the Chechen capital of Grozny, which had been bombed to ruins, and soon after declared that the major campaign was over and that the restoration of Chechnia could begin. In 2003 Russia oversaw an election for a Chechen president, but most outside observers considered the election undemocratic. Despite losing their capital and lowlands to the Russians, Chechen guerrilla forces in the more southern, mountainous Chechen regions continued scattered attacks, and in May 2004 the Russian-backed president was assassinated. In early September, Chechen rebels took residents, teachers, and schoolchildren hostage in the city of Beslan (located in the North Caucasus), and more than 300 of them were killed when Russian federal forces attempted to free them. As in Kosovo, any real and lasting peace in Chechnia remained problematic.

CHECHEN CONFLICT

Europe's Long-Established Democracies

Compared to the changes and challenges facing the former Communist countries, Europe's more established and stable democratic countries had an easier path in the 1990s and early twenty-first century. Many of these countries remained among the world's most prosperous nations.

In 1993, however, unemployment rates in Europe rose to over 10 percent and remained in double digits until almost the end of the decade. By early 2005 they were somewhat lower but still high as compared to the United States or Japan. Some European countries were much better off than others. In mid-1996, for example, Switzerland's unemployment rate was under 5 percent, Germany's was slightly over 10 percent, and Spain's was over 20 percent; three years later the percentage for each was only slightly lower. By April 2005 Spain, Germany, and France all hovered around 10 percent, but Great Britain and Ireland each had less than 5 percent unemployment.

ECONOMIC CHANGES

The costly integration of eastern Germany and the privatization of its government enterprises provided one explanation for the high German unemployment, but another explanation was a generous benefits system for workers that made it difficult for Germany to keep labor costs down and compete globally. In 1996 the German government, under the moderately conservative Helmut Kohl, passed legislation aimed at reducing the cost of benefits. During the 1990s other European governments continued to privatize previously government-owned enterprises and to become more fiscally conservative, cutting back some earlier established welfare state provisions. Where proposed cutbacks were believed to be too draconian, however, strong opposition sometimes forced governments to retreat.

SHIFTING POLITICAL POWER

In Great Britain, Conservative Party leader John Major remained in power throughout the early and mid-1990s. In the 1997 elections, however, his party was defeated in the most one-sided parliamentary election since World War II, and Labour Party leader Tony Blair became the youngest British prime minister of the century. A year later, Helmut Kohl's party in Germany was also replaced as the party in power by a less conservative party, and Social Democrat leader Gerhard Schröder became chancellor. Although both Blair and Schröder headed historically moderate socialist parties, both men had moved their parties toward the political center (as President Clinton had done with the Democrats in the United States). In 1999 the two European leaders cosigned a paper advocating a "Third Way," between socialism and capitalism. Blair's party was again victorious in the 2001 and 2005 elections, but its majority in the last election was much lower than in either of the first two. Schröder also continued in office, but by mid-2005 the popularity of his party was also declining.

In France, the neo-Gaullist Jacques Chirac was elected to replace the socialist Mitterrand in 1995. Although Chirac was forced to share power with socialist Prime Minister Lionel Jospin in 1997, the new prime minister was a pragmatic socialist similar in many ways to Blair and Schröder. After Chirac was reelected as president in 2002, with Jospin being one of the defeated candidates, Jospin resigned as prime minister and was replaced by the more conservative Jean-Pierre Raffarin, who remained in office until mid-2005. Another interesting development in French political life was a law passed in May 2000 that obligated political parties to nominate as many women as men for most elections, a significant departure from the past in a country where only 11 percent of the representatives in the lower house of parliament were women. Nevertheless by early 2005, the percentage of women in France's lower house had barely increased and remained much lower than in the Scandinavian countries, Germany, or Spain, all of whose lower houses had more than 30 percent women representatives.

EU AND EMU

Part of the stimulus to European governments' economic restraint came from the European Union and the European Monetary Union (EMU), which was established by most EU members in 1999 with the goal of creating a common currency, the Euro. In early 2002 the Euro replaced the national currencies in Belgium, Germany, Greece, Spain, France, Ireland, Italy, Luxembourg, the Netherlands, Austria, Portugal, and Finland. Of EU members only Britain, Denmark, and Sweden, plus the 10 new members of 2004, remained outside the Euro zone by mid-2005. To enter the EMU, member nations were expected to contain budget deficits, inflation, and interest rates. The increasing percentage of retired people was one major reason for budget deficits. Among EU members, declining birthrates and longer life spans meant that retired people made up an increasing percentage of the population, which in turn meant higher health care costs.

Although much less common than in the former Communist countries, ethnic tensions also troubled some western European areas, including various large cities where immigrants and their children resided (see Chapter 31). In early 1996 militant members of the Irish Republican Army (IRA), impatient with the lack of progress in Northern Ireland during a 17-month cease-fire, renewed their bombings in England. A settlement was finally reached between Northern Irish political and religious factions and the British and Irish governments in 1998. The agreement stipulated continued British rule over Northern Ireland (Ulster) but also provided for a provincial government containing both Protestant and Catholic factions that would have authority over many local matters. The agreement, however, did not bring lasting harmony, and intermittent violence and the maintaining of weapons and paramilitary groups by both Catholics and Protestants continued to hamper effective rule. After operating several years with only sporadic suspensions, the provisional government since October 2002 has been in continual suspension, relinquishing direct control back to the British government. A hopeful sign, however, did occur in July 2005 when the IRA announced it was going to abandon armed struggle.

ETHNIC TENSIONS

In Spain a guerrilla group (ETA) whose goal was Basque independence was responsible for killing hundreds of people by various means, primarily sporadic shootings and bombings, in the decades after it began such actions in 1968. In March 2004 the Spanish prime minister at first blamed ETA for coordinated bombings on trains in Madrid that killed 191 people and injured many more, but it was eventually indivduals, mostly Moroccan, with suspected links to Al Qaeda who were arrested and charged with the crime. Despite the prime minister's initial erroneous assessment, the Al Qaeda link was almost immediately suspected, and the Madrid tragedy played some role in national elections three days later (see below). In 2005, however, ETA did claim responsibility for a series of attacks and refused to lay down its weapons as a precondition for peace talks with the government.

TERRORISM

In July 2005, London's transportation system, primarily the subways, suffered coordinated attacks similar to those in Madrid, though the death toll (56 including four suicide bombers) was less than in Madrid. The bombers were residents of London's large Muslim community.

Europe and the Post–Cold War World

EU and NATO developments were certainly central to Europe and Europe's relationship to the rest of the world. Russian opposition to NATO expansion was one cause of the Russian parliament's long delay in ratifying a U.S.-Soviet START-2 treaty signed at a Moscow summit in January 1993. The delay in fulfilling the earlier U.S.-Soviet START-1 treaty of 1991 (see Chapter 31) was due more to the dispersal of nuclear weapons in Ukraine, Belarus, and Kazakhstan, as well as Russia. Only in late 1994 did Ukraine follow the example of Belarus and Kazakhstan and agree to allow the destruction of its nuclear weapons. The START-2 treaty, which pledged both sides to

RUSSIAN FOREIGN POLICIES

further drastic reductions in their long-range nuclear arsenals and to eliminate completely nuclear multiwarhead land-based missiles, was finally ratified in 2000, by which time the Russian government was more concerned and alarmed about U.S. talk of deploying an antimissile defense shield that would necessitate altering the 1972 antiballistic missile (ABM) treaty signed by the Soviet Union and the United States. This talk especially alarmed the Russians because of the state of their own military, which was greatly weakened from its Soviet-era heyday. Despite Russian objections, however, the U.S. withdrawal from the treaty occurred in 2002.

Russia's relationship with Western powers in the 1990s was also affected by Russian-Western financial dealings, concerns over the sale of arms and dispersion of nuclear materials from Russia, conflicts in Bosnia-Herzegovina and Kosovo (where Russia tended to be more sympathetic to its historic allies, the Serbs), Russia's military campaign in Chechnia, and Russia's policies relating to other countries that had been part of the U.S.S.R.

Until August 1994, when Russia pulled the last of its troops from the former Soviet Baltic republics, their presence remained a Western concern. Yet Russian resentment over citizenship requirements and other matters affecting ethnic Russians in Latvia and Estonia also caused disquiet; about 25 million ethnic Russians remained living in other parts of the former U.S.S.R.

In the Transcaucasian states, Russian policies were aimed at propping up its strategic position, maintaining a major role in controlling Caspian Sea petroleum, and preventing other nations from exercising much influence in the area. Iran and Turkey had historically been major competitors in the region, and new Caspian oil finds stimulated heightened Western interests in striking deals to help extract oil and transport it. The emergence of Muslim militant movements, often encouraged by the revolutionary Muslim regime in Iran, was another concern for Russia and Western nations. In the vast territories of the five Central Asian Soviet successor states, three major Russian concerns were the area's rich natural resources, border security, and protecting the interests of the ethnic Russians living there. Despite its natural resources, this region continued to be troubled in the 1990s by poverty and political instability as authorities attempted to limit opposition, including militant Islamic challenges.

NEW DEVELOPMENTS IN A NEW CENTURY

In the early twenty-first century, the global fight against terrorism, the U.S. invasion of Iraq, and developments in former non-Russian parts of the Soviet Union all affected Russian and European relations with the rest of the world. After the 9/11 terrorist attacks in the United States, the United States became less critical of Russian actions in Chechnia, where Russia claimed it was also battling terrorism. In late 2001, as the United States planned its attack on the Afghan Taliban, Russia shared its intelligence information and went along with the U.S. use of former Soviet air bases in Central Asia. In 2002 positive Russian-U.S. relations helped bring Russia into the former G-7 of leading global powers, transforming it into the G-8, and led to the signing of a Strategic Offensive Reductions Treaty (SORT), which pledged both countries to reduce its strategic nuclear warheads to 1,700–2,200 by December 31, 2012. The treaty, however, lacked verification procedures and allowed storage rather than the destruction of nonoperational missiles.

In early 2003, like Gerhard Schröder of Germany, Jacques Chirac of France, and the leaders of many other countries, Russia's Putin criticized the United States for failing to pursue a common UN-sponsored policy when it attacked Iraq. Even though Presidents Putin and Bush took subsequent steps to improve relations, U.S. Iraqi policies continued to feed Russian suspicions as did fears of growing U.S. influence over former Soviet areas. Of special concern was U.S influence on new NATO and EU members Estonia, Latvia, and Lithuania; on Georgia and Ukraine, where the United States had supported victorious democratic candidates; and on some of the Central Asian countries where the United States had become more influential during its war against Afghanistan's Taliban. From its side, the United States occasionally criticized what it perceived as Putin's increasing authoritarianism, as well as the help Russia gave to Iran in building a nuclear plant. Partly in a effort to prevent U.S. global dominance, Russia significantly improved relations with China.

THE UNITED STATES

After 1990 the United States continued the political shift to the right that had begun in the late 1960s and intensified during the Reagan years. In 1991, toward the end of President George H. W. Bush's term in office, the U.S. economy plunged into recession after a decade of growth. The decline eroded Bush's popularity, which rested mainly on success in the 1991 Persian Gulf War and his support of conservative social values. The public also grew alienated from the Democrat-controlled Congress, regarding lawmakers as out of touch with the needs of ordinary citizens and beholden to powerful lobbyists and special interests. One measure of the public's disenchantment with government was voter apathy: in 1988 only 50 percent of eligible voters cast their ballots, an all-time low for the modern era.

By 1992, however, voters were angry enough to unseat many incumbents. The youthful and charming six-term Democratic governor of Arkansas Bill Clinton, campaigning on a platform of change, defeated incumbent President Bush and insurgent Reform Party candidate Ross Perot. In his first two years Clinton pursued a mixed pro-business, socially liberal agenda. Chief among his free market initiatives was his support for the North American Free Trade Agreement (NAFTA) among the United States, Canada, and Mexico. Top among his efforts to enact a more socially liberal agenda was his failed bid for universal health insurance, spearheaded by First Lady Hillary Rodham Clinton. The effort galvanized the insurance industry and other powerful economic sectors against the administration's more liberal tendencies.

CLINTON'S FIRST YEARS

Clinton's social liberalism faded after the 1994 midterm elections gave Republicans a majority in both houses of Congress. Most of the new lawmakers were male, white, young, politically inexperienced, conservative, and committed to ending what they denounced as the "liberal welfare state." To shore up his chances for reelection, Clinton embraced much of their conservative agenda, which included abolishing Aid to Families with Dependent Children (AFDC) in 1996, while continuing to cast himself as a champion of Social Security, education, racial justice, and the environment.

Ironically, with the cold war ended, the nation at peace, and the economy flourishing, the tenor of political life in the 1990s grew ever-more divisive and partisan.

The causes were complex, rooted in a sensationalist media culture that increasingly blurred the line between private and public life, and in Republican disgust with aspects of Clinton's personal life and character, from his marriage to a high-profile feminist and dalliance with marijuana as a youth to his penchant for prevarication. The president from Hope, Arkansas, and his wife embodied many of the values and behaviors the New Right found intolerable.

ECONOMIC SHIFTS

Despite this political rancor, key sectors of the economy flourished through most of the 1990s, in part due to increases in productivity attributable to rapid changes in information technologies. As the computer revolution transformed the way companies did business, overall employment and profits rose while the stock market, especially its high-tech sector, reached dizzying highs. Still, structural problems underlay the boom of the 1990s, notably a continuing decline in manufacturing employment and expansion of part-time service-sector jobs with fewer benefits. These trends were epitomized in Wal-Mart, which in 2000 became the nation's largest employer, paying most of its 750,000 nonunion U.S. workers slightly more than minimum wage, and covering fewer than half of its workers by its health plan. Under Clinton inequality in income and especially wealth continued to rise, more slowly than under the Reagan and Bush administrations, while consumer and business debt mounted.

CLINTON IMPEACHMENT

In 1996 Clinton was reelected while Republicans kept control of both houses of Congress. His second term was marred by scandal, his self-confessed "improper relationship" with a White House intern becoming fodder for his Republican adversaries. The first sitting president to be impeached by the House of Representatives since Andrew Johnson in 1868, Clinton survived the scandal with a decisive Senate acquittal. Still, the episode cast a shadow over his presidency.

SIMMERING RACIAL DISCORD

It also distracted the nation from more pressing concerns, including simmering racial discord. Numerous events of the 1990s revealed the racial fault lines that continued to divide the nation. These included the 1992 uprising in Los Angeles following the acquittal of white police officers videotaped severely beating an unarmed black motorist, riots that killed more than 50 people and caused $1 billion in property damage, and the media-sensationalized trial and acquittal of black athlete and entertainer O. J. Simpson. A large majority of whites believed that Simpson had murdered his white wife and a young man, while most blacks believed him innocent and his prosecutors motivated by racism.

THE NEW IMMIGRANTS

Race relations were also becoming more complex. In the 1990s more than 9 million legal immigrants, more than 80 percent from Asia and Latin America, entered the country. By the year 2000 more than 10 percent of U.S. residents had been born outside the nation's borders. The skyrocketing Latino and Asian populations portended a future in which nonwhites would, by midcentury, outnumber whites. In 2001, with more than 35 million people in a nation of nearly 300 million, Latinos surpassed blacks to become the country's largest minority. Despite many high-profile Latinos in politics, sports, and entertainment, and a thriving middle class, most of the new immigrants, mainly from Mexico and Central America, were poor, undereducated, had few English skills, and occupied the lowest rungs of an increasingly segmented job market.

RISING RIGHT-WING MILITANCY

Surging immigration, the rise of the New Right, and creative use of old and new communications media—especially radio and the Internet—also fostered the growth of militant right-wing groups advocating white supremacy and hostility toward homosexuality, abortion, and especially the federal government. Referring to standoffs between rightist extremist groups and the FBI, a 1997 article in *Modern Militiaman* declared, "The [militia] movement was conceived at Ruby Ridge [Idaho] in 1992, [and] given birth on April 19, 1993 at Waco [Texas]." These episodes, which ended in the deaths of right-wing militants, became rallying cries for the fringe Right. In 1995, on the two-year anniversary of the FBI assault on the Branch Davidian compound in Waco, Texas, the United States experienced its deadliest domestic terror case in its history to that time, when two men linked to the militia movement blew up the federal building in Oklahoma City, killing 168 people.

Less visible than domestic terrorism but ultimately far more lethal was the emergence overseas of Al Qaeda and other fundamentalist Islamic groups dedicated to the destruction of U.S. power in Asia, the Mideast, and North Africa. The origins of Al Qaeda ("the base," or "foundation") stretch back to the rebel mujahideen victory over the Soviets in Afghanistan (see Chapter 31) and the U.S. victory in the 1991 Gulf War. After defeating Iraq the United States established military bases in Kuwait, Saudia Arabia, and other Muslim countries. Many Islamic militants interpreted these events as profoundly humiliating and degrading. From exile in Sudan in 1992 Osama bin Laden, a wealthy Saudi and head of Al Qaeda who had spent several years in Afghanistan financing a jihad, or holy war, against the Soviets, issued a fatwa, or religious edict, calling for jihad against Western "occupation" of Islamic lands. In 1996 he addressed the United States as follows:

ROOTS OF AL QAEDA

> Terrorizing you, while you carry arms on our land, is a legitimate and morally demanded duty. . . . Your example and our example is like a snake which entered a man's house and got killed by him. The coward is the one who lets you walk, carrying arms, freely on his land and provides you with peace and security. . . . The walls of oppression and humiliation cannot be demolished except in a rain of bullets.

Throughout the 1990s bin Laden and his lieutenants planned attacks on the U.S. homeland. The first came in February 1993, when a massive truck bomb exploded beneath the twin towers of the World Trade Center in New York City, injuring 1,000 and killing 6. The operative who planted the bomb later acknowledged that the attackers had hoped to destroy both towers and kill 250,000 people. A string of Al Qaeda attacks against U.S. interests in Africa and the Mideast followed, including the 1998 bombings of the U.S. embassies in Kenya and Tanzania and the 2000 attack on the USS *Cole*. Remarkably, although Al Qaeda was formed in 1988, U.S. intelligence agencies did not describe the organization in writing until 1999.

More pressing concerns, in the eyes of most U.S. citizens, erupted in spring 2000 when the dot-com bubble burst and the stock value of thousands of high-tech firms dropped through the floor. Talk of the "new economy" evaporated as stock prices slid for three straight years. The dramatic plunge in technology and other stocks was soon followed by a series of major corporate scandals and the biggest bankruptcies in U.S. history, most prominently the Enron and WorldCom fiascos. Systematic use of illegal accounting methods and other unethical business practices at the top echelons of these energy and telecommunications giants reflected a greed-infected corporate culture.

THE DOT-COM BUBBLE BURSTS

The twin towers of the World Trade Center during the September 11, 2001, attack.

THE FIRST GEORGE W. BUSH ADMINISTRATION

Meanwhile, the rancor of domestic political life intensified. In the 2000 elections, Republican George W. Bush, former Texas governor and son of former President Bush, defeated Vice President Al Gore in one of the closest and most hotly contested presidential elections in U.S. history. For six weeks the nation's attention was riveted on Florida, on whose votes the election would hinge. In a controversial decision, the Supreme Court ruled in December that Florida should cease its recount, and the next day Gore conceded defeat.

At home, President Bush aimed to extend the legacy of the Reagan Revolution by slashing taxes, especially for businesses and top income-earners, trimming the remnants of New Deal liberalism, and fulfilling his campaign pledges to the religious Right. Overseas, his administration adopted a tough unilateralist stance, declining U.S. membership in the International Criminal Court and rejecting the 1997 Kyoto Protocol mandating a reduction in greenhouse gasses to combat global warming.

THE 9/11 ATTACKS

The Bush administration's focus shifted sharply in response to the coming to fruition of Al Qaeda's plans to attack U.S. citizens on their own soil. On the morning of September 11, 2001, nineteen Al Qaeda operatives hijacked four commercial airplanes on the U.S. East Coast. Two of the planes slammed into the twin towers of the World Trade Center, destroying both, while a third rammed the Pentagon. A fourth, evidently meant to destroy the White House or Capitol building, crashed, due to the heroic actions of its passengers, in a field in Pennsylvania. Nearly 3,000 people died in the carefully planned attack.

The 9/11 attacks shocked the nation, generating an outpouring of patriotic sentiment. The assaults prompted Congress to pass the USA Patriot Act, granting federal authorities sweeping new powers in surveillance and law enforcement, and to create a new cabinet-level Department of Homeland Security. The attacks also sparked a major shift in U.S. foreign policy, with President Bush declaring the "war on terror" the nation's top national security priority. In late 2001, with UN backing, the United States invaded Afghanistan and toppled the Taliban regime, which had harbored bin Laden and Al Qaeda. More controversial was Bush's decision to invade Iraq in March 2003 to oust the regime of Saddam Hussein. Fingering the Iraqi dictator as complicit in the 9/11 attacks, and alleging a massive buildup of weapons of mass destruction that posed an imminent danger to the United States and other Western powers, the Bush administration failed, despite prodigious effort, to secure UN Security Council support for the invasion. Of the major powers only Britain under Tony Blair joined the "coalition of the willing." Never in the modern era has the United States under-taken a military action of such magnitude with so little international support.

BUSH RESPONDS TO 9/11

A massive air and land invasion ended Hussein's regime in six weeks, and on May 1, 2003, Bush declared "major combat operations" at an end. At that moment a powerful insurgency against the U.S. occupation was erupting, an insurgency that grew swiftly in scope and power and continues more than two years later (see Chapter 34 for more on Iraq). Within a year of the invasion it became clear that there was no con-nection between the Hussein regime and the 9/11 attacks and that the regime had no weapons of mass destruction. In April 2004, in an event with far-reaching implica-tions, the world learned via dozens of photographs that U.S. soldiers had tortured prisoners at Iraq's Abu Ghraib prison. World public opinion of the United States, already at an all-time low, sunk even further. At home, by mid-2005, President Bush's view that toppling the Iraqi dictator would make America safer was increasingly being challenged by a perception that the invasion had turned Iraq into a magnet and breed-ing ground for terrorists from around the world, undermined U.S. safety, and dimin-ished U.S. world standing.

THE IRAQ WAR

ABU GHRAIB

In August 2005 it was not terrorists but Hurricane Katrina that pummeled the United States, slamming into the Gulf Coast, destroying much of the city of New Orleans, rendering 1 million people homeless, and causing well over 1,000 deaths and tens of billions of dollars in damage. The worst natural disaster in U.S. history, the catastrophe in Louisiana and adjacent Gulf states revealed what many viewed as an appalling lack of planning by local, state, and federal officials, prompting vigor-ous debates on the nation's emergency preparedness as well as its continuing deep divisions of race and class.

HURRICANE KATRINA

Earlier, in 2004, with U.S. public support for the Iraq war still strong, President Bush defeated Democratic challenger John Kerry and Congress came under firm Republican control. Pledging to overhaul Social Security through "personal retirement accounts," to extend the tax cuts begun in his first term, to continue waging the war on terror with steely resolve, and to reaffirm "family values" championed by the religious Right, Bush oversaw a 2004 budget deficit of over $400 billion, the largest in U.S. history. In a few short years the largest budget surplus in U.S. history, bequeathed from the 1990s, had become the largest national debt in U.S. history. One cause was escalating military spending. In 2004–2005 the United States, with less than 5 percent of the world's population, accounted for about 50 percent of the world's total military spending—about 25 times more than Russia's and 14 times more than China's. Although business profits rose, wages and employment stagnated and consumer and business debt, like that of the government, swelled.

LATIN AMERICA

On New Year's Day 1994 a group of rebels donning black ski masks and calling themselves the Zapatista National Liberation Army (EZLN) rose in rebellion against the Mexican government in the southeastern state of Chiapas. The uprising was timed to coincide with the implementation of NAFTA. From the mountains of Chiapas Subcommander Marcos, mouthpiece of the EZLN, issued a series of blistering manifestos and communiqués explaining and justifying the rebellion, tapped out on his laptop and disseminated globally via the World Wide Web:

> We are the product of 500 years of struggle. . . . We are denied the most elementary education so that they can use us as cannon fodder and plunder our country's riches, uncaring that we are dying of hunger and curable diseases. Nor do they care that we have nothing, absolutely nothing, no decent roof over our heads, no land, no work, no health, no food, no education. . . . But TODAY WE SAY ENOUGH!

Detailing the crushing poverty and oppression suffered by southeast Mexico's majority Maya population, denouncing NAFTA and economic globalization, and insisting that Mexico's government democratize, the EZLN represented what has been described as the world's first postmodern rebellion. Harboring few illusions about actually defeating the Mexican army, the Zapatista assault was directed mainly at the hearts and minds of Mexicans and the outside world. So it remains. Twelve years on, the rebellion simmers, with the EZLN governing dozens of "autonomous municipalities" in Chiapas and widely reputed as a crafty, media-savvy, formidable force. Meanwhile, with the 2000 election of opposition party candidate Vicente Fox, the PRI was forced to relinquish its 71-year stranglehold on power.

**DEMOCRATIC
INSURGENCIES**

The Zapatista rebellion symbolized a broader move in Latin America from the late 1980s to the present toward deepened democracy and a resurgent, retooled, more pragmatic and realist Left. Demanding constitutional rights and accountable governments, ordinary citizens, through myriad political parties, organizations, and interest groups, have ousted right-wing dictatorships and forced broad democratic transitions. Demands for democratic institutions have focused mainly on free and fair elections; open mass media; an end to military impunity; judicial reform; and the institutionalized inclusion of organizations mobilized around specific issues and constituencies, especially women's rights, indigenous rights, workers' rights, public health, and the environment. This democratic resurgence compelled official truth commission reports in Argentina, Chile, El Salvador, Guatemala, and Peru, detailing human rights violations in the era of the dirty wars.

Significantly, this transition to democracy revealed a broad social consensus in many Latin American countries that forcefully rejected the neoliberalism (see Chapter 27) promoted by the United States and international financial institutions like the IMF. Instead, a solid majority of voters in the region's largest and most developed countries—including Brazil, Argentina, Chile, and Venezuela—have opted for what might be termed a pragmatic left-wing populism. The reasons behind the popular clamor for more socially activist governments seem clear. By the late 1990s the region's foreign debt loomed at nearly $700 billion, a threefold increase from 1982, while an average of nearly 50 cents of every $1 of GNP was owed to foreign creditors. Roughly one-fourth of the region's nearly 500 million people lived on less than $1 per day, while the vast urban squalor described by Carolina Maria de Jesus in her 1950s diary had only grown (see Chapter 21). People demanded full rights of citizenship and a dignified material life. Having won the former, many were poised to pursue the latter. Whether this leftward shift portends long-term change or marks but another swing in the political pendulum remains to be seen.

Examples from several countries and regions highlight these trends. In oil-rich Venezuela, ex-paratrooper Hugo Chavez, swept into office in 1998 and reelected in 2000, launched what he called the "Bolivarian Revolution" (named after the nineteenth-century hero Simón Bolívar). Funded by climbing oil revenues, Chavez's reform program included massive state spending meant to lift the urban and rural poor out of poverty (especially for nutrition, public health, housing, land ownership, and job creation); measures meant to undermine the power of the country's landowning oligarchy; and forceful opposition to free trade and the neoliberal agenda of what Chavez called "the Colossus of the North" (the United States) and its "imbecile" president. His fiery rhetoric further polarizing an already deeply divided society, Chavez was briefly ousted in 2002 in a failed U.S.-backed coup. Two years later he resoundingly survived a recall vote initiated by his opponents.

CHAVEZ IN VENEZUELA

In Brazil, the administration of Fernando Collor de Mello, which followed the military's relinquishing of power in the late 1980s, became bogged down in corruption scandals. His successor, Fernando Henrique Cardoso (1992–2000) mainly followed the economic prescriptions of the IMF, including free market reforms and steep cuts in public expenditures. Cardoso's policies corked inflation and stabilized the currency while leaving the country's poorest citizens even poorer. In 2002 Brazilians decisively elected as president Luiz Inacio Lula da Silva, or "Lula." An avowed socialist, former congressman, and leader of the country's Worker's Party, Lula pledged on his inauguration that "we will be responsible for 170 million Brazilians, and we will have to govern with all of Brazilian society to build a more fair, more brotherly, and more united country." To date he has succeeded in calming the jitters of foreign investors and creditors, who feared a return to freewheeling populism, though in 2005 a major corruption scandal threatened to undermine his administration.

BRAZIL

In Argentina, the Peronists under Carlos Saúl Menem (1989–2003) also embraced the prescriptions of the IMF and international markets. The economic medicine tamed inflation and spurred economic growth but also generated high unemployment, worsening social indices, and rising social discontent. In 2001–2002 Argentines took to the streets in protest, banging pots and pans and demanding "Everyone Must Go!" A year later voters swept into office ex-governor and reformist Peronist Néstor Kirchner.

ARGENTINA

Thumbing his nose at IMF austerity measures, Kirchner thus far has pulled Argentina out of its economic slump while deflecting popular discontent.

CHILE

In Chile, the 1990s brought a series of democratically elected governments, decisively ending 17 years of the Pinochet dictatorship (1973–1990). As Chileans grappled with the legacy of the dirty war, elected officials responded to civil society's demand for a full accounting—most notably in the 1991 report of the Commission of Truth and Reconciliation—while avoiding pushing too hard against a watchful military. Through the 1990s, neoliberal reforms generated mounting economic inequality among Chile's already deeply divided society. The 2000 victory of a center-left coalition led by socialist Ricardo Lagos marked the eclipse of Chile's authoritarian right and the emergence of a new political alignment of center-left and center-right blocs. Aging former dictator Pinochet, meanwhile, remained in the news, indicted in Spain for human rights violations committed during the dirty war.

CUBA

In Cuba, the 1991 collapse of the Soviet Union ushered in a prolonged "special period" in which Cubans struggled for the necessities of life amidst a continuing U.S. trade embargo, withered domestic markets, and an authoritarian state apparatus. Through the 1990s the million-plus Cuban exile community in Miami repeated its mantra—"next year in Havana"—while the aging Castro and his regime grappled with the country's deepening economic crises.

PERU

Peru was one of the few countries in Latin America not to undergo a democratic transition in the 1990s. Instead, the dictatorship of Alberto Fujimori battled and crushed the Maoist "Shining Path" insurgency, committing massive human rights violations while toeing the IMF line in its neoliberal reforms. In 2001 Fujimori resigned and went into exile following a corruption scandal. His democratically elected successor, Alejandro Toledo, has proven widely unpopular, though for Peruvian civil society the opening of the political system represents a hard-earned and welcome development.

ANDEAN INDIGENOUS MOVEMENTS

Elsewhere in the Andes, especially Ecuador and Bolivia, well-organized indigenous movements emerged in the 1990s as powerful motors for change. Notably, many such organizations claim a heritage and legitimacy stretching back centuries, to the height of ancient Andean civilizations. Unseating a series of presidents in these countries by sustained mass protests, and insisting on more democratic institutions and tighter restraints on multinational corporations, Andean indigenous movements, like the EZLN and other groups in Mexico, promise to play an increasingly prominent role in the political life of the Andean republics. In 2005 Amnesty International warned that the U.S.-led "war on terror" threatened to target Andean indigenous movements that stand opposed to free market neoliberal globalization. Significantly, all of them oppose it. In coming years the brewing conflicts between indigenous organizations, national governments, the U.S. government, and international capital likely will intensify.

CANADA

REGIONALISM IN CANADA

In 1980 Canada adopted a national anthem, "O Canada," declaring it the "True North, strong and free." By the 1990s, with a new world order emerging after the fall of the Soviet Union and crises once more emanating from the Middle East, many Canadians wondered if the center of this True North would hold. Regionalism, sometimes inflected with continentalism, was on the rise. Many French-speakers continued demanding separatism for Quebec. Large numbers of British Columbians felt closer ties to Seattle and San Francisco than to Toronto or Ottawa. Unhappy Albertans, sitting atop vast natural gas and petroleum reserves, launched yet another political movement to redress Westerners' grievances. Native peoples intensified their claims for more rights and autonomy. Two notable events of the 1990s, however, offered some hope that these problems could be solved. In 1995 voters rejected a referendum on Quebec sovereignty, a hairbreadth victory for national unity that nonetheless presaged a somewhat less divisive political climate. Four years later Canada established the new territory of Nunavut (which means "our land" in the Inuktitut language), a vast tract in the country's north-central region, under Native governance.

Meanwhile Canada continued its usually friendly, though sometimes contentious, relationship with the United States, a nation with 10 times its population. For Canada, the issue of its relationship with the southern neighbor remains of central importance. For the United States, in contrast, relations with its northern neighbor, despite passage of legislation such as the North American Free Trade Agreement of 1994, remained largely an afterthought. Internationally, Canada could no longer aspire to be a "middle power" in a world where the United States was the sole superpower, but generally Canada retained its global reputation as a country of humanitarian intentions.

CANADA-U.S. RELATIONS

THE AMERICAS IN THE TWENTY-FIRST CENTURY

In broader terms, recent trends across the Western Hemisphere underscore the extent to which the people of the Americas live in an increasingly borderless world. The halting hemispheric integration that began in the nineteenth century and grew exponentially in the twentieth continues to expand in the twenty-first. This is true not only for the relatively frictionless movement of capital, information, ideas, music, film, and other cultural products and forms. It is also true for people. It is evident in their patterns of migration and transmigration (going back and forth between host country and home country). It is apparent in the explosion of monetary remittances from Latin Americans working in the United States to their families and communities back home, which in many countries have displaced sugar, coffee, minerals, and other export products to become the main source of foreign exchange. It is expressed in the burgeoning tourism industry, which, along with remittances, has become the economic lifeblood of many areas, especially in the circum-Caribbean. And it is manifest in the actions and agendas of human rights, labor, women's, indigenous, environmental, and many other organizations, from Patagonia to the Arctic Circle.

In coming decades, barring some cataclysmic disruption, the integration of the Americas will continue to accelerate, with the southern and northern parts of the hemisphere mixing and combining in a kaleidoscope of ways. On whose terms this integration takes place, and to whose benefit, will likely remain among the most important questions to ask about this dynamic and diverse half of the globe.

SUMMARY

In the new post–cold war era, Europe and the Americas faced some similar adjustment problems. For Russia and other former Communist states the adjustment to a new era was greater and caused more suffering than in the long-established Western democracies; nevertheless, the latter had to readjust many of their policies, especially in foreign affairs, to account for the new reality. Throughout both Europe and the Americas important steps toward more integration occurred, such as NAFTA and the expansion of both the EU and NATO, but these integrating steps also aroused opposition on nationalistic and other grounds, both within and outside the integrating countries. Russian opposition to NATO expansion and the negative votes on a new EU constitution in 2005 by voters in France and the Netherlands were just a few examples. Although there was originally much hope that the end of the cold war would institute a more peaceful era, old ethnic and national rivalries and stepped-up terrorist activities, especially the 9/11 suicide missions against the U.S. World Trade Center and Pentagon, diminished these hopes. Fears of terrorism escalated, as did U.S. military activity abroad. Although debates continued as to whether such military actions increased or decreased the danger of terrorism on U.S. soil, they, especially the U.S. attack on Iraq in 2003, did increase tensions between the United States and several other major powers. France, Germany, Russia, and China, for example, criticized the United States for pursuing a unilateral foreign policy without UN cooperation.

SUGGESTED SOURCES

Aron, Leon. *Yeltsin: A Revolutionary Life.* 2000. A long, but insightful biography.

Baker, Peter, and Susan Glasser. *Kremlin Rising: Vladimir Putin's Russia and the End of Revolution.* 2005. A critical look at Putin and Putin's Russia by journalists stationed in Moscow from 2001 to 2004.

Behar, Ruth. *Translated Woman: Crossing the Border with Esperanza's Story.* 1993. Engaging and subtle account of an anthropologist's encounter with a Mexican street peddler and her own immigrant past.

Frankland, E. Gene. *Global Studies: Europe.* 8th ed. 2003. A good collection of essays; a new edition is due in late 2005.*

German, Tracey C. *Russia's Chechen War.* 2003. A concise analysis, especially good on the causes of the war.

Goldman, Marshall I. *The Piratization of Russia: Russian Reform Goes Awry.* 2003. A recent work by one of America's leading authorities on the Russian economy.*

Herspring, Dale R., ed. *Putin's Russia: Past Imperfect, Future Uncertain.* 2003. A good collection of essays by leading scholars.

Hitchcock, William I. *The Struggle for Europe: The Turbulent History of a Divided Continent 1945 to the Present.* Pt. 4. 2004. The best account of Europe in dealing with more than a half century's history.*

Hoffman, David E. *The Oligarchs: Wealth and Power in the New Russia.* 2002. A U.S. journalist's portrait of Russia's new capitalist tycoons.*

Jack, Andrew. *Inside Putin's Russia.* 2004. A more favorable analysis of Putin's policies than that of Baker and Glasser (see above); this British foreign correspondent who served in Russia also sees more continuity between the Yeltsin and Putin policies.*

Kagan, Robert. *Of Paradise and Power: America and Europe in the New World Order.* 2003. A slim book that stresses the present differences between U.S and European views of the world.*

Meier, Andrew. *Black Earth: A Journey through Russia after the Fall.* 2003. An excellent treatment by a journalist who traveled widely in Russia in the post-Soviet period.*

The 9/11 Commission Report: Final Report of the National Commission on Terrorist Attacks upon the United States. 2004. (Also available online at www.9-11commission.gov). Nominated for a National Book Award, a detailed and often gripping account of the history behind the 9/11 attacks, with a series of influential policy recommendations.

Richards, Charles. *The New Italians.* 1995. A readable overview by an English journalist.*

Rothschild, Joseph, and Nancy M. Wingfield. *Return to Diversity: A Political History of East Central Europe since World War II.* 3rd ed. 2000. The best overall treatment of the rise and fall of communism and the post-Communist decade in the former Soviet bloc.*

Rowe, William, and Vivian Schelling. *Memory and Modernity: Popular Culture in Latin America.* 1991. Provocative and informed exploration of Latin American popular culture in the late twentieth century.

Searching for the Roots of 9/11. Films for the Humanities and Sciences. 2003. A 47-minute video that features Thomas Friedman and a variety of international voices.

Service, Robert. *Russia: Experiment with a People.* 2003. An excellent overview of post-Soviet Russia by a leading British historian.

Shevtsova, Lilia. *Putin's Russia.* 2003*; *Yeltsin's Russia: Myths and Reality.* 1999.* These two brief books offer expert analysis by one of Russia's chief political observers.

Talbott, Strobe. *The Russia Hand: A Memoir of Presidential Diplomacy.* 2002. An insider's account of U.S.-Russian diplomacy from President Clinton's chief adviser on Russia.*

White, Stephen, Judy Batt, and Paul G. Lewis, eds. *Developments in Central and East European Politics, 3.* 3rd ed. 2003. An updating of developments in eastern and central Europe.

WEB SOURCES

www.cdi.org/russia/johnson/default.cfm. Numerous articles and pieces dealing with contemporary Russia are gathered daily and archived at this site, which is easily searchable. In mid-2005 archived materials dated back to 1997.

www.tol.cz. A gateway to a wide range of materials on 28 post-Communist countries once part of the Soviet bloc.

www2.etown.edu/vl. Provides an Internet directory of over 2,600 annotated links dealing with international relations topics. See, for example, links to Western Europe, European Union, Eastern Europe, Latin America, global environment, American foreign policy, and United States government.

www.9-11commission.gov. The website of the 9/11 Commission (National Commission on Terrorist Attacks upon the United States) with links to its report and other materials.

www.ezln.org. The official website of the Zapatista National Liberation Army.

---

*Paperback available.

34

⑥Asia, the Middle East, and Africa in a New Era

The collapse of the Soviet Union and the end of Communist regimes in Europe brought new challenges to Asia, the Middle East, and Africa. During the 1990s free market economies gained ground throughout these parts of the world, with China and India leading the way in chalking up significant growth rates, challenging Japan's lead as an economic superpower. The Communist Party maintained a monopoly of power in China, Vietnam, and North Korea, and autocratic governments remained entrenched in much of the Middle East and Africa. However democratic aspirations stirred among many peoples throughout the vast region, and many peoples, from South Africa to South Korea, began to enjoy democratic rights. Violence and the threat of violence remained high throughout the region due to unresolved political differences between North and South Korea, China and Taiwan, Palestinians and Israelis, and different ethnic and religious groups in Africa.

ASIA

Political Trends

COMMUNIST PARTIES IN CHINA, VIETNAM, AND NORTH KOREA RETAIN POWER

With the exception of Cuba, the remaining Marxist states are in Asia. In China, where Marxist economic theories were discarded with the ascent of Deng Xiaoping in 1978, the liberated economy hurtled forward, making up for lost time and opportunities of previous decades. The monopoly of political power by the Communist Party was all that remained of Marxism. Deng Xiaoping's successor, Jiang Zeming, and China's current leader, Hu Jintao, have continued his policy of rapid economic development. However the 70-million-strong Chinese Communist Party (CCP) retained a tight monopoly of political power and suppressed any form of dissent with an iron fist. Hu in fact proclaimed in 2004 that the quest for a multiparty China was a "dead end." A partial loosening of state repression did not satisfy widespread yearning for freedoms, expressed in the popularity of underground churches (versus the state-sanctioned and controlled churches) and Internet chatrooms. Without the rule of law, strikes by ill-treated workers and dispossessed farmers remained illegal in China, and dissidents continued to be locked up.

Vietnam followed China's lead in economic liberalization beginning in the late 1980s while its Communist Party continued to monopolize political power. Only North Korea retained both Marxist economic and political systems, which condemned its

China has permitted greater religious
freedom for some groups since the 1980s.
Many old places of worship have reopened,
and new ones have been built—such as
this one to the Buddhist goddess of mercy
near Guangzhou (Canton), which has
thousands of pilgrims and visitors daily.

people to isolation, extreme economic deprivation, and harsh political repression. Unlike
China and Vietnam, a Communist dynasty has ruled North Korea since its creation, in
that when Kim Il Sung died in 1994 he was succeeded by his son Kim Jong Il. The
younger Kim continued to rule North Korea in a father-son cult of personality with no
parallel anywhere else in the world. In contrast, Japan's post–World War II democratic
institutions continued to thrive; the Liberal Democratic Party has been in charge with
only one election loss during the mid-1990s. South Korea and Taiwan also continued
along democratic paths with peaceful transfers of power after each election.

Democracy continued to make gains in most of South and Southeast Asia. In
Indonesia, President Suharto was forced to resign in 1998 after ruling that country
corruptly for 32 years and bequeathing massive economic problems. Since then and
up to 2004 three national elections have elected three presidents, including one
woman, to lead this, the most populous and secular Muslim nation. India's national
elections in 1996 and 1999 resulted in the defeat of the long-dominant Congress Party
and the ascent to power of the Hindu nationalist Bharatiya Janata Party (BJP) under
prime minister Atal Behari Vajpayee. However, economic reforms under the BJP that

**ELECTIONS IN
INDONESIA
AND INDIA**

favored the middle class, not the majority, brought the Congress Party back to power in a national election in 2003. India and Indonesia were Asia's two largest democracies. Fair elections and peaceful transfers of power in both countries confirmed their democratic path. Likewise Bangladesh, Sri Lanka, Malaysia, and the Philippines continued to be governed by democratically elected leaders. The exceptions were Pakistan and Myanmar (Burma). Pakistan continued to fluctuate between ineffective and corrupt elected governments and autocratic military rule. In 1999 a coup led by the army deposed the corrupt and inept elected prime minister and brought General Pervez Musharraf to power. In Myanmar, Nobel Peace Prize laureate and elected leader Aung San Suu Kyi remained under house arrest while the military junta continued to rule.

WAR IN AFGHANISTAN

In Afghanistan a U.S.-led invasion in 2002 ousted the extremely repressive and terrorist-harboring Islamist Taliban regime. Slowly U.S. and NATO forces and United Nations peacekeepers have worked to restore order to that wrecked nation. In 2004 in the first national democratic election ever and one in which women were given the right to vote, Hamid Karzai was elected president of Afghanistan, but his government faced an uphill battle to reconstruct the war-torn and impoverished nation.

SEPARATIST MOVEMENTS IN ASIA

Separatist movements threatened the stability of authoritarian and democratic governments throughout the continent. The end of the cold war contributed to the resurfacing of old disputes and gave others new prominence. China's repression of political and religious freedom has failed to quell separatism among its Muslim minority in the northwest. This minority has been affected by the newly won independence of the five new republics in former Soviet Central Asia, which, however, were also ruled by authoritarian political systems, and the Muslim populations of these republics have also often displayed dissatisfaction with governments they believed were contrary to Muslim values. India, too, continued to be dogged by separatist movements, the most persistent and lethal being among the Muslims in Kashmir where upward of 80,000 people have died in Pakistan-aided Muslim uprisings since 1989. The Kashmir crisis and Muslim opposition in Kashmir also contributed to an upsurge in Hindu nationalism that resulted in communal riots and violence in several Indian cities. Nuclear tests by both India and Pakistan in 1998 intensified the two nations' rivalry over Kashmir that culminated in border conflicts in that disputed land in 2001–2002. In the wake of 9/11 and the global terrorist threat, however, India and Pakistan have begun to explore a peaceful settlement to their long-standing dispute. Other discontented minorities in revolt include Muslims in the Philippines and tribal groups in Myanmar.

Diplomatic and Military Uncertainties

GROWING MILITARY POWER OF CHINA AND NORTH KOREA

The collapse of the Soviet Union and the end of the cold war unleashed diplomatic and military uncertainties in Asia, as elsewhere. Russia's political instability under President Boris Yeltsin and its economic difficulties in adjusting to a capitalist system reduced its ability to influence events in Asia and globally, while China's rapid economic growth provided it with the means to compete more effectively. For example, its trade with the five former Soviet Central Asian republics increased 10-fold in a decade from the 1990s to the twenty-first century. Chinese propaganda emphasized nationalism to counter domestic dissatisfaction with the regime's human rights abuses and growing economic disparity between rich and poor. China's military budget increased over 400 percent between 1994 and 2004. At 2.5 million men in 2003, the Chinese army was the largest in the world. Despite efforts to modernize its armed forces, however, the Chinese military still lacked modern equipment and was unlikely to catch up with the United States military for a long time. In spite of a disastrous economy and the loss of the Soviet Union as patron, North Korea's army of 1.2 million men, plus nuclear weapons since 2003, continued to threaten South Korea and Northeast Asia.

With a newly vibrant and rapidly growing economy, India substantiated its claim to regional leadership in southern Asia. Thus, at a time when Russia and western European nations were dramatically reducing their military expenditures, Asian nations, both Communist and non-Communist, were increasing theirs. Japan too expanded its military budget, in response to the threat from North Korea and China's military buildup; it began to discuss amending its constitution to eliminate the no-war clause and, for the first time since World War II, sent troops beyond its shores, to Iraq in 2003. Significantly, Japan and all eastern Asia continued to depend on U.S. military might, the presence of U.S. military bases in the region, and the approximately 30,000 U.S. troops in South Korea to maintain peace and stability.

Economic Development

Despite its deep recession through much of the 1990s and its subsequent anemic recovery, Japan remained the world's second-largest economy. And despite continued underdevelopment and poverty in areas such as North Korea and much of former Soviet Central Asia, most of the Asian people experienced strong economic growth. This was especially true of the two most populous countries in the world, China and India. From the early 1980s into the early twenty-first century, China's GDP growth averaged over 9 percent per year and India's almost 6 percent. Despite China's impressive growth rate, in the early twenty-first century its GDP was still only about one-fourth that of Japan. Although slowed by widespread financial crises in the 1990s, South Korea, Taiwan, Thailand, Malaysia, Singapore, and Hong Kong (which reverted to China in 1997 but retained a measure of autonomy) renewed their strong growth by the end of the century. Singapore was especially successful. With an economic policy that fostered growth through free trade, and a highly competitive educational policy that produced a skilled labor force, it was able to adapt to ever-higher levels of technological sophistication. In 2003 Singapore's per capita income was $22,000; its citizens' standard of living trailed only Japan's in Asia. Economic liberalization and joining ASEAN (Association of South East Asian Nations), which was moving toward forming a regional free-trade zone, was even lifting the poor economies of Myanmar, Vietnam, and Cambodia.

Most of the successful East Asian economies were also the most egalitarian. In one of the world's fairest distributions of wealth, the richest fifth of South Korea's population averaged only 5.7 times more income than the poorest fifth. Although China

RAPID ECONOMIC GROWTH

BOOMING CHINESE AND INDIAN ECONOMIES

moved a record number of people out of poverty in recent decades, it became less egalitarian. By favoring rapid growth in cities at the expense of workers, it created huge disparities between rich and poor.

Experts explain Japan, South Korea, and Taiwan's economic success this way: Lacking abundant natural resources, they had to invest in their human resources, in high-quality mass education and research institutions. Well-trained labor forces in turn allowed them to produce goods for competitive world markets. Prospering economies created ever-expanding middle classes that saved and invested a large portion of their incomes, which fueled further growth.

China's rapid growth beginning in the 1980s was partly propelled by investments from Japan, Hong Kong, and Taiwan. China expanded its educational system, gutted during the Cultural Revolution; it also allowed some of its brightest students to study abroad, although the government remained ambivalent about the reliability of young people exposed to Western concepts of freedom, especially in the aftermath of the democracy movement of 1989. It also worried about the brain drain, because it feared that many of the approximately 80,000 Chinese students studying in the United States in the early 2000s would opt not to return home, attracted by higher pay and political freedom. However China's advancing economy has also led to new opportunities for the country's brightest engineering and science students. Foreign companies such as Microsoft have set up centers in China and employed some of the best Chinese graduates there. India too worried about its 60,000-plus graduate students in the United States choosing not to return, though Indians were primarily motivated by economic opportunities rather than politics in making their choice. However, reforms and deregulation of the Indian economy since the 1990s have motivated many Indians to return after studying abroad, to fuel an economic boom, especially in software and information technology industries that have created "Silicon Valleys" on the subcontinent.

CHINA AND INDIA COMPETE FOR RAW MATERIALS WORLDWIDE

China and India's booming economies and increasing needs have created shortages and pushed up prices for raw materials, especially for natural gas, petroleum, and iron ore. Each country has become a strong competitor to Japan and Europe for Russia's natural gas and petroleum and have bid for exploration rights from Indonesia to the Sudan. Their demand for iron ore and other minerals has created a boom from Brazil to Mongolia. But the increased use of energy and other resources, and hunger for more, has added to environmental degradation and pressures on the land. The enormous thirst for energy has led China to build the Three Gorges Dam on the Yangzi River at a great environmental and social cost. China has also launched a massive nuclear power generating program and begun building many nuclear power plants.

GLOBALIZING ECONOMIES

Soon after 2000 most Asian nations had joined the World Trade Organization (WTO). Increasing world trade and the irresistible forces of globalization meant that countries were competing globally as never before. In 2002 Japan produced the fastest computer yet, with the processing power of the 20 fastest American computers combined. China too, was catching up from being the "factory to the world" to becoming the "design laboratory of the world," as assembly-line and garment-making factories were moving from China to Vietnam and Cambodia where labor is even cheaper. Meanwhile, computer support and other facilities were moving from the United States and

Globalization has made English the second language of choice worldwide. Children in this preschool classroom in Mongolia are studying English.

Great Britain to India, and Japanese auto manufacturers were building more plants in the United States. Although many people's lives were lifted up by the global trend toward outsourcing, many people's jobs became obsolete and they were left behind.

Despite a slowing trend, Asia remained the continent with the greatest population growth. Although the United States pioneered in the research and development of bioengineered crops, Asia quickly adopted the technology, helping it to become the region of most rapid food-production growth. After the United States, China has developed the most advanced biotechnology programs for all kinds of food and non-food crops, followed by India, Indonesia, and Japan. Critics of genetically modified crops feared that developments in Asia could leave consumers around the world with little choice but to accept them. With decreasing supplies of land and water, scientists were racing to develop a "super rice" that is both tasty and immune to the toxic effects of herbicides. Some biologists maintained that genomics will have an earlier and greater impact in agriculture, especially in rice, than in medicine in the next 20 years because a third of the world's people rely on rice for half their calories.

Social Changes

Economic advances and the information revolution contributed to a continuing social revolution. Rising literacy rates and living standards fed demand for information. In Japan most households had at least one daily newspaper delivered to their door, with a circulation of over 10 million for its largest newspaper, the *Yomuiri Shimbun*.

MEDIA IMPACTS

A television revolution also continued, particularly in cable and satellite viewing, even in remote areas and poor countries where a television set was the most important purchase for many families. Televisions brought not only news and entertainment but also consumer demand and an awareness of the riches and comforts enjoyed by the privileged and beyond most people's reach. More recently the cellular telephone has also lifted the isolation of poor rural areas, and accessibility to the Internet has connected the educated to one another in their own countries and throughout the world. It is small wonder that North Korea banned shortwave radio, computers, and the Internet to its citizens and that China's police kept a close watch on computer websites and urban Internet cafes. Television, computers, and the Internet also increased Western influences in clothing, shopping in supermarkets (many being worldwide chains such as Wal-Mart), eating fast foods, and drinking Western liquor and wines. To cater to the yen for wine among its middle class, even officially dry India developed a growing wine-making industry with vines imported from France and California.

INTERNATIONAL AID

The dissolution of the Soviet Union ended Soviet aid to its former client states Vietnam and North Korea and to friendly states such as India. Japan and the United States remained the largest direct-aid givers and also contributed large sums to multinational aid-giving institutions. Conversely, a small-scale aid institution, called the Grameen Bank, has been notable for its success. Begun in Bangladesh by an economics

The Grameen Bank's microloans to women to start enterprises have improved the standard of living in poor countries and empowered women. Here a group of women in Bangladesh are waiting to pay installments on their loans.

professor in the 1970s and funded by the Canadian government and the Ford Foundation, it made an astonishing 3.7 million small loans across the globe by 2005, 96 percent of them to women, to start small enterprises, helping them gain financial independence. Economists from many countries have gone to Bangladesh to study the bank's working and opened Grameen Bank branches in their own lands. As a Chinese beneficiary said, "Women are more reliable. They don't smoke or drink or that kind of thing."

Although the Middle East, Africa, and Latin America had higher percentage population growth rates, Asia had higher growth in numbers because of its large base. China had 1.3 billion people in the early 2000s and India over 1 billion. A harshly enforced one-child-per-family policy has made small families the norm for the Chinese. Even without coercion, poor rural women in poor Asian countries were having fewer children due to information on contraception gained from sources such as satellite television. For example, the average Indian woman in 2002 bore just under three children, compared with six in the 1905s. Japan's birthrate is especially low, and if present trends continue its population would decrease significantly in decades to come.

Two items in Asia's demographic statistics worried planners. One was the challenge to society of an aging population. Japan had the world's highest longevity for both men and women, and that for most Asian nations was catching up. An aged population meant a potential labor shortage, even for China where in 2002 about 8 percent of the population were over 60 years, with 24 percent being projected by 2050. When fewer and fewer working people will have to support more and more aged retired people, what will happen to the social safety net? Labor shortages already plagued Japan, which could be alleviated by immigration. As in western Europe but in contrast to the United States, traditional cultural norms strongly opposed the influx of aliens. Government measures such as family subsidies, longer maternal leaves, and dating services to encourage marriage and family in Japan, Taiwan, and Singapore have failed to achieve the desired effects. The other worrisome trend is the preponderance of males over females due to bias for sons over daughters. Family-planning pressures and modern techniques that can determine the gender of the unborn resulted in the abortion of many female fetuses, and girls already born were more likely to suffer from neglect. The mid-1990s trend of approximately 114 boys for every 100 girls born in many Asian countries remained true into the twenty-first century. The cruelty of selective abortion as well as the dangerous implications of societies with surplus male populations have already led to laws in India and China (with as yet uncertain effectiveness) that prohibit selective abortion and tests on the gender of fetuses.

POPULATION GROWTH

MIDDLE EAST AND AFRICA
New Political Leaders, Wars, and Democracy

From 1990 to 2005 a new generation of leaders came to power in many Middle Eastern nations. Following the deaths of King Hussein in Jordan and King Hassan II in Morocco, their sons succeeded to the thrones as Abdullah II and Muhammad VI.

Younger rulers also came to power in several Persian Gulf states, and following Hafiz al-Asad's death in 2000, his son Bashar was declared president of Syria. Yasir Arafat's death in 2004 led to the election of Mahmud Abbas whose new presidency of the Palestine National Authority (see below) possibly signaled a new era for the Palestinians. In 2005, even the long-term ruler of Egypt, Hosni Mubarak, promised open and direct elections for president of Egypt. Many of these new leaders promised economic reforms, increases in technological education, and more jobs. However, it remained uncertain whether they would implement much-needed political reforms or whether they could successfully balance the demands by the United States to open up their economies and stamp out terrorists and the often conflicting domestic demands, particularly by Islamist forces, for political reforms.

WAR IN IRAQ

During the 1990s economic sanctions and sporadic U.S. air raids against Iraq continued, but Saddam Hussein remained firmly in power. Although the sanctions failed to remove Hussein, they were estimated to have caused the deaths of up to 500,000 Iraqi children. After the September 11, 2001, terrorist attacks in the United States and the removal of the Taliban regime in Afghanistan, the U.S. government turned its attention to Iraq, which, although not involved in the 9/11 attacks, was alleged to have weapons of mass destruction (WMD) and to harbor other terrorists. The U.S. President Bush was also determined to remove Hussein from power by any means necessary in spite of widespread international opposition. When most European nations and the United Nations refused to join in the attack on Iraq, the U.S. military with Britain and a few small European nations, launched a full-scale invasion of Iraq in 2003. The Iraqi military, weakened and demoralized by years of wars and sanctions, was quickly defeated; Iraq was totally occupied and thousands of Iraqis were imprisoned, many for alleged terrorist connections. The allied troops failed to protect many Iraqi civilians who were killed in the occupation and also failed to prevent widespread looting and destruction of Iraq's national heritage, in particular, the Iraqi National Museum with its priceless historic treasures dating back to ancient times. Stories and photographs of U.S. and British soldiers torturing Iraqi prisoners contributed to increased international and domestic opposition to U.S. policies under the Bush administration. Nor were WMD found; Saddam Hussein's sons were ultimately killed and he was captured after a protracted search.

IRAQI ELECTIONS

As months dragged on and the Iraqi infrastructure, including vital water and electricity supplies, was not reconstructed, many Iraqis, who had suffered under Hussein's brutal dictatorship, blamed the U.S. government and mounted a massive resistance against the occupying forces and the civilian contractors who supported them. The troops retaliated with massive attacks on strongholds of the resistance with heavy casualties among the troops and civilians alike. However, in spite of the violence, fairly free and open elections were held in 2005 and the Shi'i majority in Iraq, long denied power, emerged as the victors and moved to form a coalition government. Yet political and economic conditions remained extremely volatile and it seemed certain that the U.S. military would continue to maintain as many as 100,000-plus troops and numerous bases in Iraq, as well as indirect control for the foreseeable future over the nation's petroleum reserves.

Meanwhile, the neighboring oil-rich nations of Kuwait and Saudi Arabia, both absolute monarchies, made only limited gestures toward opening up their political systems. In the 1996 elections in Kuwait only 100,000 of its 700,000 citizens could vote, and women were denied the vote altogether. After protracted pressure from the United States and mounting domestic opposition, including terrorist attacks against foreigners and the government, the Saudi monarchy announced limited elections for local offices in 2005, but it also curtailed the numbers of voters and banned women from participating. Nevertheless, the future of the Saudi monarchy seemed highly precarious.

Ethnic Strife and Islamist Political Movements

As in Europe and Asia, ethnic rivalries also threatened the political stability and territorial integrity of a number of Middle Eastern nations. In Turkey, Iraq, and Iran Kurdish minorities demanded either more autonomy or complete independence. The Turkish government generally rejected these demands and retaliated with armed attacks against Kurdish insurgents. The Kurds were also plagued by internal rivalries among competing political and tribal leaders. However, the Kurdish demands for more autonomy and political power in Iraq gained force with the fall of Saddam Hussein and the 2005 elections in which they participated in large numbers.

KURDISH NATIONALISM

Similarly, ethnic disputes between Greek and Turkish Cypriots and occupying Turkish forces on Cyprus remained unresolved. Although Turkish Cypriots voted for a complex reunification plan in 2004, Greek Cypriot voters rejected the compromise. Hence, although Cyprus joined many other European nations in becoming a full-fledged member of the European Union, the island remained divided.

Islamic forces threatened the continued existence of well-entrenched regimes in Egypt, Tunisia, Algeria, and elsewhere. Islamist groups were often supported by disaffected and unemployed youth in nations whose populations were overwhelmingly young. Others supported a return to traditional values and the institution of Islamic law as a means to halt the widespread influence of U.S. military and economic power in their nations, as well as the spread of Western popular culture. Although mounting religious activism was a global phenomenon, the tensions between secular and religious forces were particularly acute in the Middle East and parts of Africa. In nations as diverse as Egypt, Algeria, Pakistan, and Afghanistan, where the populations were largely Muslim, large and exceedingly popular militant Islamist movements demanded the creation of Islamic governments and constitutions based on Islamic law; Al Qaeda and some other Islamic organizations also resorted to violence in their struggle to gain power and oust regimes they opposed.

ISLAMIST MOVEMENTS

Lebanon demonstrated the continued problems inherent in a confessional system in which a citizen's religious affiliation forms the basis of national identity and participation in political, social, and economic institutions. During the 1990s Hizballah (Party of God) launched protracted armed resistance against the continued occupation of southern Lebanon by Israel and the Israeli-backed and Israeli-trained southern Lebanese army. As Israeli casualties continued to rise, opposition to the occupation grew among the Israeli public. In spring 2000 the Israeli government somewhat hastily withdrew from

PROBLEMS IN LEBANON

Lebanon. Many Lebanese from all political and religious parties credited Hizballah with this victory. Members of Hizballah subsequently gained a number of seats in parliament and, along with Syria, which continued to maintain troops in Lebanon, became a key force in the political life of the nation. In the post-9/11 era the United States became more vociferous in its opposition to Syria and Iran, Hizballah tensions in Lebanon became more evident, and some feared a return to the bloodshed that had characterized Lebanon during the civil war in the 1970s and 1980s.

Egypt, Algeria. and Turkey were also torn between the conflicting forces of secularism and religious, political fundamentalism. In these nations Islamist movements were often opposed by both the military and entrenched, generally wealthy elites. The largely urban elites also worried that Islamic governments might crush democratic institutions. The status and rights of women were also threatened by extreme Islamist movements. However, many Muslim women in Pakistan, Turkey, and elsewhere used Islamic precepts to refute extreme policies such as those the Taliban had adopted in Afghanistan.

VIOLENCE IN ALGERIA

In the absence of other viable political movements in countries such as Egypt and Algeria, public support for the creation of an Islamic state remained high. After the military intervened to halt the fair and open 1991–1992 elections, which the Islamists were poised to win, civil war broke out in Algeria. During the resulting violence, in which civilian men, women, and children were attacked by both the Islamist and government forces, over 50,000 Algerians were killed. Islamist parties were subsequently barred from participating in elections, and some ultimately renounced the use of violence to gain power. But it remained clear that if Islamists were permitted to participate in truly free and open elections, they might well win. As one Algerian noted, "Tomorrow, perhaps, we'll get round to democracy."

ISLAMIST MOVEMENTS IN TURKEY

Even in highly secular Turkey, Islamist political parties gained in popularity especially in poor urban slums and more traditional rural areas. In the late twentieth century and early twenty-first century, Turkish Islamist parties won in open, democratic elections. However, by 2004 the Islamist party in power in Turkey had adopted exceedingly pragmatic polities on both domestic and international issues. Eager to join the European Union, Turkey moved to improve its record on human rights and treatments of minorities and made gestures regarding a settlement of the continued division of Cyprus and the Turkish military presence on the northern part of the island.

REFORMERS IN IRAN

Similarly, in Iran, reformist politicians who included some leading religious figures gained considerable support from the young, who make up the majority of voters. The young and others demanded the liberalization of many of the conservative social policies enacted by Khomeini's revolutionary government, and an outspoken proponent of liberalization was elected president in 1997. Conservatives in the clergy who controlled the judiciary retaliated by shutting down liberal newspapers, jailing writers, and advocating the continuation of a guided republic. They also criticized the West, especially the United States, for failing to understand Islam or the Islamic government in Iran. Many European governments and China sought to engage and encourage the Iranian reformers as the best means to work harmoniously with Iran and possibly to persuade it not to continue its quest to become a nuclear power. In contrast, many politicians and commentators in the United States and Israel advocated a hard line against the Islamic republic in Iran that might even involve taking military action to prevent Iran from becoming a nuclear power.

Developments in Sudan also remained highly volatile. The civil war between the north and south in Sudan, the longest ongoing war in Africa, escalated when the military regime supported by the National Islamic Front instituted rule by Islamic law. The Islamist regime further alienated Sudanese minorities, particularly Christians in the south, while its support for other Islamist movements around the world was condemned by the United States. Following protracted negotiations, an exceedingly complex settlement between the warring factions in the north and south was reached in 2005, but massacres and atrocities continued in Darfur province, where government and independent armed terror groups attacked rival tribes. Unlike much of the other Sudanese violence, that in Darfur was not based on religion, as most of those involved in both sides of the conflict were Muslim, but on tribal differences. The international community condemned the violence and bloodshed but was reluctant to step in militarily to stop it as NATO forces had done in Bosnia.

WAR IN SUDAN

Israeli–Palestinian Arab Conflict

In 1993 the Israelis and Palestinians announced a dramatic breakthrough in their protracted struggle. The September Oslo agreement promised a compromise whereby the Israelis would withdraw and turn over limited portions of the West Bank and the Gaza Strip to the Palestinian Authority led by Yasir Arafat and the Palestine Liberation Organization (PLO). The agreement called for an extremely complex series of territorial withdrawals by the Israeli occupying forces and the turnover of land to the Palestinian Authority. The Palestinian territory was disconnected geographically and was also surrounded by Israeli-held territory. Palestinians complained that the territorial arrangements resembled Swiss cheese, with the Israelis getting the cheese and the Palestinians receiving the holes.

OSLO AGREEMENT

Further agreements and withdrawals were to be negotiated in the future. The Oslo agreement was formalized with much-publicized handshakes between Arafat and the Israeli leaders, Yitzhak Rabin and Shimon Peres, on the U.S. White House lawn, with President Clinton presiding. Jordan quickly followed suit by signing a formal peace treaty with Israel in 1994. However, the Oslo agreements failed to resolve major points of disagreement, including the status of Jerusalem, the right of return for the Palestinian refugees, security issues, control of scarce and vital water resources, and the ultimate creation of an independent Palestinian state.

The Palestinians believed the process would lead to full independence, while many Israelis were fearful or totally opposed to the creation of an independent Palestinian state. Although the Israelis did withdraw from limited Palestinian territory and the PLO and Arafat handily won the 1996 elections, the new Palestine National Authority failed to solve basic economic problems or to stop all violent attacks against Israelis. As the initial euphoria faded, Palestinians faced ever-higher unemployment and saw more land confiscated by Israelis for the building of more settlements. As the peace process stalled, some observed that the negotiations seemed more about "process" than "peace."

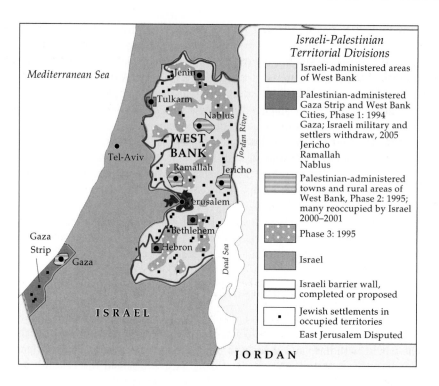

Israeli-Palestinian
Territorial Divisions

Israeli-administered areas
of West Bank

Palestinian-administered
Gaza Strip and West Bank
Cities, Phase 1: 1994
Gaza; Israeli military and
settlers withdraw, 2005
Jericho
Ramallah
Nablus

Palestinian-administered
towns and rural areas of
West Bank, Phase 2: 1995;
many reoccupied by Israel
2000–2001

Phase 3: 1995

Israel

Israeli barrier wall,
completed or proposed

Jewish settlements in
occupied territories

East Jerusalem Disputed

CYCLE OF VIOLENCE

For their part, Israelis worried about national security, and extremists on both sides opposed compromise. A fanatical Israeli settler massacred Palestinian worshipers in the Hebron mosque; and members of Hamas, the main Palestinian Islamist organization, killed Israeli civilians. Thus, the cycle of violence escalated, culminating in the 1995 assassination of Rabin, the Israeli Prime Minister and leader of the Labor Party, not by Palestinians but by an Israeli opposed to the peace process.

The Israeli Labor Party narrowly lost the subsequent elections and the hard-line Likud Party, which had opposed many of the compromises with the Palestinians, came to power. Tensions reached a boiling point when Israel opened a tunnel under the holy sites (known as the Haram as-Sharif to Muslims and the Temple Mount to Jews) in Jerusalem. Massive demonstrations by Palestinians followed as the United States continued its attempts to mediate a settlement.

Further negotiations in 2000 failed to break the deadlock. Both the Israelis and Palestinians disagreed as to the final status of the Palestinian entity, and both claimed sovereignty over parts or all of Jerusalem. The status of the city, and the right of return for Palestinians, were two of the thorniest problems of the conflict. Nor was Arafat able to devise creative suggestions to break the stalemate.

AL-AQSA INTIFADA

In fall 2000, following a provocative visit by Ariel Sharon, a military general and Likud leader, to Haram as-Sharif with its sacred al-Aqsa mosque, young Palestinians exploded into massive demonstrations. These new protracted demonstrations were quickly dubbed the al-Aqsa Intifada. Fearing further compromise, Israelis elected the hard-line Sharon as prime minister. The violence soon spread from the occupied territories into Israel as Palestinian suicide bombers attacked Israeli civilians in Tel Aviv and other cities. Israel retaliated by reoccupying most of the territory from which it had earlier withdrawn, and many more Palestinians were killed or once again made homeless. The cycle of violence worsened the economic situation in both Israel and Palestinian areas. By 2004 it was estimated that 47 percent of Palestinians lived below the poverty line of $410 per month for a family of six.

In a futile attempt to separate the two sides, Sharon's government constructed a 360-kilometer wall, twice as long and three times higher than the Berlin Wall had been. Built entirely on Palestinian land, the wall further divided Palestinian towns one from another, worsened the economic situation, and still failed to stop suicide attacks or violence in Israel and the occupied territories.

In 2005 Sharon implemented plans to withdraw Israeli troops and settlers from the Gaza Strip. This led some radical Israelis, especially among the settlers, to threaten that he might be assassinated as Rabin had been for compromising with the Palestinians. By 2005 both Israelis and Palestinians seemed exhausted by the violence and deaths and wanted a compromise and an end to the hostilities. Some intellectuals and human rights activists even urged the creation of a binational state for both Israelis and Palestinians, but the majority of the people remained firmly committed to separate states. In the aftermath of the invasion of Iraq, the U.S. reengaged in the process to mediate between the Israelis and Palestinians. Whether such moves would be successful was highly problematic, and thus the Middle East remained one of the most volatile regions of the world.

AFRICA AND THE POST–COLD WAR ERA

With the collapse of the Soviet Union and the end of the cold war, African nations, like many in Asia and Europe, experienced a resurgence of democracy and popular demands for more direct participation in solving political and economic problems. During the 1990s over 40 African nations moved toward more public participation in their governments. Long-term one-party rulers, such as Zambia's Kenneth Kaunda, were defeated in open elections, and thousands joined public demonstrations demanding political reforms in nations as diverse as Zaire, Malawi, and Kenya. But by 2005 the long-awaited elections had yet to be held for the Sahrawis (western Sahara), stonewalled by Morocco in spite of United Nations efforts to implement elections.

Political Changes in West, East, and Southern Africa

In West Africa some nations, including Ghana and others, moved toward or maintained democratic systems. A multiparty system was instituted in Ghana in 1992; with four open and fair elections by 2005 Ghana was often held up as a model for the potential of democracy in Africa. In contrast, oil-rich Nigeria swung back and forth between democracy and military dictatorships. After three postponements free elections were held in 1993, but when the candidates favored by the military lost, the military simply seized

GHANA AND NIGERIA

power and silenced political opposition. Ken Saro-Wiwa, an outspoken critic of the regime and champion of his Ogoni ethnic minority, was arrested and hanged in 1995. Although international human rights groups condemned the abuses of Nigeria's military dictatorship, the reactions of petroleum companies and Western governments with substantial economic interests in Nigeria were muted. Finally, in 2000 a fragile democratic government was put in place, but Nigeria's economy continued to suffer from huge foreign debts incurred by former regimes and massive inefficiency and corruption.

ELECTIONS IN MANY NATIONS

By 2005 the local and bloody war among rival factions in Liberia ended and neighboring Sierra Leone held elections. When the long-term dictator of Togo, who had led sub-Sahara's first postindependence military coup in 1967, died in 2005 and his son attempted to take over the government, other African nations successfully pressured him to step down. The reinstitution of Togo's constitutional government was hailed as the "African solution to African problems."

In 2004 the Carter Center, founded by former U.S. president and Nobel Peace Prize recipient Jimmy Carter, monitored free elections in Mozambique; these were the 53rd elections around the world that the Center had monitored for fairness and transparency. In describing his visit in Mozambique, Carter emphasized that people in Africa as well as around the rest of the world were tired of war and wanted peace.

WAR IN HORN OF AFRICA

Even before the end of the cold war, both superpowers had decreased their foreign aid to the desperately poor nations in the Horn of Africa. Years of civil strife, starvation, massive human migrations, and warfare had so undermined or destroyed centralized governments that the political systems were unable to respond to even the basic needs of the people. Soviet-backed regimes in the Horn of Africa collapsed, but no clear-cut political force emerged to take their place. Consequently, Ethiopia and Somalia both became battlegrounds for rival gangs and local warlords. While families faced starvation, armed gangs confiscated food donations provided by Western nations and relief organizations and terrorized civilians. By the early 1990s up to 2,000 people were dying of starvation and violence every week in Somalia, and UN peacekeeping forces, including some Americans, landed in Somalia in an attempt to provide at least minimal safety and food distribution for the civilian population. Although the troops were initially welcomed, local warlords opposed the intervention; after some peacekeepers were attacked and killed, the United States withdrew its forces and the region settled into low-level armed conflict. Sporadic border wars also broke out between Eritrea and Ethiopia but did not ignite into full-scale or protracted conflict.

KENYA AND ZIMBABWE

The picture in Kenya was equally mixed. Daniel arap Moi, whose regime was marked by massive corruption and misuse of public funds, was defeated in the 2002 elections. The new regime moved to take back land illegally taken by Moi and his supporters, but it faced the daunting task of trying to rebuild the economy and the confidence of the tourist industry on which Kenya was heavily dependant for valued foreign capital. In contrast, Robert Mugabe clung to power in Zimbabwe in spite of massive and prolonged demonstrations against his repressive and corrupt regime. Mugabe retaliated against his opponents by nationalizing land owned by white citizens, jailing black political opponents, and cracking down on the press and civil liberties. In the process, the nation's once-vibrant economy declined and agricultural productivity fell drastically.

The occurrence of refugees created by famines, war, civil strife, and ethnic cleansing has been all too frequent in the twentieth century. Here, Hutus from Rwanda await distribution of food in a makeshift refugee camp in neighboring Zaire.

Ethnic Warfare in Central Africa

In the central African nations of Rwanda and Burundi ethnic rivalries exploded into genocidal warfare. The populations of both nations were about 85 percent Hutu and 14 percent Tutsi, but in Rwanda Hutus had controlled the government since 1959 and in Burundi the Tutsi, strongly entrenched in the military, generally held political power. In 1994 the Hutu-led government in Rwanda launched a series of genocidal attacks on the Tutsi population, killing at least 500,000 people. Although Western nations supplied over half of Rwanda's budget, they did not step in to stop the killing. The Tutsi rebel army then retaliated and as they consolidated power, over 200,000 Hutus, fearing retribution for the genocide of the Tutsis, fled into neighboring Zaire where they came under the protection of the United Nations and other international humanitarian organizations. Some Hutu leaders, who had been responsible for the genocide, even used the protection of the international community to rearm, launching attacks against the Tutsis. Simultaneously, violence broke out between the Hutus and Tutsis in Burundi. By the twenty-first century, some Hutu leaders were charged and brought to trial by the International Court for crimes of ethnic cleansing, just as some Serbs were tried for similar crimes in Bosnia.

GENOCIDE IN RWANDA

As fighting in Rwanda and Burundi continued, the violence spilled over into Zaire. The corrupt and weakened Zairian dictatorship of Mobutu Sese Seko seemed unwilling to control the Hutu rebels, and civilians were caught between a rich, corrupt elite and rebel-armed bands that were often composed largely of young boys. Mobutu, who was reputed to have amassed a $4 billion fortune during his years in power, fled the country in 1997 and Laurent-Desire Kabila came to power with the support of several neighboring nations. When he was killed several years later, his son took over power in Zaire. The years of misrule and warfare had devastated the economy, and the inflation rate was estimated at an astounding 9,000 percent per year. Thus, the region remained one of enormous tension and human suffering.

The situation in oil-rich Angola was equally uncertain. When the cold war ended, so too did outside support for the socialist government and for rebels opposing it. But the rebels, who had been heavily supported by the West and South Africa, were well armed; although the 1994 Lusaka Accords promised to end 20 years of civil warfare, the fighting continued until the death of the rebel leader Jonas Savimbi in 2002. Meanwhile, economic development stalled and inflation soared. The gap between a few enormously wealthy urbanites and the impoverished peasants in Angola widened.

Progress in South Africa

The picture in South Africa was far brighter. Following his release from prison in 1990 Nelson Mandela entered into long negotiations with the white apartheid government led by F. W. de Klerk. Mandela was not embittered by his 27 years in prison and was willing to compromise with those who had imprisoned him. As a result, by 1993 Mandela and de Klerk fashioned an interim constitution that provided the framework for full and open elections for all South Africans, black and white. The 1994 elections swept Mandela and his party, the African National Congress (ANC), into office.

Once in power, Mandela proved his flexibility and political acuity, working with the rival Kwa Zulu Inkatha Party and the white National Party. Some within the ANC, including Mandela's wife Winnie, opposed compromising. Winnie Mandela had emerged as a political power in her own right during her husband's long imprisonment, but her reputation was tainted by allegations of corruption and misuse of power within the ANC and the couple later divorced.

The building of an economic infrastructure for the black majority was the most daunting task facing the new government. With a 50 percent illiteracy rate and a 45 to 50 percent unemployment rate among blacks, the government faced enormous pressure to improve education and provide new jobs. Land reform was another critical issue.

The South African government also established the Truth and Reconciliation Commission to investigate assassinations of ANC leaders and opponents of the apartheid regime. By 1996 the testimonies of several high-ranking police had implicated the white-led National Party government in the political assassinations of opponents in neighboring African states and as far away as London. Although the government was determined to bring the guilty to justice, Mandela also favored reconciliation with the 12 percent white minority. The Truth and Reconciliation Commission, with its balanced and principled stance on human rights, served as a model for demands that similar investigations and public trials be held in Guatemala, Bosnia, Rwanda, Cambodia, and other nations where repressive regimes and dictators had murdered and tortured many of their own people during the latter part of the twentieth century.

A firm champion of democracy, Mandela willingly left office when his term as president had ended and turned over the reins of power to Thabo Mbeki, a top leader in the ANC. As an elder statesman, Mandela continued diplomatic efforts to achieve peaceful settlements to a number of conflicts in Africa as well as speaking out about the threat of the HIV/AIDS epidemic.

Social and Economic Developments in Africa

As in other parts of the world, economic disparities in African nations contributed to mounting crime in urban areas, and ethnic and social struggles in rural areas. In world tours, Nelson Mandela, who enjoyed enormous popularity and respect, urged wealthy nations to invest, not only in South Africa, but throughout the continent. Robust economies would enable many new and still fragile democratic governments in Africa to deliver on promises to improve living standards for all their citizens. Relief from the crippling debts most African nations owe Western nations and banks would be of major assistance in helping African economies recover. Wealthy nations discussed and even promised debt relief during major economic conferences in the 1990s and into the twenty-first century, but by 2005 little concrete action had taken place to relieve Africa's indebtedness.

ECONOMIC PROBLEMS

The global HIV/AIDS crisis further drained the economic resources of sub-Saharan nations. By the beginning of the twenty-first century, UNICEF had declared that AIDS might be the worst catastrophe ever to hit the world. And the problems were particularly acute in many African nations where governments were slow to deal directly with the problem and the cost of life-saving drugs was prohibitive. However, by 2005 some nations, such as Namibia, were addressing the crisis, instituting educational programs on the disease, and securing drugs to combat the disease at reduced prices from Western pharmaceutical companies.

HIV/AIDS CRISIS

Other development projects held the promise of raising living standards in sub-Saharan Africa. For example, the new Trans-Sahara highway, largely funded by the Arab Fund for Economic Development and the Islamic Development Bank, will link Morocco in North Africa with Senegal in sub-Saharan Africa. This new link will bring Africa and Europe closer while facilitating trade and tourism.

Similarly, the Green Belt Movement established by Wangari Maathai, a Kenyan woman activist and 2004 Nobel Peace Prize winner, planted trees in arid areas, thereby increasing agricultural production. Like the Grameen Banks in Asia, this movement also empowered women, who are particularly vital in food production in Africa. These are creative approaches that address vital environmental concerns as well as economic needs.

SUMMARY

In the post–cold war era many nations in Asia, the Middle East, and Africa held democratic elections and new governments emerged, but in China and other nations in the Middle East and some African nations dictatorships continued in power. A few nations, such as North Korea, clung to old Communist systems, but most moved toward free enterprise and capitalism. As old-style state-planned economies were dismantled, some individuals and foreign companies prospered but many, particularly in predominantly agricultural countries, continued to live in poverty. The resulting social upheavals led to mounting violence and in Rwanda and Sudan massive massacres of some ethnic groups. Negotiations, diplomacy, and armed interventions often failed to resolve these crises.

War in Afghanistan and Iraq further destabilized the Middle East and caused continued uncertainty for their citizens as well as the international community. The Arab-Israeli conflict remained a major flashpoint, as Palestinians continued to struggle for self-determination. In contrast, the apartheid system in South Africa was dismantled, and free elections were open to all citizens. A new democratic government led by the charismatic Nelson Mandela was installed; and when his term in office was over, in contrast to many other African leaders, Mandela stepped down to make way for another elected president.

In nations with large Muslim populations, many supported the creation of Islamic regimes, and some like Al Qaeda implemented terrorist attacks against local governments and Western nations, particularly the United States, which as the sole superpower was blamed for many of the problems and cultural upheavals throughout the region. It remains unclear whether the forces of secularism or religion will triumph in nations as diverse as Algeria, Egypt, and Turkey.

SUGGESTED SOURCES

Africa: In Defiance of Democracy. Film highlighting the problem of the "Big Man" in Africa where some aging dictators have clung to power in spite of popular opposition.

Becker, Jasper. *Rogue State, Understanding North Korea and Its Continuing Threat.* 2000. Eye-opening study of the world's remaining Stalinist state.

Beilin, Yossi. *From the Oslo Agreement to a Final Agreement.* 2000. An inside account of negotiations between the Israelis and Palestinians.

Boer, Andrea M., and Valerie M. Hudson. *Bare Branches: The Security Implications of Asia's Surplus Male Population.* 2004. Controversial work on the dangerous implications of China's and India's surplus young male populations due to fetal sex-selection.

Diawara, Manthia. *An African Exile in the World.* 2003. An autobiographical account about the trials of the immigrant experience.

Gordon, April A., and Donald L. Gordon. *Understanding Contemporary Africa.* 3rd ed. 2001. Anthology with essays on key issues facing African nations and peoples.*

Huband, Mark. *The Skull beneath the Skin: Africa after the Cold War.* 2003. Balanced study of African governments, civil wars, and ethnic divisions at the end of the 20th century.*

Kepel, Gilles. *The War for Muslim Minds: Islam and the West.* 2005. Scholarly narrative on Al Qaeda, bin Laden, and other Islamist movements by a foremost expert in the field.*

Kristof, Nicholas D., and Sheryl Wu Dunn. *Thunder from the East: Portrait of a Rising Asia.* 2000. This husband-wife team of journalists who have spent 15 years in Asia provides a sweeping overview with especially strong sections on East and Southeast Asia.

Malley, Robert. *The Call from Algeria: Third Worldism, Revolution, and the Turn to Islam.* 1996. A thoughtful analysis of rising Islamist movements and bloody civil war in Algeria.*

Mandela, Nelson. *Long Walk to Freedom: The Autobiography of Nelson Mandela.* 1994. An eloquent personal account of Mandela's long struggle against apartheid and his fight for the political freedom of all South Africans.* See also *An Irresistible Vision: Mandela and the End of Apartheid,* a 50-minute film with archival footage and interviews with members of his family and fellow leaders.

New, David S. *Holy War: The Rise of Militant Christian, Jewish and Islamic Fundamentalism.* 2002. Describes how religious fundamentalism has contributed to the ongoing Arab-Israeli conflict and impeded a resolution to the problem.*

Olds, Kris, et al. *Globalization and the Asia-Pacific Contested Terrains.* 1999. Valuable book by many contributing scholars.

Rwanda: History of a Genocide. Filmakers Library. Historical overview of ethnic warfare in Rwanda, with firsthand footage; 52-minute video.

Salam Pax: The Baghdad Blog. Highly amusing and insightful firsthand account by an Iraqi living in Baghdad during the 2003 war.*

Soyinka, Wole. *Open Sore of a Continent: A Personal Narrative of the Nigerian Crisis.* 1996. A scathing critique of Nigerian politics by the Nigerian recipient of the 1986 Nobel Prize for Literature.

Wan, Ming. *Japan between Asia and the West: Economic Power and Strategic Balance.* 2001. Highly readable book, focuses on how Japan uses economic power to secure its interests.

Weaver, Mary Anne. *Pakistan in the Shadow of Jihad and Afghanistan.* 2002. Written by a reporter with two decades of experience in this part of the world.

WEB SOURCES

www2.etown.edu/vl. Provides an Internet directory of over 2,600 annotated links dealing with international relations topics. See, for example, links to Africa, Asia, and the Middle East.

www.nmhschool.org/tthornton/mehistorydatabase/mideastindex.htm. This website provides numerous links on Middle East developments in the 1990s and the twenty-first century.

www.washingtonpost.com/wp-srv/inatl/longterm/africanlives/front.htm. Excellent series of articles on the lives of Africans in the 1990s.

allafrica.com. A valuable site dealing with a wide variety of African issues such as health, the environment, the arts, conflicts, sustainable development, and women.

*Paperback available.

World Geography

INTRODUCTION

The history of every nation has been and is, to a great extent, determined by its geography. Physical geography considers landforms, climate, soils, and other natural factors that are the setting for human activities and often impose limitations on them. Cultural geography studies population, urbanization, and the significance of languages, religions, and settlement, among other phenomena, in creating the human mosaic. Finally, economic geography concerns itself with the ways in which people pursue their livelihoods. Patterns of agricultural and industrial development, resource utilization, differences in wealth and poverty, trade and transportation, and environmental impacts are analyzed with a view to understanding the complex human struggle for survival or advancement. In the following section, the world's major geographical regions are briefly summarized, with attention to their economic development, population growth, and changes in resource utilization.

WORLD POPULATION IN 1900 AND IN 2004

There were approximately 1.6 billion people in 1900, and about two-thirds lived in Asia, which, including European Russia, accounted for about one-third of the earth's land surface. Europe contained the next largest population, with nearly 400 million people. By comparison, the other land areas were sparsely populated, with 81 million in the United States and Canada, 63 million in Central and South America, 118 million in Africa, and only 6 million in Australasia and Oceania. Antarctica was (and remains) an unpopulated land. Every continent contained large areas unsuitable to human habitation because of extreme heat or cold, too much or too little rain, infertile soils, or high altitudes. As a result, approximately 90 percent of the people lived (and still live) on less than 10 percent of the land.

In 2004 the world population reached about 6.4 billion. The enormous increase was due to the doubling of life expectancy from 30 years in 1900 to about 64 years in 2004, as a result of improved hygiene and public health. At the median fertility level of 5.4 births per woman around 1970, the United Nations Population Division predicted that there would be 12 billion people by 2050. However, due to a dramatic decrease in the number of children born worldwide to 2.7 children per woman by 2000, the population bomb is currently expected to plateau at 9 billion in 2050.

The most drastic decrease in projected population was in China due to the government's one-child-per-family policy. In other areas, the slowing of the birthrate was due primarily to better education and career opportunities for women. Most European and some East Asian countries were significantly below the replacement rate, which created another set of problems.

ASIA

Asia is the largest continent and is by far the larger part of the Eurasian land mass.

Japan

Japan lies at the eastern extremity of Asia. It is an island nation the size of California, and in 1900 it had approximately 40 million people. Only 16 percent of the land was arable, and agriculture was labor-intensive. Rice was the main crop, with other cereals, tea, and mulberry for silkworms as secondary crops. As a result of government intervention and encouragement, Japan developed a core of basic and light industries. These industries were fueled by a very limited coal supply and later by abundant hydroelectricity from harnessed mountain streams. Japan lacked industrial resources and had to depend on importing raw materials and exporting manufactured products for survival. In 1900 it was the only Asian nation to have industrialized successfully, and its people enjoyed the highest standard of living in Asia. Today Japan is an industrial giant that enjoys the second-highest gross national product (GNP) among all nations, and it continues to maintain the highest standard of living in Asia and one of the highest in the world. Tokyo, the capital of Japan, and the greater metropolitan area surrounding it (including Yokohama and a few smaller cities) contain well over 30 million people, making it the largest urban conglomeration in the world.

China

China lies to the west of Japan. It is a giant nation in size and in 1900 was the most populous in the world, with over 400 million people. However, most of China was unsuitable for habitation. Great mountains rim its northwest. Mount Everest, highest peak of the towering Himalayan Mountains, bestrides its southwestern border. Its northern frontier is rimmed by the Gobi and Karakorum deserts, an area inhabited by Mongol and Turkic peoples, many of them nomads. With the building of railroads, sedentary farmers from farther south steadily settled in the marginal lands.

Only 10 percent of the land in China was arable; most of this lay along the Yellow and Yangzi (Yangtze) river valleys and near the coast. Over 80 percent of the population lived on this farmland, and, as elsewhere in Asia, most were subsistence farmers. In the cool, dry north, farmers grew wheat and other cereals. In the warmer and wetter south, rice was the main crop, and double- and triple-cropping allowed more food to be harvested from tiny farms. The diet of most Chinese was protein-poor, the result of poverty and lack of grazing land. The main source of meat was the pig, a scavenging animal. Extreme changes in weather brought floods and famine, the endemic scourge of Chinese agriculture. Farmers either owned their own land or rented. Because of the custom of equal division of land among all male heirs, there were few large estates in China. The nation had significant deposits of coal and iron ore, but in 1900 China had few modern industries and railroads, and those were mostly owned and developed by foreign nations.

By 2004, the People's Republic of China ranked third in GDP among nations of the world (after the United States and Japan) but remained an economically underdeveloped nation. It imported large quantities of petroleum, natural gas, and other raw materials to supply its growing economy. Almost 70 percent of its 1.3 billion people remained rural. Agriculture was collectivized around 1950, but returned to private cultivation after 1980 although the land remained state-owned. Water conservancy projects, most notably the Three Gorges Dam, have reduced floods.

India

India is a self-contained subcontinent, rimmed on the north by the Himalayan and the Hindu Kush ranges, south of which stretch the great Ganges-Brahmaputra and Indus valleys. Low-lying mountains and plateaus, flanked by coastal plains, cover central and southern India. Monsoon winds demarcate the seasons and provide rainfall critical to agriculture.

In 1900 about 30 percent of the land was arable, producing rice, wheat, other cereals, cotton, tea, and sugarcane. Most Indian farmers, whether tenant or landholder, were poor, illiterate, and debt ridden. Most were vegetarian because of poverty or religious prohibitions. Oxen were the chief draft animals, but many of the cattle roaming the Indian countryside and cities were "holy cows" and made little economic contribution. India had a few modern industries, mostly textile mills in Bombay and Calcutta. A system of British-built trunk roads and railroads linked the various sections of the subcontinent.

Today there are three major nations on the subcontinent: India, Pakistan, and Bangladesh. Despite ambitious economic plans, foreign aid, and local efforts, most people in each nation remain poor (see, however, Chapter 34 on India's impressive recent economic growth). All suffer from rapidly increasing populations that have defied sporadic efforts at control. Thus, increased production from irrigation projects and the green revolution (which introduced disease-resistant hybrid strains of grain crops that depend on chemical fertilizers and pesticides for their high yield) have not raised the standard of living significantly for most people, partly due to increasing population. To date, no large petroleum deposits have been found. As a result, all three nations are heavily dependent on petroleum imports and have suffered acutely from the high cost of energy.

Southeast Asia

Southeast Asia contains two regions, the Indochinese peninsula, consisting of Vietnam, Laos, Cambodia, Malaysia, Thailand, and Myanmar, and the two island groups of Indonesia and the Philippines. Accessibility from the sea makes water rather than land the primary means of transportation within the area and has made the area open to outside influence in times ancient and modern. There is also great similarity in the topography and climate of Southeast Asia. The climate is either equatorial or tropical monsoon, with abundant rainfall. As a result, living patterns tend to be similar. In 1900 most people were farmers. Rice was generally the main crop, and farmwork was done by humans. After the late nineteenth century, with Western capital and management, large areas were opened to plantation farming, most notably rubber in Malaya and Vietnam, tea and coffee in Java (an island of Indonesia), and sugarcane in Java and the Philippines. Many of the plantations depended on Chinese or Indian labor, as did newly opened mines, such as the tin mines in Malaya.

In recent decades rapid population increases have resulted in intense pressure on the land. Virgin forests are being destroyed at a rapid rate for timber and to provide cropland, without regard to ecological results. Although the green revolution has helped to increase yields, it has also squeezed out small farmers who cannot afford the improvements. The dispossessed have flocked to cities and created huge slums of unemployed. Industrialization has come too slowly to absorb the large reservoir of workers. Malaysia, with a small population and abundant resources, is relatively well off. Indonesia, with major petroleum and natural gas deposits, is also reasonably prosperous. Political and economic mismanagement mire the economies of the Philippines, Myanmar, and Vietnam.

The Middle East

The Middle East, or Southwest Asia, forms a unit because of similarities in geography and the religion of the majority of the people. Except for coastal plains, river valleys, and oases, the area tends to be arid, with much desert. Mountainous terrain dominates large parts of Persia (Iran) and Turkey and all of Afghanistan.

While in 1900 the majority of the people were farmers living in villages, a minority were, and remain, nomadic. In Persia and Afghanistan, the tribes followed their herds up and down the mountain slopes in a vertical migration pattern. They and their sedentary village neighbors wove colorful wool rugs, each tribe or village with its own distinctive pattern. Nomads called Bedouins lived in the dry plains and desert lands. They herded sheep, horses, and camels. Each group followed strictly defined migration routes; violations resulted in tribal wars. Nomads traded their animals to villagers for agricultural products.

Today, as a result of the discovery of large petroleum deposits, the Middle East has become an important region economically and strategically. Petroleum has made Iraq, Saudi Arabia, Iran, Kuwait, and other Persian Gulf states very prosperous. In some oil-rich nations per capita income exceeds that of many advanced Western nations. Lack of petroleum keeps the remaining nations poor. Oil-rich nations such as Iran, Iraq, and Saudi Arabia have spent their oil revenues lavishly for modernization, armaments, and wars. Large-scale irrigation projects have also been undertaken—for example, the Ataturk Dam in Turkey, which harnesses the water of the Euphrates River for electric power and irrigation.

AFRICA

Africa is physically dominated by plateaus and low tablelands. Such large river systems as the Nile, Congo, Niger, and Zambezi drain parts of the continent, but only sections of each of these rivers are navigable. Rainfall is sparse in the north and south and very abundant in the equatorial zones. Many regions suffer from natural disasters such as droughts and locust infestations. The continent has played a subordinate role in the modern commercial world and, with few exceptions, remains underdeveloped.

North Africa

North Africa is arid except for a relatively narrow strip along the coast and the Nile valley, where there is adequate moisture from rainfall or irrigation for agriculture. In 1900 North Africa was the most urbanized part of the continent. There were many good harbors: Alexandria, Tripoli, and Algiers, for example. The economy was a mixture of the old and the new, represented by native subsistence farms and European-organized plantations for such crops as cotton and grapes. A few nomads roamed the marginal dry lands.

Today the European-controlled plantations are gone, although most local people remain farmers. There are few modern industries because the region lacks most of the resources necessary for developing manufacturing complexes. The Aswan High Dam generates electricity and has brought more acreage into cultivation along the Nile. Egypt has a huge population and little petroleum, while Libya and Algeria have huge petroleum and natural gas reserves and small populations.

West Africa

West Africa's interior is linked by rivers, but the long coastline lacks good ports. With abundant rainfall, much of the area is suitable for tropical crops, and a reliable local labor supply made possible the development of cacao, palm oil, rubber, coconut, and cotton plantations, under European domination, in the late nineteenth and early twentieth centuries. Europeans also opened up tin, gold, bauxite, and other mines in the interior. Despite commercialization, many local peoples, especially in the interior, remained primitive subsistence farmers. Sleeping sickness and river blindness carried by the tsetse fly and mosquito made herding and farming difficult. No Europeans settled in the area.

Demand for tropical products by the outside world continued to play an important part in local economies. Minerals, including diamonds and petroleum, have generated wealth where they are found—for example, petroleum in Nigeria and diamonds in Sierra Leone. However, the general dependence of West African economies on exports have made it a victim of fluctuating world demands and prices.

East Africa

East Africa from Ethiopia in the north to Tanganyika (Tanzania) in the south has no uniform topography but forms a distinctive unit because it possesses the most favorable conditions in tropical Africa for human habitation and successful agriculture. Much is highland between 3,000 and 6,000 feet in elevation with a temperate climate. Coastal East Africa has long been known to Arabs, Indians, Chinese, and Europeans and was important through most of the nineteenth century for the export of gold, ivory, spices, and slaves.

In the late nineteenth century, British and German colonists found the area inhabited by indigenous black subsistence farmers who were dominated by Bantu herders and farmers. European settlers introduced commercial agriculture that produced sugar, coffee, tea, and tobacco. Indian laborers developed roads and railroads, and many stayed to become retailers and professional people. While some black East Africans became plantation workers, most remained herders and farmers.

After independence, Kenya and Uganda lost many skilled workers because they expelled most of their European and Indian residents. Today Kenya and Tanzania are relatively prosperous because of continued development brought about by local efforts and foreign aid. Wars, civil disturbances, and drought have extensively damaged the economies of Ethiopia, Somalia, and Uganda.

Southern Africa

Europeans modified southern Africa more than any other part of the continent. It attracted European settlers because of its equable climate and land suitable to European-style farming and grazing. It was also populated sparsely by peoples of a simple culture who were easy to subdue. By 1900 Europeans had spread from South Africa to the Rhodesias (Zambia and Zimbabwe). The discovery of gold and diamonds made the area rich and glamorous.

Today South Africa, together with Russia, mines most of the world's gold and diamonds. Together with Namibia (formerly Southwest Africa), it is also rich in silver, uranium, copper, and a host of other minerals. South Africa also has huge coal reserves. Thus, it is the wealthiest and most advanced African nation, with extensive modern mining and manufacturing centers and large cities.

EUROPE

Europe is situated on the western tip of the Eurasian landmass. Its coastal location and the belt of prevailing westerly winds give much of Europe a temperate climate and sufficient rain. However, eastern Europe suffers from the extremes of heat and cold typical of continental climates, while the Mediterranean basin has a dry summer climate. There are no deserts. Even the highest mountain ranges, such as the Alps, the Pyrenees, and the Carpathians, are relatively minor barriers compared with the Himalayas in Asia and the Rockies and Andes in North and South America. The Danube and Rhine rivers, flowing into the Black Sea and Atlantic Ocean, respectively, dominate the central and western portions of the continent. In 1900 Europe, along with the United States, had undisputed leadership in the world economy, especially in manufacturing: It supplied most of the world with machine-made goods and commanded most of its trade. Western Europe was the most advanced part of the continent.

Great Britain

In 1900 Great Britain was a leading economic power. The Industrial Revolution began in England in the eighteenth century; it was made possible by water power in Lancashire and Yorkshire and by coal mines in the Midlands and south Wales. Dominance of the seas permitted Great Britain to colonize and trade around the world and to bring food and raw materials from many lands. Great Britain became a global investor nation, and London became the financial center of the world.

After the mid-twentieth century Great Britain lost its preeminent position. The growing industrial might of the United States, Germany, Japan, and others has deprived it of old markets. It lost its empire and investments, and many of its industrial plants became outmoded. However discovery of petroleum under the North Sea has made Great Britain energy self-sufficient.

France

France, about four-fifths the size of Texas, is the largest nation in Europe after Russia and Ukraine. With frontage on both the Atlantic Ocean and the Mediterranean Sea, it has long been a link between nations of the Mediterranean and northern Europe.

Since the early nineteenth century, France has had a stable and slow-growing population and so has avoided the problems of overpopulation. This stability has been a disadvantage in France's effort to maintain its position in Europe because the populations of Great Britain, Germany, and Italy increased at a faster rate.

French agriculture enjoyed a strong tradition. France was one of the first nations to adopt modern farming practices in the nineteenth century, and these methods proved so successful that French farmers were reluctant to leave their farms for factories or to adopt twentieth-century practices. Unlike Great Britain, France was self-sufficient in its basic food needs.

In 1900 France lacked major iron ore deposits (the Lorraine ore fields were then under German control) and abundant coal. To compensate for these deficiencies, French industry focused on high-quality products. For example, although it produced all types of textiles, it was especially noted for fashion fabrics. The same focus prevailed in most other types of manufacturing, and handicrafts continued strong.

Today France has recovered from the damage of two world wars. With the loss of its empire, it is now even more dependent on imports of fuel and industrial raw materials. It is a leader in nuclear power generation. France exports textiles, automobiles, chemical and electrical equipment, weapons, and wine; the last is not high on the list by value but enjoys great prestige and is one of the oldest and steadiest earners of foreign exchange.

Germany

Germany is located east of France in the center of Europe. It occupies an exceedingly favorable position for international trade, with good land, river, and sea routes radiating in all directions. Its climate is reasonably suitable for agriculture. Above all, it is abundantly supplied with coal and minerals such as iron ore, copper, lead, and zinc. In 1900 it was the second largest European country after Russia and vied with Great Britain for economic leadership in Europe.

Germany had many industrial centers, of which the most important was and is the greater Ruhr industrial district, a focal point of world industry. The Ruhr area contains the largest deposits of high-grade coal in Europe, as well as other minerals. It is situated on the Rhine River complex of water and land routes. As a result, the Ruhr became home to huge iron and steel plants, as well as heavy-metal fabricating mills that produced locomotives, automobiles, machinery, chemicals, cement, paper, synthetics, textiles, and electrical equipment.

After 45 years of division that began with its defeat in World War II, Germany is reunified, but it has been shorn of former eastern territories, including East Prussia, and Alsace-Lorraine in the west. Partition produced dislocations in the German economy. East Germany's economy was largely integrated with that of the Soviet Union and its satellites, while the economy of the larger and more populous West Germany was integrated with those of other members of the European Economic Community, which it dominated. Since reunification in 1991 Germany has been engaged in a massive and partially successful effort to upgrade the infrastructure and productivity of the former eastern Communist sector. Germany dominates the European Union economically.

Italy

In 1900 Italy was not as strong economically as Great Britain, France, and Germany but was the leader among Mediterranean states. Mountainous Italy lacks natural resources and has little productive farmland. Its agricultural-industrial core was and is the north Italian plain and the bordering Alpine and Apennine foothills. Here, textile, metal, and chemical industries relied on hydroelectric power, or "white coal." The rest of Italy was rural and poor. Southern Italy geographically and economically was closer to other Mediterranean lands than to northern Italy. Generally speaking, the level of poverty increased as one moved south.

Italy is prosperous today due to a diversified economy. Emigration, which had been a safety value in the past, has sharply declined, as has the birthrate.

The Iberian Peninsula and Greece

Iberia includes Spain and Portugal and is a peninsula cut off from Europe by the difficult Pyrenees Mountains; it is more accessible to Africa across the Straits of Gibraltar. Much of the land in both nations is too rugged and dry for farming and more suitable to grazing. Most of the agriculture of this area and North Africa in 1900 was based on the cultivation of grapes, olives, and citrus fruits. Roads and railways were expensive to build and maintain. Lack of abundant coal or iron ore made for slow industrial development. In 1900 Greece was a poor country without modern industries.

Today Spain, Portugal, and Greece are more prosperous than before because of the integration of their economies with those of other nations of the European Community. Tourism is booming because of the mild, sunny climate and abundant historical ruins.

Eastern Europe

Broad lowlands and rivers characterize the northern section of eastern Europe, whereas much of the landscape in the Balkans to the south is cut up by rugged mountains. Poland, Hungary, Bulgaria, and Romania were traditionally grain-growing areas, but only small pockets of land were cultivable in the regions of Former Yugoslavia, Greece, and Albania.

Agriculture was the main mode of livelihood in 1900. Industries were developed only in Silesia (then Germany, now Poland) and Bohemia (then the Austro-Hungarian empire, now the Czech Republic). Before World War II, all nations in the area exported food to western Europe in exchange for industrial products.

After World War II, the Soviet Union dominated the entire region except for Austria and Yugoslavia. The result was state planning of the economy to coordinate with developments in the Soviet Union (except for Yugoslavia). Up to the 1960s the economies of Poland and Czechoslovakia in general emphasized industry, while the other nations concentrated on food crops and industrial raw materials.

With the collapse of the Soviet Union, all eastern European nations regained their independence. They are all struggling with restructuring their economies from discredited Soviet Marxist models to capitalist free market models with varying success. Many have benefited from integration with western Europe and membership in the European Community.

Northern Europe

Northern Europe consists of Scandinavia (Norway, Sweden, and Denmark) and Finland. Except for low-lying Denmark, which is suitable for farming and grazing, the area is mountainous and heavily glaciated. The nature of the terrain and the northerly latitude render most of the land unsuitable for agriculture and normal grazing. There are extensive forests, and, as a result of coastal indentations, much of the land is close to the sea. Therefore, forest industries and fishing have played, and still play, important roles in the economy.

Today Scandinavia is highly industrialized. Since the region lacks coal, most industries are fueled by hydroelectricity (except in Norway, which has developed abundant petroleum deposits beneath the North Sea). The area is notable for its effective use of natural resources, such as iron ore and uranium, and enjoys a high level of prosperity. It ranks high in the world in per capita production and in economic and cultural standards. Illiteracy is virtually unknown, and health and sanitary conditions are unsurpassed anywhere.

RUSSIA (SOVIET UNION)

Russia comprises large portions of both Europe and Asia. It is about as large as all of North America. Most of Russia is situated north of 50 degrees latitude, with the result that most of the land ranges from cool temperate to arctic in climate, although small areas near the Black Sea are subtropical. Some major rivers flow northward into the Arctic Ocean, while others, such as the Volga and Dnieper, flow into the Caspian and Black seas.

In 1900 Russia was primarily an agricultural nation. It was an exporter of grain and forest products. In Asiatic Russia the population was very sparse. There, Great Russians and other people of European descent lived in farming, mining, or penal communities, amid nomadic or seminomadic natives of Turkic and Mongolian racial background. In Central Asia, people were Muslim in religion.

The Industrial Revolution did not come to Russia until the late nineteenth century. In 1900 it was far behind Great Britain, Germany, and France in key aspects of industrial development. Moreover, Russian industries were limited to small areas close to the western extremity of the empire. They were in the St. Petersburg (Leningrad)–Baltic coastal region, where communications with the rest of Europe were best; in the Moscow region, because it was a focal point of water routes; and in the Ukraine-Crimea area to the south, rich in coal and iron ore deposits.

During the Soviet era European Russians were moved, some forcibly, to populate the rest of the Soviet Union, and in some areas they outnumbered the indigenous population. This population movement was offset, however, by larger population increases among some of the other hundred-plus nationalities that populated the Soviet Union, especially those of Muslim background in Central Asia, until the non-Russians constituted almost 50 percent of the Soviet population. European parts of the Soviet Union remained more developed and enjoyed a higher standard of living.

With its GNP second only to that of the United States, the Soviet Union became an economic giant. A succession of Five-Year Plans substantially built up Soviet industry. New industrial centers dotted the Soviet Union from the Baltic to the Pacific, and even above the Arctic Circle. The most important of these were in the Caucasus and Volga regions in Europe, in the Urals, in the Kuzbass mineralized area of Siberia, in Central Asia, and in the Baikal and Far Eastern areas of Asia. Much environmental degradation resulted from rapid and careless industrialization. Soviet agriculture was collectivized, centrally managed, and poorly mechanized; because farmworkers lacked incentive, it was inefficient and wasteful. Further, a difficult climate and bad soil conditions meant low yield per acre. As a result, the Soviet Union was not self-sufficient in grains, a basic staple crops. The standard of living of Soviet citizens was much lower than that of Europeans and North Americans.

In 1991 the Soviet Union broke up. Estonia, Latvia, and Lithuania along the Baltic Sea and Georgia in the south seceded outright. All other component republics of the former U.S.S.R. were independent but continued tenuous and unstable ties with one another in a Commonwealth of Independent States, which Georgia also joined by 1994. Russia, still the largest and strongest of the republics, is back to its approximate boundaries of the eighteenth century. Industries and agriculture are in a state of flux and disorganization in all states of the former Soviet Union as they seek to privatize agriculture and restructure their industries on capitalist principles. Many suffered a significant decline in their GNP during the last decade of the twentieth century. Russia was in 2004 the largest producer of petroleum, outstripping Saudi Arabia. The Russian economy was heavily dependent on the export of petroleum and natural gas.

NORTH AMERICA

The Western Hemisphere has three distinctive divisions: North America, Middle America, and South America. North America was the first area in the New World to experience the Industrial Revolution. As a result, it possesses the most advanced economies.

Canada

In 1900 most of Canada's 11 million people were congregated in the southeastern corner. The southern prairie lands were mostly given over to grain farming, and in the north were forests and frozen wastes. In 2004 Canada had about 32 million people. Discovery of petroleum and minerals has made it wealthy, but lack of population and capital and a formidable climate make development difficult. In 1994 Canada, the United States, and Mexico launched the North American Free Trade Agreement (NAFTA), whose goal is to end all tariffs and integrate the economies of the three nations of North America.

The United States

The United States is well endowed in assets. About two-thirds of its territory is lowland, and much of this area possesses some of the best soils for agriculture as well as favorable climates. In 1900 U.S. farming was the most efficient in the world. Out of a population of 74 million, about 13.5 million were farmers, who grew enough to export large quantities. The economic heartland region of the United States was situated in the northeast quadrant from the east bank of the Missouri to the Atlantic, and north of the Ohio and Potomac rivers. This area was noted for agriculture, mining, manufacture, and commerce. The coastal stretch between Boston and Baltimore contained a number of large urban centers. New York City was a major world center of finance and culture.

The southeastern United States was primarily agricultural, with some industries. Land west of the Missouri River up to the Rocky Mountains was sparsely populated and devoted to agriculture and ranching. Further west lay the Rocky Mountain region of rugged terrain and forests. The economy there centered on gold, silver, tin, copper, and other minerals. Along the Pacific coast, an agricultural economy was developing.

With about 295 million people at the end of 2004, the United States is the industrial giant of the world. U.S. agriculture is still the most efficient in the world, and agricultural products remain major items of export, as are machinery, manufactured goods, and technology. However, in recent years some of its manufacturers have faced stiff competition from other nations, and high labor costs have forced many industries to outsource to low-wage countries, which is a worldwide phenomenon. Dependence on foreign sources for about half its petroleum needs has restricted industrial growth. Within the United States there has been a shift of industries and population from the old centers in the northeastern frost belt to the Sunbelt in the South and Southwest and to the West Coast.

MIDDLE AMERICA

Middle America consists of Mexico, Central America, and the Caribbean islands. The former two regions are situated within a major belt of high mountains, with narrow coastal plains and some interior basins, and are populated by Amerindians and people of Spanish descent.

Mexico

In 1900 half the people in Mexico were concentrated in the areas around Mexico City, where high plateaus and valleys supported agriculture. Northern Mexico is too arid to sustain large populations, and the southern part is debilitatingly hot and humid. In 1900 corn was the staple grain, cultivated by subsistence farmers or laborers on large estates. Sugar was a major crop. There was some mining and a little manufacturing. Today Mexico has more factories and mines, and through NAFTA its economy is becoming integrated with the economies of the United States and Canada. Recent discoveries of large petroleum and natural gas fields have promoted prosperity, but population increases to 105 million people in 2004 have been too rapid for the absorption of new workers into the labor force.

Central America

Central America is broken up into numerous small nations. Rugged terrain and areas of dense rain forest prevented good land communications in 1900. Unstable governments frightened away investors. Except for enclaves of modern plantation agriculture, most people were, and remain, subsistence farmers, not much touched by modern influences. The Panama Canal, situated at the base of Central America, provides a route of communication between the Atlantic and Pacific oceans.

The Caribbean Islands

The Caribbean islands were colonized by many European powers and were mainly populated by descendants of African slaves. The economies were export oriented and were dominated by sugar and other tropical crops. Today the newly independent republics depend heavily on tourism for income.

SOUTH AMERICA

South America remained predominantly rural and underdeveloped, with poor infrastructure. Even Brazil, the continent's largest economy, accounted for less than 1 percent of global commerce in 2003.

Northern South America

Northern South America is dominated by Brazil. The rain forests of the Amazon River basin spread through much of the interior of Brazil and northern South America, which was largely underdeveloped in 1900. The population was concentrated along the coastal regions and engaged in sugar and coffee production and ranching. Brazil encouraged immigrants from both Europe and Asia. Today Brazil's economy is booming, with rapid development of industry and mining. The Amazon River valley is being rapidly developed but with severe ecological repercussions.

Other nations in northern South America are Colombia and Venezuela, plus the Guiana colonies. In 1900 most inhabitants were farmers and herders whose use of the land was dictated by the mountains. Coffee was grown, and gold, other metals, and emeralds were mined. Today coal and petroleum have provided the basis for the development of some manufacturing in Colombia and Venezuela. The Guiana colonies of Guyana, French Guiana, and Suriname remain poor.

Western or Andean South America

Consisting of Chile, Bolivia, Peru, and Ecuador, the narrow strip of land constituting Andean South America extends from the equator to 50 degrees south latitude. The rugged Andes isolated this area from the rest of South America, as few roads penetrated the mountains to connect with the rest of the continent.

Ecuador, in the north, was predominantly a land of poor Amerindians who lived on traditional farming and herding. The urban and commercial sector was dominated by mestizos (people of Amerindian-Spanish descent) and people of Spanish descent.

Foreign-owned operations played a major part in extracting Peru's mineral resources—copper, lead, zinc, coal, and more recently petroleum. Guano (fertilizer made from bird droppings) was once the main export of coastal Peru; it has been replaced by fish from the Pacific Ocean. Agriculture remained underdeveloped because of the difficult terrain and the conservative ways of the indigenous people.

Bolivia is a land-locked, high-altitude Andean nation. Very few Spaniards settled in this area, with the result that over half the people remain full-blooded Amerindians. Other than subsistence agriculture, which involved most of the population, tin mining was and continues to form the basis of Bolivia's commercial life.

Chile's favorable climate attracted many Spanish and other European settlers. In 1900 it was one of the most advanced nations in South America. Today it has modern urban centers and diversified manufacturing. It has commercial rather than subsistence farming in the temperate coastal valleys. Chilean wines have won wide acclaim.

Argentina, Uruguay, and Paraguay

Argentina, Uruguay, and Paraguay are located in southern South America. Argentina and Uruguay, on the Atlantic coast, enjoy a favorable location for trade, temperate climate, and good soils. These two nations attracted European immigrants who brought new skills and technology. Except for the Chaco waste region in the north and parts of Patagonia in the extreme south, most of the land is suitable for farming and grazing. The main products in 1900 were commercially raised maize, wheat, cattle, and sheep, which were exported to Europe. Today Argentina is an important commercial, manufacturing, and agricultural nation. In contrast, land-locked Paraguay remains underdeveloped and poor.

AUSTRALASIA

Australasia is the smallest, most recently developed, and most sparsely populated continent. The dominating feature of this region, the island continent of Australia, is too arid for intensive settlement in the interior, and in 1900 the population was concentrated along the south and east coasts. Indigenous people, small in number and called aborigines, had been largely pushed to the arid interior. First colonized by Great Britain in the late eighteenth century, most Australians were of British descent. Agriculture prevailed mostly along the east and south coasts and along some inland plains with adequate rainfall. Sheep and cattle ranching took place in the more arid parts of the interior, while the vast core of the continent remained relatively empty. Australia exports its rich minerals, natural gas, and farm products. It has also developed manufacturing industries. New Zealand, which the British colonized in the nineteenth century, remained rural and pastoral. Until the 1970s Australia and New Zealand only accepted European immigrants. Although non-European immigrants have been accepted subsequently, their number remains small. In 2004 Australia's population was 20 million, and New Zealand's was 4 million.

THE ARCTIC AND ANTARCTICA

In 1999 a United Nations convention set a 10-year deadline for countries to stake claims on the Arctic, the ice-capped sea with an imaginary point that is the North Pole. Since then Denmark, Norway, Russia, the United States, and Canada have laid claims and begun surveying missions to discover what resources—for example, oil and natural gas—lie below the polar ice. These countries are also interested in possible sea routes across the Arctic, at least in the summer, if the melting of polar ice permits it in the future, thus shortening lines of trade.

Antarctica is an ice-covered continent of over 5 million square miles surrounding the South Pole. It is uninhabited though several countries have scientific outposts on the continent.

SUMMARY

Human activities since 1900, including pollution, affected the physical world more than during any preceding comparable era. Industries and automobiles have increased carbon dioxide in the atmosphere, which has contributed to ozone depletion and global warming. The warming trend is likely to continue and threatens low-lying coastal areas worldwide, as sea levels have already risen because of the melting of sea ice. Climate changes will also change agriculture and living patterns, with incalculable benefits and problems. Increasing populations impinge on living spaces, the cutting down of irreplaceable rain forests affects global ecosystems, and overharvesting by commercial fishing, as well as pollution, depletes marine resources.

Ever-increasing human demands for food, energy, and raw materials have led to developments with unknown consequences. For example, although the Aswan High Dam built on the Nile in Egypt, the Ataturk Dam in Turkey, and the not-yet-completed Three Gorges Dam in China produce electricity and have brought more cropland under cultivation, they have also caused massive silting and damaging ecological changes along the routes of the rivers. Another example is the green revolution; it results in high-yielding crops, but the chemical fertilizers and pesticides necessary for the new seed strains are also responsible for increased pollution.

Recent advances in genetic engineering, pioneered in the United States, have modified the genetic makeup of crops and farm animals to increase yields. However, the long-term effects of such developments are not clear, and doubts about them have motivated rich western European nations to advocate caution in their application. On the other hand, developing nations such as China that have huge populations to feed are enthusiastic about the immediate good results.

Vast disparities exist, as the examples that follow demonstrate. In 2003 the world's population was around 6.3 billion; 1.2 billion people, about one-fifth of the total—mostly in south, east, and central Asia, Africa, and Central and South America—lived in dire poverty, many on less than one dollar per day per person, and accounted for only 1 percent of the world's income. The richest one-fifth of humankind, on the other hand, most of whom live in North America, western Europe, and parts of east Asia, earned 86 percent of the world's income.

Poverty, wars, and ethnic and religious turmoil have spurred huge waves of legal and illegal migration both within national borders and across borders and continents. The preferred destinations of millions of migrants seeking work and higher living standards are prosperous western Europe, North America, and Australia. While the poor nations continue to suffer from population growth, albeit at a slower rate than before, advanced nations with low fertility rates are rapidly aging. It is projected that by 2050 half of Spaniards and Italians will be over 52 years old. The decreasing number of young working-age people in countries with large aging populations will put great stress on government finances and strain the social fabric in those lands.

B

Wealthy Nations, Poor Nations, and Military Spending in the 1980s and 1990s

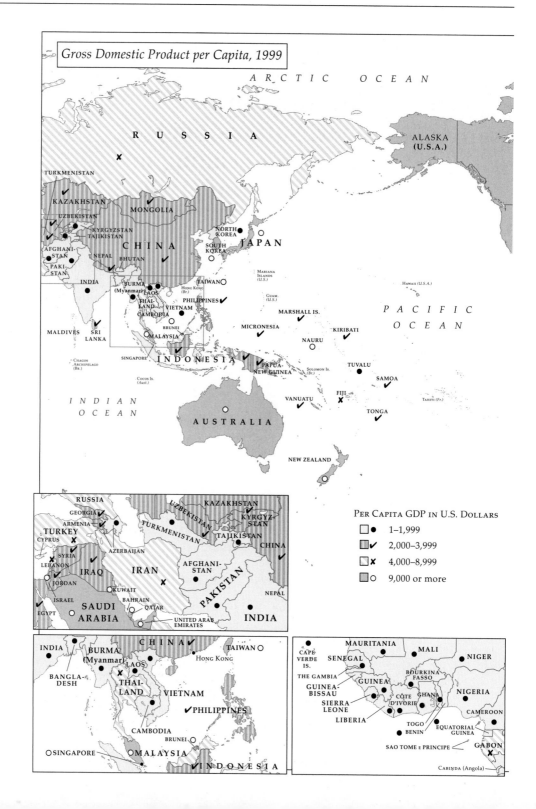

Gross Domestic Product per Capita, 1999

Per Capita GDP in U.S. Dollars

□●	1–1,999
▨✔	2,000–3,999
□✗	4,000–8,999
▨○	9,000 or more

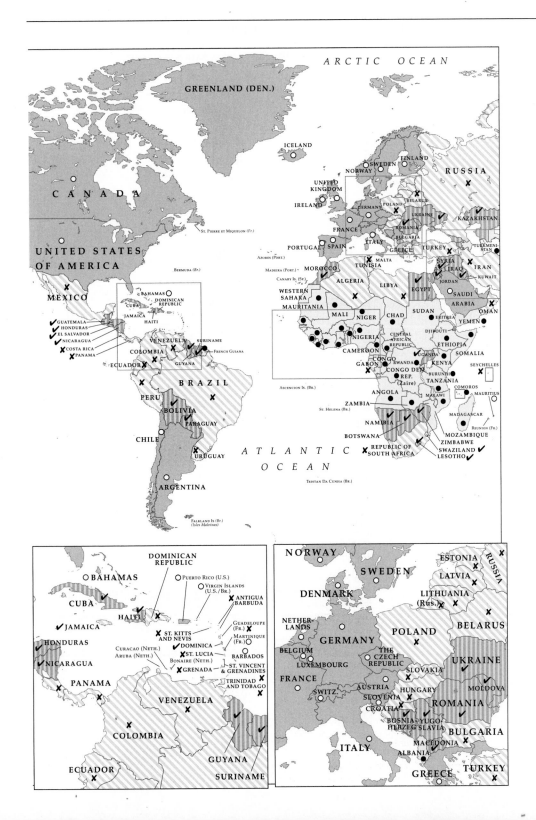

Per Capita Military Expenditures and Gross National Product by Region for 1989, 1994, and 1999 (constant 1999 dollars)

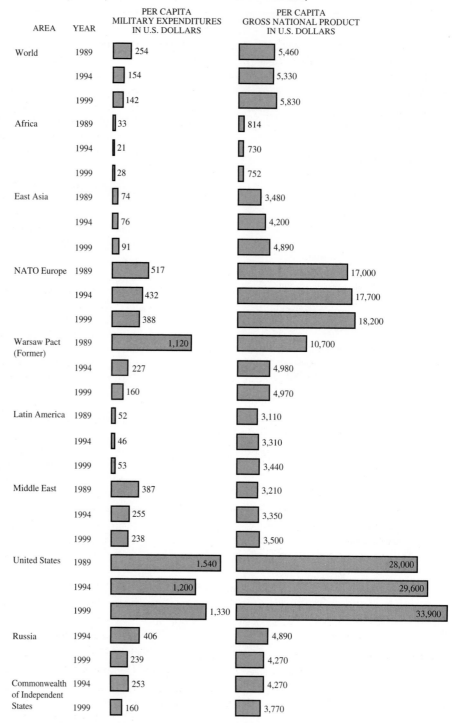

AREA	YEAR	PER CAPITA MILITARY EXPENDITURES IN U.S. DOLLARS	PER CAPITA GROSS NATIONAL PRODUCT IN U.S. DOLLARS
World	1989	254	5,460
	1994	154	5,330
	1999	142	5,830
Africa	1989	33	814
	1994	21	730
	1999	28	752
East Asia	1989	74	3,480
	1994	76	4,200
	1999	91	4,890
NATO Europe	1989	517	17,000
	1994	432	17,700
	1999	388	18,200
Warsaw Pact (Former)	1989	1,120	10,700
	1994	227	4,980
	1999	160	4,970
Latin America	1989	52	3,110
	1994	46	3,310
	1999	53	3,440
Middle East	1989	387	3,210
	1994	255	3,350
	1999	238	3,500
United States	1989	1,540	28,000
	1994	1,200	29,600
	1999	1,330	33,900
Russia	1994	406	4,890
	1999	239	4,270
Commonwealth of Independent States	1994	253	4,270
	1999	160	3,770

Figures above for 1989, 1994 and 1999 are taken from U.S. Department of State figures.

GLOSSARY

Anticolonialism/Anti-imperialism Movement for independence by African, Middle Eastern, Asian, and Latin American peoples against foreign, often Western, domination.

Anti-Semitism Anti-Jewishness.

ANZUS Australia–New Zealand–United States Treaty; one of the U.S.-led multilateral treaties designed to counter Communist expansion in Asia.

Apartheid Government-instituted policies of severe racial segregation, especially in South Africa from 1949 to c. 1991.

ARVN Army of the Republic of Vietnam; U.S.-armed and U.S.-supported South Vietnamese army that fought the Communist North Vietnamese army during the Second Indochina War.

ASEAN Association of Southeast Asian Nations; began as a group of non-Communist nations (1967) with the goal of fostering economic cooperation among members. Later joined by Communist Vietnam.

Caudillo In Spanish-speaking countries, the civil or military person who controls the government.

CCP Chinese Communist Party; founded in 1921 and came to power in 1949.

Cold war The struggle between the United States and its allies against the Soviet Union and its allies from the mid-1940s to the late 1980s; it involved many tensions and confrontations but stopped short of direct armed conflict between the two sides.

Collective security Shared responsibility for a nation's security, especially in the interwar years of the 1920s and 1930s.

Collectivization The Soviet process begun in 1929 under Stalin of forcing peasants onto collective—and, to a lesser extent, state—farms; also applied with some variations in other Communist countries.

Colonization Move by nation to settle its own people on territory outside its own borders.

Colons French-descended colonists who had settled in French possessions overseas.

Common Market See European Communities (EC).

Commonwealth of Independent States (CIS) Formed in December 1991 by all of the former Soviet republics except Estonia, Latvia, Lithuania, and Georgia. Georgia subsequently joined in 1994.

Détente The lessening of tensions during the 1970s in the cold war between the Communist bloc and NATO countries, especially between the Soviet Union and the United States.

Dirty wars The violent repression of rebels and dissidents by governments, especially by authoritarian right-wing Latin American ones during the 1960s, 1970s, and 1980s. These "wars" were characterized by mass arrests, systematic use of torture, killings, "disappearances," and other violations of human and civil rights.

Dollar diplomacy U.S. policy of using its power to aid its financial interests abroad; it sometimes involved establishing sympathetic leaders in Latin America, who in turn supported U.S. intervention in their nations' economies. This process is often called Yankee imperialism in Latin America.

European Communities (EC) Formed in 1967 when the European Economic Community (EEC, or Common Market), founded in 1957, joined with the European Coal and Steel Community and the European Atomic Energy Community to form the European Communities (EC), later the European Community. Original members of the EC included France, West Germany, Italy, Belgium, the Netherlands, and Luxembourg. Great Britain, Ireland, and Denmark became members of the EC in 1973, Greece in 1981, and Spain and Portugal in 1986. The goal of the EC was to abolish trade barriers and provide for the free movement of capital and labor between the participating nations. As the organization grew, its departments, including the Council of Ministers and the European Parliament, also increased in significance. In 1993 the EC expanded into the European Union (EU), and in 1995 Sweden, Finland, and Austria joined the organization. In 2004, 10 more countries were added. In 1999 11 of the EU members (all except Britain, Denmark, Greece, and Sweden) took a further step in integrating their economies when they put into operation the European Monetary Union (EMU), which provided for the gradual introduction of a common currency (the euro).

European Economic Community (EEC) See European Communities (EC).

European Monetary Union (EMU) See European Communities (EC).

European Union (EU) See European Communities (EC).

Evolution Darwin's theory that animal species evolve in an environment of natural selection, where the fittest, or most adaptable, survive.

Five-Year Plan   First introduced in the Soviet Union in 1928, five-year plans became characteristic of many planned economic systems, especially Communist ones in which the government decided on what types of goods and services were to be produced and in what quantities.

Free market economy   An economy in which the types and quantities of goods and services produced are determined primarily by private enterprises and consumers; the opposite of a Soviet-style command, or planned, economy.

Glasnost   A Russian word meaning openness; especially used in reference to Gorbachev's policy of more freedom of expression and less censorship and government secrecy.

Global South (the South)   In the aftermath of the cold war, those nations, mostly in the Southern Hemisphere, with low gross national products (GNPs) and massive problems of poverty and economic development.

Globalization   Process of increasing interconnectedness among the countries of the world, especially their economies. This process accelerated rapidly in the final decades of the twentieth century. In less affluent parts of the world, it is sometimes perceived as a form of Westernization and neoimperialism.

Green revolution   Modern food production techniques including the use of high-yielding seeds that greatly increase food production, especially in Asia.

Harijans   Means "children of god"; used first by M. K. Gandhi instead of *untouchable,* or *outcaste,* to denote the lowest group of Hindu Indians.

Imperialism   A country's extension of rule or authority, by force or the threat of its use, over a foreign territory. At various times in the twentieth century the term meant some combination of political, economic, cultural, or military domination by stronger powers over the peoples and nations of Africa, Asia, Latin America, and eastern Europe.

Iron curtain   A term popularized by Winston Churchill in 1946 to describe the geographic and political divide between Western Europe and the Communist Eastern bloc countries.

KMT   Kuomintang, the Nationalist Party of China; founded by Sun Yat-sen, it ruled China between 1928 and 1949 and ruled Taiwan until mid-2000.

Laissez-faire   Government noninterference in business and the economic system of a nation.

Left, left-wing   Political forces, including liberalism, socialism, and communism, that favor more government involvement and state aid to help the lower classes than does the Right. Also more inclined than the Right to favor government regulation of business. *See also* Right, right-wing.

Manifest Destiny   The belief of some Americans that it was God's will that the United States expand across North America (from the North Pole to Panama) and perhaps even across South America.

Nationalism   An emotional loyalty toward one's nation, sometimes including a belief in the superiority of that nation, regardless of whether it is also an independent country.

Nativism   The political and social force in the United States at the turn of the twentieth century that opposed the influx of immigrants from southern and eastern Europe, Africa, and Asia.

NATO   North Atlantic Treaty Organization; an alliance formed in 1949 by 12 countries from Western Europe and North America against the perceived threat of the U.S.S.R. The alliance was later expanded, and the latest additions, in 1999, of the Czech Republic, Hungary, and Poland brought the total number of member nations up to 19.

Neoliberalism   A frequent response of the last quarter century by the United States, the International Monetary Fund (IMF), the World Bank, and other economic powers to the high foreign debt and hyperinflation of less developed countries, especially in Latin America. The basic idea behind neoliberalism was to shrink state expenditures as much as possible and thereby minimize governments' "interference" in the "free" play of market forces. This often meant slashing public funding for education, health care, public transport, and other areas, while permitting the unimpeded flow of foreign capital

NEP   New Economic Policy; a Soviet economic policy from 1921 until 1928 that allowed peasants to sell their produce on the open market and permitted some small-scale private enterprise.

Perestroika   A Russian word meaning restructuring; especially used in reference to Gorbachev's policy of economic—and, to a lesser extent, political and social—restructuring.

Populism   A political force in the United States at the turn of the twentieth century that distrusted big financial and corporate powers and fought for the economic and political interests of farmers, small businessmen, and others. Among other points, populists desired the public ownership of railroads.

Progressivism An early-twentieth-century U.S. reform movement that democratized the political process for whites and addressed social and economic problems, many of them brought about or worsened by industrialization, urbanization, and relatively unregulated capitalism.

Reparations Payments demanded from the losers in World War I as compensation for damage suffered during the war; such payments have also been demanded from nations, governments, and businesses by victims of aggression in World War II and other conflicts.

Right, right-wing Political forces, including conservatism, fascism, and Nazism, that are more sympathetic than the Left to the economic interests of the upper-classes and less sympathetic to using the powers of government to assist the lower classes. *See also* Left, left-wing.

Satyagraha "Soul force" or "truth force"; a Hindu-based technique of nonviolent protest used by M. K. Gandhi against the white-dominated government of South Africa and later British rule in India.

SCAP Supreme Command Allied Powers; U.S.-dominated organization that supervised the remaking of Japan after its defeat in World War II.

SEATO Southeast Asian Treaty Organization; a U.S.-led multilateral treaty to oppose Communist expansion in Asia. Other members were Great Britain, France, Thailand, and the Philippines.

Socialism Although the term is sometimes used to include both communist and democratic socialist systems, during the twentieth century it was used primarily to identify the latter. In such a system the government was elected democratically but controlled more of the economy than did governments under capitalism, a system socialists believed favored the upper classes to the detriment of the lower classes.

Suffragists People who struggled to extend voting rights, especially to women; emerged as a political force in the West, but also in other nations including Egypt, Turkey, and China.

Swadeshi Movement in India led by the Indian National Congress to boycott British-made products and promote Indian handmade goods as a tool in the fight for independence.

Swaraj Means "self-rule"; slogan promoted by the Indian National Congress in its struggle for Indian independence.

Terrorism The unlawful use of violence, or the threat of it, against individuals, groups, or property to intimidate governments or societies, often to achieve political, religious, or ideological goals. The term is sometimes used more widely to include "state terrorism." Moreover, those labeled "terrorists" are sometimes considered "freedom fighters" by their defenders.

Third World Mostly newly independent and poor, agricultural nations in much of Asia, Africa, South America, and Latin America that during the cold war sought to steer a neutral course between the First World (the United States and its allies) and the Second World (the Soviet Union and its allies). *See also* Global South.

Total war Concept that all resources of the enemy, including their civilians producing for the effort, are subject to destruction, while, at the same time, one's own civilian population is pressured to the maximum to support the war effort.

Truman Doctrine A U.S. policy established in 1947 to "support free peoples who are resisting attempted subjugation by armed minorities or by outside pressures." Prompted by U.S. fears of Communist actions in Greece and by Soviet demands regarding the Turkish Straits, the doctrine justified sending economic aid and military equipment and advisers to areas believed threatened by communism.

Viet Cong Short for Vietnamese Communist, the North Vietnamese–led guerrillas who fought the U.S.-supported South Vietnamese government in the Second Indochinese War.

Vietminh Short for Vietnamese League for National Independence, a Communist-led movement that fought against French rule in Vietnam after World War II.

War of attrition The concept that war cannot be won quickly through the collision of military forces, but, because of military stalemates, war must be decided by long-term pressure aimed at breaking the enemy civilian population's will to fight.

Welfare state A non-Communist state in which the government has established systematic programs, policies, and regulations to provide for the various social needs of its people—for example, during sickness and unemployment. Although the term is sometimes applied to some pre–World War II states, the term first came into common usage after World War II, when Britain in 1946 made all of its citizens eligible for free medical services.

Zaibatsu Japanese word meaning "financial clique"; the banking, mining, and industrial conglomerates of Japan.

Zionism Jewish nationalism; movement to create and support an independent Jewish state, Israel.

CREDITS

Page 12, American Institute of Physics/Niels Bohr Library; 19, © Time Life Pictures/Mansell/Time Life Pictures/Getty Images; 26, U.S. Navy Department; 29, Pablo Picasso (1881–1973). *Les Demoiselles d'Avignon*. 1907. Oil on canvas, 8′ × 7′ 8″. Acquired through the Lille P. Bliss Bequest. (333.1939). The Museum of Modern Art, New York. Digital Image © The Museum of Modern Art, NY/Licensed by Scala/Art Resource, NY © 2006 Estate of Pablo Picasso/Artists Rights Society (ARS), New York; 34, 39, © Bettmann/Corbis; 45, Photograph from the Namibian National Archive/Schulmann Collection/MCT International; 52, Courtesy African Museum, Johannesburg; 58, © Hulton-Deutsch Collection/Corbis; 63, © Bettmann/Corbis; 65, © National Archives/Corbis; 73, Courtesy Museum of American China Trade, Milton, MA; 84, "Afternoon tea," © 1976 Aperture, Inc., as published in The Last Empire, Photography in British India, 1855–1911, Aperture, 1976; 93, © Culver Pictures; 97, © Bettmann/Corbis; 101, Brooklyn Eagle; 110, © Hulton-Deutsch Collection/Corbis; 113, National Archives; 128, © Underwood & Underwood/Corbis; 135, Courtesy Jack Bradley; 147, © Hulton-Deutsch Collection/Corbis; 151, Illustrated London News; 156, © Brown Brothers; 164, © The Granger Collection, New York; 177, © AP/Wide World Photos; 181, © Underwood and Underwood/Corbis; 194, © Camera Press; 207, © Hulton-Deutsch Collection/Corbis; 208, Courtesy Nehru Memorial Library; 217, © General Photographic Agency/Getty Images; 221, © Bettmann/Corbis; 223, From "A Woman Tenderfoot in Egypt" by Grace Thompson Sexton (New York: Dodd, Mead and Co., 1923; 232, © Brown Brothers; 236, © Sovfoto/Eastfoto; 243, Historical Pictures Service; 248, Photo © Giraudon/Art Resource. © 2006 Estate of Pablo Picasso/Artists Rights Society (ARS), New York; 251, Central Press Photo; 260T, YIVO Institute for Jewish Research; 260B, © Corbis; 261, © Bettmann/Corbis; 266, © AP/Wide World Photos; 270, Walter Moss; 273, © Bettmann/Corbis; 285, EPA Documerial; 289, © Sebastiao Salgado/Contact Press Images; 290, Walter Moss; 291, Courtesy CARE; 295, Courtesy Roger Swearingen; 300, Nancy Moss; 310, 319, 321, 330, 339, © Bettmann/Corbis 348, © Michael Heron/Woodfin Camp and Associates; 352, © NCNA/Camera Press; 356, © AP/Wide World Photos; 365, © Bettmann/Corbis; 374, 382, Keystone Press Agency; 387, © Bettmann/Corbis; 393, © AP/Wide World Photos; 399, © David Kubinger/Corbis; 403, 405, © Bettmann/Corbis; 408, © Larry Towell/Magnum Photos; 413, © Bettmann/Corbis; 417, Keystone Press Agency; 420T, © AP/Wide World Photos; 420B, © Lee Lockwood/Black Star; 429, © George Tames/The New York Times; 434, © Peter Menzel/Stock Boston; 447, © Bettmann/Corbis; 449, Rachel Lee/The Free China Journal; 453, © AP/Wide World Photos; 456, Keystone Press Agency; 466TL, © Robin Moyer/Getty Images/Timepix; 466TR, © Peter Charlesworth/Corbis Saba; 466B, © Bettmann/Corbis; 471, John Van Hasselt/Corbis; 482, © Georg Gerster/Photo Researchers, Inc.; 489, © David C. Turnley/Corbis; 497, 501, Walter Moss; 504, 508, © Bettmann/Corbis; 517, © Reuters/Corbis; 524, 527, © AP/Wide World Photos; 530, Courtesy Pelli Clarke Pelli Architects; 537, Walter Moss; 539, © ITAR-TASS/AFP/Getty Images; 548, © Sean Adair/Reuters/Corbis 557, Jiu-Hwa Upshur; 561, © Jae-Hyun Seok/The New York Times 562, © Rafiqur Rahman/Reuters/Corbis; 571, © AP/Wide World Photos

INDEX

Note: Page numbers in italic indicate photos. Page numbers followed by a n indicate the Suggested Sources sections. Page numbers followed by f indicate maps and illustrations.

The World in 2000

ARCTIC OCEAN

RUSSIA

ALASKA (U.S.A.)

TURKMENISTAN

KAZAKSTAN
UZBEKISTAN
KYRGHYZSTAN
TAJIKISTAN

MONGOLIA

NORTH KOREA
SOUTH KOREA

JAPAN

AFGHANI-STAN
PAKI-STAN
NEPAL
BHUTAN

CHINA

TAIWAN
HONG KONG (Br.)

MARIANA ISLANDS (U.S.)

HAWAII (U.S.A.)

INDIA

BURMA (Myanmar)
LAOS
THAIL-AND
CAMBODIA
VIETNAM
PHILIPPINES

GUAM (U.S.)

MALDIVES
SRI LANKA

MARSHALL IS.

PACIFIC OCEAN

BRUNEI
MALAYSIA

Palau
MICRONESIA

KIRIBATI

NAURU

Chagos Archipelago (Br.)

SINGAPORE
INDONESIA

PAPUA-NEW GUINEA

Solomon Is.

TUVALU

SAMOA

Cocos Is. (Aust.)

VANUATU

FIJI

TAHITI (Fr.)

INDIAN OCEAN

AUSTRALIA

TONGA

NEW ZEALAND

RUSSIA
GEORGIA
ARMENIA
TURKEY
CYPRUS
SYRIA
LEBANON
IRAQ
JORDAN
ISRAEL
EGYPT
SAUDI ARABIA

UZBEKISTAN
TURKMENISTAN
AZERBAIJAN
IRAN
KUWAIT
BAHRAIN
QATAR
UNITED ARAB EMIRATES

KAZAKSTAN
KYRGHYZ-STAN
TAJIKISTAN
CHINA
AFGHANI-STAN
PAKISTAN
NEPAL
INDIA

INDIA
BANGLA DESH
BURMA (Myanmar)
CHINA
LAOS
THAI-LAND
VIETNAM
CAMBODIA
SINGAPORE
MALAYSIA
INDONESIA

TAIWAN
HONG KONG (Br.)
PHILIPPINES

MAURITANIA
MALI
NIGER
CAPE VERDE IS.
SENEGAL
THE GAMBIA
GUINEA-BISSAU
GUINEA
BOURKINA FASSO
NIGERIA
SIERRA LEONE
CÔTE D'IVOIRE
GHANA
LIBERIA
TOGO
BENIN
EQUATORIAL GUINEA
CAMEROON
SAO TOME E PRINCIPE
GABON
CABINDA (Angola)

622

ARCTIC OCEAN

GREENLAND (DEN.)

ICELAND

CANADA

RUSSIA

SWEDEN
FINLAND
NORWAY
UNITED
KINGDOM
IRELAND

KAZAKHSTAN

GERMANY POLAND BELARUS
UKRAINE
FRANCE
RUMANIA
BULGARIA
TURKEY
TURKMENI-
STAN

UNITED STATES
OF AMERICA

PORTUGAL SPAIN
ITALY GREECE
MALTA

SYRIA
IRAQ
IRAN

St. Pierre et Miquelon (Fr.)

AZORES (PORT.)

MOROCCO
TUNISIA
JORDAN KUWAIT

MEXICO
BELIZE
BAHAMAS
Bermuda (Br.)
Madeira (Port.)
Canary Is. (Sp.)
WESTERN
SAHARA

ALGERIA
LIBYA
EGYPT
SAUDI
ARABIA
OMAN

CUBA
DOMINICAN
REPUBLIC
JAMAICA
HAITI

MAURITANIA

CAPE VERDE
IS.
MALI
NIGER
CHAD
SUDAN
ERITREA
YEMEN
DJIBOUTI

GUATEMALA
HONDURAS
EL SALVADOR
NICARAGUA
COSTA RICA
PANAMA
Canal Zone (U.S.)

SENEGAL
GUINEA
SIERRA LEONE
LIBERIA
GHANA
COTE
D'IVOIRE
NIGERIA
CENTRAL
AFRICAN
REPUBLIC
CAMEROON
GABON
CONGO
RWANDA
BURUNDI
ETHIOPIA
SOMALIA
UGANDA
KENYA

VENEZUELA
SURINAME
French Guiana

COLOMBIA
GUYANA
ECUADOR

CONGO
DEM. REP.
(ZAIRE)
TANZANIA
SEYCHELLES

BRAZIL

PERU
ANGOLA
MALAWI
COMOROS
MAURITIUS

Ascension Is. (Br.)

ZAMBIA
MADAGASCAR
Reunion (Fr.)

BOLIVIA
PARAGUAY
St. Helena (Br.)
NAMIBIA
ZIMBABWE
MOZAMBIQUE

CHILE
BOTSWANA
SWAZILAND
LESOTHO

ATLANTIC
OCEAN

REPUBLIC OF
SOUTH AFRICA

URUGUAY

Tristan Da Cunha (Br.)

ARGENTINA

Falkland Is (Br.)
(Isles Malvinas)

DOMINICAN
REPUBLIC
BAHAMAS
Puerto Rico (U.S.)
Virgin Islands
(U.S./Br.)
ANTIGUA
BARBUDA

CUBA
HAITI

JAMAICA
St. Kitts
and Nevis
Guadeloupe
(Fr.)
Martinique
(Fr.)

HONDURAS
Curacao (Neth.)
Aruba (Neth.)
DOMINICA
St. Lucia
Bonaire (Neth.)
BARBADOS
ST. VINCENT
& GRENADINES
GRENADA
TRINIDAD
AND TOBAGO

NICARAGUA

PANAMA

COSTA
RICA

CANAL ZONE
(U.S.)

VENEZUELA

COLOMBIA

ECUADOR

GUYANA

SURINAME

NORWAY

SWEDEN
ESTONIA
RUSSIA
LATVIA
LITHUANIA
(Rus.)

DENMARK

BELARUS

NETHER-
LANDS
POLAND
BELGIUM
GERMANY
THE
CZECH
REPUBLIC
UKRAINE
LUXEMBOURG
SLOVAKIA
FRANCE
SWITZ.
AUSTRIA
HUNGARY
MOLDOVA
SLOVENIA
RUMANIA
CROATIA
BOSNIA-
HERZEG
YUGO-
SLAVIA
BULGARIA
MACEDONIA
ITALY
ALBANIA
GREECE
TURKEY

623